Contemporary Controversy

READINGS FOR COMPOSITION AND DISCUSSION

edited by

MORRIS FREEDMAN
UNIVERSITY OF NEW MEXICO

PAUL B. DAVIS
UNIVERSITY OF NEW MEXICO

CHARLES SCRIBNER'S SONS   NEW YORK

Copyright © 1966 Charles Scribner's Sons

This book published simultaneously in the
United States of America and in Canada—
Copyright under the Berne Convention

All rights reserved. No part of this book
may be reproduced in any form without the
permission of Charles Scribner's Sons.

A—1.66

Printed in the United States of America
LIBRARY OF CONGRESS CATALOG CARD NUMBER 66–11193

Introduction

William Hazlitt's contention that "when a thing ceases to be a subject of controversy, it ceases to be a subject of interest" is particularly relevant to the classroom. We have found that, in reading, discussing, and writing, students respond better and perform more capably when stimulated and engaged by the controversial and the contemporary. This anthology is designed to provide such stimulation. Its contents range from disputes about the value of the new translations of the Bible to ones about whether we should land on the moon, from essays of vigorous polemic to ones of gentle persuasion. But all of the topics have two things in common—their controversy and their contemporary significance.

The four major parts of the anthology provide a survey of the diversity and complexity of contemporary issues. Part I, by way of prologue, asks "What Is College For?" The prologue is followed by three major divisions: Part II, "Arts and Humanities"; Part III, "Society"; and Part IV, "Science and Technology." These divisions, though useful, are not rigid; some subjects could have been classified as readily in one as in another. The sections "The Quick and the Dead on the American Highway" and "Smoking, Cancer, and Statistics," for example, while concerned with scientific method and technical problems, also raise significant social issues.

In our questions and assignments we have tried to emphasize narrower problems of composition and rhetoric as well as broader aesthetic, humanistic, social, and scientific issues. These broader issues are bound to overlap from one section to the next. We have occasionally noted these relationships, but we would urge instructors to point out others and to concentrate on those aspects of the anthology that best suit their own inclinations and best serve their own purposes.

In each section we have tried to represent two sides of the issue and, usually, what seems to us to be the objective position. Not all the controversies are represented by diametric oppositions; in many cases differences, though fundamental, are treated by the authors of the selections in a selective and analytical, rather than a polemical, way. Such, for example, is the character of the differences between Lewis Mumford and Peter Blake on Frank Lloyd Wright's Guggenheim Museum or those between Drs. Morrison and Fister on government-supported medical care. The objective position, too, appears in many forms. Sometimes it is embodied in the statement of one side, as in the section "Smoking, Cancer, and Statistics," in which some of the statistical evidence that Alan S. Donnahoe questions is included in his presentation. In some sections, where a dialogue is literally conducted between two sides, such objective material as there is emerges in the course of the debate—as in the television play from "The Defenders" series, "The Pill Man," in which the pro and the con arguments for making drugs available to addicts are presented during a trial. And, for some sections, the objective material exists outside this anthology (the suggestions for additional reading will aid students in finding such material)—as for the section on Hannah Arendt's reporting of the Eichmann trial, discussed here by two vehemently opposed authorities, Justice Michael A. Musmanno and Dr. Bruno Bettelheim.

The controversies we have chosen also illustrate different kinds of written English, from the technical language of the scientific report and the polished style of the *New Yorker* to the evocative rhetoric of a lawyer's defense in a capital case. In using the book the student will be confronted by widely varying degrees of concern for documentation, by different styles of footnoting and punctuation, and even by variations in spelling. Perhaps the most obvious differences are those between British and American usage in vocabulary, idiom, and spelling. More important are the differences between legal or scientific prose, with its requirements of precision, and prose intended for the general reader. We have not normalized the texts or tried to eliminate these differences. Rather we hope that the variety will give the student a more realistic view of the written language than is often provided by more conventional essay texts. Effective writing depends upon the recognition of many kinds of English and the development of the capacity to discriminate among them.

In addition to providing questions for discussion and assignments for writing, we have appended suggestions for additional reading, which, in effect, serve to make small casebooks of each section. We would suggest as well that teachers might want to place certain books on reserve in their campus libraries since they supplement our anthology closely. Among these would be Hannah Arendt's *Eichmann in Jerusalem: A Study in the Banality of Evil* (New York, 1963), copies of the new translations of the Bible, James B. Conant's *The Education of American Teachers* (New York, 1963), Jane Jacobs' *The Death and Life of Great American Cities* (New York, 1961), the Surgeon General's report *Smoking and Health* (Washington, 1964), and Arthur Koestler's *The Act of Creation* (New York, 1964).

We owe many debts in compiling this book: to members of our families, especially Mary Davis and Paul Freedman; to our indefatigable assistant, Edith Higgins; to our colleagues, friends, and students, among whom we especially wish to thank Clinton Adams, George Arms, Ernest W. Baughman, Van Deren Coke, Franklin Dickey, Nathan Glazer, Hamlin Hill, David Housman, Edwin Lieuwen, Almira Saffle, Don Schlegel, Sidney Solomon, Martin Steinmann, Dale Swihart, and David Vernon. We are, of course, alone responsible for the shortcomings of the book.

M. F.
P. B. D.

Contents

Introduction iii

I. PROLOGUE

What Is College For?
OSCAR HANDLIN   *Are the Colleges Killing Education?*   3
MORRIS FREEDMAN   *Who Judges the Judges?*   11

II. ARTS AND HUMANITIES

1. Dictionary: Pre- or De-scriber
DWIGHT MACDONALD   *The String Untuned*   25
BERGEN EVANS   *But What's a Dictionary For?*   45
JAMES SLEDD   *The Lexicographer's Uneasy Chair*   55

2. The Encyclopaedia Britannica and the Business of Knowledge
HERMAN KOGAN   *The Modern EB: How It Is Edited*   65
HARVEY EINBINDER   *The Britannica*   78
ROBERT HUTCHINS and HARVEY EINBINDER   *The Britannica*   93

3. The New Bible: God's Word or Man's
From *The Gospel According to St. Matthew (King James Version)*   99
The Sermon on the Mount (The New English Bible: New Testament)   103
CECIL NORTHCOTT   *A Sharp Sword of the Lord*   109
T. S. ELIOT   *A Scholar Finds the Beauty Wrung out of New English Bible's Verses*   113

4. Toynbee's History: Mish-Mash or Monument
ARNOLD J. TOYNBEE   *My View of History*   119
ALBERT L. GUÉRARD   *A Quest for Patterns in the Past*   126
H. R. TREVOR-ROPER   *Arnold Toynbee's Millennium*   129

5. Pop Goes the Artist
LAWRENCE ALLOWAY   *'Pop Art' Since 1949*   149
LESLIE JUDD AHLANDER   *Washington Gallery Shows Pop Art*   155

RUSSELL BAKER   *Observer*   158
PETER SELZ   *The Flaccid Art*   160

6. The Wrightness of the Guggenheim
FRANK LLOYD WRIGHT   *The Solomon R. Guggenheim Memorial*   166
PETER BLAKE   *The Guggenheim: Museum or Monument?*   167
LEWIS MUMFORD   *What Wright Hath Wrought*   174

III. SOCIETY

1. First Things First: Teaching Our Teachers
JAMES B. CONANT   *Concluding Observations*   189
FRED M. HECHINGER   *It's Teacher's Turn in the Corner*   196
HAROLD TAYLOR   *New Blood, Not Dry Words*   200

2. Young America: Beat, Bored, and Delinquent
JACK KEROUAC   *The Origins of the Beat Generation*   206
NORMAN PODHORETZ   *The Know-Nothing Bohemians*   213
ARTHUR MILLER   *The Bored and the Violent*   222
J. EDGAR HOOVER   *These Fighters Against Youth Crime Need Your Help*   230

3. The Bible and the Bill of Rights
Abington School District v. *Schempp,* 374 U.S. 204 (1962)
JUSTICE CLARK   *Opinion of the Court*   236
JUSTICE DOUGLAS   *[A Concurring Opinion]*   249
JUSTICE STEWART   *[A Dissenting Opinion]*   251

4. Society's Right to Kill
JOE W. HENRY, JR.   *Tennessee* v. *Wash Jones: The Closing Argument for the Defense*   260
JACQUES BARZUN   *In Favor of Capital Punishment*   270
From *Controversy: Mr. Barzun and Capital Punishment*   278

5. Eichmann and Evil: War Crimes or Man's Crimes
MICHAEL A. MUSMANNO   *Man with an Unspotted Conscience*   288
HANNAH ARENDT and MICHAEL A. MUSMANNO   *[Exchange of Letters]*   292
BRUNO BETTELHEIM   *Eichmann; the System; the Victims*   296
MICHAEL A. MUSMANNO and BRUNO BETTELHEIM   *[Exchange of Letters]*   312
NEW YORKER   *Notes and Comment*   315

CONTENTS

6. Drug Addiction: Illness or Crime
ALBERT RUBEN and CHARLES ECKERT   The Pill Man   318

7. The Spoils of City Planning
JANE JACOBS   Modern City Planning: The Victory Over Vitality   344
LEWIS MUMFORD   Mother Jacobs' Home Remedies   354
HERBERT J. GANS   City Planning and Urban Realities   368
WYNDHAM THOMAS   City Centres Die at Six   376

IV. SCIENCE AND TECHNOLOGY

1. The Quick and the Dead on the American Highway
WILLIAM HADDON, JR., M.D., M.P.H. and JAMES L. GODDARD, M.D., M.P.H.   An Analysis of Highway Safety Strategies   385
NATIONAL SAFETY COUNCIL   From Speed Regulation   389
ROBERT L. SCHWARTZ   The Case for Fast Drivers   396

2. Public or Private Medicine
OSCAR R. EWING   Report to the President, 1948   406
DR. GEORGE M. FISTER   The Case Against Federalized Medicine   414
LORD TAYLOR   America's Medical Future: A Briton's View   419
ROBERT S. MORISON, M.D.   New US Patterns   423

3. Smoking, Cancer, and Statistics
ADVISORY COMMITTEE TO THE SURGEON GENERAL
  From Smoking and Health   429
ALAN S. DONNAHOE   Smoking and Health: Other Side of the Report   445

4. Ethics and Population Control
HUDSON HOAGLAND   From Population Problems and the Control of Fertility   454
JOHN L. THOMAS, S.J.   The Catholic Position on Population Control   469
JOHN C. BENNETT   Protestant Ethics and Population Control   476
METROPOLITAN LIFE INSURANCE COMPANY
  American Population Growth in 1963   481

5. Psychology and Science
ARTHUR KOESTLER   The Dark Ages of Psychology   487
NEVILLE MORAY   Outside the Cave   495

6. Racing to the Moon

ROBERT JASTROW and HOMER E. NEWELL	Why Land on the Moon?	502
FRANKLIN A. LINDSAY	The Costs and the Choices	510
EDWIN DIAMOND	That Moon Trip: Debate Sharpens	516
RICHARD AUSTIN SMITH	Now It's an Agonizing Reappraisal of the Moon Race	522

I
Prologue

Prologue

What Is College For?

Are the Colleges Killing Education?

OSCAR HANDLIN

With the coming of spring, hysteria creeps across the campus. Tension mounts steadily, and even when it does not erupt in some overt form, it still disturbs the last two months of the college year. Now is the time when the steadily growing psychiatric staffs come into their own.

The young people who brood in their rooms, who forget to come down to the dining hall, and who burst out in fits of irrationality are not worrying about who will win the great game or who will come to the dance or be tapped for the fraternity. Joe College is dead, and his little anxieties are unrecognizably antique. His successors are immersed in their books and laboratories, and their concern is for the grade that an incomprehensible marking system will grind out for them.

Among the undergraduates, it is worst for the juniors. Most of the seniors are reconciled; they have by now amassed whatever capital they will possess and know it is too late to make serious changes. The sophomores are frenetically hopeful; despite the facts of the past, they feel they have a chance. The freshmen are still reeling from the shock of self-discovery but are not yet fully aware of what has hit them. The juniors are, and therefore the panic that all share to some extent is particularly intense among them.

The phenomenon is relatively recent, and it is not everywhere the same. Indeed, there may still be some refuge which is entirely unaffected, where college remains a place of learning, not a racetrack. But year by year the infection spreads, and it seems most virulent in the best institutions and among the best students.

The American college functions with a time-encrusted mechanism, much

Atlantic Monthly, CCIX (May 1962), 41–45. Reprinted by permission of Willis Kingsley Wing. Copyright © 1962, by Oscar Handlin.

of it immensely valuable because of the experience, tradition, and wisdom built into it. But some of its devices were designed for purposes long since forgotten. We do not question their presence; the grating noise they make seems a necessary part of the operation. Who can imagine that this is the sound of minds being crushed in a process that frustrates the whole educational enterprise?

Those great big beautiful A's so avidly sought, those little, miserly C's so often found, were meant for another time and another student body. They were the tools of the teacher in the day when the college was more a disciplinary than an educational institution. The miscellaneous lots of boys and young men who recited their lessons in the eighteenth- and nineteenth-century American college were indifferently prepared, only occasionally interested, and given to outbursts that took them altogether out of control. The instructor needed grades and fines and other punishments to keep them in hand.

The problems of discipline became less pressing when the college acquired its modern institutionalized form. The grading system nevertheless retained its importance. The curriculum was divided into blocks of courses, each worth a number of points, and an education was defined by the score that stood to the student's credit in the college accounting system. The grade then became critical, because it was evidence of the amount of learning deposited to his credit.

This pattern has persisted, although few remember what forces brought it into being. Yet no faculty would now maintain that education can be defined by a balance sheet of credits, or that the statistical magic that produces grade scores carried to the second decimal place is a reliable way of evaluating students.

Until recently the system was hardly effective enough to do much harm. A large percentage of the student body could afford to disregard it entirely. After the manner of the lads in Owen Wister's *Philosophy 5*, they looked down on the grinds and occupied themselves in their own ways. And the minority who were interested could study away to their hearts' content without the anxiety of involvement in a mass competition.

All that has now changed. The new students enter after a rigid selective process, they present few disciplinary problems, and they arrive after good and uniform preparation. The constant surveillance of their studies serves no useful function and only interferes with their education.

The trouble is that the students themselves do not know it. This generation has been so thoroughly harnessed to the treadmill of the examination that it accepts its servitude as a normal if strenuous condition of life. All the external pressures of society encourage that belief. Since education has become a national emergency, it is a patriotic duty to do well in algebra. The student who gets an A in physics will not only advance to a successful career in space but will also defend his country against the Russians. The talented boy has replaced the athlete as the school hero, and the letter worth getting is no longer that on the sweater but that on the report card.

The process of subversion begins almost in the first year of the best high schools. The most highly motivated students know that they are engaged in a close race; only the fleetest will enter the desirable colleges. Ahead of them loom the great goals, the College Boards and the National Merit competition. Along the way are the lesser hurdles they must surmount, and their task is to train themselves to score well.

How can their high school education have any other meaning? Admission to college comes generally in the spring of their senior year and is based on performances on tests taken a good deal earlier. Everything that comes later is totally irrelevant. Furthermore, a variety of schemes for early admission and early appraisal have pushed some of the tests back into the middle of the third year of high school. For many students, therefore, almost half of their secondary school career becomes meaningless, since it does not prepare them for the examinations. It is a rare teacher who can resist the tendency to turn his classes into extended cram sessions.

Alas, the young people finally discover that entry into college solves no problems. It only reveals the new hurdles they could not earlier see. True, the place is strange and the conditions of life new, but the race is the same, only the pace is faster. Back in those innocent high school days, these boys and girls were a select group—the brightest and best. Now they are thrown into a mass in which everyone is select and everyone had been brightest and best. In this renewed competition some who had always been winners discover that they too will have to be losers. The cruelty of the contest is clearest in courses which establish grades on the basis of a statistical distribution curve. No matter how hard they work, or how able they are, one half of the class will fall below the average. Each student, therefore, finds himself involved in a struggle with his neighbor, whose success will drag him down.

Any freshman can grasp the point of the explanation for his D on the question in Philosophy H. "No, there was nothing particularly *wrong* with the answer. But everyone else in the section did so well that the classifying apparatus sorted you out toward the lowest of the pigeonholes." He will learn thereafter to crowd his way to the top.

Meanwhile, the goal of college is the same as that of high school—the high score that will open the way to the next stage of competition. Now the students work for the grades that will admit them to the graduate or professional school. The intense haste with which they reach toward what they mistakenly believe to be narrowing opportunities shortens their vision. Tactics become pre-eminently important. These young people work hard, and they shun the snap course "which gets you nowhere." But they tiptoe gingerly through the curriculum, weighing all the angles. One will regularly carry an additional course all year, then at the last possible moment drop that in which the risk is greatest. Another sacrifices each summer vacation, not to shorten his studies, but because instructors are reputed to grow more pliable as the temperature rises. And only the reckless will dare not to know the right answers as the grader expects them, or allow questions to draw their thinking in unexpected directions.

Many students now feel unbearable pressure from their parents. The strain is not consciously applied, but it is none the less real. It is the product of a situation that leads young people to wonder whether their careers in college will jeopardize the love and affection of their parents.

Each family has hopefully groomed its own aspirants for the race. Mom and Dad often have made genuine sacrifices of time and energy to be sure their hopeful was adequately prepared. They must not be disappointed. The boy who does well advances to scholarships and jobs that will immediately have an effect upon the income of the whole family. The one who does not becomes a drag, reducing his father's chances for a new car, his little sister's prospects for an expensive education.

The solicitous letters and the regular telephone calls impress upon the student the fact that it is not he alone who is being tested, but the whole family. How proud they are when the stock rises, how concerned when it falls! The A shows the virtue of the home and school that produced the good performer. The C is not only a blow to the ego of the recipient; it is a reflection upon the adequacy of his training. Unless they rebel entirely, the young people carry to class the anxiety, lest they let down those who had invested in them. So much hangs on the outcome.

The proliferation of rewards has, paradoxically, stimulated this destructive competition. The National Science Foundation and the Woodrow Wilson fellowships have done immense good. But, at the same time, they have put undesirable pressure on the aspirants. Those who make it are free (they think); they see themselves firmly planted on the academic escalator with a regular income, security, and marriage just within reach. The attractiveness of these immediate goals obscures every other consideration.

It is in vain to point out that success in tests is not necessarily the way to achievement, that the careers of great men do not always begin with a ranking in the upper tenth percentile, that places are available, and that there are other than competitive values to education. Their whole experience points in the other direction.

The losses to the students and to society are tremendous. The distorted emphasis nullifies much of what the colleges aim to do.

I speak now not of the reconciled mass who somehow make their peace with the system, but of the ablest, among whom the qualities of excellence might be found. These young people secure an admirable training in the techniques of the correct answer. They learn to remember; to be accurate, neat, and cautious. But they are rarely called on to use their ability autonomously or speculatively, to deal with situations in which the answers are not known but must be discovered.

They cannot afford the sense of the tentativeness of knowledge, of the imperfection of existing formulations. Writing against the clock, they must always put the cross in the right box and round out the essay with an affirmative conclusion. With what pain, if ever at all, will they learn how to know what they do not know, how to probe alone beyond the limits of what is handed to them, how to be creative original thinkers! By the time they carry their diplomas away, they will have missed an education—that experience which, by the exposure of one mind to the thinking of others, creates not answers but a lifetime of questions.

We are all sufferers by the losses sustained by this generation of students. An open society like our own depends in large measure upon the educational system to evaluate those who pass through it and to channel them into the proper places in life. If the colleges fail in the process of selection, the young people with the appropriate talents will not become the doctors and teachers, the diplomats and businessmen, the physicists and engineers they should be. When the pegs do not fit the holes, the structure creaks.

Undue emphasis upon performance measured by college may have precisely that effect. These scores have only a slight predictive value and are unlikely to furnish reliable indications of future achievement. I do not mean that high-ranking students do worse than low-ranking ones. As a group, they do better. But, in the long run, not all A students do as well as they should, and not all do better than all B students; there are enough dramatic reversals of form to raise doubts about excessive reliance upon these standards. Every teacher has seen the slow starter work at his own pace, then suddenly discover himself and outdistance the front-runners.

We organize the boys and girls in classes and treat them as anonymous integers in an elaborate record system. Yet we know that each is an individual different from every other. Each has his own way of learning. To pretend that all can be classified and graded on the identical scale denies those differences and does violence to reality. Above all, it puts a premium on malleability, upon accommodation to existing expectations, upon the qualities of getting along. The good boy is he who matches up to his teachers' previously formed standards. But is he the one likely to grow into the man of achievement?

Unless he learns somehow to locate himself by his own standards, a blast of awareness, in school or later, will blow him off his course. My roommate, said the boy who was my tutee, was good at everything; there was not a blemish on the record at commencement. In his senior year, my roommate took the aptitude tests in business, medicine, and law, did well in all, and as a matter of course entered the law school, having done best in that subject. No doubt he would have been at the head of the pack in that race also, but in an unguarded moment my roommate allowed himself to wonder what being a lawyer would mean to him. He did not know the answer. He did not even know how to go about finding the answer.

In the past, the looseness and inefficiency of the educational system provided the means for rescuing talent in danger of being wasted. The boy whose interests matured late or changed as he grew up could jog along at his own rate and make up for lost time when he was ready. But the more rigid the system becomes, the less room it leaves for the variant patterns of the maverick. The species, indeed, becomes ever less likely to appear, as the habit or desire for nonconformity is stifled. The student totally absorbed in the race loses confidence in himself and accepts the premature rating as a valid measure of his ability. Then the evaluation becomes self-fulfilling. Placidly the young man tells me he would like to be a historian, and will if he earns a *magna*. If he gets only a *cum* he will go into his father's laundry business. Life becomes a play in which the first act determines the outcome of the plot.

As a result, many of the most sensitive youngsters simply throw up their hands. They turn their backs on the whole process and all too often reject all the values attached to the college. They hasten into marriage, seeking in life the reality and personal security school does not afford them. Or they simply refuse to finish; increasingly, the able students are among those who leave before graduation. The stronger or more stubborn ones stick it out for the sheepskin; the weaker or more reflective ones break down or pull out—in either case, a tragic waste of talent. For they were all good when they got to college (otherwise they would not have been admitted), and the failure is not altogether theirs.

There was a boy who had been at Harvard only one year. As a freshman in a smaller college he had done so well, and his high school record had been so good, that he had been encouraged to transfer, and a scholarship had enabled him to do so. After two semesters he was defeated and refused to go on. In the interminable calculation of pluses and minuses, he felt he was in danger of losing sight of what he had come for, and he wished to leave college to be educated. This is the stuff beats are made of. Such people do better to preserve their authenticity as persons by going away or by abstracting themselves from the routine rather than by yielding to the pressures. Yet the college loses by the inability to influence—and be influenced by—them.

She is a junior of about twenty, neat and not bad-looking; nothing distinguishes her in the rows of notetakers in the lecture hall. Now she has found the excuse for a conference in some question about the reading. She talks nervously about what is not on her mind and then blurts out what is. She will not be back to finish next year. She has taken a librarian's job in Georgia, in a small town, where she will be useful. Why? Nothing here seems worth doing; the courses she takes are all right, but she gets only B's in them. She has studied bits of philosophy and bits of government, and she is interested in the relation of ethics to politics. As she talks, life comes back to her voice and the words tumble out fluently. Well, why not go on with the subject next year? It will not make a manageable thesis. It had not occurred to her that one could learn outside the framework of the requirements.

The system favors certain character types over others, and not always the most desirable ones. For the young man who knows when he enters that he will be an actuary or a geologist or a patent attorney, the learning track runs clearly to his destination and all the stations are plainly marked. He will make few mistakes and run few risks. Even if he is not altogether docile, he operates within a limited framework and wastes no time. His schooling is likely to be uneventful; it may also be unadventurous and unimproving.

By contrast, those who come to college without specifically defined goals or who change as they learn are at a competitive disadvantage. They must make choices along the whole route, and therefore face the hazard of mistaken decisions. They are prone to turn into dead ends and to need second chances. Since what is relevant to their needs is not already marked out for them, they may gain more from looking out of the window than from taking notes. Their records will look spotty and erratic. Yet they may be growing at every stage and may, in the end, be the better for their mistakes than their fellows who never faltered. Society may be the loser by the failure to make room for the recovery of such talents. We need not only men who can get the job done, but also those who can wonder why it needs to be done.

Under the pressure of unremitting competition, a valuable sector of the educational enterprise shows signs of contraction. Since the measured blocks and units of formal instruction have clearly defined weight, it is foolhardy to expend precious energies upon activities to which no immediate reward is attached. Those who waste time by the way will lose ground in the race to the "bookers" who concentrate on the assignments. The tendency to shy away from distractions is recent and has not gone far, but it is already ominous.

Not all learning in the college community of the past was confined to the classroom. Often the students taught each other more effectively than the teachers could, gained more from extracurricular activities than from formal classwork. The experience of writing for the paper, or of managing a team, or of singing or playing, and, most of all, the undirected talk that swirled formlessly through the night have a value that cannot be recognized in grades or credits. There will be ever less time for them as the shadow of the examination falls across the college. Boys made rivals by competition will be less ready to help one another, and the immensely variegated activities of the college as it was may dry up.

Finally, the whole process thrusts an uncongenial role upon the instructor. His function as a teacher becomes subsidiary to that of the grader; he is judge rather than counselor, impartial arbiter rather than ally of the student. That, too, distorts the meaning of education. It destroys the intimacy of a relationship in which the older person conceives his role as that of helping the younger, in which the younger can turn to the older for aid and advice without fear of being evaluated in the process.

There is no simple corrective to this disorder, even were its nature clearly perceived. Much of the difficulty springs from the unprecedented demands a democratic society places upon the colleges. We cannot and should not halt the increasing size of student bodies. We need more rather than fewer fellowships. And the college should continue to play a part in career selection. These are conditions of the value we place upon equality of opportunity. Only thus can we locate ability wherever it may be found and compensate for the inequalities of family background. Yet, to the degree that we encourage these desirable trends, our institutions will become more formal, more bureaucratic, and more rigidly organized.

But we need not, in consequence, continue to encumber ourselves with outmoded methods of evaluation which frustrate the larger goals of education. It will be a long, difficult task to get away from them.

I tease myself sometimes with daydreams of how we might break out of the present situation. A few institutions have already separated the teaching and the marking functions. That is as it should be, and the result is to clarify the relationship of the teacher to his students. It would be gratifying to appear in a classroom where everyone was on the same side, where there was not one to police and the others to be policed, but all were to work toward the same end. Evidence points to the merits of a divorce between the essentially incompatible tasks of instructor and grader.

That separation of tasks would, of course, make it impossible to administer examinations and award marks for every segment of instruction. So much the better. No other system of higher education subjects its students to the endlessly badgering tests of the American college. The examinations of French and English universities are difficult, but they come where they belong, at the terminus of a stage in education. And they probe not fragments of courses, but the mastery of a whole field of knowledge, however and whenever acquired. These methods cannot be simply transferred to our own situation. But they indicate that we can safely do without the recurrent, meaningless hurdles we now set in the way of our students. We can aim at a mode of evaluation that will judge the whole man as he leaves the campus, not the bits and pieces of him we glimpse as he passes through it.

Above all, we can take the heat off by leaving these people alone. Most college freshmen are now eighteen years old. They are men and women who are, or should be, above all concerned with discovering themselves. All those prescriptions and requirements, all those efforts at surveillance and discipline, obscure the true nature of their tasks. They must learn after their own fashion, even at the cost of false starts, errors, and lost time. The college can help them, if they wish to be helped, mostly by creating an environment for discovery. The faculty can help them, if they wish to be helped, mostly through establishing the contacts, fruitful when free, of the more, with the less, experienced minds. But the stifling competitive atmosphere of the race for position, which the college itself generates by anachronistic grading methods, has no place in that environment.

Who Judges the Judges?

MORRIS FREEDMAN

One of the most frequently voiced complaints by students is about the grading system, a complaint they have been joined in by a number of prominent educators. Sometimes associated with the complaint about being constantly evaluated by their professors, is the wish to evaluate their professors. It is perhaps not as paradoxical as it seems at first for students, who complain about being judged, to want to judge their judges. In fact, one may well be considered the corollary of the other, for I sense that both come from an impulse to fuzz and blur some of the traditional character of contemporary American education. These two positions often cluster together with several others: disciplines should break down their sharp boundaries; we should have no examinations, or, at most, only final comprehensive ones; discussion should replace lecture.

David Riesman put the matter unequivocally. "Now, I am convinced," he once wrote, "that grades contaminate education—they are a kind of currency, which, like money, gets in the way of students' discovering their intellectual interests." And Oscar Handlin, also a professor at Harvard, in an article in *The Atlantic* entitled "Are the Colleges Killing Education?" put it with equal forcefulness. "The constant surveillance of their studies," he said about students, "serves no useful function and only interferes with their education." Both professors cite instances of how grades and examinations inhibit the educational process rather than aid it.

I confess that I am not only puzzled by the unmodulated way in which Professors Riesman and Handlin put their case, but also by their not seeming to see the issue in the largest possible context, that of all of the workings of a university.

Surely no one will argue that some courses, especially introductory ones but some advanced ones as well, have a fixed body of subject-matter, of concepts, of techniques of analysis, which must be learned before any student

From *Chaos In Our Colleges*, by Morris Freedman. Copyright 1963 by Morris Freedman. New York: David McKay Company, Inc. Used by permission.

can go ahead in that field to do original work. How can a student of mathematics or physics or biology go through a sequence of courses, each of them dependent on the one before, without learning a certain amount of material in each one? A student of history, without some basic foundation in the facts and concepts of historical study? Some fields in their introductory courses leave little room for subjective and imaginative response. The substance of the course must simply be learned up to a minimal level before the student can go on to other things. And how can we determine how much the student learns except by examination, and how can we indicate the level of his attainment except by grades? (Some schools fudge the issues by pretending not to give "grades"; they do not stoop to A's, B's, or F's but grade by such appraisals as "satisfactory," "superior," "adequate," and the like. But these are grades just the same, whatever they are called.)

Obviously, many fields do not have a clear body of subject matter which must be learned; they develop skills in techniques and thought. English and perhaps philosophy are such fields, although both have divisions which call for the student to learn basic material (in English, the history of literature, including dates and contents of works; in philosophy, the history of philosophical thought, including dates and major works; both, of course, also require the student to understand and be able to evaluate the substantive matter of the history). In areas where subjective response is important and encouraged, grades obviously become more uncertain guides of achievement. Students with the gift of gab, or with a faster handwriting, or with a capacity to perform on tests, or with the talent to sense a professor's weakness or personal slant, will do better than equally prepared students without these side skills. In such subjects, as Handlin says, "only the reckless will dare not to know the right answers as the grader expects them, or allow questions to draw their thinking in unexpected directions."

But it is not the subjectivity and uncertainty of grades which so disturb Messrs. Riesman and Handlin; it is the grading system itself, however much it may be refined. It is the competitiveness implicit in the "currency" value of grades that is deplored. Of course, every instructor can cite case after case of the "greasy grind," out to make grades at any cost, including, if necessary, dispensing with actual learning. I can remember classmates of mine who spent much of their time figuring out which professors to take to keep up their grade averages, and then, if they made a mistake, a great deal more time, figuring how to beat the professor at his game. For all they might have learned in such pursuits, this was a learning entirely irrelevant to college. With equal effort, they could just as easily have gotten the material of the course. And we all know students, perfectly able young men and women, cast into despair by not achieving the grades they wanted or deserved.

But I do not see what any of this proves except that an inordinate value has been put on grades; it does not mean that the grading system is in itself wrong. Riesman cites a study at the University of Chicago of the success of students. It was "concluded," he writes, "that those students frequently fared best who were not too obedient, who did not get an undiluted, uncomplicated, straight-A record. (The straight-A students, in fact, sometimes slipped away without anyone's noticing.)" Precisely: sensible academic persons know how to evaluate grades properly. They are only one of several estimates made of a student's potential.

Handlin remarks that "every teacher has seen the slow starter work at his own pace, then suddenly discover himself and out-distance the front-runners." Again: precisely. *Every teacher* of sense and experience makes allowances for all sorts of individual variation: slow starting; incapacity to take objective examinations; over-capacity for taking certain kinds of examination; brilliance that leaps beyond any anticipation; erratic originality that works elliptically and privately and, sometimes, incomprehensibly; steadiness that in itself attains a high level of ordering and understanding. And every teacher of sense and experience takes all such matters into account when evaluating a student, whether by grades or in writing a confidential estimate.

I have been intimately involved in an honors program for the past seven years. About fifteen students meet in a colloquium once a week for two hours with two professors. We all read a book a week, and the students write papers on the books to start the discussion; the papers are intended to help them crystallize their reaction. One semester, we thought that we would not grade the papers, but simply write comments on them. After all, there is no right and wrong in this sort of thing. The students asked after a while to be given grades so that they would have some notion of how relevantly, how cogently, they were reading the books. (These grades sometimes bore only a remote relation to the final one, for the final grade was based on class discussion, and on the highest rather than on the average performance, and was considered as much an estimate of the student's future success in honors as of his current work.) The point is that these students themselves, allowed and encouraged to range freely, felt that the grades gave them one quick measurement. And that's all college grades can ever do.

College proceeds by intervals, by steps of achievement. There can be no other way unless we are ready to advocate a four-year bull session, starting anywhere and ending anywhere, which I know some observers are in favor of. But if we are not ready to go to the peripatetic, free-floating, unstructured arrangement advocated so eloquently by Paul Goodman, we must recognize that the dynamics of college require grades. They help the students themselves make the ascent from one level to another. Grades will always be crude, reductive measures of students, but if they are recognized as such, as I think they are, some of their worst effects will be minimized. Not even Phi Beta Kappa asks for a straight-A average (although its practice of selecting a certain portion of the top members of a class encourages competitiveness). And the very dubious status of Phi Beta Kappa key holders today testifies to the reservations with which grades are widely regarded.

What is needed on the subject of grades, as elsewhere, is a rigorous and open investigation of their significance. The fools in the faculty and in the student body, if they cannot learn through experience the limited meaning of grades, should have some of the point made for them explicitly, if any such even moderately subtle point can penetrate their sometimes willful density. In a sensible environment, grades are used sensibly.

Perhaps equally urgent is a wider recognition that, as Handlin puts it, "not all learning in the college community of the past was confined to the classroom. Often the students taught each other more effectively than the teachers could, gained more from extracurricular activities than from formal classwork." Of course, but we cannot pretend that the classroom with all of its exigencies is really being replaced, or that we can hope to know in any practical way, for the purposes of helping a student move properly through college, just what value extra-curricular activities actually have. That value is the student's private choice and affair; it is supplementary to that of the classroom: otherwise, why bother with class at all? Why not, as indeed some students (and some faculty too) do, simply specialize in extra-curricular affairs? I do not share Professor Handlin's concern that "there will be ever less time for [students to participate in extra-curricular affairs] as the shadow of the examination falls across the college. Boys made rivals by competition will be less ready to help one another, and the immensely variegated activities of the college as it was may dry up." Campus life outside the classroom, for one thing, is likely to be far more competitive and demanding, and less fairly so, than in the classroom; for another, it is the classroom that has to fear the student union, not the union the classroom.

With students, the objection to grades has often seemed to me an objection to discipline of any sort. Why should they have to know a fixed body of material? Why, if they want to be literary critics, should they have to read, say, Dryden's criticism, or that of Wordsworth and Coleridge? Can't they work on Faulkner or Hemingway without going through all the nonsense of the past? Why can't they be original in philosophy, sociology, history, government classes? Haven't they eyes and ears, haven't they seen and heard enough to talk about anything? Why must they be subjected to endless scrutiny? They've done their reading and their thinking; why can't professors believe them? Why the constant challenge, the demand for proof, the endless measuring? Why do they have to do just what everyone else is told? Doesn't originality count as well as conformity and neatness?

These all seem like plausible challenges, and sometimes they are honest and reasonable as well. I have had students who have asked whether they might not try writing sonnets in an English class rather than doing the more conventional assignments. They have turned in interesting efforts, revealing clearly that they have wrestled with the form and have learned to understand something of the energy and labor that goes into creative work. But others have told me that they are writing a novel "in their heads," and that the work will be great. Some have developed the high art of student gamesmanship to dupe the most skeptical instructor. One bohemian type, who talked and gestured a remarkably impressive game of intimacy with modern poetry, impressing her fellows and some professors, turned out—when she was finally cornered into taking an examination, consisting of both objective and essay questions—to be both ignorant and illiterate—although not stupid.

Students often tend to rate their instructors, I think unconsciously, on how well they can con them. The instructor who can be carried away by student enthusiasms is considered "responsive" to student needs and capacities. A favorite ploy of the *luft*-student, the student who lives on air, is to divert class discussion into intriguing side roads. The instructor who generally goes along on these excursions, responding to student "interest," is much admired, especially if his examinations then proceed to examine the side issues, or if he gives no examinations, or if he gives all students high grades for "class participation."

Not all students, of course, who wish to be involved in faculty evaluation are of this sort. Many outstanding students, indeed, feel that some of their professors simply are incompetent, and they are quite likely to know this better than colleagues or administrators. But the impulse toward asking for student participation in tenure or promotion decisions of faculty comes, I think, from a fundamental wish to make over the character of college education in the direction of the continuous bull session. In part, I say this because those instances I have seen of students pressuring to have their opinions on faculty performance given heed have involved professors who have been grand discussion leaders but who, sometimes by their own admission, did not bother to cover a subject matter, or, more importantly, to be active in their chosen field, keeping up with current work, as evidenced by publication or other sorts of productivity. In larger part, however, I say this because of the philosophical and practical implications of student evaluation of faculty.

Some work has been done to show that student evaluation can be carried out effectively and meaningfully, and I am ready to stipulate that our advances in the area of all such measurements of opinion and appraisal have been so considerable that a proper evaluation would indeed reveal something of a professor's competence in the classroom. But how would such an evaluation be used? I have known professors who have used self-evaluation measures (some of them very crude ones, it is true, and some administered before final grades were assigned) simply to broadcast how high they rated; such persons had no other claim to advancement. Any system of showing evaluations only to the professors, for their own private benefit, breaks down as soon as one professor starts publicizing good results. This would be like a secret ballot in a small group in which the participants start announcing their votes; there's no way of checking, and others, more reticent, have their privacy violated.

Should an administration use such evaluation even in part to advance or to hold back a man? (I am assuming that all sorts of halo effects—the upgrading of a professor who gives high marks; the downgrading of one who gives low; etc.—have been effectively eliminated or controlled.) I think not. The value of a student estimate of a professor implies that a student can truly know how good a professor is. This seems to me a dubious proposition, at least at this stage in our knowledge of the classroom process. No matter how impeccable and extensive any measurement, it cannot tell how deeply a professor has penetrated into a student's consciousness. If, as Handlin says, we cannot say how much a student learns *outside* the classroom, how can we tell how much he learns *inside* the classroom? The student may think he has learned so much; the professor may even think he knows, roughly, how much each student has learned. But learning does not stop with the final examination. It may go on for years. An attitude of mind may be instilled which will not reach full fruition until the student has gone into the world and been there for a good period. I still respond, sometimes with a start, to things which first implanted themselves in undergraduate, let alone graduate classes. I think I may be closer now to estimating truly the effectiveness of some of my teachers, but, precisely because I am still learning from them (sometimes even negatively, as I reject some of their teaching), I would hesitate to fix an evaluation.

Now, I am not dismissing the usefulness of student evaluations, if these are devised so as to be more than popularity contests, and if they are not used by administrators as the sole criterion for a total evaluation. (I have heard of one college president who threw away all other considerations in granting tenure or salary increases or promotion, and relied entirely on a ballot of professor popularity conducted by the fraternities and sororities.) But a fair and "safe" evaluating tool, judiciously applied, may finally not offer much more evidence than is already available and may simply be too costly, in time and money, to be worth the effort. I think there are few campuses where everyone does not know who are the best and the worst teachers. And within our present system of electives and multiple section courses, students indicate their sense of good and bad teaching, a sense not wholly determined by grades or entertainment alone. (Of course, it is important for natural selection to operate that a required course, wherever possible, not be taught as a monopoly by only one person.)

Time and again the suggestion is made that the traditional curriculum ought to be revised. It is said that division of English and history courses into chronological periods or into types, or of sociology and philosophy courses into discrete areas, or of mathematics and physics into a fixed sequence, fragments learning into artificial little units, de-emphasizes the interconnectedness of a discipline, and of one discipline with another, and leads to a compartmentalization that stresses specialization to the detriment of over-all comprehension. It is true that a professor teaching the 17th century in English literature may well not be as intimately informed about the 18th as he should be, and that the specialist in European medieval history may be hazy about contemporary Latin American history. It is true that it is important for student and teacher in any field to have an over-all sense of his subject. But I am not sure that what follows is that we should jumble all our courses together.

My impression is that student and faculty "generalists" usually do not want to root themselves anywhere. They prefer to "specialize" in "things in general." Although they argue that the person who works in a larger area understands and knows more than the one who absorbs only a small one, the fact is that it is sometimes easier to talk about all history than about the history of a particular country at a particular time. The "appreciation" of history, like that of science, or of literature, or of art, is much easier to teach and to learn than is 18th century French history, or zoology, or the drama of the Restoration, or the techniques and theories of post-Impressionist painters. It is important to have large integrating courses that cut across all areas, that provide a large perspective, but only as a supplement to the traditional curriculum (which, of course, should always be subject to revision as new arrangements suggest themselves). A college devoted to things in general is finally devoted to nothing at all.

Associated with an objection to grades and the traditional curriculum is an objection to examinations. Students and faculty feel superior to the housekeeping drudgery of tests. Handlin puts this association neatly. "I tease myself sometimes," he writes, "with daydreams of how we might break out of the present situation. A few institutions have already separated the teaching and marking functions. That is as it should be, and the result is to clarify the relationship of the teacher to his students. It would be gratifying to appear in a classroom where everyone was on the same side, where there was not one to police and the others to be policed, but all were to work toward the same end. Evidence points to the merits of a divorce between the essentially incompatible tasks of instructor and grader. . . . No other system of higher education subjects its students to the endlessly badgering tests of the American college. The examinations of French and English universities are difficult, but they come where they belong, at the terminus of a stage in education. And they probe not fragments of courses, but the mastery of a whole field of knowledge, however and whenever acquired."

If Handlin really believes that examinations are *only* a form of policing, it seems to me that he altogether misconceives the intent and use of examinations. Examinations are one of the simplest ways for students to make order out of their learning; they are one of the simplest ways for an instructor to relate the learning in his classroom to his teaching. They are essential, I submit, to the teaching-learning dialogue. Students need to pause and to sort out, systematize, arrange, absorb what has been going on, not only in the classroom, but in the library and in their own discussions; frequently serious students want examinations to help them in their learning. Now, of course, examinations on different levels will have to differ as to purpose; in freshman English courses, for example, examinations may well be a form of policing, usually just to see that the brainwashing of high school misinformation is effective. But on higher levels, examinations have nothing to do with policing at all. For example, in junior, senior, and graduate courses, examinations are simply another teaching and learning aid. Too many tests are certainly a nuisance to teacher and student, but none at all will work all sorts of questionable pedagogic results: students will not keep up with the continuing work of the class, leaving it for the last minute; some few students, even when they keep up, will not really understand the work; the class will tend to descend (or ascend, I suppose) to vague discussions around the material of the course instead of engaging with the material itself. I would be delighted to have someone else mark my students, and, indeed, in introductory courses assistants have become widely available. In advanced work, however, it seems to me essential for an instructor, especially if he has larger classes, or if he lectures more than he conducts discussion, to have examinations as a way of determining how well he is communicating. Otherwise he may simply be talking to himself.

The French and English systems Handlin cites, also practiced in some places in this country (the graduate English department at Columbia, for example), have their own pitfalls. Some French and English students, particularly those who have gone through a disciplined and rigorous tutorial system beforehand, certainly produce meaningful results on such examinations. But many, skilled in testmanship and other forms of gamesmanship, use the European system merely to attain a gloss of learning, a veneer that becomes transparent when they have to deal with substance. I have known both sorts of European scholars, and the latter, while not common, suggests that the system is not without its defects. A European mathematician once confided that the system indeed encourages frauds. In the American system, someone who skims the surface of his discipline, learning to drop names of books, learning to indicate by a shrug or the raising of an eyebrow an intimacy with his subject matter that it would be vulgar to challenge, will come a cropper long before graduation if he has to take examinations along the way. At Columbia, the oral examination in English was a terrifying ordeal, traumatic and disturbing to many students, and not always the best measurement of a student's learning. No doubt the system spared the professors from the regular and tedious chore of reading periodic examinations, leaving them free to do other work, but fakers got through, the timid dropped out of school altogether (and timidity is not a reliable counter-indication for college teaching), and the experience left every candidate in some state of shock. (I must confess that, all in all, I would not change the Columbia system but simply suggest that the examination be made less catastrophic, less like the final day of judgment; I understand that improvement has taken place in recent years.)

The challenge to grading, the theory that students ought to evaluate faculty, the wish to replace the present subject and area oriented curriculum, the objection to examinations, seem to me to have at their source a misconception of the student role in college. The misconception is by no means limited to students; indeed, it may have been voiced first by professors, and it is certainly encouraged by many professors and some administrations. It has to do with conceiving of college as a world in which students are supposed *primarily* to grow up. Any learning they do is thought of as incidental, sometimes indeed (especially when examinations and grading systems are objected to) as interfering with the maturing process. Many professors when asked what they think their function is answer that it is to help students learn to think and to grow up. Few are so "old-fashioned"—or so daring—as to say "to teach" and to see that the students learn. Students, when justifying a frenetic, time and energy consuming extra-curricular life, explain that they are learning to live with the problems of the real world.

No question that life adjustment, growing up, are important processes, and, for college students, they obviously must take place on a campus. Every professor, administrator, and student should realize this. But these are extra-classroom problems, they are complementary but subordinate to the classroom process. Too many teachers take their role as surrogate parent too intensely, with sometimes uncomfortable and unhappy consequences. The teacher who is always conferring with and advising students, helping them "grow up," will not only be neglecting his first responsibility as a teacher and scholar, but will also probably not be helping the student much, for he is likely to be an amateur at any sort of counseling. Of course, on campuses without a guidance service—psychiatrists, psychologists, social workers—professors will often have to do double duty, and on any campus, there will be professors with whom students have an especially sensitive rapport. Professors—like students—are human, and situations will always arise, naturally and wholesomely, in which one person tries to help another.

But the question is one of emphasis, of orientation. Some studies of student societies make the campus seem like one huge group therapy laboratory. Classrooms are smaller units to practice group dynamics (or group therapy). Conferences are like psychoanalytic sessions. Students have to be patted on the head, held by the hand, bottle-fed (some of the campuses specializing in this big brother relationship have nearby bars, where afternoon beer sessions are popular places for carrying on this uplifting group work). And I would say that to the extent that any of this activity, however excessive and seemingly irrelevant, contributes to an intensification of genuine intellectual activity, it is justified. Much of it, of course, not only does not contribute; it interferes.

The boom in student sociology comes from outside the classroom, from personnel deans, from administrators. As I indicated earlier, it was a natural enough development as student society increased in numbers, as self-appraisal became necessary for universities growing and meeting new needs. And I think there is no doubt that when professors become aware of the buzzing, booming, swirling world of students, they cannot but be affected in their teaching. Too few professors, of course, do become aware of their students as persons; in fact, too few become aware of any of the huge amount of research done right under their noses about students. More should certainly know of the separate society that surrounds them.

But the student sociologists should not distort the landscape which they are examining. The culture they study has more than one center of activity; the only reason that students are on campus in the first place is to go to class. It is the classroom which defines a student. (I use classroom in the wide sense, to include any teaching-learning situation.) A student without a classroom has no identity as a student.

Questions

1. How do Handlin and Freedman differ on the question of the importance of grades? Would learning improve if grades were abolished?
2. Ought students be allowed to express formally their opinions on whether teachers are doing a good job? How valid is the argument that students may not know how well a teacher teaches? Would rating scales of teachers help poor teachers?
3. Where does a student learn the most important things while in college? In class? In his social life? In the dormitory? In the library? Justify your answer.
4. What is the most important thing you expect college to do for you?
5. In college, is competition truly competition? What would you replace competition with?
6. What is a "slow starter"? An "early bloomer"? A "late bloomer"? What are you? Explain.
7. To what extent should students themselves be allowed to choose freely the courses they would like to take? Should all courses be electives?
8. What is an important difference between college students and the young people discussed in part III, 2.
9. Where and how do students spend most of their public extracurricular time on your campus? Why?

Assignments

1. Write your own report on the mood of the students today. Quote or paraphrase the material in this section as appropriate. When quoting or paraphrasing material for your report (and for other papers suggested in this anthology), be sure to acknowledge your source by documenting it carefully. For examples of proper documentation, you should consult *The MLA Style Sheet*, compiled by William Riley Parker (New York, 1951), or a good handbook of English.
2. Make up a questionnaire to give to about a half dozen of your fellow students on the following matters: religious belief, political belief, attitude toward grades, vocational ambition, and attitude toward visits in dormitories by persons of the opposite sex. Analyze the results of your questionnaire.

3. In an essay of not more than 1,000 words, relate the mood of student life today to the discussions of the lives and the activities of the young people in part III, 2.

Additional Reading

An enormous number of books and studies on the college student has been issued in recent years. Many of them are technical, with a pronounced sociological slant. Few campus libraries are without a full collection of these works. Perhaps the most provocative general books, however, are David Riesman's and Paul Goodman's. Riesman's comments on college students may be found, with other selections, in his book *Individualism Reconsidered* (Glencoe, Illinois, 1954). Goodman's comments have appeared in many magazine articles, which may be located through the usual periodical indexes; and some of these articles have been collected in his book *Growing Up Absurd* (New York, 1960). Worth looking at too is Ernest Havemann and Patricia Salter West, *They Went to College* (New York, 1952), which is essentially a statistical study with interesting, often provocative, analysis.

The student disturbances in 1964 at the University of California's Berkeley campus evoked a number of interesting articles relevant to the topic of this section. Among those reporting the events at Berkeley from the perspective of administration and faculty were Lewis S. Feuer, "Rebellion at Berkeley," *New Leader*, XLVII (December 21, 1964), 3–12; Sidney Hook, "Freedom to Learn But Not to Riot," *New York Times Magazine*, January 3, 1965, pp. 8–9 ff.; and Nathan Glazer, "What Happened at Berkeley," *Commentary*, XXXIX (February 1965), 39–47. Among those reporting from the students' perspective were Paul Jacobs, "Dr. Feuer's Distortions," and Stephen Weissman, "What the Students Want" (and a reply from Feuer), *New Leader*, XLVIII (January 4, 1965), 9–17; and Paul Goodman, "Thoughts on Berkeley," *New York Review of Books*, III (January 14, 1965), 5–6. A less partisan survey of the Berkeley events is A. H. Raskin, "The Berkeley Affair: Mr. Kerr vs. Mr. Savio & Co.," *New York Times Magazine*, February 14, 1965, pp. 24–25 ff. Some exchanges, involving observers and principals, are Clark Kerr, "For the Record," and Lewis S. Feuer, "Inevitability and Institutes," *New Leader*, XLVIII (January 18, 1965), 8–10; and Paul Goodman and Nathan Glazer, "Berkeley: An Exchange," *New York Review of Books*, IV (February 11, 1965), 22–23. Issues of journals appearing after ones cited usually carried correspondence commenting on the articles. Clark Kerr, *The Uses of the University* (Cambridge, 1964), is also relevant to many of the issues raised at Berkeley.

II
Arts and Humanities

SECTION ONE | Dictionary: Pre- or De-scriber

The String Untuned

DWIGHT MACDONALD

The third edition of Webster's New International Dictionary (Unabridged), which was published last fall by the G. & C. Merriam Co., of Springfield, Massachusetts, tells us a good deal about the changes in our cultural climate since the second edition appeared, in 1934. The most important difference between Webster's Second (hereafter called 2) and Webster's Third (or 3) is that 3 has accepted as standard English a great many words and expressions to which 2 attached warning labels: *slang, colloquial, erroneous, incorrect, illiterate.* My impression is that most of the words so labelled in the 1934 edition are accepted in the 1961 edition as perfectly normal, honest, respectable citizens. Between these dates in this country a revolution has taken place in the study of English grammar and usage, a revolution that probably represents an advance in scientific method but that certainly has had an unfortunate effect on such nonscientific activities as the teaching of English and the making of dictionaries—at least on the making of this particular dictionary. This scientific revolution has meshed gears with a trend toward permissiveness, in the name of democracy, that is debasing our language by rendering it less precise and thus less effective as literature and less efficient as communication. It is felt that it is snobbish to insist on making discriminations—the very word has acquired a Jim Crow flavor—about usage. And it is assumed that true democracy means that the majority is right. This feeling seems to me sentimental and this assumption unfounded.

There have been other recent dictionaries calling themselves "unabridged," but they are to Webster's 3 as a welterweight is to a heavyweight. 3 is a massive folio volume (thirteen inches by nine and a half by four) that weighs thirteen and a half pounds, contains four hundred and fifty thousand entries—an "entry" is a word plus its definition—in 2,662 pages, cost three and a half million dollars to produce, and sells for $47.50 up, according to binding. The least comparable dictionary now in print is the New Webster's Vest Pocket Dictionary, which bears on its title page the charmingly frank notation, "This dictionary is not published by the original publishers of Webster's Dictionary or by their successors." It measures five and a half inches by two and a half by a half, weighs two and a quarter ounces, has two hundred and thirty-nine pages, and costs thirty-nine cents. The only English dictionary now in print that *is* comparable to 3 is the great Oxford English Dictionary, a unique masterpiece of historical research that is as important in the study of the language as the King James Bible has been in the use of the language. The O.E.D. is much bigger than 3, containing sixteen thousand four hundred pages in thirteen folio volumes. It is bigger because its purpose is historical as well as definitive; it traces the evolution of each word through the centuries, illustrating the changes in meaning with dated quotations. The latest revision of the O.E.D. appeared in 1933, a year before Webster's 2 appeared. For the language as it has developed in the last quarter of a century, there is no dictionary comparable in scope to 3.

The editor of 2, Dr. William A. Neilson, president of Smith College, followed lexical practice that had obtained since Dr. Johnson's day and assumed there was such a thing as correct English and that it was his job to decide what it was. When he felt he had to include a sub-standard word because of its common use, he put it in, but with a warning label: *Slang, Dial.*, or even bluntly *Illit.* His approach was normative and his dictionary was an authority that pronounced on which words were standard English and which were not. Bets were decided by "looking it up in the dictionary." It would be hard to decide bets by appealing to 3, whose editor of fifteen years' standing, Dr. Philip Gove, while as dedicated a scholar as Dr. Neilson, has a quite different approach. A dictionary, he writes, "should have no traffic with . . . artificial notions of correctness or superiority. It must be descriptive and not prescriptive." Dr. Gove and the other makers of 3 are sympathetic to the school of language study that has become dominant since 1934. It is sometimes called Structural Linguistics and sometimes, rather magnificently, just Modern Linguistic Science. Dr. Gove gives its basic concepts as:

1. Language changes constantly.
2. Change is normal.
3. Spoken language is the language.
4. Correctness rests upon usage.
5. All usage is relative.

While one must sympathize with the counterattack the Structural Linguists have led against the tyranny of the schoolmarms and the purists, who have caused unnecessary suffering to generations of schoolchildren over such matters as *shall* v. *will* and the *who-whom* syndrome—someone has observed that the chief result of the long crusade against "It's me" is that most Americans now say "Between you and I"—it is remarkable what strange effects have been produced in 3 by following Dr. Gove's five little precepts, reasonable as each seems taken separately. Dr. Gove conceives of his dictionary as a recording instrument rather than as an authority; in fact, the whole idea of authority or correctness is repulsive to him as a lexical scientist. The question is, however, whether a purely scientific approach to dictionary-making may not result in greater evils than those it seeks to cure.

When one compares 2 and 3, the first difference that strikes one is that 2 is a work of traditional scholarship and hence oriented toward the past, while 3—though in many ways more scholarly, or at least more academic, than 2—exhales the breezy air of the present. This is hardly surprising, since the new school of linguistics is non-historical, if not anti-historical. Henry Luce's *Time* rather than Joseph Addison's *Spectator* was the hunting ground for 3's illustrative quotations. There is a four-and-a-half-page list of consultants. Its sheer bulk is impressive—until one begins to investigate. One can see why James W. Perry had to be consulted on Non-numerical Computer Applications and Margaret Fulford on Mosses and Liverworts, but it seems overdoing it to have *two* consultants on both Hardware and Salvation Army, and some people might even question the one apiece on Soft Drinks, Boy Scouts, Camp Fire Girls, and Girl Guiding, as well as the enrolling of Mr. Arthur B. LaFar, formerly president of the Angostura-Wuppermann bitters company, as consultant on Cocktails. Such padding is all the more odd, considering that the editors of 3 have forgotten to appoint anybody in Philosophy, Political Theory, or Theatre. The old-fashioned 2 had six consultants on Catholic Church and Protestant Churches. 3 has only one, on Catholic Church. But it also has one on Christian Science, a more up-to-date religion.

The G. & C. Merriam Co. has been publishing Webster's dictionaries since 1847, four years after Noah Webster died. Work on 3 began the day 2 went to press, but it gathered real momentum only fifteen years ago, when Dr. Gove began building up his staff of lexicographers. The first step was to sort out the words of 2 into a hundred and nine categories, so that specialized-definition writers could deal with them. It took five women two and a half years to do this. (" 'If seven maids with seven mops swept it for half a year, Do you suppose,' the Walrus said, 'That they could get it clear?' "—*Lewis Carroll*.) After that, all that had to be done was to write new definitions for most of the three hundred and fifty thousand entries that were taken over from 2, to select and write a hundred thousand new entries, to collect four and a half million quotations illustrating word usage, and to distribute them among the definition writers. The scope of the operation may be suggested by the fact that in chemistry alone the lexicographers gathered two hundred and fifty thousand quotations and took six and a half years to write the definitions. After that, it was up to the Lakeside Press, of Chicago, to set type from a manuscript that was as bristling with revisions and interlineations, mostly in longhand, as a Proust manuscript. At first they gave the printers clean, retyped copy, but they soon found that the extra step produced an extra crop of errors. The printing was done by the Riverside Press, of Cambridge, Massachusetts, a long-established firm, like Merriam, whose dictionaries it has been printing for almost a century. But antiquity is relative. There is no one at Riverside like the compositor at Oxford's Clarendon Press who began setting type for the O.E.D. in 1884 and was still at it when the last volume came off the presses in 1928.

In seeking out and including all the commonly used words, especially slang ones, the compilers of 3 have been admirably diligent. Their definitions, in the case of meanings that have arisen since 1900 or so, are usually superior (though, because of the tiny amount of a dictionary it is possible to read before vertigo sets in, all generalizations must be understood to be strictly impressionistic). They have also provided many more quotations (this is connected with the linguistic revolution), perhaps, indeed, too many more. It is quite true, as the promotional material for 3 claims, that this edition goes far beyond what is generally understood by the term "revision" and may honestly be termed a new dictionary. But I should advise the possessors of the 1934 edition to think carefully before they turn it in for the new model. Although the publishers have not yet destroyed the plates of 2, they do not plan to keep it in print, which is a pity. There are reasons, which will presently appear, that buyers should be given a choice between 2 and 3, and that, in the case of libraries and schools, 3 should be regarded as an up-to-date supplement to 2 rather than a replacement of it.

Quantitative comparison between 2 and 3 must be approached cautiously. On the surface, it is considerably in 2's favor: 3,194 pages v. 2,662. But although 2 has six hundred thousand entries to 3's four hundred and fifty thousand, its entries are shorter; and because 3's typography is more compact and its type page larger, it gets in almost as much text as 2. The actual number of entries dropped since 2 is not a hundred and fifty thousand but two hundred and fifty thousand, since a hundred thousand new ones have been added. This incredible massacre—almost half the words in the English language seem to have disappeared between 1934 and 1961—is in fact incredible. For the most part, the dropped entries fall into very special categories that have less to do with the language than with methods of lexicography. They are: variants; "nonce words," like *Shakespearolatry* ("excessive reverence or devotion to Shakespeare"), which seemed a good idea at the time, or for the nonce, but haven't caught on; a vast number of proper names, including nearly every one in both the King James and the Douay Bibles; foreign terms; and obsolete or archaic words. This last category is a large one, since 2 includes "all the literary and most of the technical and scientific words and meanings in the period of Modern English beginning with the year 1500," plus all the words in Chaucer, while 3, in line with its modernization program, has advanced the cut-off date to 1755. A great many, perhaps most, of the entries dropped from 2 were in a section of small type at the foot of each page, a sort of linguistic ghetto, in which the editors simply listed "fringe words"—the definitions being limited to a synonym or often merely a symbol—which they thought not important enough to put into the main text. 3 has either promoted them to the text or, more frequently, junked them.

Some examples of the kinds of words that are in 2 but not in 3 are: *arrousement, aswowe* (in a swoon), *dethronize, devoration* (act of devouring), *disagreeance, mummianize* (mummify), *noyous* (annoying), *punquetto* (strumpet), *ridiculize,* and *subsign* (subscribe). Two foreign words that one might expect to find in 3 were left out because of insufficient "backing"; i.e., the compilers didn't find enough usages to justify inclusion. They were *Achtung* and *niet;* the researchers must have skipped spy movies and Molotovian diplomacy. *Pot holder* was left out, after considerable tergiversating, because (a) for some reason the compilers found little backing for it, and (b) it was held to be self-explanatory (though considering some of the words they put in . . .). If it had been considered to be a single word, it would have been admitted, since one rule they followed was: No word written solid is self-explanatory.

The hundred thousand new entries in 3 are partly scientific or technical terms, partly words that have come into general use since 1934. The sheer quantity of the latter is impressive. English is clearly a living, growing language, and in this portion of their task the compilers of 3 have done an excellent job. Merriam-Webster has compiled some interesting lists of words in 3 that are not in 2.

Some of the political ones are:

character assassination	loyalty oath
desegregation	McCarthyism
freedom of speech	segregated
globalize	red-baiting
hatemonger	shoo-in
integrationist	sit-in
welfare capitalism	subsistence economy

Among the new entries in the cocktail-party area are:

club soda	name-dropping
elbow bending	pub crawler
gate-crasher	quick one
glad-hander	rumpot
good-time Charlie	silent treatment
Irish coffee	table-hop
jungle juice	yakety-yak

The most important new aspect of 3, the rock on which it has been erected, is the hundred thousand illustrative quotations—known professionally as "citations" or "cites"—drawn from fourteen thousand writers and publications. (Another hundred thousand "usage examples" were made up by the compilers.) Most of the cites are from living writers or speakers, ranging from Winston Churchill, Edith Sitwell, Jacques Maritain, J. Robert Oppenheimer, and Albert Schweitzer to Billy Rose, Ethel Merman, James Cagney, Burl Ives, and Ted Williams. Many are from publications, extending from the Dictionary of American Biography down to college catalogues, fashion magazines, and the annual report of the J. C. Penney Company. The hundred thousand cites were chosen from a collection of over six million, of which a million and a half were already in the Merriam-Webster files; four and a half million were garnered by Dr. Gove and his staff. (The O.E.D. had about the same number of cites in its files—drawn mostly from English literary classics—but used a much larger proportion of them, almost two million, which is why it is five or six times as long as 3.) For years everybody in the office did up to three hours of reading a day—the most, it was found, that was possible without attention lag. Dr. Gove presently discovered a curious defect in this method: the readers tended to overlook the main meanings of a word and concentrate on the peripheral ones; thus a hundred and fifty cite slips were turned in for *bump* as in burlesque stripping but not one for *bump* as in a road. To compensate for this, he created a humbler task force, whose job it was to go through the gutted carcasses of books and magazines after the first group had finished with them and arbitrarily enter on a slip one word—plus its context—in the first sentence in the fourth line from the top of each surviving page. The percentage of useful slips culled by this method approximated the percentage of useful slips made out by the readers who had used their brains. Unsettling.

The cites in 2 are almost all from standard authors. Its cite on *jocund* is from Shakespeare; 3's is from Elinor Wylie. Under *ghastly* 2 has cites from Gray (two), Milton (three), Poe, Wordsworth, Shakespeare, Shelley, Hawthorne, and—as a slight concession to modernity—Maurice Hewlett. 3 illustrates *ghastly* with cites from Louis Bromfield, Macaulay, Thackeray, Thomas Herbert, Aldous Huxley, H. J. Laski, D. B. Chidsey, and J. C. Powys. For *debonair,* 2 has Milton's "buxom, blithe and debonair," while 3 has H. M. Reynolds' "gay, brisk and debonair." One may think, as I do, that 3 has dropped far too many of the old writers, that it has overemphasized its duty of recording the current state of the language and skimped its duty of recording the past that is still alive (Mr. Reynolds would hardly have arrived at his threesome had not Mr. Milton been there before). A decent compromise would have been to include both, but the editors of 3 don't go in for compromises. They seem imperfectly aware of the fact that the past of a language is part of its present, that tradition is as much a fact as the violation of tradition.

The editors of 3 have labored heroically on pronunciation, since one of the basic principles of the new linguistic doctrine is that Language is Speech. Too heroically, indeed. For here, as in other aspects of their labors, the editors have displayed more valor than discretion. Sometimes they appear to be lacking in common sense. The editors of 2 found it necessary to give only two pronunciations for *berserk* and two for *lingerie,* but 3 seems to give twenty-five for the first and twenty-six for the second. (This is a rough estimate; the system of notation is very complex. Dr. Gove's pronunciation editor thinks there are approximately that number but says that he is unable to take the time to be entirely certain.) Granted that 2 may have shirked its duty, one may still find something compulsive in the amplitude with which 3 has fulfilled its obligations. Does anybody except a Structural Linguist need to know that much? And what use is such plethora to a reader who wants to know how to pronounce a word? The new list of pronunciation symbols in 3 is slightly shorter than the one in 2 but also—perhaps for that reason—harder to understand. 2 uses only those nice old familiar letters of the alphabet, with signs over them to indicate long and short and so on. (It also repeats its pronunciation guide at the foot of each page, which is handy; 3 does not, to save space and dollars, so one has to flop over as much as thirteen and a half pounds of printed matter to refer back to the one place the guide appears.) 3 also uses the alphabet, but there is one catastrophic exception. This is an upside-down "e," known in the trade as a "schwa," which stands for a faint, indistinct sound, like the "e" in *quiet,* that is unnervingly common and that can be either "a," "e," "i," "o," or "u," according to circumstance. Things get quite lively when you trip over a schwa. *Bird* is given straight as *bûrd* in 2, but in 3 it is *bərd, bɜd,* and *bəid.* This last may be *boid,* but I'm not sure. Schwa trouble. ("Double, double schwa and trouble."—*Shakespeare.*)

Almost all 3's pictures are new or have been redrawn in a style that is superior to 2's—clearer and more diagrammatic. The new cut of "goose," with no less than twenty-four parts clearly marked, is a special triumph. The other animal illustrations, from *aardvark* to *zebu,* are less picturesque but more informative than those in 2. The illustrations are—rightly—chosen for utility rather than ornament. On facing pages we have pictures of *coracles, corbel,* and *corbiesteps,* all definitely needed, though, on another, *pail* might have been left to the imagination. One of the few illustrations repeated from 2 is *digestive organs,* and a fine bit of uncompromising realism it is, too.

I notice no important omissions in 3. *Namby-pamby* is in. However, it was coined—to describe the eighteenth-century Ambrose Philips' insipid verses—not "by some satirists of his time" but by just one of them, Henry Carey, whose celebrated parody of Philips is entitled "Namby-Pamby." *Bromide* is in ("a conventional and commonplace or tiresome person"), but not the fact that Gelett Burgess invented it. Still, he gets credit for *blurb* and *goop. Abstract expressionism* is in, but *Tachism* and *action painting* are not. The entries on Marxist and Freudian terms are skimpy. *Id* is in, but without citations and with too brief a definition. *Ego* is defined as Fichte, Kant, and Hume used it but not as Freud did. The distinction between *unconscious* and *subconscious* is muffed; the first is adequately defined and the reader is referred to the latter; looking that up, he finds "The mental activities just below the threshold of consciousness; *also:* the aspect of the mind concerned with such activities that is an entity or a part of the mental apparatus overlapping, equivalent to, or distinct from the unconscious." I can't grasp the nature of something that is overlapping, equivalent to, *or* distinct from something else. While *dialectical materialism* and *charisma* (which 2 treats only as a theological term, although Max Weber had made the word common sociological currency long before 1934) are in, there is no *mass culture,* and the full entry for the noun *masses* is "pl. of mass." There is no reference to Marx or even to Hegel under *reify,* and under *alienation* the closest 3 comes to this important concept of Marxist theory is "the state of being alienated or diverted from normal function," which is illustrated by "alienation of muscle." Marx is not mentioned in the very brief definition of *class struggle.*

The definitions seem admirably objective. I detected only one major lapse:

> McCarthyism—a political attitude of the mid-twentieth century closely allied to know-nothingism and characterized chiefly by opposition to elements held to be subversive and by the use of tactics involving personal attacks on individuals by means of widely publicized indiscriminate allegations esp. on the basis of unsubstantiated charges.

I fancy the formulator of this permitted himself a small, dry smile as he leaned back from his typewriter before trudging on to *McClellan saddle* and *McCoy* (the real). I'm not complaining, but I can't help remembering that the eponymous hero of *McCarthyism* wrote a little book with that title in which he gave a rather different definition. The tendentious treatment of *McCarthyism* contrasts with the objectivity of the definition of *Stalinism,* which some of us consider an even more reprehensible *ism:* "The political, economic and social principles and policies associated with Stalin; *esp:* the theory and practice of communism developed by Stalin from Marxism-Leninism." The first part seems to me inadequate and the second absurd, since Stalin never had a theory in his life. The definitions of *democratic* and *republican* seem fair: "policies of broad social reform and internationalism in foreign affairs" v. "usu. associated with business, financial, and some agricultural interests and with favoring a restricted governmental role in social and economic life." Though I wonder what the Republican National Committee thinks.

One of the most painful decisions unabridgers face is what to do about those obscene words that used to be wholly confined to informal discourse but that of late, after a series of favorable court decisions, have been cropping up in respectable print. The editors of 2, being gentlemen and scholars, simply omitted them. The editors of 3, being scientists, were more conscientious. All the chief four- and five-letter words are here, with the exception of perhaps the most important one. They defend this omission not on lexical grounds but on the practical and, I think, reasonable ground that its inclusion would have stimulated denunciations and boycotts. There are, after all, almost half a million other words in their dictionary—not to mention an investment of three and a half million dollars—and they reluctantly decided not to imperil the whole enterprise by insisting on that word.

Two useful features of 2 were omitted from 3: the gazetteer of place names and the biographical dictionary. They were left out partly to save money—they took up a hundred and seventy-six pages, and the biographical dictionary had to be brought up to date with each new printing—and partly because Dr. Gove and his colleagues, more severe than the easygoing editors of 2, considered such items "encyclopedic material" and so not pertinent to a dictionary. The force of this second excuse is weakened because although they did omit such encyclopedic features of 2 as the two pages on *grasses,* they put in a page-and-a-half table of currencies under *money* and three and a half pages of *dyes.* It is also worth noting that Merriam-Webster added a new item to its line in 1943—the Webster's Biographical Dictionary. While I quite understand the publishers' reluctance to give away what their customers would otherwise have to buy separately, I do think the biographical dictionary should have been included—from the consumer's point of view, at any rate.

However, the editors have sneaked in many proper names by the back door; that is, by entering their adjectival forms. *Walpolian* means "1: of, relating to, or having the characteristics of Horace Walpole or his writings," and "2: of, relating to, or having the characteristics of Robert Walpole or his political policies," and we get the death dates of both men (but not the birth dates), plus the information that Horace was "Eng. man of letters" and Robert "Eng. statesman" (though it is not noted that Horace was Robert's son). This method of introducing proper names produces odd results. Raphael is in (*Raphaelesque, Raphaelism, Raphaelite*), as are Veronese (*Veronese green*) and Giotto and Giorgione and Michelangelo, but not Tintoretto and Piero della Francesca, because they had the wrong kind of names. Caravaggio had the right kind, but the editors missed him, though *Caravaggesque* is as frequently used in art criticism as *Giottesque*. All the great modern painters, from Cézanne on, are omitted, since none have appropriate adjectives. Yeats is in (*Yeatsian*) but not Eliot, Pound, or Frost (why not *Frosty?*). Sometimes one senses a certain desperation, as when *Smithian* is used to wedge in Adam Smith. *Menckenian* and *Menckenese* get an inch each, but there is no *Hawthornean,* no *Melvillesque,* no *Twainite.* All the twentieth-century presidents are in—Eisenhower by the skin of *Eisenhower jacket*—except Taft and Truman and Kennedy. Hoover has the most entries, all dispiriting: *Hoover apron* and *Hooverize,* because he was food administrator in the First World War; *Hooverville,* for the depression shanty towns; *Hoovercrat,* for a Southern Democrat who voted for him in 1928; and *Hooverism*.

This brings up the matter of capitalization. 2 capitalized proper names; 3 does not, with one exception. There may have been some esoteric reason of typographical consistency. Whatever their reasons, the result is that they must cumbersomely and forever add *usu. cap.* (Why *usu.* when it is *alw?*)

The exception is *God,* which even these cautious linguisticians couldn't quite bring themselves to label *usu. cap. Jesus* is out because of adjectival deficiency, except for *Jesus bug,* a splendid slang term, new to me, for the waterbug ("fr. the allusion to his walking on water," the "his" being firmly lower case). He does get in via His second name, which, luckily, has given us a rather important adjective, *usu. cap.*

At first glance, 3's typography is cleaner and more harmonious. Dr. Gove estimates that the editors eliminated two million commas and periods (as after adj., n., and v.), or eighty pages' worth. A second glance shows a major and, from a utilitarian point of view, very nearly a fatal defect. Words that have more than one meaning—and many have dozens—are much easier to follow in 2, which gives a new paragraph to each meaning, than in 3, which runs the whole entry as one superparagraph. ("What! Will the line stretch out to the crack of doom?"—*Shakespeare.*) Thus 2 not only starts each new meaning of *cut* with a paragraph but also puts in an italicized heading: *Games & Sports, Bookbinding, Card Playing, Motion Pictures.* In 3 one has to look through a solid paragraph of nine inches, and there are no headings. The most extreme example I found was 3's entry on the transitive verb *take,* which runs on for a single paragraph two feet eight inches long, in which the twenty-one main meanings are divided only by boldfaced numerals; there follow, still in the same paragraph, four inches of the intransitive *take,* the only sign of this gear-shifting being a tiny printer's squiggle. *Take* is, admittedly, quite a verb. The Oxford English Dictionary gives sixty-three meanings in nine feet, but they are spaced out in separate paragraphs, as is the mere foot and a half that 2 devotes to *take.*

A second glance also suggests second thoughts about the richness of citations in 3. Often it seems *plethoric,* even *otiose* ("lacking use or effect"). The chief reason 3's entries on multiple-meaning words are so much longer than 2's is that it has so many more citations. Many are justified and do indeed enrich our sense of words, but a good thing can be overdone. The promotional material for 3 mentions the treatment of *freeze* as an improvement, but does anybody really need such illustrative richness as:

> 6a: to make (as the face) expressionless [with instructions to recognize no one; and in fact he did *freeze* his face up when an old acquaintance hailed him—Fletcher Pratt] [a look of incredulity *froze* his face . . . and his eyes went blank with surprise—Hamilton Basso] b. to preserve rigidly a particular expression on [he still sat, his face *frozen* in shame and misery—Agnes S. Turnbull]

The question is rhetorical.

One of the problems of an unabridger is where completeness ends and madness begins. The compilers of 2 had a weakness for such fabrications as *philomuse, philomythia* ("devotion to legends . . . sometimes, loquaciousness"), *philonoist* ("a seeker of knowledge"), *philophilosophos* ("partial to philosophers"), *philopolemic, philopornist* ("a lover of harlots"), and *philoso-*

pheress (which means not only a woman philosopher, like Hannah Arendt, but a philosopher's wife, like Xantippe). These are omitted by the compilers of 3, though they could not resist *philosophastering* ("philosophizing in a shallow or pretentious manner"). But why do we need *nooky* ("full of nooks") or *name-caller* ("one that habitually engages in name-calling") or all those "night" words, from *night clothes*—"garments worn in bed," with a citation from Jane Welsh Carlyle, of all people—through *nightdress, nightgear, nightgown, nightrobe, nightshirt,* and *nightwear?* What need of *sea boat* ("a boat adapted to the open sea") or *sea captain* or *swimming pool* ("a pool suitable for swimming," lest we imagine it is a pool that swims) or *sunbath* ("exposure to sunlight"—"or to a sun lamp," they add cautiously) or *sunbather* ("one that takes sunbaths")? Why *kittenless* ("having no kitten")? Why need we be told that *white-faced* is "having the face white in whole or in part"? Or that *whitehanded* is "having white hands"? (They missed *whitelipped.*)

Then there are those terrible negative prefixes, which the unwary unabridger gets started on and slides down with sickening momentum. 3 has left out many of 2's absurdities: *nonborrower, nonnervous, non-Mohammedan, non-Welsh, non-walking.* But it adds some of its own: *nonscientist, nonphilatelic, non-inbred, nondrying* (why no *nonwetting?*), *nonbank* ("not being or done by a bank"), and many other non-useful and nonsensical entries. It has thirty-four pages of words beginning with *un-*, and while it may seem carping to object to this abundance, since the O.E.D. has three hundred and eighty such pages, I think, given the difference in purpose, that many may be challenged. A reasonably bright child of ten will not have to run to Daddy's Unabridged to find the meaning of *unreelable* ("incapable of being wound on a reel"), *unlustrous* ("lacking luster"), or *unpowdered* ("not powdered"). And if it's for unreasonably dumb children, why omit *unspinnable, unshining,* and *unsanded?*

For a minor example of Gnostomania, or scholar's knee, see the treatment of numbers. Every number from *one* to *ninety-nine* is entered and defined, also every numerical adjective. Thus when the reader hits *sixty* he goes into a skid fifteen inches long. *Sixty* ("being one more than 59 in number") is followed by the pronoun ("60 countable persons or things not specified but under consideration and being enumerated") and the noun ("six tens: twice 30: 12 fives," etc.) Then comes *sixty-eight* ("being one more than 67 in number") and *sixty-eighth* ("being number 68 in a countable series"), followed by *sixty-fifth, sixty-first,* and so on. The compilers of 2 dealt with the *sixty* problem in a mere two entries totalling an inch and a half. But the art of lexicography has mutated into a "science" since then. (*"Quotation mark* . . . sometimes used to enclose . . . words . . . in an . . . ironical . . . sense . . . or words for which a writer offers a slight apology.") In reading 3 one sometimes feels like a subscriber who gets two hundred and thirty-eight copies of the May issue because the addressing machine got stuck, and it doesn't make it any better to know that the operators jammed it on purpose.

My complaint is not that 3 is all-inclusive—that is, unabridged—but that *pedantry* is not a synonym of *scholarship*. I have no objection to the inclusion of such pomposities, mostly direct translations from the Latin, as *viridity* (greenness), *presbyopic* (farsighted because of old age), *vellication* (twitching), *pudency* (modesty), and *vulnerary* (wound-healing). These are necessary if only so that one can read James Gould Cozzens' "By Love Possessed," in which they all occur, along with many siblings. And in my rambles through these 2,662 pages I have come across many a splendid word that has not enjoyed the popularity it deserves. I think my favorites are *pilpul*, from the Hebrew *to search*, which means "critical analysis and hair-splitting; casuistic argumentation;" *dysphemism*, which is the antonym of *euphemism* (as, *axle grease* for *butter* or *old man* for *father*), *subfusc*, from the Latin *subfuscus*, meaning brownish, which is illustrated with a beautiful citation from Osbert Sitwell ("the moment when the word Austerity was to take to itself a new subfusc and squalid twist of meaning")—cf. the more familiar *subacid*, also well illustrated with "a little subacid kind of . . . impatience," from Laurence Sterne; *nanism*, which is the antonym of *gigantism; mesocracy*, which is the form of government we increasingly have in this country; and *lib-lab*, which means a Liberal who sympathizes with Labor—I wish the lexicographers had not restored the hyphen I deleted when I imported it from England twenty years ago. One might say, and in fact I will say, that H. L. Mencken, whose prose was dysphemistic but never subfusc, eschewed pilpul in expressing his nanitic esteem for lib-lab mesocracy. Unfortunately, 3 omits 2's *thob* ("to think according to one's wishes"), which someone made up from *think-opinion-believe*, or else I could also have noted Mencken's distaste for thobbery.

Dr. Gove met the problem of *ain't* head on in the best traditions of Structural Linguistics, labelling it—reluctantly, one imagines—*substandard* for *have not* and *has not*, but giving it, unlabelled, as a contraction of *am not, are not*, and *is not*, adding "though disapproved by many and more common in less educated speech, used orally in most parts of the U. S. by many cultivated speakers esp. in the phrase ain't I." This was courageous indeed; when Dr. C. C. Fries, the dean of Structural Linguists today, said, at a meeting of the Modern Language Association several years ago, that *ain't* was not wholly disreputable, a teapot tempest boiled up in the press. When Dr. Gove included a reference to the entry on *ain't* in the press announcement of 3, the newspapers seethed again, from the Houston *Press* ("It Ain't Uncouth To Say Ain't Now") to the San Francisco *Examiner* ("Ain't Bad at All—In Newest Revised Dictionary") and the *World-Telegram* ("It Just Ain't True That Ain't Ain't in the Dictionary"). But moral courage is not the only quality a good lexicographer needs. Once the matter of education and culture is raised, we are right back at the non-scientific business of deciding what is correct—*stand-*

ard is the modern euphemism—and this is more a matter of a feeling for language (what the trade calls *Sprachgefühl*) than of the statistics on which Dr. Gove and his colleagues seem to have chiefly relied. For what Geiger counter will decide who is in fact educated or cultivated? And what adding machine will discriminate between *ain't* used because the speaker thinks it is standard English and *ain't* used because he wants to get a special effect? "Survival must have quality, or it ain't worth a bean," Thornton Wilder recently observed. It doesn't take much *Sprachgefühl* to recognize that Mr. Wilder is here being a mite folksy and that his effect would be lost if *ain't* were indeed "used orally in most parts of the U.S. by many cultivated speakers." Though I regret that the nineteenth-century schoolteachers without justification deprived us of *ain't* for *am not*, the deed was done, and I think the *Dial.* or *Illit.* with which 2 labels all uses of the word comes closer to linguistic fact today.

The pejorative labels in 2 are forthright: *colloquial, erroneous, incorrect, illiterate.* 3 replaces these self-explanatory terms with two that are both fuzzier and more scientific-sounding: *substandard* and *nonstandard.* The first "indicates status conforming to a pattern of linguistic usage that exists throughout the American language community but differs in choice of word or form from that of the prestige group in that community," which is academese for "Not used by educated people." *Hisself* and *drownded* are labelled *substand.*, which sounds better than *erron.*—more democratic. *Nonstandard* "is used for a very small number of words that can hardly stand without some status label but are too widely current in reputable context to be labelled *substand.*" *Irregardless* is given as an example, which for me again raises doubts about the compilers' notion of a reputable context. I think 2's label for the word, *erron. or humorous,* more accurate.

The argument has now shifted from whether a dictionary should be an authority as against a reporter (in Dr. Gove's terms, prescriptive v. descriptive) to the validity of the prescriptive guidance that 3 does in fact give. For Dr. Gove and his colleagues have not ventured to omit all qualitative discriminations; they have cut them down drastically from 2, but they have felt obliged to include many. Perhaps by 1988, if the Structural Linguists remain dominant, there will be a fourth edition, which will simply record, without labels or warnings, all words and non-words that are used widely in "the American language community," including such favorites of a former President as *nucular* (warfare), *inviduous,* and *mischievious.* But it is still 1962, and 3 often does discriminate. The trouble is that its willingness to do so has been weakened by its scientific conscience, so that it palters and equivocates; this is often more misleading than would be the omission of all discriminations.

One drawback to the permissive approach of the Structural Linguists is that it impoverishes the language by not objecting to errors if they are common enough. ("And how should I presume?"—*T. S. Eliot.*) There is a natural tendency among human beings, who are *by def.* fallible, to confuse similar-sounding words. "One look at him would turn you nauseous," Phil Silvers said on television one night, as better stylists have written before. Up to now, dictionaries have distinguished *nauseous* (causing nausea) from *nauseated* (experiencing nausea); 2 labels *nauseous* in the sense of experiencing nausea *obs.*, but it is no longer *obs.* It is simply *erron.*, a fact you will not learn from 3, which gives as its first definition, without label, "affected with or inclining to nausea." So the language is *balled up* and *nauseous* is telescoped into *nauseated* and nobody knows who means which exactly. The magisterial Fowler—magisterial, that is, until the Structural Linguists got to work—has an entry on Pairs & Snares that makes sad reading now. He calls *deprecate* and *depreciate* "one of the altogether false pairs," but 3 gives the latter as a synonym of the first. It similarly blurs the distinction between Fowler's *forcible* ("effected by force") and *forceful* ("full of force"), *unexceptional* ("constituting no exception to the general rule") and *unexceptionable* ("not open or liable to objection," which is quite a different thing). A Pair & Snare Fowler doesn't give is *disinterested* (impartial) and *uninterested* (not interested); 2 lists the *uninterested* sense of *disinterested* but adds, "*now rare;*" even such permissive lexicographers as Bergen and Cornelia Evans, in their "Dictionary of Contemporary American Usage," state firmly, "Though *disinterested* was formerly a synonym for *uninterested*, it is not now so used." But 3 gives *disinterested* as a synonym of *uninterested*.

Each such confusion makes the language less efficient, and it is a dictionary's job to *define* words, which means, literally, to set limits to them. 3 still distinguishes *capital* from *capitol* and *principle* from *principal,* but how many more language-community members must join the present sizable band that habitually confuses these words before they go down the drain with the others? Perhaps nothing much is lost if almost everybody calls Frankenstein the monster rather than the man who made the monster, even though Mrs. Shelley wrote it the other way, but how is one to deal with the *bimonthly* problem? 2 defines it as "once in two months," which is correct. 3 gives this as the first meaning and then adds, gritting its teeth, "*sometimes:* twice a month." (It defines *biweekly* as "every two weeks" and adds "2: twice a week.") It does seem a little awkward to have a word that can mean every two weeks *or* every eight weeks, and it would have been convenient if 3 had compromised with scientific integrity enough to replace its perfectly accurate *sometimes* with a firm *erroneous*. But this would have implied authority, and authority is the last thing 3's modest recorders want. ("Let this cup pass from me."—*New Testament.*)

The objection is not to recording the facts of actual usage. It is to failing to give the information that would enable the reader to decide which usage he wants to adopt. If he prefers to use *deprecate* and *depreciate* interchangeably, no dictionary can prevent him, but at least he should be warned. Thus 3 has under *transpire*—"4: to come to pass; happen, occur." 2 has the same entry, but it is followed by a monitory pointing hand: "*transpire* in this sense has been disapproved by most authorities on usage, although the meaning occurs in the writings of many authors of good standing." Fair enough. I also prefer 2's handling of the common misuse of *infer* to mean *imply*—"5: loosely and erroneously, to imply." 3 sounds no warning, and twice under *infer* it advises "compare imply." Similarly, 2 labels the conjunctive *like* "illiterate" and "incorrect," which it is, adding that "in the works of careful writers [it] is replaced by *as.*" 3 accepts it as standard, giving such unprepossessing citations as "impromptu programs where they ask questions much like I do on the air—Art Linkletter" and "wore his clothes like he was . . . afraid of getting dirt on them—*St. Petersburg (Fla.) Independent.*" *Enthuse* is labelled *colloq.* in 2 but not in 3. It still sounds *colloq.* if not *godawf.* to me, nor am I impressed by 3's citations, from writers named L. G. Pine and Lawrence Constable and from a trade paper called *Fashion Accessories*. Or consider the common misuse of *too* when *very* is meant, as "I was not too interested in the lecture." 2 gives this use but labels it *colloq.* 3 gives it straight and cites Irving Kolodin: "an episodic work without too consistent a texture;" Mr. Kolodin probably means "without a very consistent texture," but how does one know he doesn't mean "without an excessively consistent [or monotonous] texture"? In music criticism such ambiguities are not too helpful.

In dealing with words that might be considered slang, 2 uses the label wherever there is doubt, while 3 leans the other way. The first procedure seems to me more sensible, since no great harm is done if a word is labelled slang until its pretensions to being standard have been thoroughly tested (as long as it is admitted into the dictionary), while damage may be done if it is prematurely accepted as standard. Thus both 2 and 3 list such women's-magazine locutions as *galore, scads, scrumptious,* and *too-too,* but only 2 labels them slang. (Fowler's note on *galore* applies to them all: "Chiefly resorted to by those who are reduced to relieving the dullness of matter by oddity of expression.") Thus *rummy, spang* (in the middle of), and *nobby* are in both, but only 2 calls them slang.

Admittedly, the question is most difficult. Many words begin as slang and then rise in the world. Dean Swift, a great purist, objected to *mob* (from the Latin *mobile vulgus*), *banter, bully,* and *sham;* he also objected to *hyp,* which has disappeared as slang for *hypochondriac,* and *rep,* which persists for *reputation* but is still labelled slang even in 3. Some slang words have survived for centuries without bettering themselves, like the Jukes and the Kallikaks. *Dukes* (fists) and *duds* (clothes) are still slang, although they go back to the eighteenth and the sixteenth century, respectively.

The definition of *slang* in 3 is "characterized primarily by connotations of extreme informality . . . coinages or arbitrarily changed words, clipped or shortened forms, extravagant, forced, or facetious figures of speech or verbal novelties usu. experiencing quick popularity and relatively rapid decline into disuse." A good definition (Dr. Gove has added that slang is "linguistically self-conscious"), but it seems to have been forgotten in making up 3, most of whose discriminations about slang strike me as arbitrary. According to 3, *scram* is not slang, but *vamoose* is. "*Goof* 1" (to make a mistake or blunder") is not slang, but "*goof* 2" ("to spend time idly or foolishly") is, and the confusion is compounded when one finds that Ethel Merman is cited for the non-slang *goof* and James T. Farrell for the slang *goof*. "*Floozy* 1" ("an attractive young woman of loose morals") is standard, but "*floozy* 2" ("a dissolute and sometimes slovenly woman") is slang. Can even a Structural Linguist make such fine distinctions about such a word? The many synonyms for *drunk* raise the same question. Why are *oiled*, *pickled*, and *boiled* labelled slang if *soused* and *spiflicated* are not? Perhaps cooking terms for *drunk* are automatically slang, but why?

I don't mean to *imply* (see *infer*) that the compilers of 3 didn't give much thought to the problem. When they came to a doubtful word, they took a staff poll, asking everybody to check it, after reviewing the accumulated cites, as either slang or standard. This resulted in *cornball's* being entered as slang and *corny's* being entered as standard. Such scientific, or quantitative, efforts to separate the goats from the sheep produced the absurdities noted above. Professor Austin C. Dobbins raised this point in *College English* for October, 1956:

> But what of such words as *boondoggle, corny, frisk, liquidate, pinched, bonehead, carpetbagger, pleb, slush fund,* and *snide*? Which of these words ordinarily would be considered appropriate in themes written by cultivated people? According to the editors of the ACD [the American College Dictionary, the 1953 edition, published by Random House] the first five of these words are slang; the second five are established usage. To the editors of WNCD [Webster's New Collegiate Dictionary, published by Merriam-Webster in the same year] the first five of these words represent established usage; the second five are slang. Which authority is the student to follow?

Mr. Dobbins is by no means hostile to Structural Linguistics, and his essay appears in a recent anthology edited by Dr. Harold B. Allen, of the University of Minnesota, an energetic proponent of the new school. "Perhaps the answer," Mr. Dobbins concludes, "is to advise students to study only one handbook, consult one dictionary, listen to one instructor. An alternate suggestion, of course, is for our textbooks more accurately to base their labels upon studies of usage." Assuming the first alternative is ironical, I would say the second is impractical unless the resources of a dozen Ford Foundations are devoted to trying to decide the matter scientifically—that is, statistically.

Short of this Land of Cockaigne, where partridges appear in the fields ready-roasted, I see only two logical alternatives: to label all doubtful words slang, as 2 does, or to drop the label entirely, as I suspect Dr. Gove would have liked to do. Using the label sparingly, if it is not to produce bizarre effects, takes a lot more *Sprachgefühl* than the editors of 3 seem to have possessed.

Thus *horse* as a verb ("to engage in horseplay") they accept as standard. The citations are from Norman Mailer ("I never horse around much with the women") and J. D. Salinger ("I horse around quite a lot, just to keep from getting bored"). I doubt whether either Mr. Mailer or Mr. Salinger would use *horse* straight; in these cites, I venture, it is either put in the mouth of a first-person narrator or used deliberately to get a colloquial effect. Slang is concise and vivid—*jalopy* has advantages over *dilapidated automobile*—and a few slang terms salted in a formal paragraph bring out the flavor. But the user must know he *is* using slang, he must be aware of having introduced a slight discord into his harmonics, or else he coarsens and blurs his expression. This information he will not, for the most part, get from 3. I hate to think what monstrosities of prose foreigners and high-school students will produce if they take 3 seriously as a guide to what is and what is not standard English.

Whenever the compilers of 3 come up against a locution that some (me, or I) might consider simply wrong, they do their best, as Modern Linguists and democrats, to be good fellows. The softening-up process begins with substituting the euphemistic *substandard* for 2's blunt *erroneous* and *illiterate*. From there it expands into several forms. *Complected* (for *complexioned*) is *dialect* in 2, *not often in formal use* in 3. *Learn* (for *teach*) is *now a vulgarism* in 2, *now chiefly substand.* in 3. (*Chiefly* is the thin end of the wedge, implying that users of standard English on occasion exclaim, "I'll learn you to use bad English!") *Knowed* is listed as the past of *know* though *broke* is labelled substandard for *broken*—another of those odd discriminations. Doubtless they counted noses, or citation slips, and concluded that "Had I but knowed!" is standard while "My heart is broke" is substandard.

(To be entirely fair, perhaps compulsively so: If one reads carefully the five closely printed pages of Explanatory Notes in 3, and especially paragraphs 16.0 through 16.6 (twelve inches of impenetrable lexical jargon), one finds that light-face small capitals mean a cross-reference, and if one looks up know—which is given after *knowed* in light-face small capitals—one does find that *knowed* is dialect. This is not a very practical or sensible dictionary, one concludes after such scholarly labors, and one wonders why Dr. Gove and his editors did not think of labeling *knowed* as substandard right where it occurs, and one suspects that they wanted to slightly conceal the fact or at any rate to put off its exposure as long as decently possible.)

The systematic softening or omitting of pejorative labels in 3 could mean: (1) we have come to use English more loosely, to say the least, than we did in 1934; or (2) usage hasn't changed, but 3 has simply recorded The Facts more accurately; or (3) the notion of what is a relevant Fact has changed between 2 and 3. I suspect it is mostly (3), but in any case I cannot see *complected* as anything but *dialected*.

In 1947 the G. & C. Merriam Co. published a little book entitled "Noah's Ark"—in reference to Noah Webster, who began it all—celebrating its first hundred years as the publisher of Webster dictionaries. Toward the end, the author, Robert Keith Leavitt, rises to heights of eloquence which have a tinny sound now that "Webster" means not 2 but 3:

> This responsibility to the user is no light matter. It has, indeed, grown heavier with every year of increasing acceptance of Webster. Courts, from the United States Supreme Court down, rely on the *New International's* definitions as a sort of common law: many a costly suit has hinged on a Webster definition, and many a citizen has gone behind prison bars or walked out onto the streets a free man, according to the light Webster put upon his doings. The statute law itself is not infrequently phrased by legislators in terms straight out of Webster. Most daily newspapers and magazines, and nearly all the books that come off the press, are edited and printed in accordance with Websterian usage. Colleges and schools make the *New International* their standard, and, for nearly half a century, students have dug their way through pedantic obscurity with the aid of the *Collegiate*. In business offices the secretary corrects her boss out of Webster and the boss holds customers and contractors alike in line by citing how Webster says it shall be done. In thousands upon thousands of homes, youngsters lying sprawled under the table happily absorb from Webster information which teachers have striven in vain to teach them from textbooks. Clear through, indeed, to the everyday American's most trivial and jocose of doings, Webster is the unquestioned authority.

While this picture is a bit idyllic—Clarence Barnhart's American College Dictionary, put out by Random House, is considered by many to be at least as good as the Webster Collegiate—it had some reality up to 1961. But as of today, courts that Look It Up In Webster will often find themselves little the wiser, since 3 claims no authority and merely records, mostly deadpan, what in fact every Tom, Dick, and Harry is now doing—in all innocence—to the language. That freedom or imprisonment should depend on 3 is an alarming idea. The secretary correcting her boss, if he is a magazine publisher, will collide with the unresolved *bimonthly* and *biweekly* problem, and the youngsters sprawled under the table will happily absorb from 3 the information that *jerk* is standard for "a stupid, foolish, naïve, or unconventional person." One imagines the themes: "Dr. Johnson admired Goldsmith's literary talent although he considered him a jerk." The editors of the New Webster's Vest Pocket Dictionary, thirty-nine cents at any cigar store, label *jerk* as *coll*. But then they aren't Structural Linguists.

The reviews of 3 in the lay press have not been enthusiastic. *Life* and the *Times* have both attacked it editorially as a "say-as-you-go" dictionary that reflects "the permissive school" in language study. The usually solemn editorialists of the *Times* were goaded to unprecedented wit:

> A passel of double-domes at the G. & C. Merriam Company joint in Springfield, Mass. [the editorial began], have been confabbing and yakking for twenty-seven years—which is not intended to infer that they have not been doing plenty work—and now they have finalized Webster's Third New International Dictionary, Unabridged, a new edition of that swell and esteemed word book.
> Those who regard the foregoing paragraph as acceptable English prose will find that the new Webster's is just the dictionary for them.

But the lay press doesn't always prevail. The irreverent may call 3 "Gove's Goof," but Dr. Gove and his editors are part of the dominant movement in the professional study of language—one that has in the last few years established strong beachheads in the National Council of Teachers of English and the College English Association. One may grant that for the scientific study of language the Structural Linguistic approach is superior to that of the old grammarians, who overestimated the importance of logic and Latin, but one may still object to its transfer directly to the teaching of English and the making of dictionaries. As a scientific discipline, Structural Linguistics can have no truck with values or standards. Its job is to deal only with The Facts. But in matters of usage, the evaluation of The Facts is important, too, and this requires a certain amount of general culture, not to mention common sense—commodities that many scientists have done brilliantly without but that teachers and lexicographers need in their work.

The kind of thinking responsible for 3 is illustrated by Dr. Gove's riposte, last week, to the many unfavorable reviews of his dictionary: "The criticisms involve less than one per cent of the words in the dictionary." This quantitative approach might be useful to novelists who get bad reviews. It is foolproof here; a reviewer who tried to meet Dr. Gove's criterion and deal with a sizable proportion of 3's words—say, ten per cent—would need forty-five thousand words just to list them, and if his own comments averaged ten words apiece he would have to publish his five-hundred-thousand-word review in two large volumes. Some odd thinking gets done up at the old Merriam-Webster place in Springfield.

Dr. Gove's letter to the *Times* objecting to its editorial was also interesting. "The editors of *Webster's Third New International Dictionary* are not amused by the ingenuity of the first paragraph of your editorial," it began loftily, and continued, "Your paragraph obscures, or attempts to obscure, the fact that there are so many different degrees of standard usage that dictionary definitions cannot hope to distinguish one from another by status labelling." (But the *Times*' point was precisely that the editors did make such distinctions by status labelling, only they were the wrong distinctions; i.e., by omitting pejorative labels they accepted as standard words that, in the opinion of the *Times*, are not standard.) There followed several pages of citations in which Dr. Gove showed that the *Times* itself had often used the very words it objected to 3's including as standard language. "If we are ever inclined to the linguistic pedantry that easily fails to distinguish moribund traditions from genuine living usage [the adjectives here are perhaps more revealing than Dr. Gove intended] we have only to turn to the columns of the *Times*," Dr. Gove concluded. The *Times* is the best newspaper in the world in the gathering and printing of news, but it has never been noted for stylistic distinction. And even if it were, the exigencies of printing a small book every day might be expected to drive the writers and editors of a newspaper into usages as convenient as they are sloppy—usages that people with more time on their hands, such as the editors of an unabridged dictionary, might distinguish from standard English.

There are several reasons that it is important to maintain standards in the use of a language. English, like other languages, is beautiful when properly used, and beauty can be achieved only by attention to form, which means setting limits, or de-fining, or dis-criminating. Language expresses the special, dis-tinctive quality of a people, and a people, like an individual, is to a large extent defined by its past—its traditions—whether it is conscious of this or not. If the language is allowed to shift too rapidly, without challenge from teachers and lexicographers, then the special character of the American people is blurred, since it tends to lose its past. In the same way a city loses its character if too much of it is torn down and rebuilt too quickly. "Languages are the pedigrees of nations," said Dr. Johnson.

The effect on the individual is also unfortunate. The kind of permissiveness that permeates 3 (the kind that a decade or two ago was more common in progressive schools than it is now) results, oddly, in less rather than more individuality, since the only way an individual can "express himself" is in relation to a social norm—in the case of language, to standard usage. James Joyce's creative distortions of words were possible only because he had a perfect ear for orthodox English. But if the very idea of form, or standards, is lacking, then how can one violate it? It's no fun to use *knowed* for *known* if everybody thinks you're just trying to be standard.

Counting cite slips is simply not the way to go about the delicate business of deciding these matters. If nine-tenths of the citizens of the United States, including a recent President, were to use *inviduous*, the one-tenth who clung to *invidious* would still be right, and they would be doing a favor to the majority if they continued to maintain the point. It is perhaps not democratic, according to some recent users, or abusers, of the word, to insist on this, and the question comes up of who is to decide at what point change—for language does indeed change, as the Structural Linguists insist—has evolved from *slang, dial., erron.,* or *substand.* to *standard*. The decision, I think, must be left to the teachers, the professional writers, and the lexicographers, and they might look up Ulysses' famous defense of conservatism in Shakespeare's "Troilus and Cressida":

> The heavens themselves, the planets and this centre
> Observe degree, priority and place,
> Insisture, course, proportion, season, form,
> Office and custom in all line of order. . . .
> Take but degree away, untune that string,
> And, hark, what discord follows! Each thing meets
> In mere oppugnancy. The bounded waters
> Should lift their bosoms higher than the shores
> And make a sop of all this solid globe.
> Strength should be lord of imbecility
> And the rude son should strike his father dead.

> Force should be right, or rather right and wrong
> (Between whose endless jar justice resides)
> Should lose their names, and so should justice too.
> Then every thing includes itself in power,
> Power into will, will into appetite
> And appetite, a universal wolf,
> So doubly seconded with will and power,
> Must make perforce a universal prey
> And, last, eat up himself. . . .

Dr. Johnson, a dictionary-maker of the old school, defined *lexicographer* as "a harmless drudge." Things have changed. Lexicographers may still be drudges, but they are certainly not harmless. They have untuned the string, made a sop of the solid structure of English, and encouraged the language to eat up himself.

But What's a Dictionary For?

BERGEN EVANS

The storm of abuse in the popular press that greeted the appearance of *Webster's Third New International Dictionary* is a curious phenomenon. Never has a scholarly work of this stature been attacked with such unbridled fury and contempt. An article in the *Atlantic* viewed it as a "disappointment," a "shock," a "calamity," "a scandal and a disaster." The New York *Times,* in a special editorial, felt that the work would "accelerate the deterioration" of the language and sternly accused the editors of betraying a public trust. The *Journal* of the American Bar Association saw the publication as "deplorable," "a flagrant example of lexicographic irresponsiblity," "a serious blow to the cause of good English." *Life* called it "a nonword deluge," "monstrous," "abominable," and "a cause for dismay." They doubted that "Lincoln could have modelled his Gettysburg Address" on it—a concept of how things get written that throws very little light on Lincoln but a great deal on *Life.*

What underlies all this sound and fury? Is the claim of the G. & C. Merriam Company, probably the world's greatest dictionary maker, that the preparation of the work cost $3.5 million, that it required the efforts of three hundred scholars over a period of twenty-seven years, working on the largest collection of citations ever assembled in any language—is all this a fraud, a hoax?

So monstrous a discrepancy in evaluation requires us to examine basic

Atlantic Monthly, CCIX (May 1962), 57–62. Reprinted by permission of the author.

principles. Just what's a dictionary for? What does it propose to do? What does the common reader go to a dictionary to find? What has the purchaser of a dictionary a right to expect for his money?

Before we look at basic principles, it is necessary to interpose two brief statements. The first of these is that a dictionary is concerned with words. Some dictionaries give various kinds of other useful information. Some have tables of weights and measures on the flyleaves. Some list historical events, and some, home remedies. And there's nothing wrong with their so doing. But the great increase in our vocabulary in the past three decades compels all dictionaries to make more efficient use of their space. And if something must be eliminated, it is sensible to throw out these extraneous things and stick to words.

Yet wild wails arose. The *Saturday Review* lamented that one can no longer find the goddess Astarte under a separate heading—though they point out that a genus of mollusks named after the goddess is included! They seemed to feel that out of sheer perversity the editors of the dictionary stooped to mollusks while ignoring goddesses and that, in some way, this typifies modern lexicography. Mr. Wilson Follett, folletizing (his mental processes demand some special designation) in the *Atlantic,* cried out in horror that one is not even able to learn from the Third International "that the Virgin was Mary the mother of Jesus"!

The second brief statement is that there has been even more progress in the making of dictionaries in the past thirty years than there has been in the making of automobiles. The difference, for example, between the much-touted Second International (1934) and the much-clouted Third International (1961) is not like the difference between yearly models but like the difference between the horse and buggy and the automobile. Between the appearance of these two editions a whole new science related to the making of dictionaries, the science of descriptive linguistics, has come into being.

Modern linguistics gets its charter from Leonard Bloomfield's *Language* (1933). Bloomfield, for thirteen years professor of Germanic philology at the University of Chicago and for nine years professor of linguistics at Yale, was one of those inseminating scholars who can't be relegated to any department and don't dream of accepting established categories and procedures just because they're established. He was as much an anthropologist as a linguist, and his concepts of language were shaped not by Strunk's *Elements of Style* but by his knowledge of Cree Indian dialects.

The broad general findings of the new science are:

1. All languages are systems of human conventions, not systems of natural laws. The first—and essential—step in the study of any language is observing and setting down precisely what happens when native speakers speak it.

2. Each language is unique in its pronunciation, grammar, and vocabulary. It cannot be described in terms of logic or of some theoretical, ideal

language. It cannot be described in terms of any other language, or even in terms of its own past.

3. All languages are dynamic rather than static, and hence a "rule" in any language can only be a statement of contemporary practice. Change is constant—and normal.

4. "Correctness" can rest only upon usage, for the simple reason that there is nothing else for it to rest on. And all usage is relative.

From these propositions it follows that a dictionary is good only insofar as it is a comprehensive and accurate description of current usage. And to be comprehensive it must include some indication of social and regional associations.

New dictionaries are needed because English has changed more in the past two generations than at any other time in its history. It has had to adapt to extraordinary cultural and technological changes, two world wars, unparalleled changes in transportation and communication, and unprecedented movements of populations.

More subtly, but pervasively, it has changed under the influence of mass education and the growth of democracy. As written English is used by increasing millions and for more reasons than ever before, the language has become more utilitarian and more informal. Every publication in America today includes pages that would appear, to the purist of forty years ago, unbuttoned gibberish. Not that they are; they simply show that you can't hold the language of one generation up as a model for the next.

It's not that you mustn't. You *can't*. For example, in the issue in which *Life* stated editorially that it would follow the Second International, there were over forty words, constructions, and meanings which are in the Third International but not in the Second. The issue of the New York *Times* which hailed the Second International as the authority to which it would adhere and the Third International as a scandal and a betrayal which it would reject used one hundred and fifty-three separate words, phrases, and constructions which are listed in the Third International but not in the Second and nineteen others which are condemned in the Second. Many of them are used many times, more than three hundred such uses in all. The Washington *Post,* in an editorial captioned "Keep Your Old Webster's," says, in the first sentence, "don't throw it away," and in the second, "hang on to it." But the old Webster's labels *don't* "colloquial" and doesn't include "hang on to," in this sense, at all.

In short, all of these publications are written in the language that the Third International describes, even the very editorials which scorn it. And this is no coincidence, because the Third International isn't setting up any new standards at all; it is simply describing what *Life,* the Washington *Post* and the New York *Times* are doing. Much of the dictionary's material comes from these very publications, the *Times,* in particular, furnishing more of its illustrative quotations than any other newspaper.

And the papers have no choice. No journal or periodical could sell a single issue today if it restricted itself to the American language of twenty-eight years ago. It couldn't discuss half the things we are interested in, and its style would seem stiff and cumbrous. If the editorials were serious, the public—and the stockholders—have reason to be grateful that the writers on these publications are more literate than the editors.

And so back to our questions: what's a dictionary for, and how, in 1962, can it best do what it ought to do? The demands are simple. The common reader turns to a dictionary for information about the spelling, pronunciation, meaning, and proper use of words. He wants to know what is current and respectable. But he wants—and has a right to—the truth, the full truth. And the full truth about any language, and especially about American English today, is that there are many areas in which certainty is impossible and simplification is misleading.

Even in so settled a matter as spelling, a dictionary cannot always be absolute. *Theater* is correct, but so is *theatre*. And so are *traveled* and *travelled, plow* and *plough, catalog* and *catalogue*, and scores of other variants. The reader may want a single certainty. He may have taken an unyielding position in an argument, he may have wagered in support of his conviction and may demand that the dictionary "settle" the matter. But neither his vanity nor his purse is any concern of the dictionary's; it must record the facts. And the fact here is that there are many words in our language which may be spelled, with equal correctness, in either of two ways.

So with pronunciation. A citizen listening to his radio might notice that James B. Conant, Bernard Baruch, and Dwight D. Eisenhower pronounce *economics* as ECKuhnomiks, while A. Whitney Griswold, Adlai Stevenson, and Herbert Hoover pronounce it EEKuhnomiks. He turns to the dictionary to see which of the two pronunciations is "right" and finds that they are both acceptable.

Has he been betrayed? Has the dictionary abdicated its responsibility? Should it say that one *must* speak like the president of Harvard or like the president of Yale, like the thirty-first President of the United States or like the thirty-fourth? Surely it's none of its business to make a choice. Not because of the distinction of these particular speakers; lexicography, like God, is no respecter of persons. But because so widespread and conspicuous a use of two pronunciations among people of this elevation shows that there *are* two pronunciations. Their speaking establishes the fact which the dictionary must record.

Among the "enormities" with which *Life* taxes the Third International is its listing of "the common mispronunciation" *heighth*. That it is labeled a "dialectal variant" seems, somehow, to compound the felony. But one hears the word so pronounced, and if one professes to give a full account of

American English in the 1960s, one has to take some cognizance of it. All people do not possess *Life's* intuitive perception that the word is so "monstrous" that even to list it as a dialect variation is to merit scorn. Among these, by the way, was John Milton, who, in one of the greatest passages in all literature, besought the Holy Spirit to raise him to the "highth" of his great argument. And even the *Oxford English Dictionary* is so benighted as to list it, in full boldface, right alongside of *Height* as a variant that has been in the language since at least 1290.

Now there are still, apparently, millions of Americans who retain, in this as in much else, some of the speech of Milton. This particular pronunciation seems to be receding, but the *American Dialect Dictionary* still records instances of it from almost every state on the Eastern seaboard and notes that it is heard from older people and "occasionally in educated speech," "common with good speakers," "general," "widespread."

Under these circumstances, what is a dictionary to do? Since millions speak the word this way, the pronunciation can't be ignored. Since it has been in use as long as we have any record of English and since it has been used by the greatest writers, it can't be described as substandard or slang. But it is heard now only in certain localities. That makes it a dialectal pronunciation, and an honest dictionary will list it as such. What else can it do? Should it do?

The average purchaser of a dictionary uses it most often, probably, to find out what a word "means." As a reader, he wants to know what an author intended to convey. As a speaker or writer, he wants to know what a word will convey to his auditors. And this, too, is complex, subtle, and forever changing.

An illustration is furnished by an editorial in the Washington *Post* (January 17, 1962). After a ringing appeal to those who "love truth and accuracy" and the usual bombinations about "abdication of authority" and "barbarism," the editorial charges the Third International with "pretentious and obscure verbosity" and specifically instances its definition of "so simple an object as a door."

The definition reads:

> a movable piece of firm material or a structure supported usu. along one side and swinging on pivots or hinges, sliding along a groove, rolling up and down, revolving as one of four leaves, or folding like an accordion by means of which an opening may be closed or kept open for passage into or out of a building, room, or other covered enclosure or a car, airplane, elevator, or other vehicle.

Then follows a series of special meanings, each particularly defined and, where necessary, illustrated by a quotation.

Since, aside from roaring and admonishing the "gentlemen from Springfield" that "accuracy and brevity are virtues," the *Post's* editorial fails to explain what is wrong with the definition, we can only infer from "so simple" a thing that the writer takes the plain, downright, man-in-the-street attitude that a door is a door and any damn fool knows that.

But if so, he has walked into one of lexicography's biggest booby traps: the belief that the obvious is easy to define. Whereas the opposite is true. Anyone can give a fair description of the strange, the new, or the unique. It's the commonplace, the habitual, that challenges definition, for its very commonness compels us to define it in uncommon terms. Dr. Johnson was ridiculed on just this score when his dictionary appeared in 1755. For two hundred years his definition of a network as "any thing reticulated or decussated, at equal distances, with interstices between the intersections" has been good for a laugh. But in the merriment one thing is always overlooked: no one has yet come up with a better definition! Subsequent dictionaries defined it as a mesh and then defined a mesh as a network. That's simple, all right.

Anyone who attempts sincerely to state what the word *door* means in the United States of America today can't take refuge in a log cabin. There has been an enormous proliferation of closing and demarking devices and structures in the past twenty years, and anyone who tries to thread his way through the many meanings now included under *door* may have to sacrifice brevity to accuracy and even have to employ words that a limited vocabulary may find obscure.

Is the entrance to a tent a door, for instance? And what of the thing that seals the exit of an airplane? Is this a door? Or what of those sheets and jets of air that are now being used, in place of old-fashioned oak and hinges, to screen entrances and exits. Are they doors? And what of those accordion-like things that set off various sections of many modern apartments? The fine print in the lease takes it for granted that they are doors and that spaces demarked by them are rooms—and the rent is computed on the number of rooms.

Was I gypped by the landlord when he called the folding contraption that shuts off my kitchen a door? I go to the Second International, which the editor of the *Post* urges me to use in preference to the Third International. Here I find that a door is

> The movable frame or barrier of boards, or other material, usually turning on hinges or pivots or sliding, by which an entranceway into a house or apartment is closed and opened; also, a similar part of a piece of furniture, as in a cabinet or bookcase.

This is only forty-six words, but though it includes the cellar door, it excludes the barn door and the accordion-like thing.

So I go on to the Third International. I see at once that the new definition is longer. But I'm looking for accuracy, and if I must sacrifice brevity to get it, then I must. And, sure enough, in the definition which raised the *Post's* blood pressure, I find the words "folding like an accordion." The thing *is* a door, and my landlord is using the word in one of its currently accepted meanings.

We don't turn to a work of reference merely for confirmation. We all have words in our vocabularies which we have misunderstood, and to come on the true meaning of one of these words is quite a shock. All our complacency and self-esteem rise to oppose the discovery. But eventually we must accept the humiliation and laugh it off as best we can.

Some, often those who have set themselves up as authorities, stick to their error and charge the dictionary with being in a conspiracy against them. They are sure that their meaning is the only "right" one. And when the dictionary doesn't bear them out they complain about "permissive" attitudes instead of correcting their mistake.

The New York *Times* and the *Saturday Review* both regarded as contemptibly "permissive" the fact that one meaning of one word was illustrated by a quotation from Polly Adler. But a rudimentary knowledge of the development of any language would have told them that the underworld has been a far more active force in shaping and enriching speech than all the synods that have ever convened. Their attitude is like that of the patriot who canceled his subscription to the *Dictionary of American Biography* when he discovered that the very first volume included Benedict Arnold!

The ultimate of "permissiveness," singled out by almost every critic for special scorn, was the inclusion in the Third International of *finalize*. It was this, more than any other one thing, that was given as the reason for sticking to the good old Second International—that "peerless authority on American English," as the *Times* called it. But if it was such an authority, why didn't they look into it? They would have found *finalize* if they had.

And why shouldn't it be there? It exists. It's been recorded for two generations. Millions employ it every day. Two Presidents of the United States—men of widely differing cultural backgrounds—have used it in formal statements. And so has the Secretary-General of the United Nations, a man of unusual linguistic attainments. It isn't permitting the word but omitting it that would break faith with the reader. Because it is exactly the sort of word we want information about.

To list it as substandard would be to imply that it is used solely by the ignorant and the illiterate. But this would be a misrepresentation: President Kennedy and U Thant are highly educated men, and both are articulate and literate. It isn't even a freak form. On the contrary, it is a classic example of a regular process of development in English, a process which has given us such thoroughly accepted words as *generalize, minimize, formalize,* and *verbalize*. Nor can it be dismissed on logical grounds or on the ground that it is a mere duplication of *complete*. It says something that *complete* doesn't say and says it in a way that is significant in the modern bureaucratic world: one usually *completes* something which he has initated but *finalizes* the work of others.

One is free to dislike the word. I don't like it. But the editor of a dictionary has to examine the evidence for a word's existence and seek it in context to get, as clearly and closely as he can, the exact meaning that it conveys to those who use it. And if it is widely used by well-educated, literate, reputable people, he must list it as a standard word. He is not compiling a volume of his own prejudices.

An individual's use of his native tongue is the surest index to his position within his community. And those who turn to a dictionary expect from it some statement of the current status of a word or a grammatical construction. And it is with the failure to assume this function that modern lexicography has been most fiercely charged. The charge is based on a naïve assumption that simple labels can be attached in all instances. But they can't. Some words are standard in some constructions and not in others. There may be as many shades of status as of meaning, and modern lexicography instead of abdicating this function has fulfilled it to a degree utterly unknown to earlier dictionaries.

Consider the word *fetch*, meaning to "go get and bring to." Until recently a standard word of full dignity ("Fetch me, I pray thee, a little water in a vessel"—I Kings 17:10), it has become slightly tainted. Perhaps the command latent in it is resented as undemocratic. Or maybe its use in training dogs to retrieve has made some people feel that it is an undignified word to apply to human beings. But, whatever the reason, there is a growing uncertainty about its status, and hence it is the sort of word that conscientious people look up in a dictionary.

Will they find it labeled "good" or "bad"? Neither, of course, because either applied indiscriminately would be untrue. The Third International lists nineteen different meanings of the verb *to fetch*. Of these some are labeled "dialectal," some "chiefly dialectal," some "obsolete," one "chiefly Scottish," and two "not in formal use." The primary meaning—"to go after and bring back"—is not labeled and hence can be accepted as standard, accepted with the more assurance because the many shades of labeling show us that the word's status has been carefully considered.

On grammatical questions the Third International tries to be equally exact and thorough. Sometimes a construction is listed without comment, meaning that in the opinion of the editors it is unquestionably respectable. Sometimes a construction carries the comment "used by speakers and writers on all educational levels though disapproved by some grammarians." Or the comment may be "used in substandard speech and formerly also by reputable writers." Or "less often in standard than in substandard speech." Or simply "dial."

And this very accurate reporting is based on evidence which is presented for our examination. One may feel that the evidence is inadequate or that the evaluation of it is erroneous. But surely, in the face of classification so much more elaborate and careful than any known heretofore, one cannot fly into a rage and insist that the dictionary is "out to destroy . . . every vestige of linguistic punctilio . . . every criterion for distinguishing between better usages and worse."

Words, as we have said, are continually shifting their meanings and connotations and hence their status. A word which has dignity, say, in the vocabulary of an older person may go down in other people's estimation. Like *fetch*. The older speaker is not likely to be aware of this and will probably be inclined to ascribe the snickers of the young at his speech to that degeneration of manners which every generation has deplored in its juniors. But a word which is coming up in the scale—like *jazz*, say, or, more recently, *crap*—will strike his ear at once. We are much more aware of offenses given us than of those we give. And if he turns to a dictionary and finds the offending word listed as standard—or even listed, apparently—his response is likely to be an outburst of indignation.

But the dictionary can neither snicker nor fulminate. It records. It will offend many, no doubt, to find the expression *wise up,* meaning to inform or to become informed, listed in the Third International with no restricting label. To my aging ears it still sounds like slang. But the evidence—quotations from the *Kiplinger Washington Letter* and the *Wall Street Journal*—convinces me that it is I who am out of step, lagging behind. If such publications have taken to using *wise up* in serious contexts, with no punctuational indication of irregularity, then it is obviously respectable. And finding it so listed and supported, I can only say that it's nice to be informed and sigh to realize that I am becoming an old fogy. But, of course, I don't have to use it (and I'll be damned if I will! "Let them smile, as I do now, At the old forsaken bough Where I cling").

In part, the trouble is due to the fact that there is no standard for standard. Ideas of what is proper to use in serious, dignified speech and writing are changing—and with breathtaking rapidity. This is one of the major facts of contemporary American English. But it is no more the dictionary's business to oppose this process than to speed it up.

Even in our standard speech some words are more dignified and some more informal than others, and dictionaries have tried to guide us through these uncertainties by marking certain words and constructions as "colloquial," meaning "inappropriate in a formal situation." But this distinction, in the opinion of most scholars, has done more harm than good. It has created the notion that these particular words are inferior, when actually they might be the best possible words in an informal statement. And so—to the rage of many reviewers—the Third International has dropped this label. Not all labels, as angrily charged, but only this one out of a score. And the doing so may have been an error, but it certainly didn't constitute "betrayal" or "abandoning of all distinctions." It was intended to end a certain confusion.

In all the finer shades of meaning, of which the status of a word is only one, the user is on his own, whether he likes it or not. Despite *Life's* artless assumption about the Gettysburg Address, nothing worth writing is written *from* a dictionary. The dictionary, rather, comes along afterwards and describes what *has been* written.

Words in themselves are not dignified, or silly, or wise, or malicious. But they can be used in dignified, silly, wise, or malicious ways by dignified, silly, wise, or malicious people. *Egghead,* for example, is a perfectly legitimate word, as legitimate as *highbrow* or *long-haired.* But there is something very wrong and very undignified, by civilized standards, in a belligerent dislike for intelligence and education. *Yak* is an amusing word for persistent chatter. Anyone could say, "We were just yakking over a cup of coffee," with no harm to his dignity. But to call a Supreme Court decision *yakking* is to be vulgarly insulting and so, undignified. Again, there's nothing wrong with *confab* when it's appropriate. But when the work of a great research project, employing hundreds of distinguished scholars over several decades and involving the honor of one of the greatest publishing houses in the world, is described as *confabbing* (as the New York *Times* editorially described the preparation of the Third International), the use of this particular word asserts that the lexicographers had merely sat around and talked idly. And the statement becomes undignified—if not, indeed, slanderous.

The lack of dignity in such statements is not in the words, nor in the dictionaries that list them, but in the hostility that deliberately seeks this tone of expression. And in expressing itself the hostility frequently shows that those who are expressing it don't know how to use a dictionary. Most of the reviewers seem unable to read the Third International and unwilling to read the Second.

The *American Bar Association Journal,* for instance, in a typical outburst ("a deplorable abdication of responsibility"), picked out for special scorn the inclusion in the Third International of the word *irregardless.* "As far as the new Webster's is concerned," said the *Journal,* "this meaningless verbal bastard is just as legitimate as any other word in the dictionary." Thirty seconds spent in examining the book they were so roundly condemning would have shown them that in it *irregardless* is labeled "nonstand"—which means "nonstandard," which means "not conforming to the usage generally characteristic of educated native speakers of the language." Is that "just as legitimate as any other word in the dictionary"?

The most disturbing fact of all is that the editors of a dozen of the most influential publications in America today are under the impression that *authoritative* must mean *authoritarian.* Even the "permissive" Third International doesn't recognize this identification—editors' attitudes being not yet, fortunately, those of the American people. But the Fourth International may have to.

The new dictionary may have many faults. Nothing that tries to meet an ever-changing situation over a terrain as vast as contemporary English can hope to be free of them. And much in it is open to honest, and informed, disagreement. There can be linguistic objection to the eradication of proper names. The removal of guides to pronunciation from the foot of every page may not have been worth the valuable space it saved. The new method of defining words of many meanings has disadvantages as well as advantages. And of the half million or more definitions, hundreds, possibly thousands, may seem inadequate or imprecise. To some (of whom I am one) the omission of the label "colloquial" will seem meritorious; to others it will seem a loss.

But one thing is certain: anyone who solemnly announces in the year 1962 that he will be guided in matters of English usage by a dictionary published in 1934 is talking ignorant and pretentious nonsense.

The Lexicographer's Uneasy Chair

JAMES SLEDD

". . . this latest dictionary to bear the Merriam-Webster label is an intellectual achievement of the very highest order."
—Sumner Ives in *Word Study*

". . . the anxiously awaited work that was to have crowned cisatlantic linguistic scholarship with a particular glory turns out to be a scandal and a disaster."
—Wilson Follett in the *Atlantic*

"Somebody had goofed."
—Ethel Merman in *Webster's Third New International Dictionary*

But who? Is the goof trademarked, a Merriam-Webster, or is scholarship in Springfield trans-*Atlantic*? The experts will have to answer that question, and thoughtful laymen after using the new dictionary for a long time. This review has more modest aims. Mainly it examines a few issues which less inhibited critics have already raised, suggests some possible limitations of their criticisms, and urges that the serious work of serious scholars must be seriously judged.

Everyone knows that the *Third International* is an entirely new dictionary for use today. In this eighth member of a series which began in 1828, the Merriam Company has invested over $3,500,000, almost three times the cost of the 1934 *New International,* so that the statements in *Webster's Third* are backed by over a century of experience, by the evidence of more than 10,000,000 citations, and by the knowledge and skill of a large permanent staff and more than 200 special consultants. To a reviewer, those facts should be rather sobering.

College English, XXIII (May 1962), 682–687. Reprinted with the permission of the National Council of Teachers of English and James Sledd.

Some editors, however, and some reviewers have not been restrained from prompt attacks. They have criticized the *Third International* for its failure to include expected encyclopedic matter, for its technique of definition, and especially for its treatment of what is called usage; and they have charged Dr. Gove and his associates with unwise innovations motivated by the desire to destroy all standards of better and worse in the use of English. While insisting upon the responsibility of lexicographers, some of the attackers have not been equally alert to the responsibility of critics.

The question of motives can be dismissed at once. The lexicographers at the Merriam Company, it may safely be assumed, have just one motive: to make the best possible dictionaries. They may have failed, in one respect or another; but such innovations as they actually have made have not been made without the most serious and responsible consideration.

The charge of unwise innovation has two parts: first, that an innovation has been made; and second, that it is unwise. Some of the critics have assumed that the editors of the *Third International* have departed from established lexicographical custom by assuming the role of historians, not lawgivers. One reviewer, indeed, to prove his accusation that the lexicographers had abandoned authority for permissiveness, quoted a part of their statement that "the standard of English pronunciation . . . is the usage that now prevails among the educated and cultured people to whom the language is vernacular." He had not bothered to read precisely the same statement in the 1934 *New International*.

More generally, too many of the unfavorable critics have ignored the whole history of English lexicography since Samuel Johnson: they have hurried to denounce an innovation as unwise before establishing the fact of innovation. Already in the eighteenth century, the ideal of the standard and standardizing dictionary had been sharply questioned. The encyclopedist Ephraim Chambers declared his view that "the Dictionary-Writer is not supposed to have any hand in the things he relates; he is no more concerned to make the improvements, or establish the significations, than the historian" to fight the battles he describes. Even Johnson said of himself that he did not "form, but register the language," that he did not "teach men how they should think, but relate how they have hitherto expressed their thoughts"; and when Englishmen a century later set out to make the great *Oxford Dictionary*, they assumed from the beginning that the lexicographer is "an historian" of the language, "not a critic." It may be that professional lexicographers have been on the wrong track for two centuries and that in two hours an amateur can set them straight; but in that event the amateur and not the lexicographer would be the innovator. He would do well, before attempting to put his lawgiving theory into practice, to face Johnson's doubts in that magnificent "Preface" and to ask himself the unanswerable question how rational choice among the resources of a language is possible for the man who does not know what those resources are.

The relation between a dictionary and an encyclopedia is another problem whose history should have been better known to some reviewers. Few lexicographers are likely to solve it either to their own full satisfaction or to the satisfaction of all their readers. From the *Third International,* the objectors miss the gazetteer and the biographical dictionary of the 1934 volume, and they dislike the new decision to restrict the word-list "to generic words . . . as distinguished from proper names that are not generic." Other readers might just as well make opposite complaints. The hairy-nosed wombat and the hickory shuckworm do not greatly interest the average American, who has equally little need to know the incubation period of the ostrich or the gestation period of the elephant, to contemplate the drawing of a milestone marked "Boston 20 miles," or to examine a colorplate of fishes which is a slander to the catfish and the brook trout; and the occasional philologist might hope for a dictionary which explains words and leaves to the encyclopedia, as Murray said, the description of things. But who can say that he knows infallibly how such decisions should be made? Murray did not claim infallibility but admitted inconsistency in his omission of *African* and inclusion of *American.* Since man and the universe cannot be put between two covers, some things must be omitted; "selection is guided by usefulness"; and usefulness can be guessed at but not measured. Readers who can get the use of a Webster's unabridged will have access to an encyclopedia. They should consult it when they need to know about people and places. Meanwhile they may be grateful that the *Third International* has made space for as many quotations as it now includes. A dictionary without quotations is like a table of contents without a book.

There remain, of the critics' favorite subjects, the technique of definition and the matter of usage. The technique of definition is briefly explained in the editor's preface:

> The primary objective of precise, sharp defining has been met through development of a new dictionary style based upon completely analytical one-phrase definitions throughout the book. Since the headword in the definition is intended to be modified only by structural elements restrictive in some degree and essential to each other, the use of commas either to separate or to group has been severely limited, chiefly to units in apposition or in series. The new defining pattern does not provide for a predication which conveys further expository comment. . . . Defining by synonym is carefully avoided by putting all unqualified or undifferentiated terms in small capital letters. Such a term in small capitals should not be considered a definition but a cross-reference to a definition of equivalent meaning that can be substituted for the small capitals.
>
> A large number of verbal illustrations mostly from the mid-twentieth century has been woven into the defining pattern with a view to contributing considerably to the user's interest and understanding by showing a word used in context.

If it is not naively optimistic to expect most critics of a dictionary to agree on anything, general approval may be expected for careful synonymies and for the distinction between a synonym and a definition; and the value of illustrative quotations has been demonstrated by centuries of English lexicography. The objection that not many mid-century authors deserve quotation has already been answered, for it is only another form of the notion that the lexicographer should be a lawgiver and not a historian. It would, moreover, be rash to suggest either that many of the quotations are not particularly informative or that identification by the mere names of the authors makes it impossible to check the quotations or to examine them in their contexts: with 10,000,000 quotations to choose from, the editors must know the possibilities of choice more fully than any critic, and precise references would take up much valuable space.

The definitions themselves are another matter. Without advancing any claim to special competence, an ordinary reader may fairly report that he finds some of the definitions extraordinarily clumsy and hard to follow and that as an English teacher he would not encourage his students to follow the new Merriam-Webster model. The one-phrase definitions of nouns in particular may become confusing because in English it is hard to keep track of the relations among a long series of prepositional phrases, participial phrases, and relative clauses; the reader may simply forget what goes with what, if indeed he ever can find out. A less serious criticism is that the new typeface and the long entries unbroken by indentation are bad for middle-aged eyes. Real mistakes, of course, are extremely rare, but a fisherman may be pardoned an objection to the fourth numbered definition of the noun *keeper* as "a fish large enough to be legally caught." The crime is not catching but keeping an undersized or oversized fish.

Perhaps such a quibble is itself no keeper, and some criticism of the dictionary's treatment of usage has been equally frivolous. An excellent bad example appeared in *Life*, whose editors compressed a remarkable amount of confusion into a single sentence when they attacked "Editor Gove" for "saying that if a word is misused often enough, it becomes acceptable." Though one can argue how much use and by what speakers is enough, consistency would force *Life's* editors into silence. Their sacred kye are scrawnier than Pharaoh's seven kine, and it is shocking that the influence of such a magazine should force learning to debate with ignorance.

Yet so loud a stridulation of critics cannot simply be ignored. There is a real question whether the *Third International,* though justly called "the most comprehensive guide to usage currently available," has recorded usage as precisely as it might have done. Were the editors right to abandon "the status label *colloquial*"? Have they adequately reported not only what people say and write but also those opinions concerning speech and writing which properly enter into their own definitions of *standard* and of *Standard English*? Those are legitimate questions to ask of a dictionary "prepared with a constant regard for the needs of the high school and college student" and of the general reader. However diffidently and respectfully, a reviewer must give the best answers that he can.

Several reasons have been offered, by various authorities, for the abandonment of the label *colloquial*. Those reasons are not all alike. It is one thing to say that we cannot know "whether a word out of context is colloquial or not" (Gove), that lexicographers cannot distinguish the "many different degrees of standard usage" by status labels but can only suggest them by quotations (Gove), or that "the bases for discrimination are often too subtle for exact and understandable verbal statement" (Ives); it is quite another thing to argue against marking words *colloquial* because many readers have wrongly concluded that a word so marked is somehow bad (Ives). In a matter to which the editors must have given their best thought, the variety itself of these justifications and the failure to order them in any coherent and inclusive statement is somewhat puzzling; and the impertinent might be tempted to inquire how 200,000 quotations will enable the inexpert reader to do what 10,000,000 quotations did not make possible for the expert lexicographer or how a dictionary can be made at all if nothing can go into it which the ignorant might misinterpret. One reason for the widespread misinterpretation of the policy adopted is surely that the underlying theory has not been clearly explained.

And that is not all. The very defenses of the new policy appear sometimes to refute the contention that finer discriminations are not possible than those in *Webster's Third*. When the newspapers attack the dictionary for listing words like *double-dome* and *finalize* as standard, defenders reply by citing other slangy or colloquial or much reprobated terms from the columns of those same newspapers. What is the force of the attack or the defense unless the intelligent layman can draw precisely that distinction between "the formal and informal speech and writing of the educated" which the *Third International* refuses to draw for him? If he lacked that ability, both attackers and defenders would be wasting their citations.

Much can be said, of course, about the confusion of styles in modern writing. Perhaps distinctions among styles are now indeed less clear and stable than they were in a less troubled age; perhaps the clumsier writers do ignore the existing distinctions while the sophisticated use them to play sophisticated tunes; perhaps the scrupulously objective lexicographer cannot establish those distinctions from his quotation slips alone. For all that, distinctions do exist. They exist in good writing, and they exist in the linguistic consciousness of the educated. Dr. Gove's definers prove they exist when they give *egghead* as a synonym for *double-dome* but then define *egghead* in impeccably formal terms as "one with intellectual interests or pretensions" or as "a highly educated person." Such opposition between theory and practice strikes even a timid and generally admiring reviewer as rather odd, as though some notion of scientific objectivity should require the scientist to deny that he knows what he knows because he may not know how he knows it.

In the absence, then, of convincing argument to the contrary, a simple reader is left with the uneasy feeling that the abandonment of "*Colloq.*" was a mistake which the introduction of more quotations does not quite rectify and that as a teacher he must now provide foreigners and inexperienced students both with some general principles of linguistic choice and with specific instruction in instances where the new dictionary does not discriminate finely enough among stylistic variants. The dictionary leaves unlabeled many expressions which this teacher would not allow a beginning writer to use in serious exposition or argument except for clearly intended and rather special effects: (*to be caught*) *with one's pants down, dollarwise, stylewise* (*s.v. -wise*), (*to give one*) *the bird, dog* "something inferior of its kind," *to enthuse, to level* "deal frankly," *schmaltz, chintzy, the catbird seat, to roll* "rob," *to send* "delight," *shindig, shook-up, square* "an unsophisticated person," *squirrelly, to goof*, and the like. Enforcing such modest niceties will now be more difficult; for classroom lawyers and irate parents will be able to cite the dictionary which the teacher has taught Johnny how to read but which has collapsed the distinction between formal and informal Standard English. Similar difficulties could occur with various mild obscenities, such as *pissed off* and *pisspoor*, which should be marked not only as slang but with some one of the warning labels that the dictionary attaches to the almost quite adequately recorded four-letter words; and the label *slang* itself might well be more freely used with the various synonyms for *drunk—stewed, stinko, stoned, tight, tanked, sozzled, potted, pie-eyed, feeling no pain, blind, looped, squiffed, boiled, fried, high*, etc. Odzooks!

The convenience of a classroom teacher, however, is a rather petty criterion by which to judge a great dictionary, and the tiny handful of evidence here alleged must not be taken as justifying the shrill lament that *Webster's Third* is "a scandal and a disaster." The wake has been distinctly premature. Both the dictionary and the language it records are likely to survive the keening critics, whose exaggerations are something of a stumbling block themselves. The mere extent of the information in a dictionary unabridged should fix in a reviewer's mind the salutary knowledge that as no one man can make such a book, so no one man can judge it; but the popular reviews of the *Third International* have merely skimmed its surface and have said little of its technical features or substantial accomplishments. The present discussion will conclude with a few slight remarks on some such matters and with the renewed insistence that longer use and more expert study will be necessary before the dictionary can be definitively judged.

Teachers of elementary composition may be especially interested in the dictionary's three well-filled pages on English punctuation. As several recent grammarians have done, the editors attempt to establish definite relations between pointing and intonation, and they pursue that end with some care and vigor: the theory that punctuation may in part be taught by relating it to pitch-contours and to pauses here receives a better-than-average statement.

Yet the composition teacher may still be sceptical. For one thing, no account of English intonation has deserved or won universal acceptance. The editors themselves thus seem to postulate more than the three "pauses" allowed in the Trager-Smith phonology, which their description directly or indirectly follows. What is worse is the failure of the proposed relationships between speech and pointing as one moves from dialect to dialect: rules that may hold in one region do not hold in another. For much Southern American speech and for much Southern British, it is simply not the case that "the rising pause . . . is usually indicated in writing by a comma"; for many speakers and writers in many areas, an exclamation point may correspond to a *low*-pitched "terminal stress" as well as to a high one; and a colon may be used in writing not just for "a fading or sustained pause in speech" but for a "rising pause" or for no pause at all. The editors have weakened their case by stating it too simply and too strongly.

For the linguistically inclined, Mr. Edwin Artin's extensive "Guide to Pronunciation" will have a particular attraction. The "Guide" is just that—a guide; "not a treatise on phonetics" or a structural dialectologist's systematic account of American pronunciation, but an explanation of the way the editors have used their new alphabet in their transcriptions. Though the forgetful will regret that the key is no longer before them at each opening, and though a stern phonemicist might call the whole system sloppy, the new alphabet is an arguable solution to an extremely complex theoretical and practical problem and a definite improvement over the more complicated yet less accurate and more misleading diacritical key in the *Webster's* of 1934. The objective in devising the alphabet "was a set of symbols which would represent each speech sound which distinguishes one word from another and each difference in sound which is associated with some large region of the country" (Ives), so that the editors might record both the formal and the informal pronunciations actually heard in cultivated conversation from speakers of the standard dialects in the various regions. The *Third International* can thus do fuller justice than its predecessor did to regional variation and to modes of speech less artificial than the "formal platform speech" of the earlier work.

Like every competent writer on American pronunciation, Mr. Artin will be criticized as well as praised. He writes, indeed, at a particularly difficult time, when phonological theory is so unsettled that rival groups among the linguists can scarcely communicate with one another. Since pleasing one group of theorists means displeasing its opponents, since it is easily possible to please neither or none, and since Mr. Artin does not include in his "Guide" the sort of general and historical information which could be found in the corresponding section of the 1934 dictionary, perhaps he will not have so large an audience as Kenyon reached. His readers will be the kind who will argue the results of equating the medial consonants of *tidal* and *title* because in some dialects they are phonetically identical or of distinguishing them because the preceding diphthongs may be of different lengths and because the consonants of *tide* and *titular* clearly differ. Other readers, if they find the "Guide" hard going, will not risk too much confusion by limiting their study to the table of symbols and to the short section on pronunciation in the "Explanatory Notes."

Within the dictionary proper, the word-list first invites examination. Like the addenda to the later editions of the *Second,* the vexing miscellaneous entries at the bottoms of the pages are now gone from *Webster's Third,* either dropped or worked into the main alphabet; numerous obsolete words have disappeared, since the cut-off date has been advanced from 1500 to 1755; and further space for additions has been found by rejecting many no longer useful terms from the rapidly changing and never generally current technical vocabulary with which both the *Second* and the *Third International* are stuffed. This plethora of scientific and technical terms, carefully gathered in an elaborate reading program, is of course no plethora at all but only a comfortable supply for the scientist and technologist, who seem pleased with the dictionary's coverage of their fields; and a general dictionary must make room as well for some regionalisms, for a certain amount of recent slang, and for the new words in general use which so eloquently damn our culture. When all this has been done, it would be unfair to complain that perhaps not enough attention has been paid to the distinctive vocabularies of English-speaking nations other than Britain and the United States.

Beyond the word-list, neither space nor the reviewer's competence will allow him to go. He has few complaints about spelling, the only loud one being against *alright;* as far as a layman's knowledge goes, the etymologies are accurate, and beyond that point they remain clear and comprehensible; the discrimination and the arrangement of senses impose silence on the reader who has not studied them with the same care that went into their making; and the synonymies have already proved their practical value. A sweeping conclusion will not be expected of a review whose thesis is that the prematurity of sweeping conclusions has already been sufficiently exemplified, but a moderately serious examination has made a few things perfectly plain about the *Third International*. As a completely new, independent, responsibly edited, unabridged dictionary, no other work can rival it on precisely its own ground. Its merits are infinitely greater than those of the reviews which have lightly questioned them. Time and the experts will ultimately decide its just rank in the world of English lexicography, whether above, below, or alongside its predecessor; but meanwhile it can usefully fill a place in the libraries of a generation.

Questions

1. How do the approaches to *Webster's Third* of Macdonald, Evans, and Sledd differ? Which position would you choose to defend, and why?
2. What are the positions taken by Macdonald and Sledd on the entry of names? Which do you agree with?

EXERCISES 63

3. What does Evans think a dictionary is for? What does Macdonald think a dictionary is for?
4. What is the difference between a descriptive approach to putting the dictionary together and a prescriptive one? Which of these approaches did the Merriam-Webster Company follow in putting out *Webster's Third*? What evidence can you offer for your answer? (Before answering, see especially Sledd's comments on these matters.)
5. What is a nonce word? Can you give any examples of nonce words other than those quoted in the essays?
6. What is the strongest point made by Macdonald? By Evans? By Sledd? Do you agree with any of these? Why? What weakness in *Webster's Third* do at least two of the writers agree on?
7. How does Macdonald distinguish between "pedantry" and "scholarship"? Is this distinction important? Why? What do you think would be the position of Evans or Sledd on this distinction?
8. How does Evans demonstrate his point that "The difference . . . between the much-touted Second International (1934) and the much-clouted Third International (1961) is not like the difference between yearly models [of automobiles] but like the difference between the horse and buggy and the automobile. Between the appearance of these two editions a whole new science related to the making of dictionaries, the science of descriptive linguistics, has come into being."
9. What is the main difference between Macdonald's discussion of the concepts of the modern science of language and the discussions of Sledd and Evans?
10. Is the argument that a word exists a good one to justify inclusion of that word in a dictionary? Should "ain't" and "irregardless" be listed in a dictionary? If "no," why not? If "yes," how would you list them?
11. Should you not use a dictionary because it contains words that you don't like? Why do you suppose that *Webster's Third* offended so many people and so strongly? Are you offended?

Assignments

1. Make up a list of a half dozen words *not* in *Webster's Third* that are widely used in polite discourse today. These words may be technical ones from an occupation or a profession, new slang expressions, combinations of familiar words, or familiar words used in a new sense or in a sense not recorded by the dictionary. Define these words in the manner of *Webster's Third* and quote contexts in which each appears in the sense defined.
2. Translate the editorial in the New York *Times* quoted by Macdonald into "good" English. Indicate for at least three of the expressions why you have changed them.
3. Find out what lexicography Bergen Evans himself has done. Look at this work in the library and write an analysis of one aspect of it.
4. Describe the nature and the purpose of one of the various unabridged dictionaries to be found in the reference room of your college library.
5. Compare the entries for the word "money" in a desk dictionary, in *Webster's Second,* in *Webster's Third,* and in *The Oxford English Dictionary*. Which entry is the fullest? Why? In what specific ways do the several entries differ from one another? How do you account for these differences? Write a definition of "money" in your own words that would be understood by a child who has not yet entered elementary school.

6. Describe in some detail how you would go about putting together a dictionary. Referring to the articles by Macdonald, Evans, and Sledd, indicate and justify how you would follow the usual procedure and how you would depart from it.
7. Write an essay on the uses of a dictionary, referring as appropriate to Macdonald, Evans, and Sledd.
8. Write an essay comparing a foreign with an English dictionary.

Additional Reading

Following the publication of *Webster's Third*, in 1961, a vigorous, heated, and almost always controversial debate broke out in newspapers and magazines regarding not only the merits of *Webster's Third* as opposed to those of the earlier editions of the *New International*, but also the whole purpose of a dictionary. Many of these articles, editorials, and essays may be found in *Dictionaries and That Dictionary*, edited by James Sledd and Wilma R. Evans (Chicago, 1962). One of the strongest attacks was that made by Jacques Barzun, "What Is A Dictionary?" *American Scholar*, XXXII (Spring 1963), 176–181. Comments on Barzun's article may be found in the *American Scholar*, XXXII (Autumn 1963), 604–608. Interesting material on how a dictionary is put together may be found in *Young Sam Johnson*, by James L. Clifford (New York, 1955), and in Johnson's preface to his dictionary, as well as in the introductions to *Webster's Second* and *Third*. Allan Walker Read, in *"That* Dictionary or *The* Dictionary?" *Consumer Reports*, XXVIII (October 1963), 488–492, surveys the problems, the shortcomings, and the achievements of *Webster's Third*, with some reference to other unabridged dictionaries.

SECTION TWO | The Encyclopaedia Britannica *and the* Business of Knowledge

The Modern EB: *How It Is Edited*

HERMAN KOGAN

In editorial methods and procedures, the modern *Encyclopaedia Britannica*, unlike its predecessors, represents a kind of complex journalism. Its system of continuous revision, in effect since publication of the fourteenth edition, sets up rigid deadlines and strict schedules, requires constant scrutiny of its contents and a steady watchfulness on world events necessitating textual alterations, and makes imperative keeping its information as up to date as is possible in a set of books whose forty-one thousand articles comprise more than forty million words.

Vital to this system is a corps of permanent advisers, some seventy-five scholars on the faculties of the University of Chicago and other major American universities and from Great Britain's London, Cambridge, and Oxford universities. Each of these advisers has a definitely assigned function: to watch articles within his field of specialization. Each counsels the encyclopaedia's editors on the necessity for current revision of an article, the need for additions, deletions, or entirely new articles, and the contributors most competent to make such changes or to write fresh material.

By methods devised by two veteran editorial workers, Mrs. Mae MacKay and Mrs. Harriet Milburn, a large editing staff checks articles, works on the important index volume, and handles and controls the flow of copy from contributors. The task is a constant one, for to supplant the numbered editions there have been, since the fourteenth edition in 1929, new printings at least once each year and sometimes more frequently. Some changes have been

Reprinted from *The Great E.B.*, by Herman Kogan, by permission of The University of Chicago Press. © 1958 by Herman Kogan.

minor—a shift in a statistic, a change of personnel, a correction of a spelling error. But some of the larger revisions have involved changing or rewriting as many as four million words and recruiting over four hundred new contributors.

Inevitably, new information seldom fits neatly into established revision schedules. With the explosion of the atom bomb at Hiroshima and subsequent fast-moving developments, a full article on the subject was required swiftly, and to make room for it four full pages of new material were inserted in the proper volume. Made suspect, too, by the explosion, were some five hundred other articles, from "Alchemy" to "Uranium," which had to be checked—and, in many cases, altered—by editorial workers before the onrushing deadline for a scheduled new printing. When Elizabeth II became the British queen in 1952, more than a few royal biographies and articles on English history were affected. Her accession added a Roman numeral to the first Elizabeth. Further, because of the British custom of referring to virtually all government offices, official celebrations, and prizes in the name of the sovereign, all through the work were scattered references to the high court of justice known as "King's Bench Division," "His Majesty's Stationer," and "King's Scouts." These had to be changed. Yet there were exceptions to the rule, such as the "King's Cup Race," which retained its old designation. The "King's Prize" for shooting, on the other hand, had to be altered, as did the British anthem, now "God Save the Queen."

Most frequently in need of periodic revision are the scientific sections. In some scientific fields, changes can be anticipated; all articles in these classifications are scheduled for review by specified monitors at short intervals. But sometimes unexpected developments occur. In 1953, when anthropologists declared that the Piltdown man's jaw was a hoax, and thereby revised many suggested theories of modern man's origins, editor Walter Yust and his aides immediately consulted the index for references. They were relieved to find that the article on the subject did note that many experts had always expressed doubts about the find. But it also stated that the jaw represented an individual of early Pleistocene times. The article was not scheduled for full review until 1956. But to report the hoax as soon as possible, without waiting for that printing or for a special discussion of the subject in the *Book of the Year*, the editors quickly consulted one of the advisers on anthropology. And he specified how, with a minimum of patching on the actual plates from which the article was printed, interim alterations could be made immediately.

Wars have always caused drastic changes—and editorial headaches. Destroyed monuments and buildings, migrations and increases or decreases in population, new boundaries, new alliances, political shifts, the establishment of new independent states—all must be recorded in the reference work as soon as possible, for readers are quick to note such omissions. An example of how political changes can be vexatious is the checkered history of Vilnyus, the

European city also known as Wilno and Vilna. Before 1938 it was in dispute between Poland and Lithuania; then it was seized on March 17 of that year by Poland, captured by the Soviet Union in September, 1939, ceded to Lithuania a month later, taken again by the Soviet Union on June 15, 1940, lost to Germany on June 22, returned in the summer of 1944 to Soviet control, and ultimately established as the capital of the Lithuanian Soviet Socialist Republic. Doggedly, the *Encyclopaedia Britannica* editors followed and recorded the shifting fortunes of this city and of others similarly affected.

Physical catastrophes send the editors scurrying to the latest printing of their work. In 1950, researchers had just completed some three hundred editorial changes to incorporate the latest findings concerning heights of peaks, lengths of rivers, and populations of cities in the vast Himalayan mountain range. Almost simultaneously with the completion of this detailed job, heavy earthquakes were reported in that area. The mountains were said to be "crawling southward" under the influence of violent earth shocks; some peaks were abruptly rising and others were falling, rivers were changing their courses, whole villages were disappearing. All the toil that had preceded the news of these disasters had to be repeated for the next printing.

As with a newspaper, certain kinds of material can be prepared before a specific event. As soon as the Presidential candidates of all parties are nominated, for instance, assignments are instantly made for full biographies of each nominee, and appropriate photographs are assembled. At the same time, shorter biographies are also prepared. When the results of the national election are known, the full biography of the winner and the pictures are sped to the printers, as is the shorter biography of the loser. Similarly, if and when Alaska and Hawaii are admitted to statehood, the *Encyclopaedia Britannica* will be ready; changes will be necessary in at least 514 articles and in the big full-color plate now showing the forty-eight-starred American flag. Occasionally, a new edition has been held up just beyond a set deadline to record a late development. When Franklin D. Roosevelt died suddenly, the editors were able to insert this event into the work along with information about his successor, Harry S. Truman. When Pope Pius XII was critically ill, the printers were asked to hold pertinent sections of Volume XVII ("P" to "Planti") as long as possible; this was done, although the crisis was passed when the pontiff took a turn for the better and survived his illness.

II

At the heart of the complex system designed to maintain the flow of fresh material into those areas where alterations are most frequently required is the copy-control section built over the years since adoption of continuous revision. But there are essential preliminaries to the work of copy control. Two years before each new printing, Yust carefully studies the schedule of some thirty subject classifications into which the millions of words are divided. After conferences with his immediate aides and after studying recommendations from scores of editorial advisers, he selects the articles deemed in need of revision. When the lists of articles to be revised are drawn, they are dispatched to the specific advisers at American and English universities for the names of likely contributors. Generally the suggestions of these scholars on the need for change and the best possible contributors are followed, since they are all prime authorities in their respective fields. But occasionally an adviser is challenged, as when one proposed that the biographies of Octavia and Miranda Hill, nineteenth-century pioneers in British housing, be deleted for "more important matter," inasmuch as neither was especially well known outside of England. This suggestion evoked from John Armitage, the set's London editor, the protest: "I feel faint at the suggestion. Miranda may . . . depart from the title but Octavia stands second in our line of 19th century heroines to Florence Nightingale. Her name is honourably mentioned in any review of housing, and housing managers cannot pass their examinations without a knowledge of her life and work. . . . If Octavia does not rate as a great woman, there is none." The adviser was overruled and neither of the Hill sisters was eliminated.

Dates, names, and essential details about the articles to be revised are recorded by the copy-control section on large cards in a mechanical device variously known among the hundred editorial workers as "the Robot" or "the Monster." With the flick of a switch, it can disclose the precise status of every article. Indeed, every bit of data about a specific article, from the moment a prospective contributor is asked to handle it to the date on which the corrected proof is sent to the printer, is known to the Robot and remains known not only for the current edition but for those of the future. The Robot has rarely lost a challenge. A group of advisers clustered around it once defied a young lady in charge to inform them what had happened to the article on "Goldfish." She flipped a knob, looked at a card, then turned to one of the professors, saying, "Why, you've been holding it for two months and we've been trying to get it from you." Another inquired about an article in his specialty and was quickly informed, "The contributor has died and we are expecting a suggestion from you for a successor." When the adviser expressed surprise, explaining that he had only just heard of the contributor's death, he was told of another editorial worker whose task it is to examine each day's obituary notices in the *New York Times* and apprise the Robot of the demise of any contributor.

On receipt of the names of proposed contributors, letters of solicitation, specific in content and intent, are dispatched to them. They state briefly what is wanted and by what date, and that the rate of compensation is five dollars for reading each page of printed text and two cents a word for writing the revision, a rate established at the time of the publication of the fourteenth edition. The invitation is sometimes rejected, but rarely because of low payment. Most experts and scholars realize the prestige attached to being asked to contribute to the *Encyclopaedia Britannica,* and less than 2 per cent of those invited have ever declined.

An avid statistician once reckoned the number of processes from the time the copy is solicited until it appears in its proper place in the proper volume some nine months later to be 569. When the contributor accepts his assignment, a copy of the article in the latest printing is sent to him, and the date is entered on the proper card in the Robot. A favorite story in the editorial lore of the company involves the head of a history department in a western university to whom a historical article, many years unchanged, was sent. In agreeing to revise it, the professor was aroused enough to write, "I'll be glad to do this for you. The article is badly organized, inaccurate and full of errors of both omission and commission." An investigation revealed that the critic was the man who had written the earlier article years before—a discovery that remained undisclosed until the new treatise had been received at the editor's desk.

Most writers of major articles are given at least a year to prepare their manuscripts; not until a month before the scheduled delivery of the article is the author prodded to produce it. Immediately upon receipt, the words are counted and payment is promptly made. This policy was instituted because of Yust's own experiences as a free-lance writer, when quick compensation, however small, often elated him more than a delayed check, however large.

The next step for the manuscript is the Robot, where receipt is recorded and a note made of illustrations furnished or needed. Along the route, the copy is read by the specialist advisers for authenticity, then checked several times by editorial workers. After Yust and his assistant editors read it, either the manuscript is approved or a rewrite is decreed. Never is any material rewritten by anyone save the contributor himself. Any article that is difficult to read or obtuse is sent back to the writer with a request that he clarify the bothersome sections. Although few specific instructions are sent to contributors, it has been deemed wise to ask physical scientists, who often write on technical matters which cannot be explained simply, to adhere to a few general rules. The opening paragraph of these instructions reads: "Each article under each heading should begin with a clear statement in one sentence of the meaning and scope of that heading, comparable to an extended dictionary definition. The first paragraph following that heading should be an amplification of the first sentence, possibly with a discussion of subheadings and the like if the article is to be a long one. If it is to be very long with a number of sections, there should be a short list of contents by section-titles and division-titles."

An article that does not require rewriting by the author and is finally approved is turned over to typists who retype it on copy-fitting paper. Subeditors then reread and check the article. They prepare layouts of the actual page where the article will be placed. By this time it is known whether the revised article will be longer or shorter than the original. For either eventuality, a solution is ready. In a Killer-Filler file are lists of short articles that advisers have suggested can be eliminated from the page or adjoining pages without arousing protests from readers or impairing the basic purposes of the encyclopaedia, and collections of likely entries, mainly brief biographies or extended definitions, that can be inserted if a new article runs short. If the Killer-Filler file cannot produce reasonable balm for the situation, part of the new entry, if too long, is set in smaller type or, often, an additional page is inserted.

Back to the copy-control section goes the article, once it has been tailored to fit. Initials of the contributor are affixed to the manuscript, and it is then transferred to indexers who arrange their cards on a circular device they call their Lazy Susan. They not only make direct changes but also note all cross-references, "see also's," and related data that may be affected by additions, deletions, and other changes.

A few more technical steps, and the copy is ready for the linotype operators at R. R. Donnelley and Sons's Lakeside Press. This occurs after proper notations have been transmitted to the Robot about the myriad details of specific articles. Proofs are sent to the writers for final checking and last-minute changes; all proofs are read, too, by editorial experts. In previous years proofs were rarely sent to contributors, but Yust put this into effect shortly after he became editor, for he realized the importance both professionally and psychologically of such a method. He also recalled with what indignation George Bernard Shaw replied when offered not proofs but a typed copy of his fourteenth-edition article on socialism. "Do not bother about sending me a typescript," Shaw scrawled on one of his postcards. "I have the carbon duplicate of the one I sent you, besides an earlier-corrected draft from which it was fair-copied. But if I cannot have a proof (which is really shocking) at least let the printer set up from my copy and not from a copy of it; for if the printer's errors are reinforced by the typist's errors, and both edited by an American proofreader who will conclude that I must mean exactly the opposite of what I had written (accidentally omitting the nots) the result will be disastrous."

III

Shaw is one of forty-three Nobel Prize winners among the four thousand contributors to the *Encyclopaedia Britannica*. Most of them, like Shaw and Einstein and Sir Norman Angell ("Outlawry of War"), Hans Adolph Krebs ("Citric Acid"), General George C. Marshall (a section of "World War II"), and J. J. R. Macleod ("Insulin"), were asked to contribute after they had won this honor. But some were contributors even before their selection: Ralph Bunche ("Beira," "Belgian Congo," and "Nairobi"), who wrote for the set four years before he won the Nobel Prize in 1950, and Professors Linus C. Pauling ("Theory of Resonance," "Valence," and "Ice") and Glenn T. Seaborg, author of six articles from "Actinium" to "Transuranium Elements."

Shaw's article, interestingly enough, has been little altered since its publication in 1929, although some additions have been made to it. This is true of other major and minor classics written for earlier editions that remain useful to students and scholars and casual readers alike. There are among them Thomas Babington Macaulay's biographical essays on Samuel Johnson, Oliver Goldsmith, and John Bunyan; Sir Donald Francis Tovey's writings on music, more than three dozen articles from "Aria" to "Wagner, Wilhelm Richard"; G. K. Chesterton's vivid, contentious treatise on Charles Dickens; Sigmund Freud's essay on "Psychoanalysis," with additions enumerating advances in the important field in which he pioneered; and Julian Huxley's authoritative "Courtship of Animals."

IV

The exigencies of time and expense often make it impossible for the continuous revision method to include as many changes as editors and readers would like. To help fill the gaps are the *Book of the Year* and the Library Research Service, both of which have developed here and in Great Britain since their beginnings in the 1930's.

The first of these, in addition to its subject surveys, contains more than a million words in its annual one thousand articles, reporting on developments and news during the previous year in activities varying from "Accident Prevention" and "Infantile Paralysis" to "Tariffs" and "Zoology." Each issue is new in content, but the list of subjects remains essentially stable. Editorial procedures resemble those of the parent set, but the time between receipt of manuscripts and finished volume is only five months. Deadlines for contributors are spread from mid-September to mid-December, with most articles due by the end of October. As with the encyclopaedia, a multitude of details including a great deal of reading and checking of data is involved before final copies are sent to the printer.

Since its origin, the function of the Library Research Service has been to reply to readers' questions on subjects not covered either in the set or in the yearbook. Each purchaser has the right to ask a maximum of fifty questions over a period of ten years, but no replies are given to seekers of medical or legal advice or specific professional or commercial information. In its first years, the service received questions that could often be answered by reference to only one or two books. But as readers became more conversant with the privileges of the valuable department and the amount of information that it could supply, the questions grew more involved and more difficult.

The service sends its researchers for information to many institutions, from the Chicago Public Library to New York's Library of Engineering Societies to the San Francisco Public Library and, of course, to the Library of Congress. Owners of the *Encyclopaedia Britannica* receive, in answer to their inquiries, individual, single-spaced reports, from four to as many as thirty pages long, made up of extracts from the highest authorities and supplemented by a bibliography to spur further individual study.

The department has always been stubborn in its refusal to be stumped.

Actually, its rate of defeat has been about 1 per cent. On the other hand, the following is a representative list of reports sent out in a single day after researchers had collected their material:

> Admission of China to the United Nations: Pro and Con
> Security Measures and the Threat to Civil Liberties
> Communism in the Schools
> The Future of the Coal Industry
> Statistics on the Sale of Soft Drinks in Bottles and Cans
> The Guaranteed Annual Wage
> Designing Skiving Tools
> Statistical Quality Control for the Electronics Industry
> Marketing Dehydrated Alfalfa
> Organization and Operation of a Fabric Mart
> Making Decorative Tiles for Table Tops
> Construction of a Buffet Sideboard With Hutch China Cupboard
> Interplanetary Navigation
> Tibetan Concept of Morality
> Maya Indian Baptismal Rites for Children Aged 3–12
> Psychoanalytical Interpretation of the Works of Dostoevsky and Shakespeare
> Current Soviet Theories on the Origin of the Solar System
> Lanchester's Equations on the Phugoid Theory of the Flight Path
> Nature Study for Children
> Children's Fears
> Federal Aid to Education

For owners of *Britannica Junior* an adjunct to the Library Research Service is designed to aid parents and children. Pamphlets, booklets, and bibliographies are available for set owners on an extensive range of problems, from "Babies: Their Care and Training" to "Cultural Activities for Children," in addition to specific reports on questions involving quarrels among siblings, activities for rainy days, eating habits, home duties for children, vocational opportunities, and sex instruction.

v

Despite all precautions, checking and rechecking, and expert proofreading, letters complaining of errors, omissions, defects, misstatements, or misinterpretations in E B are inevitable. Keen attention—even when the writer's return address is a state mental hospital and his missive an eight-page farrago of nonsense about how to achieve perpetual motion or square the circle—is paid to all letters. Sometimes these communications provide useful clues to new information and do catch mistakes which slipped past everyone on the 569-step route from contributor's desk to printed page. Every form of criticism, whether in letters or publications, is diligently investigated; many are referred to the contributor and to the relevant adviser. In an average year the most prevalent plaints, constituting some 70 per cent of the total number received, charge errors of fact or omission, yet careful editorial checks show that less than 6 per cent of such grievances have any validity.

Charges of non-inclusion are sometimes as difficult to down as the belief that rewards are offered for finding errors; that myth has persisted since the days when the company offered a prize of a dollar to any boy or girl who found a mistake in the early editions of *Britannica Junior*. Such awards were given only for a year or two, but letter writers still cagily ask about the "big prize" before disclosing the nature of the purported error. One correspondent in Ohio, when informed that the company would be happy to learn what mistakes he claimed to have found but had to decline to pay any premium, replied, "I, as a lawyer, sell my professional services. If you do not deign my information worth at least $50, let us drop the correspondence forthwith." At that, the Ohio lawyer was comparatively mild in his request. Demands others have made include (1) a new set of the *Encyclopaedia Britannica* plus the *World Atlas* and *World Language Dictionary*, (2) $5,000, and (3) a position as an assistant editor.

VI

For many years, no critic or scholar has had cause to write about the set with such vehemence as those who attacked William Robertson Smith's treatises on religious subjects in the 1880's or as Willard Huntington Wright did in his peevish *Misinforming a Nation* in 1917. Some of the bitterest attacks in recent years have come from the Soviet Union. In 1952, when the Soviet Union was claiming Russian origin of most of the great inventions, they assailed the editors of the *Encyclopaedia Britannica* as "modern savages" because Guglielmo Marconi instead of A. S. Popov was named the inventor of the wireless telegraph and James Watt instead of I. I. Polzunov was called "father of the steam engine." This, however, was not the first assault by the Soviets. Four years earlier, William Benton received a translation of an article in Moscow's *New Times* titled, "How the *Encyclopaedia Britannica* Distorts History." It was filled with allegations that "lies and fabrications" made up the work's articles on the Union of Soviet Socialist Republics. Benton forwarded copies to Hutchins and Yust for comment. Hutchins' reply was characteristically brief and pungent: "Nuts!" But Yust made a point-by-point rejoinder, carefully refuting the charges that the work had neglected the role of the Communist party in the Russian Revolution, that there was no mention of the Stakhanov movement to reward laborers for increased production, that the heroic defense of Stalingrad received not a word of attention, and that the official *History of the Communist Party of the Soviet Union* was unlisted. Besides citing page and line in his rejoinder, Yust suggested a more careful use of the index. By 1955, relations were more tranquil. Benton, visiting the Soviet Union, interviewed the editors of the Soviet encyclopaedia and asked if they were satisfied that the *Encyclopaedia Britannica* devoted a fair amount of space to their vast country. They replied affirmatively but insisted that their encyclopaedia was superior because of its "complete objectivity," although admitting that all articles were written, as B. A. Vvedensky, editor-in-chief, asserted, "from the position of our world outlook—Marxism-Leninism." After he returned to the United States, Benton dispatched copies of the latest printing of the *Encyclopaedia Britannica* to a number of Soviet officials whom he had met, including Premier Nicolai Bulganin and Klementi Voroshilov.

Despite the fact that *Encyclopaedia Britannica* has been American-owned since 1901, charges are still made that it is "pro-British"—a charge counterbalanced by critics who deplore its "Americanization." Many such letters begin, "Of course, I would not expect to find this in a British publication, but . . ." and then proceed to ask answers to questions as farfetched as "What was the name of the Dobermann Pinscher that won the best-of-breed in New York in 1921?" or "Why can't I find the maiden name of Molly Pitcher's mother in your set?" In one instance, Yust had special satisfaction in replying to an Anglophobe who demanded to know why Washington's Farewell Address was not included. "You point out," wrote Yust, "that *Britannica* does not reprint in its entirety Washington's Farewell Address, and you ascribe this to 'British bias.' You may have noted that the Declaration of Independence and the Constitution are printed in full. If you wish a copy of Washington's Farewell Address, let me refer you to the publication, 'Speeches and Documents in U.S. History.' It was published this year by Oxford University Press, whose main address is London, England."

Although articles on religion are rarely subjected to the type of criticism encountered by similar writings in earlier editions, occasional complaints are received about bias against specific creeds. Sometimes, in interesting contrast to the outcry of certain Catholic critics against articles in the eleventh edition, objections are heard that the articles on Catholic subjects have been subjected to "clerical shearing" by high-ranking members of that faith. One hasty critic insisted that all religious articles marked "X" at the end indicated such "censorship." What he did not know—but was quickly made aware of by the editors—was that the "X" signified that a subeditor had inserted current information or had made minor revisions. Actually, the current practice is to ask leaders of religious faiths to advise and verify factual points and, in the case of controversial issues, to ask the writer to compare opposing viewpoints. Since the 1957 printing and subsequent ones, certain articles pertaining to the New Testament, which had drawn frowns from Roman Catholic and Protestant clergy, were rewritten to the satisfaction of both groups by Professor Jaroslav Jan Pelikan, a young Lutheran minister and member of the University of Chicago's Federated Theological Faculty.

VII

Other sample queries and complaints: A man in Atlantic, Iowa, demanded to know if Jesse James was still alive and added, "I'll take your word for it." The reply was soon dispatched: "We too have heard rumors that Jesse James is still alive or that he did not die in 1882 but lived to be over 100 years old. However, it seems that all of the authoritative sources agree that he was killed in 1882." A woman from El Paso, Texas, wrote to acclaim her father the inventor of slot machines, and would the *Encyclopaedia Britannica* like to acquire the patent? Back went the reply that the *Encyclopaedia Britannica* never engages in such transactions, plus a bibliography to give the woman clues as to whether anyone preceded her father in devising this boon to mankind. A man from Mylo, North Dakota, complained that, although the work he had purchased was handsome and fascinating, he was appalled to find no Mylo, North Dakota, on any of the maps. To him was sent the answer that lack of space prevents the inclusion of towns with only 110 inhabitants. Another woman insisted on a definitive answer to her query about whether a sexually inactive man is more prolific intellectually. The careful reply, based on material gleaned from the Library Research Service, was that some men can be both romantic and intellectual and some cannot—with examples from history of each. A high school sophomore wrote, "You state that all arachnida possess an endoskeleton, but my biology teacher says they possess only an exoskeleton." The question was referred to Alexander Petrunkevitch, Yale professor emeritus of biology, who replied to the student that arachnida possess both an exoskeleton and an endoskeleton.

When one of his staff members informed Bruce Gould, editor of the *Ladies' Home Journal,* that in 1768 the *Encyclopaedia Britannica* had four sentences on the atom and five pages on love but that in the current edition there were nine pages on the atom and nothing on love, Gould queried Benton, an old friend of his: "Is it true that the *Britannica* ignores love? And, if so, why?" In reply, Gould received not only a list of index references to "love" in articles ranging from "Libido" to "Ethics, History Of," but also an interesting extract from the second edition's article on the subject:

> The symptoms produced by this passion are as follows: The eye-lids often twinkle; the eyes are hollow, and yet appear as if full with pleasure; the pulse is not peculiar to the passion, but the same with that which attends solicitude and care. When the object of this affection is thought of, particularly if the idea is sudden, the spirits are confused, the pulse changes, and its force and time are very variable; in some instances, the person is sad and watchful; in others, the person, not being conscious of his state, pines away, is slothful, and regardless of food; tho' the wiser, when they find themselves in love, seek pleasant company and active entertainments. As the force of love prevails, sighs grow deeper; a tremor affects the heart and pulse; the countenance is alternately pale and red; the voice is suppressed in the sauces; the eyes grow dim; cold sweats break out; sleep absents itself, at least until the morning; the secretions become disturbed; and a loss of appetite, a hectic fever, melancholy, or perhaps madness, if not death, constitutes the sad catastrophe.

To this Yust, commenting on the fact that the original article on "Love" was dropped after the eighth edition, added, "Perhaps previous editors agreed in a sense with the young lady on our staff who suggested the following reply to a similar criticism—'Love is better experienced than read about: the opposite is true of the atomic bomb.'"

Polite replies have been sent to less reasonable correspondents, including the man who maintained angrily that the principle of the rotary engine is spurious and offered the *Encyclopaedia Britannica* all rights to his treatise, "Fallacies in Rotary Design"; the befuddled student who wrote, "I want to ask you the Constitutional Convention of what year was composed of how many men appointed by the legislatures of what several states"; and the woman who insisted that only the editor could give her the formula for inhibiting growth of mold on her set of *Encyclopaedia Britannica*. (The answer was: "Wipe them with a rag which has been wrung out in a solution of half vinegar and half water, then rub the covers with a good paste wax.")

VIII

Yust's momentary irritation at discovering that a letter writer is correct and the *Encyclopaedia Britannica* is wrong has invariably been replaced instantly by a feeling of gratitude toward the correspondent. Mary Beard, wife of the historian Charles A. Beard and herself a scholar, once protested that too much space was given to biographies of men and not enough to those of women. Yust made a count and found that Mrs. Beard was justified. Of some thirteen thousand biographies, less than eight hundred were those of women. He wrote to thank Mrs. Beard for the information—then put her to work preparing the biographies of women she thought should have a place. Another correspondent, politely, but with a slight indication of petulance that such a stupid error could be made, wrote to inquire whether a formula printed in the encyclopaedia as "Cp equals $8.81 + 0.019T + 0.00000zzzT^2$" should not really read "Cp equals $8.81 - 0.019T - 0.00000zzzT^2$?" Yust checked with the adviser and contributor and replied, "You are correct, sir, and we are grateful to you." Yust has sent similar expressions of gratitude—after appropriate checking—to writers who reported that Russia's coldest temperature was not 94° below zero at Verkhoyansk but 103° below zero at Oimyakonsk; that in Volume IV, page 22, a certain "not" should be "now" and on page 628 of Volume XVIII, "external" should read "eternal"; that in Volume XIII the latitude of Yakutsk is given as 62° 5′ and in Volume XXIII as 62° 1′; that Martha Washington was listed as "the first Lady of the Land" instead of "the first First Lady of the Land"; that Wisconsin is called the "Badger State" not because, as explained in the work, it has many badgers, but from the way—as Yust was informed in an indignant letter from a sixth-grade class in a Milwaukee school—in which miners of southwestern Wisconsin burrowed into sides of hills for metal.

Whenever Yust has found his attention called to genuine or alleged errors by the same correspondent over a period of months or years, he knows that he will soon receive from that writer a letter starting, "Dear Sir, You will be interested to know that I have just finished reading every word in all the 24 volumes of the *Britannica*. I believe I am the first person who has ever done this." Yust acknowledges the accomplishment with admiration (he, himself, has never read the set through) but advises the proud writer that others have laid similar claims. Their places in life are as varied as their names, ages, and the time it took each to do it. A. Urban Shirk, a Little Neck, Long Island, sales manager, went through the twenty-four volumes in four and a half years. A youngster named Robin Weir, of Galloping Tiger Ranch, Delray Beach, Florida, began to read the set when he was fourteen and finished when he was nearly eighteen. An architect, J. Lloyd Conrich, of San Francisco, read his set at a leisurely pace over seventeen years. "I enjoyed it all," he wrote to Yust, "even to discovering such extremely interesting things as the number of muscles in an elephant's trunk, and that people used to wean babies on warm beer." A retired minister, George Roberts, took only three years to finish his set, finding only the articles on physics and chemistry " 'hard reading,' these being uncongenial to one who never studied them and who invariably flunked mathematics in school." George F. Goodyear, a Buffalo, New York, chemist, started to read in the second volume when he was a student in Harvard Law School and wanted to learn about astronomy. He continued to read at the rate of about a thousand pages a year and finished in twenty-two years. George Bernard Shaw always claimed that in his youth he had read the complete ninth edition at the British Museum—except for the scientific articles. But to C. S. Forester, the famous British novelist and creator of Horatio Hornblower, belongs an interesting distinction: he read through two separate editions.

IX

Yust delights in hearing from all such claimants, as he does from the critics, both serious and petty. A sensible man, he recognizes that "facts" are not always incontrovertible, and he expects that there will always be questions and inquiries and complaints both from the well-meaning and the carpers. Some expect him to be an authority on everything in his encyclopaedia, but Yust can reply, as Diderot once did, "I know indeed a great enough number of things, but there is hardly anyone who does not know his subject better than I." Strong in his belief that his is the greatest of all modern encyclopaedias of a general nature, Yust is zealous in his efforts to keep that standard high. But, being a man of easy wit, he can smile with pride, knowing that a jest often expresses an evaluation as effectively as a critical essay, when he reads in a newspaper this advertisement:

> For Sale!
> Complete Set of Encyclopaedia Britannica!
> never used—My Wife Knows Everything!

The Britannica

HARVEY EINBINDER

Almost everyone at one time or another has been approached by an eager encyclopædia salesman who has promised to deliver, for a small sum down and a small remittance each month, a set of volumes containing the knowledge of the present and the wisdom of the past. Many people have been captured by this exciting prospect and have found themselves with a set of books that they later discovered was antiquated, poorly edited, and difficult to read.

The publication and distribution of encyclopædias is a large and flourishing business in the United States. Sales of reference books have risen from $106 million in 1954 to $234 million in 1958. During 1960 more than $260 million will be spent by the American public on encyclopædias—a sum that is almost as great as the total expenditure for text-books of all kinds. The sum is much greater than the dollar volume of the nation's 1,500 bookstores and it makes the twelve million dollars spent on quality paperbacks, about which there is so much ballyhoo and publicity, seem rather puny and insignificant. The sales of a single firm, the *Encyclopædia Britannica*, currently exceed $70 million which almost equals the dollar volume of all adult books sold through stores. The distribution of encyclopædias is such a large and centralised business compared with other aspects of publishing that the financial resources of companies in the field are much greater than those of even the largest hard-back publishers. This permits many encyclopædia firms to engage in other ventures. Thus Crowell-Collier, which publishes *Collier's Encyclopædia* and the *Harvard Classics*, owns radio stations in Los Angeles, San Francisco, and Minneapolis; and it has recently acquired control of the Macmillan Company, the fourth largest trade book publisher in the United States.

Although five companies enjoy large sales in America, as far as the general public is concerned, one work—the *Encyclopædia Britannica*—dwarfs all its competitors. The *Britannica* enjoys its unusual reputation thanks to an intensive programme of advertising and publicity combined with the host of famous scholars and authors who have contributed to the set. As a result, its name has become almost synonymous with the word "encyclo-

Encounter, XVI (May 1961), 16–25. Copyright © 1961 by Harvey Einbinder. Reprinted by permission of the author.

pædia." This popular image has received official sanction in a full-length history which is appropriately called *The Great EB*. The author of this extended exercise in public relations, Herman Kogan, a former Chicago newspaper man, has been suitably rewarded for his efforts—he is now Director of Company Relations for the *Britannica*.

One curious anomaly of the encyclopædia business is that its products are almost never evaluated or criticised. Each week, magazines and newspapers devote many pages to the latest novel, biography, or bit of political journalism embalmed in hard covers, but almost nothing is printed about the reference works that are a major investment of the book-buying public. The merchandising of these works is a silent business beyond the reach of criticism and its success largely depends, not on the quality of its products, but on the skill and ingenuity of its salesmen.

If text-books seldom receive critical reviews, this is understandable since they are evaluated by school administrators, teachers, and professors whose professional training presumably enables them to discriminate between competing texts. But encyclopædias are purchased primarily by laymen who can scarcely judge whether or not they are getting a fair value for their money. One significant reason why encyclopædias are seldom reviewed is that critics are intimidated by the sheer bulk of these works. As a result, whenever such works must be reviewed, critics usually avoid the arduous task of examining their contents to determine their usefulness, reliability, and accuracy. Instead they merely repeat the publicity material furnished by the publisher. Consequently most encyclopædia reviews are merely a form of free advertising. They record the obvious features of the set, but carefully omit any comparison with competing encyclopædias which would aid consumers.

If the sale of reference books to-day is a large and prosperous business, it is likely to become even more so in the near future. The mounting stress on higher education as an indispensable asset and the increasing competition for entrance into a few select American "Ivy League" colleges, which have assumed a magic aura in middle-class circles, have made the labour of encyclopædia salesmen so much the easier. They are no longer forced to persuade people that knowledge is an important commodity and reference books a valuable possession. Parents are now eager to snatch at any aid that will assist their children in acquiring the advanced education which seems essential for their future social and financial prosperity. The businessmen who publish and sell encyclopædias have recognised this shift towards a child-oriented society and are acting accordingly.

The new approach can be traced in the advertising programme of the *Encyclopædia Britannica*. Once upon a time, appeals were directed primarily to adults who were told that ownership of the *Britannica* would make them socially stimulating and intellectually respected. This was a natural approach because the *Encyclopædia* is a reference work intended for adult readers. But now this appeal has been superseded by a new, more persuasive line aimed at the parents of young children. This "new look" in encyclopædia selling can be documented by a series of advertisements that appeared in the Sunday Book Section of the *New York Times* during 1959. On February 1st parents were asked:

> "Which is more important to your child . . . .
> The size of his home or the size of his mind?"

And they were told: "The first step in enlarging the mind is knowledge, and that is why thinking parents put the acquisition of the *Encyclopædia Britannica* before any other possession." This positive statement that the ownership of a set of books—the right set of books—is just what every home needs is reassuring to anxious parents who find their children are more interested in television and comic books than in reading and studying.

On August 23rd a deeper note was struck when parents were asked:

> "Are you giving your children more than you had?"

Such a stern question can hardly fail to stimulate the sensitive nerves of suburban American mothers. Once their anxiety is aroused, they are informed that if they "want to give their children this priceless gift of knowledge—the *Encyclopædia Britannica* is an essential possession. With this world-famous treasure of knowledge in your home, your children will soon develop the habit of 'looking it up in the *Britannica*'—a habit that will help them acquire a standard of life to sustain them throughout life."

To lend further distinction to these advertisements, they appear under the name of Dr. J. Chapman Bradley, who presumably is an educator or a distinguished child psychologist. But there is some difficulty in finding out more about Dr. Bradley's credentials. He is not listed in *Who's Who in America,* or *Who's Who in American Education,* or in any of the other standard biographical reference works. Fortunately, however, his background is briefly described by Herman Kogan in *The Great EB.* Mr. Kogan relates that Dr. Bradley served as an ordained Presbyterian minister for a decade, and then was a top executive of the American Bible Society. He invented display plates for automobiles and once headed a company that sold them. Since 1946 Dr. Bradley has been with the *Britannica*—first as a salesman in the Bronx, and then as a district and finally a division manager in Chicago. Presumably Dr. Bradley's important sales position makes him an authority in describing why the *Encyclopædia* is an essential aid in educating youngsters.

The *Britannica* has gone even further in its hypnotic appeal to anxious parents. The high point was undoubtedly reached in the *New York Times* on September 27th, at the beginning of the school year, when parents were asked:

"How can you express the inexpressible love you feel for your child?"

Lest parents be at a loss for an answer, they were instructed in the EB catechism: "Probably the most concrete way in which we show a genuine concern for our children is in the concern we have for their education. . . . There can be no doubt that a respect for knowledge exists in a home where the *Encyclopædia Britannica* is a valued possession."

To make sure that this point will sink home, the message is accompanied by a touching picture of a mother and her small son—who can hardly be more than five years old. Having successfully aroused the deep-seated instincts of parental love and responsibility, sales executives can sit back and confidently await the flood of little coupons which will bring parents the booklet containing a preview of the latest edition and an inevitable visit from a smooth-talking salesman.

The fact that the *Britannica* is not intended for children, and cannot be used by children because of its scholarly and highly technical content, is immaterial as far as advertising managers are concerned. Their job is to increase sales, and the truth of their copy is secondary. Their goal is to fashion an irresistible sales message which will make the EB *appear* indispensable to any parent who is concerned for the welfare of his children. Therefore it is only natural that advertising men should play on the sensitivity of middle-class parents who are frightened by the prospect that they may be unwittingly depriving their children of some precious asset required for their future success.

Of course, encyclopædias are not the only reference works that indulge in bold claims. Collegiate dictionaries make a practice of exaggerating the number of vocabulary entries they contain. Perhaps the most striking example in this field is the *Merriam-Webster New International Dictionary.* An advertisement appearing in the February 1961 issue of *Harper's,* as well as many other magazines, extolls this dictionary by announcing that it "ANSWERS MORE QUESTIONS THAN ANY OTHER REFERENCE WORK . . . for a fraction of the price you'd expect to pay!" The advertising copy states that this unabridged dictionary "is the world's greatest 'information centre'—equivalent in printed material to an 18-volume encyclopædia . . . containing so much encyclopædic matter that it has become famous as the 'great question answerer.' It covers the entire range of man's knowledge of this eventful era."

The advertising message fails to mention, however, that the text of the *Merriam-Webster Unabridged Dictionary* was completed in 1934, and that its 2,987 pages have been reprinted without change ever since that date. The only concession to this "eventful era" is a brief Addenda of new words which occupies 40 pages in the front of the work. This sort of thing is possible because the G. & C. Merriam Company has no effective competition in the field of unabridged dictionaries. Consequently it can offer the public its somewhat antiquated "question answerer" without any fear of losing sales. The Company once followed the same policy with its *Collegiate Dictionary* by reprinting the text without change for years—with the exception of a brief introductory section containing New Words. But now Merriam-Webster has abandoned this policy because two competing publishers are producing college dictionaries that are continually revised.

The marketing of encyclopædias in the U.S.A. is one of the last strongholds of direct selling. To attract likely prospects, many interesting techniques have been devised. One of the oldest is a phone call from a salesman who announces the good news that you have been selected to receive a set free of charge because you are such a distinguished leader in your community. Later when the salesman arrives to discuss the matter, he tells you, oh yes, there is a small charge (of several hundred dollars), but he assures you the cost is far below what an ordinary consumer can buy the encyclopædia for. The figure mentioned, of course, is exactly the same that everyone else pays.

This technique was described in detail by E. H. Powell, who served for many years as the *Britannica's* chief executive officer, in an article appearing in the *Saturday Evening Post* on July 28th, 1945. When Mr. Powell first discovered that EB salesmen were using this devious approach, he was appalled and ordered a thorough reform of the sales staff to eliminate this unethical practice. But Mr. Powell left the *Britannica* in 1948. As many Americans have learned, this ancient method has been revived by salesmen and executives whose desire for additional income has overcome their moral scruples.[1]

Aggressive salesmanship coupled with continued economic prosperity has resulted in an enormous increase in *Britannica* sales during the last eight years. Income from the *Encyclopædia* alone has risen from $12 million in 1952 to $55 million in 1959. The Company also markets the *Great Books of the Western World* (containing the *Syntopicon*), a Dictionary, an Atlas, and a

---

[1] The dubious sales tactics employed by the Company have attracted the attention of the United States Government. In 1952, the Federal Trade Commission in Washington issued a "Cease and Desist Order" to halt the Company's "School Advancement Programme," which was being used to sell the *Britannica Junior*, because this programme was falsely represented to consumers as a means of aiding schools when it was really a device for selling books. In July 1958, hearings were held by the F.T.C. in Chicago to investigate charges that the *Britannica* was being offered to consumers at special prices. The Initial Decision of the Hearing Examiner was released to the public in September, 1960: it stated that *Britannica* prices for a combination of books and research material had been falsely advertised. The examiner found that the advertised price of $511.50 contained in a typical brochure furnished to salesmen "is fictitiously padded in the amount of $120." This Initial Decision has been disputed by the *Britannica*, and a spokesman for the Company has stated that the examiner's findings will be appealed to the full commission because the *Encyclopædia* has always adhered to the highest selling standards.

bookcase to house the *Britannica*. Consumers are reminded in advertisement after advertisement of the benefits of this increased sales volume. Thus they are told in a lavish two-page colour spread in *Life* magazine (November 21st, 1960):

> The latest edition of the *Britannica* . . . is the greatest in our almost 200-year publishing history. An *enormous printing* materially reduces our costs and under an unusual direct-from-the-publisher plan, we pass these savings on to you.

Despite this claim and the fact that almost 200,000 sets are now sold each year, the price of the *Britannica* has remained unchanged since 1949. The savings from this enormous printing are not all passed on to consumers —some of them are being shared by salesmen, executives, and the owners. This is confirmed by an interview published in the *New York Times* in which Mr. William Benton stated that a good salesman can earn $20,000 a year selling the *Britannica;* district sales managers receive about $70,000 a year.[2]

The lavish rewards offered to sales personnel are a familiar aspect of the encyclopædia business—the meagre payments made to editorial contributors follow inevitably from the emphasis placed on salesmanship rather than scholarship. Generally, encyclopædias like to boast about the vast sums they spend in preparing new editions while remaining reticent about their payments to authors. The *Britannica*, however, is an exception: it makes a special point of the fact that its contributors are paid only 2 cents a word. It likes to recall that Bernard Shaw received only $68.50 for his essay on "Socialism" and Albert Einstein $86.50 for his article on "Space-Time." If one is to believe the *Encyclopædia's* editors, they have never had difficulty in recruiting contributors even at these low rates. According to *The Great EB,* "Many experts and scholars realise the prestige attached to being asked to contribute to the *Encyclopædia Britannica* and less than 2 per cent of those invited have ever declined." Apparently, scientists and scholars have little interest in being paid in cash for their efforts—nebulous honours and prestige are sufficient. It is interesting to note that although the *Britannica* publicly boasts that it has paid contributors at the rate of 2 cents a word ever since 1929, it always neglects to mention that the set cost only $129.50 in 1929, while to-day its price is $298.

Many encyclopædias make elaborate claims about their coverage, accuracy, and completeness, even though their owners concentrate on selling the work rather than on improving its contents. Consequently the quality of such encylopædias is often far from impressive. Sometimes they neglect important contemporary developments despite their practice of annual revision. The *Britannica*'s lapses are particularly striking because of its great reputation for

---

[2] Within the last two years, the Company has reorganised its sales organisation and increased the commission of its salesmen from 15 to 25 per cent. Consequently, U. S. salesmen now receive $75 for each set they sell.

scholarship, reliability, and modernity. The editors claim that every article in the *Encyclopædia* is considered for revision at least once every five years, yet the 1960 edition does not mention the Lascaux Cave Paintings discovered in 1940. There is no reference in the text or the index to Strontium-90, and there is nothing of substance on radioactive fall-out—a subject which has been a matter of grave international concern for the past six years—yet Norman Cousins and Adlai Stevenson, who are members of the *Britannica*'s Board of Editors, have repeatedly stressed the importance of this issue. Despite the current excitement over satellites, sputniks, and space flight, the article on Mars has remained unchanged for the last thirty years; yet Dr. Robert Hutchins, Chairman of the *Encyclopædia*'s Board of Editors, has stated recently, "One thing can be said with certainty, and that is that the *Britannica* reflects modern scholarship."

Despite Dr. Hutchins's confident assurance, many articles in the 1960 edition are one, two, and three generations old, an aspect of the work that is not widely publicised. Among the articles reprinted from the eleventh edition of 1910–1911 are the entries on Dante, Chaucer, and Cervantes; Pope, Byron, Swift, and Swinburne; Goethe, Baudelaire, Verlaine, and Rimbaud; as well as those on Bach, Mozart, Beethoven, Schumann, and Wagner. So many of these articles are pedestrian factual accounts that it is difficult to believe they have been retained because of their literary or critical excellence.

Even more surprising is the presence of material taken from the ninth edition, which was first issued in individual volumes over a period of fourteen years from 1875 to 1889. Such ancient articles, which are from seventy-one to eighty-four years old, include the current entries on Sophocles, Aristophanes, and Pindar; Thackeray, Congreve, Coleridge, and Shelley, as well as those on Voltaire, Michelangelo, Rubens, and Rembrandt. Originally many of these articles were in fact distinguished literary essays, but they have been sharply condensed to make room for additional material in science and technology; they now appear as dry, arid accounts whose facts have often been corrected by later research.[3]

The zenith of the *Britannica*'s evolution as a reference work was reached when the eleventh edition was issued in twenty-nine monumental volumes in 1910–1911. This edition was largely the work of English and Scottish professors—of 1,500 contributors, only 120 were Americans. A decade after the eleventh edition appeared, Sears Roebuck, a Chicago mail order house, acquired control of the *Encyclopædia*; and when it published the fourteenth edition in 1929, a new American influence became evident as the *Britannica*

---

[3] The entry on the Duke of Wellington still carries a footnote listing two possible places and dates for his birth. This footnote was first attached to the original article when it appeared in the ninth edition seventy years ago, and it has been retained for three generations, even though it has long been established by the evidence of contemporary Irish newspapers and the sworn testimony of Wellington's parents that he was born in Merrion Street in Dublin on May 1st, 1769.

was popularised, "humanised," and adulterated to reach a wider audience. In 1943, a former advertising executive, William Benton, and the University of Chicago gained possession of the work, and they succeeded in turning the set into a veritable gold mine. The *Britannica* has yielded more than $20 million in profits and royalties during the last eighteen years, and it now earns more than $3 million a year for its fortunate owners.

The *Book of the Year* is issued annually in separate English and American editions to keep *Encyclopædia* subscribers abreast with current developments. It contains biographical notices on leading personalities associated with the *Britannica* who are not sufficiently important to merit insertion in the *Encyclopædia* itself. Such individuals include William Benton, Robert Hutchins, and Lawrence Kimpton, Chancellor of the University of Chicago. Sir Geoffrey Crowther joined this select circle after he was appointed Chairman of the Encyclopædia Britannica Ltd. in 1956. His biography appears in the 1957 and 1958 *Book of the Year* and reports he is "bringing to this essentially Anglo-American enterprise a firm belief in the indispensability of the transatlantic alliance." [4]

When the eleventh edition was published in 1910–1911, the British Empire was at its zenith and the "English way of life" was being emulated around the world. The *Encyclopædia* was issued under the auspices of Cambridge University, and as a vehicle of English learning and culture, it was natural that the set should emphasise the nation's literature, history, and tradition. This insular point of view was accentuated because the work was the first major edition of the *Britannica* to include entries on living persons. The result was a flood of notices on contemporary English notables whose achievements were recorded at great length so that the *Encyclopædia* became a virtual Who's Who of British life.

This national bias was attacked in 1917 by Willard Huntington Wright who pointed out in a book, *Misinforming a Nation*, that many major European figures including Van Gogh, Gauguin, and Cezanne were omitted from the eleventh edition. Despite Wright's criticism, it is surprising to discover that many forgotten Victorians still occupy valuable space in the 1960 edition. Their biographies have been reprinted from the eleventh edition, even though the modern set has only 38 million words compared with the 44 million words of the 1911 edition. Such "famous" Victorians include the composers, John Hatten, Joseph Barnby, and Sterndale Bennett; the painters, William Etty, George Watts, and John Gilbert; as well as the Victorian poets, Charles Wells and John Davidson. Each of these British "notables" receives an entry, but there are no articles on Benjamin Britten, W. H. Auden, or Jackson Pollock.

[4] However, in November, 1959, Sir Geoffrey was replaced as Chairman of EB Ltd. by Senator William Benton, who is also Chairman of the American company; thus assuring that "this essentially Anglo-American enterprise" will be properly directed from the Senator's Madison Avenue office in New York. Needless to say, the biographical entry on Sir Geoffrey no longer appears in the American *Book of the Year*.

In many instances, the modern *Encyclopædia* has retained the reverent, respectful treatment of eminent Victorians adopted by the eleventh edition. A good example is the article on Sir Jonathan Hutchinson (1828–1913), a distinguished Harley Street physician who served as president of the Royal College of Surgeons. The article describes one of Sir Jonathan's leading medical contributions in the following words:

> His book, *Leprosy and Fisheating* (1906), exposed many popular errors, though his conclusion regarding a definite connection between the disease and the eating of salted fish has not been generally accepted.

Although the eleventh edition was widely acclaimed as a monument of British scholarship, it was not immune from criticism. An article appearing in *Science* in 1912 pointed out that the history of non-Euclidean geometry furnished by A. N. Whitehead and Bertrand Russell contained several significant errors. In particular, undue prominence was given to Gauss who never published anything on the subject, and an attempt was made to link Gauss and Bolyai who actually worked independently. Furthermore, Gauss' formula for the circumference of a circle was printed incorrectly. It is somewhat disconcerting to find these errors reproduced in the 1960 edition which has reprinted Whitehead and Russell's contribution.[5]

Scientific subjects were often treated in the eleventh edition in a hopelessly technical manner. Frequently entries were filled with mathematical formulas and technical details far beyond the comprehension of the general reader. To-day such articles, with their dense array of equations, recall the atmosphere of the Cambridge Mathematical Tripos, and they may remind older scientists of the ponderous English mathematical texts of their youth (*cf.* Hobson's *Spherical Harmonics*). Since the eleventh edition, great progress has been made in presenting scientific subjects in a manner that can be grasped by an educated layman, and many contemporary articles in the *Britannica* are masterly examples of scientific exposition. Sometimes, however, an author forgets the needs of the public and decides to provide instruction for his colleagues rather than the ordinary reader. A good example is the article on "Logic" which begins by enunciating Lukasiewicz's axioms of the propositional calculus,

1. $p \supset q \supset \blacksquare q \supset r \supset \blacksquare p \supset r$
2. $\sim p \supset p \supset p$
3. $p \supset \blacksquare \sim p \supset q$

---

[5] The only difference is that their historical treatment of non-Euclidean geometry has been sharply condensed and the initials identifying them as the authors have disappeared. As a result, neither Russell nor Whitehead is listed as a contributor—an omission that seems rather strange considering the *Encyclopædia*'s penchant for boasting about the number of Nobel Prize-winners who have contributed to the work.

and then proceeds to derive a number of logical theorems with the aid of the symbolism and operations of the propositional calculus. The presence of such a highly-technical article is hard to explain, particularly when *Britannica* editors firmly remind contributors that they are writing for "a person of average education who is in search of clear and simple information." Despite this admonition, the desire to impress other specialists is often victorious. This is illustrated by the entry on "Topology" which is filled with mathematical material of a singularly advanced type. Its character may be suggested by a single definition:

> The 1-dimensional "Betti number modulo 2 of K," denoted by $p^1(K, 2)$ (or simply p^1 when the modulo 2 algebraic operations are understood to be used without explicit mention), is the greatest number of 1-cycles $Z_1^1, Z_2^1, \ldots, Z_{p_1}^1$ of K that satisfy no homology of the form $a_1^1 Z_1^1 + \ldots + a_i^1 Z_i^1 + \ldots a_{p_1}^1 Z_{p_1}^1 \sim 0$ modulo 2, where the coefficients a_i^1 are all 0 or 1 but not all 0 (we make the convention that $0 \sim 0$).

Is such mathematical exposition really "suitable for children" who are supposed to find the *Encyclopædia* a storehouse of useful information?

Any shortcomings that may exist in the *Britannica* are discreetly ignored in its promotional material which asks the public to accept the authority of its articles without question. An advertisement appearing in the September 27th, 1960, issue of *Look* Magazine boldly announces: "*It is truth. It is unquestionable fact. And it is the beginning, the support, and the constant touchstone of education.*" Yet the article on Galileo, which has just been revised for the 1960 edition, repeats the discredited story that Galileo gave all the professors and students of the university a visual demonstration from the Leaning Tower of Pisa that different weights fall with the same velocity. This fanciful legend was first reported by the biographer Viviani in 1654, more than sixty years after the experiment was supposed to have occurred.

Its utility as a "constant touchstone of education" may be suggested by the entry on Shakespeare which contains no discussion of his plays and the survey article on "Sculpture" which fails to note the existence of abstract sculpture as exemplified by the creative activity of Brancusi, Calder, and Henry Moore. The 1960 edition continues to reprint eccentric and out-dated opinions of Sir Donald Francis Tovey on modern music that now furnish more amusement than critical insight. His essay on "Chamber Music" reports:

> The trombone and side-drums in the chamber music of Stravinsky will do well enough in a very smart house-party where all the conversation is carried on in an esoteric family slang, and the guests are expected to enjoy the booby-traps.

Tovey curtly dismisses Schönberg's early theory of added fourths in the article on "Harmony" by stating:

> Arnold Schönberg's harmonic theory is often masterly in its analysis of classical music; but it is extremely disappointing in its constructive aspect. . . . Schönberg's theory rests on no observation at all. . . . To find the composer of the *Gurrelieder* fathering such theories is as disconcerting as to discover Einstein telling fortunes in Bond Street.

These are by no means the only outlandish examples that can be discovered in the *Encyclopædia*'s pages. Careful examination soon reveals remnants from the Victorian era. A telling example is the current article on Rabelais, which was written originally by George Saintsbury for the ninth edition. Saintsbury, as a good Victorian, is forced to deal with the "great blemish of *Gargantua and Pantagruel*—their extreme coarseness of language and imagery." He explains that Rabelais' errors looked at from an absolute standard are, of course, unpardonable—but, judged relatively, he may be excused because:

> Rabelais's coarseness, disgusting as it is, has nothing of the corruption of refined voluptuousness about it, and nothing of the sniggering corruption which disgraces men like Pope, like Voltaire, and like Sterne. The general taste having been considerably refined since, Rabelais has in parts become nearly unreadable—the worst and most appropriate punishment for his faults.

Saintsbury's initials have long since disappeared from this article, which has been revised recently. The revision consisted in adding a new bibliography and reprinting Saintsbury's 19th-century text—a rapid and economical method that is often employed by editors to bring the *Britannica* "up-to-date."

One can not only find the prudery of the Victorian era in the latest edition, but also some of the fanciful beliefs of an earlier age. An amusing illustration is the essay on "Spiritualism" by Sir Oliver Lodge: it reports that careful investigators of the Society for Psychical Research, founded in London, "have accumulated a great mass of evidence" in favour of spiritualism. Sir Oliver describes the powerful force of "exteriorised protoplasm now generally known as ectoplasm" in the following terms:

> The force exerted by ectoplasm can be quite considerable. For instance, a table can be raised completely off the ground; and the weight of a man clambering on the table need not be sufficient to bring it down. The forces have sometimes been measured by spring balances. . . . In quoting such assertions it is not supposed that they are as yet fully accepted; but they indicate the lines on which the investigation should proceed.

Sir Oliver's rambling essay on Spiritualism has been reprinted for the last generation. Fortunately, however, the 1960 edition also contains an article on "Psychical Research" which is far more critical and scientific in character.

Such inconsistency between different entries is the bane of encyclopædia editors. It frequently occurs whenever the index of a reference work fails to record all the information in its pages. Thus the 1960 *Britannica* contains a long article on the "Dead Sea Scrolls," but the discussion of the "Manuscripts of the Bible" ignores the discovery of an Isaiah roll among the Dead Sea Scrolls which is more than a thousand years older than the traditional Hebrew Masoretic text. There is a major entry on the "Minoan Linear Scripts" which describes how the British scholar Michael Ventris succeeded in unravelling the Linear B Script without the aid of a bi-lingual text by means of a brilliant hypothesis that the script is a form of archaic Greek. Yet the essay on "Aegean Civilisation" in the first volume states that Minoan records "are undeciphered and likely to remain so, except in the improbable event of the discovery of a long bi-lingual text, partly couched in some familiar script and language."

It is bad enough when different articles contradict each other, but what can one say when the same entry offers contradictory information? A striking instance is the article on "Richard III": it wavers between the popular tradition created by Tudor historians that depicts Richard as a mis-shapen monster whose name is synonymous with wickedness, and the subdued portrait presented by modern scholars who have rehabilitated his reputation. The article reports in its final paragraph:

> Tradition represents Richard as deformed. It seems clear that he had some physical defect, though not so great as has been alleged. Extant portraits show an intellectual face characteristic of the early Renaissance, but do not indicate any deformity.

Earlier in the article, however, this judicious caution is thrown aside as the Tudor version of the tumultuous events of 1483 is recorded:

> On June 13 came the famous scene when Richard appeared suddenly in the council baring his withered arm and accusing Jane Shore and the Queen of sorcery; Hastings, Morton, and Stanley were arrested and the first-named at once beheaded.

Thus Richard suddenly appears in the article as a monster with a withered arm! Shakespeare employs this incident to create an exciting scene in which Richard cries,

> *Look how I am bewitch'd; behold, mine arm*
> *Is like a blasted sapling, wither'd up.*
> *And this Edward's Wife, that monstrous witch,*
> *Consorted with that harlot strumpet Shore,*
> *That by their witchcraft thus have marked me.*

This striking scene was invented by Sir Thomas More and copied by Shakespeare. Actually, Richard had Hastings seized and beheaded for treason, not witchcraft, yet the *Britannica* zealously repeats the story as if it were unquestionably true.[6]

If a British reader is disturbed by the treatment of Richard III, what is an American to think when he examines the entry of Franklin Delano Roosevelt and discovers that it was written by Allan Nevins twenty-five years ago and has been reprinted ever since? The only change has been to add two brief paragraphs on the presidential elections of 1936, 1940, and 1944. There is no bibliography attached to the article, and for information on Roosevelt's second and third terms, the reader is directed to the entry on the "United States." One might suspect that this inadequate notice has been retained because F.D.R. is still a controversial figure in certain American circles, but surely this seems rather far-fetched since William Benton and Adlai Stevenson, both Liberal Democrats, are members of the *Britannica*'s Board of Editors. A much more plausible explanation is the fact that if the 1¾-page article on Franklin Roosevelt were expanded to include the events of his second and third terms, it would be necessary to disturb the "classic" five-page article on Theodore Roosevelt which has been reprinted for the last thirty years.

It would be easy to multiply illustrations of the *Encyclopædia*'s failure to live up to its exalted popular image, but it may be rather futile to attack the *Britannica*'s contents in a brief article. When I offered a critical appraisal last winter in the *Columbia University Forum,* Dr. Robert Hutchins complained in a published communication in the Spring issue that my criticism was superficial because I singled out only 90 of the *Encyclopædia*'s 42,000 entries. Such partial coverage is inevitable in a short article, and it offers an easy way in which to neutralise any unfavourable comment.[7]

The profit instinct has always been a powerful motive in stimulating the efforts of encyclopædia publishers. In the past, publishers have been content to leave editors with a free hand once they allocated the necessary funds. Robertson Smith, who served as an editor of the ninth edition, stated that he seldom heard from the owners—his principal contact was by letters which would arrive at periodic intervals containing a long slip of paper. At the top of the slip was printed THE BANK OF ENGLAND, and at the bottom was the signature of A. & C. Black. Matters are quite different to-day when publishers carefully regulate every step in the production of reference works—from their initial inception to their final manufacture, promotion, and sale. Often, one could infer, they are guided as businessmen, not by the requirements of

---

[6] This assurance extends to the greatest mystery of English history—the fate of the "little Princes." According to the *Encyclopædia*, "There seems no reasonable doubt that early in August, Edward V and his brother Richard . . . were murdered by their uncle's orders"; but this certainty is not shared by modern scholars.

[7] This has made it necessary for me to prepare a full-length book to document fully the disparity that exists between the *Britannica*'s popular reputation and its actual contents.

scholarship, but by the findings of "market research" as they consciously strive to launch reference works that will appeal to a broad group of consumers.

The importance of isolating the commercial spirit from the objectives of scholarship is clearly demonstrated by the history of the *Britannica*. When the great eleventh edition was issued fifty years ago, the work was owned by two shrewd and aggressive Americans, Horace Hooper and Walter Jackson. They promoted the set with a bold and vigorous advertising campaign that overwhelmed the resistance of consumers. But editorial control over the work rested firmly in the hands of the London *Times*, which had been receiving royalties ever since 1898. Hooper and Jackson were unable to exert any influence on the contents of the set because *The Times* assumed full responsibility for the preparation of the eleventh edition, and the editor of *The Times*, Moberly Bell, would not allow the reputation of his newspaper to be compromised by commercial considerations. Matters are quite different to-day. The *Encyclopædia* is owned jointly by William Benton and the University of Chicago,[8] and one is driven to conclude that they seem content to measure the success of their enterprise by the number of sets sold.

The mediocre quality of many of our contemporary American reference works confirms the truism that the goals of scholarship and the aims of salesmanship are not synonymous. At best, sound works are produced when there is active competition and a large well-defined market. This is the case with collegiate dictionaries and junior encyclopædias. But the commercial spirit is incapable of providing an incentive for scaling the heights of scholarship. Massive projects, such as the *Oxford English Dictionary* which took seventy years to complete, would never have been carried through if they depended on their commercial prospects. Such enterprises can never hope to compete with popular works intended for a large audience; yet the progress of learning depends on such scholarly undertakings.

This situation has become more than a matter of private concern to professors and scholars. To-day knowledge has become a vital instrument in the expression of national policy. This has been recognised for some time in the Soviet Union. The editors of the second edition of *The Great Soviet Encyclopædia* were given explicit instructions by the Council of Ministers for their work to be written from a Marxist-Leninist viewpoint to show the "superiority of Socialist culture" and the "degeneracy of capitalist society." The resulting fifty-one volume Russian encyclopædia completed in 1958 faithfully reflects the communist belief that truth and objectivity must be subservient to the political interests of the Communist Party. If this

---

[8] For tax purposes, Sears and Roebuck gave the University of Chicago complete ownership of the *Britannica* as a gift; and the University transferred two-thirds of its interest to William Benton in return for $100,000 in working capital which he advanced.

encyclopædia truly represents the spirit of the Soviet Union, what must we say of the patched-up, makeshift *Encyclopædia Britannica*? [9]

The emphasis on business goals rather than scholarship during the past decade may help to explain some of the surprising lapses that have occurred in the set. Until the 1954 edition, the *Britannica* offered a rather astonishing prophecy in an article on "Pacific Ocean Questions." It stated: "One of the most interesting of Pacific questions is how far Bolshevik Russia will succeed in the Orient. In China its propaganda is probably doomed to failure because of the almost universal peasant-proprietorship." The *Encyclopædia*'s neglect of contemporary developments has, on occasion, led to foreign protests. Late in 1958, a Singapore newspaper editor complained about the article on the "Malays" which reported:

> The Malays are indolent, pleasure-loving, improvident, fond of bright clothing, of comfort, of ease, and dislike toil exceedingly. They have no idea of money, and little notion of honesty where money is concerned. . . . They are addicted to gambling, and formerly were much given to fighting, but their courage is not high judged by European standards. The sexual morality of the Malays is very lax. . . .

This passage was written by a British colonial official for the eleventh edition and has been reprinted for almost fifty years. According to *Time* magazine, when John V. Dodge, Managing Editor of the *Britannica*, was asked about this passage his abashed reply was: "I wish to say we are embarrassed by the paragraph you quote. . . . It obviously should have been replaced long ago—and I cannot say why it was not."

The newly-independent nations of Asia and Africa look to Britain and America for more than pounds and dollars: they seek technical skills and specialised knowledge that will assist them in passing from backward countries into industrialised societies. It is important that the leaders of these countries gain an understanding of the achievements of western culture and its values of personal freedom and free intellectual inquiry. An encyclopædia can play a significant role in this educational task because it synthesises the whole circle of learning within the confines of a single set of volumes. As a vehicle for the communication of knowledge and ideas, it can be readily transported to the far corners of the earth, and its wealth of information makes the work particularly valuable in backward countries which lack adequate library facilities and institutions of higher learning. In view of the current competition between the East and the West for "the minds of men," may it not be a hazardous luxury to accept the present state of the

---

[9] The relative weight accorded to scholarship and sales promotion may be suggested by the following consideration. At the current rate of 2 cents a word, if all the words in the *Britannica* were to be replaced, the total payment to contributors would be less than $800,000. This sum is far smaller than the *Encyclopædia*'s annual U. S. advertising budget, which now equals four million dollars a year.

Encyclopædia Britannica merely because "it is the best there is"? I suggest that the English-speaking community to-day requires something far better: a work that will truly represent the persistent and unfettered search for truth that is a distinguishing mark of a free society.

The Britannica

ROBERT HUTCHINS AND HARVEY EINBINDER

It is too bad that before printing his article "A Straight Look at the Encyclopaedia Britannica" in your Winter issue, you or Dr. Harvey Einbinder did not show his paper to somebody who knows something about how the *Encyclopaedia Britannica* is edited.

If this had been done, Dr. Einbinder's article could not have been written. He might in fact have been moved to quite different conclusions.

He might have asked who formulates the editorial policies of the *Britannica*. The answer is the Board of Editors, of which I have been chairman for twelve years. The other members are former Senator William Benton; Norman Cousins; Sir Geoffrey Crowther; Clifton Fadiman; Professor Richard P. McKeon; David Owen, Executive Chairman of the Technical Assistance Board of the United Nations; Professor Thomas Park, President-elect of the American Association for the Advancement of Science; George N. Shuster; Adlai Stevenson; and Ralph W. Tyler, Director of the Center for Advanced Study in the Behavioral Sciences. These men meet regularly for intensive two-day sessions devoted to the discussion of policies and plans for the long-term development of the *Britannica* and immediate editorial problems of the sort Dr. Einbinder implies are left unexamined. The board's existence is an expression of the *Britannica's* constant concern for the maintenance of its editorial traditions.

How are the editorial policies recommended by the board carried out? Specifically, this is the job of the *Britannica's* editorial staff of 225 in England and the United States. Under the direction of John V. Dodge as executive editor, this staff works closely with 160 advisers, each of whom is an acknowledged authority in the field for which he is responsible. The advisers are selected in consultation with the members of a committee of the faculty of the University of Chicago of which Professor Park is chairman. No article goes into the set until it has first received the specific approval of an adviser.

Columbia University Forum, III (Spring 1960), 40–42. © 1960 by Columbia University. Reprinted by permission of the publisher.

One thing can be said with certainty, and that is that the *Britannica* reflects modern scholarship. In the 1960 edition there are articles by forty winners of the Nobel Prize.

What are the revisions recently made or now going on? If Dr. Einbinder had inquired, he would have discovered that the number of words revised in the 1960 printing was 7,250,000, the rough equivalent of seventy books of the ordinary size. In the ten years from 1950 to 1959 inclusive, 34,000,000 words were revised in 49,000 articles. The total number of words in the *Britannica* is 40,000,000; the total number of articles is 42,000; many articles during the ten years referred to were revised several times.

Dr. Einbinder disparages only 90 of the *Britannica's* 42,000 articles, although it is not impossible that there are others which he might consider worthy of censure. Of these ninety, thirteen have been revised since 1940. In the 1960 printing, nine of the articles specifically mentioned by Dr. Einbinder have been completely rewritten or substantially revised, along with scores of others which he has not. If Dr. Einbinder had asked, he could have found out about these changes.

What is an encyclopaedia? Dr. Einbinder appears to think that it is a combination of classical articles and a daily newspaper. He wants literary distinction and current information. Every encyclopaedia editor wants literary distinction, and the Board of Editors of the *Britannica* has spent more time on this subject than on any other. No encyclopaedia editor in his senses, however, would try to compete with *The New York Times* or *Time* magazine. I find it [extraordinary] that Dr. Einbinder makes no reference to the *Britannica Book of the Year,* issued annually by the Company to help *Britannica* owners keep up to date. The *Book of the Year,* by the way, contained an article on the Dead Sea Scrolls in 1956. That article served to keep *Britannica* owners up to date on that particular subject until the appearance, in the 1960 printing of the *Britannica,* of Millar Burrows' major article on the topic.

Is the *Britannica* perfect? Certainly not. When the editor of the Third Edition had finished his labors, he took pains to point out in his preface that despite the great attention and industry that had gone into it, he was more aware than any of his readers could ever be that "the work passes from our hands in a state far from perfection." The Board of Editors and the editorial staff are spending a good deal of time, effort and money on improving the *Britannica* every year. If Dr. Einbinder had taken a less superficial, and somewhat straighter, look at the *Britannica,* he would have been impressed by the work that is being done to maintain and to raise, if possible, the standards of a great institution.

ROBERT M. HUTCHINS
Chairman, Board of Editors
The Encyclopaedia Britannica
Chicago, Illinois

Harvey Einbinder writes:

Dr. Hutchins in his letter makes no effort to dispute my factual findings. Rather he claims: "One thing can be said with certainty, and that is that the *Britannica* reflects modern scholarship." Yet the 1960 edition (the newest) contains articles on major literary and artistic figures reprinted from the Ninth Edition and written seventy-one to eighty-five years ago; and it contains a large number of entries taken from the Eleventh Edition of 1911 which perpetrate antiquated intellectual and critical ideas. A great deal of the elaborate program of revision for which Dr. Hutchins has given such impressive statistics consists in merely cutting and patching old entries, adding a few lines here and there, to bring them "up-to-date."

The article on the Dead Sea Scrolls noted by Dr. Hutchins appeared in the 1958, not the 1956, *Book of the Year*—eleven years after the discovery of the Scrolls. The article lacks a bibliography that would serve as a useful guide to the vast literature on the Dead Sea Scrolls because bibliographies are not included in the *Book of the Year,* which is essentially a journalistic production, and not a work of scholarship.

Dr. Hutchins makes no attempt to defend Mr. Benton's practice of making bold public statements advocating greater monetary rewards for scientists and educators while privately paying contributors 2 cents a word as publisher of the *Encyclopaedia Britannica*. Dr. Hutchins says nothing about the morality of an organization that pays such a niggardly rate to contributors while *Britannica* salesmen earn $20,000 and district sales managers $70,000 a year. Presumably Dr. Hutchins' silence means that he and his colleagues endorse the principle that scientists and scholars should donate their services to the *Britannica,* while salesmen and executives reap the benefits from its current financial success.

Dr. Hutchins regrets I did not show my paper to somebody who knows how the *Britannica* is edited; he claims if this had been done, my article could not have been written. Unfortunately for Dr. Hutchins' argument, the *Saturday Review* had a copy of a similar article by me, "Outmoded Critical Views in the *Encyclopaedia Britannica*" in its files for eight months—from February 18 to October 1, 1959. The editor of the *Saturday Review,* Norman Cousins, told me he was extremely impressed by this article, but that he could not publish it because he was attempting to institute a thorough reform of the *Encyclopaedia's* editorial organization. But he insisted that I write for the *Saturday Review*. As a result of his request, I prepared a critique of the *Encyclopaedia of World Art* which served as the feature article in the *Saturday Review's* Reference Book Issue of March 19, 1960. Mr. Cousins would hardly have given me this assignment if he were not impressed with my criticism of the *Britannica.*

Dr. Hutchins appears to have great faith in the ability of the Board of Editors to formulate long-range policies and deal with immediate editorial problems during intensive two-day sessions. However, he does not explain how any group of men can intelligently guide the destinies of an encyclopedia unless they are intimately aware of its contents. It can easily be demonstrated that Board members do not possess such knowledge. A single example may suffice.

Radioactive fallout has been an issue of grave international concern ever since twenty-three Japanese fishermen were poisoned by radioactive debris in the Pacific six years ago. Norman Cousins, as co-chairman of the Committee for a Sane Nuclear Policy, has been an active and energetic leader in the campaign to warn the nation of the serious dangers of continued nuclear bomb tests. The subject is obviously of great importance, yet there seems to be nothing of substance on radioactive fallout or strontium-90 in the 1960 *Britannica*.

Adlai Stevenson, who has been a member of the *Encyclopaedia's* Board of Editors since 1955, made the cessation of hydrogen bomb testing a major issue in his 1956 Presidential campaign. On October 15th he promised that if he were elected, his first order of business would be to seek world agreement to halt bomb tests because they released "something called strontium-90, which is the most dreadful poison in the world." Yet I could find no information about fallout or strontium-90 in the 1960 *Britannica*, despite the 7,250,000 words that have been revised for this edition.

The *Book of the Year* virtually passes over the ominous effects of radioactive fallout. The 1959 volume contains a photograph of Linus Pauling and Edward Teller debating whether the United States should continue testing nuclear weapons, but the accompanying text fails to explain the issues behind the debate. The 1960 volume disregards the wide differences of opinion expressed by leading scientists on the dangers of radioactive fallout. Instead it accepts without question the optimistic claim of the AEC that the effects of strontium-90 are insignificant compared with those of other sources of radiation.

Apparently Mr. Cousins and Mr. Stevenson, as busy public personalities, have not discovered that fallout and strontium-90 are ignored in the *Encyclopaedia Britannica* and, in my view, confidently dismissed in the *Book of the Year*. If Mr. Cousins and Mr. Stevenson have never noticed this failure to deal adequately with an issue which has been intimately associated with their public careers, are they likely to find time to evaluate the *Britannica's* deficiencies in the fields of art, literature, history, music, and archeology?

Dr. Hutchins is quite right in claiming that my look at the *Britannica* was superficial. It only mentioned ninety articles in a brief six-page essay. At best, it merely noted a few of the *Encyclopaedia's* glaring faults. This short-coming will soon be rectified. I am now writing a book, *The Myth of the Britannica*, which will demonstrate how an inadequate reference work has been elevated into a national legend. Its findings should come as a surprise to those who believe in this "great institution," not as a result of first-hand study, but because of the exaggerated claims of promoters and publicists.

Questions

1. Does Einbinder's description of Kogan's book as an "extended exercise in public relations" accurately describe the section of that book reprinted here?
2. Where does Einbinder explain his reasons for writing his essay "The Britannica"?
3. Can Einbinder's discussion of Dr. J. Chapman Bradley be considered an *ad hominem* argument?
4. What is the reason for the section about dictionaries in Einbinder's article?
5. Does Hutchins' definition of "modern scholarship" differ from Einbinder's? Cite the texts.
6. What does Einbinder conceive an encyclopedia to be? Is Hutchins' description of Einbinder's conception accurate?
7. Einbinder criticizes, in particular, the article on Franklin D. Roosevelt, but Kogan mentions that special care is taken to keep articles on presidents current. Go to the encyclopedia and evaluate the currentness of articles about contemporary political figures.
8. Kogan speaks favorably of a number of articles, particularly those about writers and artists, which are unrevised classics from past editions. Einbinder, however, attacks these classics. What should be the primary criteria in editing such articles?
9. Kogan says that "Every form of criticism . . . is diligently investigated." Have the errors that Einbinder has pointed out been corrected in recent editions?
10. Do the different general encyclopedias have different aims? To what extent could Einbinder's criticisms be considered criticisms of the basic aims of any encyclopedia?
11. Does Kogan's discussion of the critics of the *Britannica* answer indirectly some of Einbinder's criticisms?

Assignments

1. Compare the ways a number of standard general encyclopedias treat a subject of which you have some knowledge. Which encyclopedia best handles the subject? Which is most up to date? Do the different encyclopedias seem to be intended for different audiences?
2. Defend or attack the proposition that in this age of specialization the general encyclopedia is a relic of the past.
3. Discuss the limits to the use of an encyclopedia for reference, even a completely modern and completely accurate one.
4. Trace an article through a number of editions of the same encyclopedia. Discuss the ways in which it has been revised and suggest the reasons for such revision.

Additional Reading

Einbinder's promised book, *The Myth of the Britannica* (New York, 1964), appeared four years after its mention in the *Columbia University Forum* article reprinted here.

Reviews of the book can be located through the periodical indexes and the *Book Review Digest*. Einbinder's original article about the *Britannica,* which appeared in the *Columbia University Forum,* III (Winter 1960), 20–25, provides an interesting comparison with the article which is reprinted here from *Encounter;* the changes in the later article suggest the ways in which Einbinder's ideas were developing. Another interesting attack on the *Britannica* is Willard Huntington Wright's *Misinforming a Nation* (New York, 1917), which, while out of print, may still be available in some libraries.

SECTION THREE
The New Bible: God's Word or Man's

From *The Gospel According to* ST. MATTHEW

And seeing the multitudes, he went up into a mountain: and when he was set, his disciples came unto him:
 [2] And he opened his mouth, and taught them, saying,
 [3] Blessed are the poor in spirit: for their's is the kingdom of heaven.
 [4] Blessed are they that mourn: for they shall be comforted.
 [5] Blessed are the meek: for they shall inherit the earth.
 [6] Blessed are they which do hunger and thirst after righteousness: for they shall be filled.
 [7] Blessed are the merciful: for they shall obtain mercy.
 [8] Blessed are the pure in heart: for they shall see God.
 [9] Blessed are the peacemakers: for they shall be called the children of God.
 [10] Blessed are they which are persecuted for righteousness' sake: for their's is the kingdom of heaven.
 [11] Blessed are ye, when men shall revile you, and persecute you, and shall say all manner of evil against you falsely, for my sake.
 [12] Rejoice, and be exceeding glad: for great is your reward in heaven: for so persecuted they the prophets which were before you.
 [13] Ye are the salt of the earth: but if the salt have lost his savour, wherewith shall it be salted? it is thenceforth good for nothing, but to be cast out, and to be trodden under foot of men. [14] Ye are the light of the world. A city that is set on an hill cannot be hid. [15] Neither do men light a candle, and put it under a bushel, but on a candlestick; and it giveth light unto all that are

[The Sermon on the Mount], Matthew V-VII, *New Testament* (King James Version).

in the house. [16] Let your light so shine before men, that they may see your good works, and glorify your Father which is in heaven.

[17] Think not that I am come to destroy the law, or the prophets: I am not come to destroy, but to fulfil. [18] For verily I say unto you, Till heaven and earth pass, one jot or one tittle shall in no wise pass from the law, till all be fulfilled. [19] Whosoever therefore shall break one of these least commandments, and shall teach men so, he shall be called the least in the kingdom of heaven: but whosoever shall do and teach them, the same shall be called great in the kingdom of heaven. [20] For I say unto you, That except your righteousness shall exceed the righteousness of the scribes and Pharisees, ye shall in no case enter into the kingdom of heaven.

[21] Ye have heard that it was said by them of old time, Thou shalt not kill; and whosoever shall kill shall be in danger of the judgment: [22] but I say unto you, That whosoever is angry with his brother without a cause shall be in danger of the judgment: and whosoever shall say to his brother, Raca, shall be in danger of the council: but whosoever shall say, Thou fool, shall be in danger of hell fire. [23] Therefore if thou bring thy gift to the altar, and there rememberest that thy brother hath ought against thee; [24] leave there thy gift before the altar, and go thy way; first be reconciled to thy brother, and then come and offer thy gift. [25] Agree with thine adversary quickly, whiles thou art in the way with him; lest at any time the adversary deliver thee to the judge, and the judge deliver thee to the officer, and thou be cast into prison. [26] Verily I say unto thee, Thou shalt by no means come out thence, till thou hast paid the uttermost farthing.

[27] Ye have heard that it was said by them of old time, Thou shalt not commit adultery: [28] but I say unto you, That whosoever looketh on a woman to lust after her hath committed adultery with her already in his heart. [29] And if thy right eye offend thee, pluck it out, and cast it from thee: for it is profitable for thee that one of thy members should perish, and not that thy whole body should be cast into hell. [30] And if thy right hand offend thee, cut it off, and cast it from thee: for it is profitable for thee that one of thy members should perish, and not that thy whole body should be cast into hell. [31] It hath been said, Whosoever shall put away his wife, let him give her a writing of divorcement: [32] but I say unto you, That whosoever shall put away his wife, saving for the cause of fornication, causeth her to commit adultery: and whosoever shall marry her that is divorced committeth adultery.

[33] Again, ye have heard that it hath been said by them of old time, Thou shalt not forswear thyself, but shalt perform unto the Lord thine oaths: [34] but I say unto you, Swear not at all; neither by heaven; for it is God's throne: [35] nor by the earth; for it is his footstool: neither by Jerusalem; for it is the city of the great King. [36] Neither shalt thou swear by thy head, because thou canst not make one hair white or black. [37] But let your communication be, Yea, yea; Nay, nay: for whatsoever is more than these cometh of evil.

[38] Ye have heard that it hath been said, An eye for an eye, and a tooth

for a tooth: [39] but I say unto you, That ye resist not evil: but whosoever shall smite thee on thy right cheek, turn to him the other also. [40] And if any man will sue thee at the law, and take away thy coat, let him have thy cloke also. [41] And whosoever shall compel thee to go a mile, go with him twain. [42] Give to him that asketh thee, and from him that would borrow of thee turn not thou away.

[43] Ye have heard that it hath been said, Thou shalt love thy neighbour, and hate thine enemy. [44] But I say unto you, Love your enemies, bless them that curse you, do good to them that hate you, and pray for them which despitefully use you, and persecute you; [45] that ye may be the children of your Father which is in heaven: for he maketh his sun to rise on the evil and on the good, and sendeth rain on the just and on the unjust. [46] For if ye love them which love you, what reward have ye? do not even the publicans the same? [47] And if ye salute your brethren only, what do ye more than others? do not even the publicans so? [48] Be ye therefore perfect, even as your Father which is in heaven is perfect.

Take heed that ye do not your alms before men, to be seen of them: otherwise ye have no reward of your Father which is in heaven. [2] Therefore when thou doest thine alms, do not sound a trumpet before thee, as the hypocrites do in the synagogues and in the streets, that they may have glory of men. Verily I say unto you, They have their reward. [3] But when thou doest alms, let not thy left hand know what thy right hand doeth: [4] that thine alms may be in secret: and thy Father which seeth in secret himself shall reward thee openly.

[5] And when thou prayest, thou shalt not be as the hypocrites are: for they love to pray standing in the synagogues and in the corners of the streets, that they may be seen of men. Verily I say unto you, They have their reward. [6] But thou, when thou prayest, enter into thy closet, and when thou hast shut thy door, pray to thy Father which is in secret; and thy Father which seeth in secret shall reward thee openly. [7] But when ye pray, use not vain repetitions, as the heathen do: for they think that they shall be heard for their much speaking. [8] Be not ye therefore like unto them: for your Father knoweth what things ye have need of, before ye ask him. [9] After this manner therefore pray ye:

Our Father which art in heaven, Hallowed be thy name. [10] Thy kingdom come. Thy will be done in earth, as it is in heaven. [11] Give us this day our daily bread. [12] And forgive us our debts, as we forgive our debtors. [13] And lead us not into temptation, but deliver us from evil: For thine is the kingdom, and the power, and the glory, for ever. Amen.

[14] For if ye forgive men their trespasses, your heavenly Father will also forgive you: [15] but if ye forgive not men their trespasses, neither will your Father forgive your trespasses.

[16] Moreover when ye fast, be not, as the hypocrites, of a sad countenance: for they disfigure their faces, that they may appear unto men to fast.

Verily I say unto you, They have their reward. [17] But thou, when thou fastest, anoint thine head, and wash thy face; [18] that thou appear not unto men to fast, but unto thy Father which is in secret: and thy Father, which seeth in secret, shall reward thee openly.

[19] Lay not up for yourselves treasures upon earth, where moth and rust doth corrupt, and where thieves break through and steal: [20] but lay up for yourselves treasures in heaven, where neither moth nor rust doth corrupt, and where thieves do not break through nor steal: [21] for where your treasure is, there will your heart be also. [22] The light of the body is the eye: if therefore thine eye be single, thy whole body shall be full of light. [23] But if thine eye be evil, thy whole body shall be full of darkness. If therefore the light that is in thee be darkness, how great is that darkness!

[24] No man can serve two masters: for either he will hate the one, and love the other; or else he will hold to the one, and despise the other. Ye cannot serve God and mammon. [25] Therefore I say unto you, Take no thought for your life, what ye shall eat, or what ye shall drink; nor yet for your body, what ye shall put on. Is not the life more than meat, and the body than raiment? [26] Behold the fowls of the air: for they sow not, neither do they reap, nor gather into barns; yet your heavenly Father feedeth them. Are ye not much better than they? [27] Which of you by taking thought can add one cubit unto his stature? [28] And why take ye thought for raiment? Consider the lilies of the field, how they grow; they toil not, neither do they spin: [29] and yet I say unto you, That even Solomon in all his glory was not arrayed like one of these. [30] Wherefore, if God so clothe the grass of the field, which to day is, and to morrow is cast into the oven, shall he not much more clothe you, O ye of little faith? [31] Therefore take no thought, saying, What shall we eat? or, What shall we drink? or, Wherewithal shall we be clothed? [32] (For after all these things do the Gentiles seek:) for your heavenly Father knoweth that ye have need of all these things. [33] But seek ye first the kingdom of God, and his righteousness; and all these things shall be added unto you. [34] Take therefore no thought for the morrow: for the morrow shall take thought for the things of itself. Sufficient unto the day is the evil thereof.

Judge not, that ye be not judged. [2] For with what judgment ye judge, ye shall be judged: and with what measure ye mete, it shall be measured to you again. [3] And why beholdest thou the mote that is in thy brother's eye, but considerest not the beam that is in thine own eye? [4] Or how wilt thou say to thy brother, Let me pull out the mote out of thine eye; and, behold, a beam is in thine own eye? [5] Thou hypocrite, first cast out the beam out of thine own eye; and then shalt thou see clearly to cast out the mote out of thy brother's eye.

[6] Give not that which is holy unto the dogs, neither cast ye your pearls before swine, lest they trample them under their feet, and turn again and rend you.

[7] Ask, and it shall be given you; seek, and ye shall find; knock, and it shall be opened unto you: [8] for every one that asketh receiveth; and he that

seeketh findeth; and to him that knocketh it shall be opened. [9] Or what man is there of you, whom if his son ask bread, will he give him a stone? [10] Or if he ask a fish, will he give him a serpent? [11] If ye then, being evil, know how to give good gifts unto your children, how much more shall your Father which is in heaven give good things to them that ask him? [12] Therefore all things whatsoever ye would that men should do to you, do ye even so to them: for this is the law and the prophets.

[13] Enter ye in at the strait gate: for wide is the gate, and broad is the way, that leadeth to destruction, and many there be which go in thereat: [14] because strait is the gate, and narrow is the way, which leadeth unto life, and few there be that find it.

[15] Beware of false prophets, which come to you in sheep's clothing, but inwardly they are ravening wolves. [16] Ye shall know them by their fruits. Do men gather grapes of thorns, or figs of thistles? [17] Even so every good tree bringeth forth good fruit; but a corrupt tree bringeth forth evil fruit. [18] A good tree cannot bring forth evil fruit, neither can a corrupt tree bring forth good fruit. [19] Every tree that bringeth not forth good fruit is hewn down, and cast into the fire. [20] Wherefore by their fruits ye shall know them.

[21] Not every one that saith unto me, Lord, Lord, shall enter into the kingdom of heaven; but he that doeth the will of my Father which is in heaven. [22] Many will say to me in that day, Lord, Lord, have we not prophesied in thy name? and in thy name have cast out devils? and in thy name done many wonderful works? [23] And then will I profess unto them, I never knew you: depart from me, ye that work iniquity.

[24] Therefore whosoever heareth these sayings of mine, and doeth them, I will liken him unto a wise man, which built his house upon a rock: [25] and the rain descended, and the floods came, and the winds blew and beat upon that house; and it fell not: for it was founded upon a rock. [26]And every one that heareth these sayings of mine, and doeth them not, shall be likened unto a foolish man, which built his house upon the sand: [27] and the rain descended, and the floods came, and the winds blew, and beat upon that house; and it fell: and great was the fall of it. [28] And it came to pass, when Jesus had ended these sayings, the people were astonished at his doctrine: [29] for he taught them as one having authority, and not as the scribes.

The Sermon on the Mount

5 When he saw the crowds he went up the hill. There he took his seat, and
2 when his disciples had gathered round him he began to address them. And this is the teaching he gave:

Matthew V–VII, from *The New English Bible: New Testament.* © The Delegates of the Oxford University Press and The Syndics of the Cambridge University Press 1961. Reprinted by permission.

3	'How blest are those who know that they are poor; the kingdom of Heaven is theirs.
4	How blest are the sorrowful; they shall find consolation.
5	How blest are those of a gentle spirit; they shall have the earth for their possession.
6	How blest are those who hunger and thirst to see right prevail;[a] they shall be satisfied.
7	How blest are those who show mercy; mercy shall be shown to them.
8	How blest are those whose hearts are pure; they shall see God.
9	How blest are the peacemakers; God shall call them his sons.
10	How blest are those who have suffered persecution for the cause of right; the kingdom of Heaven is theirs.

11,12 'How blest you are, when you suffer insults and persecution and every kind of calumny for my sake. Accept it with gladness and exultation, for you have a rich reward in heaven; in the same way they persecuted the prophets before you.

13 'You are salt to the world. And if salt becomes tasteless, how is its saltness to be restored? It is now good for nothing but to be thrown away and trodden underfoot.

14,15 'You are light for all the world. A town that stands on a hill cannot be hidden. When a lamp is lit, it is not put under the meal-tub, but on the lamp-stand, where it gives light to everyone in the house.

16 And you, like the lamp, must shed light among your fellows, so that, when they see the good you do, they may give praise to your Father in heaven.

17,18 'Do not suppose that I have come to abolish the Law and the prophets; I did not come to abolish, but to complete. I tell you this: so long as heaven and earth endure, not a letter, not a stroke, will disappear from the Law until all that must happen has happened.[b]

---

[a] Or to do what is right. [b] Or before all that it stands for is achieved.

19,20 If any man therefore sets aside even the least of the Law's demands, and teaches others to do the same, he will have the lowest place in the kingdom of Heaven, whereas anyone who keeps the Law and teaches others so will stand high in the kingdom of Heaven. I tell you, unless you show yourselves far better men than the Pharisees and the doctors of the law, you can never enter the kingdom of Heaven.

21 'You have learned that our forefathers were told, "Do not commit murder; anyone who commits murder must be brought to judgement."

22 But what I tell you is this: Anyone who nurses anger against his brother*a* must be brought to judgement. If he abuses his brother he

[a] *Some witnesses insert* without good cause.

must answer for it to the court; if he sneers at him he will have to answer for it in the fires of hell.

23,24 'If, when you are bringing your gift to the altar, you suddenly remember that your brother has a grievance against you, leave your gift where it is before the altar. First go and make your peace with your brother, and only then come back and offer your gift.

25 'If someone sues you, come to terms with him promptly while you are both on your way to court; otherwise he may hand you over to the judge, and the judge to the constable, and you will be put in jail.
26 I tell you, once you are there you will not be let out till you have paid the last farthing.

27 'You have learned that they were told, "Do not commit adultery."
28 But what I tell you is this: If a man looks on a woman with a lustful eye, he has already committed adultery with her in his heart.

29 'If your right eye leads you astray, tear it out and fling it away; it is better for you to lose one part of your body than for the whole of it
30 to be thrown into hell. And if your right hand is your undoing, cut it off and fling it away; it is better for you to lose one part of your body than for the whole of it to go to hell.

31 'They were told, "A man who divorces his wife must give her a
32 note of dismissal." But what I tell you is this: If a man divorces his wife for any cause other than unchastity he involves her in adultery; and anyone who marries a woman so divorced commits adultery.

33 'Again, you have learned that they were told, "Do not break your
34 oath", and, "Oaths sworn to the Lord must be kept." But what I tell you is this: You are not to swear at all—not by heaven, for it is God's
35 throne, nor by earth, for it is his footstool, nor by Jerusalem, for it is
36 the city of the great King, nor by your own head, because you cannot
37 turn one hair of it white or black. Plain "Yes" or "No" is all you need to say; anything beyond that comes from the devil.

38 'You have learned that they were told, "An eye for an eye, and
39 a tooth for a tooth." But what I tell you is this: Do not set yourself against the man who wrongs you. If someone slaps you on the right
40 cheek, turn and offer him your left. If a man wants to sue you for your
41 shirt, let him have your coat as well. If a man in authority makes you
42 go one mile, go with him two. Give when you are asked to give; and do not turn your back on a man who wants to borrow.

43 'You have learned that they were told, "Love your neighbour, hate
44 your enemy." But what I tell you is this: Love your enemies*a* and pray

[a] *Some witnesses insert* bless those who curse you, do good to those who hate you.

45 for your persecutors;*b* only so can you be children of your heavenly

46 Father, who makes his sun rise on good and bad alike, and sends the rain on the honest and the dishonest. If you love only those who love you, what reward can you expect? Surely the tax-gatherers do as much
47 as that. And if you greet only your brothers, what is there extraordinary
48 about that? Even the heathen do as much. You must therefore be all goodness, just as your heavenly Father is all good.

6 'Be careful not to make a show of your religion before men; if you do, no reward awaits you in your Father's house in heaven.

2 'Thus, when you do some act of charity, do not announce it with a flourish of trumpets, as the hypocrites do in synagogue and in the streets to win admiration from men. I tell you this: they have their
3 reward already. No; when you do some act of charity, do not let your
4 left hand know what your right is doing; your good deed must be secret, and your Father who sees what is done in secret will reward you.°

5 'Again, when you pray, do not be like the hypocrites; they love to say their prayers standing up in synagogue and at the street-corners, for everyone to see them. I tell you this: they have their reward already.
6 But when you pray, go into a room by yourself, shut the door, and pray to your Father who is there in the secret place; and your Father who sees what is secret will reward you.ᵈ

---

[b] *Some witnesses insert* and those who treat you spitefully. [c] *Some witnesses add* openly. [d] *Some witnesses add* openly.

---

7 'In your prayers do not go babbling on like the heathen, who imagine that the more they say the more likely they are to be heard.
8 Do not imitate them. Your Father knows what your needs are before you ask him.
9 'This is how you should pray:

    "Our Father in heaven,
    Thy name be hallowed;
10   Thy kingdom come,
    Thy will be done,
    On earth as in heaven.
11   Give us today our daily bread.ᵃ
12   Forgive us the wrong we have done,
    As we have forgiven those who have wronged us.
13   And do not bring us to the test,
    But save us from the evil one." ᵇ

---

[a] *Or* our bread for the morrow. [b] *Some witnesses add* For thine is the kingdom and the power and the glory, for ever. Amen.

---

14 For if you forgive others the wrongs they have done, your heavenly
15 Father will also forgive you; but if you do not forgive others, then the wrongs you have done will not be forgiven by your Father.

16 'So too when you fast, do not look gloomy like the hypocrites: they make their faces unsightly so that other people may see that they
17 are fasting. I tell you this: they have their reward already. But when
18 you fast, anoint your head and wash your face, so that men may not see that you are fasting, but only your Father who is in the secret place; and your Father who sees what is secret will give you your reward.

19 'Do not store up for yourselves treasure on earth, where it grows
20 rusty and moth-eaten, and thieves break in to steal it. Store up treasure in heaven, where there is no moth and no rust to spoil it, no thieves to
21 break in and steal. For where your wealth is, there will your heart be also.

22 'The lamp of the body is the eye. If your eyes are sound, you will
23 have light for your whole body; if the eyes are bad, your whole body will be in darkness. If then the only light you have is darkness, the darkness is doubly dark.

24 'No servant can be slave to two masters; for either he will hate the first and love the second, or he will be devoted to the first and think nothing of the second. You cannot serve God and Money.

25 'Therefore I bid you put away anxious thoughts about food and drink to keep you alive, and clothes to cover your body. Surely life is
26 more than food, the body more than clothes. Look at the birds of the air; they do not sow and reap and store in barns, yet your heavenly
27 Father feeds them. You are worth more than the birds! Is there a man
28 of you who by anxious thought can add a foot to his height [a]? And why be anxious about clothes? Consider how the lilies grow in the fields;
29 they do not work, they do not spin;[b] and yet, I tell you, even Solomon

[a] Or a day to his life. [b] One witness reads Consider the lilies: they neither card nor spin, nor labour.

30 in all his splendour was not attired like one of these. But if that is how God clothes the grass in the fields, which is there today, and tomorrow is
31 thrown on the stove, will he not all the more clothe you? How little faith you have! No, do not ask anxiously, "What are we to eat? What
32 are we to drink? What shall we wear?" All these are things for the heathen to run after, not for you, because your heavenly Father knows
33 that you need them all. Set your mind on God's kingdom and his justice
34 before everything else, and all the rest will come to you as well. So do not be anxious about tomorrow; tomorrow will look after itself. Each day has troubles enough of its own.

7 1,2 'Pass no judgement, and you will not be judged. For as you judge others, so you will yourselves be judged, and whatever measure you
3 deal out to others will be dealt back to you. Why do you look at the speck of sawdust in your brother's eye, with never a thought for the

4   great plank in your own? Or how can you say to your brother, "Let me take the speck out of your eye", when all the time there is that plank in
5   your own? You hypocrite! First take the plank out of your own eye, and then you will see clearly to take the speck out of your brother's.

6   'Do not give dogs what is holy; do not feed your pearls to pigs: they will only trample on them, and turn and tear you to pieces.

7   'Ask, and you will receive; seek, and you will find; knock, and the
8   door will be opened. For everyone who asks receives, he who seeks finds, and to him who knocks, the door will be opened.

9   'Is there a man among you who will offer his son a stone when he
10, 11 asks for bread, or a snake when he asks for fish? If you, then, bad as you are, know how to give your children what is good for them, how much more will your heavenly Father give good things to those who ask him!

12 'Always treat others as you would like them to treat you: that is the Law and the prophets.

13 'Enter by the narrow gate. The gate is wide that leads to perdition,
14 there is plenty of room on the road,ᵃ and many go that way; but the gate that leads to life is small and the road is narrow,ᵇ and those who

---

[a] *Some witnesses read* The road that leads to perdition is wide with plenty of room.
[b] *Some witnesses read* but the road that leads to life is small and narrow.

---

find it are few.

15 'Beware of false prophets, men who come to you dressed up as
16 sheep while underneath they are savage wolves. You will recognize them by the fruits they bear. Can grapes be picked from briars, or
17 figs from thistles? In the same way, a good tree always yields good
18 fruit, and a poor tree bad fruit. A good tree cannot bear bad fruit,
19 or a poor tree good fruit. And when a tree does not yield good fruit
20 it is cut down and burnt. That is why I say you will recognize them by their fruits.

21 'Not everyone who calls me "Lord, Lord" will enter the kingdom of Heaven, but only those who do the will of my heavenly Father.
22 When that day comes, many will say to me, "Lord, Lord, did we not prophesy in your name, cast out devils in your name, and in your name
23 perform many miracles?" Then I will tell them to their face, "I never knew you: out of my sight, you and your wicked ways!"

24 'What then of the man who hears these words of mine and acts upon them? He is like a man who had the sense to build his house on
25 rock. The rain came down, the floods rose, the wind blew, and beat upon that house; but it did not fall, because its foundations were on
26 rock. But what of the man who hears these words of mine and does not act upon them? He is like a man who was foolish enough to build his

27 house on sand. The rain came down, the floods rose, the wind blew, and beat upon that house; down it fell with a great crash.'
28 When Jesus had finished this discourse the people were astounded
29 at his teaching; unlike their own teachers he taught with a note of authority.

A Sharp Sword of the Lord

The New English Bible is not a translation for the connoisseur of literary phrases and elegant turns of language; rather it is one which stands ready for action as an agent of evangelization.

CECIL NORTHCOTT

For three and a half centuries the translators of the Bible appointed by the high and mighty King James have breathed faith and fervor into the souls of English-speaking peoples. Their sonorous cadences, musical eloquences and memorable diction have been the Bible for both believer and unbeliever. During the last decade King James has been notably supported by his heirs and assigns, the men of the American Revised Standard Version who screened out many of his archaisms and generally gave him a new look yet were careful not to depart too sharply from the loved and familiar biblical image bequeathed to the English-speaking peoples by the pious monarch of the 17th century.

King James will always be with us. He will be handled with loving faithfulness as long as the English tongue lasts. He adorns the throne of speech, and his very infelicities and oddities have won an abiding affection for themselves. They are built into the Word of God with such an eternal certainty that come all the machinations of principalities and powers, this rock of the ages will endure for the comfort and edification of mankind.

I

But King James is King James. In 1946 the General Assembly of the Church of Scotland, provoked by an overture from the presbytery of Stirling and Dunblane, looked His Majesty squarely in the face, as only an assembly of Scots can do, and said enough is enough; the time has come "that a translation of the Bible be made in the language of the present day." From

Christian Century, LXXVIII (March 15, 1961), 320–321. Copyright © 1961 Christian Century Foundation. Reprinted by permission from the *Christian Century*.

then on the process of organization and translation has moved with stately and efficient precision, presided over by a committee of the main churches of Great Britain and Ireland with appropriate panels of translators and under the general direction of C. H. Dodd, sometime Norris-Hulse professor of divinity in the University of Cambridge, a Congregationalist, and the first non-Anglican to hold a chair of divinity in the ancient universities of England.

In the introduction to the New Testament of the New English Bible (Oxford and Cambridge University presses, $4.95) the translators say, "We have conceived our task to be that of understanding the original as precisely as we could (using all available aids), and then saying again in our native idiom what we believed the author to be saying in his." There in a sentence is the key to this masterly achievement. The translators further state: "In doing our work we have constantly striven to follow our instructions and render the Greek, as we understood it, into the English of the present day, that is, into the natural vocabulary, constructions, and rhythms of contemporary speech. We have sought to avoid archaism, jargon and all that is either stilted or slipshod." In their efforts to render the Bible into English as it is spoken the translators have had the assistance of a literary panel whose members include A. T. P. Williams, the present Bishop of Winchester; Basil Willey, professor of English language and literature at Cambridge; W. F. Oakeshott, now rector of Lincoln College, Oxford, and for some years headmaster of Winchester College (one of the great public schools of England); and A. L. P. Norrington, now president of Trinity College, Oxford, and for years associated with Oxford University Press and the making of the Oxford English dictionary.

In the view of the translators, "only those who have meditated long upon the Greek original are aware of the richness and subtlety of meaning that may lie even within the most apparently simple sentence, or know the despair that attends all efforts to bring it out through the medium of a different language." That is a disarming apologia for a translation which takes the reader at once into the timeless New Testament world, where he is no longer cluttered and clothed with biblical language as the centuries have known it but is confronted with English of Attic clarity, English that sparkles crisply in the 20th century air.

II

I open this superbly printed and presented book with (I hope) something of the reverent excitement felt by a subject of King James handling the printed pages of his Bible three and a half centuries ago. I am the English ploughboy. I am the London dilettante in the crypt of Old St. Paul's. I am the parishioner of St. John's-by-the-Gas Station turning the Bible pages of the mid-20th century. And I read:

> This then is my word to you, and I urge it upon you in the Lord's name. Give up living like pagans with their good-for-nothing notions. Their wits are beclouded, they are strangers to the life that is in God, because ignorance pre-

vails among them and their minds have grown hard as stone. Dead to all feeling, they have abandoned themselves to vice, and stop at nothing to satisfy their foul desires. But that is not how you learned Christ. For were you not told of him, were you not as Christians taught the truth as it is in Jesus?—that leaving your former way of life, you must lay aside that old human nature which, deluded by its lusts, is sinking towards death. You must be made new in mind and spirit, and put on the new nature of God's creating, which shows itself in the just and devout life called for by the truth. Then throw off falsehood; speak the truth to each other, for all of us are the parts of one body. [Ephesians 4:17–25]

For I reckon that the sufferings we now endure bear no comparison with the splendour, as yet unrevealed, which is in store for us. For the created universe waits with eager expectation for God's sons to be revealed. It was made the victim of frustration, not by its own choice, but because of him who made it so, yet always there was hope, because the universe itself is to be freed from the shackles of mortality and enter upon the liberty and splendour of the children of God. [Romans 8:18–21]

Before God, and before Christ Jesus who is to judge men living and dead, I adjure you by his coming appearance and his reign, proclaim the message, press it home on all occasions, convenient or inconvenient, use argument, reproof, and appeal, with all the patience that the work of teaching requires. For the time will come when they will not stand wholesome teaching, but will follow their own fancy and gather a crowd of teachers to tickle their ears. They will stop their ears to the truth and turn to mythology. But you yourself must keep calm and sane at all times; face hardship, work to spread the Gospel, and do all the duties of your calling. [II Timothy 4:1–5]

These three examples from the Epistles show the easy, flowing style of the translation with its freedom from the tyrannous versification which has throttled the life of the Bible since the 16th century. Without straining for effect the translators have permitted the English language to run its course through the Greek.

The result is not just a good, near-rendering of the original but a translation which is taut, resilient and deeply satisfying in the English tongue of today. The pitfalls of the paraphraser are avoided, and there is no reaching out for Bible language which in itself has become a heavy curse to the free course of the Word of God. Here is the Bible not simply in a new dress draped over the old physical frame but in a renewed body alive and vigorous with all the strong internal vitality of the Word of God.

In the world of the Gospels there is the same clear radiance, and if the test of this translation is whether it effectively introduces the reader to Jesus Christ, then the result is triumphant:

They were on the road, going up to Jerusalem, Jesus leading the way; and the disciples were filled with awe; while those who followed behind were afraid. He took the Twelve aside and began to tell them what was to happen to him. 'We are now going to Jerusalem,' he said; 'and the Son of Man will be given up to the chief priests and the doctors of the law; they will condemn him to death and hand him over to the foreign power. He will be mocked and spat upon, flogged and killed; and three days afterwards, he will rise again.' [Mark 10:32–34]

> Our Father in heaven,
> Thy name be hallowed;
> Thy kingdom come,
> Thy will be done,
> On earth as in heaven.
> Give us today our daily bread.
> Forgive us the wrong we have done,
> As we have forgiven those who have wronged us.
> And do not bring us to the test,
> But save us from the evil one. [Matthew 6:9–13]
>
> But on the Sunday morning very early they came to the tomb bringing the spices they had prepared. Finding that the stone had been rolled away from the tomb, they went inside; but the body was not to be found. While they stood utterly at a loss, all of a sudden two men in dazzling garments were at their side. They were terrified, and stood with eyes cast down, but the men said, 'Why search among the dead for one who lives? Remember what he told you while he was still in Galilee, about the Son of Man: how he must be given up into the power of sinful men and be crucified, and must rise again on the third day.' Then they recalled his words and, returning from the tomb, they reported all this to the Eleven and all the others. [Luke 24:1–9]

Here is the diamond-like hardness of the Gospels as they bear witness to Christ and his work which are the heart of the world of faith and experience. This is not a translation for the connoisseur of literary phrases and elegant turns of language. The Bible has suffered too much from the literary gents of the last three centuries who between them have contributed to its suffocation as the witness to the supremacy and saviorhood of God in Christ. The new translation stands stripped for action as an evangelizing weapon—evangelization being its sole purpose. I am ready to hear from my American friends that this is a British-English translation and that there are phrases and allusions in it which will not travel the Atlantic. I am ready to be told that it lacks the comforting grace and sentimental associations which are part of the communication system of truth itself, and which are to be found in the King James-Authorized Version. We take in what is warm and emotional; we tend to reject what may be stringently austere. For many millions the Bible was born in 1611. What the New English Bible asserts without saying so is that the Bible is born in every generation, to every age, to every man. It is universal yet personal, timeless yet contemporary, and on these grounds the New English Bible takes its place as a treasure to be discovered and loved.

III

Writing in the London *Observer* on the first day of 1961, C. H. Dodd said: "Complete success is not to be expected; translation is in the end an impossible art. But it is hoped that the new translation will do something to make the New Testament more generally understood, so far as understanding depends on language; to make it . . . as intelligible to our contemporaries as the original was to those who first read it in their own homely 'Common Greek.' That it is as relevant, and important, to us as to them is the conviction which lies behind the present enterprise."

That is the modest aim of an enterprise which may be of revolutionary significance for 20th century Christianity. For the final test of the new Bible—and we must wait some years for the Old Testament and the Apocrypha—will be not only in personal reading but in its impact on the present generation both outside and inside the life of the church. A new instrument of mission is being forged for the Christian faith, a sharp sword of the Lord whose thrust is in a language that is becoming the present-day universal tongue spoken in many lands and under many skies. King James and his men translated for their confined world of old England, and their masterpiece is secure. The New English Bible is at once universal, and its appearance may well mark a turning point in the world mission of the Christian church.

A Scholar Finds the Beauty Wrung out of New English Bible's Verses

T. S. ELIOT

There are three points of view from which any translation of the Bible may be examined: that of doctrine, that of accuracy of translation, and that of English prose style. In what follows I am concerned only with the question of style.

The translation of the Bible undertaken over 350 years ago at the suggestion of King James I was made by the best scholars in the kingdom. It was a revision of previous translations; the task was parcelled out between six committees, and a general committee spent over two years in revising the work of the six.

In the preparation of THE NEW ENGLISH BIBLE, of which only the New Testament has been completed and published, an equally careful procedure has been followed. There have been four "panels," of which one has been responsible for the New Testament, and another is responsible for "the literary revision of the whole."

Again, the committees have been enlisted from among the best scholars in the kingdom, and, this time, with complete freedom of choice: for denominational considerations have played no part.

Errors of Taste

The age covered by the reigns of Elizabeth I and James I was richer in writers of genius than is our own, and we should not expect a translation made in our time to be a masterpiece of our literature or, as was the Authorised Version of 1611, an exemplar of English prose for successive generations of writers.

We are, however, entitled to expect from a panel chosen from among the most distinguished scholars of our day at least a work of dignified mediocrity. When we find that we are offered something far below that modest level, something which astonishes in its combination of the vulgar, the trivial and the pedantic, we ask in alarm, "What is happening to the English language?"

I shall give a few quotations in illustration, before examining the principles of translation adopted by the translators, as set forth in the Introduction: principles which seem to me to take us some way towards understanding the frequent errors of taste in the translation itself.

The translation of a passage may be subjected to criticism on several grounds. I can illustrate this very well by examining a sentence in St. Matthew (hereinafter referred to as "Matthew" in conformity with "The New English Bible") the earlier version of which will be a familiar quotation to many even of those who are ignorant of the Scriptures: "Do not feed your pearls to pigs."

We notice, first, the substitution of "pigs" for "swine." The Complete Oxford Dictionary says that "swine" is now "literary" but does not say that it is "obsolete." I presume, therefore, that in substituting "pigs" for "swine" the translators were trying to choose a word nearer to common speech, even if at the sacrifice of dignity.

I should have thought, however, that the word "swine" would be understood, not only by countryfolk who may have heard of "swine fever," but even by the urban public, since it is still applied, I believe, to human beings as a term of abuse.

Next, I should have thought that the sentence would be more in accordance with English usage if the direct and indirect objects were transposed, thus: "Do not feed pigs upon your pearls." To make "pearls" the direct object is, if I am not mistaken, an Americanism, and my belief is confirmed, rather than dispelled, by the examples of this usage given in the Oxford English Dictionary.

The most unfortunate result, however, is that the substitution of "feed" for "cast" makes the figure of speech ludicrous. There is all the difference in the world between saying that pigs do not *appreciate* the value of pearls, and saying, what the youngest and the most illiterate among us know, that they cannot be *nourished* on pearls.

This is not the only instance in which a figure of speech, or illustration, has been ruined; though in some other places rather by literalness, as "no man can be slave to two masters," which ceases to carry any admonition, and becomes merely a flat statement about the condition of slavery.

London *Sunday Telegraph*, December 16, 1962, p. 7. Reprinted by permission of the *Sunday Telegraph*.

"Or how can you say to your brother, 'Let me take the speck out of your eye,' when all the time there is that plank in your own?" may be literally accurate but will certainly, if it is read in church, raise a giggle among the choirboys. As for the house built upon sand, "down it fell with a great crash!"

As for clarity, I find some passages more puzzling in "The New English Bible" than in the Authorised Version. Surely others besides myself will take no comfort from being told, as the first beatitude: "How blest are those who know that they are poor." (The translator of Luke is more nearly in accord with the Authorised Version here.)

And the unlearned, on being told that "a man who divorces his wife must give her a note of dismissal", will marvel at the apparent facility with which the Hebrews could get rid of their wives. "Bill of divorcement," even though it gives no clear notion of the process required by Jewish law, at least sounds ceremonious.

The foregoing examples are all taken from "the Gospel according to Matthew," an Evangelist who seems to have been especially unlucky in his translator. The other Gospels, however, conform to the same style (or absence of style) in their monotonous inferiority of phrasing.

I wish nevertheless to quote one brief passage in order to give the translator of "Luke" his due (Luke iii, 14–15). To the soldiers who ask what they should do John the Baptist replies: "No bullying; no blackmail; make do with your pay!"

I admit gladly that lapses of taste are less offensive when committed against a "Letter"—that is to say, against what we have known heretofore as an "Epistle"—than when committed against a Gospel. And there is much more justification, I will even say *need*, for modern translations of the Epistles than for modern translations of the Gospels.

Some years ago Dr. J. H. Oldham lent me the translation of St. Paul's Epistles made by Gerald Warre Cornish (who fell in action, I believe, in the First World War). It struck me as admirable and very useful. To imagine, however, that a modern translation can make St. Paul's meaning clear is an exaggeration: what it can make clear is what the familiarity of the Authorised Version may disguise from us—the fact that St. Paul is a difficult writer.

A modern translation makes it easier for us to get to grips with the thought of St. Paul: it does not relieve us of the necessity of using our own minds, any more than can a translation of Kant's "Critique of Pure Reason."

And if the translations of Paul in "The New English Bible" did not offend our taste with Boeotian absurdities similar to those in the translations of the Gospels (e.g. Paul "formulated the charge" that Jews and Greeks alike are all under the power of sin) they might take a respectable place among modern translations.

I do not propose to prolong my inventory of verbal infelicities in "The New English Bible." The *Times Literary Supplement* of March 24, 1961, had an excellent article on "Language in the New Bible"; and the Trinitarian Bible

Society has issued, as a leaflet, a useful list of specimens of bad taste, compiled by the Rev. Terence H. Brown and available at the price of one penny.

The instances I have given will suffice to prepare the way for an examination of the principles which the translators have set before themselves. These find their statement in the Introduction. I do not think that this Introduction has yet received enough attention.

According to the Introduction, the translators have set before themselves several aims: fidelity to what the author wrote; clarity; finer shades of idiom (than in the Authorised Version); to say in our own native idiom what they believed the author to be saying in his; and contemporaneity.

We are told that the language of the Authorised Version is "even more definitely archaic, and less generally understood, than it was 80 years ago" (when the Revised version was prepared) *"for the rate of change in English usage has accelerated."*

I put this clause in italics, because it seems to me significant—and ominous. The English usage of 80 years ago, we are told, is out of date. And if the rate of change has accelerated, is it not likely to continue the acceleration? What is likely to be the fate of "The New English Bible" 80 years hence?

We are then told that for a version more modern than that of 1881 "an attempt should be made consistently to use the idiom of contemporary English to convey the meaning of the Greek." This requirement of contemporaneity is emphasised at the end of the same paragraph: "The present translators have been *enjoined* (italics mine) to replace Greek constructions and idioms by those of contemporary English."

Change for Worse

No attempt is made to substantiate the assertion that the rate of change of English usage has accelerated, or to inform us in what respects English usage is changing. It does not seem to have occurred to the mind of the anonymous author of this Introduction that change can sometimes be for the worse, and that it is as much our business to attempt to arrest deterioration and combat corruption of our language, as to accept change.

Nor are we given any definition of "contemporaneity." Is it to be found in the writing of the best contemporary writers of English prose, and if so, who are they and who is to decide who they are? Or is it to be found in colloquial speech, and if so at what level of literacy?

Will the readers who find "sweated all day in the blazing sun" suits them better than "borne the burden and heat of the day" be the same as those who find "extirpate" more "contemporary" than "destroy"?

When we turn to the description on the jacket we find that the aim was "to be in style neither traditional nor modernistic." If style is to be contemporary without being modernistic, the words "contemporary" and "modernistic" should be carefully defined.

For Whose Use?

At the time when "The New English Bible" was published, it seems that Dr. Dodd appeared in a television programme and explained the purposes for which it was designed. As I did not hear him on that occasion, I quote from the article in the *Times Literary Supplement* to which I referred earlier:

> In a helpful television programme . . . Dr. Dodd, the director of the enterprise, told viewers whom the new Bible was intended for: it was, he said, for people who do not go to church, for a rising generation less well educated than formerly in classical and literary traditions, and for churchgoers so well accustomed to the language of the Authorised Version that they may have come to find it soothing rather than meaningful.

So long as "The New English Bible" was used only for private reading, it would be merely a symptom of the decay of the English language in the middle of the 20th century. But the more it is adopted for religious services the more it will become an active agent of decadence.

There may be Ministers of the Gospel who do not realise that the music of the phrase, of the paragraph, of the period is an essential constituent of good English prose, and who fail to understand that the life of a reading of Gospel and Epistle in the liturgy is in this music of the spoken word.

The first appearance of "The New English Bible" in churches has, I believe, been in the reading of the Epistle for the day. Nothing will be gained, for the new version will be just as hard to grasp, when read in church, as the Authorised Version, and it will lack the verbal beauty of the Authorised Version.

To understand any version we must study it at home, or under direction. And if use of "The New English Bible" "Letters" in churches is followed by adoption of "The New English Bible" Gospels, must we not look forward to the day when the Collects of Cranmer are revised for use in Anglican churches, to make them conform to "contemporary English"?

It is good that those who aspire to write good English prose or verse should be prepared by the study of Greek and Latin. It would also be good if those who have authority to translate a dead language could show understanding and appreciation of their own.

Questions

1. In what sense does Northcott consider the New English Bible a "sharp sword of the Lord"? Is his title appropriate? Does it contain a Biblical allusion? How can one trace Biblical allusions?
2. Why does Northcott use the phrase "machinations of principalities and powers"?

3. Explain the meaning of Northcott's phrase "English of Attic clarity."
4. In what sense does Northcott suggest that versification has "throttled the life of the Bible"? Would Eliot agree?
5. What does Northcott mean when he says: "For many millions the Bible was born in 1611"?
6. What is the function of the paragraph in Eliot's essay which begins "I admit gladly. . ."?
7. What does Eliot mean by the phrase "Boeotian absurdities"? Explain his use of the word "period" in the sentence about the "music . . . of the period."
8. Would Eliot's statement that "it is as much our business to attempt to arrest deterioration and combat corruption of our language, as to accept change" be likely to make him sympathetic or unsympathetic with the aims of the editors of *Webster's Third*? (See part II, 1.)
9. Identify Cranmer (mentioned in Eliot's essay).
10. Do the quotations used in Northcott's essay bear out Eliot's points?
11. Define the area of disagreement between Eliot and Northcott.
12. What are the qualities of a good translation? Of a good Bible translation?

Assignments

1. Compare the two translations—one from the King James Bible and one from the New English Bible—of the passage given in this section.
2. Referring to the material in this section, write an extended definition of "style."
3. Read the translators' introductions to a number of modern Bible translations. Write an essay discussing the points of agreement and disagreement or the most important considerations in Bible translation.
4. Obtain two modern translations of the same Bible passage (other than the one in this section) or of any work of foreign literature (for example, *The Cherry Orchard*, by Anton Chekhov; *Hedda Gabler*, by Henrik Ibsen). Discuss the merits and the deficiencies of each.

Additional Reading

The New English Bible created sharp lines of attack and defense. The titles of the reviews suggest that in this discussion, as perhaps in all discussions of religious questions, there is no middle ground. Some of the reviews of the new translation are F. L. Lucas, "Greek Word Was Different," *Saturday Review*, XLIV (April 1, 1961), 12–14; Bergen Evans, "Thou Shalt Not or You Shall Not," *New York Times Magazine*, March 26, 1961, p. 28; G. Wells, "Water in the Wine," *National Review*, X (May 6, 1961), 284–285; J. C. Maxwell, "Designed to Be Read as the Bible," *Spectator*, No. 6925 (March 17, 1961), p. 370; V. S. Pritchett, "Finalised Version," *New Statesman*, LXI (March 17, 1961), 425–426; Dwight Macdonald, *Against the American Grain* (New York, 1962), pp. 262–288.

An interesting comparison of recent Bible translations appears in C. Razor, "Comparison of the Style of Four Recent Translations of the New Testament with that of the King James Version," *Journal of Religion*, XLI (April 1961), 73–90.

SECTION FOUR | *Toynbee's History: Mish-Mash or Monument*

My View of History

ARNOLD J. TOYNBEE

My view of history is itself a tiny piece of history; and this mainly other people's history and not my own; for a scholar's life-work is to add his bucketful of water to the great and growing river of knowledge fed by countless bucketfuls of the kind. If my individual view of history is to be made at all illuminating, or indeed intelligible, it must be presented in its origin, growth, and social and personal setting.

There are many angles of vision from which human minds peer at the universe. Why am I a historian, not a philosopher or a physicist? For the same reason that I drink tea and coffee without sugar. Both habits were formed at a tender age by following a lead from my mother. I am a historian because my mother was one before me; yet at the same time I am conscious that I am of a different school from hers. Why did I not exactly take my mother's cue?

First, because I was born by my mother into the next generation to hers, and my mind was, therefore, not yet set hard when history took my generation by the throat in 1914; and, secondly, because my education was more old-fashioned than my mother's had been. My mother—belonging as she did to the first generation, in England, of university women—had obtained an up-to-date education in modern Western history, with the national history of England itself as the principal guide-line. Her son, being a boy, went to an old-fashioned English public school and was educated, both there and at Oxford, almost entirely on the Greek and Latin classics.

For any would-be historian—and especially for one born into these

From *Civilization on Trial*, by Arnold J. Toynbee. Copyright 1948 by Oxford University Press, Inc. Reprinted by permission.

times—a classical education is, in my belief, a priceless boon. As a training-ground, the history of the Graeco-Roman world has its conspicuous merits. In the first place, Graeco-Roman history is visible to us in perspective and can be seen by us as a whole, because it is over—in contrast to the history of our own Western world, which is a still-unfinished play of which we do not know the eventual ending and cannot even see the present general aspect from our own position as momentary actors on its crowded and agitated stage.

In the second place, the field of Graeco-Roman history is not encumbered and obscured by a surfeit of information, and so we can see the wood—thanks to a drastic thinning of the trees during the interregnum between the dissolution of the Graeco-Roman society and the emergence of our own. Moreover, the conveniently manageable amount of evidence that has survived is not overweighted by the state papers of parochial principalities, like those which, in our Western world, have accumulated, ton upon ton, during the dozen centuries of its pre-atomic-bomb age. The surviving materials for a study of Graeco-Roman history are not only manageable in quantity and select in quality; they are also well-balanced in their character. Statues, poems, and works of philosophy count here for more than the texts of laws and treaties; and this breeds a sense of proportion in the mind of a historian nursed on Graeco-Roman history; for—as we can see in the perspective given by lapse of time more easily than we can see it in the life of our own generation—the works of artists and men of letters outlive the deeds of business men, soldiers, and statesmen. The poets and the philosophers outrange the historians; while the prophets and the saints overtop and outlast them all. The ghosts of Agamemnon and Pericles haunt the living world of to-day by grace of the magic words of Homer and Thucydides; and, when Homer and Thucydides are no longer read, it is safe to prophesy that Christ and the Buddha and Socrates will still be fresh in the memory of (to us) almost inconceivably distant generations of men.

The third, and perhaps greatest, merit of Graeco-Roman history is that its outlook is oecumenical rather than parochial. Athens may have eclipsed Sparta and Rome Samnium, yet Athens in her youth made herself the education of all Hellas, while Rome in her old age made the whole Graeco-Roman world into a single commonwealth. In Graeco-Roman history, surveyed from beginning to end, unity is the dominant note; and, when once I had heard this great symphony, I was no longer in danger of being hypnotized by the lone and outlandish music of the parochial history of my own country, which had once enthralled me when I listened to my mother telling it to me in instalments, night by night, as she put me to bed. The historical pastors and masters of my mother's generation, not only in England but in all Western countries, had been eagerly promoting the study of national history in the mistaken belief that it had a closer bearing on their countrymen's lives and was, therefore, somehow more readily accessible to their understanding than the history of other places and times (although it is surely evident that, in reality, Jesus' Palestine and Plato's Greece were more potently operative than Alfred's or Elizabeth's England in the lives of English men and women of the Victorian age).

Yet, in spite of this misguided Victorian canonization—so alien from the spirit of the father of English history, the Venerable Bede—of the history of the particular country in which one happened to have been born, the unconscious attitude of the Victorian Englishman towards history was that of someone living outside history altogether. He took it for granted—without warrant—that he himself was standing on *terra firma*, secure against being engulfed in that ever-rolling stream in which Time had borne all his less privileged sons away. In his own privileged state of being emancipated, as he supposed, from history, the Victorian Englishman gazed with curiosity, condescension, and a touch of pity, but altogether without apprehension, at the spectacle of less fortunate denizens of other places and periods struggling and foundering in history's flood—in much the same way as, in a mediaeval Italian picture, the saved lean over the balustrade of Heaven to look down complacently at the torments of the damned in Hell. Charles the First—worse luck for him—had been in history, but Sir Robert Walpole, though threatened with impeachment, had just managed to scramble out of the surf, while we ourselves were well beyond high-water mark in a snug coign of vantage where nothing could happen to us. Our more backward contemporaries might, perhaps, still be waist-high in the now receding tide, but what was that to us?

I remember, at the beginning of a university term during the Bosnian crisis of 1908–9, Professor L. B. Namier, then an undergraduate at Balliol and back from spending a vacation at his family home just inside the Galician frontier of Austria, saying to us other Balliol men, with (it seemed to us) a portentous air: 'Well, the Austrian army is mobilized on my father's estate and the Russian army is just across the frontier, half-an-hour away.' It sounded to us like a scene from *The Chocolate Soldier,* but the lack of comprehension was mutual, for a lynx-eyed Central European observer of international affairs found it hardly credible that these English undergraduates should not realize that a stone's-throw away, in Galicia, their own goose, too, was being cooked.

Hiking round Greece three years later on the trail of Epaminondas and Philopoemen and listening to the talk in the village cafés, I learnt for the first time of the existence of something called the foreign policy of Sir Edward Grey. Yet, even then, I did not realize that we too were still in history after all. I remember feeling acutely homesick for the historic Mediterranean as I walked, one day in 1913, along the Suffolk coast of a grey and uneventful North Sea. The general war of 1914 overtook me expounding Thucydides to Balliol undergraduates reading for *Literae Humaniores,* and then suddenly my understanding was illuminated. The experience that we were having in our world now had been experienced by Thucydides in his world already. I was re-reading him now with a new perception—perceiving meanings in his words, and feelings behind his phrases, to which I had been insensible until I, in my turn, had run into that historical crisis that had inspired him to write his work. Thucydides, it now appeared, had been over this ground before. He and his generation had been ahead of me and mine in the stage of historical experience that we had respectively reached; in fact, his present had been my future. But this made nonsense of the chronological notation which registered my world as 'modern' and Thucydides' world as 'ancient.' Whatever chronology might say, Thucydides' world and my world had now proved to be philosophically contemporary. And, if this were the true relation between the Graeco-Roman and the Western civilizations, might not the relation between all the civilizations known to us turn out to be the same?

This vision—new to me—of the philosophical contemporaneity of all civilizations was fortified by being seen against a background provided by some of the discoveries of our modern Western physical science. On the timescale now unfolded by geology and cosmogony, the five or six thousand years that had elapsed since the first emergence of representatives of the species of human society that we label 'civilizations' were an infinitesimally brief span of time compared to the age, up to date, of the human race, of life on this planet, of the planet itself, of our own solar system, of the galaxy in which it is one grain of dust, or of the immensely vaster and older sum total of the stellar cosmos. By comparison with these orders of temporal magnitude, civilizations that had emerged in the second millennium B.C. (like the Graeco-Roman), in the fourth millennium B.C. (like the Ancient Egyptian), and in the first millennium of the Christian era (like our own) were one another's contemporaries indeed.

Thus history, in the sense of the histories of the human societies called civilizations, revealed itself as a sheaf of parallel, contemporary, and recent essays in a new enterprise: a score of attempts, up to date, to transcend the level of primitive human life at which man, after having become himself, had apparently lain torpid for some hundreds of thousands of years—and was still, in our day, so lying in out-of-the-way places like New Guinea, Tierra del Fuego and the north-eastern extremity of Siberia, where such primitive human communities had not yet been pounced upon and either exterminated or assimilated by the aggressive pioneers of other human societies that, unlike these sluggards, had now, though this only recently, got on the move again. The amazing present difference in cultural level between various extant societies was brought to my attention by the works of Professor Teggart of the University of California. This far-going differentiation had all happened within these brief last five or six thousand years. Here was a promising point to probe in investigating, *sub specie temporis*, the mystery of the universe.

What was it that, after so long a pause, had so recently set in such vigorous motion once again, towards some new and still unknown social and spiritual destination, those few societies that had embarked upon the enterprise called civilization? What had roused them from a torpor that the great majority of human societies had never shaken off? This question was simmering in my mind when, in the summer of 1920, Professor Namier—who had already put Eastern Europe on my map for me—placed in my hands Oswald Spengler's *Untergang des Abendlandes*. As I read those pages teeming with firefly flashes of historical insight, I wondered at first whether my whole inquiry had been disposed of by Spengler before even the questions, not to speak of the answers, had fully taken shape in my own mind. One of my own cardinal points was that the smallest intelligible fields of historical study were whole societies and not arbitrarily insulated fragments of them like the nation-states of the modern West or the city-states of the Graeco-Roman world. Another of my points was that the histories of all societies of the species called civilizations were in some sense parallel and contemporary; and both these points were also cardinal in Spengler's system. But when I looked in Spengler's book for an answer to my question about the geneses of civilizations, I saw that there was still work for me to do, for on this point Spengler was, it seemed to me, most unilluminatingly dogmatic and deterministic. According to him, civilizations arose, developed, declined, and foundered in unvarying conformity with a fixed time-table, and no explanation was offered for any of this. It was just a law of nature which Spengler had detected, and you must take it on trust from the master: *ipse dixit*. This arbitrary fiat seemed disappointingly unworthy of Spengler's brilliant genius; and here I became aware of a difference in national traditions. Where the German *a priori* method drew blank, let us see what could be done by English empiricism. Let us test alternative possible explanations in the light of the facts and see how they stood the ordeal.

Race and environment were the two main rival keys that were offered by would-be scientific nineteenth-century Western historians for solving the problem of the cultural inequality of various extant human societies, and neither key proved, on trial, to unlock the fast-closed door. To take the race theory first, what evidence was there that the differences in physical race between different members of the *genus homo* were correlated with differences on the spiritual plane which was the field of history? And, if the existence of this correlation were to be assumed for the sake of argument, how was it that members of almost all the races were to be found among the fathers of one or more of the civilizations? The black race alone had made no appreciable contribution up to date; but, considering the shortness of the time during which the experiment of civilization had been on foot so far, this was no cogent evidence of incapacity; it might merely be the consequence of a lack of opportunity or a lack of stimulus. As for environment, there was, of course, a manifest similarity between the physical conditions in the lower Nile valley and in the lower Tigris-Euphrates valley, which had been the respective cradles of the Egyptian and Sumerian civilizations; but, if these physical conditions were really the cause of their emergence, why had no parallel civilizations emerged in the physically comparable valleys of the Jordan and the Rio Grande? And why had the civilization of the equatorial Andean plateau had no African counterpart in the highlands of Kenya? The breakdown of these would-be scientific impersonal explanations drove me to turn to mythology. I took this turning rather self-consciously and shamefacedly, as though it were a provocatively retrograde step. I might have been less diffident if I had not been ignorant, as I was at that date, of the new ground broken by psychology during the war of 1914–18. If I had been acquainted at the time with the works of C. G. Jung, they would have given me the clue. I actually found it in Goethe's *Faust,* in which I had fortunately been grounded at school as thoroughly as in Aeschylus' *Agamemnon.*

Goethe's 'Prologue in Heaven' opens with the archangels hymning the perfection of God's creation. But, just because His works are perfect, the Creator has left Himself no scope for any further exercise of His creative powers, and there might have been no way out of this *impasse* if Mephistopheles—created for this very purpose—had not presented himself before the throne and challenged God to give him a free hand to spoil, if he can, one of the Creator's choicest works. God accepts the challenge and thereby wins an opportunity to carry His work of creation forward. An encounter between two personalities in the form of challenge and response: have we not here the flint and steel by whose mutual impact the creative spark is kindled?

In Goethe's exposition of the plot of the *Divina Commedia,* Mephistopheles is created to be diddled—as the fiend, to his disgust, discovers too late. Yet if, in response to the Devil's challenge, God genuinely puts His created works in jeopardy, as we must assume that He does, in order to win an opportunity of creating something new, we are also bound to assume that the Devil does not always lose. And thus, if the working of challenge-and-response explains the otherwise inexplicable and unpredictable geneses and growths of civilizations, it also explains their breakdowns and disintegrations. A majority of the score of civilizations known to us appear to have broken down already, and a majority of this majority have trodden to the end the downward path that terminates in dissolution.

Our *post mortem* examination of dead civilizations does not enable us to cast the horoscope of our own civilization or of any other that is still alive. *Pace* Spengler, there seems to be no reason why a succession of stimulating challenges should not be met by a succession of victorious responses *ad infinitum*. On the other hand, when we make an empirical comparative study of the paths which the dead civilizations have respectively travelled from breakdown to dissolution, we do here seem to find a certain measure of Spenglerian uniformity, and this, after all, is not surprising. Since breakdown means loss of control, this in turn means the lapse of freedom into automatism, and, whereas free acts are infinitely variable and utterly unpredictable, automatic processes are apt to be uniform and regular.

Briefly stated, the regular pattern of social disintegration is a schism of the disintegrating society into a recalcitrant proletariat and a less and less effectively dominant minority. The process of disintegration does not proceed evenly; it jolts along in alternating spasms of rout, rally, and rout. In the last rally but one, the dominant minority succeeds in temporarily arresting the society's lethal self-laceration by imposing on it the peace of a universal state. Within the framework of the dominant minority's universal state the proletariat creates a universal church, and after the next rout, in which the disintegrating civilization finally dissolves, the universal church may live on to become the chrysalis from which a new civilization eventually emerges. To modern Western students of history, these phenomena are most familiar in the Graeco-Roman examples of the *Pax Romana* and the Christian Church. The establishment of the *Pax Romana* by Augustus seemed, at the time, to have put the Graeco-Roman world back upon firm foundations after it had been battered for several centuries by perpetual war, mis-government, and revolution. But the Augustan rally proved, after all, to be no more than a respite. After two hundred and fifty years of comparative tranquillity, the Empire suffered in the third century of the Christian era a collapse from which it never fully recovered, and at the next crisis, in the fifth and sixth centuries, it went to pieces irretrievably. The true beneficiary of the temporary Roman Peace was the Christian Church. The Church seized this opportunity to strike root and spread; it was stimulated by persecution until the Empire, having failed to crush it, decided, instead, to take it into partnership. And, when even this reinforcement failed to save the Empire from destruction, the Church took over the Empire's heritage. The same relation between a declining civilization and a rising religion can be observed in a dozen other cases. In the Far East, for instance, the Ts'in and Han Empire plays the Roman Empire's part, while the rôle of the Christian Church is assumed by the Mahayana school of Buddhism.

If the death of one civilization thus brings on the birth of another, does not the at first sight hopeful and exciting quest for the goal of human endeavours resolve itself, after all, into a dreary round of vain repetitions of the Gentiles? This cyclic view of the process of history was taken so entirely for granted by even the greatest Greek and Indian souls and intellects—by Aristotle, for instance, and by the Buddha—that they simply assumed that it was true without thinking it necessary to prove it. On the other hand, Captain Marryat, in ascribing the same view to the ship's carpenter of HMS *Rattlesnake,* assumes with equal assurance that this cyclic theory is an extravaganza, and he makes the amiable exponent of it a figure of fun. To our Western minds the cyclic view of history, if taken seriously, would reduce history to a tale told by an idiot, signifying nothing. But mere repugnance does not in itself account for effortless unbelief. The traditional Christian beliefs in hell fire and in the last trump were also repugnant, yet they continued to be believed for generations. For our fortunate Western imperviousness to the

Greek and Indian belief in cycles we are indebted to the Jewish and Zoroastrian contributions to our *Weltanschauung*.

In the vision seen by the Prophets of Israel, Judah, and Iran, history is not a cyclic and not a mechanical process. It is the masterful and progressive execution, on the narrow stage of this world, of a divine plan which is revealed to us in this fragmentary glimpse, but which transcends our human powers of vision and understanding in every dimension. Moreover, the Prophets, through their own experience, anticipated Aeschylus' discovery that learning comes through suffering—a discovery which we, in our time and circumstances, have been making too.

Shall we opt, then, for the Jewish-Zoroastrian view of history as against the Graeco-Indian? So drastic a choice may not, after all, be forced upon us, for it may be that the two views are not fundamentally irreconcilable. After all, if a vehicle is to move forward on a course which its driver has set, it must be borne along on wheels that turn monotonously round and round. While civilizations rise and fall and, in falling, give rise to others, some purposeful enterprise, higher than theirs, may all the time be making headway, and, in a divine plan, the learning that comes through the suffering caused by the failures of civilizations may be the sovereign means of progress. Abraham was an émigré from a civilization *in extremis;* the Prophets were children of another civilization in disintegration; Christianity was born of the sufferings of a disintegrating Graeco-Roman world. Will some comparable spiritual enlightenment be kindled in the 'displaced persons' who are the counterparts, in our world, of those Jewish exiles to whom so much was revealed in their painful exile by the waters of Babylon? The answer to this question, whatever the answer may be, is of greater moment than the still inscrutable destiny of our world-encompassing Western civilization.

A Quest for Patterns in the Past

ALBERT L. GUÉRARD

This completes D. C. Somervell's masterly epitome of a masterpiece, Arnold J. Toynbee's ten-volume "A Study of History." The words are almost exclusively Toynbee's, and the work has received the author's unreserved blessing. Every

---

New York Times Book Review, February 24, 1957, pp. 1, 32. © 1957 by The New York Times Company. Reprinted by permission.

step in the argument has been carefully preserved. The drastic condensation affects only the detailed illustrations.

It is well known that Toynbee's erudition is fabulous. He is a one-man Royal Institute for the Study of All Things Knowable, and not a few others besides. But we should not be overawed by sheer bulk. Erudition may well be waste or bluff. It would be easy to pile up a random twenty doctoral dissertations which in their array of recondite facts would match Toynbee's ten volumes, and yet be vacuous of thought. On the other hand, Houston Stewart Chamberlain and Oswald Spengler pontifically assert crude hypotheses and bolster them up with haphazard third-hand documentation. Toynbee's range and depth of knowledge is overwhelming, but what is impressive in his work is the quality of his thought.

Familiar from childhood with classical antiquity, a specialist in the Near and Middle East, well acquainted with India and China, he is able to use the "General and Comparative" method which has proved so fruitful in biology, sociology and literature. If we ignore the fact that certain patterns recur at many historical moments and in widely different places, we are apt to ascribe local or personal causes to such phenomena. But if we are aware of feudalism in Japan, of monasticism in Tibet, we shall be less tempted to explain feudalism in terms of certain virtues in the Goths or monasticism through the genius of St. Benedict.

The "study of history" is the quest for such patterns. Toynbee's terminology—societies or civilizations as historical units, challenge and response, withdrawal and return, dominant minorities, internal and external proletariat, times of trouble, universal states, universal churches—has already become familiar. But the acquisition of a few pat formulas is not the benefit we seek. The essential point in this enormous effort is the *study*, the quest. It is not simply an intelligent narrative, like Voltaire's, H. G. Wells' or Will Durant's: it is an honest and infinitely patient probing. This is the lesson, and this is the reward. We are sitting at one end of a log, and Arnold Toynbee at the other.

History is something to be studied. The actual course of events, man's consciousness of those events, their recording, their interpretation, are inseparable; and all four combine to constitute history. But they are not identical. To seek with the nineteenth-century historian Ranke how "it" actually happened posits a conception of the "it" that is worth investigating. And such a conception is the man himself. The most scrupulous history is the portrait of the author projected on the neutral screen of mankind's multitudinous experience.

Take Toynbee's twenty-one (or twenty-three, or twenty-eight) civilizations. They exist—in Toynbee's mind, just as a definite number of "propensities" existed in the mind of Gall the Phrenologist, a fixed number of "passions" in the mind of Fourier the Phalansterian; and the study of these Toynbeean myths is highly rewarding. But we could shake the kaleidoscope. One example: societies, when they are "affiliated," continuous and over the same area, are to a large extent identical with periods. But periods have no objective existence.

The world had to learn from the first Arnold Toynbee (1852–83) that it had gone through the Industrial Revolution (and I am not certain that Sir Winston Churchill has fully absorbed that knowledge). Our present Toynbee recognizes the great Renaissance of the sixteenth century (named 300 years after the event) and alludes to the faint, abortive Carolingian Renaissance, a false dawn. But he ignores the perhaps greater and still unnamed Renaissance of the eleventh century, although he admits that "there was at that time an amazing outburst of Western energies."

To borrow terms from William James and Jacques Barzun, "all things (including civilizations) are constructs held together by names," which is strictly medieval nominalism. Without the names, and the name-givers, we should have chaos. Every "society" is, not a living organism, but a historical junkshop and a confused utopia. So is every man's mind: try to catalogue your most cherished habits and beliefs, and assign a date to them. You too, in a less familiar sense, "belong to the ages." But the order we impose upon the chaos of events is of our own making.

So the image of world history we get from this monumental work is the image of Arnold Toynbee: a learned, kindly and very wise British gentleman. His mind is a fascinating Yea-and-Nay, like the British Constitution and the Thirty-nine Articles of the Established Church. He rejects the mental anarchism of H. A. L. Fisher, who refuses to recognize patterns, and above all design, in history. But he condemns even more emphatically the providentialism of Bossuet, who so grandly unfolded God's own plan.

He brands as absurd the present state of religious parochialism, and looks forward to a universal Church Militant that will harmonize the four "higher religions." But he himself professes a theodicy which, if not narrowly parochial, is far from universal: a personal (therefore anthropomorphic) God; Creation (although not, as Archbishop Ussher had it, "at 6 P.M. on the evening before Oct. 23, 4004 B.C."); the Fall and the Original Sin; the Incarnation and the Atonement.

In his prophecy of the Universal State, he balances neatly—almost too neatly for comfort—the claims of the United States and those of the U.S.S.R. But he minimizes the power of the judicial mind, which refuses partisan commitments; and that mind is strongly represented, not only in India and Western Europe, but even in our own country.

To spend many hours of strenuous delight with Toynbee is not to master history but to study history. The reward is, in Matthew Arnold's terms, "to turn a stream of fresh and free thought upon our stock notions and habits"—and upon Arnold Toynbee's as well. And this is the very essence of culture, the pursuit—ever frustrated, ever ennobling—of our total perfection.

Arnold Toynbee's Millennium

H. R. TREVOR-ROPER

Arnold Toynbee's Bible—for so one can reasonably describe his ten-volume *Study of History*—has not been well received by the professional historians. I agree with them in regarding it as untrue, illogical and dogmatic. But in this essay I do not intend to argue its historical truth or falsehood, its logical coherence or incoherence, its empirical validity or invalidity. I intend to consider its significance as a document of our time. For true or false, logical or illogical, empirical or abstract, this book has excited a great deal of attention. Although every chapter of it has been shot to pieces by the experts, and although it is written in a style compared with which that of Hitler or Rosenberg is of Gibbonian lucidity, it has been hailed by the unprofessional public, at least in America, as "an immortal masterpiece," "the greatest work of our time," "probably the greatest historical work ever written." As a dollar-earner, we are told, it ranks second only to whisky. Its success has carried its already much-travelled author round and round the globe, lecturing, flower-crowned, from China to Peru. Surely this phenomenon requires some explanation. It is not enough to say that the work is intellectually erroneous. We must ask why such error has such a vogue. What is the meaning of Toynbee's message in the context of our time? To answer this question we must look at Toynbee's message in a different spirit from that in which most of his critics have regarded it. They were primarily concerned with its truth. They tested the validity of his arguments. I am now concerned with his meaning. What kind of a future does Toynbee (rightly or wrongly) envisage? What part, in the unfolding of history, does he invite us to play?

To understand Toynbee's message, it is important to remember the stages in which it was delivered and the events which were happening in the world at that time. For Toynbee's Bible was not delivered to the world all at once. It consists of two Testaments, separated from each other by some fifteen years—fifteen years which included the war of 1939–45. The Old Testament,

Encounter, VIII (June, 1957), 14–28; also in *Encounters: An Anthology from the First Ten Years of Encounter Magazine*. Reprinted by permission of *Encounter* Magazine.

which comprises volumes 1–6, appeared between 1932 and 1939. The New Testament, which comprises volumes 7–10, was published in 1954. Moreover, the New Testament ends with a remarkable volume, which sheds a great deal of light on the purpose and character of the whole work, volume 10 or the Book of Revelation. If we are to understand the message of Toynbee fully, we must examine his Bible in the order in which it was written, beginning with Genesis and ending with Revelation.

Now Toynbee's general message, the message of his Old Testament, is simple and reasonable clear. His Book of Genesis is the story of the Fall of Civilisations. All civilisations, according to Toynbee, are comparable; all pass through similar stages; all flourish and decay according to the same general laws, the same general time-scale of growth and change; all ultimately die. There may be different forms of death. Some civilisations die sudden, violent deaths without living out their time; others may seem to linger on, but in reality they are dead, mere fossils of themselves. For there is no exemption from the law of mortality. Always there is an end, and our own Western Civilisation, which we once thought unique and immortal, is in fact no different from the others. It too must die. As a matter of fact, it must die very soon. Has it not already shown all the signs of senility, as diagnosed by the scientific doctor of civilisations? Did it not reach its peak 400 years ago? Are not 400 years the time invariably allotted, by the mystical mathematics of History, to the "Time of Troubles" which precedes the death of a civilisation? Is not our civilisation already visible in dissolution? Surely its end is near.

Such is Toynbee's general message. It is a determinist message. But it has another characteristic too. It is also a fundamentally obscurantist message. For although Toynbee, in analysing civilisations, claims to be dispassionate and scientific, in fact his whole analysis is governed by strong emotional prejudice. In spite of its Hellenic training, his mind is fundamentally anti-rational and illiberal. Everything which suggests the freedom of the human reason, the human spirit, is to him odious. This illiberalism again and again distorts his own logic. Terms which, for his "scientific" purpose, should be neutral, like "decline" or "decay," are by him given a moral significance and arbitrarily equated with the processes which he happens to dislike—i.e. the growth of liberalism or rationalism. So, in his Book of Genesis, the Fall of our Civilisation is dated from the time when our ancestors ate the fruit of the Tree of Knowledge and sought to be like gods, knowing good and evil—the time of the Renaissance. To Toynbee the Renaissance was the beginning of the irreversible decline of the West, and every further manifestation of human reason is to him yet another milestone on the road to ruin. Europe's greatest centuries, the centuries of the Reformation, the New Philosophy of the 17th century, the Enlightenment, the gradual conquest of disease and famine, are to him its darkest ages. The European Enlightenment of the 18th century, that incomparable period of human emancipation, the age of Bach and

Mozart, Gibbon and Voltaire, is to him merely "a spell of low ideological temperature," a weary lull in the otherwise fatal course of Europe's disintegration and decay, a brief respite between "a first and a second paroxysm of its deadly seizure." The seizure, we may note in passing, was already deadly even before the lull. Europe's death was already decreed, not when industrialism or communism or the hydrogen bomb arose to threaten it, but when the Renaissance, that great spiritual disaster, descended like a fatal curse upon us. It was then that disintegration set in, then that that sentence of death was passed which is now, after the preordained term of 400 years, about to be executed upon us.

Is there then no hope? Can nothing stay our doom? No, says Toynbee, nothing. The best we can do is to find our way back into that Paradise of medieval innocence from which, by our fatal presumption, we have been expelled. Since it was the Renaissance and the Reformation which, by opening the eyes and the mind of man, set us on the 400-year slope leading to destruction, let us now seek to go back behind those fatal episodes, deny them and their consequences, pretend that they have never been. Let us confess that, for the last four centuries, we have all been miserable sinners. We have broken the holy eggshell of Catholic unity in which we had been happily and innocently enclosed, insulted the primitive taboos which before had kept us there, and crept out into the fresh, clear light of day. But now, thanks to the inspired "science" of the Prophet Toynbee, we have discovered that the daylight is misleading, the open air cold. Let us then, with devout hands, piece together the festering relics of that cosy shell and creep back again into its warm darkness. Who knows but that holy old hen, Mother Rome, though understandably somewhat stand-offish after such long insubordination, may consent to sit again upon her naughty but now penitent brood? We shall not reverse the iron laws of History, but perhaps we shall mitigate our doom. By sin came death. We cannot now escape the decree of death; but at least let us repent of our sin.

Such, in general, was the message of Toynbee's Old Testament. It is worth while to consider briefly its pedigree and its application to current affairs. For there is nothing very original about it, except the monstrous systemisation to which everything is subjected. The "decline of the West" is, relatively at least, an obvious fact—though with certain limitations to which Toynbee pays little attention. That is to say, the technical conquest and organisation of great land-masses by railways, motor power, and air transport has deprived the small maritime powers of Europe of one of their advantages and has mobilised instead the naturally far greater resources of huge, but previously unorganised, countries like America and Russia. But this shift in the balance of power has, of course, nothing whatever to do with the mere flow of time, the "ageing" of cultures, or the corroding effects of the Renaissance. It was remarked by geographers like Sir Halford Mackinder before Toynbee seized upon the same fact and, separating it from its real causes, ascribed it instead to the cosmic processes which he assumed. These cosmic processes have in turn another pedigree.

It is a German pedigree. The theory that all history is predetermined and that the stages between one predetermined phase and another are marked by catastrophic convulsions seems to be a peculiar product of the German mind. It was advanced by Hegel, by Marx, by Nietzsche; and in the 20th century, when great catastrophes seemed to be descending with particular force on Germany, it became, in varying ways, the orthodoxy of various German schools. For after the defeat of the First World War, in the aftermath of that exhausting struggle, surrounded by the *débris* of ancient empires, and faced with terrible social problems, it was easy and even natural for Germans to draw on these native ideas and imagine a universal catastrophe. So the Marxists, hating the "capitalist" West, announced with glee that a whole age was over. The West, with its culture, was finished, and must be transformed by conquest: conquest which must come from the new, non-Western power that had accepted the German doctrine of Marxism, Soviet Russia. Theirs was a confident message, because they hoped to be the heirs of the West, the beneficiaries and rulers of the new age. On the other hand conservative German intellectuals, drawing on the same tradition, accepted the same conclusions with much less glee. It was with wailing and gnashing of teeth that Oswald Spengler declared that the turn of the West had come: that "civilisations" were comparable and all mortal; and that the hour of dissolution for our civilisation was at hand.

It was at this point that Toynbee came in. An English amateur, tagging somewhat incongruously along behind these German professionals, he repeated Spengler's general theory. He was also a conservative, and as a classical scholar he loved the past: it was therefore with some sorrow that he envisaged the crumbling of an ancient order. On the other hand, as an obscurantist, moved by a detestation of human reason and its works, he clearly enjoyed a certain Germanic *Schadenfreude* in equating the decline of the West with the rise of rationality. This equation, one may add, was not new: it was a favourite equation of the obscurantist school of writers—Belloc, Chesterton, T. E. Hulme. Incidentally it is also inconsistent with Toynbee's general theory. For since Toynbee ascribes an equal time-span to all civilisations, regardless of their relative rationality, it is clear that decay, to him, is a function of age, not of reason. Still, it pleased Toynbee to make this equation: it enabled him to wring his hands with more prophetic gusto if he could say to a dying civilisation not only, "You are old, you have one foot in the grave, you shall surely die," but also, "You have sinned, your sins have found you out, you deserve to die! I told you so! Repent."

Thus Toynbee's Old Testament, like the ponderous vaticinations of Spengler, can be seen as the obverse of Germanic radicalism, as the despairing wail of conservative defeatism. "The old order is perishing," cried the radicals, "it is doomed to perish. Let us give it one more knock, and it will be finished. Then the reign of the new ruling class will begin." Such has been the cry of radical revolutionaries at all times. It was the cry of the Anabaptists of Münster in the 16th century, of the English Saints in the 17th century. However, society is a good deal tougher than radicals suppose, as the Anabaptists and the Saints quickly found. When radicals scream that victory is indubitably theirs, sensible conservatives knock them on the nose. It is only very feeble conservatives who take such words as true and run round crying for the last sacraments.

For these reasons Toynbee's Old Testament was not taken very seriously in England. It was still only in Germany that such catastrophic views enjoyed any currency. And indeed in Germany they soon achieved a new lease of life. For although the Marxists proved unable to realise their dream of conquering Germany, another anti-Western radical party, which had stolen the Marxist thunder, was soon able to exploit the theory of "the Decline of the West." Adolf Hitler, like Spengler and Toynbee, was a student of history. Like them he ranged over the centuries and crammed such facts as he found it convenient to select into a monstrous system. The true facts of geography joined the rubbish of the philosophers in his head, and he saw himself as the Phœnix of centuries, the Messiah who would roll up one age of history and open out a new. The West, he said, was finished; but Germany was not, or at least need not be—if only it would repudiate the West. He would revive Germany by detaching it from the embraces of a dying civilisation. He would breathe into it a primitive, barbarian, irrational spirit. He would wrest from Marxist Russia the leadership of the new, non-Western, non-capitalist, non-rational age and establish a new empire over the ruins of the West. To demoralise his intended victims he assured them that the iron laws of "historical necessity" were on his side; and having demoralised as many as were frightened by such words, he gathered up his forces and, in 1939, he struck.

When the German legions marched over Europe, trampling on its liberties, it must have seemed to many that Toynbee's dismal prophecies were coming true. Surely this was the end of the West. Was it not written in the Holy Writ? Then if defeat was certain, was it not most sensible to accept it in its least painful form, by prompt surrender? So everywhere in Europe a class of men appeared who were not Nazis, or pro-Nazis, who did not relish the prospect before them, who were in fact conservatives, but who accepted as inevitable "the New Order" that was threatened from Berlin. The West, they said, was finished: why should it not surrender in the hope of saving at least those elements of Western Civilisation which were worth preserving? Freedom of all kinds could be sacrificed, provided the essentials of civilisation—the social hierarchy and the Church—were saved. We have sinned, such men cried, we have eaten the forbidden fruit; let us repent and retire out of history, leaving the future to the Nazi Millennium. In future let us be good and let who will be clever; we shall not try to think, but only to pray. The patron saint of such men throughout Europe was Marshal Pétain. He was the patron of all those whose will had been sapped by the messianic claims of Hitler and the dismal certitudes of Toynbee. For Toynbee, in so far as he had any influence, was the unconscious intellectual ally of Hitler in the non-Nazi world, the true prophet of European Pétainism.

I say 'unconscious' because in fairness to Toynbee we must admit that he has no particular preference for a German conquest of Europe. He seems not to care who destroys the West, so long as the West is destroyed and thus vindicates his theory. Nor has he ever prophesied who will be its destroyer. Certainly he never foresaw that it might be Hitler. In 1936, after a long interview with Hitler, Toynbee declared himself "convinced of his sincerity in desiring peace in Europe." Even in 1939 he was blind, or indifferent, to the particular threat of Nazi Germany. For civilisations, he maintains, always succumb to internal age, not external blows; or at least external blows are only the occasion, not the cause of their dissolution. Even the Incas were not really destroyed by the Spaniards but because their civilisation had reached its logical term when the Spaniards arrived. The apparent destroyer is in fact not a destroyer but merely a demonstrator of internal rottenness. Still, by 1940, Hitler had proved himself a demonstrator of some capacity. If the West was really so rotten that it was about to crumble through natural decay, it was reasonable to expect that the first external knock would complete the process. This is what the Pétainists believed. It was naturally mortifying to them when, in spite of all the blows which it received, in spite of historical necessity, and in spite of the combined eloquence of Hitler and themselves, the West did not merely not crumble: it resisted; it was victorious; it survives.

What was Toynbee to do when faced with this unexpected survival of the civilisation whose doom he had so confidently pronounced? Change his views? That is too much to expect of any prophet. A slight reinterpretation is the most we can reasonably require. And sure enough, this is what we get. In 1954, after fifteen years of silence, Toynbee published his New Testament, and, in publishing it, admitted not indeed error—he has never admitted to any error—but a certain development in his views. In the past fifteen years, he writes, "my inner world had been undergoing changes which, on the miniature scale of an individual life, were for me of proportionate magnitude" to the vast changes which the great war of 1939–45 had caused in the world without.

What were these inner changes? Something of them had already been revealed, obliquely, in a public discussion which Toynbee had held in 1948 with the most formidable of his critics, the distinguished Dutch historian Professor Geyl. In this discussion Geyl had described Toynbee, on the basis of his Old Testament, as a determinist. To his surprise, he found that Toynbee now indignantly repudiated the charge. "With the awful warning of Spengler's dogmatic determinism before my eyes," Toynbee declared, "I always have been and shall be mighty careful, for my part, to treat the future of our civilisation as an open question." It was in vain that Geyl protested that this suspension of judgment simply does not exist in Toynbee's book: indeed "as regards the future, in one place in your book you are very near to drawing, as you put it, 'the horoscope of our civilisation' from the fate of other civilisations, and you suggest repeatedly that we have got into the disintegration stage which you picture to us so elaborately in your book as leading inevitably to catastrophe." Toynbee simply refused to admit this conclusion. All his arguments might lead thither, but now, suddenly, he refused to pronounce the final doom. He did not give any reason for this refusal to accept the only conclusion to which all his "laws" seem infallibly to lead. All he would say was that although he had established the laws under which all other civilisations have perished, and although he had shown that our civilisation too is subject to those laws and has now reached the stage at which death can hardly be postponed, nevertheless—who knows? Something may yet turn up. What? we ask. But we receive no answer. All we are told is that Toynbee is not a determinist. And he adds ("somewhat testily" we are told), "I suppose I must be the last judge of what my own beliefs are." To which one can only answer, "No doubt: but not of the rationality or consistency of those beliefs."

What was the escape-clause which Toynbee, by 1948, had discovered in his own determinist system? For answer, we look to his New Testament, which he was meditating at that time in the light of those profound inner changes caused by the war, and which, six years later, was to be published to the world as volumes 7–10 of his *Study of History*. These volumes do indeed add a very significant message to the message of the Old Testament: a message not this time of despair but of hope—of a kind.

It is not that Toynbee sees any prospect of the survival of Western Civilisation as we understand it. On that point his message is unchanged. Not even the events of 1939–45 can change his eagerness to see "the West" destroyed, and indeed he seems at times positively impatient with those events for their obstinate non-conformity with his theory. Why, he seems to overhear us asking, did the West not crumble finally before the might of Hitler? Poof! he answers. Hitler was no threat at all—how could he have been if even the rotten West did not crumble at his touch? Hitler's armies were phantom armies only: it was only the decadent pacifism of Europe which made him appear formidable. He had not made Germany a military power, he had merely "coaxed, duped, and flogged" it "into being one degree less unwarlike than its neighbours." "In the realm of the blind the one-eyed man is king." Nor does Toynbee allow the war of 1939–45 to be a real war—had he not already committed himself to the assertion that the war of 1914–18 was the last major war of which enfeebled Europe, according to the Toynbeean Tables, was capable? So Hitler's war is dismissed as a mere "supplementary war," beneath the notice of the historical scientist, and therefore unable to disturb the perfect symmetry of those Tables. And finally, if the feeble Hitler let the Professor down by failing to establish universal domination over the ruins of Europe, let us not suppose that that was due to any resistance by the still feeble Europe. No. That was due to "a chapter of lucky accidents" such as no historian could or indeed should be expected to prophesy, and such—Toynbee adds with relish—as cannot conceivably occur again. Thus Hitler's war, which Toynbee had not predicted in 1939, was written off, after it was over, as an irrelevant "secondary war," a mere airshot which does not in the least invalidate the general theory that the West is ripe for conquest. It is inconceivable, we are assured, that our next assailant will repeat the "accidental combination of incidental errors" which led to Hitler's failure. Therefore let us not lose faith—faith in the gospel of our own inevitable defeat.

Where then, we may ask, is the novelty of Toynbee's New Testament? Where is that escape-clause at which he had hinted in his discussion, in 1948, with Professor Geyl? The answer is that the glad tidings of great joy which Toynbee now offers is not that Western civilisation as we know it can be saved. It is that something far more important than our rotten civilisation can be born out of its ruin. In the 1930's Toynbee had lamented the impending death of our civilisation because then, along with much that was rational and therefore bad, the good, irrational elements must also perish. He had therefore hoped against hope that by some modification, some deliberate weakening of the rational and strengthening of the irrational elements, the structure might be preserved. But now Toynbee has admitted the fragility, the logical weakness of any such hope. He has yielded at last to the pressure of his own determinist system. But he has been able to do so without reluctance because he has discovered a new, a very important and—to him—a consoling truth.

The truth which dawned on Toynbee in the years of Hitler's war, the years between the Old Testament and the New, is basically very simple. It is that human civilisations are not, after all, organic wholes. Their elements are detachable and can survive, as vital and vivifying parts, in other civilisations, in the "universal states" which shall succeed them. Why then, he asks, should we not separate the essential from the inessential elements, the good from the bad, and, having done that,

> [. . .] *let determin'd things to Destiny*
> *Hold unbewail'd their way?*

Why should not our Western Civilisation go to its doom, the sooner the better, carrying with it the rubbish with which human reason has by now fatally deformed it, provided that the valuable parts of it, its primitive pre-Reformation faith, can be preserved as one of the vitalising ingredients of the new "universal state"? Surely this is a more logical, more positive, and (to some) more cheering conclusion than that desperate, defeatist proposal so feebly tacked on to Toynbee's Old Testament. Now there is no question of mere reaction. Now salvation will come not by forlorn retreat into the shrivelled womb of Mother Church, but by moving onwards on our predetermined path, which proves not to be so fatal after all. Our civilisation shall indeed perish; but what, after all, is civilisation? "Civilisations," we are now told, "have forfeited their historical significance except in so far as they minister to the progress of religion." Therefore, what does it matter how soon or by whom Western humanity is decimated, Western justice mocked, Western art and letters snuffed out, Western freedom abolished? Our religion—or rather, one strand of it: for Toynbee still seems to reject Protestantism—shall survive, not indeed alone or exclusive, but as part of a higher religion, the religion of a universal state.

Such is Toynbee's new Dispensation. It is, of course, not entirely new; for Toynbee's whole system is by definition repetitive. Therefore this new Dispensation too has a historical precedent. The precedent is taken, as always, from Græco-Roman civilisation. For although Toynbee claims to base his system on a number of past civilisations, in fact, as the critics have often pointed out, it is based on Græco-Roman civilisation only—the only civilisation which Toynbee has really studied and to whose pattern, as he interprets it, all other civilisations are now arbitrarily told to conform. So now the decline of the West must be made to resemble the decline of Greece and Rome, and the new universal Church, of which Toynbee is the prophet, must resemble the old Christian Church, in the days when it was new. The wheel of history has once again come full circle. The future is once again made clear by the past.

For did not the ancient pagan civilisation of the Hellenic world, obedient to the Toynbeean Laws, duly decompose? Were not its political forms—the independent Greek cities, the Hellenistic monarchies, the Roman republic itself—utterly extinguished? Did not the memory of its poets and philosophers happily fade away, burnt out of human recollection by the purifying fires of clerical bigotry, until the rot of the Renaissance allowed them to return? But did not the more essential parts of that civilisation, its mysteries and mummeries, its sacraments and sacrifices, Isis and Adonis and Mithras, happily survive, gathered up and preserved in that new syncretist religion, "that quaint Alexandrian *tutti-frutti*," as Norman Douglas once described it, Christianity? Even so, Toynbee tells us, our Western civilisation is now fast decomposing. We shall be conquered, destroyed, absorbed. Our political forms, our liberties, our culture shall be crushed out. But what of that? For our religious beliefs, which alone matter, will be preserved, pickled as one of the ingredients of a new syncretist religion, a new *tutti-frutti*, "a mish-mash," as one commentator has described it, "of the Virgin Mary and Mother Isis, of St. Michael and Mithras, of St. Peter and Muhammad, of St. Augustine and Jalalad-Din Mawlana." Such, we are now assured, is to be the new "universal religion" which will render political conquest a positive boon and will replace for all mankind the use of human reason and the remembrance of its great landmarks, the Renaissance, the Reformation, the New Philosophy, the Enlightenment.

But how is this new Dispensation to come in? Will our conquerors themselves bring it in? Certainly not. The Roman Emperors did not invent Christianity, they merely created a political system within which it was able to spread. The beginning of the new religion was quite separate. At a certain point in time during the decomposition of Hellenic society there arose a Messiah. The Messiah preached a Word, a Message, which altered the immutable sentence of the Book of Genesis and gave to mankind, predetermined to physical death, a new hope of spiritual life. Around this Message the disciples of the Messiah afterwards assembled and crystallised the miscellaneous mythology of other religions. Even so today the necessity of a new religion requires the appearance of a new Messiah: a new Messiah who, incidentally, has certain advantages over the old. For the old Messiah acted naïvely: he uttered his message, and his disciples slowly did the rest of the work, so that the new religion grew up, as it seemed, spontaneously, over centuries, obedient to impersonal laws. But the new Messiah can do better than that. Knowing the laws, he can himself operate them, or at least further their operation, much more expeditiously. He knows in advance what the final form of the new religion must be. He can foreshorten the centuries of change and preach the new religion, the new *tutti-frutti*, "the Mish-mash of the Virgin Mary and Mother Isis" all at once.

And who is to be this new Messiah? It surprises me that among so many commentators of Toynbee's work, none (so far as I know) has publicly posed or answered this question. And yet the answer seems to emerge clearly—only too clearly—from the text. It is true the Messiah is never explicitly named; even on this point the Prophet does not deviate into clarity; but discreetly and repeatedly, as the great work nears its end, he is identified until finally, there can be no mistake. In the tenth volume of his work, the last book of his Bible, his Book of Revelation, the secret is laid bare: the Messiah steps forth: he is Toynbee himself.

I know that this statement will seem outrageous to some. It will be said that Toynbee is personally a modest and humble man and that this is to ascribe to him *hybris* and blasphemy. I do not wish to ascribe anything to him which does not seem to me to emerge inescapably from his published work. I shall therefore try to document the conclusion I have expressed.

First of all I should say that I am not impressed by Toynbee's alleged "humility." It is perfectly true that he himself often praises this virtue. "Spiritual humility," he says, is one of the distinctive signs of the great historian, and he congratulates himself on being free from that "blight of egocentricity" which has prevented other historians from seeing as far as he has done. This "contrite humility, the first of Christian virtues," has, he says, fortified him throughout his superhuman task, and it has also guided his hand in everything he has written; for "in the writing of a book, as in every other human endeavour, the worst of all vices is the *hybris* that is the nemesis of self-conceit. An author is convicting himself of being past praying for if ever he allows the Old Adam in him to close his mind to a suggestion for some modification of his first draft by answering, What I have written I have written."

Now this is all very well, but when we look further into Toynbee's work we find it very difficult to discover this "humility" of which he so regularly boasts. For instance, when has Toynbee ever modified his text in answer to criticism? Some very formidable criticisms were made of some of the arguments used in his early volumes. Has Toynbee ever paid the slightest attention to them or made the slightest modification of those arguments or their conclusions? His only reply has been to include, in his later volumes, a chapter of abuse against those purblind modern historians who, enslaved by a barren devotion to the minutiæ of their technique, have had the *"hybris,"* the "sin," not to admit the validity of his historical laws. As for his claim to be free from "the blight of egocentricity," it is instructive to look at his last volume of all. There, in the index, it will be found that whereas the entry "History," which is, after all, the subject of the whole work, occupies only five column-inches, the entry "Toynbee, Arnold Joseph" occupies twelve column-inches, and there are separate entries for twelve other members of the Toynbee family who owe this distinction entirely to their relationship with the Professor. The "Acknowledgements and Thanks," too, which cover thirty pages, are awarded not only to the usual suppliers of information, correctors of proofs, and benevolent publishers, but to all who, since the beginning of History, have deserved immortality by contributing, each according to his capacity, to that ultimate creation of the ages, the mind of Toynbee. Æschylus, Pindar, Aristotle are there; the Bible, St. Augustine, Fra Angelico have done their bit; thanks are conveyed to "the glory of God" and, on either side of it, to the also beneficent city of York and uncle William Toynbee. Plato is thanked for teaching the Professor "when, in a mental voyage, I found myself at the upper limit of the atmosphere accessible to Reason, not to hesitate to let my imagination carry me up into the stratosphere on the wings of a myth." William of Wykeham is thanked for having founded Winchester College and having thoughtfully "made this provision for me 507 years before I was elected a scholar of his college." It is clear, from such evidence, that Toynbee regards himself as a portent no less significant than his work. All creation has been groaning and travailing to produce him; Winchester College has at last, in him, achieved its purpose; the ultimate bounds of human reason have at last, by him, been pierced.

All this being so, I do not think we are obliged to ascribe to Toynbee that almost unnatural humility which he so often goes out of his way to claim. Or, at least, his humility must be relative: his own greatness must seem to him so clearly superhuman that it shows remarkable condescension in him to claim, in public, no more than unique mortal genius. As for the humility which he preaches as a necessary virtue of the historian, we are forced to conclude that he is not really thinking of himself at all: he is thinking of his critics. If only *they* were more humble, how much better it would be! Then they would not presume to criticise one who had so splendidly outsoared the shadow of their night.

Thus I do not consider it *a priori* inconceivable that Toynbee should regard himself as the Messiah. And in fact, if we examine the autobiographical part of his work in a little more detail, we can hardly help observing the repeated evidence that this is how he does regard himself. In fact we shall discover that Toynbee, unlike previous Messiahs who were lamentably careless in this respect, has made scrupulous provision for his future devotees. Having himself (since History—as he has shown—repeats itself) tasted almost all the experiences of his prototype, he has contrived so to record these experiences, their dates and places, that there will be no danger of heresy or error in such important matters. Tucked away in the corners of his New Testament, we can find the authentic record of everything that matters in his Life: the minor prophets who dimly heralded his coming; the Holy Family; the precocious Infancy; the youthful Temptations; the missionary Journeys; the Miracles; the Revelations; the Agony. Moreover, looking forward as well as back, he has, by considerately recording the places he has visited and the objects he has touched, made provision for a constant traffic in those pilgrimages and relics upon which the religion of the Mish-Mash, like all true religion, must depend.

Am I serious? Alas, I am. Toynbee's truly monstrous self-adulation, combined with his fundamental obscurantism, do indeed emotionally repel me. But let us not give out all the heat we may feel. Perhaps the subject is best treated with detachment, even if it requires an artificial detachment. So let us interpose the cooling concept of an imaginary century. Let us transport ourselves, in imagination, a century or so onward in time, so that we can look back calmly upon the phenomenon before us. Let us suppose that all has worked according to plan. The Time of Troubles is over. Western Civilisation, long declining, has now at last (thank God) foundered, and all that is good in it, and in other civilisations, has been preserved and pickled in the universal world-state with its universal world-religion of Mish-Mash. From this vantage post I invite my readers to look coolly back at the figure of Toynbee as it will then emerge from his own New Testament and from the glosses with which his disciples, in the course of a century, will naturally have enriched it.

It is noon. The drowsy doggerel of the Founder's Litany "Mother Mary, Mother Isis, Mother Cybele, Mother Ishtar, Mother Kwanyin, have compassion on us . . ." is rhythmically sounding in all the Churches of Mish-Mash. We know the history of this Litany of course: how the Disciples asked the Master to teach them to pray, and how in "London, at 6.25 p.m. on 15th June 1951, after looking once more, this afternoon, at Fra Angelico's picture of the Beatific Vision," the Master obliged by uttering this formula (Vol. X, p. 143). As the unintelligible sounds issue mechanically from his lips, the worshipper will, of course, allow his eyes to stray. Perhaps they will light on a stained-glass window, illuminated from without by the rational daylight. What will it represent? That, of course, will vary with the locality. At Abersoch, in Wales, for instance, a richly painted window will naturally illustrate the great local miracle of the Epiphany: how the Founder, at the age of two, already driven forward by intellectual curiosity and a philosophy of action, "took and carried out a decision to run into the sea in order to find out what would happen," and was haled back by an anxious nurse who, though she sprained her ankle in the act, has since been amply compensated by her official beatification. The church at Abersoch is now rich, thanks to the resort of pilgrims eager to baptise their children in those now curative seawaves, so the window is a fine one, and the artist has not failed to point the moral of the incident. How could he, when the Master has himself so clearly emphasised it: "There was no benevolently officious nurse to pull him back from the intellectual plunge that he made, six years later, into the Ocean of History" (X. 19).

"Six years later," the inattentive worshipper may well muse, "that means that our Founder took his first decisive intellectual plunge at the age of eight. When? Where? In what parish church or rural shrine is this great event worthily commemorated?" On this point, unfortunately, the Scriptures are ambiguous. For the Founder himself tells us (X. 218) that he was only seven when he read, in the Book of Genesis, about Noah's three sons and thence precociously took note of "the differentiation of the Human Race into divers groups and sub-groups and the historical problems raised by the question how these groups are related to one another"; and again (X. 235) that he was not yet eight when he read *Paradise Lost* in three days and imbibed from it "the idea of a theodicy"; and it was at the age of seven, too, he tells us, that he received from his mother the inscribed copy of her *True Stories from Scottish History* "which stands behind his shoulder in his study at No. 45 Pembroke Square, London," and which he has "just now" taken down (X. 18). . . .

How thoughtful, incidentally, of the Founder always to identify the placing of his books! These helpful details have made it possible to reconstitute his study exactly as he kept it, even down to that translation by Gilbert Murray which he took out of the row on May 11th, 1951 (X. 217); and Aunt Gertrude Toynbee's copy of Mommsen which he received from her in September 1906, which he read in the summer of "A.D. 1907" (now A.T. 18) and which was "here on my desk in May 1951" (X. 229); and the four volumes of *The Story of the Nations*, with the bookplate of grandmother (now the Blessed) Harriet Toynbee in them, which were "all four of them on my table on this 21st day of February 1951" (X. 219); and the map of Greece which he used on April 26th, 1912, and is still "lying at his elbow at this moment" on September 23rd, 1952; and the forty-two sheets of an early MS. by himself which, "as he wrote these words, he took out of a drawer in a bookcase given him by his mother in his study at 45 Pembroke Square, Kensington, London" (X. 22). The study, of course, is now no longer in Pembroke Square. Like the Virgin's House at Bethlehem, which miraculously migrated to Loreto in Italy, it has now been removed intact to the great Toynbeeum in California, and a mere replica has replaced it in Kensington. But London is not entirely without original relics. The three volumes of Grote's work on Plato, for instance, which the Founder "took down from the shelf in the Athenæum Club" are now preserved in the club in a jewelled reliquary and exposed for the worship of members on the anniversary of the day, April 23rd, 1951 (formerly St. George's Day), on which the Founder records that he touched them (X. 20).

Meanwhile, in other churches throughout the world, similar thoughts must be occurring to other worshippers. At Dunwich, Suffolk, a statue of Mother and Child naturally commemorates the Founder's Mother giving him, when he was five years old, that sagacious tip ("the Wisdom of Dunwich") which enabled him, five years later, to write a better essay than the other boys in his school (X. 41). At the school itself, Wootton Court near Canterbury (now a training college for the Mish-Mash clergy), a splendid church is of course dedicated to the Confounding of the Elders in the matter of the Parthian Cataphracts (X. 224). Further afield, in Osaka, Japan, a rich temple marks the spot where the Founder, in November 1929, was inspired by a puppet-show to entertain profound thoughts about determinism and free-will (X. 231). In Greece, in the wild country between Káto Vezáni and Ythion, a rural shrine marks the spot where, on April 26th, 1912, the Founder drank dysentery from an infected stream and thus escaped the dangers of military service. (The lucky stream now cures the disease it then inflicted.) At 12 Westbourne Terrace, London, a fine wallpainting depicts the Founder there listening to his great-uncle Captain (now St.) Henry Toynbee discoursing on the rig of sailing ships (X. 213); and at Arezzo the old daubs by Piero della Francesca have been painted over with more truly devotional frescos representing the Founder fruitfully questioning the rector of the church on "the affinities of certain forms of headgear" (X. 239). The spot where the Founder swam the Euphrates (IX. 38) is of course a great place of pilgrimage, pickpockets, and baksheesh. In Yorkshire, the less ambitious tourist will find, on Slingsby Moor, the barrow where the Messiah was able to catch "still unspent reverberations of waves of psychic events" since unrecorded time; and, at Ampleforth Abbey, a noble altar-piece commemorating the Founder's famous Dream in "A.D. 1936" (A.T. 47) of clinging to the Crucifix: the premonition of his later Passion (IX. 634).

Of these lesser shrines there is no end. For the Founder not only excelled St. Paul and St. Francis Xavier in his travels, he was also considerate enough to supply the faithful with a very detailed record of them. The mere list of places visited by him fills, in his index, three and a half column-inches. But some reference must be made to the seven great centres of the new religion, the Steven Stations as they are now called, where the Founder had his seven direct historical revelations—such an improvement on "the sole flash of inspiration with which Gibbon was ever visited" (X. 103)—when he was "rapt into a momentary communion" with incidents in the distant past. The first Station was at Oxford (now Arnoldopolis) in "A.D. 1911" (A.T. 22). Others were on a peak of Pharsalus on January 10th, 1912 (conducted tours on the anniversary); at Monemvasía on April 23rd, 1912, where "the quietly browsing goats" (X. 136) are now stylised figures in local art, like the ox and the ass of Bethlehem in Italian painting; and on a peninsula in the Gulf of Chihli on November 24th, 1929, where, in spite of this important event, the ungrateful natives are unhappily not yet settled in the new faith. But the great revelation is the seventh, which took place near Victoria (now "the Seventh") Station in London. On that occasion the Master "found himself in communion not just with this or that episode in History, but with all that had been, and was, and was to come. In that instant he was directly aware of the passage of History gently flowing through him in a mighty current and of his own life welling like a wave in the flow of this vast tide" (X. 139). How unfortunate that the Founder "failed to record the exact date" of this experience. In the absence of evidence the Church has had to name a conventional date for its annual commemoration: the Day of Toynbee's Transfiguration is now kept on December 25th (formerly Christmas).

Of course the Founder's life was not without its frustrations. In his early days there was the Temptation in Buckinghamshire when the Devil, in the form of Uncle Paget Toynbee ("*vivebat* A.D. 1855–1932"—for the Founder always gives these useful biographical data about the Holy Family) and Aunt Helen Toynbee ("*née* Helen Wrigley, of Bury, Lancs.") sought to divert him at age of seventeen into "a wrong intellectual turning." "Your Aunt Nellie and I," said this plausible old uncle, "have come to the conclusion that you have been dispersing your interests too widely, and our advice to you is to make your choice of some single subject and to concentrate hereafter on that." Fortunately the young Messiah had an "instantaneous conviction that this advice was bad." He put Satan firmly behind him, and continued to pursue the superficial omniscience which he afterwards so triumphantly attained. Then there was the sad case of the Betrayal, when the Master was "wholesomely shocked" by the defection of his supposed disciple G. L. Iscariot Cheesman. Cheesman, we are told, so far yielded to "the dismal orthodox cult of specialisation" that he insisted on learning thoroughly the subject which he was employed to teach. Fortunately the Master survived all these dangers, and now his "narrow escape from intellectual perdition" (X. 35) is the theme of many a vivid fresco (and many a dull sermon) in the new age. During the years of his mission he was of course past the danger of temptation, although he was never free from carping critics whom, by one of his happy historical parallels, he would designate as "Scribes and Pharisees." This, however, was to be expected. Even in his schooldays he had premonitions of his future Agony, "though I had not yet tasted the cup for myself" (X. 235); nor had he yet—as he was afterwards, like St. Francis of Assisi, to do—received "Christ's stigmata" (IX. 644).

However, all that is now over. The words, the very names of the critics are now extinct, except in so far as the Master has deigned to take note of them. . . . And here, no doubt, our worshipper's mind will again digress to commend the providence of the Founder who salvaged so much of past literature (in so far as he approved of it) from the wholesome conflagration of the pre-Mish-Mash culture. Readers of Toynbee today sometimes object to his numerous and (to a superficial view) irrelevant quotations from ancient and modern literature. And why, they ask, all these careful references: may one not remark that human projects sometimes "gang agley" without appending a footnote reference to "Burns, Robert: to a Mouse, stanza 7"? May not one use the phrase "eyes that see not" without giving chapter and verse for the nine passages of the (Christian) Bible in which it occurs? A moment's thought should silence these impertinent questioners. Do they not realise that the Master is not writing for us but for our descendants in the Half-Baked Millennium of which he is the Prophet? By then all previous "pagan" literature will of course have been destroyed, so that only those passages which are, as it were, pickled in the new Bible can participate in its immortality; just as fragments of Hebrew secular literature survive embalmed in the Christian Scriptures. Naturally such detached gobbets from the lost literature of the past will need an explanatory apparatus which to us, who still know the originals, may well seem otiose. Instead of cavilling at the overcrowded pages, we should express our gratitude to Toynbee for allowing so much of pre-Toynbeean literature to enter, in these stormy times, into the Noah's Ark of his Holy Writ.

I have said enough. The temptation of fantasy is irresistible when dealing with this huge, presumptuous, and utterly humourless work, and perhaps I have gone a little further than the orthodox Toynbeean priesthood may go. But the quotations I have given are really enough to prove my point. Has any other writer, however apocalyptic his message, taken such pains to acquaint the public with the trivial details of his own life, the successive signs of his Election, or to represent himself personally as the culminating end-product of one civilisation, the herald, law-giver, and prophet of another? Has any other Christian scholar thus applied to himself the successive incidents of the Christian myth? If the conclusions were stated without the evidence, they would be rejected as incredible. Such egotism leaves the claim of Mohammed, to be the unique prophet of God, nowhere. But then Mohammed, as Toynbee says, was "a conspicuously unsuccessful prophet." He only spread his message from China to Nigeria, from Indonesia to Spain. Toynbee, it is clear, is the Messiah of a much wider world.

But let us forget these details. It is not the content of Toynbee's work that interests me. To me it is a matter of indifference whether he read some unimportant book in the library of the Athenæum Club or in No. 45 Pembroke Square, in the summer of 1907 or in September 1952. I am interested in the character, not the content of his work; and I am interested in it because, fundamentally, I find it not merely erroneous—that is not a matter for emotion—but hateful. For Toynbee does not only utter false arguments and dogmatic statements, calling them "scientific" and "empirical"; he does not only preach a gospel of deliberate obscurantism; he seems to undermine our will, welcome our defeat, gloat over the extinction of our civilisation, not because he supports the form of civilisation which threatens us, but because he is animated by what we can only call a masochistic desire to be conquered. If Hitler and Stalin rejoiced in the prospect of destroying the West, theirs at least was a crude, intelligible rejoicing. They smacked their lips because they looked for plunder. Toynbee has no such clear interest in supporting a conqueror. He hungers spiritually not for this or that conquest, but for our defeat.

Defeat by whom? Toynbee does not care. To him it does not matter whether it is Hitler's New Order or World Communism which provides the irrelevant secular structure for the religion of Mish-Mash. And so there have been various claimants. For instance, in 1947–51, the American ex-Marxist James Burnham, having swallowed Toynbee's Old Testament whole, declared that "Western civilisation has reached the stage in its development that calls for the creation of its Universal Empire" and urged the American government to seize its chance by rising and destroying the Russian government, "if necessary by total war." This ambition was not very different from that of Hitler. Indeed, if we look closer at Mr. Burnham's policy, we find that it is very like that of Hitler: for he declared that the value of European allies was to be measured not by their attachment to any liberal values, but solely by their hatred of communism. Consequently he rejected all other national leaders except General Franco, General Chiang-kai-Shek, General de Gaulle, and the Pope. If this is the measure of virtue, it seems a pity that Hitler had not been left in peace. He was, after all, incontestably anti-communist; and he might have been necessary to reinforce Mr. Burnham's seedy army of crusaders. As it is, it seems unlikely that these three generals and the Pope would make much of a showing against the Red Army, and therefore it is a Russian conquest of Europe that Toynbee must envisage. He envisages it without apparent dismay. The essential thing to him is that a world empire should be established. The secular details are irrelevant. Christianity needed the secular framework of the Roman Empire: what did it matter whether the emperor was Augustus or Nero, Elagabalus or Diocletian? Perhaps in the end, after three centuries, there will even be a Constantine.

Thus Toynbee is still the philosophic ally of any conqueror who will destroy the West. And this, I think, is the explanation of a paradox which certain critics have noted in his work. For although Toynbee always presents himself as a "gentle" figure, a "pilgrim" humbly seeking universal understanding, in fact his history is primarily concerned with dynasties and conquests. He is uninterested in the arts and sciences, in trade and industry, in administration and finance. His mind prefers to dwell among the horrors of war, the march of armies, the seizure of empires, the founding of tyrant houses. "Such preoccupation with violence," says one critic, "might seem puzzling in so pronounced a pacifist and humanitarian if Freud had not taught us the meaning of ambivalence." In fact, I fear, the explanation is simple. Like many intellectuals, Toynbee seems fascinated by brute power and longs to surrender to it. And since he identifies himself with the History of the world which he has felt "gently flowing through him like a mighty current," he wants the whole world to surrender to it too.

Such, I believe, is Toynbee's philosophy. It is a doctrine of messianic defeatism. Toynbee detests Western civilisation because it is basically liberal and rational. Detesting it, he wishes to see it destroyed, and he does not care who destroys it. On its ruins he envisages a new society, or rather, the religion only of a new society. The new society itself, as far as he is concerned, can be the nightmare society of 1984, provided that the religion is the religion of Mish-Mash, of which he is the prophet and Messiah. And this he calls a great hope for the West! Is it any wonder that the greatest of his critics has called it "a blasphemy against the West."

For in fact there is no reason to fold our hands and resign ourselves to the inevitable death of Western civilisation. There is, of course, a relative decline in the power of Western Europe: a decline due to the technical achievements of Western Europe in mobilising the resources of the much greater areas which now overshadow it. It is not now conceivable that Western Europe—that is, Britain, France, the Low Countries, and Italy—should dominate the world to the extent that they have done in the past. But who regards "domination" as an essential mark of civilisation? And anyway this real decline is relative not absolute: it is quite improper to ascribe a "disease" to a man who, while as healthy as ever, has been outgrown by a giant. Moreover, if we compare Western Europe today with Western Europe in the 1930's, we find that in some respects it is positively healthier today. In the 1930's Germany and Italy were lost to the West. Today all Italy and half Germany are firmly recovered. In the 1930's the social situation throughout Western Europe was rendered precarious by "the contradictions of capitalism" which both Hitler and Stalin sought to exploit. Today those contradictions have been so largely resolved that no Western country seriously fears revolution. Indeed, the boot is on the other leg. It is in the communist countries of Eastern Europe that the contradictions of communism are now threatening revolution, and the intellectuals of Poland, Hungary, and Russia itself look to Western "social capitalism" as the answer. In such circumstances to talk of the West as if it were not merely reduced in relative power but a diseased civilisation is not only incorrect: it is absurd.

Those who look to history for lessons should look to both sides of it. They will then find that the West has "declined" before now. For instance, in the early 16th century, Christendom saw itself reduced to frontiers almost as narrow as any it had known since the fall of the Western Roman Empire. The once Christian cities of Asia and North Africa had long been lost; now the Turks had advanced into the heart of Europe. The long Christian islands of the Mediterranean, the Christian cities of Belgrade and Budapest were all lost. When, men asked, would the remorseless conquest be stayed? Europe only survived, they said, thanks to the Sophy of Persia, who distracted the Turks in Asia. And then, on top of these disasters, came the great schism of the Protestant Reformation. What wonder that the Toynbee of those days, Pope Clement VII, believed that the Last Days predetermined in the Apocalypse were about to come and, in this mood, commissioned Michael Angelo to paint, on the wall of the Sistine Chapel, the Last Judgment? And yet, looking back, it is not this aspect of the 16th century which seems to us significant. The 16th century, to us, is the beginning of the greatness of the West. Even to Toynbee, who regards the greatness of the West as its decay, the 16th century is the beginning, not the end, of the process.

A similar point could be made about the early 17th century. Then, too, certain sad spirits supposed that the world was coming to an end. Nature, they said, was in decay, and while enthusiasts looked eagerly for the Millennium, defeatist spirits, repeating, like Sir Thomas Browne, that " 'tis too late to be ambitious, the great mutations of the world are over," resigned themselves to the impending doom. And yet this was the age of Bacon and Descartes, the beginning of those scientific discoveries which had enriched and alleviated the life of man!

Therefore, let us hear no more of the Decline of the West. Speaking absolutely, not relatively, the phrase has no meaning. The Toynbeean tables are about as relevant to modern historical knowledge as the chronology of Archbishop Ussher. And as for the Messiah and the Millennium, if we think of them at all, let it be only as a bogey. If the politics of 1984 and the religion of the Mish-Mash are all that our new prophet can offer us as the reward of acquiescence in the "inevitable" ruin which he "scientifically" predicts, that at least should spur us to throw this Jonah overboard and resist. After all, as some sage philosopher once observed, the irresistible is very often merely that which has not been resisted.

Questions

1. What is the "cyclic view of the process of history" that Toynbee speaks of? What is the difference between "the Jewish-Zoroastrian view of history" and "the Graeco-Indian"?
2. What is a classical education? Why does Toynbee say that a classical education is desirable? Would one be as useful today as it was to Toynbee?
3. What is the tone of Toynbee's essay? What does Trevor-Roper say about Toynbee's humility?

4. What is a determinist? Does Trevor-Roper define the term in the course of using it? How does he apply the term to Toynbee? Who else described Toynbee as a determinist? What was Toynbee's response to that description?
5. Why does Trevor-Roper call Toynbee "Messiah"? "Founder"? How does he use the phrase "German pedigree" with reference to Toynbee?
6. What is Guérard's attitude toward Toynbee? Does he support his generalizations? How does Guérard's way of writing about Toynbee differ from Trevor-Roper's? How do you account for the difference? Who is more convincing, Trevor-Roper or Guérard? Why?
7. Does Toynbee's essay support Trevor-Roper's thesis or Guérard's? In what ways?
8. How would you describe each man's style? Whose is the most vigorous? The most languid? The most gentlemanly?
9. "We are sitting at one end of a log, and Arnold Toynbee at the other." What is Guérard referring to in this sentence? How does this description apply to your reading of Toynbee?
10. How do you account for the extravagance of expression in both Trevor-Roper and Guérard? How is it that a theory of history can rouse such strong feeling?

Assignments

1. Identify or otherwise define all the words and phrases in italics in Toynbee's essay.
2. Summarize Trevor-Roper's evaluation of Toynbee, then Guérard's; and analyze the two as to forcefulness, number and variety of illustrations, and generalizations.
3. Speculate on how a theory of history might affect politics, diplomacy, religion, science, or education.
4. Argue either that history repeats itself or that it does not, referring extensively to the material in this section.
5. Define "history," "millennium," and "messiah" for an elementary-school dictionary; or explain them in about 150 words each for an elementary-school encyclopedia.

Additional Reading

Dozens of essays and books have been written in recent years on the nature of modern historical method. One of the most interesting books is that by Ved Mehta, *Fly and The Fly Bottle* (Boston, 1963), which includes interviews with Toynbee, Trevor-Roper, and Peter Geyl. Peter Geyl himself has two books on the major historians of our time, *Debates With Historians* (Cleveland, 1956) and *Use and Abuse of History* (New Haven, 1955). One of the most important recent books analyzing contemporary historical method and philosophy is by H. Stuart Hughes, *History as Science and Art* (New York, 1963). The study by Herbert J. Muller, *Uses of the Past* (New York, 1954), offers the perspective of a nonprofessional historian; and the anthology edited by Fritz Stern, *Varieties of History* (Cleveland, 1956), provides a thorough survey of the subject.

SECTION FIVE | *Pop Goes the Artist*

'Pop Art' since 1949

LAWRENCE ALLOWAY

The term 'pop art' has been popular this year, welcomed by critics who think that the use of a slogan will confer awareness on their sluggish prose and by dealers who always prefer a trend to a single artist. But the term is not all that new in London: in the recent history of pop art I detect at least three phases. The term refers to the use of popular art sources by fine artists: movie stills, science fiction, advertisements, games boards, heroes of the mass media. In itself this is not new: one of Max Ernst's earliest paintings has the distinctive outline of Charlie Chaplin in it. In the early nineteen-fifties de Kooning called one of his women paintings 'Marilyn Monroe'. Such use of the popular arts is incidental to the *main* purpose of these artists, however; it is merely one of the possibilities that can occur in the act of painting.

    Pop art begins in London about 1949 with work by Francis Bacon. He used, in screaming heads that he painted at this time, a still from an old movie, *The Battleship Potemkin*. This image, of the nurse wounded in the eye in the Odessa steps sequence, though mixed with other elements, was central to the meaning of the work. About 1951 Bacon extended his use of these sources to include Eduard Muybridge's photographs, whose motion-studies of people and animals, made in the eighteen-nineties, provided Bacon with motives. The difference between Bacon's use of quotations from the mass media and other, earlier uses, is this: recognition of the photographic origin of a part of his image is central to his intention. In fact, his painting has often de-

---

The Listener, December 27, 1962, pp. 1085–1087. Reprinted by permission of the author.

pended on being stretched between the style of the grand manner and topical, pop-art derived, incidents of violence.

Pop art, after Bacon, got linked with technology, and this was the first phase of pop. It was at this time that I became involved in it. Influential in London about ten years ago were three books which were certainly known to the artists who were to use pop sources. Ozenfant's *Foundations of Modern Art,* Siegfried Giedion's *Mechanization Takes Command,* and Moholy-Nagy's *Vision in Motion.* What I liked in those books (and I know it rang a bell with other people then in their twenties) was their acceptance of science and the city. Science fiction, because it was pro-technology, but highly fantastic, was popular at this time. I remember that science fiction magazines and paper books used to be handed around and swapped a great deal. The three books I mentioned were also being read by the British constructivists, but the artists I am speaking of valued the illustrations more than the texts which we thought perpetuated a good many clichés. You know the kind of thing: they called for a 'modern spirit', 'the integration of the arts', and so on. It was the visual abundance of these books which was influential, the choice of illustrations that ranged freely across the borders of art and non-art. The visual explosion of the twentieth century, with its wealth of vivid imagery, became a direct source of art.

There were two exhibitions which reflected this situation and indeed furthered its understanding in London, in 1953 and 1955. Both were held at the Institute of Contemporary Arts, which has been a centre for the investigation of the relations between fine and pop art. First was 'Parallel of Life and Art' arranged by Eduardo Paolozzi, Peter Smithson (the architect), and Nigel Henderson (the photographer). A hundred blown-up photographs of motion studies, ethnographical material, child art, micro-photographs, blended technology, and fantasy in wild profusion. Then in 'Man, Machine and Motion', Richard Hamilton explored the intimate contact of men and machines and the extensions of speed and reach which resulted. He used photographs which were valued not solely as documentary records, though they were that, but also as imaginative fantasy. In this way properties usually reserved for the fine arts were associated with photographs. Hamilton, later in the 'fifties, used pop art elements in his own paintings which look like versions of Marcel Duchamp's glass ordered by Maidenform Bra or General Electric as part of a very soft sell campaign. Hamilton has stated, and it is important to get this clear about the use of pop art sources in general, that his paintings are not 'a sardonic comment on our society . . . I would like to think of my purpose as a search for what is epic in everyday objects and everyday attitudes'.

Typical of this first phase of pop art in England is the work of Eduardo Paolozzi, whose bronze sculptures of the 'fifties carry allusions to obsolescent robots as well as to the Frankenstein monster. As a boy Paolozzi had seen Karloff monster movies, and retained the massive, lumbering contours in his memory until it returned in his sculptures of the human image. Paolozzi and I used to go to the London Pavilion, which was the first-run house for monster movies in the 'fifties. And our feeling was never that we were slumming, or getting away from it all, or not being serious. It was our assumption that what we felt at, say, *Tarantula*, was as serious and interesting and worthwhile as our other aesthetic feelings. What happened was that these emotionally charged images from the mass media dramatically reduced aesthetic distance. In place of Roger Fry's 'disinterested contemplation', in place of Sir Herbert Read's elaborate theoretical schemes, which were the main aesthetic systems available in London at the time, something intimate and simple was offered.

An appeal to common experience was central to the first phase of pop art. It lasted, strongly, from about 1951 to 1958. All the art of this phase was figurative, with references to pop art which could be demonstrated. John McHale, for example, made collages in 1955 out of the then-fresh post-war colour-printed American magazines. These bright printed fragments were assembled into squat human figures consisting of signs of all the goods and services we consume. They were, in effect, portraits of consumers. First phase pop art had its casualties and perils: McHale, for instance, became so engrossed by the non-art material that he failed to forge it into traditionally defined art.

The second phase of pop art, which overlaps the first, is abstract and begins about 1957. The effort, now, was to align abstract painting with pop art. The problem was to preserve, however elliptically, the basis in common experience that both Bacon and Paolozzi had demonstrated, but without specifying their sources so legibly. The 'humble' sources had to feed the art in another way. This was the time when we compared big paintings, whether Monet's murals of lily ponds in the Orangerie or the giant easel paintings of Jackson Pollock, with CinemaScope. The big-screen revolution in the cinema started in 1954 and gave a polemical point of reference to discussions of art in terms of intimacy and 'spectator participation'.

Richard Smith, one of the artists who linked abstract to pop art, wrote three years ago: 'Current technology, gossip column hearts and flowers, Eastman-color features, have no direct pin-pointable relation to my work of the moment, but they are not alien worlds'. Thus, abstract painting is linked, not to the absolute (as it was by Mondrian), not even to the rational economy of industrial production (as by Malevich), but to the sensuous world of leisure. As paintings expanded to environmental scale, they were likened not only to the big screens, but also to bill boards. The references were highly allusive, as by colour-cues: for instance, the colour used in a painting might be the green identified with menthol cigarettes. Big scale and brilliance of colour were the two main means of connecting the mass media with abstract painting. William Green, who, a few years back, was a hero of the mass media, because he rode a bicycle over his paintings, had an exhibition which he called 'Errol Flynn'. It is not that the sticky, bituminous paintings were about Errol Flynn, in any referential sense, but that this was the kind of meaning that Green assigned to his art, in accordance with his other interests. In Paris, on a similar principle of arbitrariness, Mathieu used feudal history and genealogy for titles. In London, Green, Smith, and others declared their allegiance with the public by evoking the instantaneously shared themes of mass communications. In 1960 four Cambridge undergraduates, master-minded by Robert Freeman, staged an exhibition in London with throwaway, pin-up material, mingled equally with their own abstract art. Thus they situated their art within the communications-soaked world we all shared. They represented art as one of the battery of messages in the world today, not as an act in relation to an absolute.

So the painters of the first phase used, objectively, popular material that modified the image of man with which they were all concerned. But the artists of phase two (most of whom were friendly with their immediate predecessors) shifted the emphasis to the man-made environment. The basic assumption was that our idea of nature has changed because of the bombardment of our sense by the signs, colours, and lights of the mass media. Hence it was supposed to be possible to create an analogue of the man-made environment that we all participate in, by means of a non-verbal but highly topical imagery. In *Life* magazine, once, a solemn red Rothko was compared to a colour photograph of a sunset. This certainly has nothing to do with Rothko, but it demonstrates the kind of relation sought for between abstract painters and the environment. It was not the sunset the abstract painters wanted, but the flow of neon, the dazzle of high-style fashion, the envelopment of big-screen cinema, realized not by one-to-one references but by colour and scale.

The second phase of pop-based abstract art has not continued as a strong force. Other aspects of the tradition of abstract art have resumed the role played briefly by pop art references. It was in 1961 that the third wave of pop art appeared, in the 'Young Contemporaries' exhibition. That marked the beginning of the situation in which we now find ourselves. Pop art is now figurative again but drawing not on a single source, such as movies or science fiction, but on a medley of popular techniques. Peter Phillips uses symbols of the pin-table, the leather jacket set, and playing-card eroticism. Derek Boshier mingles images from cereal packets, weather maps, and transfers; and David Hockney mingles graffiti and child art. Pop art is, perhaps, part of a general revival of interest in iconography, in figurative imagery as a means of expression. Iconography, the study of visual meanings in art, has been very influential through the 'fifties until now. It was a favourite word of Paolozzi's, and I used to use iconographical methods in my art criticism as a way of writing about art while getting away from over-refined formal analysis. By means of iconography, too, one could discover shared themes between advertisements and art, movies and sculpture, science fiction and constructivism.

In England, the paintings of American-born R. B. Kitaj continue the iconographical theme. His paintings include pop references, but only as one of a number of sources, which also include, for example, ancient cosmogonies. The Journals of the Smithsonian and the Warburg Institutes are among the sources that he coaxes, with his remarkably acute pictorial sense, into diagrammatic, yet painterly, displays. He has been a decisive influence on recent uses of pop art, but his followers have all neglected the essential breadth of his work.

Paolozzi, in a lecture given at the Institute of Contemporary Arts in 1958, observed: 'The evolution of the cinema monster from Meliès onwards is necessary study for the fabricator of idols or gods containing elements which press in the direction of the victims' nerve-senses'. The study of pop art, growing out of his spontaneous enjoyment of it, is to aid in the fabrication of 'idols or gods'. Thus a traditional role of the sculptor, the forging of heroic figures, is not abandoned; only the base upon which it is to be established has been widened.

This power to connect diverse sources into a unified pictorial structure is missing from most of the third-phase painters. Derek Boshier and David Hockney, for instance, seem unable to translate their awkward arrays of different kinds of signs into one coherent format. A reason for this, I suspect, is the fact that they take their standards from graphic art rather than from painting. In graphic art anything goes, measured only by an unchecked and mobile standard of vividness and charm. Hence the flips in scale in their imagery, and the loose chains of form that zig-zag episodically over the field of the painting. American painters of the same age-groups who use this kind of imagery, have a stronger painting tradition to measure their performance by. They have not abandoned the high standards of the older American abstract painters, though they have moved decisively away from abstraction as such. Thus, there is a continuity between recent and current work, which confers a certain formal strength on what is new. England, not supplying any standard of comparable rigour, has, in a way, let these artists down.

One who has solved the problem of painterly coherence, Peter Phillips, has another difficulty. Gifted painter though he is, he lacks Kitaj's or Paolozzi's sense of pop art as the latest resonance of long iconographical traditions. He seems to use pop art literally, believing in it as teenagers believe in the 'top twenty'. In a sense, the appeal to common sources within a fine art context, one of the strongest original motives for using pop art, has been lost. The new pop art painters use the mass media in the way that teenagers do, to assert, by their choice of style and goods, their difference from their elders and others. Thus the third wave of pop artists use their imagery to differentiate themselves from the regular audience for art, instead of, as earlier, to reach it. Hockney's paintings, abounding in autobiographical graffiti, are like a diary kept jointly by Holden Caulfield and Baron Corvo. Peter Blake, a prestigeful figure in the circle, also relies more on the charm of his personality than on the production of substantial works.

Hockney wrote recently: 'I paint what I like, when I like, and where I like'; and this freedom is his right and his pleasure. He went on to list some of his 'sources': 'landscapes of foreign lands, beautiful people, love, propaganda, and major incidents (of my own life)'. Given this programme one can see that a rambling and discursive kind of art is likely to follow, unless governed by a firm formal control. In a way, Hockney is not to blame for not reaching this level of control. The fault lies not with the talented young but with the store of information, called tradition, that is available to them. The older painters and the younger do not mix and do not discuss their work in any serious or sustained way. Fey elements of the romantic, the amateur, and the graphic are officially praised in preference to sophistication and professionalism. The importance of the abstract painters of the 'Situation' group, which showed twice, once in 1960, once in 1961, lay in their high level of professionalism. They rejected the purely local standards of English art and aimed at mastery of the international tradition of abstract painting. Too many of the current wave of pop artists, though benefiting from the environmental openness of some of the 'Situation' painters, are content with negligent and permissive formal standards. The odd and the cute, the whimsical and the queer, are threatening British art again, under the guise of topicality. What is needed is an attitude more like, say, Allan Jones's, who uses pop art themes, but not exclusively. As he wrote: 'I don't mind a picture having a story as long as the beginning and the end exist within the four edges of the canvas', which is a way of asserting the sufficient formality of the painting. Too many of his contemporaries, on the other hand, make their art open-ended, and everything passes through it.

We tend, because of the simplicity everybody likes to impose on our lives and culture, to think of post-war art as overwhelmingly abstract. However, parallel with the abundance and high quality of abstract art is a greal deal of what one may call iconographical art. Let me remind you of a few names: Bacon, Balthus, Giacometti, Dubuffet, Asger Jorn, de Kooning. The real condition of modern art is diversity, and theories or arguments that nominate one tendency over the others impoverish our culture. In historical terms, pop art is part of this iconographical line which runs alongside, coexists with, abstract art. One piece of evidence to support this is the contribution of Dubuffet to artists of the first and third phases in England. Dubuffet influenced Paolozzi, in his human figures, and his influence is implicit also in the textures and graffiti of David Hockney. My point is that pop art is an episode, a thread, in a general tradition of iconographical art which has exploded since the late nineteenth century, when the riches of visual material, in many styles, were first recognized.

Pop artists of the third and current phase deny this historical setting by the use they make of pop art elements. The effect of the first and second phases of pop was (and this was badly needed in the 'fifties) to reduce the idealism and snobbery of English aesthetics and art criticism. Now, however, happy in the playground of the opened-out situation, pop artists lack a grasp of the history their art belongs to, as well as a sense of the internal rigour necessary to art. Instead of contributing to the expanded communications system, which is nineteenth- and twentieth-century art, they are coasting along and relaxing. Pop art in England has become a game for those who want to tell themselves that they 'think young'.—*Third Programme*

Washington Gallery Shows Pop Art

LESLIE JUDD AHLANDER

Throughout history art has been a reflection of its times, mirroring faithfully the world around it, even when that art has been abstract. Man is a part of the time, space and culture that surrounds him, and he has no possible way of getting outside that world—or himself—in order to see it objectively. Being part of it, he himself mirrors it. The act of looking involves the total personality of the spectator, and he is affected by who and what and where he is whether he wants it so or not.

Since the Renaissance, with its consistent portrayal of Biblical themes, a misunderstanding of the role of art has arisen that has created great confusion in the public mind. The public has become convinced that art mirrors what should be, rather than what is. Thus the ideal, not the life around him, is considered the correct subject for the artist.

Yet the artist, being a part of that life, reflects his surroundings regardless of the apparent subject of his paintings. When we see a Renaissance portrayal of the "Madonna and Child," we seldom stop to consider that the Madonna is usually clothed in the most sumptuous of Renaissance clothing, that her hair is done in the most sophisticated style of the day and that she is usually laden with jewelry. How would the Madonna really have been dressed? In rags, probably, or a simple flowing robe and shawl. How often a crenellated Renaissance fortress is shown in the background of the Holy picture, with gardens laid out in Renaissance style, depicting clipped trees and hedges and formal flower beds. The truth? Somewhat different. The austere and barren land of ancient Jerusalem.

The sitter for the Madonna may have been the artist's mistress, the wife of some duke, or just a woman brought in from the streets. Her personal life could have been anything but virtuous. Yet we accept this vision of the

This is a slightly revised version of the original article, which appeared in the Washington *Post*, April 21, 1963, p. G6. Reprinted by permission of the Washington *Post* and the author.

Madonna without once stopping to think that she is in fact a reflection of her time and place, her country and her station in life, and is therefore more truly a picture of life in Renaissance Italy than of Jerusalem some 1500 years or so earlier.

With the rise of the middle classes art began to reflect this level of society, and we find the prosperous Dutch burgher and his wife, for instance, rather than kings and princes, as subjects for art. In the 19th century with the French Revolution we find the lower classes taking their place, and Daumier paints the ordinary citizen in work or play; Van Gogh chooses the postman rather than the titled ruler, and so on. The 20th century has been called "The Age of the Common Man," and much of our art has reflected him, his surroundings, his interests and his dreams.

With two succeeding 20th century wars, art has reflected the turmoil, the upheaval, the destruction of old conventions and ideals. After World War I, Dada became an art movement of great importance. Its need to destroy the old values in order to set up new ones created an "anti-art" where objects were taken out of their old surroundings and resituated to give them a pristine value. Surrealism also contributed to this reassessment of old values by its irrational juxtaposition of objects, based on the visions of the subconscious.

Since World War II there has been a further steady revision of old standards. The theater, poetry and literature reflected this rejection of the past most clearly in the anti-theater, anti-poetry and anti-literature movements, where generally accepted standards of composition, language and form were totally discarded. "Waiting for Godot" and "The Rhinoceros" are examples of this revision. Mastroianni became the "anti-hero" of the movies, the common man caught in a world, alas, very much of his own making.

As "The Rhinoceros" and Mastroianni reflect our world as it is, not as it should be, so a new group of young artists has emerged who reflect our visual world as it is, not as it should be. Their work may be seen in a new show just opened at the Washington Gallery of Modern Art. Their thesis is anti-thesis; their philosophy, anti-philosophy; their technique, anti-technique. They say: here it is, the life around you, we present it without comment, for it needs no comment. Draw your own lessons, your own conclusions. You will get out of it only what you put into it. If you see in it an indictment of the times you live in, it is because you know (even though you won't admit it, perhaps) that our work does indeed reflect the crass, vulgar, cheap, mass-produced anti-art.

Yet, at the same time, they point to the fact that there is beauty of a kind in commercial art and in the life around us. And they play with art and reality, balancing or mixing them, creating art and at the same time presenting the unvarnished fact, in the same sort of interchangeable state that we sense around us on all sides.

What are the ideals of the common man? Let us take Tom Wesselman's

"Still Life No. 28," (and subtitle it, "The American Dream"). Here are Lincoln the Great Emancipator (in a cheap cromo-lithograph), and the stars and stripes around him (though the stripes are used as a tablecloth). The Nation's Capitol looms in the background (This Glorious Democracy of Ours). A real television set is placed on the painted table, and the spectator may turn it on if he wishes: the old American gimmick of audience participation, dear to TV. A cold beer or two for when the commercial comes on; some idealized fruit looking as it never does at the supermarket (our glossy, sleek, commercial art with which we are surrounded); a bowl of flowers and leaves (plastic? of course!), and the family cat. Is this not the American dream?

These artists do not care to reject the world around them. They are in reaction to the school of abstract expressionism, which is a personal, introspective art, given to the sensibility of the artist and his commitment to the act of painting. They are in reaction to this art form just as the Ashcan painters at the beginning of the century revolted against the official, idealized Salon art of its time. The Ashcan artists turned to the man in the street, painting the life around them, trying to see it as it existed, not as it should be. Pop Art, which could in this sense be called neo-Ashcan (a title which should please these artists with its combination of pretentiousness and common words), again asks the spectator to look around him and see what is, not what should be.

Two of the artists in the Pop Art show should be thought of as transitional rather than clearly a part of this particular movement. They are Robert Rauschenberg and Jasper Johns, whose leadership consisted in finding a way back to the image as it exists, and to the ambiguity of art in its relation to reality. Their work remains painterly, in the sense that the surface of the painting reflects the artist's use of traditional means. It is in their subject matter that they bridge the gap between abstract expressionism (the act of painting) and the world around them. They are still concerned with the relationship of forms in space, with the picture plane and the projection of the image upon it. Yet they use recognizable objects, and indeed, insist upon the total clarity of their subject, even to the point of labeling it. Is a painted broom more or less a broom than an actual broom mounted upon a canvas? What is the nature of reality? Is reality a hamburger, a TV set and a glass of beer, or is it paint on canvas, or "The Rape of Europe"?

The Age of the Common Man is not an age of gods and heroes and there is no reason why its art should be about heroics and myths. If the true American dream that brought our forefathers to these shores has vanished in a welter of juke boxes, hamburgers, commercialism and rampant materialism, we have no right to ask our artists to paint what is not so, what is in fact a lie. If we do not have the courage to face reality as it exists, we have no right to ask the artists to paint us a dream world that we have somehow destroyed. It is not important that the Pop Artists refuse to articulate a philosophy. To anyone with eyes to see (and ears to hear, for there is plenty of noise in the show, just as there is in our own lives) the lessons and philosophy of Pop Art will be abundantly clear. Let the spectator beware.

Popular art of quite another kind is currently on view at the Pan American Union. Here a small but choice group of primitive paintings by untutored artists of North and South America has been brought together. These artists are untrained, and their vision is common to such artists everywhere: a stress on pattern and design, clear, bright colors and an eye for detail that often misses the forest for the trees. Several works borrowed from the Garbisch Collection of the National Gallery of Art show early work done in the United States, and this is followed by a handsome painting by John Kane, famous 20th century American primitive.

Among the Latin Americans the Haitians are particularly colorful and charming, with their acute sense of color and flattened patterns. A handsome portrait of Simon Bolivar from Venezuela is a beautifully stylized design. An amusing picture of the Pan American Union with the artists of the Americas bringing their treasures as offerings not only recalls early paintings of the Magi bringing gifts to the Christ Child, but also pays tribute to the great role the Pan American Union has played in making the arts of the Americas known and appreciated.

Observer

RUSSELL BAKER

WASHINGTON, April 21—The big news in American culture these days is "pop art." Many culture insiders believe it may be a bigger craze than folk singing before the summer is out, and no wonder.

Art Goes Popular

The highly publicized exhibition which opened here the other day at the Gallery of Modern Art demonstrated that "pop art" is not only more fun than anything since the Keystone Kops, but also an exhilarating tonic for the ego. A lot of people who have been standing around modern art galleries for

New York *Times* (Western Edition), April 23, 1963, p. 10. © 1963 by The New York Times Company. Reprinted by permission.

years feeling scared and bourgeois are going to go away from this show convinced that almost anybody can be an artist.

For example, consider the effect on the viewer of Jim Dine's brooding black study, "Shovel With Long Handle." What Jim did was to take a canvas seven feet long and cover it with black paint. He then took a coalshovel seven feet long and covered that with black paint. Then, he attached the shovel to the canvas!

The viewer's first response is: "I could do that if I had some canvas, a shovel and black paint." He realizes only gradually that it is not so simple as that. The effect of "Shovel With Long Handle," he senses, is dependent upon its subtle relationship to two other Dine works in the same room.

Black, Black, Black

These are "Black Backroom"—a sink stuck on canvas on which a good bit of black paint has been indiscriminately smeared around—and "Black Window." "Black Window," as its title suggests, is a black window—sill, sash, frame and glass—to which several pieces of hardware are audaciously attached to the top. These include an axe, pliers, a wrench, a can opener, an egg beater and a carving knife.

In a different vein, there is George Brecht's "Stool." Brecht has taken a stool and placed a bag of oranges on it. The gallery has arranged matters so that the viewer comes to "Stool" immediately after the emotional shock of Claes Oldenburg's "Pants." "Pants" is an oversize pair of bright blue men's trousers made of sailcloth and hung on an outsized clothes hanger.

One moves, confused and shaken, from "Pants" to the cool serenity of "Stool," with its bag of oranges, and finds himself subtly led to reminiscences about oranges he has seen on stools in other times, other places.

Artistic Repair Bill

The viewer moves with continuing pleasure through a constant series of surprises. Here, for example, is "Starchief," by Robert Watts. It is a green dashboard from a Pontiac Starchief. Plugged into an electrical outlet, it makes monotonous noises while its odometer clicks off the miles at a rate which indicates the thing is supposed to be moving at 300 miles per hour.

And here is Robert Rauschenberg's "Black Market," a big rectangle of canvas on which the artist has placed a bedspring, a 1959 Ohio license plate, four metal-jacketed notebooks on which the public may express itself, and a one-way street sign with a dog leash dangling from the arrow tip.

The leash leads to a box on the floor containing a green comb, several yellow pencils, some inking pads and stamps, and the car repair bill of one C. V. West for brake work by the Temple Motor Company of Alexandria, Va., last

Tuesday. The bill was for $53.60. Among the public expressions recorded in the notebooks this weekend was one stating, "Rauschenberg, you are mad."

The Return to the Cellar

In an essay for the exhibit program, Alan R. Solomon takes a very somber view of all this, arguing that it has something to do with the fact that modern man "sees himself in his art . . . as a disrupted, contorted victim of the modern cataclysm, torn by forces of a magnitude beyond his comprehension, a grim figure, full of despair and anguish, entirely without hope."

This may be so, but if it is why does the visitor leave the exhibition feeling relaxed, pleased and full of interior giggles?

If "pop art" catches on with the public, as it very well may, American cellars this summer will be the scene of more welding and sawing and hammering and soldering than at any time since the do-it-yourself craze subsided. And it won't be contorted victims of cataclysm stripping the hardware stores, but a bunch of optimists pursuing the will-o-the-wisp of art.

The Flaccid Art

PETER SELZ

Ten years ago painting in America was largely dominated by Abstract Expressionism. Today there is a wider range of possibility in both style and subject matter. The older Abstract Expressionists are doing some of their finest work and Rothko has just completed a series of impressive murals for Harvard University. But, in addition, the Hard Edge painters are successfully synthesizing Mondrian and the New York School; a group of painters from Washington, Morris Louis and Kenneth Noland among them, have achieved new images by staining their canvases with simple shapes of decorative color; a rising generation of figure painters—Diebenkorn, Golub, and Oliveira —depict the ruined and isolated human beings of a disaffected society. Also the detritus of our culture is being re-assembled with often stunning and mordantly amusing results by the "junk artists." But the trend

Originally published as "Pop Goes the Artist," *Partisan Review*, XXX (Summer 1963), 313–316. Reprinted by permission of *Partisan Review* and the author.

which has been most widely publicized and discussed during the past year is Pop Art.

Artists who make use of images and articles from popular culture—H. C. Westermann, Edward Kienholz, Marisol, Tinguely—are not necessarily practitioners of Pop Art. Westermann's metaphorical statements about the violent and ambiguous quality of contemporary life, Kienholz's incisively bitter social satire, or Marisol's sophisticated and humorous primitivism, the highly inventive constructions of Jean Tinguely, which have electrified and motorized our esthetic concepts, all differ significantly from Pop art works. It is true that Pop Artists owe a great debt to Rauschenberg, but his Combine Paintings transform ordinary objects by fusing them provocatively with Abstract Expressionism.

The Pop Artists, some of whom came out of the advertising world, some out of the world of painting, stand apart as a group in that they not only take their subject matter from mass-production sources in our culture—magazines, billboards, comic strips, television—but they frequently employ commercial techniques as well: the airbrush, silkscreen reproductions, imitated benday screens. Sometimes, as in pictures by Dine and Wesselmann, actual objects are incorporated in the manner of collage. There is no theoretical reason why such popular imagery, or even the use of commercial art processes, should not produce works of real interest and value. After fifty years of abstract art, nobody could propose an academic hierarchy of subject matter; after fifty years of brilliant invention in collage and assemblage, nobody would be justified in suggesting that any technique is taboo. The reason these works leave us thoroughly dissatisfied lies not in their means but in their end: most of them have nothing at all to say. Though they incorporate many forms and techniques of the New York School (there is a particular debt to de Kooning's women) and the Hard Edge painters, these forms have been emptied of their content and nothing has been added except superficial narrative interest. People who ought to know better have compared Pop Art to the work of Chardin, because it depicts actual objects among familiar surroundings: an eighteenth-century still life, a twentieth-century billboard—why not? Leo Steinberg in the Museum of Modern Art's symposium on Pop Art goes so far as to suggest parallels to the realism of Caravaggio and Courbet. But Chardin, Caravaggio and Courbet created worlds of their own in which the reality of the subject was transformed into an esthetic experience. The interpretation or transformation of reality achieved by the Pop Artist, insofar as it exists at all, is limp and unconvincing. It is this want of imagination, this passive acceptance of things as they are that make these pictures so unsatisfactory at second or third look. They are hardly worth the kind of contemplation a real work of art demands. If comparisons are in order, one might more appropriately be made to the sentimental realism of nineteenth-century painters like Meissonier, Decamps, or Rosa Bonheur—all exceedingly popular and high-priced in their day.

When I was a teacher in the 1950's, during and after the McCarthy period, the prevailing attitude among students was one of apathy and dull acceptance. We often wondered what sort of art would later be produced by these young men and women, who preferred saying, "Great, man!" to "Why?" or possibly even, "No!" Now that the generation of the Fifties has come of age, it is not really surprising to see that some of its members have chosen to paint the world just as they are told to see it, on its own terms. Far from protesting the banal and chauvinistic manifestations of our popular culture, the Pop painters positively wallow in them. "Great, man!"

In the symposium on Pop Art at the Museum of Modern Art, Henry Geldzahler, an enthusiastic supporter of the trend, clarified both the attitudes of these artists and the reason for their prompt acceptance by the art world when he said, "The American artist has an audience, and there exists a machinery—dealers, critics, museums, collectors—to keep things moving. . . . Yet there persists a nostalgia for the good old days when the artist was alienated, misunderstood, unpatronized."

But I doubt that nostalgia is at issue here. What we have instead is a school of artists who propose to show us just how nice everything is after all. A critical examination of ourselves and the world we inhabit is no longer hip: let us, rather, rejoice in the Great American Dream. The striking abundance of food offered us by this art is suggestive. Pies, ice cream sodas, coke, hamburgers, roast beef, canned soups—often triple life size—would seem to cater to infantile personalities capable only of ingesting, not of digesting nor of interpreting. Moreover, the blatant Americanism of the subject matter—packaged foods, flags, juke boxes, slot machines, Sunday comics, mammiferous nudes—may be seen as a willful regression to parochial sources just when American painting had at last entered the mainstream of world art.

Only in the Pop Artist's choice of subject matter is there an implicit taking of sides. Essentially he plays it cool. He makes no commitments; for a commitment in either love or anger might mean risking something. Aline Saarinen in the April issue of *Vogue* (such magazines are an important part of the machinery that creates art-fashion) aptly says of Warhol: "He seems to love everything and love it equally. . . . I suspect that he feels not love but complacency and that he sees not with pleasure or disgust but with acquiescence."

What is so objectionable about Pop Art is this extraordinary relaxation of effort, which implies further a profound cowardice. It is the limpness and fearfulness of people who cannot come to grips with the times they live in. The Abstract Expressionists dedicated their lives to art and made a point of doing so. And who could have been more committed than Caravaggio, Chardin, and Courbet? But the Pop painters, because of their lack of stance, their lack of involvement, are producing works that strike the uninfatuated viewer as slick, effete, and chic. They share with all academic art—including, by the way, Nazi and Soviet art—the refusal to question their complacent acquiescence to the values of the culture. And most ironic of all is the fact that this art of abject conformity, this extension of Madison Avenue, is presented as *avant garde*.

In his brief introduction to the catalog of the Recent Acquisitions for Brandeis University, Sam Hunter suggests that Pop Art uses many of the compositional devices of the "purer expressions of our times." Indeed it does. It uses them in the same manner that a Hollywood movie vulgarized and banalized the teachings of Freud, or, at best, as Truman Capote has popularized and sensationalized Faulkner. It is what Dwight Macdonald calls "Midcult," the exploitation of the discoveries of the *avant garde*. "It is a more dangerous opponent to High Culture than Academicism," he says, "because it incorporates so much of the *avant garde*." This, I believe, exactly describes the relation of Pop Art to the tradition of modern art.

What we are dealing with then is an art that is easy to assimilate—much too easy; that requires neither sensibility nor intellectual effort on the part of either artist or audience; that has no more personal idiom than rock and roll music or the standard mystery story or soap opera. It is as easy to consume as it is to produce and, better yet, is easy to market, because it is loud, it is clean, and you can be fashionable and at the same time know what you're looking at. Eager collectors, shrewd dealers, clever publicists, and jazzy museum curators, fearful of being left with the rear guard, have introduced the great American device of obsolescence into the art world. For one thing, many of these objects simply won't last physically, but—more important—they will soon be old-fashioned because "styling" has been substituted for style, and promotion has taken the place of conviction. Like all synthetic art, when its market collapses it will collapse for good.

For this is not a folk art, grown from below, but *Kitsch*, manufactured from above and given all the publicity Madison Avenue dealers have at their disposal. The creator of such objects is not permitted to mature as an artist, for he has allowed himself to be thrust into a role he previously rejected (though it paid well it was demeaning), i.e., that of the designer of tail fins for General Motors. Allan Kaprow, the author of environments and happenings, prophesies that art dealers may indeed turn into art directors, and he actually looks forward to this development with relish.

It has been suggested of Pop Art that "something good may come of it—just give it time." I am not a prophet, but as an historian I must point out that earlier movements of this century—Cubism, Constructivism, Dada, Surrealism, Abstract Expressionism—produced much of their best work at the outset. It is possible that artists of conviction and ability may use some of the imagery of Pop Art in genuine works of art. Some have already done so. But that is a different question.

Questions

1. Alloway speaks of the uses of quotations from the mass media as one of the elements of pop art. Can you think of other works of art in which quotations are used? In any of T. S. Eliot's poems?
2. "An appeal to common experience was central to the first phase of pop art," writes Alloway. What does he mean by this? Give some examples. What is the difference between a pop artist's version of a comic strip and the original comic strip?
3. Is Selz favorably or unfavorably disposed toward pop art? Why does he call it "flaccid"?
4. If you happen to be favorably disposed to pop art, how do you justify it to someone for whom it is strange? If you disapprove of it and share the sentiments of those who believe that the whole movement is a fraud, how do you account for the seriousness with which art critics and art historians take the movement?
5. What should the role of a museum or of a university department of art be in relation to new movements in art? Should it be to encourage them? Should it be to wait until artists and movements become established and values fixed before exhibiting new work?
6. Should an artist always know what he is doing? Why?
7. Would you go out of your way to see an exhibition of pop art? Why? Why not? Do you see any exhibitions of art? Why? Why not?
8. How does pop art differ in seriousness from rock n' roll music? Is it fair to compare these two forms?

Assignments

1. Take either the pro or the con position on the following proposition: Pop art cannot properly be called "art" because anyone can create it.
2. Examine an advertisement in a magazine of general circulation (for example, *New Yorker, Saturday Evening Post, Ladies' Home Journal, Redbook*). Discuss the esthetic merit of the advertisement in not more than 500 words.
3. Prepare a glossary including the following expressions: "abstract expressionism," "dada," "surrealism," "esthetic distance," and "cubism." You will probably have to use a history of art, an unabridged dictionary, an encyclopedia, and the selections printed here.
4. Find out what kinds of painting at least three of the following artists are known for and relate their styles to pop art: Courbet, Caravaggio, Breugel, Picasso, De Kooning, Matisse, Francis Bacon, Duchamps, and Dubuffet.
5. Relate pop art to the beat movement (see part III, 2).
6. Make your own work of pop art and then explain it.

Additional Reading

Pop art is so current a phenomenon that the subject keeps coming up regularly in periodicals almost as a news item. *Time* and *Newsweek* magazines, for example, have run stories on pop art together with illustrations. *Arts Magazine*, X (April 1963), 36–45, contains the text of a public symposium on pop art held at the

Museum of Modern Art on December 13, 1962. *Art News*, LXII (November 1963), 24–25, contains statements by several leading pop artists about their work. The *New Yorker*, XL (February 29, 1964), 39–105, contains a profile of Robert Rauschenberg, one of the pioneer pop artists, which gives a good account of the beginning of the movement and of its rationale. "Pop Art Sells On and On—Why?" *New York Times Magazine*, May 31, 1964, p. 7 ff., examines the interesting question of the financial success of pop art.

SECTION SIX | The Wrightness of the Guggenheim

The Solomon R. Guggenheim Memorial

FRANK LLOYD WRIGHT

Mr. Guggenheim's desire to leave to his city something other than just the conventional museum lives after him—if it can find sympathetic appreciation of his often expressed and now manifested desire. His choice of myself as his architect was based upon the assumption that "the rectilinear frame of reference" for the exhibition of a painting referred more to the frame than to the painting.

He also (and with my complete sympathy) declared that a painting should be seen as nearly as possible as the painter saw it—in the continuation of artificial light managed to suit the exhibitor, and the natural daylight in which in all probability it was painted. To accomplish this, the museum in which to see a painting in an atmosphere suited to inspire the beholder with its beauty—meant a new order of architecture for this purpose.

That is why I went to work for Mr. Guggenheim—to give him a building creating an atmosphere instead of a frame in which to show the painting—incorporating it as a feature of the structure of the edifice in such manner as to reveal its properties of color and design more freely—less constructed and restricted than the bolt-upright canvas on a perpendicular wall under electric light from above.

It is true that most efforts to nature-daylight the artists' creations have not had sufficient study or intelligent modification. To do this under contributing factors in a building is this edifice provided for in The Solomon R. Guggenheim Will—a project he amply endowed and which has greatly increased since his death owing to the wise management of his trustees.

Architectural Record, CXXIII (May 1958), 182. Reprinted by permission of the *Architectural Record*.

The subject, however, presents a problem which directly challenges the conventional museum director. But the stakes we play for are important. The success of the museum means the liberation of the picture from the exploitation of the picture-broker and puts the painting more at ease according to its nature and the nature of the observer.

No mere drawings (or photographs either) convey this affair of "atmosphere." No model can show it or words express it. Only in the presence of it can fair judgment be uttered.

In the type of architecture represented there is no outside independent of the inside—the two are as one—organic—integral.

The trustees may or may not regard their duty as completed when the building stands there on the avenue proudly in the name of Solomon R. Guggenheim.

Mr. Guggenheim wanted his people to see a picture much as the artist himself saw it in changing light and whoever owned it might see it. But the very heart of his memorial as he saw it and left money to provide—might go out when the museum as a business came in.

What the museum as a business of trading, collecting, circulating, exchange and purchase, shipping in and shipping out requires is an office building and Mr. Guggenheim left no money to build one. This can be added to the present memorial without harm if so decided.

What stands there now in his name is envisioned as a unique quiet retreat where the collection of the "non objective" (so called) art he believed in and made could be greatly extended. He saw his museum as it is built to his will—thanks to his trustees. He did not want an office building or anything like one and left no money to build one. He envisioned a museum pretty much as it stands. Unique, a genuine intelligent experiment in museum-culture where pictures could be better seen with less discomfort in an atmosphere peculiarly belonging to the free forms of art he loved for itself—a true friend of the future.

The Guggenheim: Museum or Monument?

PETER BLAKE

"The critic is no respecter of an original source of information," Frank Lloyd Wright said some years ago. In all the excited comment that has attended the opening of the Guggenheim Museum, "the original source of in-

Architectural Forum, III (December 1959), 86–94. Copyright 1959 *Architectural Forum*. Reprinted by permission of the *Architectural Forum*.

formation"—which is Wright's work over more than 60 years—has been largely ignored as an aid to understanding the building.

The Guggenheim building is, by this time, reasonably familiar to most people, both in New York and elsewhere. Although much of the impact of its astonishing spaces cannot be captured by the camera, enough has been published to give everybody a rough idea of what the structure is like.

It is, of course, an extremely complex structure. "They'll still try and figure this one out 100 years from now," Wright used to say, grinning wickedly. Any attempt to evaluate the building is bound to be complex also, for such an evaluation should try and answer these questions: first, what sort of structure and what sort of space was Wright trying to create? Second, does this sort of structure and this sort of space make for a good museum—and what is a good museum, anyway? And, third—intent and function aside—is the Guggenheim Museum a beautiful piece of architecture?

Wright operated on an architectural level reserved for very few men in each generation. On this level—the level of pure art—architects like Phidias, Brunelleschi, Michelangelo, and Wren produced forms and spaces that have become significant parts of our cultural heritage. In all likelihood, these forms and spaces were judged, initially, according to whether or not they were practical; but over the centuries the work of such men has become important to us because it possessed less tangible qualities that seemed more significant in the long run. Any critical evaluation of the Guggenheim Museum must therefore deal both with its immediate, practical aspects and with its long-term implications.

What sort of structure and what sort of space?

The most remarkable fact about the Guggenheim Museum is that it represents, literally, the summing up of almost everything Wright tried to do in his lifetime. Within the huge body of his work—both completed buildings and projects—the museum reveals a consistency and singleness of purpose that should be an important lesson to many younger architects who have been bouncing around from "new concept" to "new concept" as fast as a bevy of jittery Ping-pong balls. What Wright tried to do over the years, in logical order and with utter dedication, was this: first, the creation of open rectangular structures that contained open spaces; next, the manipulation of space so that it began to move within structures—horizontally outward and inward, as well as up and down; then the development of *fluid* structures to complement fluid space—fluid structures not unlike those found in sea shells; and finally, the complete marriage of fluid structure and fluid space. The Guggenheim Museum is the most important fruit of that marriage.

Wright's first attempt to break away from rectangular structure and to create a sort of fluid composition of interlocking planes was in that charming little windmill at Taliesin East, which he built in 1896 and which, for some mysterious reason, he insisted upon calling "Romeo and Juliet." The plan of that little structure is almost identical with the plan of the Guggenheim administration wing completed this year! Wright's first effort to manipulate space so that it would move up and down as well as sideways came in the Larkin Building in Buffalo, 1904. "I think I first *consciously* began to try to beat the box in the Larkin Building," he wrote later. Like the Guggenheim Museum, the Larkin Building was lit, primarily, through a huge skylight above a central well; like the Guggenheim Museum, the Larkin Building had galleries at several levels, all open to the great, central space; and like the Guggenheim Museum, the Larkin Building had all vertical circulation in towers pushed out beyond the central space.

But the Larkin Building was still a rectangular structure—and so were some of the other buildings that belong into this astonishingly consistent chronology: the skylit Unity Church of 1906, the open-to-the-sky Midway Gardens of 1914, the multi-level lobby of the Imperial Hotel, completed in 1922. All these shared a great, central idea: the idea that space could be made to break down floors as well as walls, and that the flow of space—"the great reality of the building," as Wright called it—could take place in three and four dimensions.

The first completed structure that went beyond the Larkin concept was the S. C. Johnson office complex of 1936. Here, in this curvilinear building, Wright permitted his fluid spaces to mold the enclosing structure. The result was a remarkable space, full of premonitions of the Guggenheim: a space lit, again, from above, and ringed at different levels by galleries which, in turn, followed the curvilinear pattern of the plan. The "module" of the building was the circle.

Still, Wright had felt for some years prior to the Johnson Wax Building that the only way truly to experience space in motion was to let people "glide" effortlessly through the spaces so conceived. The most effective way of conveying that experience, Wright felt, was to create curvilinear structures in *three* dimensions—i.e., to build spiral structures rather than flat circles. His theory was this: as people moved along the path of the spiral, the space around them would seem to revolve gently, and unfold in thousands of ever changing views and vistas. The spiral form—the sea-shell form—became an obsession with him: in 1925, in the Gordon Strong Planetarium project, Wright turned the top of Sugar Loaf Mountain into a majestic spiral ramp, ascending to the planetarium proper. Years later, after World War II, he finally built his first spiral—the lovely Morris Store in San Francisco, whose elegant ramp plays the most amazing tricks upon any visitor used to the straightforward experience of boxy spaces. At about the same time Wright, still obsessed by the spiral device, designed a self-service garage for Pittsburgh which used the spiral effectively to solve an eminently practical problem. By this time the Guggenheim Museum project was well under way: from its inception, the building had been a spiral shape lit from above through a glass dome. Somehow Wright, one of the great salesmen in the history of architecture, had persuaded Solomon R. Guggenheim that the spiral was just the thing for his museum.

It may be argued that the application of so obviously preconceived a form to just about any problem—planetarium, store, parking garage, or museum—is a complete denial of Sullivan's "Form follows function." Probably so. But Wright had denied that maxim almost from the start (and Sullivan himself had qualified it repeatedly). Wright always felt that an architectural form that grew out of some truth in nature would, more often than not, challenge preconceived notions of function, and force men to re-examine such notions in the light of a new architectural truth. That certainly became necessary in the Guggenheim Museum.

How good a museum?

The most extreme opposite in concept to Wright's museum is Mies van der Rohe's museum project designed for the *Architectural Forum* in 1942. Mies's project is, in some respects, the realization of every museum director's dream: it is a large, open space, practically without columns, and so utterly anonymous in character that Mies himself, in presenting it, simply composed a series of *collages* showing paintings and sculpture floating in a space that was barely defined by a few, near-invisible lines. The paintings and the sculpture were King. Nothing in the architecture was permitted to impinge upon the experiencing of the works of art displayed. Moreover, since no one could possibly predict what sort of art might, someday, be displayed in the museum, the installation was made infinitely flexible.

The Guggenheim Museum has little of this flexibility. Wright did prepare several sketches showing ways in which he thought the paintings could be displayed; but, if anything, these sketches emphasize the fact that the spiral-ramp museum did not allow very much flexibility of installation. Wright argued that the outward-slanting walls would make the paintings look as if they sat on easels—a rationalization that no experienced museum director could take very seriously. The fact is that it is extremely difficult to display paintings on the Guggenheim's spiral ramps: to start with, the viewer stands on an incline; next, the wall slopes away from him at another angle; then the principal source of light (as conceived by Wright) would tend to light the viewer rather than the painting; and, finally, because of the absence of all verticals and horizontals in the structure—and the prevalence of lines and planes slanting in all directions—no painting would ever look as if it had been hung straight.

In the face of so much adversity, the Guggenheim's director, James Johnson Sweeney, developed an installation scheme that comes close to pure genius: he "floated" all paintings on single, steel arms that project about 4 feet out from the slanting walls; he balanced Wright's strong back-lighting with even stronger front-lighting; and he removed all frames from the canvases. The result is an extraordinarily airy and spacious installation in which the paintings seem totally removed from the powerful architecture that surrounds them, and are given a chance to speak clearly for themselves. The display of sculpture has proved to be more difficult: Sweeney has placed most of it in the center of the great, circular well, where it is dwarfed by the space above. (In any event, Wright had meant the well to be a sitting area.) The small side gallery on the second level might offer a solution as installation techniques are further perfected.

Loyal partisans of Wright are critical of Sweeney's installation for three reasons: first, because he painted the background walls white instead of leaving them cream-colored as Wright wanted them to be. (But paintings do not look well when seeming to float in lobster bisque.) Second, because he lit the walls so brightly that the ramps and the people on them are thrown into silhouette. (But to divorce the paintings from the overwhelmingly powerful architecture, Sweeney had to suspend them between front- and back-lighting of almost equal intensity.) And, third, because several of Sweeney's installation techniques (e.g., the big lighting troughs along ceilings) tend to violate the integrity of Wright's forms and spaces. (This problem remains to be resolved—and Sweeney might well feel that it was not his job to resolve it.)

But despite the complaints of the loyalists, it is quite possible that Wright would have been delighted by many of Sweeney's improvisations. Although the two men did not subscribe to the same esthetic principles, they have tended to complement one another: Sweeney's lighting made Wright's room look even more spacious than it would have looked otherwise; and Wright's architecture—though self-assertive in the extreme—gave Sweeney a museum that, as G. E. Kidder Smith put it recently, "glorifies art."

To glorify and dramatize art—that certainly has been one of the chief functions of a good museum ever since museums were first built. And, quite frequently, this important requirement has produced buildings that tend to overshadow the works of art displayed inside them. At times this has been a blessing; but at no time has a dramatic building ever succeeded in overshadowing a really great painting or work of sculpture. Some of today's painters and sculptors who have criticized the Guggenheim Museum as an attack upon their art may be simply (and justly) insecure about the power of their own work. The Miros and Kandinskys now on display in the Guggenheim Museum do not seem to be having the slightest trouble. . . .

Still, there is no denying that the Guggenheim Museum will be an everlasting challenge to its directors. But if all its future directors respond to the challenge as creatively as Sweeney has responded to it, the result may be a good deal more stimulating than the "easy" exhibitions made possible in any "ideal" museum.

How beautiful a building?

Although the external form of the Guggenheim cannot be divorced from its interior spaces, the two are, of course, read separately and can be judged separately.

Almost all of Wright's city buildings were, in a sense, attacks upon the city *as it is*. The Guggenheim is no exception: it is in deliberate conflict with its neighbors, and in deliberate conflict with the street on which it stands. At a time when we are becoming increasingly concerned with *coherence* in our townscape, this may justly be criticized. Paul Rudolph, the architect who heads Yale's School of Architecture, has recently talked about the difference between "background" and "foreground" buildings, and the need for both. Wright's building is, of course, a "foreground" building—and correctly so. The trouble is that it does not, at present, have a decent background. But in the ever changing pattern of Manhattan building, Wright might have been justified to hope for a decent background in the near future. (Indeed, several neighboring buildings have been torn down since the Guggenheim was completed.) Ideally, of course, the museum should have been located in an open park; for any rounded structure needs to be seen *in the round*—and needs plenty of space to be so seen. And, perhaps, the building will be seen that way at some future time. In any event, if the Guggenheims had wanted a building that was polite to its Manhattan neighborhood, they should have gone to another architect. In every respect, the Guggenheim denies its surroundings: it does not look out at them, but is centered upon itself and open only to the sky.

Seen as an isolated form, the building has great force and beauty. But, oddly enough, it has practically no scale. The great surprise that awaits a visitor coming into the museum for the first time is the breath-taking *size* of the circular space within. Nothing on the outside has prepared him to expect so huge an interior! It may be argued that Wright wanted to create precisely that dramatic effect, but his earlier work tends to deny that. Here, in the Guggenheim, there might have been a real place for Wright's exterior ornament to give pattern, texture, and scale to the great, sculptural forms. It is possible that the planting (ivy, etc.), when completed, will provide this texture and scale; but at present it is absent.

Inside the museum is a collection of two or three major spaces, all of them hugely successful. The great, circular, spiral-enclosed room is, quite simply, one of those spaces that no one will ever forget. It is a space of such grandeur that all the many, justifiable criticisms of the building *as a museum* seem to become insignificant by comparison.

It is impossible to describe the impact of this space; it must be experienced to be understood. It is sufficient to say that if Wright had built nothing else, this space would assure him a special place in the history of architecture.

But it *is* possible to isolate a few details that reveal Wright's genius. Landis Gores, the Connecticut architect, has pointed out that a lesser man would have made the spiral a continuous, uninterrupted corkscrew. Such a scheme would have been boring as well as confusing, for it would lack points of reference that would give a visitor a chance to orient himself. Wright, by reversing the flow of the ramp near the elevator stack, made the spiral infinitely more interesting and dramatic.

The dome above the great, central well is less successful as executed than as originally designed. Wright's first details of the dome showed a division into circles very similar to that used at the Johnson Wax Building; the present dome is a little less elegant and its ribs (especially as lit up from inside the building) seem a little too thick. Wright's original design ran into cost problems, and the present dome represents a compromise.

A second space inside the museum is easily missed—and should not be. This is the circular, 277-seat auditorium in the basement. This intimate room is, quite possibly, the most delightful auditorium built anywhere in recent years. The circular (but not symmetrical) plan establishes a sense of intimacy between audience and stage that is lacking in most theaters and auditoriums today. Once the museum's program gets under way, this auditorium should become one of the finest public assets Manhattan can boast.

The third, important space inside the museum is the administration block, a circular building with a central well, a skylight, and galleries at every floor. Except for the fact that the galleries are level and there is no ramp, the administration block is a "baby-Guggenheim," and a pretty one at that.

Eero Saarinen has said that one test of a fine piece of architecture is whether it is "all one thing." The Guggenheim theme is, of course, the circle; and this theme is ever present: it appears in the circular pattern of the terrazzo floor, in the windows of the office block, in the friezes, gates, and screens. There is hardly a false note in the detail supplied by Wright (though later additions are, occasionally, out of character). There is, however, some unfortunately crude workmanship, especially where different planes and curves intersect. Wright might have been well-advised to take one small leaf from Le Corbusier's book, and to contrast deliberately brutal surfaces with smoothly finished details elsewhere. But this would have been asking too much.

The Guggenheim Museum is the only permanent building in New York City to have been designed by Wright. It is an extraordinarily personal statement in the midst of a conformist city. It contains at least one of the most beautiful spaces created in this century. It is a dramatic glorification of the paintings and sculpture housed within it. It is not the most practical building in the world—but neither, one suspects, is the Pantheon. It will be remembered and debated long after its more efficient contemporaries have been forgotten. It is, undoubtedly, the most valuable piece in the Guggenheim collection. And it will be a constant admonition to all those who see it—and especially to architects, painters, and sculptors—that creation is, among other things, a constant process of challenging and questioning accepted notions, everywhere.

What Wright Hath Wrought

LEWIS MUMFORD

There are many ways of approaching the new Solomon R. Guggenheim Museum, and perhaps the best is the roundabout route that has been opened up by the timely appearance of Frank Lloyd Wright's *Drawings for a Living Architecture* in a monumental volume published for the Bear Run Foundation and the Edgar J. Kaufmann Charitable Foundation by Horizon Press. With its generous format and with reproductions of exquisite faithfulness, this is not merely a grand cross-section of Wright's work but the most intimate means of coming in contact with his mind and genius. It is not unusual for an architect to be a man of talent in the kindred arts of painting and sculpture; that, indeed, was almost the classic preparation for an architect in the early Renaissance, and architects like Le Corbusier have probably spent as much of their time at the easel as at the drawing board. What is unusual about Wright is that the sketches and the finished presentation drawings of his buildings are works of art in their own right, carrying his unmistakable signature. Both his crayon sketches and his plans express in the most sensitive way the exhilarating and positively liberating effect of his genius. The drawings show—sometimes more clearly even than the actual buildings—the combination of formal discipline and effulgent feeling, the union of the audacious engineer, enthralled by the possibilities of technology, and the highly individualized artist, that were the man himself. The color reproductions are particularly good. Wright used one of the most difficult of media, the colored crayon, as well as water color, in renderings whose handling of landscape and foliage sometimes reminds one of Dürer's sketches, yet the drawings have a kind of architectural firmness because of the use of fine straight lines, seemingly ruled, to convey an underlying sense of geometric structure, in sky or background as well as in building. But the color, even when used to embellish the plans, remains delicately lyrical, with an early-morning freshness.

© 1959 by Lewis Mumford. First published in *The New Yorker*. Reprinted from his volume, *The Highway and The City* by permission of Harcourt, Brace & World, Inc.

Here, before his plans and elevations were transformed into buildings, are examples of Wright's creative intentions at their purest. If not a single one of these projects had been carried out, one would still know him for the original artist that he was, the inexhaustible creator, whose formal structures and images, far from shrinking into a convention, were unfolding until the very moment of his death and were far more rich and free in the last third of his life than in his early years. Who but Wright could have conceived the fabulous setting of his proposed Baghdad Opera House, placed in a large, circular garden, which in turn was to be walled in by a low, circular 'ziggurat' with parking space for over fourteen hundred cars?

There are many vital aspects of Wright's architecture—above all, those produced by movement through space—that cannot be translated into perspective drawings, so one must not think of such renderings, however evocative, as an equivalent for the experience of the buildings themselves. But these imagined forms are unique for their immediate revelation of Wright's personality, with his fingertip sensitiveness, his expansive response to nature, his delight in the intricate play of natural and fabricated forms, his immense, unflagging vitality—the vitality that enabled him, like his Imperial Hotel in Tokyo, to sustain earthquake blows that would have shattered another personality.

Wright's architectural work was just such a defiant break with the past, just such an attempt to establish a firm American core as Whitman had conceived half a century earlier: his whole accomplishment could be described, from first to last, as a 'Song of Myself.' In these plans and renderings, one has Wright the poet without any disturbing afterthoughts about the relation of his architectural fantasies to the needs and functions they served, or the conditions of climate and weather they had to meet, or their responsibility to the neighborhood or the community, or the precedent that they helped establish—or failed to establish—for other buildings. Here, in fact, in terms of an old definition of architecture, is pure 'Delight,' dwarfing all considerations of 'Commodity' and 'Firmness.' Wright's drawings live in their own world, self-begotten, self-enclosed, often breathtaking in their originality and endearing in their loveliness. When his designs fail esthetically—as I feel that his design for the Rogers Lacy Hotel in Dallas, the garish Golden Beacon skyscraper in Chicago, and the Marin County public buildings all deplorably fail—it is usually because the artist was led astray by his sheer technical exuberance, which tempted him to ignore his own sense of fitness and to flout other human responses.

Just because of its direct, unembarrassed presentation of Wright's personality with a minimum of textual explication, his *Drawings* is, I think, the most satisfactory monograph that has been published on his architecture, though I would not belittle the pioneer studies published by Wasmuth and Wijdeveld. Any building of Wright's must be viewed within the frame of his life's work that this book provides, and any lapse must be placed within the perspective of his long series of triumphs in a career pursued without regard for historical conventions or chic contemporary stereotypes. By the same token, when Wright failed, he failed with originality and decision—the inverted triumph of a great acrobat who so despises the safety nets that he would rather break his neck than rely on them.

Wright dared greatly in all that he undertook, and above all he dared to be himself. Loving Emerson, he must have recognized a special personal blessing in Emerson's statement that "whoso would be a man must be a nonconformist." Wright lived to see the confident, self-reliant America of Emerson and Whitman, even the mugwump America of Howells, turn into that meek, tame, glossily corrupt totalitarian 'democracy' which now lives—or half lives—in the shadow world of the television screen. To one who had the audacity to sin against the conventions of this society in almost every way except its love for exhibitionism and publicity, much may be forgiven.

Frank Lloyd Wright was a chip off the old American block. In the sense in which the term still applied before the Civil War, he might be called one of the last Americans—a distinction he shared with such a profoundly different personality as Robert Frost. In his unique development, both the good and the bad qualities one associates with that role were exaggerated: on one hand his isolationism, his anti-Europeanism, his belligerence, his lightly triggered arrogance, his colossal self-admiration, but over against this his originality, his freshness, his gay generosity, his boundless affirmation of life, his belief that the world need not remain decayed and corrupt but might be made over anew in the morning.

These thoughts on his life and character temper all that I am bound, out of my respect for Wright's greatness as an artist, to say about the Guggenheim Museum, the only example of his architecture in New York. If I have occasion to speak severely, remember that I am talking about a true artist, one of the most richly endowed geniuses this country has produced—an artist who has no need for the apologetic leniency one might accord to a lesser talent. For the most serious flaws in Wright's work, it may be that our country fully shares reproof with the artist. Had we had the proud understanding, when he was in mid-career, to encourage him with great commissions, we would have earned the right to challenge his narcissism and his complacent egocentricity and to require a more sober perfection than he, in the sheer willfulness of his genius, was prepared to achieve. Wright was at his best with appreciative but self-reliant clients, and in an equally appreciative America he might have risen to our more searching demands and thrown away the shallow showmanship that on too many occasions marred his architecture no less than his public relations.

The Guggenheim Museum is a formidable, ponderous, closed-in concrete structure of almost indescribable individuality; the main element, the art gallery, might be called an inverted ziggurat that tapers toward the bottom—not the Mesopotamian kind, which stood on a square base, but

Bruegel's round version in his 'Tower of Babel.' Functionally, this museum, which occupies a whole block front on Fifth Avenue, from Eighty-eighth to Eighty-ninth Street, divides into two parts—at the south end a low, telescoped tower (the ziggurat) crowned by a wired-glass dome visible solely from the air, and at the north end an attached administration building only half its height, a combination of rectangular and circular forms, with portholes for windows, opening on viewless balconies with solid parapets. The ground floor of the tower is recessed under the overhanging second floor to create a deep shadow, so that the tower appears to be set on a strong horizontal base formed by the continuous concrete band of the second-floor wall, which seems, because of the shadow, to float in space.

In many of Wright's later designs, such as the unexecuted group of funeral chapels in San Francisco, such a broad horizontal base serves both to bring together separate elements and to set the building apart from the immediate landscape, as was done in such Renaissance designs as the villas in Frascati. In the Museum, the base seems wholly detached and esthetic—not functional, as in the case of Wright's early prairie houses, which rested, without the usual cellar and foundations, on a low pedestal. The main mass, the tower, is set back from the building lines at the southwest corner, where the second-story wall bulges out into a bay that emphasizes, in profile, the wider curve and sloping sides of the ziggurat.

Despite its dull color, a sort of evaporated-milk ochre, this great monolith stands out boldly from the flat, anonymous apartment houses in the neighborhood, the positiveness of the form offsetting the all too congenial mediocrity of tone. The building is so definitely a thing apart, so different from every other one on Fifth Avenue, that the sprawling, pale-green letters (along the lower edge of the second-story wall) that identify it may almost be forgiven for their feebleness because they are actually not needed at all. As an external symbol of contemporary abstract art, this building has a genuine fitness in its severe rationality of form. But Wright had, out of respect for the materials and constructive elements he chose, denied himself the more enlivening resources of which he was master. This building is non-traditional, non-representational, non-historical abstract art in its own right; indeed, it not merely coincides with the contents, it supersedes them. You may go to this building to see Kandinsky or Jackson Pollock; you remain to see Frank Lloyd Wright.

From the moment I examined the preliminary drawings I was disturbed and puzzled by its design, and I am still disturbed, though further reflection and observation have revealed a little of Wright's intentions and decisions. At that, almost every part of this design leads to a critical question mark. Let us first consider the exterior, and, to begin with, the choice of monolithic concrete. Whether it is in the raw state imprinted by the mold, or whether it is smoothed and painted, concrete remains a sullen material. If left in the rough, as in Le Corbusier's Maison de l'Unité d'Habitation, in Marseille, or in Louis

Kahn's Yale Art Gallery, it is tolerable only at a distance; if it is smooth, unless it is mixed and poured with extreme care, cracks and splotches are bound to show from the beginning, and if the smoothness is covered with a cement paint, as in this case, it lacks texture and character. Worst of all, the flawed surface denies the solidity of the material, as if it were hastily done in plaster over canvas.

Wright was a master of texture, in brickwork no less than in stone. Yet in this building, by its nature a showpiece, he was content to emphasize the sheer elephantine solidity of the heavy concrete walls. Is it possible that this structure, seemingly designed from the foundations up as if it were a fortification, was meant to be precisely that—as indestructible as he could make it? There would be at least a strong subjective justification behind this folly. Two of Wright's early buildings, among the best of his first twenty-five years as an architect, were prematurely demolished—the Midway Gardens in Chicago and the Larkin office building in Buffalo—and now the Imperial Hotel seems doomed. Did he design the Guggenheim Museum as a super-pillbox that would resist vandalism or demolition as effectively as those surviving concrete bunkers Hitler's minions built along the Channel coast? Wright is reported to have said that if a nuclear bomb destroyed New York, his building, on its cushioned foundation, would merely bounce with the shock and survive. Thus Wright would be left, in effect, surveying the ruins, ironically triumphing over the city that had waited till the end of his life to give him this one opportunity. He may have been consoled by the thought, but, apparently to insure that triumph, he sacrificed the purposes of the Museum and created an empty monument as the sole prospective occupant of an untenanted world. In his plan for the Baghdad Opera House garage, Wright turned an embarrassment—the eventual need for motorcar parking—into a magnificent opportunity, but in the Guggenheim Museum he turned an opportunity into an obstacle. Even as a fortress, even as a bomb shelter, it falls short of perfection.

His seeming decision to leave behind an indestructible monument should perhaps enlist our sympathy, but the result does not merit our approval. From this error all the worst features of the exterior design spring. It is formidably *im*pressive, but it is not *ex*pressive of anything except the desire for monumental solidity. Montgomery Schuyler, our best nineteenth-century architectural critic, said that H. H. Richardson's overponderous buildings were defensible solely in a military sense, and the gibe applies equally to Wright's museum. Only in the intimate touches do the more lovable features of Wright's imagination emerge, such as the banks of green foliage that provide a flare of living color and texture along the Fifth Avenue approach. There is nothing else in this exterior to reduce the sense of grim military self-sufficiency, and the office wing is just as massive and as sparing of windows as the main structure. Except for the wealth of greenery—particularly effective in the motor court, which is framed by the entrance—there is nothing of Wright's specific imprint in the outward structure but the circular form.

In using rounded forms, Wright shares honors with Eric Mendelsohn, who first suggested the special plastic quality of concrete in the imaginative architectural sketches he published after the end of the First World War. Ever since Wright designed the Ralph Jester house, in Palos Verdes, California, back in the thirties, he was fascinated by rounded forms, curving ground plans, and circular enclosures, and he continued, with increasing felicity, to explore these architectural resources. His circular houses, such as the one he designed for his son, David, are among the best examples of his later work. But in accenting the massiveness of monolithic concrete by replacing windows with mere narrow horizontal slots between the floors of the Museum tower, Wright introduced an inflexible element into his design, for he proposed to make the amount of natural illumination, as well as the inner space, unalterable.

Again one searches for some reason besides Wright's assertion of his own ego. His circular tower creates an exhibition room whose dimensions in no way can be modified to suit the needs of a particular showing. This is an all-or-nothing building; one takes it on Wright's terms or one does not take it at all. In planning it, what Wright did was to redesign his enchanting V. C. Morris shop building, in San Francisco, which has the same system of interior circulation; but he hollowed out the interior and replaced the flat Morris façade with an exterior that would properly correspond with the circular interior of the Museum. Unfortunately, his interior scheme, a brilliant one for a shop, because it increases the temptations to buy by spreading all the merchandise before the eye, is a ruinous one for a museum, in which the works of art, surely, should impose their needs on the building. But Wright never had a place for the painter in any of his buildings, and it was perhaps too much to hope that there would be a place for him even in an art museum.

For all that the exterior of the Museum is contemporary abstract art, in creating it Wright hid his light, so to speak, under a concrete funnel; so that it is only in the interior that one may see it burning—in such a dazzling fashion, in fact, that it negates its function by obscuring all the other works of art that a museum supposedly exists to display. If the outside of the building says Power—power to defy blast, to resist change, to remain as immune to time as the Pyramids—the interior says Ego, an ego far deeper than the pool in which Narcissus too long gazed. On the outside, Wright's composition puts this architecture under the wing of the New Brutalist school; on the inside, he is the old Romanticist, singing—as if he were alone in the wilderness—the Song of Myself, but without communicating the sense of speaking for all other men and inviting their contributions, and enhancing their personalities, too, that made Whitman's swelling ego so lovable.

Thus, though the exterior of the Museum is far from negligible as 'building,' it is a feat for which the contractors and workers deserve heartier congratulations than the architect. More than one builder shied away from this difficult task, and the architectural pleasure evoked by the massive concrete forms is unduly small when one considers the immense effort and expense involved. For while, as in all of Wright's buildings, the interior and exterior are conceived as organically one, in this case the outer expression is mere 'building' or 'engineering,' while Wright's special gifts—and his sometimes defiant weaknesses as an architect—do not come to life until one gains the interior. In lesser degree this is true of many other domed structures, like the Pantheon, in Rome, and Santa Sophia, in Istanbul: but this distinction particularly applies to the Guggenheim Museum.

Yet once you come close to the Guggenheim Museum, Wright has you in his hold. From the time you scrape your feet on the unmistakably Wright grating in the vestibule and grasp the bronze bar that, serving as handle, stretches from top to bottom of the glass door, you are under his enchantment. Entering, you are in a monumental hall of exalted proportions. The form is circular, and the spiralling ramp that ascends it—broken by a bulging bay on each floor—creates a rotating band of light and dark, of solid and void, that terminates in the opaque, almost flat wired-glass dome. This dome, a combination of broken-spider-web space divisions and strong supporting forms, is in Wright's characteristic manner, though uncharacteristically, it closes out the sky as completely as the concrete structure closes out the landscape. As for the strong curve of the bays, it not merely enhances the dynamism of the helical ramp, which widens with each floor, but makes it psychologically overpowering—if not physiologically almost unbearable. For the abrupter fall of the ramp on this sharp curve adds to the muscular tensions created by the form of the structure and its dizzy impact on the eye. This is not a tall building—only six stories—but it gives the effect of great height. Without ornament, without texture, without positive color, in a design as smoothly cylindrical as a figure by Fernand Léger—this is how Wright shows himself here a master of the abstract resources of modern form. Here is the freedom that Mendelsohn dreamed of and first brought into existence in the Einstein Tower, in Potsdam, but here, too, is the disciplined movement that the baroque architects sometimes weakened in the exuberance of their ornament. In the very restraint of this composition, Wright, like a good disciple of Lao-tse, dramatizes its essential element—the central void, filled with light. It takes an effort to turn away from this striking composition, modelled with such boldness yet with such discipline and with such a vivid interplay of form between the curving ramp and the circular 'utility stacks,' which house the closets and small lavatories on each level, rising against the wall on either side of the elevator to visually tie all the floors together.

As an object by itself, the Guggenheim Museum interior is, like the exterior, a remarkable example of abstract sculpture; indeed, it is a new kind of mobile sculpture, whose dynamic flow is accentuated by the silhouettes of the spectators, who form a moving frieze against the intermittent spots of painting on the walls. Thus Wright permitted the requirements of his composition to dominate both the works of art and the freedom of the viewer. They are needed to complete it, but apart from this they do not signify. Those who respond to the interior do proper homage to Wright's genius. If the purpose of the Museum is solely to exhibit Wright, the interior has magnificent justification for its existence. And if the spectator forgets the other works of art it contains, the building is—for him if not for the neglected artists—a compensation and a unique reward. What other monumental interior in America produces such an overwhelming effect?

But architecture is not simply sculpture, and this building was meant also to serve as a museum. In that context, it is an audacious failure. Wright has allotted the paintings and sculptures on view only as much space as would not infringe upon his abstract composition. It is an open secret that he paid no attention to the program set before him and over-rode every attempt to make this great shell workable as a museum. The dominating conception would have needed complete revision if the building were to be anything but a display of Wright's virtuosity. With all the willfulness of genius, he created the minimum amount of gallery space at the maximum cost and the all but complete sacrifice of the Museum's essential requirements. This architect who stood for organic forms, who continually preached the lessons of life and growth and change, created a shell whose form had no relation to its function and offered no possibility of any future departure from his rigid preconceptions. Except for a single high-ceilinged, triangular side room opposite the main entrance, on the first floor, the sole exhibition space is that great circular wall within the tower. The continuous ribbon of promenade that winds along this wall has, for a museum, a low ceiling—nine feet eight inches—so only a picture well within the vertical boundaries thus created can be shown. The wall provided by Wright slanted outward, following the outward slant of the exterior wall, and paintings were not supposed to be hung vertically or shown in their true plane but were to be tilted back against it. The interior, under Wright's direction, was painted the same dull cream as the rest of the Museum. To make matters worse, he interposed a sloping shelf between the wall and the spectator, so that anyone interested in a closer view—whether because of myopia or a curiosity about brush stroke and treatment—could not get near a canvas. Nor could he escape the light shining in his eyes from the narrow slots in the wall. Only on the first two floors, where there are no light slots, did he forgo this embarrassing embankment.

Short of insisting that no pictures at all be shown, Wright could not have gone much further to create a structure sublime in its own right but ridiculous as a museum of art. The most pretentious Renaissance palace could hardly have served a modern artist worse. There is not a mistake in rigidity of plan, in scale, or in setting made by the pompous academic temple museums of the past that Wright did not reproduce or actually cap. Even the sculpture on view has difficulty in surviving Wright's treatment; it is in hopeless competition with the overwhelming sculptural force of the building itself. It is as if Wright had only one condition to impose on all rival artists—unconditional surrender.

With infinite labor, the Museum has since sought to neutralize Wright's blunders and to salvage the concept of the Museum as a public place for viewing works of art. But there are errors that no ingenuity can overcome, and one of them is the ramp. With it, the whole building is in motion, and the spectator must be in motion, too—part of a moving procession of people, with no place to sit down except a side bench at each floor, no place to retreat to, no possibility of changing his relation to the object viewed, except by viewing it at a distance, from the opposite side of the hall. The worst feature of the old-fashioned museum was the continuous corridor, and it is not improved here by being made a spiral. It remains only for some pious machine-minded disciple of Wright's to go one step farther and place the pictures on a moving belt, so that the spectator may remain seated. The sloping ramp and ceiling, and the slanting vertical members that divide the wall into segments, magnify the problem—the annoying distortion of view—by destroying parallels and right angles for anyone who has come to look at pictures. Who has not felt an excruciating necessity to readjust a picture when it is hung even slightly out of kilter?

In short, in the state Wright left the Museum in, it was magnificent but unusable, and the very worst service James Johnson Sweeney, its director, could have done Wright's reputation would have been to open the Museum without making any changes. That might have been a justifiable revenge in return for Wright's dismissal of all suggestions that lessened his sense of omnicompetence and omnipotence, but I am glad that the Museum did not avail itself of it. Failing to enlist Wright's understanding collaboration, the Museum authorities made a gallant effort to treat this formidable shell the way an engineer might treat a mountain he cannot remove but can circumvent by a tunnel. They called in Alfred Binder, a lighting engineer, and in association with Mr. Sweeney he evolved a system of back illumination that diffuses the natural light from Wright's narrow slots in the wall and supplements it with artificial light—front lighting that focusses directly on the pictures instead of on the spectator. The cream of the interior was changed to white, and the pictures, instead of being propped against the wall, jut forth from it, supported by adjustable steel rods, as much as four feet. This device spares the visitor, as far as possible, the distortion of view caused by Wright's interior plan and presents the pictures under an intense illumination, full of radiance but not without glare. Thus the lighted wall becomes the real frame of the pictures.

My first impressions of this ingenious rectification were highly favorable, apart from my residual doubts about the value of constant artificial illumination of such intensity. But further visits have disclosed that when the sun pours through the dome the brilliance of the lighting is unkind to paintings of any subtlety, and that the glass-covered channels of the back lighting above the pictures are so near the paintings as to be distracting. Only when one sees the paintings across the wide void of the gallery, from the other side of the ramp, with the wall lighting troughs cut out by the impending ramp, does one view them in a satisfactory light. Though the present arrangement is doubtless better than Wright's cavalier treatment, it needs to be modified and perfected. Even in the high triangular exhibition room, the lights that face the spectator are irritatingly obtrusive.

Wright might have felt that these innovations ruined the architectural effect of his great spiral, but their sole effect, as far as I can see, is to alter the relation of light and dark, and sharpen the dramatic effect of the winding ribbons of space and wall. The method of displaying the pictures at a distance from the wall was employed, I understand, at the big Picasso exhibition in Rome, and it makes use of technical resources and concepts that belong as properly to our particular age as the lushly carved gilt picture frames did to the palatial mansions and pompous ceremonies they were part of. Very likely this 'framing in light' will be copied by museums that do not have to meet the difficulties that Wright gratuitously imposed. On a plot as generous as this one, with Central Park to provide both a contrasting outer view and the maximum of natural light, he had a rare chance to evolve a solution that would do full justice to the art, to the museum visitor, and not least to his own imagination and invention. But by committing himself to the continuous ramp and the closed shell of the building he turned his back on that open landscape and the varied natural light that were his for the asking. As if to emphasize this perversity, he wasted half the imposing frontage on the administration offices and enclosed them in a wall as nearly windowless as the gallery. The fact that Wright threw away such advantages—which lent themselves to many alternative solutions in forms just as bold as the present one—is the bitterest pill this box holds for at least one of his admirers. Even in creating a place in which to exhibit himself as supreme master of abstract art, he hardly did justice to himself, for the self he put on display was his worse self, the exhibitionist and the autocrat, not the poetic creator of form who could evolve a hundred fresh architectural images while his rivals were painfully trying to evolve a single one.

In every aspect of architecture, except as an abstract composition in interior space, one's final judgment of Wright's Guggenheim Museum must, then, be a sadly unfavorable one, such a judgment as only an old friend may in fear and trembling impart to the living and only a life-long admirer feel free to deliver over the work of the dead. In coming to this verdict, I pass over the minor flaws—the absence of sufficient storeroom space, so that one whole floor of the spiral must be devoted to storage, and the lecture hall, too wide for its purpose, too lacking in facilities to serve as a little theatre, since it has none of the flexibility of function and seating that such a room might easily have had—for in some degree these shortcomings are all counterbalanced by many ingratiating touches. So, too, I ignore the administration building, with faults even more flagrant than those in the Museum itself, and I blame the city's building code, rather than Wright, for the lowness of the balustrade that lines the outer edge of the ramp—a lowness that seems scarcely adequate to its protective function.

There are two dominant types of architecture today, both anti-functional, both meretricious—that of the package and that of the Procrustean bed. This museum is a Procrustean structure; the art in it must be stretched out or chopped off to fit the bed Wright prepared for it. The building magnifies Wright's greatest weakness as an architect: the fact that once he fastened on a particular structural form (a triangle, a hexagon, a circle), he imposed it upon every aspect of his design, with no regard for the human purposes it presumably served. He thus sometimes turned a too strict logic into a hollow rhetoric. Despite all the sculptural strength the interior of the Guggenheim Museum boasts, the building as a whole fails as a work of architecture. And it is ironic to find that this failure is of exactly the same order—and because of the same kind of arrogance and willfulness—as that of Le Corbusier's equally ambivalent Maison de l'Unité d'Habitation. In both cases the plan is arbitrary, the interior space is tortured, and the essential functions are frustrated in order to comply with the architect's purely formal esthetic choices. This is not architectural originality but academicism.

The architects who pursue their formal aims so intently without consideration of all the public functions they serve are really claiming the privileges of the painter and the sculptor without fully accepting the responsibilities of their own profession. And they do this to their own disadvantage, for they forget that even minor irritations arising from functional deficiencies may seriously lower the esthetic vitality of their form. In the case of the Guggenheim Museum, the lapses are not minor, and Wright's hollow triumph is all the worse because he was lending the weight of his genius to the fashionable aberration of the moment—the curious belief that the functional aspects of architecture are unimportant. Instead of showing, as he well might have, how a great modern architect does justice to every aspect of a building, and not least the esthetic—without making timid compromises or irrational sacrifices or frivolous omissions—Wright turned his back on that challenge. He thus defeated his own purpose by producing a building that in order to function at all could not remain what he had planned it to be long enough to be formally opened. The old should not set such a bad example to the young, and the greatest of our architectural masters should not, while still hale and of sound mind, have added such a codicil to his last will and testament.

I can think of only one way of fully redeeming Wright's monumental and ultimately mischievous failure—that of turning the building into a museum of architecture. This would be in keeping with the form of the building and would cover up most of its mistakes. Could it be that it was this, and not abstract painting, that Wright had in mind, at least unconsciously, all the time? If so, the joke is on us, for this is the great master's monument to both his art and to himself. Its absurdities as a museum thus become its ultimate glory as a work of art: a work designed to outlast the transitory modes of contemporary art and even the city in which it is set.

Questions

1. Wright has often been accused of attempting to "put painting in its place" by overwhelming it with the museum building. In his essay, what does he consider the functions of a museum to be?
2. Would Wright be better described as a functionalist or an organic architect? Why?
3. What does Wright mean by "atmosphere"? By "frame"?
4. What function does the third paragraph in Blake's essay perform?
5. Explain the meaning of Blake's statement that Wright wanted a building to "take place in three and four dimensions."
6. Why does Blake place quotation marks around "easy" and "ideal" in the sentence: "But if all its future directors respond to the challenge as creatively as Sweeney has responded to it, the result may be a good deal more stimulating than the 'easy' exhibitions made possible in any 'ideal' museum"?
7. Why does Mumford begin with a general discussion of Wright's work? Does this discussion perform the same function in Mumford's essay as Blake's discussion of the stages in Wright's development as an architect?
8. Would Blake agree with Mumford's judgment that "there is nothing of Wright's specific imprint in the outward structure but the circular form"? Explain.
9. Identify Narcissus, "Song of Myself," Fernand Léger, Lao-tse, and the Procrustean bed. What do Mumford's references to these things and people add to his essay?
10. State the difference between (a) "building" or "engineering" and (b) "architecture" as Mumford employs the terms.
11. What does Mumford mean when he describes the spectators in the museum as "a moving frieze"?
12. To what buildings might Mumford refer when he speaks of "pompous academic temple museums"?
13. Explain Mumford's sentence: "He thus sometimes turned a too strict logic into a hollow rhetoric."
14. What does the use of metaphor add to Mumford's essay? Give some examples.
15. What aspects of the museum do Blake and Mumford disagree about? Do these disagreements arise from basic differences in approach?
16. Comparing Mumford's essay in this section with the one in part III, 7, discuss the stylistic features that are found in both.
17. Would the Guggenheim be an appropriate museum in which to display pop art?

Assignments

1. What are the purposes of a museum?
2. Choose some building on your campus that is particularly interesting. Write an architectural critique of it, discussing its relationship to its environment.

3. Take a building which, like the Guggenheim, might be considered a landmark in architecture and describe the peculiar aspects of its greatness.
4. Discuss the relationship of architecture to the other arts. Is it, as Wright suggests, the "mother art"?
5. Compare Wright as a modern architect with another modern architect.
6. The Huntington Hartford Gallery of Modern Art in New York was built after the Guggenheim Museum. Locate articles about the Hartford Gallery through a periodical index. Write an essay showing which museum—the Guggenheim or the Hartford—better fulfills the purposes of a museum.

Additional Reading

Among the provocative comments on the Guggenheim are William Barrett's, "Frank Lloyd Wright's Pictorama," *Commentary*, XXIX (March 1960), 205–216; Russell Lynes's, "Mr. Wright's Museum," *Harper's*, CCXIX (November 1959), 96 ff.; and Francis Steegmuller's, "Battle of the Guggenheim," *Holiday*, XXVIII (September 1960), 60–61 ff.

Frank Lloyd Wright possessed a personality as exceptional and a reputation as controversial as any of his buildings. In his writings one finds a ranging intellect, occasionally cantankerous but never dull. In such books as *The Living City* (New York, 1958), *The Natural House* (New York, 1954), and *A Testament* (New York, 1957), he developed his ideas about architecture, city planning, government, and many other subjects.

Some of Mumford's other work is cited in the additional readings to part III, 7. Peter Blake's recent book, *God's Own Junkyard* (New York, 1964), provides a stimulating discussion of the whole topic of man's physical environment.

III
Society

SECTION ONE | *First Things First: Teaching Our Teachers*

Concluding Observations

JAMES B. CONANT

I began this volume by introducing the reader to a long-standing quarrel among educators. I close by collecting in one chapter my recommendations, whose acceptance I believe might end the quarrel. If my findings are correct, neither side in the conflict has developed as coherent and consistent a position as the battle cries would lead the hearer to expect. In any discussion about the idea of a liberally educated man, one encounters differences of opinion as to what this expression means; and there is a great variety of programs reflecting these diverse opinions. A cynic might be tempted to define a liberal education as a four-year exposure to an experience prescribed by a group of professors, each of whom has prime allegiance to his own academic discipline. The programs in many institutions seem to have been developed not by careful consideration of a group but by a process that might be called academic logrolling. (I am not unfamiliar with the bargaining between departments when it comes to dividing up a student's time.) In any event, one finds a complete lack of agreement on what constitutes a satisfactory general education program for future teachers. As to the education in a specific field which the college student expects to teach, there is a far greater degree of unanimity. But about the amount of time to be devoted to such studies in college and the level of competence to be demanded, opinions differ.

When one examines the courses in education, one finds almost as much confusion as exists in general education. Here the cynic might well say that

From *The Education of American Teachers*, by James B. Conant. Reprinted by permission of the author.

the professors are jealous of their share of the student's time but are ill prepared to use it well.

Academic professors and professors of education are in complete agreement only on one point: that practice teaching, if well conducted, is important. Aside from practice teaching and the accompanying methods course, there is little agreement among professors of education on the nature of the corpus of knowledge they are expected to transmit to the future teacher.

In view of the great diversity of opinions and practices to be found in the leading institutions, I conclude that neither a state authority nor a voluntary accrediting agency is in a position to specify the amount of time to be devoted to either academic or educational courses. What is needed is on the one hand for the state to allow freedom for institutions to experiment, and on the other for the academic professors and professors of education in each institution to take joint responsibility for the reputation of their college or university in training teachers.

Recognizing that the 27 recommendations distributed throughout various chapters of the book may be difficult to recall, I have arranged them in five categories according to the persons most likely to be involved in bringing about their adoption.

GROUP A. RECOMMENDATIONS REQUIRING ACTION EITHER BY A CHIEF STATE SCHOOL OFFICER, A STATE BOARD OF EDUCATION OR A LEGISLATURE.

1. Certification requirements

   For certification purposes the state should require only (a) that a candidate hold a baccalaureate degree from a legitimate college or university, (b) that he submit evidence of having successfully performed as a student teacher under the direction of college and public school personnel in whom the state Department has confidence, and in a practice-teaching situation of which the state Department approves, and (c) that he hold a specially endorsed teaching certificate from a college or university which, in issuing the official document, attests that the institution as a whole considers the person adequately prepared to teach in a designated field and grade level.

5. Programs of practice teaching

   The state should approve programs of practice teaching. It should, working cooperatively with the college and public school authorities, regulate the conditions under which practice teaching is done and the nature of the methods instruction that accompanies it. The state should require that the colleges and public school systems involved submit evidence concerning the competence of those appointed as cooperating teachers and clinical professors.

6. State information service

    State Departments of Education should develop and make available to local school boards and colleges and universities data relevant to the preparation and employment of teachers. Such data may include information about the types of teacher-education programs of colleges or universities throughout the state and information concerning supply and demand of teachers at various grade levels and in various fields.

7. Assignment of teachers by local boards

    The state education authorities should give top priority to the development of regulations insuring that a teacher will be assigned only to those teaching duties for which he is specifically prepared, and should enforce these regulations rigorously.

10. Certification reciprocity among states

    Whenever a teacher has been certified by one state under the provisions of Recommendations 1 and 2, his certificate should be accepted as valid in any other state.

GROUP B. RECOMMENDATIONS INVOLVING APPROPRIATIONS BY STATE LEGISLATURES.

4. State financial responsibility for practice teaching

    The state should provide financial assistance to local boards to insure high-quality practice teaching as part of the preparation of teachers enrolled in either private or public institutions.

12. Loan policy for future teachers

    Each state should develop a loan policy for future teachers aimed at recruiting into the profession the most able students; the requirements for admission to the teacher-training institutions within the state should be left to the institution, but the state should set a standard for the recipients in terms of scholastic aptitude; the amount of the loan should be sufficient to cover expenses, and the loan should be cancelled after four or five years of teaching in the public schools of the state.

GROUP C. RECOMMENDATIONS REQUIRING ACTION BY A LOCAL SCHOOL BOARD, EITHER ACTING ALONE OR IN CONJUNCTION WITH STATE ACTION.

3. Cooperating teachers in practice teaching

    Public school systems that enter contracts with a college or university for practice teaching should designate, as classroom teachers working with practice teaching, only those persons in whose competence as teachers, leaders, and evaluators they have the highest confidence, and should give such persons encouragement by reducing their work loads and raising their salaries.

11. Initial probationary period of employment

    During the initial probationary period, local school boards should take specific steps to provide the new teacher with every possible help in the form of: (a) limited teaching responsibility; (b) aid in gathering instructional materials; (c) advice of experienced teachers whose own load is reduced so that they can work with the new teacher in his own classroom; (d) shifting to more experienced teachers those pupils who create problems beyond the ability of the novice to handle effectively; and (e) specialized instruction concerning the characteristics of the community, the neighborhood, and the students he is likely to encounter.

23. Revision of salary schedule by local boards

    School boards should drastically revise their salary schedules. There should be a large jump in salary when a teacher moves from the probationary status to tenure. Any salary increments based on advanced studies should not be tied to course credits earned (semester hours), but only to the earning of a master's degree, based normally on full-time residence or four summer sessions in which the program is directed toward the development of the competence of the teacher as a teacher. Such a salary increment should be made mandatory by state law.

24. Financial assistance to teachers for study in summer schools

    School boards or the state should provide financial assistance so that teachers may attend summer school after enrolling in a graduate school for the purpose of completing a program of the type stated in Recommendation 23.

25. Leaves of absence for further education of teachers

    School boards should provide leave of absence with salary for a full-time semester residence at a university to enable teachers to study toward a master's program, provided this program is designed to increase the competence of the teacher; state funds should be available for this purpose.

27. In-service education of teachers

    To insure that the teachers are up to date, particularly in a period of rapid change (as in mathematics and physics), a school board should contract with an educational institution to provide short-term seminars (often called workshops) during the school year so that all the teachers, without cost to them, may benefit from the instruction. Such seminars or workshops might also study the particular educational problems of a given school or school district. (No credit toward salary increases would be given.)

GROUP D. RECOMMENDATIONS REQUIRING ACTION BY THE FACULTIES, ADMINISTRATIVE OFFICERS AND TRUSTEES OF AN INSTITUTION ENGAGED IN EDUCATING TEACHERS FOR THE PUBLIC ELEMENTARY AND SECONDARY SCHOOLS.

2. Collegiate or university responsibility

Each college or university should be permitted to develop in detail whatever program of teacher education it considers most desirable, subject only to two conditions: first, the president of the institution in behalf of the entire faculty involved—academic as well as professional —certifies that the candidate is adequately prepared to teach on a specific level or in specific fields, and second, the institution establishes in conjunction with a public school system a state-approved practice-teaching arrangement.

13. The all-university approach to teacher training

If the institution is engaged in educating teachers, the lay board trustees should ask the faculty or faculties whether in fact there is a continuing and effective all-university (or interdepartmental) approach to the education of teachers, and if not, why not?

14. Requirements for collegiate or university teacher-education programs

The board of trustees should ask the faculty to justify the present requirements for a bachelor's degree for future teachers with particular reference to the breadth of the requirements and to spell out what in fact are the total educational exposures (school and college) demanded now in the fields of (a) mathematics, (b) physical science, (c) biological science, (d) social science, (e) English literature, (f) English composition, (g) history, (h) philosophy.

15. Foreign language preparation

If courses are required in a foreign language, evidence of the degree of mastery obtained by fulfilling the minimum requirement for a degree should be presented to the board of trustees.

16. The establishment of "clinical professors"

The professor from the college or university who is to supervise and assess the practice teaching should have had much practical experience. His status should be analogous to that of a clinical professor in certain medical schools.

17. Basic preparation of elementary teachers

    (a). *The program for teachers of kindergarten and grades 1, 2, and 3 should prepare them in the content and methodology of all subjects taught in these early school years. Depth in a single subject or cluster of subjects is not necessary.*

    (b). *The program for teachers of grades 4, 5, and 6 should provide depth of content and methods of teaching in a specific subject or cluster of subjects normally taught in these grades, with only an introduction to the remaining elementary school subjects.*

18. Practice teaching for elementary teachers

    All future elementary teachers should engage in practice teaching for a period of at least 8 weeks, spending a minimum of 3 hours a day in the classroom; the period must include at least 3 weeks of full responsibility for the classroom under the direction of a cooperating teacher and the supervision of a clinical professor.

19. Adequate staffing of small colleges training elementary teachers

    Those responsible for financing and administering small colleges should consider whether they can afford to maintain an adequate staff for the preparation of elementary school teachers. Unless they are able to employ the equivalent of three or four professors devoting their time to elementary education, they should cease attempting to prepare teachers for the elementary schools.

20. Single field diploma for secondary school teachers

    An institution should award a teaching certificate for teachers in grades 7 to 12 in one field only.

21. Clinical professors in institutions educating secondary teachers

    Every institution awarding a special teaching certificate for secondary school teachers should have on the staff a clinical professor for each field or combination of closely related fields.

22. Teaching diploma for art, music and physical education teachers

    An institution offering programs in art or music or physical education should be prepared to award a teaching diploma in each of these fields without grade designation; institutional programs should not attempt to develop competency in more than one field in four years.

26. Master's degree programs

    The graduate schools of education or their equivalent (in universities organized without such separate degree-granting schools) should devise a program for increasing the competence of teachers as teachers with the following characteristics:

(1) *It should be open to any graduate of the same institution in the same field of endeavor (e.g., elementary education, secondary school social studies, etc.).*

(2) *Courses should be allowed for credit toward the 30 semester hours whether or not the courses are of an elementary nature, provided they are clearly courses needed to increase the competence of the teacher.*

(3) *No credit toward the degree should be given for extension courses or courses taken on campus while the teacher is engaged on a full-time teaching job.*

(4) *Passing of a comprehensive examination should be required for the master's degree, as is now the case in some institutions.*

(5) *The summer-school sessions should be arranged so that four summer residences will complete the degree requirements, or two summers plus one full-time semester residence.*

(6) *If the offering in the arts and sciences is not wide enough to provide meaningful work in the summer session (as it would not be in some state colleges), arrangements should be made for the transfer of credit from a university summer school with a good offering of courses in subject-matter fields.*

(7) *For elementary teachers, the degree should be master of education in elementary education; for secondary teachers, master of education in English (or science, or social science or modern languages or mathematics).*

GROUP E. CONCERNING VOLUNTARY ACCREDITING AGENCIES.

8. Composition of NCATE

   The governing boards of NCATE and the regional associations should be significantly broadened to give greater power to (a) representatives of scholarly disciplines in addition to professional education, and to (b) informed representatives of the lay public.

9. Function of NCATE

   NCATE and the regional associations should serve only as advisory bodies to teacher-preparing institutions and local school boards. They should, on the request of institutions, send in teams to study and make recommendations concerning the whole or any portion of a teacher-education program. They should, on the request of local boards, evaluate employment policies. They should provide a forum in which issues concerning teacher education and employment are debated.

If I were to try to characterize in two words the conclusion of my study, these words would be "freedom" and "responsibility." The state should allow each college and university the maximum degree of freedom to develop its own program. Each institution should assume the maximum degree of responsibility for those graduates it certifies as being competent to teach. In the chapters dealing with the preparation of elementary and secondary teachers and in-service education, I have suggested the kinds of programs I have in mind when I refer to an institution's certifying the specific competence of a future teacher. Yet these chapters are not to be taken as blueprints of the one and only way of preparing classroom teachers. Rather, they are submitted as evidence of my contention that teachers can be adequately prepared for initial employment in four years. There may well be alternative programs which would be as good or better.

What I have been arguing for in essence is a competition to see which institution will quickly earn a high reputation for preparing well-trained teachers. Once free competition becomes possible in any state, there will be every reason for the academic professors and the professors of education in each college or university within that state to join hands to enhance the reputation of their particular institution. Before that day arrives, however, laymen will certainly have to enter into the fray in many states, and public opinion must be aroused. Yet in any such endeavor the quarrel among educators must not be made more bitter; the goal is not victory for either side but mutual respect and complete cooperation. Thus while this volume is a call for action, it is also a call for reconciliation. Once the quarreling educators bury their hatchets, the layman may put his present worries aside. That united efforts to prepare better teachers would result in better schools requires no argumentation; that the nation would be the beneficiary of such a revolution is a self-evident proposition.

It's Teacher's Turn in the Corner

FRED M. HECHINGER

A year ago James B. Conant said jokingly that he would not let "The Education of American Teachers" be published before he had a chance to leave the country, "possibly for good." * It is easy to see why: this new book is academic dynamite. It may well turn out to be as revolutionary in the field of teacher education as was the 1910 report by Abraham Flexner, "Medical Education in the United States and Canada," in hastening much needed reforms in American medical schools.

---

* It turned out just that way. Mr. Conant is now in West Berlin as special European educational representative of the Ford Foundation.

New York Times Book Review, September 15, 1963, pp. 1, 52. © 1963 by The New York Times Company. Reprinted by permission.

Few debates about what is wrong with American education have been concluded without angry blasts at the low quality of the teaching of teachers, the mediocrity of professors of education and "those dreadful teachers' colleges." "Academic" professors—the members of the arts and science faculty—talk about the education specialists as licensed physicians talk about quacks, and the educationists reply contemptuously that a Ph.D. does not make a man a teacher.

The name-calling, occasionally interrupted by a truce (usually when both the academicians and the educationists are in trouble), has rarely led to honest self-appraisal and never to far-reaching reforms. The news that Mr. Conant—former Harvard president and gentle, conservative, pragmatic reformer of the public schools—had turned his analytical mind to an examination of the teacher-training enterprise was greeted with the comfortable anticipation that comes from hope for a remedy without painful surgery.

Contrary to such smug expectations, "The Education of American Teachers" recommends not therapy but a drastic operation. Instead of trying diplomatically to renovate the old system, it urges what really amounts to a completely new start.

Why? When Dr. Conant had a close look at the actual facts of teacher education and certification, he was appalled by the weakness and chaos he found. Past attacks and ridicule had failed to describe, much less come to grips with, the real issues.

There is truth in much of the criticism, of course. Some teachers' colleges, as in the familiar parodies, offer courses on the philosophy of education, taught by people who have never studied philosophy. Colleges have permitted doctoral "research" on such subjects as "The Relative Effect of Mental Practice and Physical Practice on Learning the Tennis Forehand and Backhand Drives." In some schools teachers are able to get a salary increase simply by taking any subject that happens to be given at a convenient hour in the afternoon at a nearby college and requires no time-consuming study.

Yet the real causes that make teacher education a shambles go far deeper. They begin with the fact that too large a percentage of the young people who prepare for teaching come from the bottom rather than the top of the barrel of talent. This basic weakness is made worse by an ill-suited, badly supervised plan of studies, not only at the professional teacher-training institutions but at the liberal-arts colleges and all-purpose universities that, contrary to popular belief, actually turn out more of today's teachers than do the teachers' colleges. These deficiencies are aggravated because few of the professors who teach tomorrow's teachers have any real idea of what actually happens in an elementary or high-school classroom. The most devastating criticism to be made of a great number of those who teach teaching is that they are guilty of abominable methods in their own teaching.

Even this is not—as Mr. Conant sees it—the heart of the matter.

Teachers are certified by the separate education departments of each of the 50 states. Every state sets its own standards. In recent years, under the impact of Sputnik, the state-education authorities have tried to toughen standards by tightening the rules—especially by increasing the specific "academic" or "subject-matter" courses required for certification. In practice, these paper rules are often nothing more than a paper tiger.

Many states, for example, added to the number of hours of language study required for the certification of language teachers. Yet even today only two states require proof of speaking competence—rather than of mere course credits—for the accreditation of foreign-language teachers. More serious, most states permit teachers, once they are accredited in one field, to teach just about anything else, regardless of their training. In New York, for instance, a principal may assign a history teacher to one course a day in science, mathematics, or any other subject for which a teacher is needed. As a result of such juggling of the rules the country over, more than one-third of all 7th-grade mathematics classes are taught by teachers who have had less than two general courses of college mathematics.

Noting these and other conditions, Mr. Conant calls the existing certification system "bankrupt." He discovered that "some of our generally best institutions do a very poor job of supervising practice teaching"—even though everybody, whether a partisan of the teachers college or of the arts-and-science faction, agrees that this is the most vital aspect of teacher training.

"In most cases all that the public can know is that the teacher somehow rang up the required number of credits in courses whose catalog descriptions appear to some state education officer to meet the state specifications for courses in professional education, general education, and a field of specialization," the author writes. As for the foundation courses, designed to introduce future teachers to sociology, philosophy, political theory and educational ideology, the kindest word found for them is "pathetic." They lead the young teacher to "the most dangerous of misunderstandings: that he knows what he is talking about when, in fact, he does not."

These were some of the symptoms Mr. Conant discovered. The shock appears to have been responsible for a startling transformation in the man who, after a career as scientist, educator and ambassador, became a kind of national Minister of Educational Renaissance. Superficially he uses the same technique in "The Education of American Teachers" that made "The American High School Today" (1959) the all-American do-it-yourself school-improvement kit. There is the same courteous tolerance for the motives of even those with whom he emphatically disagrees. There is the same device of clearly-stated specific recommendations, almost in cookbook fashion. Yet here the resemblance to the earlier Conant ends.

Instead of attempting to patch up the system, he calls for radical change. Since the state certification rules have failed to offer real quality control and, in fact, often serve as a mere camouflage for inferior performance, Mr. Conant believes they should be scrapped.

The new philosophy proposed in this remarkable book is one of free competition in the training of teachers, combined with clearly pinpointed responsibility for the quality of the product. Once the state certification shibboleth is swept away, three quality-control centers would have to be strengthened:

(1) The colleges and universities, though free to determine the educational program, would vouch with their reputation for every new teacher graduated by their total faculty—the professors of education and the academicians together.

(2) The local school boards, jointly with the colleges and universities, would be held responsible for making expertly supervised practice-teaching and on-the-job training the heart and soul of the specialized professional preparation of teachers.

(3) The state education authorities would keep a watchful eye on the quality of such local internship—and help pay for it. Once fully certified—based on at least four years' carefully observed performance in the classroom—the new teacher would be licensed to teach anywhere in the United States.

The author has borrowed heavily from the experience of medicine. He is convinced that salvation (after selecting candidates among the upper-third of high-school seniors) is in sweeping away pseudo-methodology and shoddy indoctrination, substituting for it the experience of the expert practitioner. He even suggests the new position of "Clinical Professor of Education"—a superior school teacher who never abandons his own classroom but adds to it the practical and theoretical training of the new generation of teachers.

In this classroom-minded scheme of things there is no longer room for the sham of letting school boards pretend that "an odd lot of late-afternoon" extension courses can improve a teacher's real value in the classroom. Mr. Conant knows that his suggestion to do away with such courses would put a stop to one of education's most lucrative boondoggles, but he sees no way of upgrading the continuing education of teachers without abolishing the credit-mills now run by some of the most prestigious institutions.

It would be naive to predict that the author's recommendations for surgery in teacher education will be accepted as readily as was his prescription of vitamins for the high schools. Quite aside from the vested interests that will recognize the threat to their security and power, some dispassionate and legitimate doubts may arise. It may be asked, for instance, to what extent some existing colleges and universities can be trusted to uphold standards of education, if thrown entirely on their sense of professional honor.

Whatever specific details of the Conant program may be rejected or modified, the opening of a national debate is assured. The author's eminence will make impossible the kind of silent treatment with which the Establishment has so often disposed of unfavorable critics. Fortunately, too, Mr. Conant has survived long years in academia with his power of plain English unimpaired, thus making it possible for the layman to join in the discussion.

New Blood, Not Dry Words

HAROLD TAYLOR

American education is in the midst of a crisis deeper than it knows, a crisis many of whose elements are hidden by an intellectual and moral lethargy within the culture and obscured by a driving national ambition for technological, military and economic power. Other elements of the crisis are overt and have expressed themselves in radical form.

The education of the Negro people has now revealed itself as a national scandal, and the evidence of years of neglect is now exploding into public consciousness. It is clear that at least one-third of the entire population, white and black, is receiving a third-rate education, suited to a poor and backward society. We now have thousands of young men and women roaming the slum streets of our big cities, uneducated, unemployed and unemployable. The favored youth of the suburbs drifts on a tide of affluence to the twin ports of status and security. The general level of teaching in our colleges and universities is such that the best students are bored with it and the rest suffer from intellectual malnutrition.

It is therefore with hope and expectation that one turns to the work of one of our most prominent educators for guidance and leadership in solving the problem which lies beneath all other educational problems, the education of the American teacher. The teacher is the source of energy through which every society creates and recreates itself, and the education of the teacher is crucial to the development of that energy.

To those in expectation of leadership, Mr. Conant's new book, written with a staff after two years of investigation and research, will give no comfort. The book has to do not so much with the education of American teachers as with the bookkeeping and administrative arrangements for courses and requirements in the colleges and universities where teachers are being prepared. There are 1,000 of these institutions—public, private, teachers' colleges (100 now exist), universities, liberal arts colleges. They graduate 150,000

New York *Herald Tribune*, Book Week Section, September 15, 1963, pp. 1, 32. Reprinted by permission of the New York *Herald Tribune*.

teachers each year, or nearly one-third of all the graduating students of the country. Mr. Conant and his staff visited a wide cross-section of 77 institutions in 22 states.

"Knowing that the field was highly controversial, I undertook the task with some reluctance," says Mr. Conant in his preface, raising a question in the reader's mind as to whether reluctance to deal with controversy is an appropriate mood for a subject as important as this one. The reluctance shows itself in a number of ways, in the cautious committee-style of the writing (*"much to criticize on both sides of the fence"* [author's italics], "it would be unwise to discount the soundness of at least some of the reasoning") and particularly in the avoidance of all substantive questions in the political, economic or social problems of education and American culture.

The difference in educational preparation between Negro and white teachers, a matter of serious national concern, is given a single footnote to say that it will not be dealt with. The preparation of teachers who will cope with the cruel problems of the slum school receives a single reference in one sentence, "if he [the teacher-candidate] is teaching in a slum school I would advocate that some time be spent on sociology and those aspects of political science and economics which bear on school problems and urban conditions." Elsewhere Mr. Conant refers to the study of the philosophy, history and sociology of education as advisable but not essential components in the education of the teacher—advisable, that is, if taught by regular departmental members of an academic faculty in arts and sciences and not by educators who have specialized in the field.

Mr. Conant's is thus an academic approach to the teacher, and he deliberately restricts himself to the role of, in his words, "an advisor to an all-university committee" and to the task of recommending rearrangements of the customs and rules of the present academies and educational systems.

The major controversy in education, says Mr. Conant, is between the members of the academic faculties of the universities and those professional educators who are linked to the educational establishment—that is, to the professional organizations, accrediting bodies, the colleges for teachers, and the state departments of education. The latter groups are so interlocked that state requirements for obtaining a teaching certificate are usually set by tacit or explicit agreement with the accrediting agencies, and the curriculum for teacher preparation is frozen into rigid and often meaningless patterns.

"What happened after sputnik," says Mr. Conant, "might be characterized as the entry of the layman in force into a battle of professors. What is now involved is more than a quarrel among educators."

What is their quarrel?

It is a quarrel over who sets the requirements for certifying that a candidate is qualified to teach in American public schools. The private schools can appoint any person they believe to be qualified. The public schools are bound by state regulations which, in fact, they manage to avoid by a variety of ruses whenever the pressure of teacher shortages makes compliance difficult.

Mr. Conant's solution is a good one. The present policy of chaotic state requirements, differing from state to state, is bankrupt. It does not insure that there are or will be qualified teachers in the American classroom (for example, near half of all classes in high school biology are now being taught by teachers who have taken three courses or less in the field). It merely guarantees the continuation of many courses which should never have been taught in the first place.

Therefore, says Mr. Conant, reduce to three the requirements for the public school teaching certificate:

1. A baccalaureate degree from a legitimate college.

2. Evidence that the candidate has learned to teach in a practice-teaching program approved by the state department of education.

3. A teaching certificate from a college or university which certifies that it considers the candidate prepared to teach in a designated field and at a given grade level.

At one stroke this would make the institutions responsible for the quality of their own graduates and the content of their education, give greater freedom to faculties and institutions to experiment with better ways of preparing teachers, and create new standards in the public and in the profession for judging the worth of individual institutions.

The only consensus Mr. Conant could find among the academics and the professional educators on the requirements for certifying a teacher was that the teacher should "know his subject" and that he should have had experience in teaching it before he takes his first post. Mr. Conant has found for the professional educators and against the academics—that instruction in the methods of teaching is a crucial part of the preparation of teachers.

His recommendations for learning the methods would eliminate most methods courses and draw upon some of the best work being done in the teacher-training fields. The center of effort must be, he says, in the practice of teaching in the classroom, under the supervision of an experienced member of the teaching staff, chosen for his competence, rewarded for his efforts and freed from other duties. In addition, a member of the university faculty who is a competent scholar in a given field, who teaches in that field at least half his time, and who is fully aware, through experience, of the problems of method and instruction which the student will meet in the classroom, must take responsibility for conducting seminars and individual conferences in methods and materials with the student-teachers, and will certify those who have learned how to teach successfully. An institution which sets out to prepare teachers must have at least three or four such "clinical" professors on its faculty, paid at the regular faculty scale and involved fully in the university life. Otherwise the institution should not try to prepare teachers.

With the basic question of certification out of the way, Mr. Conant turns to the variety of practical problems facing the school systems, the state departments of education, and the institutions where teachers are prepared. In a set of 27 recommendations, ranging from salary scales (larger increases for career teachers) to master's-degree programs, Mr. Conant provides what amounts to a sound manual of instruction for the various parties concerned.

On reading the summary of the recommendations, one is struck by the fact that they record ideas and sentiments which have been in circulation for some time among the more intelligent members of the educational community, and that Mr. Conant has done a service by arguing at such length and so carefully for the necessity of putting such recommendations into effect. The summary can therefore be read with profit, as can the valuable appendix, without reference to the book, and can serve to support reforms and changes which improve the structure of American education.

When he turns to the content of the education of teachers, Mr. Conant is less helpful. Having removed from state departments of education the authority for requiring courses and credits, and having deplored and condemned the American habit of thinking of all education in terms of required courses taken and credits garnered, Mr. Conant immediately sets out to bring back new sets of requirements, which, as he describes them, would be mandatory for all teachers. In the case of the science teachers, Mr. Conant sees no room for anything but regular courses in a four-year program; things are too serious here for electives, or for courses in history, philosophy, sociology, or political science. Psychology is reserved for elementary school teachers; for any other candidates it becomes highly dubious, on the grounds that it does not help the teacher to predict behavior and is thus not scientific.

But Mr. Conant's curricular ideas are at their most hilarious when he comes to the question of the arts. These are included in a catch-all entitled "Foreign Languages, Art, Music and Physical Education." Dance, theater, design, sculpture, painting, writing (except for composition and grammar) are not mentioned. Graduate work in art and music is considered unwise on the grounds that the institutions of education are not yet ready to do advanced work in these fields. It is clear that by music Mr. Conant means blowing trumpets and conducting choral groups, and that art is something one does in art appreciation courses. It is also clear that although Mr. Conant knows, and says he knows, that "liberal education" as practiced in the colleges and universities is a meaningless term (". . . an experience prescribed by a group of professors each of whom has prime allegiance to his academic discipline . . ."), his recommendations for its improvement are to do more of the same while restricting further the freedom of the student to choose his own way.

To do most of the things Mr. Conant wants to do, Federal and state aid on a massive scale is essential. He does not mention it. To install the curriculum

Mr. Conant wants to install would inhibit further those parts of the present curriculum not already paralyzed by convention and regulation.

What is needed is an infusion of new blood into the tired organism of American education, a chance for those who love poetry, theater, science, philosophy or history to teach it to children, a chance for those who wish to enter fully into the life of their time to learn how to do so through teaching. Mr. Conant has tidied up the administrative details and has added the weight of his considered opinion to the side of progress. For this we can only be grateful. But we still need some light on the question of how to educate the American teacher.

Questions

1. Does Hechinger agree or disagree with the burden of Conant's recommendations? What is Taylor's position? Can you find evidence from your own experience to support either Hechinger or Taylor? Be specific.
2. What are the most important recommendations made by Conant? Will Conant's recommendations necessarily result in better teachers? Why? Why not? How would you go about trying to determine whether a person will make a good or a bad teacher?
3. What basic criticism does Taylor make of the language of the Conant report? Is this criticism justified? Be specific.
4. Why does Hechinger label his article "It's Teacher's Turn in the Corner"?
5. What in American education is Conant for or against? Be specific.

Assignments

1. Think of three good teachers you have had (A, B, and C) and of three bad ones (X, Y, and Z). Write a paper in which you describe the qualities in common (if any) the good teachers had and those in common the bad ones had. Discuss briefly whether some of these qualities might be predicted.
2. In three passages of about 150 words each, describe from your own experience the ideal elementary-school teacher, the ideal high-school teacher, and the ideal college teacher.
3. Examine your college catalogue to find, first, the number of persons whose highest degree is the Ph.D.; then, the M.A.; and, finally, the B.A. Tabulate these findings by departments, colleges, or such broad areas as education, arts and humanities, social science, science and technology. Then answer such questions as the following: Are there more Ph.D.'s in one field than another? More B.A.'s? Speculate on the meaning of your findings.
4. Discuss in what significant ways the education of a teacher of music or of painting differs from that of a teacher of physics or of geology.
5. Using your college catalogue, analyze the differences in the required curriculum for elementary-school teachers, high-school teachers, pre-medical or pre-dental students, and pre-law students.

Additional Reading

American education has been widely discussed in recent years. The two extremes on the subject may be said to be represented by the professional educationists and by the anti-educationists. The point of view of the educationists may be found in almost any issue of the *NEA Journal,* the official organ of the National Education Association; that of the anti-educationists may be found in a number of books sponsored by the Council for Basic Education. Admiral Hyman Rickover has written a number of articles and books attacking American education. James Koerner has written *The Miseducation of American Teachers* (Boston, Mass., 1963); and of course James B. Conant, in *The Education of American Teachers* (the conclusion of which is reprinted in this section), has taken up the problem in its various aspects. A symposium on Conant's book, by persons involved in many aspects of education, appeared in the *Journal of Teacher Education,* XV (March, 1964), 5–49. A discussion of the main arguments of both sides may be found in Morris Freedman, "Educationist, Anti-Educationist: A Plague on Both Your Houses," *Confessions of a Conformist* (New York, 1961), pp. 114–132.

SECTION TWO

Young America: Beat, Bored, and Delinquent

The Origins of the Beat Generation

JACK KEROUAC

This article necessarily'll have to be about myself. I'm going all out.

That nutty picture of me on the cover of *On the Road* results from the fact that I had just gotten down from a high mountain where I'd been for two months completely alone and usually I was in the habit of combing my hair of course because you have to get rides on the highway and all that and you usually want girls to look at you as though you were a man and not a wild beast but my poet friend Gregory Corso opened his shirt and took out a silver crucifix that was hanging from a chain and said "Wear this and wear it outside your shirt and don't comb your hair!" so I spent several days around San Francisco going around with him and others like that, to parties, arties, parts, jam sessions, bars, poetry readings, churches, walking talking poetry in the streets, walking talking God in the streets (and at one point a strange gang of hoodlums got mad and said "What right does he got to wear that?" and my own gang of musicians and poets told them to cool it) and finally on the third day *Mademoiselle* magazine wanted to take pictures of us all so I posed just like that, wild hair, crucifix, and all, with Gregory Corso, Allen Ginsberg and Phil Whalen, and the only publication which later did not erase the crucifix from my breast (from that plaid sleeveless cotton shirtfront) was *The New York Times*, therefore *The New York Times* is as beat as I am, and I'm glad I've got a friend. I mean it sincerely, God bless *The New York Times* for not erasing the crucifix from my picture as though it was something distasteful. As a matter of fact, who's *really* beat around here, I mean if you wanta talk of Beat as "beat down" the people who erased the crucifix are really the "beat down" ones and not *The New York Times*, myself, and Gregory Corso the poet. I am not ashamed to wear the crucifix of my Lord. It is because I am Beat, that is, I believe in beatitude and that God so loved the world that he gave his only begotten son to it. I am sure no priest would've condemned me for wearing the crucifix outside my shirt everywhere and *no matter where* I went, even to have my picture taken by *Mademoiselle*. So you people don't believe in God. So you're all big smart know-it-all Marxists and Freudians, hey? Why don't you come back in a million years and tell me all about it, angels?

Recently Ben Hecht said to me on TV "Why are you afraid to speak out your mind, what's wrong with this country, what is everybody afraid of?" Was he talking to me? And all he wanted me to do was speak out my mind *against* people, he sneeringly brought up Dulles, Eisenhower, the Pope, all kinds of people like that habitually he would sneer at with Drew Pearson, *against* the world he wanted, this is his idea of freedom, he calls it freedom. Who knows, my God, but that the universe is not one vast sea of compassion actually, the veritable holy honey, beneath all this show of personality and cruelty. In fact who knows but that it isn't the solitude of the oneness of the essence of everything, the solitude of the actual oneness of the unbornness of the unborn essence of everything, nay the true pure foreverhood, that big blank potential that can ray forth anything it wants from its pure store, that blazing bliss, *Mattivajrakaruna* the Transcendental Diamond Compassion! No, I want to speak *for* things, for the crucifix I speak out, for the Star of Israel I speak out, for the divinest man who ever lived who was a German (Bach) I speak out, for sweet Mohammed I speak out, for Buddha I speak out, for Lao-tse and Chuang-tse I speak out, for D. T. Suzuki I speak out . . . why should I attack what I love out of life. This is Beat. Live your lives out? Naw, *love* your lives out. When they come and stone you at least you won't have a glass house, just your glassy flesh.

That wild eager picture of me on the cover of *On the Road* where I look so Beat goes back much further than 1948 when John Clellon Holmes (author of *Go* and *The Horn*) and I were sitting around trying to think up the meaning of the Lost Generation and the subsequent Existentialism and I said "You know, this is really a beat generation" and he leapt up and said "That's it, that's right!" It goes back to the 1880s when my grandfather Jean-Baptiste Kerouac used to go out on the porch in big thunderstorms and swing his kerosene lamp at the lightning and yell "Go ahead, go, if you're more powerful than I am strike me and put the light out!" while the mother and the children cowered in the kitchen. And the light never went out. Maybe since I'm supposed to be the spokesman of the Beat Generation (I *am* the originator of the term, and around it the term and the generation have taken shape) it should be pointed out that all this "Beat" guts therefore goes back to my ancestors who were

Bretons who were the most independent group of nobles in all old Europe and kept fighting Latin France to the last wall (although a big blond bosun on a merchant ship snorted when I told him my ancestors were Bretons in Cornwall, Brittany, "Why, we Wikings used to swoop down and steal your nets!") Breton, Wiking, Irishman, Indian, madboy, it doesn't make any difference, there is no doubt about the Beat Generation, at least the core of it, being a swinging group of new American men intent on joy . . . Irresponsibility? Who wouldn't help a dying man on an empty road? No and the Beat Generation goes back to the wild parties my father used to have at home in the 1920s and 1930s in New England that were so fantastically loud nobody could sleep for blocks around and when the cops came they always had a drink. It goes back to the wild and raving childhood of playing the Shadow under windswept trees of New England's gleeful autumn, and the howl of the Moon Man on the sandbank until we caught him in a tree (he was an "older" guy of 15), the maniacal laugh of certain neighborhood madboys, the furious humor of whole gangs playing basketball till long after dark in the park, it goes back to those crazy days before World War II when teenagers drank beer on Friday nights at Lake ballrooms and worked off their hangovers playing baseball on Saturday afternoon followed by a dive in the brook—and our fathers wore straw hats like W. C. Fields. It goes back to the completely senseless babble of the Three Stooges, the ravings of the Marx Brothers (the tenderness of Angel Harpo at harp, too).

It goes back to the inky ditties of old cartoons (Krazy Kat with the irrational brick)—to Laurel and Hardy in the Foreign Legion—to Count Dracula and his *smile* to Count Dracula shivering and hissing back before the Cross—to the Golem horrifying the persecutors of the Ghetto—to the quiet sage in a movie about India, unconcerned about the plot—to the giggling old Tao Chinaman trotting down the sidewalk of old Clark Gable Shanghai—to the holy old Arab warning the hotbloods that Ramadan is near. To the Werewolf of London a distinguished doctor in his velour smoking jacket smoking his pipe over a lamplit tome on botany and suddenly hairs grown on his hands, his cat hisses, and he slips out into the night with a cape and a slanty cap like the caps of people in breadlines—to Lamont Cranston so cool and sure suddenly becoming the frantic Shadow going mwee hee hee ha ha in the alleys of New York imagination. To Popeye the sailor and the Sea Hag and the meaty gunwales of boats, to Cap'n Easy and Wash Tubbs screaming with ecstasy over canned peaches on a cannibal isle, to Wimpy looking X-eyed for a juicy hamburger such as they make no more. To Jiggs ducking before a household of furniture flying through the air, to Jiggs and the boys at the bar and the corned beef and cabbage of old woodfence noons—to King Kong his eyes looking into the hotel window with tender huge love for Fay Wray—nay, to Bruce Cabot in mate's cap leaning over the rail of a fogbound ship saying "Come aboard." It goes back to when grapefruits were thrown at crooners and harvestworkers at bar-rails slapped burlesque queens on the rump. To when fathers took their sons to the Twi League game. To the days of Babe Callahan on the waterfront, Dick Barthelmess camping under a London street-lamp. To dear old Basil Rathbone looking for the Hound of the Baskervilles (a dog big as the Gray Wolf who will destroy Odin)—to dear old bleary Doctor Watson with a brandy in his hand. To Joan Crawford her raw shanks in the fog, in striped blouse smoking a cigarette at sticky lips in the door of the waterfront dive. To train whistles of steam engines out above the moony pines. To Maw and Paw in the Model A clanking on to get a job in California selling used cars making a whole lotta money. To the glee of America, the honesty of America, the honesty of oldtime grafters in straw hats as well as the honesty of oldtime waiters in line at the Brooklyn Bridge in *Winterset*, the funny spitelessness of old bigfisted America like Big Boy Williams saying "Hoo? Hee? Huh?" in a movie about Mack Trucks and slidingdoor lunchcarts. To Clark Gable, his certain smile, his confident leer. Like my grandfather this America was invested with wild selfbelieving individuality and this had begun to disappear around the end of World War II with so many great guys dead (I can think of half a dozen from my own boyhood groups) when suddenly it began to emerge again, the hipsters began to appear gliding around saying "Crazy, man."

When I first saw the hipsters creeping around Times Square in 1944 I didn't like them either. One of them, Huncke of Chicago, came up to me and said "Man, I'm beat." I knew right away what he meant somehow. At that time I still didn't like bop which was then being introduced by Bird Parker and Dizzy Gillespie and Bags Jackson (on vibes), the last of the great swing musicians was Don Byas who went to Spain right after, but then I began . . . but earlier I'd dug all my jazz in the old Minton Playhouse (Lester Young, Ben Webster, Joey Guy, Charlie Christian, others) and when I first heard Bird and Diz in the Three Deuces I knew they were serious musicians playing a goofy new sound and didn't care what I thought, or what my friend Seymour thought. In fact I was leaning against the bar with a beer when Dizzy came over for a glass of water from the bartender, put himself right against me and reached both arms around both sides of my head to get the glass and danced away, as though knowing I'd be singing about him someday, or that one of his arrangements would be named after me someday by some goofy circumstance. Charlie Parker was spoken of in Harlem as the greatest new musician since Chu Berry and Louis Armstrong.

Anyway, the hipsters, whose music was bop, they looked like criminals but they kept talking about the same things I liked, long outlines of personal experience and vision, nightlong confessions full of hope that had become illicit and repressed by War, stirrings, rumblings of a new soul (that same old human soul). And so Huncke appeared to us and said "I'm beat" with radiant light shining out of his despairing eyes . . . a word perhaps brought from some wildwest carnival or junk cafeteria. It was a new language, actually spade (Negro) jargon but you soon learned it, like "hung up" couldn't be a more economical term to mean so many things. Some of these hipsters were raving mad and talked continually. It was jazzy. Symphony Sid's all-night modern jazz and bop show was always on. By 1948 it began to take shape. That was a wild vibrating year when a group of us would walk down the street and yell hello and even stop and talk to anybody that gave us a friendly look. The hipsters had eyes. That was the year I saw Montgomery Clift, unshaven, wearing a sloppy jacket, slouching down Madison Avenue with a companion. It was the year I saw Charley Bird Parker strolling down Eighth Avenue in a black turtleneck sweater with Babs Gonzales and a beautiful girl.

By 1948 the hipsters, or beatsters, were divided into cool and hot. Much of the misunderstanding about hipsters and the Beat Generation in general today derives from the fact that there are two distinct styles of hipsterism: the cool today is your bearded laconic sage, or schlerm, before a hardly touched beer in a beatnik dive, whose speech is low and unfriendly, whose girls say nothing and wear black: the "hot" today is the crazy talkative shining eyed (often innocent and openhearted) nut who runs from bar to bar, pad to pad looking for everybody, shouting, restless, lushy, trying to "make it" with the subterranean beatniks who ignore him. Most Beat Generation artists belong to the hot school, naturally since that hard gemlike flame needs a little heat. In many cases the mixture is 50–50. It was a hot hipster like myself who finally cooled it in Buddhist meditation, though when I go in a jazz joint I still feel like yelling "Blow baby blow!" to the musicians though nowadays I'd get 86d for this. In 1948 the "hot hipsters" were racing around in cars like in *On the Road* looking for wild bawling jazz like Willis Jackson or Lucky Thompson (the early) or Chubby Jackson's big band while the "cool hipsters" cooled it in dead silence before formal and excellent musical groups like Lennie Tristano or Miles Davis. It's still just about the same, except that it has begun to grow into a national generation and the name "Beat" has stuck (though all hipsters hate the word).

The word "beat" originally meant poor, down and out, deadbeat, on the bum, sad, sleeping in subways. Now that the word is belonging officially it is being made to stretch to include people who do not sleep in subways but have a certain new gesture, or attitude, which I can only describe as a new *more*. "Beat Generation" has simply become the slogan or label for a revolution in manners in America. Marlon Brando was not really first to portray it on the screen. Dane Clark with his pinched Dostoievskyan face and Brooklyn accent, and of course Garfield, were first. The private eyes were Beat, if you will recall. Bogart. Lorre was Beat. In *M*, Peter Lorre started a whole revival, I mean the slouchy street walk.

I wrote *On the Road* in three weeks in the beautiful month of May 1951 while living in the Chelsea district of lower West Side Manhattan, on a 100-foot roll and put the Beat Generation in words in there, saying at the point where I am taking part in a wild kind of collegiate party with a bunch of kids in an abandoned miner's shack "These kids are great but where are Dean

Moriarty and Carlo Marx? Oh well I guess they wouldn't belong in this gang, they're too *dark,* too strange, too subterranean and I am slowly beginning to join a new kind of *beat* generation." The manuscript of *Road* was turned down on the grounds that it would displease the sales manager of my publisher at that time, though the editor, a very intelligent man, said "Jack this is just like Dostoievsky, but what can I do at this time?" It was too early. So for the next six years I was a bum, a brakeman, a seaman, a panhandler, a pseudo-Indian in Mexico, anything and everything, and went on writing because my hero was Goethe and I believed in art and hoped some day to write the third part of *Faust,* which I have done in *Doctor Sax.* Then in 1952 an article was published in *The New York Times* Sunday magazine saying, the headline, " 'This is a Beat Generation' " (in quotes like that) and in the article it said that I had come up with the term first "when the face was harder to recognize," the face of the generation. After that there was some talk of the Beat Generation but in 1955 I published an excerpt from *Road* (melling it with parts of *Visions of Neal*) under the pseudonym "Jean-Louis," it was entitled *Jazz of the Beat Generation* and was copyrighted as being an excerpt from a novel-in-progress entitled *Beat Generation* (which I later changed to *On the Road* at the insistence of my new editor) and so then the term moved a little faster. The term and the cats. Everywhere began to appear strange hepcats and even college kids went around hep and cool and using the terms I'd heard on Times Square in the early Forties, it was growing somehow. But when the publishers finally took a dare and published *On the Road* in 1957 it burst open, it mushroomed, everybody began yelling about a Beat Generation. I was being interviewed everywhere I went for "what I meant" by such a thing. People began to call themselves beatniks, beats, jazzniks, bopniks, bugniks and finally I was called the "avatar" of all this.

Yet it was as a Catholic, it was not at the insistence of any of these "niks" and certainly not with their approval either, that I went one afternoon to the church of my childhood (one of them), Ste. Jeanne D'Arc in Lowell, Mass., and suddenly with tears in my eyes and had a vision of what I must have really meant with "Beat" anyhow when I heard the holy silence in the church (I was the only one in there, it was five P.M., dogs were barking outside, children yelling, the fall leaves, the candles were flickering alone just for me), the vision of the word Beat as being to mean beatific . . . There's the priest preaching on Sunday morning, all of a sudden through a side door of the church comes a group of Beat Generation characters in strapped raincoats like the I.R.A. coming in silently to "dig" the religion . . . I knew it then.

But this was 1954, so then what horror I felt in 1957 and later 1958 naturally to suddenly see "Beat" being taken up by everybody, press and TV and Hollywood borscht circuit to include the "juvenile delinquency" shot and the horrors of a mad teeming billyclub New York and L.A. and they began to call *that* Beat, *that* beatific . . . bunch of fools marching against the San Francisco Giants protesting baseball, as if (now) in my name and I, my childhood ambition to be a big league baseball star hitter like Ted Williams so that when Bobby Thomson hit that home-run in 1951 I trembled with joy and couldn't get over it for days and wrote poems about how it is possible for the human spirit to win after all! Or, when a murder, a routine murder took place in North Beach, they labeled it a Beat Generation slaying although in my childhood I'd been famous as an eccentric in my block for stopping the younger kids from throwing rocks at the squirrels, for stopping them from frying snakes in cans or trying to blow up frogs with straws. Because my brother had died at the age of nine, his name was Gerard Kerouac, and he'd told me "Ti Jean never hurt any living being, all living beings whether it's just a little cat or squirrel or whatever, all, are going to heaven straight into God's snowy arms so never hurt anything and if you see anybody hurt anything stop them as best you can" and when he died a file of gloomy nuns in black from St. Louis de France parish had filed (1926) to his deathbed to hear his last words about Heaven. And my father too, Leo, had never lifted a hand to punish me, or to punish the little pets in our house, and this teaching was delivered to me by the men in my house and I have never had anything to do with violence, hatred, cruelty, and all that horrible nonsense which, nevertheless, because God is gracious beyond all human imagining, he will forgive in the long end . . . that million years I'm asking about you, America.

And so now they have beatnik routines on TV, starting with satires about girls in black and fellows in jeans with snapknives and sweatshirts and swastikas tattooed under their armpits, it will come to respectable m.c.s of spectaculars coming out nattily attired in Brooks Brothers jean-type tailoring and sweater-type pull-ons, in other words, it's a simple change in fashion and manners, just a history crust—like from the Age of Reason, from old Voltaire in a chair to romantic Chatterton in the moonlight—from Teddy Roosevelt to Scott Fitzgerald . . . So there's nothing to get excited about. Beat comes out, actually, of old American whoopee and it will only change a few dresses and pants and make chairs useless in the livingroom and pretty soon we'll have Beat Secretaries of State and there will be instituted new tinsels, in fact new reasons for malice and new reasons for virtue and new reasons for forgiveness . . .

But yet, but yet, woe, woe unto those who think that the Beat Generation means crime, delinquency, immorality, amorality . . . woe unto those who attack it on the grounds that they simply don't understand history and the yearnings of human souls . . . woe unto those who don't realize that America must, will, is, changing now for the better I say. Woe unto those who believe in the atom bomb, who believe in hating mothers and fathers, who deny the most important of the Ten Commandments, woe unto those (though) who don't believe in the unbelievable sweetness of sex love, woe unto those who are the standard bearers of death, woe unto those who believe in conflict and horror and violence and fill our books and screens and livingrooms with all that crap, woe in fact unto those who make evil movies about the Beat Generation where innocent housewives are raped by beatniks! Woe unto those who are the real dreary sinners that even God finds room to forgive . . . woe unto those who spit on the Beat Generation, the wind'll blow it back.

The Know-Nothing Bohemians

NORMAN PODHORETZ

Allen Ginsberg's little volume of poems, *Howl*, which got the San Francisco renaissance off to a screaming start a year or so ago, was dedicated to Jack Kerouac ("new Buddha of American prose, who spit forth intelligence into eleven books written in half the number of years . . . creating a spontaneous bop prosody and original classic literature"), William Seward Burroughs ("author of *Naked Lunch*, an endless novel which will drive everybody mad"), and Neal Cassady ("author of *The First Third*, an autobiography . . . which enlightened Buddha"). So far, everybody's sanity has been spared by the inability of *Naked Lunch* to find a publisher, and we may never get the chance to discover what Buddha learned from Neal Cassady's autobiography, but thanks to the Viking and Grove Presses, two of Kerouac's original classics, *On the Road* and *The Subterraneans*, have now been revealed to the world. When *On the Road* appeared last year, Gilbert Milstein commemorated the event in the New York *Times* by declaring it to be "a historic occasion" comparable to the publication of *The Sun Also Rises* in the 1920's. But even before the novel was actually published, the word got around that Kerouac was the spokesman of a new group of rebels and Bohemians who called themselves the Beat Generation, and soon his photogenic countenance (unshaven, of course, and topped by an unruly crop of rich black hair falling over his forehead) was showing up in various mass-circulation magazines, he was being interviewed earnestly on television, and he was being featured in a Greenwich Village nightclub where, in San Francisco fashion, he read specimens of his spontaneous bop prosody against a background of jazz music.

Though the nightclub act reportedly flopped, *On the Road* sold well enough to hit the best-seller lists for several weeks, and it isn't hard to understand why. Americans love nothing so much as representative documents, and what could be more interesting in this Age of Sociology than a novel that speaks for the "young generation?" (The fact that Kerouac is

Partisan Review, XXV (Spring 1958), 305–311, 313–316, 318. Reprinted by permission of the *Partisan Review* and the author.

thirty-five or thereabouts was generously not held against him.) Beyond that, however, I think that the unveiling of the Beat Generation was greeted with a certain relief by many people who had been disturbed by the notorious respectability and "maturity" of post-war writing. This was more like it—restless, rebellious, confused youth living it up, instead of thin, balding, buttoned-down instructors of English composing ironic verses with one hand while changing the baby's diapers with the other. Bohemianism is not particularly fashionable nowadays, but the image of Bohemia still exerts a powerful fascination—nowhere more so than in the suburbs, which are filled to overflowing with men and women who uneasily think of themselves as conformists and of Bohemianism as the heroic road. The whole point of *Marjorie Morningstar* was to assure the young marrieds of Mamaroneck that they were better off than the apparently glamorous *luftmenschen of* Greenwich Village, and the fact that Wouk had to work so hard at making this idea seem convincing is a good indication of the strength of prevailing doubt on the matter.

On the surface, at least, the Bohemianism of *On the Road* is very attractive. Here is a group of high-spirited young men running back and forth across the country (mostly hitch-hiking, sometimes in their own second-hand cars), going to "wild" parties in New York and Denver and San Francisco, living on a shoe-string (GI educational benefits, an occasional fifty bucks from a kindly aunt, an odd job as a typist, a fruit-picker, a parking-lot attendant), talking intensely about love and God and salvation, getting high on marijuana (but never heroin or cocaine), listening feverishly to jazz in crowded little joints, and sleeping freely with beautiful girls. Now and again there is a reference to gloom and melancholy, but the characteristic note struck by Kerouac is exuberance:

> We stopped along the road for a bite to eat. The cowboy went off to have a spare tire patched, and Eddie and I sat down in a kind of homemade diner. I heard a great laugh, the greatest laugh in the world, and here came this rawhide oldtimes Nebraska farmer with a bunch of other boys into the diner; you could hear his raspy cries clear across the plains, across the whole gray world of them that day. Everybody else laughed with him. He didn't have a care in the world and had the hugest regard for everybody. I said to myself, Wham, listen to that man laugh. That's the West, here I am in the West. He came booming into the diner, calling Maw's name, and she made the sweetest cherry pie in Nebraska, and I had some with a mountainous scoop of ice cream on top. "Maw, rustle me up some grub afore I have to start eatin myself or some damn silly idee like that." And he threw himself on a stool and went hyaw hyaw hyaw hyaw. "And throw some beans in it." It was the spirit of the West sitting right next to me. I wished I knew his whole raw life and what the hell he'd been doing all these years besides laughing and yelling like that. Whooee, I told my soul, and the cowboy came back and off we went to Grand Island.

Kerouac's enthusiasm for the Nebraska farmer is part of his general readiness to find the source of all vitality and virtue in simple rural types and in the dispossessed urban groups (Negroes, bums, whores). His idea of life in New

York is "millions and millions hustling forever for a buck among themselves . . . grabbing, taking, giving, sighing, dying, just so they could be buried in those awful cemetery cities beyond Long Island City," whereas the rest of America is populated almost exclusively by the true of heart. There are intimations here of a kind of know-nothing populist sentiment, but in other ways this attitude resembles Nelson Algren's belief that bums and whores and junkies are more interesting than white-collar workers or civil servants. The difference is that Algren hates middle-class respectability for moral and political reasons—the middle class exploits and persecutes—while Kerouac, who is thoroughly unpolitical, seems to feel that respectability is a sign not of moral corruption but of spiritual death. "The only people for me," says Sal Paradise, the narrator of *On the Road*, "are the mad ones, the ones who are mad to live, mad to talk, mad to be saved, desirous of everything at the same time, the ones who never yawn or say a commonplace thing, but burn, burn, burn like fabulous yellow roman candles exploding like spiders across the stars. . . ." This tremendous emphasis on emotional intensity, this notion that to be hopped-up is the most desirable of all human conditions, lies at the heart of the Beat Generation ethos and distinguishes it radically from the Bohemianism of the past.

The Bohemianism of the 1920's represented a repudiation of the provinciality, philistinism, and moral hypocrisy of American life—a life, incidentally, which was still essentially small-town and rural in tone. Bohemia, in other words, was a movement created in the name of civilization: its ideals were intelligence, cultivation, spiritual refinement. The typical literary figure of the 1920's was a midwesterner (Hemingway, Fitzgerald, Sinclair Lewis, Eliot, Pound) who had fled from his home town to New York or Paris in search of a freer, more expansive, more enlightened way of life than was possible in Ohio or Minnesota or Michigan. The political radicalism that supplied the characteristic coloring of Bohemianism in the 1930's did nothing to alter the urban, cosmopolitan bias of the 1920's. At its best, the radicalism of the 1930's was marked by deep intellectual seriousness and aimed at a state of society in which the fruits of civilization would be more widely available— and ultimately available to all.

The Bohemianism of the 1950's is another kettle of fish altogether. It is hostile to civilization; it worships primitivism, instinct, energy, "blood." To the extent that it has intellectual interests at all, they run to mystical doctrines, irrationalist philosophies, and left-wing Reichianism. The only art the new Bohemians have any use for is jazz, mainly of the cool variety. Their predilection for bop language is a way of demonstrating solidarity with the primitive vitality and spontaneity they find in jazz and of expressing contempt for coherent, rational discourse which, being a product of the mind, is in their view a form of death. To be articulate is to admit that you have no feelings (for how can real feelings be expressed in syntactical language?), that you can't respond to anything (Kerouac responds to everything by saying "Wow!"), and that you are probably impotent.

At the one end of the spectrum, this ethos shades off into violence and criminality, main-line drug addiction and madness. Allen Ginsberg's poetry, with its lurid apocalyptic celebration of "angel-headed hipsters," speaks for the darker side of the new Bohemianism. Kerouac is milder. He shows little taste for violence, and the criminality he admires is the harmless kind. The hero of *On the Road*, Dean Moriarty, has a record: "From the age of eleven to seventeen he was usually in reform school. His specialty was stealing cars, gunning for girls coming out of high school in the afternoon, driving them out to the mountains, making them, and coming back to sleep in any available hotel bathtub in town." But Dean's criminality, we are told, "was not something that sulked and sneered; it was a wild yea-saying overburst of American joy; it was Western, the west wind, an ode from the Plains, something new, long prophesied, long a-coming (he only stole cars for joy rides)." And, in fact, the species of Bohemian that Kerouac writes about is on the whole rather law-abiding. In *The Subterraneans*, a bunch of drunken boys steal a pushcart in the middle of the night, and when they leave it in front of a friend's apartment building, he denounces them angrily for "screwing up the security of my pad." When Sal Paradise (in *On the Road*) steals some groceries from the canteen of an itinerant workers' camp in which he has taken a temporary job as a barracks guard, he comments, "I suddenly began to realize that everybody in America is a natural-born thief"—which, of course, is a way of turning his own stealing into a bit of boyish prankishness. Nevertheless, Kerouac is attracted to criminality, and that in itself is more significant than the fact that he personally feels constrained to put the brakes on his own destructive impulses.

Sex has always played a very important role in Bohemianism: sleeping around was the Bohemian's most dramatic demonstration of his freedom from conventional moral standards, and a defiant denial of the idea that sex was permissible only in marriage and then only for the sake of a family. At the same time, to be "promiscuous" was to assert the validity of sexual experience in and for itself. The "meaning" of Bohemian sex, then, was at once social and personal, a crucial element in the Bohemian's ideal of civilization. Here again the contrast with Beat Generation Bohemianism is sharp. On the one hand, there is a fair amount of sexual activity in *On the Road* and *The Subterraneans*. Dean Moriarty is a "new kind of American saint" at least partly because of his amazing sexual power: he can keep three women satisfied simultaneously and he can make love any time, anywhere (once he mounts a girl in the back seat of a car while poor Sal Paradise is trying to sleep in front). Sal, too, is always on the make, and though he isn't as successful as the great Dean, he does pretty well: offhand I can remember a girl in Denver, one on a bus, and another in New York, but a little research would certainly unearth a few more. The heroine of *The Subterraneans*, a Negro girl named Mardou Fox, seems to have switched from one to another member of the same gang and back again ("This has been an incestuous group in its time"), and we are given to understand that there is nothing unusual about such an arrangement. But the point of all this hustle and bustle is not freedom from ordinary social restrictions or defiance of convention (except in relation to homosexuality, which is Ginsberg's preserve: among "the best minds" of Ginsberg's generation who were destroyed by America are those "who let themselves be _____ in the _____ by saintly motorcyclists, and screamed with joy, / who blew and were blown by those human seraphim, the sailors, caresses of Atlantic and Caribbean love"). The sex in Kerouac's book goes hand in hand with a great deal of talk about forming permanent relationships ("although I have a hot feeling sexually and all that for her," says the poet Adam Moorad in *The Subterraneans*, "I really don't want to get any further into her not only for these reasons but finally, the big one, if I'm going to get involved with a girl now I want to be permanent like permanent and serious and long termed and I can't do that with her"), and a habit of getting married and then duly divorced and re-married when another girl comes along. In fact, there are as many marriages and divorces in *On the Road* as in the Hollywood movie colony (must be that California climate): "All those years I was looking for the woman I wanted to marry," Sal Paradise tells us. "I couldn't meet a girl without saying to myself, What kind of wife would she make?" Even more revealing is Kerouac's refusal to admit that any of his characters ever make love wantonly or lecherously—no matter how casual the encounter it must always entail sweet feelings toward the girl. Sal, for example, is fixed up with Rita Bettencourt in Denver, whom he has never met before. "I got her in my bedroom after a long talk in the dark of the front room. She was a nice little girl, simple and true [naturally], and tremendously frightened of sex. I told her it was beautiful. I wanted to prove this to her. She let me prove it, but I was too impatient and proved nothing. She sighed in the dark. 'What do you want out of life?' I asked, and I used to ask that all the time of girls." This is rather touching, but only because the narrator is really just as frightened of sex as that nice little girl was. He is frightened of failure and he worries about his performance. For *performance* is the point—performance and "good orgasms," which are the first duty of man and the only duty of woman. What seems to be involved here, in short, is sexual anxiety of enormous proportions—an anxiety that comes out very clearly in *The Subterraneans*, which is about a love affair between the young writer, Leo Percepied, and the Negro girl, Mardou Fox. Despite its protestations, the book is one long agony of fear and trembling over sex:

> I spend long nights and many hours making her, finally I have her, I pray for it to come, I can hear her breathing harder, I hope against hope it's time, a noise in the hall (or whoop of drunkards next door) takes her mind off and she can't make it and laughs—but when she does make it I hear her crying, whimpering, the shuddering electrical female orgasm makes her sound like a little girl crying, moaning in the night, it lasts a good twenty seconds and when it's over she moans, "O why can't it last longer," and "O when will I when you do?"—"Soon now I bet," I said, "you're getting closer and closer"—

Very primitive, very spontaneous, very elemental, very beat.

For the new Bohemians interracial friendships and love affairs apparently play the same role of social defiance that sex used to play in older Bohemian circles. Negroes and whites associate freely on a basis of complete equality and without a trace of racial hostility. But putting it that way understates the case, for not only is there no racial hostility, there is positive adulation for the "happy, true-hearted ecstatic Negroes of America."

> At lilac evening I walked with every muscle aching among the lights of 27th and Welton in the Denver colored section, wishing I were a Negro, feeling that the best the white world had offered was not enough ecstasy for me, not enough life, joy, kicks, darkness, music, not enough night. . . . I wished I were a Denver Mexican, or even a poor overworked Jap, anything but what I was so drearily, a "white man" disillusioned. All my life I'd had white ambitions. . . . I passed the dark porches of Mexican and Negro homes; soft voices were there, occasionally the dusky knee of some mysterious sensuous gal; and dark faces of the men behind rose arbors. Little children sat like sages in ancient rocking chairs.

It will be news to the Negroes to learn that they are so happy and ecstatic; I doubt if a more idyllic picture of Negro life has been painted since certain Southern ideologues tried to convince the world that things were just as fine as fine could be for the slaves on the old plantation. Be that as it may, Kerouac's love for Negroes and other dark-skinned groups is tied up with his worship of primitivism, not with any radical social attitudes. Ironically enough, in fact, to see the Negro as more elemental than the white man, as Ned Polsky has acutely remarked, is "an inverted form of keeping the nigger in his place." But even if it were true that American Negroes, by virtue of their position in our culture, have been able to retain a degree of primitive spontaneity, the last place you would expect to find evidence of this is among Bohemian Negroes. Bohemianism, after all, is for the Negro a means of entry into the world of the whites, and no Negro Bohemian is going to cooperate in the attempt to identify him with Harlem or Dixieland. The only major Negro character in either of Kerouac's two novels is Mardou Fox, and she is about as primitive as Wilhelm Reich himself.

The plain truth is that the primitivism of the Beat Generation serves first of all as a cover for an anti-intellectualism so bitter that it makes the ordinary American's hatred of eggheads seem positively benign. Kerouac and his friends like to think of themselves as intellectuals ("they are intellectual as hell and know all about Pound without being pretentious or talking too much about it"), but this is only a form of newspeak. Here is an example of what Kerouac considers intelligent discourse—"formal and shining and complete, without the tedious intellectualness":

> We passed a little kid who was throwing stones at the cars in the road. "Think of it," said Dean. "One day he'll put a stone through a man's windshield and the man will crash and die—all on account of that little kid. You see what I

mean? God exists without qualms. As we roll along this way I am positive beyond doubt that everything will be taken care of for us—that even you, as you drive, fearful of the wheel . . . the thing will go along of itself and you won't go off the road and I can sleep. Furthermore we know America, we're at home; I can go anywhere in America and get what I want because it's the same in every corner, I know the people, I know what they do. We give and take and go in the incredibly complicated sweetness zigzagging every side."

You see what he means? Formal and shining and complete. No tedious intellectualness. Completely unpretentious. "There was nothing clear about the things he said but what he meant to say was somehow made pure and clear." *Somehow*. Of course. If what he wanted to say had been carefully thought out and precisely articulated, that would have been tedious and pretentious and, no doubt, *somehow* unclear and clearly impure. But so long as he utters these banalities with his tongue tied and with no comprehension of their meaning, so long as he makes noises that came out of his soul (since they couldn't possibly have come out of his mind), he passes the test of true intellectuality.

Which brings us to Kerouac's spontaneous bop prosody. This "prosody" is not to be confused with bop language itself, which has such a limited vocabulary (Basic English is a verbal treasurehouse by comparison) that you couldn't write a note to the milkman in it, much less a novel. Kerouac, however, manages to remain true to the spirit of hipster slang while making forays into enemy territory (i.e., the English language) by his simple inability to express anything in words. The only method he has of describing an object is to summon up the same half-dozen adjectives over and over again: "greatest," "tremendous," "crazy," "mad," "wild," and perhaps one or two others. When it's more than just mad or crazy or wild, it becomes "really mad" or "really crazy" or "really wild." (All quantities in excess of three, incidentally, are subsumed under the rubric "innumerable," a word used innumerable times in *On the Road* but not so innumerably in *The Subterraneans*.) The same poverty of resources is apparent in those passages where Kerouac tries to handle a situation involving even slightly complicated feelings. His usual tactic is to run for cover behind cliché and vague signals to the reader. For instance: "I looked at him; my eyes were watering with embarrassment and tears. Still he stared at me. Now his eyes were blank and looking through me. . . . Something clicked in both of us. In me it was suddenly concern for a man who was years younger than I, five years, and whose fate was wound with mine across the passage of the recent years; in him it was a matter that I can ascertain only from what he did afterward." If you can ascertain what this is all about, either beforehand, during, or afterward, you are surely no square.

In keeping with its populistic bias, the style of *On the Road* is folksy and lyrical. The prose of *The Subterraneans,* on the other hand, sounds like an inept parody of Faulkner at his worst, the main difference being that Faulkner usually produces bad writing out of an impulse to inflate the commonplace while Kerouac gets into trouble by pursuing "spontaneity." Strictly speaking, spontaneity is a quality of feeling, not of writing: when we call a piece of writing spontaneous, we are registering our impression that the author hit upon the right words without sweating, that no "art" and no calculation entered into the picture, that his feelings seem to have spoken themselves, seem to have sprouted a tongue at the moment of composition. Kerouac apparently thinks that spontaneity is a matter of saying whatever comes into your head, in any order you happen to feel like saying it. It isn't the *right* words he wants (even if he knows what they might be), but the first words, or at any rate the words that most obviously announce themselves as deriving from emotion rather than cerebration, as coming from "life" rather than "literature," from the guts rather than the brain. (The brain, remember, is the angel of death.) But writing that springs easily and "spontaneously" out of strong feelings is *never* vague; it always has a quality of sharpness and precision because it is in the nature of strong feelings to be aroused by specific objects. The notion that a diffuse, generalized, and unrelenting enthusiasm is the mark of great sensitivity and responsiveness is utterly fantastic, an idea that comes from taking drunkenness or drug-addiction as the state of perfect emotional vigor. The effect of such enthusiasm is actually to wipe out the world altogether, for if a filling station will serve as well as the Rocky Mountains to arouse a sense of awe and wonder, then both the filling station and the mountains are robbed of their reality. Kerouac's conception of feeling is one that only a solipsist could believe in—and a solipsist, be it noted, is a man who does not relate to anything outside himself.

Solipsism is precisely what characterizes Kerouac's fiction. *On the Road* and *The Subterraneans* are so patently autobiographical in content that they become almost impossible to discuss as novels; if spontaneity were indeed a matter of destroying the distinction between life and literature, these books would unquestionably be It. "As we were going out to the car Babe slipped and fell flat on her face. Poor girl was overwrought. Her brother Tim and I helped her up. We got in the car; Major and Betty joined us. The sad ride back to Denver began." Babe is a girl who is mentioned a few times in the course of *On the Road;* we don't know why she is overwrought on this occasion, and even if we did it wouldn't matter, since there is no reason for her presence in the book at all. But Kerouac tells us that she fell flat on her face while walking toward a car. It is impossible to believe that Kerouac made this detail up, that his imagination was creating a world real enough to include wholly gratuitous elements; if that were the case, Babe would have come alive as a human being. But she is only a name; Kerouac never even describes her. She is in the book because the sister of one of Kerouac's friends was there when he took a trip to Central City, Colorado, and she slips in *On the Road* because she slipped that day on the way to the car. What is true of Babe who fell flat on her face is true of virtually every incident in *On the Road* and *The Subter-*

raneans. Nothing that happens has any dramatic reason for happening. Sal Paradise meets such-and-such people on the road whom he likes or (rarely) dislikes; they exchange a few words, they have a few beers together, they part. It is all very unremarkable and commonplace, but for Kerouac it is always the greatest, the wildest, the most. What you get in these two books is a man proclaiming that he is *alive* and offering every trivial experience he has ever had in evidence. Once I did this, once I did that (he is saying) and by God, it *meant* something! Because I *responded*! But if it meant something, and you responded so powerfully, why can't you explain what it meant, and why do you have to insist so?

I think it is legitimate to say, then, that the Beat Generation's worship of primitivism and spontaneity is more than a cover for hostility to intelligence; it arises from a pathetic poverty of feeling as well. The hipsters and hipster-lovers of the Beat Generation are rebels, all right, but not against anything so sociological and historical as the middle class or capitalism or even respectability. This is the revolt of the spiritually underprivileged and the crippled of soul—young men who can't think straight and so hate anyone who can; young men who can't get outside the morass of self and so construct definitions of feeling that exclude all human beings who manage to live, even miserably, in a world of objects; young men who are burdened into death with the specially poignant sexual anxiety that America—in its eternal promise of erotic glory and its spiteful withholding of actual erotic possibility—seems bent on breeding, and who therefore dream of the unattainable perfect orgasm, which excuses all sexual failures in the real world. Not long ago, Norman Mailer suggested that the rise of the hipster may represent "the first wind of a second revolution in this century, moving not forward toward action and more rational equitable distribution, but backward toward being and the secrets of human energy." To tell the truth, whenever I hear anyone talking about instinct and being and the secrets of human energy, I get nervous; next thing you know he'll be saying that violence is just fine, and then I begin wondering whether he really thinks that kicking someone in the teeth or sticking a knife between his ribs are deeds to be admired. History, after all—and especially the history of modern times—teaches that there is a close connection between ideologies of primitivistic vitalism and a willingness to look upon cruelty and blood-letting with complacency, if not downright enthusiasm. The reason I bring this up is that the spirit of hipsterism and the Beat Generation strikes me as the same spirit which animates the young savages in leather jackets who have been running amuck in the last few years with their switch-blades and zip guns. What does Mailer think of those wretched kids, I wonder? What does he think of the gang that stoned a nine-year-old boy to death in Central Park in broad daylight a few months ago, or the one that set fire to an old man drowsing on a bench near the Brooklyn waterfront one summer's day, or the one that pounced on a crippled child and orgiastically stabbed him over and over and over again even after he was good and dead? Is that what he means by the liberation of instinct and the mysteries of being? Maybe so. At least he says somewhere in his article that two eighteen-year-old hoodlums who bash in the brains of a candy-store keeper are murdering an institution, committing an act that "violates private property"—which is one of the most morally gruesome ideas I have ever come across, and which indicates where the ideology of hipsterism can lead. I happen to believe that there is a direct connection between the flabbiness of American middle-class life and the spread of juvenile crime in the 1950's, but I also believe that juvenile crime can be explained partly in terms of the same resentment against normal feeling and the attempt to cope with the world through intelligence that lies behind Kerouac and Ginsberg. Even the relatively mild ethos of Kerouac's books can spill over easily into brutality, for there is a suppressed cry in those books: Kill the intellectuals who can talk coherently, kill the people who can sit still for five minutes at a time, kill those incomprehensible characters who are capable of getting seriously involved with a woman, a job, a cause. How can anyone in his right mind pretend that this has anything to do with private property or the middle class? No. Being for or against what the Beat Generation stands for has to do with denying that incoherence is superior to precision; that ignorance is superior to knowledge; that the exercise of mind and discrimination is a form of death. It has to do with fighting the notion that sordid acts of violence are justifiable so long as they are committed in the name of "instinct." It even has to do with fighting the poisonous glorification of the adolescent in American popular culture. It has to do, in other words, with being for or against intelligence itself.

The Bored and the Violent

ARTHUR MILLER

If my own small experience is any guide, the main difficulty in approaching the problem of juvenile delinquency is that there is very little evidence about it and very many opinions as to how to deal with it. By evidence I do not mean the news stories telling of gang fights and teen-age murders—there are plenty of those. But it is unknown, for instance, what the actual effects are on the delinquent of prison sentences, psychotherapy, slum-clearance projects, settlement-house programs, tougher or more lenient police attitudes, the general

Harper's, CCXXV (November 1962), 50–56. © 1962 Harper's Magazine. Reprinted by permission Ashley-Steiner-Famous Artists, Inc.

employment situation, and so on. Statistics are few and not generally reliable. The narcotics problem alone is an almost closed mystery.

Not that statistical information in itself can solve anything, but it might at least outline the extent of the disease. I have it, for instance, from an old and deservedly respected official—it is his opinion anyway—that there is really no great increase in delinquent acts but a very great intensification of our awareness of them. He feels we are more nervous now about infractions of the social mores than our ancestors, and he likes to point out that Shakespeare, Boccaccio, and other writers never brought on stage a man of wealth or station without his bravos, who were simply his private police force, necessary to him when he ventured out of his house, especially at night. He would have us read *Great Expectations, Oliver Twist, Huckleberry Finn*, and other classics, not in a romantic mood but in the way we read about our own abandoned kids and their depredations. The difference lies mainly in the way we look at the same behavior.

The experts have only a little more to go on than we have. Like the surgeon whose hands are bloody a good part of the day, the social worker is likely to come to accept the permanent existence of the delinquency disease without the shock of the amateur who first encounters it.

A new book on the subject, *All the Way Down*,* reports the experience of a social worker—of sorts—who never got used to the experience, and does not accept its inevitability. It is an easy book to attack on superficial grounds because it has no evident sociological method, it rambles and jumps and shouts and curses. But it has a virtue, a very great and rare one, I think, in that it does convey the endless, leaden, mind-destroying boredom of the delinquent life. Its sex is without romance or sexuality, its violence is without release or gratification—exactly like the streets—movies and plays about delinquency notwithstanding.

Unlike most problems which sociology takes up, delinquency seems to be immune to the usual sociological analyses or cures. For instance, it appears in all technological societies, whether Latin or Anglo-Saxon or Russian or Japanese. It has a very slippery correlation with unemployment and the presence or absence of housing projects. It exists among the rich in Westchester and the poor in Brooklyn and Chicago. It has spread quickly into the rural areas and the small towns. Now according to Harrison Salisbury, it is the big problem in the Soviet Union. So that any single key to its causation is nowhere visible. If one wants to believe it to be essentially a symptom of unequal opportunity—and certainly this factor operates—one must wonder about the Russian problem, for the Soviet youngster can, in fact, go right up through the whole school system on his ability alone, as many of ours cannot. Yet the gangs are roaming the Russian streets, just as they do in our relatively permissive society.

So no one knows what "causes" delinquency. Having spent some months

* By Vincent Riccio and Bill Slocum. Simon and Schuster, $3.75.

in the streets with boys of an American gang, I came away with certain impressions, all of which stemmed from a single, overwhelming conviction—that the problem underneath is boredom. And it is not strange, after all, that this should be so. It is the theme of so many of our novels, our plays, and especially our movies in the past twenty years, and is the hallmark of society as a whole. The outcry of Britain's so-called Angry Young Men was against precisely this seemingly universal sense of life's pointlessness, the absence of any apparent aim to it all. So many American books and articles attest to the same awareness here. The stereotype of the man coming home from work and staring dumbly at a television set is an expression of it, and the "New Wave" of movies in France and Italy propound the same fundamental theme. People no longer seem to know why they are alive; existence is simply a string of near-experiences marked off by periods of stupefying spiritual and psychological stasis, and the good life is basically an amused one.

Among the delinquents the same kind of mindlessness prevails, but without the style—or stylishness—which art in our time has attempted to give it. The boredom of the delinquent is remarkable mainly because it is so little compensated for, as it may be among the middle classes and the rich who can fly down to the Caribbean or to Europe, or refurnish the house, or have an affair, or at least go shopping. The delinquent is stuck with his boredom, stuck inside it, stuck to it, until for two or three minutes he "lives"; he goes on a raid around the corner and feels the thrill of risking his skin or his life as he smashes a bottle filled with gasoline on some other kid's head. In a sense, it is his trip to Miami. It makes his day. It is his shopping tour. It gives him something to talk about for a week. It is *life*. Standing around with nothing coming up is as close to dying as you can get. Unless one grasps the power of boredom, the threat of it to one's existence, it is impossible to "place" the delinquent as a member of the human race.

With boredom in the forefront, one may find some perspective in the mélange of views which are repeated endlessly about the delinquent. He is a rebel without a cause, or a victim of poverty, or a victim of undue privilege, or an unloved child, or an overloved child, or a child looking for a father, or a child trying to avenge himself on an uncaring society, or whatnot. But face to face with one of them, one finds these criteria useless, if only because no two delinquents are any more alike than other people are. They do share one mood, however. They are drowning in boredom. School bores them, preaching bores them, even television bores them. The word rebel is inexact for them because it must inevitably imply a purpose, an end.

Other people, of course, have known boredom. To get out of it, they go to the movies, or to a bar, or read a book, or go to sleep, or turn on TV or a girl, or make a resolution, or quit a job. Younger persons who are not delinquents may go to their room and weep, or write a poem, or call up a friend until they get tired talking. But note that each of these escapes can only work if the victim is sure somewhere in his mind, or reasonably hopeful, that by so doing he will overthrow his boredom and with luck may come out on the other side where something hopeful or interesting waits. But the delinquent has no such sense of an imminent improvement. Most of the kids in the Riccio and Slocum book have never known a single good day. How can they be expected to project one and restrain themselves in order to experience such joy once more?

The word rebel is wrong, too, in that it implies some sort of social criticism in the delinquent. But that would confuse him with the bourgeois Beatnik. The delinquent has only respect, even reverence, for certain allegedly bourgeois values. He implicitly believes that there are good girls and bad girls, for instance. Sex and marriage are two entirely separate things. He is, in my experience anyway, deeply patriotic. Which is simply to say that he respects those values he never experienced, like money and good girls and the Army and Navy. What he has experienced has left him with absolute contempt, or more accurately, an active indifference. Once he does experience decency—as he does sometimes in a wife—he reacts decently to it. For to this date the only known cure for delinquency is marriage.

The delinquent, far from being the rebel, is the conformist par excellence. He is actually incapable of doing anything alone, and a story may indicate how incapable he is. I went along with Riccio and the gang in his book to a YMCA camp outside New York City for an overnight outing. In the afternoon we started a baseball game, and everything proceeded normally until somebody hit a ball to the outfield. I turned to watch the play and saw ten or twelve kids running for the catch. It turned out that not one of them was willing to play the outfield by himself, insisting that the entire group hang around out there together. The reason was that a boy alone might drop a catch and would not be able to bear the humiliation. So they ran around out there in a drove all afternoon, creating a stampede every time a ball was hit.

They are frightened kids, and that is why they are so dangerous. But again, it will not do to say—it is simply not true—that they are therefore unrelated to the rest of the population's frame of mind. Like most of us, the delinquent is simply doing as he was taught. This is often said but rarely understood. Only recently a boy was about to be executed for murder in New York State. Only after he had been in jail for more than a year after sentencing did a campaign develop to persuade the Governor to commute his sentence to life imprisonment, for only then was it discovered that he had been deserted by his father in Puerto Rico, left behind when his mother went to New York, wandered about homeless throughout his childhood, and so on. The sentencing judge only learned his background a week or two before he was to be officially murdered. And then what shock, what pity! I have to ask why the simple facts of his deprivation were not brought out in court, if not before. I am afraid I know the answer. Like most people, it was probably beyond the judge's imagination that small children sometimes can be treated much worse than kittens or puppies in our cities.

Gangs in Suburbia

It is only in theory that the solution seems purely physical—better housing, enlightened institutions for deserted kids, psychotherapy, and the rest. The visible surfaces of the problem are easy to survey—although we have hardly begun even to do that.

More difficult is the subterranean moral question which every kind of delinquency poses. Not long ago a gang was arrested in a middle-class section of Brooklyn, whose tack was to rob homes and sell the stuff to professional fences. Many of these boys were top students, and all of them were from good, middle-class backgrounds. Their parents were floored by the news of their secret depredations, and their common cry was that they had always given their sons plenty of money, that the boys were secure at home, that there was no conceivable reason for this kind of aberration. The boys were remorseful and evidently as bewildered as their parents.

Greenwich, Connecticut, is said to be the wealthiest community in the United States. A friend of mine who lives there let his sons throw a party for their friends. In the middle of the festivities a gang of boys arrived—their own acquaintances who attend the same high school. They tore the house apart, destroyed the furniture, pulled parts off the automobile and left them on the lawn, and split the skulls of two of the guests with beer cans.

Now if it is true that the slum delinquent does as he is taught, it must be true that the Greenwich delinquent does the same. But obviously the lines of force from example to imitation are subtler and less easily traced here. It is doubtful that the parents of this marauding gang rip up the furniture in the homes to which they have been invited. So that once again it is necessary to withhold one's cherished theories. Rich delinquency is delinquency but it is not the same as slum delinquency. But there is one clear common denominator, I think. They do not know how to live when alone. Most boys in Greenwich do not roam in gangs but a significant fraction in both places find that counterfeit sense of existence which the gang life provides.

Again, I think it necessary to raise and reject the idea of rebellion, if one means by that word a thrust of any sort. For perspective's sake it may be wise to remember another kind of youthful reaction to a failed society in a different era. In the 'thirties, for instance, we were also contemptuous of the given order. We had been brought up to believe that if you worked hard, saved your money, studied, kept your nose clean, you would end up made. We found ourselves in the Depression, when you could not get a job, when all the studying you might do would get you a chance, at best, to sell ties in Macy's. Our delinquency consisted in joining demonstrations of the unemployed, pouring onto campuses to scream against some injustice by college administrations, and adopting to one degree or another a Socialist ideology. This, in fact, was a more dangerous kind of delinquency than the gangs imply, for it was directed against the social structure of capitalism itself. But, curiously, it was at the same time immeasurably more constructive, for the radical youth of the 'thirties, contemptuous as he was of the social values he had rejected, was still bent upon instituting human values in their place. He was therefore a conserver, he believed in *some* society.

Gide wrote a story about a man who wanted to get on a train and shoot a passenger. Any train, any passenger. It would be a totally gratuitous act, an act devoid of any purpose whatever, an act of "freedom" from purpose. To kill an unknown man without even anger, without unrequited love, without love at all, with nothing in his heart but the sheerly physical contemplation of the gun barrel and the target. In doing this one would partake of Death's irreproachable identity and commit an act in revolt against meaning itself, just as Death is, in the last analysis, beyond analysis.

To think of contemporary delinquency in the vein of the 'thirties, as a rebellion toward something, is to add a value to it which it does not have. To give it even the dignity of cynicism run rampant is also overelaborate. For the essence is not the individual at all; it is the gang, the herd, and we should be able to understand its attractions ourselves. It is not the thrust toward individual expression but a flight from self in any defined form. Therefore, to see it simply as a protest against conformism is to stand it on its head; it is profoundly conformist but without the mottoes, the entablature of recognizable, "safe" conformism and its liturgy of religious, patriotic, socially conservative credos.

The Greenwich gang, therefore, is also doing as it was taught, just as the slum gang does, but more subtly. The Greenwich gang is conforming to the hidden inhumanity of conformism, to the herd quality in conformism; it is acting out the terror-fury that lies hidden under father's acceptable conformism. It is simply conformity sincere, conformity revealing its true content, which is hatred of others, a stunted wish for omnipotence, and the conformist's secret belief that nothing outside his skin is real or true. For which reason he must redouble his obeisance to institutions lest, if the act of obeisance be withheld, the whole external world will vanish, leaving him alone. And to be left alone when you do not sense any existence in yourself is the ultimate terror. But this loneliness is not the poet's, not the thinker's, not the loneliness that is filled with incommunicable feeling, insufficiently formed thought. It is nonexistence and must not be romanticized as it has been in movies and some of the wishful Beat literature. It is a withdrawal not from the world but from oneself. It is boredom, the subsidence of inner impulse, and it threatens true death unless it is overthrown.

All of which is said in order to indicate that delinquency is not the kind of "social problem" it is generally thought to be. That is, it transcends even as it includes the need for better housing, medical care, and the rest. It is our most notable and violent manifestation of social nihilism. In saying this, however, it is necessary to short-circuit any notion that it is an attempt by the youth to live "sincerely." The air of "sincerity" which so many writers have given the delinquent is not to be mistaken as his "purpose." This is romanticism and solves nothing except to sentimentalize brutality. The gang kid can be sincere; he can extend himself for a buddy and risk himself for others but he is just as liable, if not more so than others, to desert his buddies in need and to treat his friends disloyally. Gang boys rarely go to visit a buddy in jail excepting in the movies. They forget about him. The cult of sincerity, of true human relations uncontaminated by money and the social rat race, is not the hallmark of the gang. The only moment of truth comes when the war starts. Then the brave show themselves, but few of these boys know how to fight alone, and hardly any without a knife or a gun. They are not to be equated with matadors or boxers or Hemingway heroes. They are dangerous pack hounds who will not even expose themselves singly in the outfield.

Flight from Nothingness

If, then, one begins to put together all the elements, this "social problem" takes on not merely its superficial welfare aspects but its philosophical depths, which I think are the controlling ones. It is not a problem of big cities alone but of rural areas too; not of capitalism alone but of socialism as well; not restricted to the physically deprived but shared by the affluent; not a racial problem alone or a problem of recent immigrants, or a purely American problem. I believe it is in its present form the product of technology destroying the very concept of man as a value in himself.

I hesitate to say what I think the cure might be, if only because I cannot prove it. But I have heard most of the solutions men have offered, and they are spiritless, they do not assume that the wrong is deep and terrible and general among us all. There is, in a word, a spirit gone. Perhaps two world wars, brutality immeasurable, have blown it off the earth; perhaps the very processes of technology have sucked it out of man's soul; but it is gone. Many men rarely relate to one another excepting as customer to seller, worker to boss, the affluent to the deprived and vice versa—in short, as factors to be somehow manipulated and not as intrinsically valuable persons.

Power was always in the world, to be sure, and its evils, but with us now it is strangely, surrealistically masked and distorted. Time was, for example, when the wealthy and the politically powerful flaunted themselves, used power openly as power, and were often cruel. But this openness had the advantage for man of clarity; it created a certain reality in the world, an environment that was defined, with hard but touchable barriers. Today power would have us believe—everywhere—that it is purely beneficent. The bank is not a place which makes more money with your deposits than it returns to you in the form of interest; it is not a sheer economic necessity, it is not a business at all. It is "Your Friendly Bank," a kind of welfare institution whose one prayer, day and night, is to serve your whims or needs. A school is no longer a place of mental discipline but a kind of day-care center, a social gathering where you go through a ritual of games and entertainments which insinuate knowledge and the crafts of the outside world. Business is not the practice of buying low and selling high, it is a species of public service. The good life itself is not the life of struggle for meaning, not the quest for union with the past, with God, with man that it traditionally was. The good life is the life of ceaseless entertainment, effortless joys, the air-conditioned, dust-free languor beyond the Mussulman's most supine dream. Freedom is, after all, comfort; sexuality is a photograph. The enemy of it all is the real. The enemy is conflict. The enemy, in a word, is life.

My own view is that delinquency is related to this dreamworld from two opposing sides. There are the deprived who cannot take part in the dream; poverty bars them. There are the oversated who are caught in its indefiniteness, its unreality, its boring hum, and strike for the real now and then—they rob, they hurt, they kill. In flight from the nothingness of this comfort they have inherited, they butt against its rubber walls in order to feel a real pain, a genuine consequence. For the world in which comfort rules is a delusion, whether one is within it or deprived of it.

There are a few social theorists who look beyond poverty and wealth, beyond the time when men will orient themselves to the world as breadwinners, as accruers of money-power. They look to the triumph of technology, when at least in some countries the physical struggle to survive will no longer be the spine of existence. Then, they say, men will define themselves through varying "styles of life." With struggles solved, nature tamed and abundant, all that will be left to do will be the adornment of existence, a novel-shaped swimming pool, I take it, or an outburst of artistic work.

It is not impossible, I suppose. Certainly a lot of people are already living that way—when they are not at their psychiatrists'. But there is still a distance to go before life's style matters very much to most of humanity in comparison to next month's rent. I do not know how we ought to reach for the spirit again but it seems to me we must flounder without it. It is the spirit which does not accept injustice complacently and yet does not betray the poor with sentimentality. It is the spirit which seeks not to flee the tragedy which life must always be, but seeks to enter into it, thereby to be strengthened by the fullest awareness of its pain, its ultimate non sequitur. It is the spirit which does not mask but unmasks the true function of a thing, be it business, unionism, architecture, or love.

Riccio's and Slocum's book, with all its ugliness, its crudeness, its lack of polish and design, is good because it delivers up the real. It is only as hopeless as the situation is. Its implied solutions are good ones: reform of idiotic narcotics laws, a real attempt to put trained people at the service of bewildered, desperate families, job-training programs, medical care, reading clinics—all of it is necessary and none of it would so much as strain this economy. But none of it will matter, none of it will reach further than the spirit in which it is done. Not the spirit of fear with which so many face delinquency, nor the spirit of sentimentality which sees in it some virtue of rebellion against a false and lying society. The spirit has to be that of those people who know that delinquents are a living expression of our universal ignorance of what life ought to be, even of what it is, and of what it truly means to live. Bad pupils they surely are. But who from his own life, from his personal thought has come up with the good teaching, the way of life that is joy? This book shows how difficult it is to reach these boys; what the country has to decide is what it is going to say if these kids should decide to listen.

These Fighters Against Youth Crime Need Your Help

J. EDGAR HOOVER

This nation is hurtling toward a frightful internal crisis. Indeed, I am convinced that we have already reached a crossroads we have been heading for since the beginning of World War II; and that if we fail to admit the deadly nature of this crisis and to meet it quickly and aggressively, we will pay with the life of our republic.

The crisis manifests itself in what some call juvenile delinquency, and what I call youthful criminality, for that is what it is. I refer to the vicious acts of vandalism, wanton brutality and mounting savagery which typify today's arrogant teen-age gangs.

One night last summer, five youths between the ages of 15 and 18 viciously attacked two families in a Chicago park. After beating both husbands senseless with baseball bats, stabbing them with switchblade knives and robbing them, these five terrorists turned upon the two pregnant mothers and brutally raped them while the two children of one mother—aged three and one-and-a-half—watched, weeping and horrified.

"They held a knife at my throat and threatened to kill my two little children if I resisted," one of the women said. "We pleaded with them, but they paid no attention."

From *Reader's Digest*, LXXVIII (April 1961), 145–152. Copyright © 1961 by The Reader's Digest Assn., Inc. Reprinted by permission of the *Reader's Digest* and the author.

Convicted of rape and assault, each of the five young thugs received 65-year sentences. The sentencing judge recommended that the youths never be paroled.

Tragically, similar acts of brutal violence are perpetrated daily across the country by rampaging teen-age criminals. Blazing headlines of murder, sadism and gang warfare toll the depredations of youthful criminals. An 18-year-old California art student obtained money to purchase books by robbing elderly people. Known as the "mugger bandit," he committed six vicious attacks on elderly victims which netted him $70. Two of the victims, both elderly men, subsequently died as the result of the violent assaults. In describing his actions, the youth commented, "I picked on old men because they could not fight back."

Today youthful offenders account for one half of the burglary and larceny arrests in this country and nearly two thirds of the arrests for automobile thefts. And their rate of participation in more serious crimes—assault, robbery, rape, murder—is steadily rising.

If we are to continue living in a free and decent society, we must do much more than halt this trend; we must reverse it. Preoccupied with the pursuit of wealth and luxury, we seem to have lost touch with our basic traditions—work, discipline, duty, honor. But if this nation is to survive, we must give our youngsters more chance to know and revere the spiritual concepts which are the real sinews of greatness.

We can help them best by committing ourselves unreservedly to a battle that an all-too-small vanguard of dedicated Americans has been fighting for us for years—the professional leaders and part-time volunteer workers of such groups as the Boys' Clubs of America, Girl Scouts and Boy Scouts, YMCA and YWCA, Police Athletic Leagues, and Catholic, Protestant and Jewish youth organizations. The results these groups achieve continually reaffirm my faith in the strength and appeal of the American idea, and my conviction that American youth, if given the opportunity, will eagerly accept honorable challenge.

Here are some heartening examples:

During the eight years following World War II there was a 61-percent increase in juvenile crime in Louisville, Ky. But during the same period there was a 52-percent *decrease* in one of Louisville's poorest, toughest areas. No new industry moved into this neighborhood to upgrade incomes; there was no decrease in the youth population; housing conditions were not improved. One thing happened: a Boys' Club was established there.

Within five years after a Boys' Club was organized in a delinquency-ridden area of Schenectady, N.Y., there was an 80-percent decrease in youthful crime in that neighborhood. Results like these can be found in many of the 383 cities where 575 Boys' Clubs of America serve 600,000 lads.

The formula is simple. It consists of a genuine, active adult interest in youth; a deep respect and sympathy for the individual boy and girl, tempered with rigid, tough-minded adherence to the legal and moral principles which are the cornerstones of any decent society; and, above all, an unwavering faith in our youth, and Job-like patience in helping every youngster realize the best that is in him.

This formula has worked countless times. At the end of World War II one neighborhood just west of Chicago's Loop was virtually an armed camp, torn by bloody juvenile gang wars. The streets were not safe for women, night or day; children could not be sent to the grocery store with cash.

For ten years various social agencies tried to deal with these gangs with little success. Then, in 1955, a young Boys' Club extension worker whom we shall call Richard West began hanging about the pool halls and candy stores where the dominant, most vicious gang met. For months he studied the boys, listened to them, tried to talk with them. It wasn't easy. These boys came from homes filled with fearful frictions. Most had quit school. The gang was their refuge from the hostile world around them.

Rebuffed and threatened time and again, West doggedly shadowed the gang. When members were arrested, he would appear in court with them and speak in their behalf. He made the gang aware that arresting officers and judges listened to him. He was on call day and night for advice and whatever help he could provide.

Finally, one by one, gang members began coming to him with their problems. They found he could arrange loans when there was serious need—medical or dental problems, lack of food in the home. West kept watching, waiting for a display of interest he could seize on as a foundation for launching these youngsters into productive lives. Then he found it. Several times each week they would wander to a nearby high school to watch in absorbed silence as an ROTC unit performed military drill. Talking with the boys, West found they had deep respect for the kind of discipline which could produce precision drill. Here was a chance to get them active in a field in which they could win what they needed and wanted most desperately and had never had—adult support and praise.

From government surplus West obtained Army uniforms. Combat helmets were painted bright blue and white. Drums and bugles were provided. The boys learned fast. As a gang this group had flourished under iron discipline. Now the same discipline drove them toward perfection in military drill. Interest in gang feuds and hoodlumism faded. They concentrated on mastering the fast, tricky cadences of the drill repertoire. Soon they were taking part in civic parades, performing at sports events and on television.

Their success as a drill team fired the imagination of rival gangs. Before long the drill teams in this area included more than 400 youngsters who had once belonged to 17 different gangs. A Boys' Club was built in the center of the area. Here boys worked off excess energy in all kinds of sports and discovered new interests in handicrafts, science, photography and drama. Gang structures disintegrated. Boys' Club workers stayed in close touch with parents, kept pointing to the worth and potentialities of their sons, awakened parental enthusiasm for the boys.

As a result of concerted adult direction and encouragement, many of these boys returned to high school; others found jobs and completed their high-school requirements during evenings in the Boys' Club library.

Today this Boys' Club thrives with a membership of more than 1000. This area, five years ago a spawning ground for big-time crime, is now a respectable neighborhood whose citizens can walk the streets unafraid, with pride in their children and hope for the future.

Some communities have done much to combat youthful criminality through wholesome recreational programs for their children. Great progress is being made in areas where men and women care enough to do something about the problem. Seven years ago, the vast Surrey Lane area of St. Louis, Mo., faced with a growing juvenile-crime problem, did not have a single park or community center. Parents and youngsters of Surrey Lane went into action. With great effort and hard work they converted a tract of land, once a swamp, into a recreational area covering 31 acres. They raised money, cleared the land, built roads and constructed recreational facilities. And they did it as a family project—father and son, mother and daughter, young and old alike, united in the common endeavor. Today, with over 2000 youths participating in recreational activities, Surrey Lane's juvenile-crime rate is practically nil. Last year, the Freedoms Foundation at Valley Forge, Pa., honored Surrey Lane with the nation's first-place award for a community program.

The Boy Scout movement, too, has proved that when a worthy challenge is promoted among youngsters, it takes. In one year the crime rate in East Harlem was more than double that of any other section of New York City. Youthful gangs kept the 64-square-block area in terror. Scouters moved in. First they sold Scouting to the ruler of the ruling gang, an 18-year-old whom police suspected of organizing the gang wars which racked the community. Soon that gang—11 boys—was a Scout troop, dedicated to the principle of helping people instead of hurting them.

More than 150 police departments in the United States now sponsor Boy Scout units, with some police officers serving as Scout leaders. We in the FBI are proud of the fact that nearly 50 percent of our FBI agents are former Boy Scouts.

In no instance have the Boys' Clubs of America or Boy Scouts designed "special programs" for dealing with problem boys. They have succeeded simply by providing adult friendship, guidance, worthy challenge, a desire for the rewards of disciplined living. Their achievements are a monument to the intrinsic worth of our youngsters, and a powerful lesson for us all.

It is long past time that every one of us understood the deadly nature of the sickness in our society and went to work on the cure. Each one of us must help turn back the tide of moral laxity and public apathy which threatens us. Our youth movements have proved it can be done. We must get interested in our children again—in what they read, see, hear and do.

And we must get tough with ourselves. We must stop governing our lives by expediency. Nothing is so infectious as example. We must measure our every act by the same single, simple, stringent criterion that made us a great nation: *"Is it right?"*

Questions

1. What are the significant differences among the attitudes of Kerouac, Podhoretz, Miller, and Hoover toward the problem of our youth? Who is most realistic? Most idealistic? Why?
2. Who among the four tries to understand the underlying causes for the behavior of young people in terms of looking at society as a whole? Who seems to be most hostile toward beatniks and delinquents? Most punitive? Most sympathetic?
3. What evidence is offered in the articles in this section to indicate that delinquency, independence, or rebellion is not necessarily related to poverty or to broken homes?
4. Do you agree with Hoover's proposed solution for youth crime? Do Miller and Podhoretz support Hoover or contradict him? How would you fight youth crime? Bohemianism? Would you fight them at all?
5. Why does Miller call his article "The Bored and the Violent"? What connection does he see between boredom and violence? What does Miller mean when he writes that a temporary delinquency "is not the thrust toward individual expression but a flight from self in any defined form"? How does this relate to what Podhoretz and Kerouac have to say? What does Miller mean when he calls contemporary delinquency "profoundly conformist"?

Assignments

1. Describe your own contacts with or awareness of delinquency or any type of nonconformism when you went to high school.
2. Interview some person in your community who has been active in some way in fighting juvenile delinquency. Report the substance of the interview and then compare the point of view expressed in it with that in one of the articles in this section.
3. Interview three students who have not read the articles in this section on their notions of the causes and the cures for juvenile rebelliousness or boredom. You might ask them the following questions: Do you think boredom leads to violence? Do you think delinquency is the result of a drive toward being part of a group? Do you think that boys' clubs or girls' clubs can significantly reduce the amount of delinquency in a community? Have you belonged to any such groups? Do you think that coming from well-to-do homes might contribute to a young person's becoming involved in delinquent or rebellious activity of one sort or another? What do you think makes a beatnik? Is a beatnik another type of delinquent?
4. Summarize each of the articles, discussing the tone as well as emphasizing the main points of the article.
5. Relate some of the points mentioned in the section "What Is College For?" with those mentioned in this section. Try to consider specifically the connections between college students, beatniks, and juvenile delinquents.

6. Discuss the underlying issues in the section on the pop art movement (part II, 5) and in this section. Do pop artists, the beat writers, and juvenile delinquents have a common attitude toward established society?

Additional Reading

A number of studies in recent years, both specialized and popular, have been published on the subject of juvenile delinquency. Among the most original and provocative of these is the book of essays by Paul Goodman, *Growing Up Absurd* (New York, 1960). *All the Way Down* by Vincent Riccio and Bill Slocum (New York, 1962) is referred to in Miller's essay. *Teenage Tyranny* by Grace and Fred Hechinger (New York, 1963) is a survey of the problem of juvenile delinquency in this country; its title suggests the slant. An insider's discussion of the beatnik movement can be found in Lawrence Lipton's *The Holy Barbarians* (New York, 1962). A collection, *A Casebook on the Beat,* edited by Thomas Parkinson (New York, 1961), includes representative beat literature as well as essays discussing the movement.

SECTION THREE
The Bible and the Bill of Rights

Abington School District v. Schempp

OPINION OF THE COURT

MR. JUSTICE CLARK delivered the opinion of the Court.

Once again we are called upon to consider the scope of the provision of the First Amendment to the United States Constitution which declares that "Congress shall make no law respecting an establishment of religion, or prohibiting the free exercise thereof. . . ." These companion cases present the issues in the context of state action requiring that schools begin each day with readings from the Bible. While raising the basic questions under slightly different factual situations, the cases permit of joint treatment. In light of the history of the First Amendment and of our cases interpreting and applying its requirements, we hold that the practices at issue and the laws requiring them are unconstitutional under the Establishment Clause, as applied to the States through the Fourteenth Amendment.

I

The Facts in Each Case: No. 142. The Commonwealth of Pennsylvania by law 24 Pa. Stat. § 15–1516, as amended, Pub. Law 1928 (Supp. 1960) Dec. 17, 1959, requires that "At least ten verses from the Holy Bible shall be read, without comment, at the opening of each public school on each school day. Any child shall be excused from such Bible reading, or attending such Bible reading, upon the written request of his parent or guardian." The Schempp family, husband and wife and two of their three children, brought suit to enjoin enforcement of the statute, contending that their rights under the

Fourteenth Amendment to the Constitution of the United States are, have been, and will continue to be violated unless this statute be declared unconstitutional as violative of these provisions of the First Amendment. They sought to enjoin the appellant school district, wherein the Schempp children attend school, and its officers and the Superintendent of Public Instruction of the Commonwealth from continuing to conduct such readings and recitation of the Lord's Prayer in the public schools of the district pursuant to the statute. A three-judge statutory District Court for the Eastern District of Pennsylvania held that the statute is violative of the Establishment Clause of the First Amendment as applied to the States by the Due Process Clause of the Fourteenth Amendment and directed that appropriate injunctive relief issue. 201 F. Supp. 815.[1] On appeal by the District, its officials and the Superintendent, under 28 U. S. C. § 1253, we noted probable jurisdiction. 371 U. S. 807.

The appellees Edward Lewis Schempp, his wife Sidney, and their children, Roger and Donna, are of the Unitarian faith and are members of the Unitarian Church in Germantown, Philadelphia, Pennsylvania, where they, as well as another son, Ellory, regularly attend religious services. The latter was originally a party but having graduated from the school system *pendente lite* was voluntarily dismissed from the action. The other children attend the Abington Senior High School, which is a public school operated by appellant district.

On each school day at the Abington Senior High School between 8:15 and 8:30 A.M., while the pupils are attending their home rooms or advisory sections, opening exercises are conducted pursuant to the statute. The exercises are broadcast into each room in the school building through an intercommunications system and are conducted under the supervision of a teacher by students attending the school's radio and television workshop. Selected students from this course gather each morning in the school's workshop studio for the exercises, which include readings by one of the students of 10 verses of the Holy Bible, broadcast to each room in the building. This is followed by the recitation of the Lord's Prayer, likewise over the intercommunications system, but also by the students in the various classrooms, who are asked to stand and join in repeating the prayer in unison. The exercises are closed with the flag salute and such pertinent announcements as are of interest to the students. Participation in the opening exercises, as directed by the statute, is voluntary. The student reading the verses from the Bible may select the passages and read from any version he chooses, although the only copies furnished by the school are the King James version, copies of which

---

[1] The action was brought in 1958, prior to the 1959 amendment of § 15–1516 authorizing a child's nonattendance at the exercises upon parental request. The three-judge court held the statute and the practices complained of unconstitutional under both the Establishment Clause and the Free Exercise Clause. 177 F. Supp. 398. Pending appeal to this Court by the school district, the statute was so amended, and we vacated the judgment and remanded for further proceedings. 364 U. S. 298. The same three-judge court granted appellees' motion to amend the pleadings, 195 F. Supp. 518, held a hearing on the amended pleadings and rendered the judgment, 201 F. Supp. 815, from which appeal is now taken.

were circulated to each teacher by the school district. During the period in which the exercises have been conducted the King James, the Douay and the Revised Standard versions of the Bible have been used, as well as the Jewish Holy Scriptures. There are no prefatory statements, no questions asked or solicited, no comments or explanations made and no interpretations given at or during the exercises. The students and parents are advised that the student may absent himself from the classroom or, should he elect to remain, not participate in the exercises.

It appears from the record that in schools not having an intercommunications system the Bible reading and the recitation of the Lord's Prayer were conducted by the home-room teacher,[2] who chose the text of the verses and read them herself or had students read them in rotation or by volunteers. This was followed by a standing recitation of the Lord's Prayer, together with the Pledge of Allegiance to the Flag by the class in unison and a closing announcement of routine school items of interest.

At the first trial Edward Schempp and the children testified as to specific religious doctrines purveyed by a literal reading of the Bible "which were contrary to the religious beliefs which they held and to their familial teaching." 177 F. Supp. 398, 400. The children testified that all of the doctrines to which they referred were read to them at various times as part of the exercises. Edward Schempp testified at the second trial that he had considered having Roger and Donna excused from attendance at the exercises but decided against it for several reasons, including his belief that the children's relationships with their teachers and classmates would be adversely affected.[3]

Expert testimony was introduced by both appellants and appellees at the first trial, which testimony was summarized by the trial court as follows:

"Dr. Solomon Grayzel testified that there were marked differences between the Jewish Holy Scriptures and the Christian Holy Bible, the most obvious of which was the absence of the New Testament in the Jewish Holy Scriptures. Dr. Grayzel testified that portions of the New Testament were offensive to Jewish

---

[2] The statute as amended imposes no penalty upon a teacher refusing to obey its mandate. However, it remains to be seen whether one refusing could have his contract of employment terminated for "wilful violation of the school laws." 24 Pa. Stat. (Supp. 1960) § 11-1122.

[3] The trial court summarized his testimony as follows:

"Edward Schempp, the children's father, testified that after careful consideration he had decided that he should not have Roger or Donna excused from attendance at these morning ceremonies. Among his reasons were the following. He said that he thought his children would be 'labeled as "odd balls" ' before their teachers and classmates every school day; that children, like Roger's and Donna's classmates, were liable 'to lump all particular religious difference[s] or religious objections [together] as "atheism" ' and that today the word 'atheism' is often connected with 'atheistic communism,' and has 'very bad' connotations, such as 'un-American' or 'anti-Red,' with overtones of possible immorality. Mr. Schempp pointed out that due to the events of the morning exercises following in rapid succession, the Bible reading, the Lord's Prayer, the Flag Salute, and the announcements, excusing his children from the Bible reading would mean that probably they would miss hearing the announcements so important to children. He testified also that if Roger and Donna were excused from Bible reading they would have to stand in the hall outside their 'homeroom' and that this carried with it the imputation of punishment for bad conduct." 201 F. Supp., at 818.

tradition and that, from the standpoint of Jewish faith, the concept of Jesus Christ as the Son of God was 'practically blasphemous.' He cited instances in the New Testament which, assertedly, were not only sectarian in nature but tended to bring the Jews into ridicule or scorn. Dr. Grayzel gave as his expert opinion that such material from the New Testament could be explained to Jewish children in such a way as to do no harm to them. But if portions of the New Testament were read without explanation, they could be, and in his specific experience with children Dr. Grayzel observed, had been, psychologically harmful to the child and had caused a divisive force within the social media of the school.

"Dr. Grayzel also testified that there was significant difference in attitude with regard to the respective Books of the Jewish and Christian Religions in that Judaism attaches no special significance to the reading of the Bible *per se* and that the Jewish Holy Scriptures are source materials to be studied. But Dr. Grayzel did state that many portions of the New, as well as of the Old, Testament contained passages of great literary and moral value.

"Dr. Luther A. Weigle, an expert witness for the defense, testified in some detail as to the reasons for and the methods employed in developing the King James and the Revised Standard Versions of the Bible. On direct examination, Dr. Weigle stated that the Bible was non-sectarian. He later stated that the phrase 'non-sectarian' meant to him non-sectarian within the Christian faiths. Dr. Weigle stated that his definition of the Holy Bible would include the Jewish Holy Scriptures, but also stated that the 'Holy Bible' would not be complete without the New Testament. He stated that the New Testament 'conveyed the message of Christians.' In his opinion, reading of the Holy Scriptures to the exclusion of the New Testament would be a sectarian practice. Dr. Weigle stated that the Bible was of great moral, historical and literary value. This is conceded by all the parties and is also the view of the court." 177 F. Supp. 398, 401–402.

The trial court, in striking down the practices and the statute requiring them, made specific findings of fact that the children's attendance at Abington Senior High School is compulsory and that the practice of reading 10 verses from the Bible is also compelled by law. It also found that:

"The reading of the verses, even without comment, possesses a devotional and religious character and constitutes in effect a religious observance. The devotional and religious nature of the morning exercises is made all the more apparent by the fact that the Bible reading is followed immediately by a recital in unison by the pupils of the Lord's Prayer. The fact that some pupils, or theoretically all pupils, might be excused from attendance at the exercises does not mitigate the obligatory nature of the ceremony for . . . Section 1516 . . . unequivocally requires the exercises to be held every school day in every school in the Commonwealth. The exercises are held in the school buildings and perforce are conducted by and under the authority of the local school authorities and during school sessions. Since the statute requires the reading of the 'Holy Bible,' a Christian document, the practice . . . prefers the Christian religion. The record demonstrates that it was the intention of . . . the Commonwealth . . . to introduce a religious ceremony into the public schools of the Commonwealth." 201 F. Supp., at 819.

No. 119. In 1905 the Board of School Commissioners of Baltimore City adopted a rule pursuant to Art. 77, § 202 of the Annotated Code of Maryland.

The rule provided for the holding of opening exercises in the schools of the city, consisting primarily of the "reading, without comment, of a chapter in the Holy Bible and/or the use of the Lord's Prayer." The petitioners, Mrs. Madalyn Murray and her son, William J. Murray III, are both professed atheists. Following unsuccessful attempts to have the respondent school board rescind the rule, this suit was filed for mandamus to compel its rescission and cancellation. It was alleged that William was a student in a public school of the city and Mrs. Murray, his mother, was a taxpayer therein; that it was the practice under the rule to have a reading on each school morning from the King James version of the Bible; that at petitioners' insistence the rule was amended [4] to permit children to be excused from the exercise on request of the parent and that William had been excused pursuant thereto; that nevertheless the rule as amended was in violation of the petitioners' rights "to freedom of religion under the First and Fourteenth Amendments" and in violation of "the principle of separation between church and state, contained therein. . . ." The petition particularized the petitioners' atheistic beliefs and stated that the rule, as practiced, violated their rights

> "in that it threatens their religious liberty by placing a premium on belief as against non-belief and subjects their freedom of conscience to the rule of the majority; it pronounces belief in God as the source of all moral and spiritual values, equating these values with religious values, and thereby renders sinister, alien and suspect the beliefs and ideals of your Petitioners, promoting doubt and question of their morality, good citizenship and good faith."

The respondents demurred and the trial court, recognizing that the demurrer admitted all facts well pleaded, sustained it without leave to amend. The Maryland Court of Appeals affirmed, the majority of four justices holding the exercise not in violation of the First and Fourteenth Amendments, with three justices dissenting. 228 Md. 239, 179 A.2d 698. We granted certiorari. 371 U. S. 809.

II

It is true that religion has been closely identified with our history and government. As we said in *Engel* v. *Vitale*, 370 U. S. 421, 434 (1962), "The history of man is inseparable from the history of religion. And . . . since the beginning of that history many people have devoutly believed that 'More things are wrought by prayer than this world dreams of.'" In *Zorach* v. *Clauson*, 343 U. S. 306, 313 (1952), we gave specific recognition to the

---

[4] The rule as amended provides as follows:
"Opening Exercises. Each school, either collectively or in classes, shall be opened by the reading, without comment, of a chapter in the Holy Bible and/or the use of the Lord's Prayer. The Douay version may be used by those pupils who prefer it. Appropriate patriotic exercises should be held as a part of the general opening exercise of the school or class. Any child shall be excused from participating in the opening exercises or from attending the opening exercises upon the written request of his parent or guardian."

proposition that "[w]e are a religious people whose institutions presuppose a Supreme Being." The fact that the Founding Fathers believed devotedly that there was a God and that the unalienable rights of man were rooted in Him is clearly evidenced in their writings, from the Mayflower Compact to the Constitution itself. This background is evidenced today in our public life through the continuance in our oaths of office from the Presidency to the Alderman of the final supplication, "So help me God." Likewise each House of the Congress provides through its Chaplain an opening prayer, and the sessions of this Court are declared open by the crier in a short ceremony, the final phrase of which invokes the grace of God. Again, there are such manifestations in our military forces, where those of our citizens who are under the restrictions of military service wish to engage in voluntary worship. Indeed, only last year an offical survey of the country indicated that 64% of our people have church membership, Bureau of the Census, U. S. Department of Commerce, Statistical Abstract of the United States (83d ed. 1962), 48, while less than 3% profess no religion whatever. *Id.*, at p. 46. It can be truly said, therefore, that today, as in the beginning, our national life reflects a religious people who, in the words of Madison, are "earnestly praying, as . . . in duty bound, that the Supreme Lawgiver of the Universe . . . guide them into every measure which may be worthy of his [blessing. . . .]" Memorial and Remonstrance Against Religious Assessments, quoted in *Everson v. Board of Education,* 330 U. S. 1, 71–72 (1947) (Appendix to dissenting opinion of Rutledge, J.).

This is not to say, however, that religion has been so identified with our history and government that religious freedom is not likewise as strongly imbedded in our public and private life. Nothing but the most telling of personal experiences in religious persecution suffered by our forebears, see *Everson v. Board of Education, supra,* at 8–11, could have planted our belief in liberty of religious opinion any more deeply in our heritage. It is true that this liberty frequently was not realized by the colonists, but this is readily accountable by their close ties to the Mother Country.[5] However, the views of Madison and Jefferson, preceded by Roger Williams,[6] came to be incorporated not only in the Federal Constitution but likewise in those of most of our States. This freedom to worship was indispensable in a country whose people came from the four quarters of the earth and brought with them a diversity of religious opinion. Today authorities list 83 separate religious bodies, each

---

[5] There were established churches in at least eight of the original colonies, and various degrees of religious support in others as late as the Revolutionary War. See *Engel v. Vitale, supra,* at 428, n. 10.

[6] "There goes many a ship to sea, with many hundred souls in one ship, whose weal and woe is common, and is a true picture of a commonwealth, or human combination, or society. It hath fallen out sometimes, that both Papists and Protestants, Jews and Turks, may be embarked in one ship; upon which supposal, I affirm that all the liberty of conscience I ever pleaded for, turns upon these two hinges, that none of the Papists, Protestants, Jews, or Turks be forced to come to the ship's prayers or worship, nor compelled from their own particular prayers or worship, if they practice any."

with membership exceeding 50,000, existing among our people, as well as innumerable smaller groups. Bureau of the Census, *op. cit., supra,* at 46–47.

III

Almost a hundred years ago in *Minor v. Board of Education of Cincinnati,*[7] Judge Alphonso Taft, father of the revered Chief Justice, in an unpublished opinion stated the ideal of our people as to religious freedom as one of

> "absolute equality before the law, of all religious opinions and sects. . . .
>
> . . . . .
>
> "The government is neutral, and, while protecting all, it prefers none, and it *disparages* none."

Before examining this "neutral" position in which the Establishment and Free Exercise Clauses of the First Amendment place our Government it is well that we discuss the reach of the Amendment under the cases of this Court.

First, this Court has decisively settled that the First Amendment's mandate that "Congress shall make no law respecting an establishment of religion, or prohibiting the free exercise thereof" has been made wholly applicable to the States by the Fourteenth Amendment. Twenty-three years ago in *Cantwell v. Connecticut,* 310 U. S. 296, 303 (1940), this Court, through Mr. Justice Roberts, said:

> "The fundamental concept of liberty embodied in that [Fourteenth] Amendment embraces the liberties guaranteed by the First Amendment. The First Amendment declares that Congress shall make no law respecting an establishment of religion or prohibiting the free exercise thereof. The Fourteenth Amendment has rendered the legislatures of the states as incompetent as Congress to enact such laws. . . ."[8]

In a series of cases since *Cantwell* the Court has repeatedly reaffirmed that doctrine, and we do so now. *Murdock v. Pennsylvania,* 319 U. S. 105, 108 (1943); *Everson v. Board of Education, supra; Illinois ex rel. McCollum v. Board of Education,* 333 U. S. 203, 210–211 (1948); *Zorach v. Clauson, supra; McGowan v. Maryland,* 366 U. S. 420 (1961); *Torcaso v. Watkins,* 367 U. S. 488 (1961); and *Engel v. Vitale, supra.*

---

[7] Superior Court of Cincinnati, February 1870. The opinion is not reported but is published under the title, The Bible in the Common Schools (Cincinnati: Robert Clarke & Co. 1870). Judge Taft's views, expressed in dissent, prevailed on appeal. See *Board of Education of Cincinnati v. Minor,* 23 Ohio St. 211, 253 (1872), in which the Ohio Supreme Court held that:
"The great bulk of human affairs and human interests is left by any free government to individual enterprise and individual action. Religion is eminently one of these interests, lying outside the true and legitimate province of government."

[8] Application to the States of other clauses of the First Amendment obtained even before *Cantwell.* Almost 40 years ago in the opinion of the Court in *Gitlow v. New York,* 268 U. S. 652, 666 (1925), Mr. Justice Sanford said: "For present purposes we may and do assume that freedom of speech and of the press—which are protected by the First Amendment from abridgment by Congress—are among the fundamental personal rights and 'liberties' protected by the due process clause of the Fourteenth Amendment from impairment by the States."

Second, this Court has rejected unequivocally the contention that the Establishment Clause forbids only governmental preference of one religion over another. Almost 20 years ago in *Everson, supra*, at 15, the Court said that "[n]either a state nor the Federal Government can set up a church. Neither can pass laws which aid one religion, aid all religions, or prefer one religion over another." And Mr. Justice Jackson, dissenting, agreed:

> "There is no answer to the proposition . . . that the effect of the religious freedom Amendment to our Constitution was to take every form of propagation such as had prevailed in England and some of the colonies. Necessarily it made public business and thereby be supported in whole or in part at taxpayers' expense. . . . This freedom was first in the Bill of Rights because it was first in the forefathers' minds; it was set forth in absolute terms, and its strength is its rigidity." *Id.,* at 26.

Further, Mr. Justice Rutledge, joined by Justices Frankfurter, Jackson and Burton, declared:

> "The [First] Amendment's purpose was not to strike merely at the official establishment of a single sect, creed or religion, outlawing only a formal relation such as had prevailed in England and some of the colonies. Necessarily it was to uproot all such relationships. But the object was broader than separating church and state in this narrow sense. It was to create a complete and permanent separation of the spheres of religious activity and civil authority by comprehensively forbidding every form of public aid or support for religion." *Id.,* at 31–32.

The same conclusion has been firmly maintained ever since that time, see *Illinois ex rel. McCollum, supra,* at pp. 210–211; *McGowan v. Maryland, supra,* at 442–443; *Torcaso v. Watkins, supra,* at 492–493, 495, and we reaffirm it now.

While none of the parties to either of these cases has questioned these basic conclusions of the Court, both of which have been long established, recognized and consistently reaffirmed, others continue to question their history, logic and efficacy. Such contentions, in the light of the consistent interpretation in cases of this Court, seem entirely untenable and of value only as academic exercises.

IV

The interrelationship of the Establishment and the Free Exercise Clauses was first touched upon by Mr. Justice Roberts for the Court in *Cantwell* v. *Connecticut, supra,* at 303–304, where it was said that their "inhibition of legislation" had

> "a double aspect. On the one hand, it forestalls compulsion by law of the acceptance of any creed or the practice of any form of worship. Freedom of conscience and freedom to adhere to such religious organization or form of worship as the individual may choose cannot be restricted by law. On the other hand, it safeguards the free exercise of the chosen form of religion. Thus the Amendment embraces two concepts,—freedom to believe and freedom to act. The first is absolute but, in the nature of things, the second cannot be."

A half dozen years later in *Everson* v. *Board of Education, supra,* at 14–15, this Court, through MR. JUSTICE BLACK, stated that the "scope of the First Amendment . . . was designed forever to suppress" the establishment of religion or the prohibition of the free exercise thereof. In short, the Court held that the Amendment

> "requires the state to be a neutral in its relations with groups of religious believers and non-believers; it does not require the state to be their adversary. State power is no more to be used so as to handicap religions than it is to favor them." *Id.,* at 18.

And Mr. Justice Jackson, in dissent, declared that public schools are organized

> "on the premise that secular education can be isolated from all religious teaching so that the school can inculcate all needed temporal knowledge and also maintain a strict and lofty neutrality as to religion. The assumption is that after the individual has been instructed in worldly wisdom he will be better fitted to choose his religion." *Id.,* at 23–24.

Moreover, all of the four dissenters, speaking through Mr. Justice Rutledge, agreed that

> "Our constitutional policy . . . does not deny the value or the necessity for religious training, teaching or observance. Rather it secures their free exercise. But to that end it does deny that the state can undertake or sustain them in any form or degree. For this reason the sphere of religious activity, as distinguished from the secular intellectual liberties, has been given the twofold protection and, as the state cannot forbid, neither can it perform or aid in performing the religious function. The dual prohibition makes that function altogether private." *Id.,* at 52.

Only one year later the Court was asked to reconsider and repudiate the doctrine of these cases in *McCollum* v. *Board of Education.* It was argued that "historically the First Amendment was intended to forbid only government preference of one religion over another . . . . In addition they ask that we distinguish or overrule our holding in the *Everson* case that the Fourteenth Amendment made the 'establishment of religion' clause of the First Amendment applicable as a prohibition against the States." 333 U. S., at 211. The Court, with Mr. Justice Reed alone dissenting, was unable to "accept either of these contentions." *Ibid.* Mr. Justice Frankfurter, joined by Justices Jackson, Rutledge and Burton, wrote a very comprehensive and scholarly concurrence in which he said that "[s]eparation is a requirement to abstain from fusing functions of Government and of religious sects, not merely to treat them all equally." *Id.,* at 227. Continuing, he stated that:

> "the Constitution . . . prohibited the Government common to all from becoming embroiled, however innocently, in the destructive religious conflicts of which the history of even this country records some dark pages." *Id.,* at 228.

In 1952 in *Zorach* v. *Clauson, supra,* MR. JUSTICE DOUGLAS for the Court reiterated:

"There cannot be the slightest doubt that the First Amendment reflects the philosophy that Church and State should be separated. And so far as interference with the 'free exercise' of religion and an 'establishment' of religion are concerned, the separation must be complete and unequivocal. The First Amendment within the scope of its coverage permits no exception; the prohibition is absolute. The First Amendment, however, does not say that in every and all respects there shall be a separation of Church and State. Rather, it studiously defines the manner, the specific ways, in which there shall be no concert or union or dependency one on the other. That is the common sense of the matter." 343 U. S., at 312.

And then in 1961 in *McGowan* v. *Maryland* and in *Torcaso* v. *Watkins* each of these cases was discussed and approved. CHIEF JUSTICE WARREN in *McGowan*, for a unanimous Court on this point, said:

"But, the First Amendment, in its final form, did not simply bar a congressional enactment *establishing a church;* it forbade all laws *respecting an establishment of religion.* Thus, this Court has given the Amendment a 'broad interpretation . . . in the light of its history and the evils it was designed forever to suppress. . . .'" 366 U. S., at 441–442.

And MR. JUSTICE BLACK for the Court in *Torcaso*, without dissent but with Justices Frankfurter and HARLAN concurring in the result, used this language:

"We repeat and again reaffirm that neither a State nor the Federal Government can constitutionally force a person 'to profess a belief or disbelief in any religion.' Neither can constitutionally pass laws or impose requirements which aid all religions as against non-believers, and neither can aid those religions based on a belief in the existence of God as against those religions founded on different beliefs." 367 U. S., at 495.

Finally, in *Engel* v. *Vitale,* only last year, these principles were so universally recognized that the Court, without the citation of a single case and over the sole dissent of MR. JUSTICE STEWART, reaffirmed them. The Court found the 22-word prayer used in "New York's program of daily classroom invocation of God's blessings as prescribed in the Regents' prayer . . . [to be] a religious activity." 370 U. S., at 424. It held that "it is no part of the business of government to compose official prayers for any group of the American people to recite as a part of a religious program carried on by government." *Id.,* at 425. In discussing the reach of the Establishment and Free Exercise Clauses of the First Amendment the Court said:

"Although these two clauses may in certain instances overlap, they forbid two quite different kinds of governmental encroachment upon religious freedom. The Establishment Clause, unlike the Free Exercise Clause, does not depend upon any showing of direct governmental compulsion and is violated by the enactment of laws which establish an official religion whether those laws operate directly to coerce non-observing individuals or not. This is not to say, of course, that laws officially prescribing a particular form of religious worship do not involve coercion of such individuals. When the power, prestige and financial support of government is placed behind a particular religious belief, the indirect coercive pressure upon religious minorities to conform to the prevailing officially approved religion is plain." *Id.*, at 430–431.

And in further elaboration the Court found that the "first and most immediate purpose [of the Establishment Clause] rested on the belief that a union of government and religion tends to destroy government and to degrade religion." *Id.*, at 431. When government, the Court said, allies itself with one particular form of religion, the inevitable result is that it incurs "the hatred, disrespect and even contempt of those who held contrary beliefs." *Ibid.*

V

The wholesome "neutrality" of which this Court's cases speak thus stems from a recognition of the teachings of history that powerful sects or groups might bring about a fusion of governmental and religious functions or a concert or dependency of one upon the other to the end that official support of the State or Federal Government would be placed behind the tenets of one or of all orthodoxies. This the Establishment Clause prohibits. And a further reason for neutrality is found in the Free Exercise Clause, which recognizes the value of religious training, teaching and observance and, more particularly, the right of every person to freely choose his own course with reference thereto, free of any compulsion from the state. This the Free Exercise Clause guarantees. Thus, as we have seen, the two clauses may overlap. As we have indicated, the Establishment Clause has been directly considered by this Court eight times in the past score of years and, with only one Justice dissenting on the point, it has consistently held that the clause withdrew all legislative power respecting religious belief or the expression thereof. The test may be stated as follows: what are the purpose and the primary effect of the enactment? If either is the advancement or inhibition of religion then the enactment exceeds the scope of legislative power as circumscribed by the Constitution. That is to say that to withstand the strictures of the Establishment Clause there must be a secular legislative purpose and a primary effect that neither advances nor inhibits religion. *Everson* v. *Board of Education, supra; McGowan* v. *Maryland, supra,* at 442. The Free Exercise Clause, likewise considered many times here, withdraws from legislative power, state and federal, the exertion of any restraint on the free exercise of religion. Its purpose is to secure religious liberty in the individual by prohibiting any invasions thereof by civil authority. Hence it is necessary in a free exercise case for one to show the coercive effect of the enactment as it operates against him in the practice of his religion. The distinction between the two clauses is apparent—a violation of the Free Exercise Clause is predicated on coercion while the Establishment Clause violation need not be so attended.

Applying the Establishment Clause principles to the cases at bar we find that the States are requiring the selection and reading at the opening of the school day of verses from the Holy Bible and the recitation of the Lord's Prayer by the students in unison. These exercises are prescribed as part of the curricular activities of students who are required by law to attend school. They are held in the school buildings under the supervision and with the participation of teachers employed in those schools. None of these factors, other than compulsory school attendance, was present in the program upheld in *Zorach* v. *Clauson.* The trial court in No. 142 has found that such an opening exercise is a religious ceremony and was intended by the State to be so. We agree with the trial court's finding as to the religious character of the exercises. Given that finding, the exercises and the law requiring them are in violation of the Establishment Clause.

There is no such specific finding as to the religious character of the exercises in No. 119, and the State contends (as does the State in No. 142) that the program is an effort to extend its benefits to all public school children without regard to their religious belief. Included within its secular purposes, it says, are the promotion of moral values, the contradiction to the materialistic trends of our times, the perpetuation of our institutions and the teaching of literature. The case came up on demurrer, of course, to a petition which alleged that the uniform practice under the rule had been to read from the King James version of the Bible and that the exercise was sectarian. The short answer, therefore, is that the religious character of the exercise was admitted by the State. But even if its purpose is not strictly religious, it is sought to be accomplished through readings, without comment, from the Bible. Surely the place of the Bible as an instrument of religion cannot be gainsaid, and the State's recognition of the pervading religious character of the ceremony is evident from the rule's specific permission of the alternative use of the Catholic Douay version as well as the recent amendment permitting nonattendance at the exercises. None of these factors is consistent with the contention that the Bible is here used either as an instrument for nonreligious moral inspiration or as a reference for the teaching of secular subjects.

The conclusion follows that in both cases the laws require religious exercises and such exercises are being conducted in direct violation of the rights of the appellees and petitioners.[9] Nor are these required exercises mitigated by the fact that individual students may absent themselves upon parental request, for that fact furnishes no defense to a claim of unconstitutionality under the Establishment Clause. See *Engel* v. *Vitale, supra,* at 430. Further, it is no defense to urge that the religious practices here may be

---

[9] It goes without saying that the laws and practices involved here can be challenged only by persons having standing to complain. But the requirements for standing to challenge state action under the Establishment Clause, unlike those relating to the Free Exercise Clause, do not include proof that particular religious freedoms are infringed. *McGowan* v. *Maryland, supra,* at 429–430. The parties here are school children and their parents, who are directly affected by the laws and practices against which their complaints are directed. These interests surely suffice to give the parties standing to complain. See *Engel* v. *Vitale, supra.* Cf. *McCollum* v. *Board of Education, supra; Everson* v. *Board of Education, supra.* Compare *Doremus* v. *Board of Education,* 342 U. S. 429 (1952), which involved the same substantive issues presented here. The appeal was there dismissed upon the graduation of the school child involved and because of the appellants' failure to establish standing as taxpayers.

relatively minor encroachments on the First Amendment. The breach of neutrality that is today a trickling stream may all too soon become a raging torrent and, in the words of Madison, "it is proper to take alarm at the first experiment on our liberties." Memorial and Remonstrance Against Religious Assessments, quoted in *Everson, supra,* at 65.

It is insisted that unless these religious exercises are permitted a "religion of secularism" is established in the schools. We agree of course that the State may not establish a "religion of secularism" in the sense of affirmatively opposing or showing hostility to religion, thus "preferring those who believe in no religion over those who do believe." *Zorach* v. *Clauson, supra,* at 314. We do not agree, however, that this decision in any sense has that effect. In addition, it might well be said that one's education is not complete without a study of comparative religion or the history of religion and its relationship to the advancement of civilization. It certainly may be said that the Bible is worthy of study for its literary and historic qualities. Nothing we have said here indicates that such study of the Bible or of religion, when presented objectively as part of a secular program of education, may not be effected consistently with the First Amendment. But the exercises here do not fall into those categories. They are religious exercises, required by the States in violation of the command of the First Amendment that the Government maintain strict neutrality, neither aiding nor opposing religion.

Finally, we cannot accept that the concept of neutrality, which does not permit a State to require a religious exercise even with the consent of the majority of those affected, collides with the majority's right to free exercise of religion.[10] While the Free Exercise Clause clearly prohibits the use of state action to deny the rights of free exercise to *anyone*, it has never meant that a majority could use the machinery of the State to practice its beliefs. Such a contention was effectively answered by Mr. Justice Jackson for the Court in *West Virginia Board of Education* v. *Barnette*, 319 U. S. 624, 638 (1943):

> "The very purpose of a Bill of Rights was to withdraw certain subjects from the vicissitudes of political controversy, to place them beyond the reach of majorities and officials and to establish them as legal principles to be applied by the courts. One's right to . . . freedom of worship . . . and other fundamental rights may not be submitted to vote; they depend on the outcome of no elections."

The place of religion in our society is an exalted one, achieved through a long tradition of reliance on the home, the church and the inviolable citadel of the individual heart and mind. We have come to recognize through bitter experience that it is not within the power of government to invade that citadel, whether its purpose or effect be to aid or oppose, to advance or retard.

---

[10] We are not of course presented with and therefore do not pass upon a situation such as military service, where the Government regulates the temporal and geographic environment of individuals to a point that, unless it permits voluntary religious services to be conducted with the use of government facilities, military personnel would be unable to engage in the practice of their faiths.

In the relationship between man and religion, the State is firmly committed to a position of neutrality. Though the application of that rule requires interpretation of a delicate sort, the rule itself is clearly and concisely stated in the words of the First Amendment. Applying that rule to the facts of these cases, we affirm the judgment in No. 142. In No. 119, the judgment is reversed and the cause remanded to the Maryland Court of Appeals for further proceedings consistent with this opinion.

It is so ordered.

[A CONCURRING OPINION]

Mr. Justice Douglas, concurring.

I join the opinion of the Court and add a few words in explanation.

While the Free Exercise Clause of the First Amendment is written in terms of what the State may not require of the individual, the Establishment Clause, serving the same goal of individual religious freedom, is written in different terms.

Establishment of a religion can be achieved in several ways. The church and state can be one; the church may control the state or the state may control the church; or the relationship may take one of several possible forms of a working arrangement between the two bodies.[1] Under all of these arrangements the church typically has a place in the state's budget, and church law usually governs such matters as baptism, marriage, divorce and separation, at least for its members and sometimes for the entire body politic.[2] Education, too, is usually high on the priority list of church interests.[3] In the past schools were often made the exclusive responsibility of the church. Today in some state-church countries the state runs the public schools, but compulsory religious exercises are often required of some or all students. Thus, under the agreement Franco made with the Holy See when he came to power in Spain, "The Church regained its place in the national budget. It insists on baptizing all children and has made the catechism obligatory in state schools." [4]

---

[1] See Bates, Religious Liberty: An Inquiry (1945), 9–14, 239–252; Cobb, Religious Liberty in America (1902), 1–2, cc. IV, V; Gledhill, Pakistan, The Development of its Laws and Constitution (8 British Commonwealth, 1957), 11–15; Keller, Church and State on the European Continent (1936), c. 2; Pfeffer, Church, State, and Freedom (1953), c. 2; I Stokes, Church and State in the United States (1950), 151–169.

[2] See III Stokes, *op. cit., supra*, n. 1, 42–67; Bates, *op. cit., supra*, n. 1, 9–11, 58–59, 98, 245; Gledhill, *op. cit., supra*, n. 1, 128, 192, 205, 208; Rackman, Israel's Emerging Constitution (1955), 120–134; Drinan, Religious Freedom in Israel, America (Apr. 6, 1963), 456–457.

[3] See II Stokes, *op. cit., supra*, n. 1, 488–548; Boles, The Bible, Religion, and the Public Schools (2d ed. 1963), 4–10; Rackman, *op. cit., supra*, n. 2, at 136–141; O'Brien, The *Engel* Case from A Swiss Perspective, 61 Mich. L. Rev. 1069; Freund, Muslim Education in West Pakistan, 56 Religious Education 31.

[4] Bates, *op. cit., supra*, n. 1, at 18; Pfeffer, *op. cit., supra*, n. 1, at 28–31; Thomas, The Balance of Forces in Spain, 41 Foreign Affairs 208, 210.

The vice of all such arrangements under the Establishment Clause is that the state is lending its assistance to a church's efforts to gain and keep adherents. Under the First Amendment it is strictly a matter for the individual and his church as to what church he will belong to and how much support, in the way of belief, time, activity or money, he will give to it. "This pure Religious Liberty" "declared . . . [all forms of church-state relationships] and their fundamental idea to be oppressions of conscience and abridgments of that liberty which God and nature had conferred on every living soul." [5]

In these cases we have no coercive religious exercise aimed at making the students conform. The prayers announced are not compulsory, though some may think they have that indirect effect because the nonconformist student may be induced to participate for fear of being called an "oddball." But that coercion, if it be present, has not been shown; so the vices of the present regimes are different.

These regimes violate the Establishment Clause in two different ways. In each case the State is conducting a religious exercise; and, as the Court holds, that cannot be done without violating the "neutrality" required of the State by the balance of power between individual, church and state that has been struck by the First Amendment. But the Establishment Clause is not limited to precluding the State itself from conducting religious exercises. It also forbids the State to employ its facilities or funds in a way that gives any church, or all churches, greater strength in our society than it would have by relying on its members alone. Thus, the present regimes must fall under that clause for the additional reason that public funds, though small in amount, are being used to promote a religious exercise. Through the mechanism of the State, all of the people are being required to finance a religious exercise that only some of the people want and that violates the sensibilities of others.

The most effective way to establish any institution is to finance it; and this truth is reflected in the appeals by church groups for public funds to finance their religious schools.[6] Financing a church either in its strictly religious activities or in its other activities is equally unconstitutional, as I understand the Establishment Clause. Budgets for one activity may be technically separable from budgets for others.[7] But the institution is an inseparable whole, a living organism, which is strengthened in proselytizing when it is strengthened in any department by contributions from other than its own members.

Such contributions may not be made by the State even in a minor degree without violating the Establishment Clause. It is not the amount of public funds expended; as this case illustrates, it is the use to which public funds are put that is controlling. For the First Amendment does not say that some forms

---

[5] Cobb, *op. cit., supra*, n. 1, at 2.
[6] See II Stokes, *op. cit., supra*, n. 1, at 681–695.
[7] See Accountants' Handbook (4th ed. 1956) 4.8–4.15.

of establishment are allowed; it says that "no law respecting an establishment of religion" shall be made. What may not be done directly may not be done indirectly lest the Establishment Clause become a mockery.

[A DISSENTING OPINION]

MR. JUSTICE STEWART, dissenting.

I think the records in the two cases before us are so fundamentally deficient as to make impossible an informed or responsible determination of the constitutional issues presented. Specifically, I cannot agree that on these records we can say that the Establishment Clause has necessarily been violated.[1] But I think there exist serious questions under both that provision and the Free Exercise Clause—insofar as each is imbedded in the Fourteenth Amendment—which require the remand of these cases for the taking of additional evidence.

I

The First Amendment declares that "Congress shall make no law respecting an establishment of religion, or prohibiting the free exercise thereof . . . ." It is, I think, a fallacious oversimplification to regard these two provisions as establishing a single constitutional standard of "separation of church and state," which can be mechanically applied in every case to delineate the required boundaries between government and religion. We err in the first place if we do not recognize, as a matter of history and as a matter of the imperatives of our free society, that religion and government must necessarily interact in countless ways. Secondly, the fact is that while in many contexts the Establishment Clause and the Free Exercise Clause fully complement each other, there are areas in which a doctrinaire reading of the Establishment Clause leads to irreconcilable conflict with the Free Exercise Clause.

A single obvious example should suffice to make the point. Spending federal funds to employ chaplains for the armed forces might be said to violate the Establishment Clause. Yet a lonely soldier stationed at some faraway outpost could surely complain that a government which did *not* provide him the opportunity for pastoral guidance was affirmatively prohibiting the free exercise of his religion. And such examples could readily be multiplied. The short of the matter is simply that the two relevant clauses of the First Amendment cannot accurately be reflected in a sterile metaphor

---

[1] It is instructive, in this connection, to examine the complaints in the two cases before us. Neither complaint attacks the challenged practices as "establishments." What both allege as the basis for their causes of actions are, rather, violations of religious liberty.

which by its very nature may distort rather than illumine the problems involved in a particular case. Cf. *Sherbert* v. *Verner, post,* p. 398.

II

As a matter of history, the First Amendment was adopted solely as a limitation upon the newly created National Government. The events leading to its adoption strongly suggest that the Establishment Clause was primarily an attempt to insure that Congress not only would be powerless to establish a national church, but would also be unable to interfere with existing state establishments. See *McGowan* v. *Maryland,* 366 U. S. 420, 440–441. Each State was left free to go its own way and pursue its own policy with respect to religion. Thus Virginia from the beginning pursued a policy of disestablishmentarianism. Massachusetts, by contrast, had an established church until well into the nineteenth century.

So matters stood until the adoption of the Fourteenth Amendment, or more accurately, until this Court's decision in *Cantwell* v. *Connecticut,* in 1940. 310 U. S. 296. In that case the Court said: "The First Amendment declares that Congress shall make no law respecting an establishment of religion or prohibiting the free exercise thereof. The Fourteenth Amendment has rendered the legislatures of the states as incompetent as Congress to enact such laws." [2]

I accept without question that the liberty guaranteed by the Fourteenth Amendment against impairment by the States embraces in full the right of free exercise of religion protected by the First Amendment, and I yield to no one in my conception of the breadth of that freedom. See *Braunfeld* v. *Brown,* 366 U. S. 599, 616 (dissenting opinion). I accept too the proposition that the Fourteenth Amendment has somehow absorbed the Establishment Clause, although it is not without irony that a constitutional provision evidently designed to leave the States free to go their own way should now have become a restriction upon their autonomy. But I cannot agree with what seems to me the insensitive definition of the Establishment Clause contained in the Court's opinion, nor with the different but, I think, equally mechanistic definitions contained in the separate opinions which have been filed.

III

Since the *Cantwell* pronouncement in 1940, this Court has only twice held invalid state laws on the ground that they were laws "respecting an establishment of religion" in violation of the Fourteenth Amendment. *McCollum* v. *Board of Education,* 333 U. S. 203; *Engel* v. *Vitale,* 370 U. S. 421. On the other hand, the Court has upheld against such a challenge laws establishing Sunday as a compulsory day of rest, *McGowan* v. *Maryland,* 366 U. S. 420, and a law authorizing reimbursement from public funds for the trans-

---

[2] 310 U. S., at 303. The Court's statement as to the Establishment Clause in *Cantwell* was dictum. The case was decided on free exercise grounds.

portation of parochial school pupils. *Everson v. Board of Education*, 330 U. S. 1.

Unlike other First Amendment guarantees, there is an inherent limitation upon the applicability of the Establishment Clause's ban on state support to religion. That limitation was succinctly put in *Everson v. Board of Education*, 330 U. S. 1, 18: "State power is no more to be used so as to handicap religions than it is to favor them."³ And in a later case, this Court recognized that the limitation was one which was itself compelled by the free exercise guarantee. "To hold that a state cannot consistently with the First and Fourteenth Amendments utilize its public school system to aid any or all religious faiths or sects in the dissemination of their doctrines and ideals does not . . . manifest a governmental hostility to religion or religious teachings. A manifestation of such hostility would be at war with our national tradition as embodied in the First Amendment's guaranty of the free exercise of religion." *McCollum v. Board of Education*, 333 U. S. 203, 211–212.

That the central value embodied in the First Amendment—and, more particularly, in the guarantee of "liberty" contained in the Fourteenth—is the safeguarding of an individual's right to free exercise of his religion has been consistently recognized. Thus, in the case of *Hamilton v. Regents*, 293 U. S. 245, 265, Mr. Justice Cardozo, concurring, assumed that it was ". . . *the religious liberty* protected by the First Amendment against invasion by the nation [which] is protected by the Fourteenth Amendment against invasion by the states." (Emphasis added.) And in *Cantwell v. Connecticut, supra,* the purpose of those guarantees was described in the following terms: "On the one hand, it forestalls compulsion by law of the acceptance of any creed or the practice of any form of worship. Freedom of conscience and freedom to adhere to such religious organization or form of worship as the individual may choose cannot be restricted by law. On the other hand, it safeguards the free exercise of the chosen form of religion." 310 U. S., at 303.

It is this concept of constitutional protection embodied in our decisions which makes the cases before us such difficult ones for me. For there is involved in these cases a substantial free exercise claim on the part of those who affirmatively desire to have their children's school day open with the reading of passages from the Bible.

It has become accepted that the decision in *Pierce v. Society of Sisters,* 268 U. S. 510, upholding the right of parents to send their children to nonpublic schools, was ultimately based upon the recognition of the validity of the free exercise claim involved in that situation. It might be argued here that parents who wanted their children to be exposed to religious influences in

---

³ See also, in this connection, *Zorach v. Clauson,* 343 U. S. 306, 314: "Government may not finance religious groups nor undertake religious instruction nor blend secular and sectarian education nor use secular institutions to force one or some religion on any person. But we find no constitutional requirement which makes it necessary for government to be hostile to religion and to throw its weight against efforts to widen the effective scope of religious influence."

school could, under *Pierce*, send their children to private or parochial schools. But the consideration which renders this contention too facile to be determinative has already been recognized by the Court: "Freedom of speech, freedom of the press, freedom of religion are available to all, not merely to those who can pay their own way." *Murdock* v. *Pennsylvania*, 319 U. S. 105, 111.

It might also be argued that parents who want their children exposed to religious influences can adequately fulfill that wish off school property and outside school time. With all its surface persuasiveness, however, this argument seriously misconceives the basic constitutional justification for permitting the exercises at issue in these cases. For a compulsory state educational system so structures a child's life that if religious exercises are held to be an impermissible activity in schools, religion is placed at an artificial and state-created disadvantage. Viewed in this light, permission of such exercises for those who want them is necessary if the schools are truly to be neutral in the matter of religion. And a refusal to permit religious exercises thus is seen, not as the realization of state neutrality, but rather as the establishment of a religion of secularism, or at the least, as government support of the beliefs of those who think that religious exercises should be conducted only in private.

What seems to me to be of paramount importance, then, is recognition of the fact that the claim advanced here in favor of Bible reading is sufficiently substantial to make simple reference to the constitutional phrase "establishment of religion" as inadequate an analysis of the cases before us as the ritualistic invocation of the nonconstitutional phrase "separation of church and state." What these cases compel, rather, is an analysis of just what the "neutrality" is which is required by the interplay of the Establishment and Free Exercise Clauses of the First Amendment, as imbedded in the Fourteenth.

IV

Our decisions make clear that there is no constitutional bar to the use of government property for religious purposes. On the contrary, this Court has consistently held that the discriminatory barring of religious groups from public property is itself a violation of First and Fourteenth Amendment guarantees. *Fowler* v. *Rhode Island*, 345 U. S. 67; *Niemotko* v. *Maryland*, 340 U. S. 268. A different standard has been applied to public school property, because of the coercive effect which the use by religious sects of a compulsory school system would necessarily have upon the children involved. *McCollum* v. *Board of Education*, 333 U. S. 203. But insofar as the *McCollum* decision rests on the establishment rather than the Free Exercise Clause, it is clear that its effect is limited to religious instruction—to government support of proselytizing activities of religious sects by throwing the weight of secular authority behind the dissemination of religious tenets.[4]

The dangers both to government and to religion inherent in official

---

[4] "This is beyond all question a utilization of the tax-established and tax-supported public school system to aid religious groups *to spread their faith.*" *McCollum* v. *Board of Education*, 333 U. S. 203, 210. (Emphasis added.)

support of instruction in the tenets of various religious sects are absent in the present cases, which involve only a reading from the Bible unaccompanied by comments which might otherwise constitute instruction. Indeed, since, from all that appears in either record, any teacher who does not wish to do so is free not to participate,[5] it cannot even be contended that some infinitesimal part of the salaries paid by the State are made contingent upon the performance of a religious function.

In the absence of evidence that the legislature or school board intended to prohibit local schools from substituting a different set of readings where parents requested such a change, we should not assume that the provisions before us—as actually administered—may not be construed simply as authorizing religious exercises, nor that the designations may not be treated simply as indications of the promulgating body's view as to the community's preference. We are under a duty to interpret these provisions so as to render them constitutional if reasonably possible. Compare *Two Guys* v. *McGinley,* 366 U. S. 582, 592–595; *Everson* v. *Board of Education,* 330 U. S. 1, 4, and n. 2. In the *Schempp* case there is evidence which indicates that variations were in fact permitted by the very school there involved, and that further variations were not introduced only because of the absence of requests from parents. And in the *Murray* case the Baltimore rule itself contains a provision permitting another version of the Bible to be substituted for the King James version.

If the provisions are not so construed, I think that their validity under the Establishment Clause would be extremely doubtful, because of the designation of a particular religious book and a denominational prayer. But since, even if the provisions are construed as I believe they must be, I think that the cases before us must be remanded for further evidence on other issues—thus affording the plaintiffs an opportunity to prove that local variations are not in fact permitted—I shall for the balance of this dissenting opinion treat the provisions before us as making the variety and content of the exercises, as well as a choice as to their implementation, matters which ultimately reflect the consensus of each local school community. In the absence of coercion upon those who do not wish to participate—because they hold less strong beliefs, other beliefs, or no beliefs at all—such provisions cannot, in any view, be held to represent the type of support of religion barred by the Establishment Clause. For the only support which such rules provide for religion is the withholding of state hostility—a simple acknowledgment on the part of secular authorities that the Constitution does not require extirpation of all expression of religious belief.

V

I have said that these provisions authorizing religious exercises are properly to be regarded as measures making possible the free exercise of religion.

---

[5] The Pennsylvania statute was specifically amended to remove the compulsion upon teachers. Act of December 17, 1959, P. L. 1928, 24 Purdon's Pa. Stat. Ann. § 15–1516. Since the Maryland case is here on a demurrer, the issue of whether or not a teacher could be dismissed for refusal to participate seems, among many others, never to have been raised.

But it is important to stress that, strictly speaking, what is at issue here is a privilege rather than a right. In other words, the question presented is not whether exercises such as those at issue here are constitutionally compelled, but rather whether they are constitutionally invalid. And that issue, in my view, turns on the question of coercion.

It is clear that the dangers of coercion involved in the holding of religious exercises in a schoolroom differ qualitatively from those presented by the use of similar exercises or affirmations in ceremonies attended by adults. Even as to children, however, the duty laid upon government in connection with religious exercises in the public schools is that of refraining from so structuring the school environment as to put any kind of pressure on a child to participate in those exercises; it is not that of providing an atmosphere in which children are kept scrupulously insulated from any awareness that some of their fellows may want to open the school day with prayer, or of the fact that there exist in our pluralistic society differences of religious belief.

These are not, it must be stressed, cases like *Brown* v. *Board of Education*, 347 U. S. 483, in which this Court held that, in the sphere of public education, the Fourteenth Amendment's guarantee of equal protection of the laws required that race not be treated as a relevant factor. A segregated school system is not invalid because its operation is coercive; it is invalid simply because our Constitution presupposes that men are created equal, and that therefore racial differences cannot provide a valid basis for governmental action. Accommodation of religious differences on the part of the State, however, is not only permitted but required by that same Constitution.

The governmental neutrality which the First and Fourteenth Amendments require in the cases before us, in other words, is the extension of evenhanded treatment to all who believe, doubt, or disbelieve—a refusal on the part of the State to weight the scales of private choice. In these cases, therefore, what is involved is not state action based on impermissible categories, but rather an attempt by the State to accommodate those differences which the existence in our society of a variety of religious beliefs makes inevitable. The Constitution requires that such efforts be struck down only if they are proven to entail the use of the secular authority of government to coerce a preference among such beliefs.

It may well be, as has been argued to us, that even the supposed benefits to be derived from noncoercive religious exercises in public schools are incommensurate with the administrative problems which they would create. The choice involved, however, is one for each local community and its school board, and not for this Court. For, as I have said, religious exercises are not constitutionally invalid if they simply reflect differences which exist in the society from which the school draws its pupils. They become constitutionally invalid only if their administration places the sanction of secular authority behind one or more particular religious or irreligious beliefs.

To be specific, it seems to me clear that certain types of exercises would present situations in which no possibility of coercion on the part of secular officials could be claimed to exist. Thus, if such exercises were held either before or after the official school day, or if the school schedule were such that participation were merely one among a number of desirable alternatives,[6] it could hardly be contended that the exercises did anything more than to provide an opportunity for the voluntary expression of religious belief. On the other hand, a law which provided for religious exercises during the school day and which contained no excusal provision would obviously be unconstitutionally coercive upon those who did not wish to participate. And even under a law containing an excusal provision, if the exercises were held during the school day, and no equally desirable alternative were provided by the school authorities, the likelihood that children might be under at least some psychological compulsion to participate would be great. In a case such as the latter, however, I think we would err if we *assumed* such coercion in the absence of any evidence.[7]

VI

Viewed in this light, it seems to me clear that the records in both of the cases before us are wholly inadequate to support an informed or responsible decision. Both cases involve provisions which explicitly permit any student who wishes, to be excused from participation in the exercises. There is no evidence in either case as to whether there would exist any coercion of any kind upon a student who did not want to participate. No evidence at all was adduced in the *Murray* case, because it was decided upon a demurrer. All that we have in that case, therefore, is the conclusory language of a pleading. While such conclusory allegations are acceptable for procedural purposes, I think that the nature of the constitutional problem involved here clearly demands that no decision be made except upon evidence. In the *Schempp* case the record shows no more than a subjective prophecy by a parent of what he thought would happen if a request were made to be excused from participation in the exercises under the amended statute. No such request was ever made, and there is no evidence whatever as to what might or would actually happen, nor of what administrative arrangements the school actually might or could make to free from pressure of any kind those who do not want to participate in the exercises. There were no District Court findings on this

---

[6] See, *e. g.*, the description of a plan permitting religious instruction off school property contained in *McCollum* v. *Board of Education,* 333 U. S. 203, 224 (separate opinion of Mr. Justice Frankfurter).

[7] Cf. "The task of separating the secular from the religious in education is one of magnitude, intricacy and delicacy. To lay down a sweeping constitutional doctrine as demanded by complainant and apparently approved by the Court, applicable alike to all school boards of the nation, . . . is to decree a uniform, rigid and, if we are consistent, an unchanging standard for countless school boards representing and serving highly localized groups which not only differ from each other but which themselves from time to time change attitudes. It seems to me that to do so is to allow zeal for our own ideas of what is good in public instruction to induce us to accept the role of a super board of education for every school district in the nation." *McCollum* v. *Board of Education,* 333 U. S. 203, 237 (concurring opinion of Mr. Justice Jackson).

issue, since the case under the amended statute was decided exclusively on Establishment Clause grounds. 201 F. Supp. 815.

What our Constitution indispensably protects is the freedom of each of us, be he Jew or Agnostic, Christian or Atheist, Buddhist or Freethinker, to believe or disbelieve, to worship or not worship, to pray or keep silent, according to his own conscience, uncoerced and unrestrained by government. It is conceivable that these school boards, or even all school boards, might eventually find it impossible to administer a system of religious exercises during school hours in such a way as to meet this constitutional standard—in such a way as completely to free from any kind of official coercion those who do not affirmatively want to participate.[8] But I think we must not assume that school boards so lack the qualities of inventiveness and good will as to make impossible the achievement of that goal.

I would remand both cases for further hearings.

Questions

1. Why does Justice Clark describe (and why in such great detail) the practices followed in the Abington schools? Does this description have relevance to the rest of his argument?
2. What is the purpose of part II in Justice Clark's statement?
3. Justice Clark states that the "rule's specific permission of the alternative use of the Catholic Douay version" indicates the "pervading religious character of the ceremony." What does he mean? What does Justice Stewart say on this point?
4. What is the purpose of footnote 10 in Justice Clark's statement? What would Justice Stewart say on this point?
5. What does Justice Douglas' statement add to Justice Clark's?
6. What does Justice Stewart refer to as "a sterile metaphor"? What does he mean by the phrase?
7. What does Justice Stewart mean, in part II, by the term "mechanistic"?
8. Succinctly state the argument, made by those who oppose the decision of the court, that this decision established a "religion of secularism." What would be the Court's response to this accusation?
9. How would the Court rule on the constitutionality of a course about the Bible as literature?

Assignments

1. Lawyers are often attacked for using legal jargon that laymen cannot understand. Make a list of the specialized expressions used by the three justices. Defend or criticize the use of these expressions.
2. Outline the argument of Justice Clark.
3. Take one of the important cases that justices refer to as a basis for their opinions, such as *Engel* v. *Vitale, Everson* v. *Board of Education,* or *McGowan* v.

---

[8] For example, if the record in the *Schempp* case contained proof (rather than mere prophecy) that the timing of morning announcements by the school was such as to handicap children who did not want to listen to the Bible reading, or that the excusal provision was so administered as to carry any overtones of social inferiority, then impermissible coercion would clearly exist.

EXERCISES

Maryland. Read the opinions in that case and discuss the ways in which it has been used as a precedent in *Abington School District* v. *Schempp.*
4. Attack or defend one of the following propositions:
   a. Public high schools should offer courses on the Bible.
   b. The decision in *Abington School District* v. *Schempp* establishes a "religion of secularism."
   c. The Constitution should be changed to allow Bible reading in public schools.
5. Analyze the major constitutional issues involved in one of the following issues:
   a. Whether taxes should purchase transportation (or texts) for parochial school pupils
   b. Whether government loans should be made to parochial schools
   c. Whether the words "in God we trust" should appear on United States currency and the phrase "under God" be included in the Pledge of Allegiance.
6. Make a study of the attitudes toward the decision by groups and prominent individuals and describe the rationale of those who support and those who condemn the Court's decision.

Additional Reading

Besides stirring up threats of constitutional amendment in Congress, the decision on Bible reading elicited considerable discussion among educators and religious leaders. Educators have been primarily concerned with the basis of the Court's decision and with the effects that the decision might have on classroom activities. Among the discussions of the educational implications of the decision are W. W. Brickman, "Bible Reading, Prayers, and Public Schools," *School and Society,* XCI (October 5, 1963), 272; H. L. Hurwitz, "Jefferson's Wall and the Schools," *Senior Scholastic,* LXXXIV (February 7, 1964), 9; A. W. Steinhilber, "Bible Reading in the Public Schools," *School Life,* XLVI (October 1963), 13–16; "Supreme Court Decision on Bible Reading and Prayer Recitation," *NEA Journal,* LII (September 1963), 55–56.

Among the diverse religious opinions on the decision are "Court Decides Wisely: School Prayer," *Christian Century,* LXXX (July 3, 1963), 851; "Equal Justice, Lord's Prayer and Bible Reading Cases," *America,* CVIII (May 18, 1963), 704; W. B. Ball, "Implications of Supreme Court Decisions for Contemporary Church-State Problems," *Catholic World,* CXCVII (August 1963), 296–305; J. O'Gara, "Religion and the Court," *Commonweal,* LXXVIII (July 5, 1963), 391; "Churches and the Public Schools: A Policy Statement Adopted by General Board on June 7, 1963 in New York City, National Council of Churches of Christ in the United States of America," *International Journal of Religious Education,* XL (September 1963), 22–23.

SECTION FOUR: Society's Right to Kill

Tennessee v. Wash Jones: The Closing Argument for the Defense

JOE W. HENRY, JR.

May it please the Court:

Fifty-three years ago, in a bleak and barren and God-forsaken building on the banks of the Cumberland River at 5:00 o'clock in the morning, a Negro man, made in God's own image, bearing the name of Julius Morgan, and from Dyer County, Tennessee, became the first citizen of our state to be legally murdered by electrocution.

Two years later, on July 8, 1918, *the second kilowatt killing* was conducted. This time the hapless victim was one, J. D. Williams, a Negro citizen, of Giles County.

The third time the stench of searing and scorched human flesh came out of our penitentiary was that same July day in 1918, when Eddie Olsup met his Maker at the hands of the civilized State of Tennessee and in order to preserve the peace and dignity of the state. He, too, was from Giles County.

In all, 123 persons have walked that last mile.

One hundred twenty-three times we have turned our backs upon the command of the Decalogue: Thou shalt not kill.

One hundred twenty-three times we have arrogated to ourselves the right to destroy the image of God on earth.

One hundred twenty-three times we have disputed the sacred idea that no man is beyond redemption.

One hundred twenty-three times we have reverted to our primitive and savage origin bred in generations in the jungle.

One hundred twenty-three times we have closed the door on a man's life and sent him to his Maker with a crime on his soul and guilt in his heart and denied him his God-given right to repentance, redemption and forgiveness.

One hundred twenty-three times we have usurped the divine authority of heaven.

One hundred twenty-three prosecutors have sung their hymns of hate as hapless human beings prepared to hang down their heads and die.

One hundred twenty-three times we have proclaimed to the world that state government has no obligation to be civilized.

Who were these 123 men?

Their names are unimportant, but I have a list that shows them all—the roll of horror.

One cannot look at this yellow sheet—significantly it is yellow—the color denoting cowardice, the color of the Army's Dishonorable Discharge, the color that describes the worst fever known to man, the color that describes the jacket of the pestiferous hornet, the color that describes the worst brand of journalism—one cannot look at it without thinking of all the widows and orphans we have made, of all the tears that were shed in their memory and of the God who loved them, but who was thrust from their hearts by the cold hand of vengeance.

Ten men and two women sit upon this jury. Five of you owe your spiritual allegiance to the Methodist Church; two to the Church of Christ; two to the Cumberland Presbyterian, and one to the Baptist Church.

All of you stated on your examination that you believed in God, that you accepted Jesus Christ as your personal Saviour, that you subscribed to the precepts of the Christian religion, believed in the set of ethical standards proclaimed by Christ, believed in a future system of rewards and punishment, the forgiveness of sins, the resurrection of the body and the life everlasting.

In short, you are Christians and civilized citizens.

You have all—some reluctantly—expressed your belief in capital punishment.

As you follow my argument, I ask that you search your souls in an effort to arrive at a rational and Christian conclusion based upon a fresh look at the evidence.

I ask that you erase from your minds any opinion that you may have on capital punishment until I have presented the case against capital punishment and have reviewed the issues and separated superstition from fact.

Essentials of Punishment

It is generally accepted that there are *three essential ingredients* of all punishment. All must be present and if any one is missing the punishment is defective.

First, the punishment of the offender;

Second, the rehabilitation of the offender and his restoration to useful and productive citizenship;

Third, the protection of society by deterring others from the commission of like offenses.

We may dispose summarily, and without discussion, of the first two, because I will readily admit that death by electrocution definitely fulfills the essential ingredient of punishment. I am sure that the district attorney and his associate, likewise, will concede that death is fairly permanent and when the penalty of death is imposed rehabilitation and restoration are impossible. Thus, it is, at the very outset, one of the essentials of punishment is missing.

Deterrence

This leaves for consideration the major ingredient and the one that completely overshadows the first two, *i.e.*, deterrence. *Does the death penalty serve as a warning to others? Does it keep them from committing similar crimes?*

There are those who contend that we are living in an age when we have witnessed more brutality and slaughter than all our ancestors since the birth of Christ; that this is perhaps why we don't worry too much about the death of one man, that we have become inoculated to brutality and immune to human suffering.

My whole being rebels at any such philosophy. I am morally persuaded that throughout the history of time each generation has been successively better and upon the rungs of its progress we are steadily climbing the ladder that ultimately leads to a perfect order of existence.

Men of good will recognize it to be incontestably true that we are our brothers' keepers, and just as a pebble cannot be thrown into the ocean without disturbing every drop of water in the sea, so one man cannot be abandoned and sacrificed upon the altar of society's sometimes unreasonable demands without disturbing all mankind.

Yes, we have made great progress.

Throughout the recorded history of time the human race has devised many and varied means of punishing those guilty of infractions of good order, and while we have not reached perfection, our progress has been praiseworthy.

There was a time when society thought that criminals should be beheaded, burned, boiled or buried alive; when men were strangled, stoned, skinned or starved to death; when they were torn asunder by trees fastened to their limbs, or devoured by wild beasts; when they were forced to drink poison, crucified, or drowned; when they were chopped in two while still alive, or eaten alive by insects or sewn in a bag with snakes—all of this in the name of justice and all because it was *"the law of the state."*

As odious and savage as these practices sound to us today, let's face the fact that a hundred years from now when capital punishment has long vanished from the American scene as it has in most of the other civilized countries of the world—electrocution will be listed as another barbarous punishment along with drawing and quartering—for I submit to you any punishment that takes the very life of a human being is barbarous, cruel, un-Christian, and uncivilized and a throwback to the Dark Ages.

Time was when pigs, horses and cattle were tried and executed for murder. *It was the law of the state.*

In 1474 a rooster was tried for the heinous and unnatural crime of laying an egg and sentenced, together with the egg, to be burned at the stake. *It was the law of the state.*

There is another, in 1801 of a British child being hanged for stealing a spoon. *It was the law of the state.*

There is a recorded case in England of a 9-year-old girl being hanged for stealing two pennies worth of salt. *It was the law of the state.*

There is another in 1748 of a boy of 10 who was executed for murder. *It was the law of the state.*

There is the case of the 12-year-old American boy who was hanged for stealing a sheep. *It was the law of the state.*

I am sickened every time I hear a prosecutor apologetically asking for the death penalty and offering the pitiful excuse *"It's the law of the state"*.

In England during the reign of Henry VIII, there were over two hundred crimes, ranging from shooting rabbits to associating with Gypsies for which the death penalty was exacted and during this period, to the shame and disgrace of our mother country, 72,000 *Englishmen were executed.* This, however, did not seem to deter Englishmen from committing crimes.

During the reign of Queen Elizabeth I, *19,000 Englishmen were executed* but the crime rate continued to rise.

No doubt bloody Queen Mary was actuated by the noblest motives, but for all the blood she drew, crime continued unabated in Merry England.

Peter I, Tsar of Russia, issued an edict against men wearing beards and, in order to enforce it, in 1728, *put to death 8,000 Russians,* and yet today we can hardly think of a Russian without a bearded image flashing before our eyes.

There was a time in England when pickpockets were hanged and when the public hangings took place the pickpockets gathered and picked the pockets of those who came to witness the execution.

The death penalty did not deter the 7,000 people in America who committed murders in 1958.

Crime has a tendency to beget crime, and bizarre punishments have always adversely affected law enforcement.

One of the most famous of all English hangmen was John Price, who was himself hanged for murder, as was Hangman Dennis and Mr. Hespel.

Then there is the interesting story of a former head hangman at the Oklahoma State Prison, who was tried for murder himself on no less than four occasions.

Ordinary prudence and common judgment will tell us that if the imposition of the death penalty is to operate as a deterrent, executions must be performed publicly so that all may see what a horrible and hideous fate awaits the wrongdoer. Criminals should have front seats; it should be carried on television; movies should be made; the penalty made more brutal, and sheer, stark terror should be stricken into the hearts of all the people so that they, in heat of passion, or while temporarily insane, will stop and think of the gruesome fate that is theirs.

Non-justifiable murders can take only two forms:

First, those in heat of passion.

Second, those premeditated and planned.

In the first group the murderer has lost all reason and all control of his faculties and, therefore, the consequences of his deed do not enter his mind.

In the second group, the murderer thinks he has planned the perfect crime and will not be apprehended, and so he gives no thought to punishment.

Again, where is the deterrence?

The State of Delaware has just become the eighth state to outlaw capital punishment. Among the reasons assigned for this action by the Prisoners' Aid Society of Delaware were:

> 1. The evidence clearly shows that execution does not act as a deterrent to capital offenses.
> 2. The serious offenses are committed, except in rare instances, by those suffering from mental disturbances; are impulsive in nature; and are not the acts of the "criminal" class.
> 3. More convictions with less delays are obtained because the reluctance of juries to convict where the death sentence is involved is removed as a factor.
> 4. Unequal application of the law takes place because those executed are the poor, the ignorant, and the unfortunate without resources.
> 5. Conviction of the innocent does occur and death makes a miscarriage of justice irrevocable. Human judgment cannot be infallible.
> 6. The state sets a bad example when it takes a life. Imitative crimes and murder are stimulated by executions.
> 7. Legally taking a life is useless and is demoralizing to the general public. It is also demoralizing to the public officials who, dedicated to rehabilitating individuals, must callously put a man to death.

Perhaps one of the most illuminating studies on capital punishment was made by the British Royal Commission on capital punishment during the period 1949–1953. After a four-year study, and hearing expert witnesses from many parts of the world, they came to this interesting conclusion:

The general conclusion which we have reached is that there is no clear evidence in any of the figures we have examined that the abolition of capital punishment has led to an increase in the homicide rate, or that its re-introduction has led to its fall.

A California legislative committee reported in 1957:

A world-wide survey shows that nowhere has the abolition of the death penalty led to an increase in the number of homicides.

In the face of these and numerous other studies, and against all the evidence to the contrary, there are those who still insist that the death penalty is a deterrent and that its abolition would result in an increase in crime.

Let's take a look at the record.

The death penalty has been abolished in the following *countries of Europe:* Austria, Denmark, Finland, Holland, Italy, Norway, Portugal, Rumania, Spain, Sweden, Switzerland, West Germany; *of South and Central America:* Argentina, Brazil, Colombia, Costa Rica, Dominican Republic, Ecuador, Honduras, Mexico, Panama, Peru, Puerto Rico, Uruguay, Venezuela; *elsewhere:* Greenland, Iceland, Israel, New Zealand and Turkey.

In the United States it has been abolished in: Maine, Michigan, Minnesota, North Dakota, Rhode Island, Wisconsin, Alaska, Delaware, Hawaii.

In all of the foreign countries, for which I have the figures, their murder rate went down after the abolition.

In the United States during the ten-year period 1931–1940, the average rate of murders was 8.1 per 100,000, whereas, in the states that did not have capital punishment, the rate was only 2.3 *or only one fourth as high.*

It is significant that the State of Maine which abolished capital punishment in 1887 after an innocent man was executed, has one of the lowest murder rates in the United States, whereas *Georgia with fourteen crimes for which the death penalty may be exacted has the highest murder rate in the nation.*

So much for the argument that capital punishment serves to deter others from the commission of crimes. The record completely refutes this argument.

Convictions by Mistake

To me, one of the most compelling arguments against capital punishment is the possibility of mistake. Moreover, every lawyer and judge knows that bold, bald, unblushing perjury all too frequently stalks into our courts and makes a mockery of that intangible commodity we call justice.

All America has harked to the saga of Tom Dooley, the folk song imploring a gay blade headed for the gallows to hang his head in shame before he was executed, but I wonder how many know that the song was written about a North Carolina man named Tom Dula, who was convicted of murdering a young lady acquaintance and was hanged because *it was the law of the state*.

Unfortunately for Tom Dula it was a number of years later before the real murderer confessed.

So many times have the innocent been mistakenly convicted or wrongfully convicted on what later developed to be perjured testimony that a number of books have been written about numerous of these cases.

Biblical Precedents

Then, there are the great cases of recorded history where, even though it was the law, the death penalty was not inflicted.

God, Himself, set the first precedent. Cain gazed upon the beaten and bleeding body of his own brother. The denunciation of Heaven was ringing in his ears. He expected to find vengeance at every hand. But God did not visit capital punishment on him. Instead, He banished him from society, placed a mark upon him—a mark of his crime, but also a mark that would warn the rest of mankind against his destruction. *This was the judgment of Almighty God in dealing with the first murderer and I submit that it is exempt from any possibility of error.*

Then, there is *the case of David,* who was responsible for the death of Uriah the Hittite, and who was not executed but continued, in spite of his heinous crime, to grow in favor with God and man and the holy writ tells us that he was "a man after God's own heart".

The case of Moses is in point—Moses who slew the Egyptian in a fit of anger and who became a fugitive from justice, and yet, God sought him out and, from the burning bush to the heights of Pisgah, from the Red Sea to the mountain peak whence he was taken by God to survey the Promised Land from Dan to Beersheba, he, a murderer, was the right hand of God Almighty.

What if David and Moses had been executed because *"It is the law of the state?"*

The Noachin Laws

Those who urge the continuance of capital punishment forget all these things. Instead, their delight is in quoting from obsolete scripture, taken out of context and bodily lifted from the circumstances surrounding their utterance. Just as patriotism is the last refuge of a scoundrel, so the Bible is the favorite stamping ground of those who enjoy quoting scripture for their own purpose. With fiendish glee and triumphant manner they turn to the ninth chapter and sixth verse of the Book of Genesis and chant: "Whosoever sheddeth man's blood, by man shall his blood be shed."

But circumstances alter cases. Let us look at the circumstances under which this law was laid down. The world had gotten so evil that God repented that he had made man (Gen. 6:6), the great flood came, the former race of mankind with all their laws and customs had been swept away and destroyed by the waters of death.

In gratitude the little family of Noah gathered about the altar and received the seven precepts or laws, we know then as the Noachin laws, for their government. They were few in number and temporary in nature. They embraced only the subjects necessary in their peculiar situation.

All of these seven laws were aimed at repopulating a destroyed earth. Two of the seven laws read "be ye fruitful and multiply". The little family of Noah was a germ from which all the future nations of the earth were to vegetate. Every possible care therefore had to be taken for its preservation. So the right was expressly given directly by God to take away the life of its members, there being no other possible means of effectuating the purposes of heaven in their preservation. But no such direct and divine authority has been given the three and one-half million people of Tennessee.

The Mosaic Law

Then, there are those who look to the Mosaic Law and cite it as authority to show that God's power over life and death has been committed to His creatures. They overlook a number of significant factors. First of all, the law delivered to Moses amid the fire and flame and the smoke at Mt. Sinai was divided into three parts—moral, political and judicial. The moral law, the Ten Commandments, is universal in its operation and perpetual in its obligation. But the political and judicial laws are only of interest from a standpoint of Biblical history. They constituted a civil and criminal code for the government of the Jews only.

Their authority commanding the infliction of capital punishment is no more binding on a Christian nation than the laws of the Medes and the Persians, or of the various tribes that were driven from Canaan by the sword of the Lord and of Gideon.

Strong measures were needed to bring the headstrong, moody and murmuring people of the children of Israel across the Wilderness. Every student of the Bible knows how they taxed the combined authority of both God and Moses. Never before or since has there been such a rebellious tribe of people and never were such extraordinary measures required to keep a nation in subjection. Even as Moses was on the mountain receiving these very laws amidst the most sublime and awful and awesome demonstrations of the power and grandeur of God, this wayward people set themselves to dancing, in idolatrous worship, around an image made of gold.

I wish that time permitted me to delve more deeply into this with you, but it does not.

The Law of Christ

Ladies and gentlemen of the jury, centuries after the Mosaic Law and almost 2,000 years ago, a solitary wayfarer walked the shores of the Sea of Galilee, healing the sick and casting out the demons that possessed the mentally ill. Persecuted by the mighty Roman Empire, crucified by the edict of a court composed of His own countrymen, denied thrice by one of His trusted disciples in His hour of greatest need, and betrayed by the traitorous deed of another, mocked, spat upon and ridiculed, He, a victim of capital punishment, died the most ignominious death known to His day, and yet He was not deterred and His teachings of faith, hope, charity, courage and love have endured unto this day and wherever free men have instituted free government, the very cornerstone has been the ethical standards taught by Jesus of Nazareth.

There are those who forget:
The mild benevolence of His precepts,
The meekness of His spirit,
The philanthropy that breathes in all His words,
The Golden Rule which He established,
The Christian charity which He taught.

When they quote the Bible as a sanction for the death penalty, they pervert the spirit of His holy and merciful religion.

If I were inclined to support my opinion by arguments drawn from religion, the whole New Testament would be my text, for if it teaches anything, it teaches the forgiveness of sin and, therefore, a system of reform rather than extirpation.

Since so many of you are Methodists, as am I, may I read the position of our church from its official discipline: (Page 633, Par. 2020, Sec. 90, 1956)

> We stand for the application of redemptive principle to the treatment for offenders against the law . . . for this reason *we deplore the use of capital punishment* . . .

May I read you the resolution by the American Baptist Convention, adopted in Cincinnati, Ohio, June 16, 1957:

> 1. Because human agencies and legal justice are fallible, and innocent men have been put to death, and,
> 2. Because the Christian believes in the inherently sacred quality of all life as a gift of God, and,
> 3. Because the deterrent effects of capital punishment are not clearly supported by the available evidence, and,
> 4. Because the emphasis in modern penology is upon the process of creative, redemptive rehabilitation rather than primitive retribution, we, therefore,
> *Recommend the abolition of capital punishment in those states which still practice it.*

Next, I cite the resolution passed by the Protestant Episcopal Church, at its 59th General Convention, on October 9, 1958:

WHEREAS, The Church, following the faith of our Lord Jesus Christ holds that each individual is sacred as a child of God and the object of his redemptive love and that to legalize the killing of one such child who is a criminal offender conflicts with this basic Christian concept; and,

WHEREAS, The conscience of many church people has been aroused by the condemnation to death of individuals who may be innocent; and

WHEREAS, There is a growing body of public opinion which believes that capital punishment is archaic and ineffective to protect society and as a deterrent to crime; and

WHEREAS, The death penalty appears to fall for the most part on obscure, impoverished, friendless or defective individuals; and

WHEREAS, Resolutions urging abolition of the death penalty have been recently adopted by six dioceses, one missionary district and the synod of the eighty provinces, and now

THEREFORE, BE IT RESOLVED, The House of Bishops concurring, that this 59th general convention of the Protestant Episcopal Church in the United States of America record its conviction that the death penalty ought to be abolished.

How the State Kills

You have been told in great detail just precisely how Wash Jones killed and murdered Wes Howard. Now let us see how the State of Tennessee would kill and murder Wash Jones.

At about 5:30 in the afternoon of the eve of the execution the prisoner is shaved, bathed and his head is clipped. He must be clean so that it is unnecessary to bathe his body after the electrocution. His head must be clipped so they can apply the electrode.

Then they give him a new shirt and a new pair of pants, without a belt, and shoes without laces. No belt and no shoes laces. After all he must not hang or strangle himself and cheat the chair.

Next, the minister of his choice visits him to offer whatever words of assurance and solace he can conjure up.

Then the condemned man is given an opportunity to eat a hearty meal of his choice.

Then his family is permitted to visit with him until midnight. Then at about ten minutes to five the warden and the guards and the execution party come and they start to walk the last mile down the dim-lit corridor, which leads to the chamber of horrors to the electric chair.

They place him in the chair, roll up his trouser legs in order to clamp the electrode to his right leg. Then to his clipped head they clamp the other electrode.

Then they ask him for his last words. Only the prisoner, the warden and God are present in the room. The warden is doing his statutory duty, the prisoner paying his debt to society and as to him, I am sure he feels that God has forgotten him.

Then they place the mask upon his face—not for his benefit, but to keep the witnesses from looking upon the hideous countenance of the dying man as his facial features contort in pain and agony.

The warden looks through the little window at the man who throws the switch—$25.00 the state pays for this service—the warden has a stop watch in his hands and upon his signal the switch is thrown. Then, there comes the sound from the electrician's niche—a sound like that that comes from an X-ray machine, a crackle, a whine, a buzz as 2,300 volts, for thirty seconds and then 500 for one and one half minutes are sent circulating through his body as it convulsively jerks and writhes.

And then when his body has cooled off enough to touch, the physician applies his stethoscope and pronounces him dead.

He is then placed in cold storage in a deep freeze—because the state does not embalm. Now another name is added to the yellow list—the roll of horror—the state has got another pound of flesh. But it is the law of the state.

I ask you in the name of all that is sacred and holy, how can such a spectacle as this ever magnify the law or make it honorable or preserve the peace and dignity of the state?

And they say that Wash Jones killed in cold blood.

Wash didn't lock Wes Howard in a room, keep him there for weeks and months, announce ahead of time the date and time of his death, and leave the condemned man to die a thousand deaths.

Ladies and gentlemen, you and you alone can send Wash Jones to the electric chair. There can be no division of responsibility, you can never say that the rest overpowered you. It must be your deliberate, cool, premeditated act. It takes your vote.

I plead for human consideration, for charity, for mercy. Man was truly created in God's image, but humane treatment of our fellow man is necessary in order that the divine image may not be obscured.

I hope and pray that the Tennessee legislature will at this session veto the unconscionable decree of blood and write for the state, as the state has written for its citizens, the injunction—at once rational, scriptural, salutary and humanitarian: *"Thou shalt not kill."*

In Favor of Capital Punishment

JACQUES BARZUN

A passing remark of mine in the *Mid-Century* magazine has brought me a number of letters and a sheaf of pamphlets against capital punishment. The letters, sad and reproachful, offer me the choice of pleading ignorance or being proved insensitive. I am asked whether I know that there exists a worldwide movement for the abolition of capital punishment which has everywhere enlisted able men of every profession, including the law. I am told that the death penalty is not only inhuman but also unscientific, for rapists and murderers are really sick people who should be cured, not killed. I am invited to use my imagination and acknowledge the unbearable horror of every form of execution.

I am indeed aware that the movement for abolition is widespread and articulate, especially in England. It is headed there by my old friend and publisher, Mr. Victor Gollancz, and it numbers such well-known writers as Arthur Koestler, C. H. Rolph, James Avery Joyce and Sir John Barry. Abroad as at home the profession of psychiatry tends to support the cure principle, and many liberal newspapers, such as the *Observer,* are committed to abolition. In the United States there are at least twenty-five state leagues working to the same end, plus a national league and several church councils, notably the Quaker and the Episcopal.

The assemblage of so much talent and enlightened goodwill behind a single proposal must give pause to anyone who supports the other side, and in the attempt to make clear my views, which are now close to unpopular, I start out by granting that my conclusion is arguable; that is, I am still open to conviction, *provided* some fallacies and frivolities in the abolitionist argument are first disposed of and the difficulties not ignored but overcome. I should be glad to see this happen, not only because there is pleasure in the spectacle of an airtight case, but also because I am not more sanguinary than my neighbor and I should welcome the discovery of safeguards—for society *and* the criminal—other than killing. But I say it again, these safeguards must really meet, not evade or postpone, the difficulties I am about to describe. Let me add before I begin that I shall probably not answer any more letters on this arousing subject. If this printed exposition does not do justice to my cause, it is not likely that I can do better in the hurry of private correspondence.

I readily concede at the outset that present ways of dealing out capital punishment are as revolting as Mr. Koestler says in his harrowing volume, *Hanged by the Neck.* Like many of our prisons, our modes of execution should change. But this objection to barbarity does not mean that capital punishment—or rather, judicial homicide—should not go on. The illicit jump we find here, on the threshold of the inquiry, is characteristic of the abolitionist and must be disallowed at every point. Let us bear in mind the possibility of devising a painless, sudden and dignified death, and see whether its administration is justifiable.

The four main arguments advanced against the death penalty are: 1. punishment for crime is a primitive idea rooted in revenge; 2. capital punishment does not deter; 3. judicial error being possible, taking life is an appalling risk; 4. a civilized state, to deserve its name, must uphold, not violate, the sanctity of human life.

I entirely agree with the first pair of propositions, which is why, a moment ago, I replaced the term capital punishment with "judicial homicide."

The uncontrollable brute whom I want put out of the way is not to be punished for his misdeeds, nor used as an example or a warning; he is to be killed for the protection of others, like the wolf that escaped not long ago in a Connecticut suburb. No anger, vindictiveness or moral conceit need preside over the removal of such dangers. But a man's inability to control his violent impulses or to imagine the fatal consequences of his acts should be a presumptive reason for his elimination from society. This generality covers drunken driving and teen-age racing on public highways, as well as incurable obsessive violence; it might be extended (as I shall suggest later) to other acts that destroy, precisely, the moral basis of civilization.

But why kill? I am ready to believe the statistics tending to show that the prospect of his own death does not stop the murderer. For one thing he is often a blind egotist, who cannot conceive the possibility of his own death. For another, detection would have to be infallible to deter the more imaginative who, although afraid, think they can escape discovery. Lastly, as Shaw long ago pointed out, hanging the wrong man will deter as effectively as hanging the right one. So, once again, why kill? If I agree that moral progress means an increasing respect for human life, how can I oppose abolition?

I do so because on this subject of human life, which is to me the heart of the controversy, I find the abolitionist inconsistent, narrow or blind. The propaganda for abolition speaks in hushed tones of the sanctity of human life, as if the mere statement of it as an absolute should silence all opponents who have any moral sense. But most of the abolitionists belong to nations that spend half their annual income on weapons of war and that honor research to perfect means of killing. These good people vote without a qualm for the political parties that quite sensibly arm their country to the teeth. The West today does not seem to be the time or place to invoke the absolute sanctity of human life. As for the clergymen in the movement, we may be sure from the experience of two previous world wars that they will bless our arms and pray for victory when called upon, the sixth commandment notwithstanding.

"Oh, but we mean the sanctity of life *within* the nation!" Very well: is the movement then campaigning also against the principle of self-defense? Absolute sanctity means letting the cutthroat have his sweet will of you, even if you have a poker handy to bash him with, for you might kill. And again, do we hear any protest against the police firing at criminals on the street—mere bank robbers usually—and doing this, often enough, with an excited marksmanship that misses the artist and hits the bystander? The absolute sanctity of human life is, for the abolitionist, a slogan rather than a considered proposition.

Yet it deserves examination, for upon our acceptance or rejection of it depend such other highly civilized possibilities as euthanasia and seemly suicide. The inquiring mind also wants to know why the sanctity of *human* life alone? My tastes do not run to household pets, but I find something less than admirable in the uses to which we put animals—in zoos, laboratories and space machines—without the excuse of the ancient law "Eat or be eaten."

It should moreover be borne in mind that this argument about sanctity applies—or would apply—to about ten persons a year in Great Britain and to between fifty and seventy-five in the United States. These are the average numbers of those executed in recent years. The count by itself should not, of course, affect our judgment of the principle: one life spared or forfeited is as important, morally, as a hundred thousand. But it should inspire a comparative judgment: there are hundreds and indeed thousands whom, in our concern with the horrors of execution, we forget: on the one hand, the victims of violence; on the other, the prisoners in our jails.

The victims are easy to forget. Social science tends steadily to mark a preference for the troubled, the abnormal, the problem case. Whether it is poverty, mental disorder, delinquency or crime, the "patient material" monopolizes the interest of increasing groups of people among the most generous and learned. Psychiatry and moral liberalism go together; the application of law as we have known it is thus coming to be regarded as an historic prelude to social work, which may replace it entirely. Modern literature makes the most of this same outlook, caring only for the disturbed spirit, scorning as bourgeois those who pay their way and do *not* stab their friends. All the while the determinism of natural science reinforces the assumption that society causes its own evils. A French jurist, for example, says that in order to understand crime we must first brush aside all ideas of Responsibility. He means the criminal's and takes for granted that of society. The murderer kills because reared in a broken home or, conversely, because at an early age he witnessed his parents making love. Out of such cases, which make pathetic reading in the literature of modern criminology, is born the abolitionist's state of mind: we dare not kill those we are beginning to understand so well.

If, moreover, we turn to the accounts of the crimes committed by these unfortunates, who are the victims? Only dull ordinary people going about their business. We are sorry, of course, but they do not interest science on its march. Balancing, for example, the sixty to seventy criminals executed annually in the United States, there were the seventy to eighty housewives whom George Cvek robbed, raped and usually killed during the months of a career devoted to proving his virility. "It is too bad." Cvek alone seems instructive, even though one of the law officers who helped track him down quietly remarks: "As to the extent that his villainies disturbed family relationships, or how many women are still haunted by the specter of an experience they have never disclosed to another living soul, these questions can only lend themselves to sterile conjecture."

The remote results are beyond our ken, but it is not idle to speculate about those whose death by violence fills the daily two inches at the back of respectable newspapers—the old man sunning himself on a park bench and beaten to death by four hoodlums, the small children abused and strangled, the middle-aged ladies on a hike assaulted and killed, the family terrorized by a released or escaped lunatic, the half-dozen working people massacred by the sudden maniac, the boatload of persons dispatched by the skipper, the mindless assaults upon schoolteachers and shopkeepers by the increasing horde of dedicated killers in our great cities. Where does the sanctity of life begin?

It is all very well to say that many of these killers are themselves "children," that is, minors. Doubtless a nine-year-old mind is housed in that 150 pounds of unguided muscle. Grant, for argument's sake, that the misdeed is "the fault of society," trot out the broken home and the slum environment. The question then is, What shall we do, not in the Utopian city of tomorrow, but here and now? The "scientific" means of cure are more than uncertain. The apparatus of detention only increases the killer's antisocial animus. Reformatories and mental hospitals are full and have an understandable bias toward discharging their inmates. Some of these are indeed "cured"—so long as they stay under a rule. The stress of the social free-for-all throws them back on their violent modes of self-expression. At that point I agree that society has failed—twice: it has twice failed the victims, whatever may be its guilt toward the killer.

As in all great questions, the moralist must choose, and choosing has a price. I happen to think that if a person of adult body has not been endowed with adequate controls against irrationally taking the life of another, that person must be judicially, painlessly, regretfully killed before that mindless body's horrible automation repeats.

I say "irrationally" taking life, because it is often possible to feel great sympathy with a murderer. Certain *crimes passionnels* can be forgiven without being condoned. Blackmailers invite direct retribution. Long provocation can be an excuse, as in that engaging case of some years ago, in which a respectable carpenter of seventy found he could no longer stand the incessant nagging of his wife. While she excoriated him from her throne in the kitchen—a daily exercise for fifty years—the husband went to his bench and came back with a hammer in each hand to settle the score. The testimony to his character, coupled with the sincerity implied by the two hammers, was enough to have him sent into quiet and brief seclusion.

But what are we to say of the type of motive disclosed in a journal published by the inmates of one of our Federal penitentiaries? The author is a bank robber who confesses that money is not his object:

> My mania for power, socially, sexually, and otherwise can feel no degree of satisfaction until I feel sure I have struck the ultimate of submission and terror in the minds and bodies of my victims. . . . It's very difficult to explain all the queer fascinating sensations pounding and surging through me while I'm holding a gun on a victim, watching his body tremble and sweat. . . . This is the moment when all the rationalized hypocrisies of civilization are suddenly swept away and two men stand there facing each other morally and ethically naked, and right and wrong are the absolute commands of the man behind the gun.

This confused echo of modern literature and modern science defines the choice before us. Anything deserving the name of cure for such a man presupposes not only a laborious individual psychoanalysis, with the means to conduct and to sustain it, socially and economically, but also a re-education of the mind, so as to throw into correct perspective the garbled ideas of Freud and Nietzsche, Gide and Dostoevski, which this power-seeker and his fellows have derived from the culture and temper of our times. Ideas are tenacious and give continuity to emotion. Failing a second birth of heart and mind, we must ask: How soon will this sufferer sacrifice a bank clerk in the interests of making civilization less hypocritical? And we must certainly question the wisdom of affording him more than one chance. The abolitionists' advocacy of an unconditional "let live" is in truth part of the same cultural tendency that animates the killer. The Western peoples' revulsion from power in domestic and foreign policy has made of the state a sort of counterpart of the bank robber: both having power and neither knowing how to use it. Both waste lives because hypnotized by irrelevant ideas and crippled by contradictory emotions. If psychiatry were sure of its ground in diagnosing the individual case, a philosopher might consider whether such dangerous obsessions should not be guarded against by judicial homicide *before* the shooting starts.

I raise the question not indeed to recommend the prophylactic execution of potential murderers, but to introduce the last two perplexities that the abolitionists dwarf or obscure by their concentration on changing an isolated penalty. One of these is the scale by which to judge the offenses society wants to repress. I can for example imagine a truly democratic state in which it would be deemed a form of treason punishable by death to create a disturbance in any court or deliberative assembly. The aim would be to recognize the sanctity of orderly discourse in arriving at justice, assessing criticism and defining policy. Under such a law, a natural selection would operate to remove permanently from the scene persons who, let us say, neglect argument in favor of banging on the desk with their shoe. Similarly, a bullying minority in a diet, parliament or skupshtina would be prosecuted for treason to the most sacred institutions when fists or flying inkwells replace rhetoric. That the mere suggestion of such a law sounds ludicrous shows how remote we are from civilized institutions, and hence how gradual should be our departure from the severity of judicial homicide.

I say gradual and I do not mean standing still. For there is one form of barbarity in our law that I want to see mitigated before any other. I mean imprisonment. The enemies of capital punishment—and liberals generally—seem to be satisfied with any legal outcome so long as they themselves avoid the vicarious guilt of shedding blood. They speak of the sanctity of life, but have no concern with its quality. They give no impression of ever having read what it is certain they have read, from Wilde's *De Profundis* to the latest account of prison life by a convicted homosexual. Despite the infamy of concentration camps, despite Mr. Charles Burney's remarkable work, *Solitary Confinement,* despite riots in prisons, despite the round of escape, recapture and return in chains, the abolitionists' imagination tells them nothing about the reality of being caged. They read without a qualm, indeed they read with rejoicing, the hideous irony of "Killer Gets Life"; they sigh with relief instead of horror. They do not see and suffer the cell, the drill, the clothes, the stench, the food; they do not feel the sexual racking of young and old bodies, the hateful promiscuity, the insane monotony, the mass degradation, the impotent hatred. They do not remember from Silvio Pellico that only a strong political faith, with a hope of final victory, can steel a man to endure long detention. They forget that Joan of Arc, when offered "life," preferred burning at the stake. Quite of another mind, the abolitionists point with pride to the "model prisoners" that murderers often turn out to be. As if a model prisoner were not, first, a contradiction in terms, and second, an exemplar of what a free society should not want.

I said a moment ago that the happy advocates of the life sentence appear not to have understood what we know they have read. No more do they appear to read what they themselves write. In the preface to his useful volume of cases, *Hanged in Error*, Mr. Leslie Hale, M.P., refers to the tardy recognition of a minor miscarriage of justice—one year in jail: "The prisoner emerged to find that his wife had died and that his children and his aged parents had been removed to the workhouse. By the time a small payment had been assessed as 'compensation' the victim was incurably insane." So far we are as indignant with the law as Mr. Hale. But what comes next? He cites the famous Evans case, in which it is very probable that the wrong man was hanged, and he exclaims: "While such mistakes are possible, should society impose an irrevocable sentence?" Does Mr. Hale really ask us to believe that the sentence passed on the first man, whose wife died and who went insane, was in any sense *revocable*? Would not any man rather be Evans dead than that other wretch "emerging" with his small compensation and his reasons for living gone?

Nothing is revocable here below, imprisonment least of all. The agony of a trial itself is punishment, and acquittal wipes out nothing. Read the heartrending diary of William Wallace, accused quite implausibly of having murdered his wife and "saved" by the Court of Criminal Appeals—but saved for what? Brutish ostracism by everyone and a few years of solitary despair. The cases of Adolf Beck, of Oscar Slater, of the unhappy Brooklyn bank teller who vaguely resembled a forger and spent eight years in Sing Sing only to "emerge" a broken, friendless, useless, "compensated" man—all these, if the dignity of the individual has any meaning, had better have been dead before the prison door ever opened for them. This is what counsel always says to the jury in the course of a murder trial and counsel is right: far better hang this man than "give him life." For my part, I would choose death without hesitation. If that option is abolished, a demand will one day be heard to claim it as a privilege in the name of human dignity. I shall believe in the abolitionist's present views only after he has emerged from twelve months in a convict cell.

The detached observer may want to interrupt here and say that the argument has now passed from reasoning to emotional preference. Whereas the objector to capital punishment *feels* that death is the greatest of evils, I *feel* that imprisonment is worse than death. A moment's thought will show that feeling is the appropriate arbiter. All reasoning about what is right, civilized and moral rests upon sentiment, like mathematics. Only, in trying to persuade others, it is important to single out the fundamental feeling, the prime intuition, and from it to reason justly. In my view, to profess respect for human life and be willing to see it spent in a penitentiary is to entertain liberal feelings frivolously. To oppose the death penalty because, unlike a prison term, it is irrevocable is to argue fallaciously.

In the propaganda for abolishing the death sentence the recital of numerous miscarriages of justice commits the same error and implies the same callousness: what is at fault in our present system is not the sentence but the fallible procedure. Capital cases being one in a thousand or more, who can be cheerful at the thought of all the "revocable" errors? What the miscarriages point to is the need for reforming the jury system, the rules of evidence, the customs of prosecution, the machinery of appeal. The failure to see that this is the great task reflects the sentimentality I spoke of earlier, that which responds chiefly to the excitement of the unusual. A writer on Death and the Supreme Court is at pains to point out that when that tribunal reviews a capital case, the judges are particularly anxious and careful. What a left-handed compliment to the highest judicial conscience of the country! Fortunately, some of the champions of the misjudged see the issue more clearly. Many of those who are thought wrongly convicted now languish in jail because the jury was uncertain or because a doubting governor commuted the death sentence. Thus Dr. Samuel H. Sheppard, Jr., convicted of his wife's murder in the second degree is serving a sentence that is supposed to run for the term of his natural life. The story of his numerous trials, as told by Mr. Paul Holmes, suggests that police incompetence, newspaper demagogy, public envy of affluence and the mischances of legal procedure fashioned the result. But Dr. Sheppard's vindicator is under no illusion as to the conditions that this "lucky" evader of the electric chair will face if he is granted parole after ten years: "It will carry with it no right to resume his life as a physician. His privilege to practice medicine was blotted out with his conviction. He must all his life bear the stigma of a parolee, subject to unceremonious return to confinement for life for the slightest misstep. More than this, he must live out his life as a convicted murderer."

What does the moral conscience of today think it is doing? If such a man is a dangerous repeater of violent acts, what right has the state to let him loose after ten years? What is, in fact, the meaning of a "life sentence" that peters out long before life? Paroling looks suspiciously like an expression of social remorse for the pain of incarceration, coupled with a wish to avoid "unfavorable publicity" by freeing a suspect. The man is let out when the fuss has died down; which would mean that he was not under lock and key for our protection at all. He *was* being punished, just a little—for so prison seems in the abolitionist's distorted view, and in the jury's and the prosecutor's, whose "second-degree" murder suggests killing someone "just a little." *

If, on the other hand, execution and life imprisonment are judged too severe and the accused is expected to be harmless hereafter—punishment being ruled out as illiberal—what has society gained by wrecking his life and damaging that of his family?

What we accept, and what the abolitionist will clamp upon us all the more firmly if he succeeds, is an incoherence, which is not remedied by the belief that second-degree murder merits a kind of second-degree death; that a doubt as to the identity of a killer is resolved by commuting real death into intolerable life; and that our ignorance whether a maniac will strike again can be hedged against by measuring "good behavior" within the gates and then releasing the subject upon the public in the true spirit of experimentation.

These are some of the thoughts I find I cannot escape when I read and reflect upon this grave subject. If, as I think, they are relevant to any discussion of change and reform, resting as they do on the direct and concrete perception of what happens, then the simple meliorists who expect to breathe a purer air by abolishing the death penalty are deceiving themselves and us. The issue is for the public to judge; but I for one shall not sleep easier for knowing that in England and America and the West generally a hundred more human beings are kept alive in degrading conditions to face a hopeless future; while others—possibly less conscious, certainly less controlled—benefit from a premature freedom dangerous alike to themselves and society. In short, I derive no comfort from the illusion that in giving up one manifest protection of the law-abiding, we who might well be in any of these three roles—victim, prisoner, licensed killer—have struck a blow for the sanctity of human life.

Controversy: Mr. Barzun and Capital Punishment

Comments by Jerome Nathanson, Gerzson Warga, Robert Heilbroner, and S. G. Morley on Jacques Barzun's article, "In Favor of Capital Punishment."

In the last issue of the *Scholar* Jacques Barzun presented his case in favor of capital punishment. I miss in his presentation any serious argument in behalf

---

* The British Homicide Act of 1957, Section 2, implies the same reasoning in its definition of "diminished responsibility" for certain forms of mental abnormality. The whole question of irrationality and crime is in utter confusion, on both sides of the Atlantic.

From *American Scholar*, XXXI (Summer 1962), 436–447. Copyright © 1962 by the United Chapters of Phi Beta Kappa. By permission of the publishers.

of his own case. I find instead a series of undocumented proclamations. The only way I know how to respond (except by ignoring his piece completely and presenting an independent case for abolition) is to comment on his "arguments" *seriatim*.

First, though, I must deal with Mr. Barzun's declaration that his views "are now close to unpopular." When I read this I wondered if he and I live in the same United States. How close is close? Is it close enough to believe that the death penalty will soon be abolished in the forty-two states that now have it in their penal codes? Is the cause of abolition as popular as this? Is this what accounts for the fact that not long ago the voters of Oregon rejected abolition after it had been recommended to them by both the legislature and the Governor? Partly because of this the Governor of Ohio—himself a strong enough believer in abolition to have paroled murderers on his household staff—has refused to submit the question to popular vote.

A few years ago a special Massachusetts commission recommended abolition of the death penalty, whereupon the legislature promptly voted against its own commission. A few years ago Delaware abolished capital punishment. Subsequently, as has happened elsewhere, an especially outrageous crime led to a demand for its restoration. The legislature responded favorably to the demand, the Governor vetoed the measure, and it was passed again over his veto. The Governor of California is a supporter of abolition, but there is hardly the ghost of a chance, after the furor over the Chessman case, that it will be realized during his administration, even if he is elected to another term in office.

In March of 1961 the New York Legislature called for the appointment of a special commission to study the state's entire penal code which, incidentally, is thought by highly regarded criminologists to be one of the most antiquated and barbaric in the world. The death penalty is included in the study. The Governor was requested to declare a moratorium on all executions until the commission brings in its report. He summarily refused to do so—even though, mind you, it was not a request for abolition but simply for temporary suspension.

One could go on and on, all too unhappily from my point of view. I hope these instances are sufficient to dispose of Mr. Barzun's *ex cathedra* declaration that his views are "close to unpopular." After working a number of years in behalf of abolition, I have the contrary impression that the preponderance of popular sentiment is on his side. I stress popular *sentiment*. It is my conviction, although I cannot prove it, that most people have never reflected seriously and dispassionately upon this question. It is my hope that if they do they will reach the conclusion that capital punishment is wrong if anything is wrong. This is why I believe that the primary task of abolitionist groups at present is educational.

Mr. Barzun refers to a French jurist who says that "in order to understand crime we must first brush aside all ideas of Responsibility." In context the implication is not clear: whether some, many or all advocates of abolition share this view. I surely do not. It is my belief that human beings *are* morally responsible. We have to realize that whatever the background of the individual offender the crime itself is no less a crime because of that. As every judge knows, he would violate his own responsibility if he did not face this fact. This is what Justice Cardozo meant when he remarked, "The justice which is due the defendant is due the community, as well."

Yet we also have to realize that this is only a starting point in dealing with problems of crime, especially with capital cases. It is not likely that we are going to find easy answers, or that any answers will be convincing to everyone. But surely we ought to reach answers more civilized than those presently embodied in our penal codes.

Let us turn now to what Mr. Barzun calls the four main arguments of the proponents of abolition. The first one, he writes, is that "punishment for crime is a primitive idea rooted in revenge," and he entirely agrees with this. I have never heard this argument advanced by an abolitionist with whom I have worked. Furthermore, while Mr. Barzun agrees with it, I do not. One of the reasons I am against capital punishment is that I do not agree with it.

To be sure, punishment is often motivated by vengeance. Is there no punishment not so motivated? Is punishment never ethically justifiable? I think that punishment is never ethically justified when it is vindictive or retributive. But I think it is ethical when its intent is educative, rehabilitative, re-forming. Every good child psychiatrist knows that it is the completely permissive parent, not the justly punishing one, who damages the child. I think this consideration equally valid with respect to criminals. If they are not disturbed personalities requiring medical treatment, then they should be punished. Obviously in a civilized society there would be no attempt to make the punishment fit the crime. It should fit the individual. And it should be motivated by an honest desire to reeducate that individual. An overwhelming number of our penal institutions, of course, instead of effectively making this effort, breed more crime. This is a criticism of all of us who permit it, but it is no argument against the principle.

That properly motivated punishment is ethically justifiable is precisely what makes capital punishment not only ethically offensive but a contradiction in terms. For if the intent of punishment should be reeducation and reformation, then the person whose brains boil over in the electric chair or whose neck is broken by the noose is not likely to learn much from his "punishment."

The second main argument Mr. Barzun attributes to abolitionists is that "capital punishment does not deter" and, once again, he agrees. I wish I could, too, since contrary to Mr. Barzun I think it would be a clincher for the abolitionist case. Obviously the death penalty is no deterrent for professional killers, since they seldom receive it because "the organization" protects them. But for others guilty of murder the available statistics do not provide an incontrovertible case for either side. All they show is that in adjacent and sociologically comparable states, with and without capital punishment, there is little difference in the homicide rate. Since the deterrent value of the death penalty cannot be clearly demonstrated, the state places an awful burden on the conscience of its citizens cold-bloodedly to commit "judicial homicide," to use Mr. Barzun's euphemism.

The third argument, with which Mr. Barzun disagrees, is that "judicial error being possible, taking life is an appalling risk." He thinks rather that mistakes of this character point to "the need for reforming the jury system, the rules of evidence, the customs of prosecution, the machinery of appeal." One can agree with the need for some such reforms, as I do, without seeing the logical bearing of the point on the initial argument, as I do not. We know of many instances in which the state has committed "judicial homicide" upon persons subsequently found to be indubitably innocent. Human fallibility being what it is, I do not think the possibility of judicial error in capital cases should be brushed aside. But judgment about this rests upon the next point.

For the sanctity of human life, and what one means by it, is the crux of the matter. Here Mr. Barzun carries off a bit of sleight of hand. He attributes to abolitionists not only a belief in the sanctity of human life, which I assume is shared by all civilized people, but a belief in its *absolute*, that is unconditional, sanctity. On this basis he finds us "inconsistent, narrow or blind" in supporting armaments. Apart from anything else, he does scant justice to the many Friends who are simultaneously abolitionists and pacifists. And surely he deals unjustly with those of us who are not absolutists in our view. I can believe in the sanctity of human life, as I do, and still believe that it was right for us to fight for the preservation of democracy against fascism, as I believe it right to defend democracy from communism.

We must be clear about another matter that Mr. Barzun beclouds. He speaks of the "elimination from society" of certain classes of individuals. Depending upon the meaning of "elimination," I know of no abolitionist who would oppose this point in principle. No sensible person of my acquaintance advocates freedom of society for those guilty of antisocial behavior, especially of a vicious nature. I would in fact urge the amendment of our penal codes so that potentially violent persons—for example, certain psychotics—would not, in Mr. Barzun's language, "be guarded against by judicial homicide before the shooting starts," but would be isolated from society for treatment before a crime is committed. But if I read Mr. Barzun correctly, this is not what he means. By "elimination" he means "extermination," which is something quite different.

Mr. Barzun writes: "The victims are easy to forget. Social science tends steadily to mark a preference for the troubled, the abnormal, the problem case." He surely cannot doubt that many abolitionists are as deeply concerned about victims, as well as with the families and friends of victims, as he is. Surely any healthy-minded person is revolted by the rape-murder of a little girl. Is there one who does not feel deep compassion for her parents? Unfortunately the question is not one of our revulsion or compassion. The question is what we can do about it. We ought to do everything we can to prevent the occurrence of such crimes. No one can bring the child back to life. No one can ever really make amends to the parents. At the same time, can anyone honestly believe that the person capable of committing so horrible a crime is not very sick? Extermination doubtless brings emotional satisfaction to many people, but is this synonymous with justice? Even the father of "the Cape Man's" victim in New York asked the Governor to extend clemency to him. Mr. Barzun asks, "Where does the sanctity of life begin?" This is not the basic question. What must be asked is, When if at all does the sanctity of life end, and who is to be the judge of when it should?

Mr. Barzun writes, once more *ex cathedra:* "The 'scientific' means of cure are more than uncertain. . . . Reformatories and mental hospitals are full and have an understandable bias toward discharging their inmates[!]. Some of these are indeed 'cured'—so long as they stay under a rule. The stress of the social free-for-all throws them back on their violent modes of self-expression." But what is the fact? In those states in which a sentence of life imprisonment for convicted murderers permits parole eligibility for good behavior, the paroled murderers have the best record of any class of criminals not only for not repeating what they earlier did, but for not violating their parole in any way.

Another citation: "The enemies of capital punishment—and liberals generally—seem to be satisfied with any legal outcome as long as they themselves avoid the vicarious guilt of shedding blood. They speak of the sanctity of life, but have no concern with its quality. . . . They read without a qualm, indeed they read with rejoicing, the hideous irony of 'Killer Gets Life'; they sigh with relief instead of horror." I think Mr. Barzun should be challenged to produce a single healthy-minded abolitionist who reads "with rejoicing" that a person has been sentenced to imprisonment for the rest of his natural life.

The question of life imprisonment, which is quite literal in New York, for example, unless the Governor intervenes, demands clarification. There are some district attorneys who prefer it to the death penalty because, in their experience, some jurors who have no theoretical objection to capital punishment find, when they are actually sitting in a case, that they cannot bring in such a verdict without violating their consciences. They therefore vote for acquittal, even though they may have reason to think that the person on trial is guilty of the crime charged. The district attorneys who hold this view accordingly believe that fewer guilty people would be found not guilty if the "extreme penalty" were not mandatory where it is. Some legislators and others who are convinced abolitionists propose life imprisonment as an alternative not because they believe in it, but because they think that the people of their states and their legislative representatives would be unwilling to accept anything less. Many of the rest of us are convinced that mandatory life imprisonment without parole eligibility is not punishment but barbarism.

A word about the role of forensic psychiatry in murder trials is in order. I think it demeaning to the members of the psychiatric profession to be party to such procedure. Prosecution and defense will frequently produce their respective specialists to testify under M'Naghten's rule of knowing right from wrong about a given person's "sanity" or "insanity"—words no good doctor will even use in his own practice! It is hard for me to understand how a conscientious doctor can be an "advocate" of an individual's sickness or health. And the rule itself is antiquated, since many compulsive or obsessive individuals do know right from wrong but can't help themselves from doing what they know to be wrong. I believe, rather, that a person charged with a crime, certainly a major crime, should be tried for his guilt or innocence regardless of the state of his health. If found guilty, he should then be subject to medical examination, as able and objective as the state can provide. If he is sick, he should be treated accordingly. If he is not, he should be punished in whatever manner is likely to help him be an acceptable member of society.

But to return to Mr. Barzun. He remarks: "The detached observer may want to interrupt here and say that the argument has now passed from reasoning to emotional preference. . . . A moment's thought will show that feeling is the appropriate arbiter." The fact is that for anyone acquainted with intellectual history, more especially the history of ethical philosophy, "a moment's thought" will not necessarily show anything of the kind, nor do I doubt that Mr. Barzun is aware of this. To be sure, more moral philosophers, chief among them David Hume, have grounded ethical judgment in sentiment—to say nothing of contemporary "emotivists" who declare that so-called ethical judgment is really an expression of like or dislike. For a contrary and brilliantly expressed point of view I recommend to interested readers Brand Blanshard's recently published Gifford Lectures on *Reason and Goodness*.*

As astonishing as anything else in his case are Mr. Barzun's reflections on the person sentenced to life imprisonment who is eligible for parole. He writes: "What is, in fact, the meaning of a 'life sentence' that peters out long before life? Paroling looks suspiciously like an expression of social remorse for the pain of incarceration, coupled with a wish to avoid 'unfavorable publicity' by freeing a suspect." I find this a truly elegant piece of sophistry. For insofar as I am able to follow the logic of his entire position, it reduces itself to this: If a person is sentenced to life imprisonment he ought to be imprisoned for the rest of his life; but life imprisonment is worse than death; therefore, it is better both for him and society to exterminate him.

* Macmillan. $ 7.75.

Mr. Barzun appears to take it for granted that for the criminal "judicial homicide" is clearly preferable to imprisonment. He observes: "I shall believe in the abolitionist's present views only after he has emerged from twelve months in a convict cell." I confess that I have never "done time." But I doubt that Mr. Barzun has, either. I do know a man, however, who as a relative youngster was condemned to death for felony murder. He was in the death house and was, literally, within hours of dying when the Governor intervened and saved his life. Today he is a free man and a responsible citizen and, despite Mr. Barzun's theorizing, glad still to be alive.

JEROME NATHANSON
Chairman, New York Committee to
Abolish Capital Punishment, and
Chairman, Fraternity of Leaders,
American Ethical Union

. . . .

You may not receive many congratulatory letters on your recent article, "In Favor of Capital Punishment," but this one at least is such a letter. It takes great courage today to take Mr. Barzun's stand if one is aspiring to be counted among the "intellectuals." Congratulations to him both for his courage and for his article.

One minor point left me somewhat dissatisfied. When he deals with the four arguments against the death penalty advanced by its opponents, he does not demolish the second, namely, that "capital punishment does not deter." I think this argument, attractive as it may appear, is easily shown to be a fallacy:

1. I have read accounts of bank robberies where the criminal used a toy gun not because he was unable to procure a real one, but because he did not want to risk being sentenced for murder in case things went "wrong."
2. In California, where 190 murders were committed during a single year, only five convicted murderers were executed. Less than three per cent! How can we expect the death penalty to be of full deterrent force?
3. If capital punishment is no deterrent, then by logical extension punishment is no deterrent. Let us carry this to the logical but absurd conclusion: No crime must be punished because punishment is no deterrent!

DR. GERZSON WARGA
Chevy Chase, Maryland

The authorities have delivered to me the recent issue of your publication in which Dr. Barzun delivers his humane defense of capital punishment. As I read this article the scales fell from my eyes and I realized how meretricious had been my attempt, while on earth, to do away with this form of social punishment. Nevertheless old ideas die hard, even in my present position *au dessus de la mêlée*. Therefore I suggest the following, to which I am certain Dr. Barzun will be quick to agree:

1. All prison sentences are henceforth to contain these alternatives (a) the right to commit suicide, in decent privacy and with appropriate means furnished by the authorities, and (b) the right to opt for legal execution at any time when the sentence becomes unendurable.
2. Purely as a legal formality, since it will assuredly not be availed of, all death sentences are to contain the option, exerciseable solely at the prisoner's discretion, of commutation to life imprisonment (with rights under (1) above unimpaired).

It occurs to me that this might also provide something of a test for the relative humaneness of the punishments offered. Eh, M. Barzun? D'accord?

ALBERT CAMUS*

. . . .

May I express complete agreement with Mr. Barzun's article on capital punishment?

Are you acquainted with the passage in Alexis Carrel's *Man, the Unknown* (Harpers, 1935) on this subject? I think it would interest you, and provide a good supporting quote for Mr. Barzun.

> There remains the unsolved problem of the immense number of defectives and criminals. They are an enormous burden for the part of the population that has remained normal. As already pointed out, gigantic sums are now required to maintain prisons and insane asylums and protect the public against gangsters and lunatics. Why do we preserve these useless and harmful beings? The abnormal prevent the development of the normal. This fact must be squarely faced. Why should society not dispose of the criminals and the insane in a more economical manner? We cannot go on trying to separate the responsible from the irresponsible, punish the guilty, spare those who, although having committed a crime, are thought to be morally innocent. We are not capable of judging men. However, the community must be protected against troublesome and dangerous elements. How can this be done? Certainly not by building larger and more comfortable prisons, just as real health will not be promoted by larger and more scientific hospitals. Criminality and insanity can be prevented only by a better knowledge of man, by eugenics, by changes in education and in social conditions. Meanwhile, criminals have to be dealt with effectively. Perhaps prisons should be abolished. They could be replaced by smaller and less expensive institutions. The conditioning of petty criminals with the whip, or some more scientific procedure, followed by a short stay in hospital, would probably suffice to insure order. Those who have murdered, robbed while armed with automatic pistol or machine gun, kidnapped children, despoiled the poor of their savings, misled the public in important matters, should be humanely and economically disposed of in small euthanasic institutions supplied with proper gases. A similar treatment could be advantageously applied to the insane, guilty of criminal acts. Modern society should not hesitate to organize itself with reference to the normal individual. Philosophical systems and sentimental prejudices must give way before such a necessity. The development of human personality is the ultimate purpose of civilization.

S. G. MORLEY
University of California

* [Robert Heilbroner. Editors' note.]

Questions

1. Why does Henry begin his argument by giving a history of capital punishment in Tennessee? How does he make this historical introduction effective?
2. Describe the uses that Henry makes of repetition. Is this repetition effective?
3. Notice the number of allusions to religion and to the Bible in Henry's argument. Why are these allusions used? Are they effective? Are Henry's Biblical arguments at the end of his defense effective?
4. Identify examples of understatement in Henry's defense. Is this device effective?
5. What effect does Henry achieve by concluding his list of examples of non-deterrence with the case of the Oklahoma State Prison head hangman?
6. How valid is the evidence that Henry raises against the deterrence argument?
7. What elements of Henry's argument are appropriate to it as a speech? In what ways does Henry indicate an awareness of his audience (the jury)?
8. Is Barzun writing for an audience different from Henry's? In what ways does Barzun indicate an awareness of *his* audience?
9. Barzun summarizes four main arguments against capital punishment. Does Henry use all four? How? Does Henry use other arguments?
10. With which of Henry's three ingredients of punishment is Barzun most concerned?
11. How does Barzun employ specific examples? Is his use of past cases rhetorically similar to Henry's?
12. Could Barzun's fullest argument be seen as one *against* the prison system rather than one *for* capital punishment? Explain.
13. Do Henry or the correspondents answering Barzun exhibit the confused state of mind that Barzun suggests is representative of modern thinking about crime and punishment?
14. Why does Nathanson describe "judicial homicide" as a euphemism? What are Barzun's reasons for choosing the term?
15. Why does Nathanson end with the example of the reprieved man?
16. Are Warga's arguments for the deterrent effects of capital punishment valid?
17. Why does Heilbroner choose the *nom-de-plume* of Albert Camus? Is his suggestion serious? (See *Additional Reading* for this section.)

Assignments

1. Analyze the arguments on both sides of the issue of capital punishment and summarize the more important arguments on each side.
2. Write a letter to the editor of the *American Scholar* answering Barzun or one of the correspondents who wrote about Barzun's article.
3. Argue for or against one of these propositions:
   a. Capital punishment should not be abolished unless as a part of a thorough reform of the prison system.
   b. The law should not be modified because of the discoveries of psychiatry.
   c. Life imprisonment is worse than death.
4. The press is sometimes accused of prejudging a capital case and thus contributing to the judging of the criminal. Investigate and analyze the press coverage of a particular capital case.
5. Analyze the arguments for and against the deterrent effects of capital punishment. Are they logically sound? Do they validly interpret the evidence?

Additional Reading

The writing on capital punishment has been voluminous (although most recent considerations have opposed the death penalty). Some of the most recent books on the subject include James A. Joyce, *The Right to Life: A World View of Capital Punishment* (London, 1962); A. Gardiner, *Capital Punishment as a Deterrent, and the Alternative* (London, 1956); Victor Gollancz, *Capital Punishment: The Heart of the Matter* (London, 1955); Lord Longford, *The Idea of Punishment* (London, 1961); Elizabeth Tuttle, *The Crusade Against Capital Punishment* (London, 1961); Grant S. McClellan, *Capital Punishment* (New York, 1960); John Howard Yoder, *The Christian and Capital Punishment* (Newton, Kansas, 1961); Jack Kevorkian, *Medical Research and the Death Penalty* (New York, 1960); John Laurence, *A History of Capital Punishment* (New York, 1963).

Many cases have raised ethical and legal questions about capital punishment. The two most recent ones that have focused attention have been the Caryl Chessman case in California in the 1950's and the Timothy Evans-John Christie case in London in the 1940's. Both cases elicited considerable newspaper and magazine coverage and both have occasioned a number of books.

Barrett E. Prettyman, Jr.'s *Death and the Supreme Court* (New York, 1961) gives interesting and vivid descriptions of the Supreme Court's consideration of a number of capital cases. The most famous contemporary essay opposing capital punishment is Albert Camus' "Reflections on the Guillotine," which appears in his *Resistance, Rebellion, and Death* (New York, 1963).

An anthology of materials about capital punishment, *The Death Penalty* (Boston, 1964), has been edited by Edward G. McGehee and William H. Hildebrand.

SECTION FIVE | *Eichmann and Evil: War Crimes or Man's Crimes*

Man with an Unspotted Conscience

MICHAEL A. MUSMANNO

Adolf Eichmann, one of Hitler's principal instruments in the Nazi program to exterminate the Jews of Europe, was hanged on May 31, 1962, but in this book he is very much alive. We see him energetically striding from page to page, we observe him in shining, black-leather boots stamping into governmental, military and diplomatic offices in all parts of Europe. We follow him, his ornamented cap at a sharp angle, storming into hotels, concentration camps, railroad trains, human abattoirs and emerging with neither a dirty spot on his immaculate uniform, nor—according to Eichmann, with Hannah Arendt apparently supporting his boast—a dirty spot on his conscience.

That is what this book is principally about: Adolf Eichmann's conscience. The author covered the trial of Eichmann in Jerusalem for The New Yorker, and the series of articles in that magazine, which form the bulk of this book, stirred controversy as a strong wind agitates the waters of a lake. The book, which follows the articles as a gale succeeds a rising wind, will probably evoke a great deal of pensive reflection; Eichmann was no ordinary criminal, and his deeds were not the subject of the ordinary court of assizes.

There will be those who will wonder how Miss Arendt, after attending the Eichmann trial and studying the record and pertinent material, could announce, as she solemnly does in this book, that Eichmann was not really a Nazi at heart, that he did not know Hitler's program when he joined the Nazi party, that the Gestapo were helpful to the Jews in Palestinian immigration, that Himmler (Himmler!) had a sense of pity, that the Jewish gas-killing

New York Times Book Review, May 19, 1963, pp. 1, 4D–5D. © 1963 by the New York Times Company. Reprinted by permission.

program grew out of Hitler's euthanasia program and that, all in all, Eichmann was really a modest man.

Miss Arendt devotes considerable space to Eichmann's conscience and informs us that one of Eichmann's points in his own defense was "that there were no voices from the outside to arouse his conscience." How abysmally asleep is a conscience when it must be aroused to be told there is something morally wrong about pressing candy upon a little boy to induce him to enter a gas chamber of death?

The author believes that Eichmann was misjudged in Jerusalem and quotes, with astounding credulity, his statement: "I myself had no hatred for the Jews." Sympathizing with Eichmann, she laments: "Alas, nobody believed him." Should anyone be blamed for lifting an eyebrow to the suggestion that Eichmann loved the Jews? At the end of the war he exclaimed: "I shall laugh when I jump into the grave, because of the feeling that I killed five million Jews. This gives me a lot of satisfaction and pleasure."

Miss Arendt defends Eichmann against his own words here, arguing that it would be "preposterous" to believe he personally slew five million people. But his guilt did not depend on personal physical annihilation. The District Court of Jerusalem specified: "The legal and moral responsibility of him who delivers the victim to his death is, in our opinion, no smaller, and may even be greater, than the liability of him who does the victim to death." Eichmann headed the incredibly monstrous project to exterminate cold-bloodedly a segment of the human race. He rounded up his victims in cities, villages and the remotest corners of a continent; he had them jammed, herring fashion, into box cars; he had a hand in supplying the gas which eventually killed them.

If, in recalling the period, one could shut one's eyes to the scenes of brutal massacre and stop one's ears to the screams of horror-stricken women and terrorized children as they saw the tornado of death sweeping toward them, one could almost assume that in some parts of the book the author is being whimsical. For instance, she says that Eichmann was a Zionist and helped Jews to get to Palestine. The facts, as set forth in the judgment handed down by the District Court of Jerusalem, are entirely to the contrary. As far back as November, 1937, after an espionage trip into the Middle East he reported that the plan for emigration of Jews to Palestine "was out of the question," it being "the policy of the Reich to avoid the creation of an independent Jewish State in Palestine."

Then, in 1944, even when Hitler (Hitler!) ordered that a few thousand Hungarian Jews be allowed to emigrate to Palestine (not out of sympathy, of course, but as part of a plan of his own), Eichmann opposed his Fuehrer, expostulating, as reported by Reich Plenipotentiary Veesenmayer, that the Jews are "important biological material, many of them veteran Zionists, whose emigration to Palestine is most undesirable."

Miss Arendt says that the only time Eichmann gave an "order to kill" was in the autumn of 1941 when he "proposed killing by shooting" of 8,000

Serbian Jews. This is quibbling. While heading the "Eichmann Special Operation Unit" in Hungary, he shipped, in less than two months, 434,351 Jews in 147 trains of sealed freight cars to Auschwitz where the gas chambers had to work at full capacity to kill the human cargoes. These 434,351 Jews died as the result of Eichmann's orders as much as if he had personally directed the gassing and the cremating crews.

In mid-summer, 1944, Horthy, regent of Hungary, compelled the return of a train loaded with 1,500 Jews, which Eichmann had dispatched to Auschwitz. Eichmann ordered his SS men to reload the Jews after they had detrained in Hungary and, by diabolical cunning, got them back across the Hungarian border and into the ovens of Auschwitz. Miss Arendt says Eichmann did not have the "guts" to kill. Eichmann killed those 1,500 Jews as much as if he had individually strangled them with his own hands.

The author finds in Eichmann's history a solicitude for "young Jews." He was not so solicitous in July, 1942, when 4,000 French-Jewish children, all under 16 and detached from their parents, were held in the concentration camp at Drancy. His representative, Theodor Dannecker, asked Eichmann what should be done. Eichmann's reply was to order transports for the children, and soon they were on their way as appetizers for the ravenous beast of Auschwitz.

The disparity between what Miss Arendt states, and what the ascertained facts are, occurs with such disturbing frequency in her book that it can hardly be accepted as an authoritative historical work. She says Eichmann never "actually attended a mass execution by shooting" or watched a "gassing process." Eichmann himself spoke of attending a mass shooting and described seeing "marksmen . . . shooting into the pit." The pit was "full of corpses." The Court, in its final judgment, described Eichmann at Treblinka, one of the death camps in the East, watching "the naked Jews being led to the gas chambers along paths surrounded by barbed wire."

According to Miss Arendt, Eichmann never saw "the killing installations" at Auschwitz, although she admits he went to this charnel house "repeatedly." Her observation is like saying that one repeatedly sojourned at Niagara Falls but never noticed the falling water. Eichmann dispatched over two million Jews into the Auschwitz "destruction machinery" of which, Miss Arendt admits, he saw "enough to be fully informed."

The author supports Eichmann's incredible claim that he was ignorant of the *Kristalnacht* or Night of Broken Glass, even though the whole world knew of the conflagration of hatred which burned down synagogues, smashed 7,500 Jewish shop windows and drove 20,000 Jews into concentration camps.

Another unfortunate feature of this book is that the author, an eminent scholar, should reveal so frequently evidences of purely private prejudice. She attacks the State of Israel, its laws and institutions, wholly unrelated to the Eichmann case; she pours scorn on Prime Minister Ben-Gurion. Later she speaks contemptuously of a man whom the Court lauded, with moving appropriateness, as "one of the just men of the world." Miss Arendt apparently did not like this elderly, gentle, snowy-haired pastor of a German Protestant church, Heinrich Grüber, because he described Eichmann, whom he knew in his all-powerful hey-day, as a "block of ice" and "like marble." She perhaps saw something warm about Eichmann, because, she said, the evidence showed he was "rather decent toward his subordinates." Pastor Grüber had pleaded with Eichmann in behalf of persecuted Jews, and, for his pains, was thrown into a concentration camp where SS guards knocked out his teeth and inflicted other serious physical damage.

Miss Arendt deals rather intemperately and certainly injudiciously, with Gideon Hausner, the Attorney General of Israel, perhaps because, in cross-examining Eichmann, Mr. Hausner made mincemeat of the previously self-assured defendant. Mr. Hausner was not only an extremely able attorney general, but he is distinguished for his masterful legal ability at the world bar. The judges, who certainly knew more of Mr. Hausner than Miss Arendt, declared in their final judgment that Mr. Hausner "conducted the prosecution in all its stages as a jurist and on a very high professional level. In his brilliant opening speech which was eloquent and broad in perspective, and again in his concluding statement, he gave vent also to the deep feelings which stir the entire nation." President Kennedy complimented Mr. Hausner on "a job well done." People throughout the world, where humanity is felt and justice revered, echo that sentiment.

Miss Arendt says that Eichmann, "to a truly extraordinary degree," received the "cooperation" of the Jews in their own destruction. This astonishing conclusion is predicated on statements of others that some Jewish leaders dealt with Eichmann, and that, in certain instances, Jews took part in police work. The fact that Eichmann with threats of death coerced occasional Quislings and Lavals into "cooperation" only adds to the horror of his crimes. And then, Jewish councils of elders, who were required to supply lists of Jews under the false assurances that the lists were intended for "resettlement" purposes, because of war conditions, were themselves taken before the Einsatzgruppen rifles or thrown under the hissing gas "showers." But none of the author's arguments in this respect can dim the luster of martyrdom of the defenseless millions who marched bravely to their doom under the guns of the most satanic force that ever defiled the earth. The Warsaw Ghetto uprising, where 56,000 perished in a last-ditch fight for freedom, shows that the Jews did not lack the stuff of courage.

Miss Arendt declares the Eichmann trial a "failure," specifying that the Court did not give "a valid definition of the 'crime against humanity.'" In point of simple optical arithmetic, the Court validly defined and described crimes against humanity not once but a dozen times, citing the Nuremberg Charter, the basis for the Israeli law. She says that the Nuremberg Charter defines "crimes against humanity" as merely "inhuman acts." She could not be more in error. The Charter, Article 6 (c) defines Crimes Against Humanity, *inter alia*, as: "*murder, extermination, enslavement, deportation,* and other inhumane acts committed against any civil population, before or during the war. . . ." A mountain of evidence overwhelmingly convicted Eichmann beyond every reasonable doubt of the charges in the indictment of crimes against humanity.

In summing up her long thesis, Miss Arendt assures the suffering world that it is possible that crimes similar to Eichmann's "may be committed in the future." And with this comforting picture assuaging the apprehensions of the reader, she adds that "no punishment has ever possessed enough power of deterrence to prevent the commission of crimes." This, in effect, says it was a terrible mistake to punish Eichmann at all!

Then, donning judicial robes, she dictates what the judges should have said when they sentenced Eichmann, if they wanted the "justice" of what was done to emerge so as to "be seen by all." They should have said to Eichmann, according to Miss Arendt, "no member of the human race can be expected to want to share the earth with you. That is the reason, *and the only reason,* you must hang." (Emphasis supplied.) In the first place, this statement would, of course, be false: there were many people who would gladly share the earth with Eichmann. There were his wife and children; there were also the thousands of bloodthirsty accomplices who enthusiastically shared Eichmann's desires to kill off "inferior" peoples. In the second place, the utterance Miss Arendt would put into the mouths of the venerable, distinguished, wise judges who tried Eichmann would make of the eight-month trial an act of sheer vengeance—instead of the meticulously fair and legally accurate proceeding which it has been recognized to be in all responsible circles, where there is a true understanding of the sanctity of law and the conscientious calm of even-handed justice.

[Exchange of Letters]

HANNAH ARENDT AND MICHAEL A. MUSMANNO

A Statement From Miss Arendt

TO THE EDITOR:
You asked for a statement on Judge Musmanno's review of my book "Eichmann in Jerusalem." I find it hard to comply for two reasons: One is that the interesting point of this matter is your choice of a reviewer rather than the

New York Times Book Review, June 23, 1963, pp. 4–5. © 1963 by the New York Times Company. Reprinted by permission.

review itself. And the other reason is that the predictable result of your choice produced a "criticism" of a book which, to my knowledge, was never either written or published.

The choice of the reviewer was bizarre, because I had characterized Mr. Musmanno's views on totalitarian government in general and on Eichmann's role in it in particular as "dangerous nonsense."[1] Mr. Musmanno, even though he is a judge, chose not to mention the fact that he was writing *pro domo*. But this was no secret, and it is hard to understand why you did not supply this information. You mention yourself that the reviewer was "a witness at the Eichmann trial," hence he was likely to be mentioned in a report on it. The book's index could have shown you in a few minutes all you needed to know. If, on the other hand, you chose your reviewer in full *connaissance de cause*, this would constitute such a flagrant break with normal editorial procedures as to make it much more interesting than the review itself.

I shall assume that you were ignorant of the pertinent facts in your choice. Still, I find it hard to understand that the review itself did not surprise you. Obviously, you never read the book and therefore could not be aware of the over-all misrepresentation.[2] (I realize that no book editor can read, or even glance at, all books which are reviewed in his magazine, but to spot elementary falsifications—distortions, which are not matters of opinion—belongs, perhaps unjustly, among his normal duties.) However, the review contains a number of statements, so startling as to arouse editorial curiosity even in an editor who knows nothing about the book, or its author, or his reviewer. Eichmann, your reviewer wrote, was represented by me as a "Zionist" who "loved Jews" (sic!) and "was ignorant of the *Kristallnacht* or Night of Broken Glass, *even though the whole world knew of*" it. (My italics.) (The truth about the last point is that Eichmann said he had not been informed of the *preparations* for the pogrom of November, 1938. We possess a great many documents dealing with the *Kristallnacht*. Eichmann's name is nowhere mentioned. The Jerusalem court cleared him on this count.)

If the editorial offices of The New York Times Book Review had taken the trouble to check such obvious fantasies, it might even have recognized its reviewer's curious habit of lifting whole sentences out of the book, of rephrasing them slightly to avoid quotation marks, and of thus saying with great emphasis *against* the author what in actual fact was said *by* the author. Thus, your reviewer's point that Eichmann's "guilt did not depend on personal physical annihilation" and the qualifying quotation from the district court's judgment is not at all your reviewer's viewpoint but the point of the author.

It would be too tiresome to list even the most flagrant falsifications of

---

[1] The reasons for the selection of Judge Musmanno are stated accurately by Judge Musmanno in a letter that follows.

[2] Miss Arendt is wrong. The book was read by the Book Review editor and one of his assistants before the assignment was made.

your reviewer. Instead, I shall give you an example of one of the more subtle distortions. Your reviewer states that I "solemnly announce" that "Eichmann did not know Hitler's program when he joined the Nazi party." I said: "When Eichmann told the Jerusalem court that he had not known Hitler's program he very likely spoke the truth: *'The Party program did not matter, you knew what you were joining.'*" The point here is that totalitarian movements do not depend upon their program—in contrast to Continental parties. But even a reader who is unable to understand that the second part of my sentence, which is a quote from Eichmann, reveals Eichmann's totalitarian mentality, should be able to see that the first part of the sentence is qualified by its second part. This is a matter of grammar.

To repeat: The point of the matter is not the review but the fact that a paper like The New York Times published it. After having printed and, presumably, read the biographical sketch of the author, it is inconceivable that you could believe what the review said—that I "sympathized" with Eichmann and had written his defense. Moreover, do you really think it very likely that The New Yorker would have run a series in defense of Eichmann of all people, or that The Viking Press would have published it as a book?

HANNAH ARENDT.

Rome, Italy.

A Reply From Judge Musmanno

TO THE EDITOR:

I will comment on Miss Arendt's letter point by point. Where she refers to the same subject more than once I will make but one observation.

There was nothing "bizarre" about The New York Times Book Review asking me to write the review on "Eichmann in Jerusalem." Everyone knows that the Book Review endeavors to select as reviewers those individuals who are, because of profession or experience, more generally familiar than others with the subject of the book to be reviewed. The editors assumed that I qualified in this respect because I was a judge at three of the war crimes trials in Nuremberg. I testified at the Eichmann trial, have been a judge for 32 years, and for 18 years have studied the documentation on war crimes and crimes against humanity.

Miss Arendt errs as to what her book contains. She did not characterize "views on totalitarian government" and "Eichmann's role in it" as "dangerous nonsense." In fact the subject of totalitarian government was not even mentioned. What she characterized as "dangerous nonsense" was a feature of the decision of the Israel Supreme Court on the subject of "superior orders" and they said that my testimony supported it. In the first place, Miss Arendt is not qualified to condemn so crassly the solemn judgment of the highest court of a nation. In the second place, I did not testify that Eichmann never had superior orders. I testified that Eichmann dealt with Himmler and others of the murderous oligarchy.

My review was not *pro domo*. It was *pro bono publico*. It was imperative that the public know of Miss Arendt's many misstatements of facts in the Eichmann case, because that case has taken an important place in the history of the world and the human spirit. Thus, I pointed out, for instance, that Miss Arendt said that Eichmann never attended a mass execution by shooting, when he actually described such an attendance himself. She says my review contained misrepresentations, but she has made no attempt to support her utterance that Eichmann did not attend an execution.

There were no misrepresentations of any kind in my review. I merely picked up a long ruler and pointed to the blackboard of evidence and showed where Miss Arendt departed from the facts. Every statement made by me is verifiable from the official record.

I did not say that Miss Arendt said Eichmann loved the Jews. The plain purport of my statement on this subject was that I contested her statement that Eichmann did not hate the Jews. I now declare categorically that the official record proves beyond any syllable of contradiction that Eichmann hated the Jews and put his hatred into sanguinary fulfillment by murdering them—the old, the crippled, the maimed, the young, the babies—at every chance.

Miss Arendt gives further evidence of forgetting what is in her book when she indicates she never said Eichmann was a Zionist. Here are her words (p. 36): "A certain von Mildenstein . . . required him [Eichmann] to read Theodor Herzl's *Der Judenstaat*, the famous Zionist classic, which converted Eichmann promptly and *forever* to Zionism." (Italics throughout mine.)

Miss Arendt accuses me of misrepresenting her statements regarding the *Kristallnacht* or Night of Broken Glass when the Nazis smashed 75,000 Jewish shop windows, burned down synagogues and drove 20,000 Jews into concentration camps. She says now that Eichmann was not informed of the "preparations" for the dastardly affair and defends him on that basis, but in her book she said he was wholly *ignorant* of it. Here are her words (p. 189): "He [Eichmann] certainly knew nothing at the time [of the *Kristallnacht*] and, even in Jerusalem knew considerably less than the least well-informed student of the period." My comment was: "The author [Miss Arendt] supports Eichmann's incredible claim that he was ignorant of the *Kristallnacht* or Night of Broken Glass, even though the whole world knew" of it.

If Miss Arendt did not take up Eichmann's view that he was not guilty of physical murder, why did she say (p. 19), after referring to the message, "Eichmann proposes shooting," "This turned out to be the only 'order to kill,' *if that is what it was*, for which there existed even a shred of evidence"? To refer to the mountain of proof of Eichmann's orders to kill as a "shred of evidence" is like referring to the Atlantic Ocean as a brook.

Miss Arendt says that Eichmann *"very likely spoke the truth* when he said that he did not know Hitler's program when he joined the Nazi Party." Miss Arendt must be rather undiscerning if she cannot see in this Eichmann statement one of his most blatant falsehoods. To say this Hitler idolater did not know of Hitler's mania on the subject of Jews is simply ludicrous and not worthy of any extended discussion. Eichmann was introduced into the party and the S. S. by Ernst Kaltenbrunner, his fellow-townsman, who was hanged at Nuremberg as one of the most vicious of all the Nazi murderers.

In her letter Miss Arendt says I said she " 'sympathized' with Eichmann and had written his defense." I did not put it that way. But I will accept her challenge and assert that that is exactly what her book is. She says in her book, that Eichmann " 'personally' never had anything against the Jews." Commenting on this she said: "Alas, nobody believed him." Is that not sympathizing? She says that Eichmann was misjudged, misrepresented, misunderstood, that he was a victim of "hard luck." Is that not sympathizing?

MICHAEL A. MUSMANNO.
Pittsburgh, Pa.

Eichmann; the System; the Victims

BRUNO BETTELHEIM

Hannah Arendt's *Eichmann in Jerusalem: A Report on the Banality of Evil* is largely a reprint of articles that appeared in *The New Yorker*. Still, I recommend it even to those who read the articles, not because the book's content is very different, but because the impact is even more powerful in its unbroken sequence. The task she sets for herself far transcends the crimes of one man since it deals with the greatest problem of our time and not merely with genocide, one of its ugliest outcroppings. Totalitarianism in one form or another is the most important issue of our day, and if the trial had dealt only with that it would truly have been the trial of the century, for it is also totalitarianism when a nation plans for atomic destruction on a grand scale, even if that nation is democratic and plans only for defense. This is because such plans fail to set limits within the human scope. To entertain the possibility of risking atomic destruction for millions is to toy with totalitarianism because it implies the right of a state to pursue its goals no matter what.

Review of Hannah Arendt, *Eichmann in Jerusalem: A Report on the Banality of Evil* (New York: Viking, 1963); from *New Republic*, CXLVIII (June 15, 1963), 23–33. © 1963 by *New Republic*. Reprinted by permission of the *New Republic*.

This then is the virtue of Arendt's book—that it views Eichmann and his trial as posing the problem of the human being within a modern totalitarian system. But in a way it is also its shortcoming: the issues are so vast that we do not seem able yet to cope with them intellectually, though her book is certainly a most serious and in part successful effort to do so.

In order to deal with totalitarianism on a human scale she had somehow to reduce it to its human basis. This she does by pursuing three basic threads of the problem: the man Eichmann; the impossibility of judging totalitarianism from our traditional system of thought, including our legal system; and the hapless victims. But so interwoven are these three issues because of the nature of the subject and the way the trial was conducted, that neither I nor Dr. Arendt can deal with them separately.

Hannah Arendt's previous contributions to our understanding of *The Human Condition* and of *The Origins of Totalitarianism* find her singularly well equipped to understand how Eichmann's deed, his trial, and his victims, are all part of the same problem. So while her book is nominally about Eichmann in Jerusalem and though the trial is discussed in a very personal, erudite, and critical way, in a deeper sense it is not even an essay on the banality of evil, as the subtitle suggests; though it is an essay on that too. Essentially it is a book about the incongruity of it all, greatest of which is the fact that by all "scientific" standards Eichmann was a "normal" person. "Half a dozen psychiatrists had certified him as 'normal'—'More normal, at any rate, than I am after having examined him', one of them was said to have exclaimed, while another found that his whole psychological outlook, his attitude toward his wife and children, mother and father, brothers, sisters, and friends, was 'not only normal but most desirable'—and finally the minister who paid regular visits to him in prison . . . reassured everybody by declaring Eichmann to be 'a man with very positive ideas'." Obviously our standards of normality do not apply to behavior in totalitarian societies.

It is the incongruity of the murder of millions, and of one man being accused of it all. It is so obvious that no one man can exterminate millions. The incongruity is between all the horrors recounted, and this man in the dock, when essentially all he did was to talk to people, write memoranda, receive and give orders from behind a desk. It is essentially the incongruity between our conception of life and the bureaucracy of the total state. Our imagination, our frame of reference, even our feelings, are simply not up to it.

We can witness this every day. If one individual suffers, or a few—as in an airplane crash, a mine explosion, or typically as when a neighbor's child falls in a well—immediately our sympathy is roused to the quick. We feel for the victims, and their relatives. We anxiously wait for further news. We all hope and some pray. We feel compelled to do something to help. But let thirty thousands be killed by a volcano erupting, where we are not on the scene to see it—then we are not deeply moved. We may collect money, we may talk and read about it, but we still are not really shaken up inside. Our emotions are still the emotions of the small clan or clique. We react with deep feeling to what we see and can feel in ourselves, to what is immediately before our eyes, or what we can understand from personal experience. We have not yet learned to deal with the experience of the total mass state. We simply cannot think except in terms of the individual, not in terms of millions—or at least most of us cannot. A few screams evoke in us deep anxiety and a desire to help. Hours of screaming without end lead us only to wish that the screamer would shut up.

This, then, is a book about our inability to comprehend fully how modern technology and social organization, when made use of by totalitarianism, can empower a normal, rather mediocre person to play so crucial a role in the extermination of millions. By the same incongruity, it becomes theoretically possible for a minor civil servant—say a lieutenant colonel, to keep the parallel to Eichmann—to start the extermination of most of us by pressing a button. It is an incongruity between the image of man we still carry—rooted though it is in the humanism of the Renaissance and in the liberal doctrines of the 18th Century—and the realities of human existence in the middle of our current technological revolution. Had this revolution not permitted us to view the individual as a mere cog in the complex machinery, dispensable, a mere instrument, Eichmann would never have been possible. But neither would have been the slaughter at Stalingrad, Russia's slave labor camps, the bombing of Hiroshima, or the current planning for nuclear war. It is the contradiction between the incredible power technology has put at our disposal, and how unimportant the individual has become just because of it.

It is the incongruity between the banality of an Eichmann, and that only such a banal person could effect the destruction of millions. Had he been more of a man, his humanity would have kept him from his evil work; had he been less of a man, he would not have been effective at his job. His is exactly the banality of a man who would push the button when told, concerned only with pushing it well, and without any regard for who was pushed by it, or where.

Even our language has become incongruous; it fails us because our words are symbols for events occurring in an entirely different context; they refer only to matters of a different magnitude. To kill applies to the murder of an enemy in war, or for personal gain, or out of personal hate. It implies something akin to a face to face encounter. Dillinger was a killer. Eichmann was an instrument in the destruction of millions; anything that he did not consider strictly legal revolted him. As he truthfully stated, he never killed a man. Legalized mass murder, by order of the state—this he did not mind; on the contrary, he could enjoy the efficiency, the "scientific" attitude with which he executed his duty. His "expert" knowledge of the Jewish problem was in all respects woefully inadequate, as Arendt describes in detail; it mainly consisted of his having read two books. But to him this seemed a scientific approach to the problem of emigration and extermination. This again is of crucial importance, because without such legalistic or scientific detachment, the inhumanity of totalitarianism cannot be understood. It was not simply one person's pseudo-scientism leading him astray. These facts are amply documented by the legalized, murderous "scientific" experiments carried out by persons to whom, according to their training and position, the qualification of scientist could not be denied. I am referring here to the physicians who engaged in human experimentation, as described in the Nuremberg Trials and many other reports. These were—in many cases—prominent physicians, distinguished university professors and what not, all trained in pre-Nazi times, all sworn to the Hippocratic oath. And some of the greatest physicians of Germany knew and officially approved of what their colleagues were doing. They too did what they did only because it all seemed perfectly legal; all was in order within the frame of reference of the totalitarian state. Certainly it is misleading to apply to these doctors the old-fashioned term of physician or healer. But neither does the old-fashioned term murderer apply to them, or to Eichmann, because it is a term remaining within the human orientation.

Despite the judges' efforts to fit Eichmann into the old categories, his location in history, like the magnitude of his deeds, defied their efforts. That is why they tried to establish in vain that he had once killed a Jewish boy, as if that would have made any difference when he had helped to exterminate millions. But if they had been able to prove he had murdered one person, he would somehow have done a deed we could comprehend and punish within existing law and our familiar concept of retribution.

Our language is just as inadequate for discussing the victims. By now an entire literature has sprung up glorifying the martyrdom of the Jewish victims. Yet the term martyrdom applies to them as little as the ordinary term murderer applies to an Eichmann, or to the plane crews who dropped atomic bombs. Had Japan been victorious, they would probably have been tried as murderers.

According to Webster, a martyr is a person "who voluntarily suffers death as the penalty of witnessing to and refusing to renounce his religion or a principle." In this sense the early Christians were martyrs, not because they were murdered—that only makes them victims of the state—but because they could have saved their lives by embracing the state religion, and chose not to. Arendt is right not to grant the murdered Jews the sainthood of martyrs, and to view them simply as men. To those who claim they were martyrs, this is a sacrilegious position, and whoever holds that their actions may have contributed to their fate is accused of wishing to assert that the Jews were guilty—or that the Nazis were not.

If I should choose to walk unarmed at night in Central Park and get robbed there, it does not mean that my attacker is less guilty, nor that I am guilty. All it means is that I am not very smart and have failed to inform myself of the dangers I was risking. And if I get killed, I am not a martyr to the inequality of our society, the lack of police protection, or the upbringing of slum children, although my death may be due to these causes. I am merely dead. This does not change the guilt of the killer. But discussing how I contributed to my fate may prevent others from repeating my mistakes and is hence of greater use than merely bewailing my death or trying to make of me a martyr.

Whether one believes it serves no purpose to raise this question, or whether one is convinced that the issue needs the most careful scrutiny—this depends on whether one believes that a totalitarianism of Hitler's type is unique and that we shall never see it again. Arendt believes, and so do I, that some of the characteristics of the Third Reich are inherent in modern totalitarianism, while others more peculiar to it can fortunately remain so. Today as then, for example, we still respond to devices used by the modern mass state for exerting control through the impersonal bureaucracy, impersonal tastemakers, and impersonal sources of information; all hide individual responsibility behind a screen of objectivity and service to the community. This is why Arendt is not satisfied with studying the personality of an Eichmann as a unique phenomenon, but devotes equal attention to the system and what it did to its victims.

Those who wish to learn from these events for the future must accept not only the possibility, but the probability, that most people are neither heroes nor martyrs—that under great stress and misery a few become heroes, but most people deteriorate rather rapidly, and that inhumanity could be found both among Nazis and their victims. Students of society or of man have learned to take for granted that nobody, including the students themselves, are ever free of human failings. Just because we know that none of us is entirely free from guilt for what has happened, we can afford to investigate even the guilt of the victims. This Hannah Arendt tries to do around the specific event of the Eichmann trial, as others have tried to do around the concentration camp.

When in 1939, fresh out of the concentration camp, I tried to tell Americans about my experiences, I was told by most, including psychiatrists, that my views were incorrect, or that I was suffering from a prisoner psychosis, because I warned that the SS were not demented sadists or (in the words of the Eichmann trial) monsters, but in the vast majority mediocre men—banal, to use Arendt's term—but nonetheless deadly effective. I was told to let the after-effects of my camp experience subside before I said any more, because my theories were apt to mislead Americans. To believe that the SS acted according to purposeful plan ran so counter to what most people then wished to believe, that it was also unacceptable to them when I said that the camps had a crucial role in the master plan of the Reich. When I spoke about a concentration camp society and how it was intended to break the individual's ability to resist, once he was caught, this too met with little acceptance. It was just too contrary to our humanistic frame of reference.

I mention it here because Arendt's book may well meet with similar reactions. Those who will view it as an account of the trial—critical, highly personal, perhaps even biased in part—will be dismayed by it because they will miss what her book has to teach. Yet to write the history of just another prominent Nazi was hardly worth her effort, nor to describe a trial that served propaganda as much as justice. If only one more miserable political criminal was being tried, then it would have seemed petty to take the court to task for the way it conducted the trial, because the accused's guilt was clear to begin with, and he admitted to it. Or why drag into her account of the trial that Jews, and even Jewish leaders, lent an unwilling heavy hand in the extermination of Jews? This had nothing whatever to do with trying the accused. His guilt was not an iota less because they did so.

Many will harp on all this because they fail to grasp the real issue. Judge Musmanno, who reviewed her book in *The New York Times Book Review*, could see it only as a most unfair account of a trial, as if the trial itself had been her topic. He failed to see that the issue was not Eichmann, but totalitarianism. He writes, for example, that "Miss Arendt devotes considerable space to Eichmann's conscience and informs us that one of Eichmann's points in his own defense was 'that there were no voices from the outside to arouse his conscience'." Musmanno adds, "How abysmally asleep is a conscience when it must be aroused to be told there is something morally wrong about pressing candy upon a little boy to induce him to enter a gas chamber of death?" To ask such a rhetorical question is playing up to the gallery, or the emotions of the audience, as did Attorney General Hausner (according to Arendt) because it was never proved that Eichmann did such a thing, or knew about it. Of course, he knew about the killings; he never denied it. But what Arendt was talking about was the dreadful situation that in a totalitarian state there were no voices from the outside to arouse one's conscience. This is the important issue she deals with, as Musmanno's emotionally loaded question tries to make us forget. For us who were not Nazis, the issue is the absence of these voices, our voices. This is what makes living in a totalitarian society so desperate, because there is nobody to turn to for guidance, and there are no voices from the outside.

How silent one's voice becomes under totalitarianism is well known by those who were inside concentration camps. They did not raise their voices to tell about it as long as they remained within range of the system. Maybe my conscience was "abysmally asleep," but when I was released from the camp I did not tell about it, not as long as I or my mother were still on German soil. All I did tell others was to get out of Germany in a hurry, or they would perish.

That is how little my conscience spoke as long as I had to fear being returned to the camp.

To prove that Eichmann could have heard the voice of conscience, Judge Musmanno quotes the story of Pastor Grueber, whom the court lauded as "one of the just men of the world." Undoubtedly he is a wonderful man, and like everyone else, I too admire his courage and moral convictions. But Arendt's account shows how softly even this man's voice spoke. On one occasion he asked Eichmann to let unleavened bread be sent to the Jews in Hungary for Passover. And he intervened on behalf of those Jews who had been wounded in World War I, of those who had received high war decorations, and of the widows of men killed in that war. But when asked by the court directly if he had tried to influence Eichmann, when asked "Did you, as a clergyman, try to appeal to his feelings, preach to him and tell him that his conduct was contrary to morality?" he had to answer that he had not, because "words would have been useless." And so indeed they might have been. If conscience spoke so little and so softly out of the mouth of one of the most courageous men, how can one doubt that Eichmann felt that no voices spoke up to reproach him? That they did not is no excuse for Eichmann. Those who think that Arendt quotes all this to exculpate him will dismiss the book, as Judge Musmanno did. But this is not her point. Her point is that even a saintly man like Probst Grueber spoke so softly that his voice remained inaudible, and that this is the tragedy of the honest man in a totalitarian society. This is why a Pasternak remained quiet under Stalin, while the Ehrenburgs praised him.

This is also why Arendt goes to some length to discuss a different attitude toward the handing over of Jews and how it affected Nazi functionaries in countries like Denmark or Bulgaria, where there was strong resistance to it not only among the population but also among high government and church officials. She speaks of the slow erosion of doctrinaire Nazi attitudes in these Germans because they were exposed to voices that objected to Nazi morality, voices that were loud and clear enough and numerous enough to make themselves heard.

Since Arendt views the importance of the trial as revealing the nature and the still very present dangers of totalitarianism, she is critical of the legal basis of this trial. She does not accuse the judges or Attorney General Hausner because they failed in meting out justice, or for failing to conduct a trial that was as fair as one could expect it to be under the circumstances. She is critical because the court vacillated between trying a man and trying history, and to this she objects.

To try Eichmann for the deeds of the state which he carried out—this the legal system by which he was tried did not permit. Had that been attempted, then hundreds of thousands of others would have had to be tried too. All the Germans, and many Jews too, who in some fashion helped in the killing of

Jews. As those who arranged for the Nuremburg Trials recognized, it was nearly impossible to bring to justice all who participated in the crimes against humanity. For when such crimes are committed, where is one to draw the line? A lieutenant colonel, such as Eichmann, stands neither very high nor very low in the hierarchy. Since he in particular was on trial, was the line to be drawn at the level of captain? And if so, why this arbitrary cut-off point?

To avoid all these and many other difficulties, Eichmann had to be tried as a person. But to do so required that he be viewed as a man of extraordinary qualities; that is, as a monster. This Eichmann certainly was, but as part of a monstrous system; as a man, he was blatantly not. That is why neither Arendt nor the court were able to restrict themselves to the trial of one man, but resorted to "painting the broader picture." To the court this larger picture was that of anti-Semitism, and Arendt is critical of the court on this score (or so it seemed to me), because it obfuscates the fact that only one individual was on trial for his life, and to mix up his trial with that of a system is questionable if one wishes to uphold individual responsibility.

That is, both the prosecuting attorney and the judges wanted to see Eichmann's deed as horrendous—which it was—but not as something radically different from other persecutions of the Jews. That is why, as far as the prosecution was concerned, "it is not an individual that is in the dock at this historic trial, and not the Nazi regime alone, but anti-Semitism throughout history." And this is why Israel's Attorney General Hausner began his opening address with Pharoah in Egypt, and with Haman's edict, "To destroy, to slay, and to cause them to perish." Not by the farthest stretch of imagination could Eichmann be justly put to death for Pharoah's deeds. Nor can any court within our legal system try an idea, such as anti-Semitism, nor can events in the history of man, such as the history of anti-Semitism, be tried. If we begin to try ideas, we end up with witch-hunts; or condemnations without due process, such as characterized the McCarthy era in America.

Why, then, were all these images evoked? The court did so because it viewed Hitlerism as a chapter, though the most lurid chapter, of anti-Semitism. But in Arendt's opinion, which I share, this was not the last chapter in anti-Semitism but rather one of the first chapters in modern totalitarianism. For this reason it is unfortunate, as Arendt stresses, that Eichmann was not tried by an international tribunal. To ensure against further chapters, as much as a writer can, Arendt tries to show the full horrors of totalitarianism, which go very far beyond those of anti-Semitism. A full understanding of totalitarianism requires that we see Eichmann as basically a mediocrity whose dreadful importance is derived only from his more or less chance position within the system.

To believe otherwise, to believe that there exists true freedom of action for the average individual within such system, is so contrary to fact that neither prosecuting attorney nor judges attempted to show that Eichmann enjoyed such a freedom. Only the extraordinary person, at great risk to himself, retains limited freedom in such a state.

It is in this sense that totalitarianism exists wherever the state abrogates the rights of the individual and makes state reason the supreme principle. That principle in the Hitler state was to make the German people supreme, and to eliminate all racial impurity from the soil of the greater German Reich. Toward this end he exterminated not only Jews but also millions of Poles and Russians, and virtually the entire gypsy population of Europe. Individuals counted for nothing, and if they hampered the unfolding of this supreme goal they were exterminated—not to serve individual hatred or personal advantage, but to obey the supreme law. Hence Eichmann's revulsion at those who enriched themselves, and his outrage at what he considered the barbarity of the Rumanian pogroms. Hence also, as Rousset has pointed out, the requirement of the state that wherever possible, the victims should acquiesce to their destruction so that they, too, like victims in some barbarous rite, should be part of the universal effort to do what is best for the state.

Thus if one translates the extermination of the Jews as part of the history of anti-Semitism, then Eichmann and his kind are indeed the greatest anti-Semitic monsters of all. And this the court tried to establish. If, on the other hand, the extermination of the Jews was merely one part of the master plan to create the thousand year totalitarian Reich, then Eichmann becomes a cog, sometimes an important one, sometimes less so, depending on his position in the over-all machinery. In this case the cog was of such personal mediocrity that he really could not quite comprehend his role. Arendt shows again and again how he was beholden to clichés, was in many ways unable to form opinions or think on his own, was carried away by his own phrases.

At least one of these clichés is deeply significant here. Again and again Eichmann spoke of *Kadavergehorsam*, freely translated: the obedience of a corpse. This was by no means a term born under Hitler. It was taken over from the Imperial Prussian Army tradition. This corpse-like obedience was expected of every good German soldier. It was considered one of his greatest virtues. If this was so in the German Army of pre-Hitler days, when at least some shreds of democratic thinking were afloat, and when autocracy was tempered by some nodding acquaintance with humanistic ideals, how much more powerful did it become under Hitler, that throwback to the creed of the god-emperor who brooked rival deities even less than his Imperial Roman antecedents.

And it is true: whoever embraces such *Kadavergehorsam* in regard to anything his supervisors may require is no longer a man but a living corpse. Here the obedient servant of Hitler and the prisoner who walked to the gas chamber became alike as true symbols of the total state. Rewarded servant and prisoner to be murdered, each had lost his free will, his ability to act out of personal conviction. The difference is that the Eichmanns were delighted with such conditions and felt it their duty to impose it on others. That the first made the choice of his own will, while the latter were herded into it by police and fellow prisoners, is the radical difference. But in the end result, the corpse-like existence, the difference is much smaller. That Eichmann not only chose such flagrant denial of anything that we consider human—worse, that he imposed it on others—this is reason enough to judge him. But let us also remember how at one time in this country such *Kadavergehorsam* was imposed on many men and considered their most desirable attitude—those whom arbitrary fate had condemned to the role of slave.

One could wish that the court had this issue in mind when it went way beyond the trying of Eichmann to discuss Jewish failure to resist. To decide whether or not Eichmann was guilty of the crime he was accused of, this was supposedly the purpose of the trial. He admitted his guilt, which was also well established through corroborating evidence. Then why call all these witnesses for the prosecution? For the trial it was immaterial to discuss why Jews did not fight back. Yet the court asked witness after witness: "Why did you not protest?" "Why did you board the train?" "Fifteen thousand people were standing there and hundreds of guards facing you. Why didn't you revolt and charge and attack?"

Arendt is probably correct about the motives of the court. She believes that these questions were asked to convince all Jews that there can be no strength in Jewry unless it is vested in the state of Israel. She feels that by dragging out the lack of Jewish resistance, the Israeli authorities were trying to show that no such resistance was possible because no Jewish state existed to support it. If this was the reason of the court, perhaps it was also why the same court neglected to shed light on the unfortunate and desperate cooperation of Jewish leadership with the SS.

Because, like the court in Israel, it was the misfortune of the Jews of Europe that they too saw Hitlerism as only the worst wave of anti-Semitism. They therefore responded to it with methods that in the past had permitted them to survive. That is why they got involved with executing the orders of the state; that is why the Jewish leaders and elders, with heavy hearts, cooperated in arranging things for the Nazi masters. Arendt claims, and her thesis will long be fought over, that without this collaboration Hitler could never have succeeded in killing so many Jews.

This is the part of her book that will be most widely objected to. I do not claim to know whether she is right or wrong in her argument: that if the Jewish organizations had not existed, the extermination of the Jews could never have attained such tremendous proportions. But she certainly makes her point effectively. No doubt the stories of the ghettos would have been different if most Jews and their leadership had not been more or less willing, out of anxiety, to cooperate with the Germans, if they had not opposed the small minority that called for resistance at all costs, including violent fighting back. No doubt many Jews would have been quicker to support the pitifully small fighting minority had they been told what lay in store for them by Jewish leaders who knew, or should and could have known, what fate awaited them. Many others might have tried to escape. It is another question whether more Jews could have been saved if no Jewish organizations had existed, as Arendt claims.

Here too, objections will be raised against the book. Because of her concentration on the injustice bred by totalitarianism, Arendt at times creates an ambiguity in her evaluation of guilt. Thus on cursory reading she seems to plead that Eichmann was a victim and that Jewish leaders were heavy with guilt. In fact, Arendt saw rightly that Eichmann was not the greatest villain of all. But to say so leaves her open to the misunderstanding that she did not think him much of a villain, which she certainly thought he was.

Conversely, there seems little doubt that Jewish leaders who made up lists of those to be shipped to the gas chambers became accessories to Eichmann's crimes. Others who made up similar lists, not knowing about the extermination policy and thinking their choices were merely being shipped East, acted less reprehensibly. Again others concerned with saving their own lives and those of relatives were ready to sacrifice the lives of others. Finally there were those who gave the SS a helping hand only because they believed that in doing so they reduced hardship; they may merely have been lacking in foresight, in understanding of the situation, in courage. The terrible tragedy was that they, no less than those who collaborated fully with the SS, were helping Eichmann to perpetrate his crimes.

But again, these issues are immaterial in trying one individual for the crimes he committed. Why then did Hannah Arendt spend such a large part of her book on a discussion of Jewish willingness to cooperate and on the Jews' contribution to their own extermination?

I believe that her purpose was to paint the broader context of the trial as she saw it, which went far beyond that of anti-Semitism. This was of greatest interest to me, because it has to do with the much more important issue: how and where can an individual resist, or fight back in a totalitarian society? Jewish witnesses who testified seemed to think that nobody could, certainly not the persecuted Jews. Arendt's point—and it is well taken—is that any organization within a totalitarian society that compromised with the system became immediately ineffectual in opposing it and ended up helping it. "The gravest omission from the 'general picture' [that the court tried to paint of the extermination of the Jews] was that of a witness to testify to the cooperation between Nazi rulers and the Jewish authority." Eichmann himself asserted that without such cooperation the extermination would have run into serious difficulties. He said, "The formation of the Jewish Council and the distribution of business was left to the discretion of the Council. . . . These functionaries with whom we were in constant contact—well, they had to be treated with kid gloves. They were not ordered around, for the simple reason that . . . that would not have helped matters any. If the person in question does not like what he is doing, the whole works will suffer." "Judge Halevi found out from Eichmann in cross examination that the Nazis had regarded this cooperation as 'the very cornerstone' of their Jewish policy."

That the SS state could not have functioned without the cooperation of the victims, to this I can testify from my camp experience. The SS would have been unable to run the concentration camps without the cooperation of many of the prisoners—usually a willing one, in some cases reluctant, but all too often an eager cooperation.

This cooperation the court deliberately refrained from bringing to light, though it freely brought out the absence of resistance. To quote Arendt, the court did not raise the question, "Why did you cooperate in the destruction of your own people?" but this question was shouted by spectators who were only too familiar with the contribution of prominent Jews to the Jewish fate. When the former Baron Philip von Freudiger, formerly of Budapest, gave testimony, this question was screamed at him, so that the court had to interrupt the session. Arendt reports: "Freudiger, an orthodox Jew of considerable dignity, was shaken: 'There are people here who say they were not told to escape. But fifty percent of the people who escaped were captured and killed—as compared with ninety-nine percent, for those who did not escape.'" A fateful comment on the consequences of Jews being kept in the dark by Jewish leaders.

From this and much more Arendt concludes that, "If the Jewish people had really been unorganized and leaderless, there would have been chaos and plenty of misery but the total number of victims would hardly have been between four-and-a-half and six million people."

Thus only fighting partisans or those who went underground had a chance to survive; only those who made no effort to compromise, to meet the oppressor half way, those who shunned such principles as that by sacrificing thousands one might save tens of thousands. Because accepting such principles implied some cooperation with the enemy in the sacrifice of the thousands.

In retrospect it is quite clear that only utter non-cooperation on the part of the Jews could have offered a small chance of forcing a different solution on Hitler. This conclusion is not an indictment of Jews living or dead—but an empirical finding of history. To deny or ignore it may open the door to the genocide of other races or minority groups. Active resistance arouses strong admiration, permits most of us to put it out of our minds fairly soon.

Perhaps an example from the American scene may illustrate. Many of us are impressed by the way Negroes in Birmingham marched, singing and upright, to jail. But much deeper feelings are aroused in us when we see pictures of a solitary Negro being dragged down by policemen because he refuses to march to jail on his own. This experience did not often confront the German people. Certainly from my experience in the concentration camps, and with German civilians there, it made a difference. The reaction of the German people to the crimes committed against the Jews might have been very different if each Jew who was taken had to be dragged down the street, or shot down on the spot. Again and again when German citizens witnessed utter brutality against Jews, there was at least some reaction among the civilian population; and the Nazis were extremely sensitive to it.

At least one program that was very much a part of Hitler's essential demands for the purity of the German race met with so much popular resistance that it had to be discontinued. I refer to the "euthanasia" program for the extermination of the mentally sick. Later the gas that could no longer be used to exterminate mental patients because of the resistance among the German population was then used to gas Jews. (As early as 1935 Hitler had told his Reich medical leader, that "if war came he would take up and carry out this question of euthanasia because it was easier to do so in war time." This was long before he had told anyone about the extermination of the Jews. As soon as the war began the decree was carried out, and between September, 1939, and August, 1941, about 50,000 mentally-sick Germans were killed with carbon monoxide gas in institutions where the death rooms were disguised exactly as they were later in Auschwitz—that is, as shower rooms and bathrooms.)

Arendt also tells of how two small actions against Jews were used for testing out what the popular reaction might be. Perhaps if these Jews had not, on their own, packed their things and marched themselves to the train that took them away, if they had had to be openly shot, or dragged down the streets, the Nazis might have learned that such methods aroused too much resistance. There is little doubt that they were astonished at the lack of popular opposition to the extermination program. But there was also little reaction because the Jews cooperated so smoothly, following the advice of their own leaders.

When, then, or at which point, is an individual still able to save his soul and perhaps also his life, although enveloped by a totalitarian society? Interestingly enough, this very point could be identified clearly in the Eichmann trial. Arendt pays great attention to it. One can only regret that the court did not. This moment of choice came when Eichmann for the very first time visited the extermination camps and saw what happened to the Jews. He nearly fainted. But instead of heeding his emotional reaction, he pushed it down to go on with the task that he had been assigned and that he embraced as his own obligation. This was Eichmann's point of no return. Then and there he abdicated from reacting as a human being and made himself a mere tool of the state. Interestingly enough we find a similar story in the life of Höss, the commander of Auschwitz. His moment of truth came when one of his best friends, another SS man, was unjustly executed for failing to carry out an order. Such, I believe, are the moments when the vital decision has to be made, because these are situations where one is confronted in a personal, immediate way, not an abstract one, with the issue of the human being versus the totalitarian state.

For all too few Germans it came as Hitler gained power; for others it happened around the euthanasia program. For more Germans it came with Stalingrad. Not surprisingly, this decision faced American soldiers too in the war against Hitler. Perhaps typical is an American friend, a major in the air force, who for two years bombed Germany. He never questioned but that what he did was helping to bring an end to an inhuman regime, though he saw little of what he did at close range. Immediately after Hitler's collapse, he and a small group traversed Europe by jeep. He now saw close up and with his own eyes the leveling of human centers of habitation to a heap of broken rubble—but also a human rubble. In a moment of truth he saw how there was no clean division in war between those who destroy and those who battle the destroyers. He could no longer remain in the army.

Such a moment of truth came certainly to every prisoner in the concentration camps, when he was confronted with the problem of whether or not to cooperate with the SS and help in the running of the camp. It came to many Germans, and it must have come to many Jews, particularly to Jewish leaders. My thesis is that if one does not stand up to this experience, if one takes the first step in cooperating with the totalitarian system at the expense of one's convictions and sentiments, one is caught in a web that tightens with each step of cooperation until it becomes impossible to break free.

I have spoken about the incongruity of it all. There was no less incongruity in the trial itself. Here was a lieutenant-colonel, who admitted his guilt, but also that he had done nothing but his duty. And here was all the machinery of a state, trying to convict him of a crime he had admitted to begin with.

Initially I said this was not the trial of the century, though it dealt with the crime of the century. At one time the crime of Leopold and Loeb was rightly called the "crime of the century," but since then it has been superseded by crimes such as Eichmann's. These two boys committed a most inhumane act, not for gain or out of hatred, but to assert principles. It was a crime committed because of the most inhumane principles and to assert their superiority. To their crime too the old legal maxim, *"Cui bono?"* did not apply. Neither Leopold nor Loeb profited from their crime, nor did Eichmann in any appreciable way. He recognized that his advancement on the front or through other services probably would have been quicker, though he was certainly serving the principles of his masters, and in part to get his promotions.

Loeb and Leopold's trial was the trial of the century because, thanks to Darrow, the incredible inhumanity of their deed was put within the broad context of human nature. The result was that despite our revulsions at their crime enough empathy was aroused with these errant human beings so that the trial left us not only shaken with helpless indignation but also aroused in us the determination to create a better society, one that could not and would not produce another Leopold and Loeb.

Eichmann's trial was not the trial of the century, because as a trial it had altogether too many shortcomings. It was a trial where the witnesses had their day in court, but hardly the accused. It was a trial where there was no balance between the machinery available to the prosecuting attorney when compared to that of the defense. It was a trial where important witnesses for the defense were prevented from appearing in court because they were given no assurance of immunity. (Obviously only those who had intimate knowledge of Eichmann's work could have borne witness on his behalf as to whether or not he wanted the Jews exterminated, or was only following orders. But the only ones who could solve these questions were those who had seen him at his gruesome work, because they had been his collaborators. Hence they risked prosecution under the same Nazi Collaborator Law that Eichmann was tried under. They could have come to Israel and appeared as witnesses only if immunity had been granted them. This Israel refused to do, depriving Eichmann of his chance to produce witnesses on his own behalf.) It was a trial where most of the time was spent on issues that had no direct bearing on the guilt of the accused.

It was a trial where the state spoke with rightful moral indignation about crimes against humanity, to an accused it had kidnaped in violation of international law. The legal background of this trial also illustrates the incongruity of our legal concepts for dealing with 20th Century totalitarianism. And here again I speak not as an expert or as a lawyer, but rather as a citizen concerned with what our laws can, and cannot do for us all.

The basic principle underlying the law under which Eichmann was tried is derived from the charter of the Nuremberg Trials. They served as precedent, for example, for convicting a man without his having been found guilty by a jury of his peers. According to this charter of the Nuremberg Trials the greatest crime of all was the crime against peace which was called "the supreme international crime . . . in that it contains within itself the accumulated evil of the whole: war crimes, and crimes against humanity." Of those who sat in judgment at Nuremberg, at least one nation had engaged in unprovoked aggressive war against Finland, while two had committed crimes against humanity according to this charter; one by using slave labor. (In addition, that nation has been accused of the killing of 15,000 Polish officers at Katyn Forest. This was never proved, or disproved, because it was never brought to trial.) Another nation had clearly acted against the Hague convention by dropping atomic bombs, indiscriminately killing civilians. Still, these things happened before the Nuremberg Trials.

Since then, Israel, together with France and England, have waged war against Egypt and hence, according to the charter, committed the supreme international crime. But no court has tried them. While England and France could at least claim that Egypt had abrogated certain of their rights, Israel could not even make this claim. Crimes against humanity are unfortunately still tried only by the victors, with only the vanquished as the accused.

Such are the realities of political life in our 20th Century. I regret them but I do not object to them, because I know that these same realities induced me (in my more optimistic moments I like to think, forced me) to do things in the concentration camp (and probably outside as well) that would not stand up too well under closest scrutiny.

Unlike Arendt—and despite her cogent argument for an international court—I do not object to Israel's trying Eichmann, or to their trying him the way that they did, because I believe we must deal in some fashion with the Eichmanns of this world. That our legal procedures are not adequate for doing so does not mean they should go untried. I mean only to show that our existing laws are as incongruous for dealing with totalitarianism as we are unprepared as individuals to meet its challenge. Despite my many objections to details, if I were asked whether I preferred the trial to Eichmann's remaining free, I have no doubt that I am glad there was a trial.

Arendt seems to object to the trial as propaganda. This to me is its main justification, given the irregularities of the trial and Eichmann's having been kidnaped. Personally I would have preferred the solution Arendt suggests, that Eichmann should have been killed by a Jew, as Tindelian killed Talaat Bey (the great killer in the Armenian pogroms of 1915) and Schwartzbard killed Simon Petlyura (who was responsible for the pogroms during the Russian civil war). If such executioner of Eichmann had then been tried, through that trial all the crimes of Eichmann could have been forced on the conscience of the world without extraneous questions such as kidnaping and legality of the trial interfering with the clear message of the murderous nature of totalitarianism. If Eichmann's trial did not serve justice well, it did something much more important, and this for the living rather than for the dead: It brought the world face to face with those dangers of totalitarianism that it seems all too willing to avoid examining.

So while I would recommend this book for many reasons, the most important one is that our best protection against oppressive control and dehumanizing totalitarianism is still a personal understanding of events as they happen. To this end Hannah Arendt has furnished us with a richness of material.

[Exchange of Letters]

MICHAEL A. MUSMANNO AND BRUNO BETTELHEIM

SIRS:

Bruno Bettelheim writes a long philosophic, psychological cogitative thesis on Hannah Arendt's book, *Eichmann in Jerusalem* in the June 15 *New Republic*. He supports her proposition that somehow, some way, Eichmann was abused and treated badly. The fact remains that six million civilian corpses were strewn over Europe; the fact remains that Eichmann headed the organization whose objective it was to turn six million (even more, if possible) inoffensive, unarmed, helpless human beings into those six million corpses, but this does not bother Professor Bettelheim at all. He spreads over these corpses words, words, words. He speaks of totalitarianism, psychiatry, *kadavergehorsam*.

Who was responsible for this mass butchery which should sicken the stomach of anyone who has a stomach, and a heart, and a brain to understand responsibility? Bettelheim does not exclude the possibility that the victims themselves were somehow at fault, as if they might perhaps have locked themselves up in freight cars, shipped themselves to the gassing halls and there thrust the fatal nozzles into their throats.

Bettelheim cannot understand how Eichmann was much at fault. He says that "essentially all he did was to talk to people, write memoranda, receive and give orders from behind a desk." Can anything be more absurd? What were those orders of which Bettelheim speaks so casually? They were orders to kill innocent human beings! What did Adolf Hitler do but sit behind a desk and give orders to murder the peace and, with it, vast populations and a civilization we may never know again. Would Professor Bettelheim excuse Hitler because it was not proved that he ever actually individually took the life of a human being with his own hands?

Professor Bettelheim says that Eichmann did not know that what he was doing was wrong because there were no voices to arouse his conscience. Rudolf Hoess, the commandant of Auschwitz, testified in Nuremberg that he knew when the people in the gas chambers were dead when they no longer screamed. Eichmann saw Jews marching into gas chambers of death. What

New Republic, CXLVIII (June 29, 1963), 29–31. © 1963 by *New Republic*. Reprinted by permission of the *New Republic*.

kind of a hearing aid did he need so that their screams would register on his conscience and inform him they had done nothing for which to die? Professor Bettelheim says that if he heard a few screams, this would evoke in him "deep anxiety and a desire to help," but if he heard "hours of screaming without end," this would lead him "only to wish that the screamer would shut up." The screamers did eventually shut up. Six million of them.

And now Professor Bettelheim quarrels because there are people in Israel and in Jewish as well as non-Jewish homes throughout the world who look upon those six million as having suffered martyrdom. He says this is wrong because Webster defines a martyr as a person "who voluntarily suffers death as the penalty of witnessing to and refusing to renounce his religion or a principle." If Professor Bettelheim will look up the word "martyrdom" in Webster's dictionary he will find that Webster says that martyrdom is "the suffering of death on account of adherence to the Christian faith, *or to any cause.*" The six million died because they were *Jews,* and for no other reason. And non-Jews as well as Jews should place the blame where blame belongs for this unspeakable outrage against humanity and not seek to evade facts by speaking of orientation, images and all the metempirical abstruseness and nebulosities, looking to minimizing a crime without parallel in all the annals of the law.

In his metaphysical speculations, Bettelheim stumbles over the most obvious facts, and the most conspicuous realities. He says, for instance, that the trial had many shortcomings, specifying that "the witnesses had their day in court, but *hardly the accused.*" This can only be termed educated poppycock. The fact of the matter is that Eichmann was on the witness stand from June 20 to July 24, 1961, for a total of thirty-three and a half sessions! And he could have remained there longer if he had anything more to say. Never was a defendant given a greater opportunity to exculpate himself.

Thus, whatever philosophical conclusions Bettelheim intends to project in his article can have but little consequence in appraising the Eichmann case because of facts he has ignored and others he has misinterpreted. I believe that Bettelheim could have written a shorter article and one more vastly interesting if he had directly answered the inevitable but simple question: What would he have done with Adolf Eichmann?

MICHAEL A. MUSMANNO
Pennsylvania Supreme Court

IN REPLY:

Justice Musmanno has written a very emotional letter in reaction to a review that I tried to keep as rational as I could. While I believe that emotions in this case are more than justified, they are likely to prevent us from seeing a phenomenon in its true perspective. Considering Hitler's and Eichmann's deeds, it comes naturally to want to cry out, "Murder most foul . . . cruel and unnatural," but those who wish to learn from past events for the future cannot afford to permit themselves the luxury of being carried away by their feelings.

As in his original *New York Times* review of Arendt's book, Justice Musmanno accuses a writer of having said what he did not say, and then proceeds to demolish him on the basis of such erroneous claim. For example, he accuses me of having implied that the victims shipped themselves to the gas chambers, while my entire thesis was that one has to take a stand long before such a point has been reached. I wrote my book, *The Informed Heart,* and I wrote the review, because of my conviction that we all must recognize that once we permit ourselves to be rounded up, we are no longer able to fight and we have made ourselves into passive victims. That is why I discussed the problem: "At which point is an individual still able to save his soul and perhaps also his life, although enveloped by a totalitarian society?"

Justice Musmanno equally distorts what I wrote about the absence of voices. Any comparison between my review and his interpretation of it will show this.

As far as the reading of *Webster's Dictionary* is concerned, I would suggest that Justice Musmanno reconsult *Webster's Third New International Dictionary of the English Language, Unabridged* (1963). I used *martyr* as a noun, and I herewith quote in full *Webster's* definition (italics mine):

> "1: one who *voluntarily* suffers death as the penalty of witnessing to and refusing to renounce his religion or a tenet, principle, or practice belonging to it; modern-day missionary martyrs; 2: one who sacrifices his life, station, or what is of great value *for the sake of principle* or to sustain a cause; 3a: a great or constant sufferer (as from disease); a martyr to rheumatism; b: one who adopts a specious air of suffering or deprivation esp. as a means of attracting sympathy or attention."

In this sense I claimed that the Jews were not *martyrs*. Justice Musmanno refers to a definition of *martyrdom,* but this definition too rests on the meaning of the word martyr, since *Webster's* defines martyrdom as follows: "1: the state of being a martyr . . ." This is what happens when a man as familiar as Justice Musmanno must be with the rules of evidence gets carried away by emotions. First he exchanges martyrdom for martyr, then disregards *Webster's* definition of *martyr* on which his definition of *martyrdom* rests, and finally provides his own unacknowledged emphasis to the last four words in a definition, in this way misreading *Webster's*. I as a scientist cannot afford to do so.

Similarly, Justice Musmanno overlooks the fact that I never claimed to have been present at the trials or to have studied the trial records. It is the reviewer's privilege to believe that which he feels was convincingly demonstrated in the book he reviews. I reviewed Arendt's book and in so doing drew occasionally on my own experiences. It is Arendt's opinion, as I read her book, that Eichmann's trial was not the fairest as trials go, and that the witnesses had their days in court. What is important is not the number of sessions

Eichmann was in the witness stand to be questioned by his accusors, but the fact that the witnesses for the prosecution were given very wide scope while many potential witnesses for the defense were not granted the immunity they would have needed to appear in court at all.

That Justice Musmanno is curious about what I would have done with Eichmann only suggests that his emotionalism prevented him from reading all of my article, because I very clearly state in the second to the last paragraph what would have been my solution to the problem.

BRUNO BETTELHEIM
University of Chicago

Notes and Comment

Now and again, in the most unlikely places, there appears a little paradigm of the sort of misunderstanding between men of presumably good faith and sound intelligence which, in personal or international affairs, brings on catastrophe. Such a paradigm was presented recently in the pages of the *Times Book Review*. Hannah Arendt had written for this magazine, and for publication in book form, an account of the trial of Adolf Eichmann in Jerusalem. No one was more qualified than Miss Arendt to undertake such a work; her experience as German Jew, historian, philosopher, and humanist enabled her to approach her subject with feeling, with reason, and with knowledge. She outlined precisely and brilliantly the structure of the Nazi hierarchy. She analyzed the character of Eichmann, a member of that hierarchy, and found him, despite the scope of the horror that it was within his power to inflict, a man without depth of character, of passion, or of intelligence; six million victims could not have been executed without the dogged efficiency of such simpletons as he. She recorded the behavior of individuals and of nations, and found within her story a moral for Germans, for citizens of other Western countries, and for Jews—in descending order of responsibility: It is evil to assent actively or passively to evil, as its instrument, as its observer, or as its victim. She criticized the Israeli handling of the case for its lapses into histrionics at a moment that called for calm analysis and for the rendering of justice to an individual who reflected the almost total collapse of conscience in a formerly civilized nation. One of the assumptions underlying her work was that, while compassion is one enemy of evil, a stronger and more reliable force for good is

New Yorker, XXXIX (July 20, 1963), 17. Reprinted by permission; © 1963 The New Yorker Magazine, Inc.

reason, for the dictates of reason in moral questions are likely to coincide with the demands of conscience. She was concerned with all the sins of omission and commission that contributed to the disaster, and, concluding that evil is never grand but (an infinitely more terrible thought) unremittingly trivial, she subtitled her work "A Report on the Banality of Evil."

But, with the perversity that often interrupts even the most lucid and brilliant discussion of ethics and historiography, Michael A. Musmanno, a Justice of the Supreme Court of Pennsylvania, chose, in the pages of the *Times*, to misunderstand. In reviewing her book, he accused Miss Arendt of an excess of sympathy for Eichmann (her condemnation of the Nazi leaders was far more withering than any that had been made before) and of a lack of sympathy for the Jews (her sorrow over their suffering was far more eloquent than the Justice's own). He ignored all Miss Arendt's ironies (referring to her "Alas, nobody believed him," unmistakably ironic in context, as a "lament" for Eichmann). He accused her of indifference to "the screams of horror-stricken women and terrorized children as they saw the tornado of death sweeping toward them," although an important purpose of her inquiry was to determine the causes of those screams, so that they might never be heard again. To Miss Arendt's quiet, moral, rational document he opposed such rhetorical exclamations as "Himmler!," "Hitler!," as though these were enlightening statements in the philosophy of history. When, in a letter solicited by the *Times*, Miss Arendt attempted to clarify her already clear position, Justice Musmanno, in a reply, simply distorted it again, in such a way as to make fruitful discussion of "Eichmann in Jerusalem" almost impossible. The *Times* published this unsymmetrical exchange without comment, and, evidently no more sensitive to irony than Justice Musmanno himself, added to the confusion by presenting a letter written in Miss Arendt's defense as though its author, Irving J. Weiss, had taken the side of Justice Musmanno. The refusal to *listen*, the frightening breakdown of communication, is nothing new; we have grown accustomed to it in life and in the headlines. But the very essence of literature is communication, and to find such a breakdown in the literary section of a major newspaper is profoundly disappointing.

Questions

1. What are the main points of disagreement between Musmanno and Miss Arendt? Between Musmanno and Bettelheim? What are the main points of agreement between Bettelheim and Miss Arendt?
2. In [Exchange of Letters] by Miss Arendt and Musmanno, what are meant by the terms *"pro domo"* and *"pro bono publico"*? Can you determine the meanings from the context? Why does Miss Arendt say Musmanno is arguing *"pro domo,"* and why does he reply that he was reviewing her book *"pro bono publico"*?
3. Do the disagreements on facts really matter in the discussion? Can you, from Bettelheim's review and from Miss Arendt's statement, suggest, first, why she subtitled her book *A Report on the Banality of Evil*, and, second, what it is that she and Musmanno really disagree about?

4. What does Bettelheim mean by the following statement: "This then is the virtue of Miss Arendt's book—that it views Eichmann and his trial as posing the problem of the human being within a modern totalitarian system"?
5. Is a mass murderer entitled to the same rules of trial procedure as someone who murders in passion or in self-defense? Would you apply the arguments against capital punishment (part III, 4) to Eichmann?
6. How does Bettelheim apply his own concentration-camp experience to his analysis of Miss Arendt's book?
7. What is the issue raised by Bettelheim and Musmanno about the definition of "martyrdom"?
8. Is the next to last paragraph in Bettelheim's review well reasoned?

Assignments

1. Write a dialogue between someone taking Bettelheim's position and someone taking Musmanno's. Try to do justice to each side.
2. Summarize the philosophical, the moral, the ethical, the legal, or the religious issues raised in the reviews and exchanges by Musmanno, Bettelheim, and Miss Arendt.
3. Without taking one side or the other, summarize the two sides of the Eichmann question. This summary may be in the form of a report for a weekly newspaper or newsmagazine.
4. Using the arguments from one of the essays in the section on capital punishment, prepare an argument for or against the execution of Eichmann.
5. Summarize the arguments that appear in this section for and against considering Eichmann a *major* criminal.
6. Argue against an important point made by either Musmanno or Bettelheim.

Additional Reading

From the time Eichmann was located in Argentina, kidnapped, and prepared for trial in Israel, dozens, perhaps hundreds, of articles have appeared concerned with the legal and the moral implications of the kidnapping itself and the judicial procedure planned. Eichmann's involvement in the mass killing of German Jews under Hitler was never itself in question. The question, as is plain from the reviews, had to do with the nature and the extent of his guilt. The actual trial was covered by Hannah Arendt for the *New Yorker* and the articles collected in her book *Eichmann in Jerusalem: A Report on the Banality of Evil* (New York, 1963). That book in itself provoked a storm of response, with most persons either defending or attacking it vigorously, very few finding a position between.

Two of the earliest and least complicated examinations of the book appear in this section, those by Judge Michael A. Musmanno and Dr. Bruno Bettelheim. The *New York Times Book Review* for June 23, 1963, pp. 4–5, which carried the exchange between Miss Arendt and Judge Musmanno reprinted here, also carried several pages of letters in support of one or the other.

Among the many significant comments on the book may be listed Norman Podhoretz' "Hannah Arendt on Eichmann: A Study in the Perversity of Brilliance," *Commentary*, XXXVI (September 1963), 201–208, which is anti-Arendt, and Mary McCarthy's "Hue and Cry," *Partisan Review*, XXXI (Winter 1964), 82–94, which is pro-Arendt.

SECTION SIX
Drug Addiction: Illness or Crime

The Pill Man

ALBERT RUBEN AND CHARLES ECKERT

Cast of Characters

LAWRENCE PRESTON
KENNETH PRESTON
EDDIE CLARK
ANNE CLARK
TOM GRAFTON
ASST. D. A. SAM WOLFE
PHIL MACY
DETECTIVE DEWEY

DR. ROBERT HARTOG
DETECTIVE ROSS
WOMAN DETECTIVE
JUDGE
DR. WILLIAM NELSON
STANLEY
FOREMAN

Prologue

(*Interior drugstore. Night.* TOM GRAFTON *enters. Seventeen, ivy league, quick movements. He moves directly to the back counter where* EDDIE CLARK *is finishing waiting on a customer. En route, he passes a* WOMAN, *her hair in curlers under a scarf, examining some shelves at the front of the store.* TOM *waits until* EDDIE *gives the customer her change.*)

EDDIE (*to customer*): Thank you. Call again, please. (*Customer leaves.*)
TOM: Hello, Mr. Clark.
EDDIE: Hello, Tom.
TOM: My prescription ready?

Production #88 of *The Defenders*, created by Reginald Rose. Reprinted by permission of CBS Television Network, Plautus Productions, Inc. (producer), and the authors.

EDDIE (*nodding toward woman*): That lady is next.
TOM: Oh—sorry.
WOMAN: There's no rush . . . you go ahead and finish what you're doing. I don't know what I want yet. Some kind of hand lotion.
EDDIE (*eyeing the woman, to* TOM): I'm afraid I haven't quite finished making up your prescription yet. Could you come back in a—
TOM (*tensely*): I'd rather wait . . . (*under his breath*) Please.
(EDDIE *studies him closely, sees the boy's desperation, leaves for the prescription counter in back.* TOM—*beginning to wander about nervously. Seeing the soda fountain . . .*)
TOM: Mr. Clark, can I have a soda?
EDDIE (*offstage*): I'll be right out.
TOM: I can fix it myself. (*He waits for an answer.*) Okay?
EDDIE (*offstage*): Okay.
(TOM *goes behind the soda fountain. Fixes himself a drink.*)
TOM: By the way, my father said to send his regards. He and I were away, you know. Two week fishing trip . . . he's still away. I had to come back, though. (*He carries the drink with him as he emerges from behind the counter. He sips his drink nervously.*) How's Mrs. Clark?
EDDIE (*off stage*): Fine, thank you.
TOM: Give her my regards, will you?
EDDIE: I will.
(TOM *moves around the store, getting more jittery than ever. He moves close to the* WOMAN *scrutinizing the shelves.*)
TOM (*trying to be jocular but not quite succeeding*): Out of all those hand lotions, can't you find one?
WOMAN: That's what's so confusing. There are so many to choose from.
(TOM *downs the soda in long nervous gulps, walks to the counter with the glass, shaking so he has difficulty putting the glass down without rattling it. He looks around at the* WOMAN, *but she's paying no attention to him. He wipes his mouth with the back of his hand.* EDDIE—*entering from back of store with package.* TOM'S *face lightens as he hurries toward him.*)
EDDIE: Here you are, Tom.
TOM: Thanks. Put it on our bill. Thanks, Mr. Clark.
(*Beyond them, the* WOMAN *adjusts her scarf.* TOM *starts toward the front door and is met by two detectives,* DEWEY *and* ROSS, *as they enter.*)
DEWEY: We're police officers. We want to see what's in that package.
TOM (*almost shaking by now as he tries to keep the package*): Nothing— just some medicine. Honestly.
DEWEY: We'd like to see it, please.
TOM: Look. Please. Someone in my family's very sick. They're waiting for this. They need it very badly . . . (TOM *suddenly pushes* DEWEY *into* ROSS *and starts to run out. As he reaches the* WOMAN, *he stops as he sees her pointing a revolver at him. Slowly, he raises his hands.* DEWEY

comes over and takes the package from TOM's *upraised hand. Then he crosses to the back counter where* EDDIE *has watched this in horror.*)
DEWEY: Have you got a prescription for this stuff? (*He holds up the package.* EDDIE *barely shakes his head.*) Come on. (EDDIE *starts to come around the counter and they all start out.*)

ACT ONE

(*Interior interview room. Tombs. Day.* LAWRENCE *and* KEN PRESTON *are seated facing* EDDIE CLARK. *He has spent a sleepless night, needs a shave. His mood is taciturn, spiritless, reflecting his sense of defeat and despair.* LAWRENCE *is more hostile than we are accustomed to seeing him. Nothing really overt, but it's there.*)
LAWRENCE: When she telephoned, your wife said all she knew was you'd been arrested. Didn't you tell her what you're charged with?
EDDIE: No. How did she sound when you spoke to her?
KEN: Pretty upset, but I think that's natural under the circumstances.
EDDIE: When can I see her?
LAWRENCE: We'll arrange it. The police say they caught you selling narcotics without a prescription. Is that so?
(EDDIE *only nods.*)
LAWRENCE: Have you any explanation for it?
EDDIE: No. (*Beat.*) I mean I did it, and I got caught. What good are explanations going to do?
LAWRENCE: For one thing, they might help us prepare your defense.
EDDIE: What defense? I'm guilty.
LAWRENCE: Does that mean you want to plead guilty?
EDDIE: I . . . don't know. I don't see what else to do.
KEN: Have you ever been picked up before on a narcotics charge?
EDDIE: No.
KEN: Any previous convictions of any kind?
EDDIE: No.
LAWRENCE: In a way, you can consider yourself lucky. If you'd been caught by Federal agents instead of State agents, you'd be facing a much stiffer penalty. The Federal law is much stronger on it.
EDDIE: How long a prison sentence will I get?
LAWRENCE: That's hard to say. Who were you selling it to when they caught you?
EDDIE: A seventeen year old boy.
KEN: That's not going to help shorten your sentence.
(EDDIE *doesn't offer this as a defense, he just feels called up to say something.*)
EDDIE (*mumbling*): He's a sick boy.
(LAWRENCE *is annoyed at* CLARK's *cryptic answers. He is repulsed by the man's crime and skeptical of his explanation—such as it is.*)

LAWRENCE: How did you happen to take the boy on as a patient? How did you . . . shall we say . . . make the connection?
(EDDIE *betrays signs of conflict. His feeling of being without hope clashes with his more normal desire to answer the Prestons' questions, to explain to them, perhaps even persuade them.*)
EDDIE: More or less the same way as the others.
LAWRENCE: What others?
EDDIE: The others I helped to get . . . drugs . . .
KEN: How many of these others are there?
EDDIE: Five.
KEN: Do you mean you only have six customers?
EDDIE (*nodding*): That's right. Six illegal customers.
(*There is a moment of silence. The Prestons aren't quite sure what they're up against—this quiet man who seems so sure of himself and yet apparently resigned to his fate.*)
EDDIE: I'd like to see my wife.
(LAWRENCE *has been thoughtful. Now he leans forward.*)
LAWRENCE: Let me ask you something, Mr. Clark. What drugs did you supply to these six people?
EDDIE: Morphine and morphine derivatives. Some synthetics.
LAWRENCE: How much did you sell it for?
EDDIE: What it cost me.
KEN: Do you mean you didn't make any money selling this stuff?
EDDIE: No.
KEN: Then what did you do it for?
EDDIE: If . . . I say I did it because I felt sorry for them and wanted to help them . . . it sounds like I'm some kind of fanatic or something, doesn't it?

(*Interior, District Attorney's office. Day.* SAM WOLFE, *an assistant D.A., regards* LAWRENCE *with a certain deference.*)
D.A.: You don't really believe that story, do you?
LAWRENCE: Why not? What's so incredible about a man defying the law? Thoreau wouldn't pay his taxes. We know segregation statutes are being defied all over the place. It happens.
D.A.: I know, but those are things involving personal rights. You can understand why people feel strongly about things like that. But narcotics . . .
LAWRENCE: Look, even acknowledging your right to be skeptical, the fact still remains he's willing to plead guilty.
D.A.: Yeah, but to a misdemeanor. A couple of months and he'll be back in business.
LAWRENCE: Not if you take his license away.
D.A.: So he'll get it someplace else.
LAWRENCE: But that isn't what he deals in. He's not a heroin pusher. He's a

druggist who happened to get some confused ideas about a few people being sick and needing drugs he had in his shop.

D.A.: Look, Larry, the guy's been pushing dope. I don't care if he did it in a back alley or from behind a counter wearing a white coat. He's still a pusher and that's still as rotten a crime as I can think of. Especially when committed by a man who's supposed to be a respectable businessman. He's not even hooked himself—and that somehow makes it even dirtier. He doesn't deserve anything but having the book thrown at him. And that's just what he's going to get—the biggest book I can find.

ACT TWO

(*Interior. Preston's office. Day. Present are* LAWRENCE, KEN, *and* EDDIE CLARK.)

KEN (to EDDIE): When he granted bail, the judge made it conditional that you stay away from your store until after the trial.

LAWRENCE (*to* EDDIE): My advice is to abide by the judge's ruling. Can you get someone in to run the store?

EDDIE: Yes, I can do that.

LAWRENCE: I'm afraid the district attorney refused our proposal that you plead guilty to a reduced charge. The trouble is he's skeptical about the whole thing. He simply doesn't believe you didn't profit from your narcotic sales. Also he asked for a reason why you feel so strongly about addicts . . . why you're willing to risk your neck to help them. It's a fair question, Mr. Clark.

EDDIE: I thought I told you.

LAWRENCE: No, you didn't. When I asked the same question yesterday, all you said was you happened to know some addicts who were decent people and you wanted to help them.

EDDIE: That's right.

LAWRENCE: That's not enough. Not for a jury.

EDDIE (*flaring*): Why not? Is it so incredible when one human being wants to help out another?

LAWRENCE: How do you expect me to convince a jury that all you were doing was lending a helping hand to some deserving people?

EDDIE: They are, believe me.

LAWRENCE: I can understand. But what will a jury believe unless these people come in and testify for us.

EDDIE (*firmly*): No.

LAWRENCE: We don't have much else—

EDDIE: I can't do it to them. As soon as other people know they're on drugs, what happens to them? (*to* KEN) Well, you said it. Suddenly they are considered dope fiends. And even worse than that, the police'll hound them until they catch them with some pills, and then they go to prison. I mean how can I do that to anybody?

KEN: What about the Grafton boy? He's up on a narcotics charge anyway. At least may we talk to him?

(EDDIE *thinks it over, then:*)

EDDIE: I guess if he wants to testify for me, he can't get into any more trouble than he's in now.

(*Interior Grafton home. Day. A pleasant room in an uptown apartment. Not lavish, but comfortable and tasteful.* KEN *is seated opposite* TOM.)

TOM: Just tell me how. I'll do anything to help Mr. Clark.

KEN: How much did you pay him for the morphine he sold you?

TOM: Practically nothing. I think it was whatever it cost him.

KEN: How did you happen to go to him . . . you know the first time?

TOM: My dad's a friend of his. I don't know, they went to school together or something like that. Anyway, when Dad . . . you know . . . found out about me, he took me to a doctor. (*remembering—amused*) I never saw anybody so eager to get rid of me in my life.

KEN: The doctor.

TOM: He just said I should see a psychiatrist and . . . held the door open.

KEN: Did you go to a psychiatrist?

TOM: I'm still going. For a while I just tried to kick the habit, but I couldn't do it. And I told my dad I couldn't.

KEN: What did the psychiatrist say about that?

TOM: I don't know . . . I mean I sort of had the feeling he didn't know what to say. He was sure he could help me and I said I'd go to him and do anything he said, but I couldn't do it unless I had something. He said he couldn't give it to me. He . . . just couldn't, that's all. So there we were. I guess you might call it the perfect stalemate. That's when my dad took me to see Mr. Clark.

KEN: After that, when you started going to your doctor . . . did he know how you worked it out?

TOM: He never said anything but I'm sure he did.

KEN: Do you think you could make it on the stand if we asked you to be a witness for Mr. Clark?

TOM (*after a beat*): I think so. I'd sure try.

(*Interior Clark living room. Day.* ANNE, KEN, LAWRENCE. ANNE *seems very nervous and ill-at-ease.*)

ANNE: I'm so sorry Eddie's not back yet. He said he wouldn't be more than an hour.

LAWRENCE: It's our fault, Mrs. Clark. We should have phoned. But since we were in the neighborhood, we thought we could save your husband a trip downtown.

ANNE: You went to see the Grafton boy, didn't you?

LAWRENCE: Yes. You knew that the boy was being supplied drugs by your husband.

ANNE: Because Tom is an addict and—
LAWRENCE: But you knew.
ANNE: Yes.
LAWRENCE: Did you know of any others Mr. Clark was helping?
ANNE: Yes. Why?
LAWRENCE: It would be very helpful to us if those people would be defense witnesses.
KEN: And your husband refuses to involve them in any way.
ANNE: You want me to give you their names?
LAWRENCE: Or convince Mr. Clark how necessary their testimony will be to his defense.
ANNE: I don't know. . . . What about Tom? You said he was willing to appear for Eddie.
LAWRENCE: One witness only carries one-fifth the weight of five witnesses. And your husband is going to need all the weight he—
(EDDIE—*just entering at the front door.*)
EDDIE: Annie, are you—? (*He stops, his face clouding, as he sees the Prestons.*)
ANNE: You're late, Eddie. I told these gentlemen you'd be home any minute.
(LAWRENCE *and* KEN *have risen.*)
LAWRENCE: We've been having a very pleasant visit.
EDDIE (*furiously*): What are you doing here?
KEN: We were in the neighborhood and I wanted to tell you that Grafton agreed to testify.
EDDIE (*to* ANNE): Have they been asking you questions?
ANNE: I didn't mind, Eddie. They should ask . . .
EDDIE: No. They shouldn't. They should only do as I ask. (*to* LAWRENCE) You have no right to come here and snoop behind my back, frighten my wife.
LAWRENCE: Somebody in this family should be frightened before it's too late. You're in big trouble, Mr. Clark, and we want to help you despite the fact that you've done nothing but hide and conceal the truth from us.
EDDIE: You know the truth!
LAWRENCE: Not enough of it.
EDDIE: I'll tell you anything but names. Anything!
LAWRENCE: All right, Mr. Clark. Are you a drug addict?
(*The question produces startled reactions from everybody.*)
EDDIE: No. I'm not.
LAWRENCE: Were you ever an addict?
EDDIE: No. Never.
ANNE: I am. I'm an addict.
EDDIE: Anne!
(KEN *and* LAWRENCE *are shocked as* ANNE, *greatly agitated, gets to her feet. She is rigid with determination despite her husband's attempts to silence her.*)
ANNE: I'm a drug addict, Mr. Preston.
EDDIE: Oh God, Anne! Stop it! Please!

ANNE: That's how Eddie got into this. Because of me. If it hadn't been for me, he wouldn't be in any trouble. That's what you wanted to know isn't it? Why he did it? He did it because of me.
(KEN *has moved to* ANNE'S *side. He takes her arm.*)
KEN: Why don't you sit down, Mrs. Clark?
(EDDIE *sits slumped with his head in his hands, groans.* ANNE *now moves to console her husband, caressing his cheek.*)
ANNE: Shh, Honey . . . it's all right. Don't you see I want to do it? I want to help you.
EDDIE: Anne, you don't know what you're saying.
LAWRENCE: Do you mind if I ask you some questions, Mrs. Clark?
ANNE: I don't mind. I want you to.
EDDIE (*vehemently*): She's not going to say anything in court! I hope that's clear!
ANNE: What do you want to know, Mr. Preston?
LAWRENCE: How long have you been using drugs?
ANNE: About a year.
LAWRENCE: How did you get started?
ANNE: Eddie and I got married late . . . you know, compared to most people. He was over forty and I was over thirty, but we both wanted very much to have a child.
EDDIE (*in anguish*): Anne . . . I can't stand this . . .
(*It pierces* ANNE, *but she steadies herself, goes on.*)
ANNE: Eddie, I can. I'm sorry. Well, we . . . didn't. There wasn't anything wrong . . . I just didn't get pregnant. At least that's what the doctor said at first. Then he said there was something a little bit wrong with the way I was inside and everything, and maybe that was the reason. So I had an operation to correct it. In the hospital I was very nervous and . . . tense, I guess, and they gave me a lot of sedatives to help me get through it. Well, the operation went fine, and when I got home I felt really very good. But then . . . nothing happened. (ANNE *stares blankly. A long silence.*)
LAWRENCE: Mrs. Clark . . . ?
ANNE: I got . . . I started not feeling well.
EDDIE: She had a nervous breakdown. Is that so terrible?
LAWRENCE (*to* ANNE): I suppose you were given drugs again as part of your treatment.
ANNE (*nodding*): After a while the doctor said I didn't need them any more, but . . . (*She simply shrugs.*)
LAWRENCE (*to* EDDIE): And you supplied her.
EDDIE: I couldn't figure out any other way. I mean her only chance of getting straightened out was with the doctor, but she couldn't even go see him unless she had something to take. Why did you have to say it, Anne? Why?
LAWRENCE: What about the others?

EDDIE: That all came later. Anne?
ANNE: Eddie, I couldn't help it. Please. I want you to be all right . . .
LAWRENCE: Were they friends or . . . people who knew about your wife or . . . what?
EDDIE: No. Nobody knows about Anne . . . except the doctors. No, they were . . . just people. Some of them old and good friends, some just people I'd hear about.
LAWRENCE: I'm sorry, but I still don't see how you and they got together, unless you went out of your way to find them.
EDDIE (*shaking his head*): Believe me, I didn't have to go out of my way. Nobody does. You want to find a drug addict right now. Go uptown, downtown, I don't care where, chances are you'll run into a drug addict. It's funny how when you don't really know about any of this, it just seems like one of those problems that's got nothing to do with you. And then as soon as it hits you personally suddenly it seems like everywhere you turn you bump into somebody who's in the same trouble you are. People you've known for years and never thought . . . you know. I don't know how it started. I didn't want to do it. No, I didn't go out of my way. But each one who came to me seemed to be more desperate than the one before. I'd think about Anne . . . about how terrible it is for her without it . . . I just couldn't turn them down, that's all.
KEN: Did you get any help, Mrs. Clark—when you first tried to stop?
EDDIE: She's been in two sanitariums. She still goes three times a week to the psychiatrist. But she doesn't need doctors nearly so much as she needs a baby.
KEN: What about adopting a child? Have you tried that?
EDDIE (*bitterly*): Have we tried? Do you know what it's like for people our age to adopt a child?
KEN: I know it's not easy.
(ANNE *begins softly to cry.*)
ANNE (*to* EDDIE): We don't have to worry about that any more, do we? Can't you see the adoption agency giving a baby to a middle-aged couple where the mother's an addict and the father sells dope? (*She is close to hysteria, but it is too much for* EDDIE. *He can't go to her.*)
LAWRENCE (*sharply*): Mrs. Clark. (*His tone brings her out of it. She begins to dab at her eyes with a handkerchief.*)
ANNE: What?
LAWRENCE: Do you think you can repeat what you just told us in a courtroom?
EDDIE: No, she can't! And anyway I won't let her!
(*With considerable effort,* ANNE *gains control of herself.*)
ANNE (*to* LAWRENCE): How long until the trial?
LAWRENCE: Several weeks.
EDDIE: You see? She shouldn't be put under the emotional strain of testifying.

ANNE: How many weeks?
LAWRENCE: Two. Maybe three.
ANNE: Three? Three weeks?
EDDIE: You don't have enough morphine for three weeks, Anne. And I can't get you any more.
(ANNE *looks at* EDDIE *a long time, then comes to a difficult decision. She never takes her eyes from* EDDIE's *face as she addresses* LAWRENCE.)
ANNE: All right, Mr. Preston. I'll be ready to testify whenever you need me. I promise you. I'll be ready.

ACT THREE

(*Interior courtroom. Day. The* JUDGE *on the bench, Detective* DEWEY *on the stand, the* D. A. *on his feet before the bench, the* PRESTONS *and* EDDIE *at the defense counsel's table.* ANNE *is seated in the first row of spectators—who are few.*)
D. A.: Did the accused make any attempt to protest when you arrested him?
DEWEY: No.
D. A.: Did he say anything in fact?
DEWEY: No, he just came along.
D. A.: Almost as though he'd been expecting you.
DEWEY: Yes, sir.
LAWRENCE (*overlapping*): Objection.
JUDGE: Sustained.
D. A.: That's all. Thank you.
LAWRENCE: No questions.
(DR. WILLIAM NELSON *from the Coroner's Office.*)
D. A.'S VOICE: Did you do a laboratory test to find out what was in this bottle —Exhibit three?
DR. NELSON: Yes, I did.
D. A.: And what was your conclusion?
NELSON: The pills in the bottle are morphine sulphate, a narcotic drug.
D. A.: Thank you, Doctor. (*He returns to his seat, replaced by* LAWRENCE.)
LAWRENCE: Is morphine sulphate an addictive drug, Doctor?
NELSON: Oh, absolutely.
LAWRENCE: How would you define an addictive drug?
NELSON: Well . . . it's one that creates a dependence on it . . . and a need for increased doses to get the same effect.
LAWRENCE: What kind of dependence?
NELSON: Psychological certainly, and physiological probably.
LAWRENCE: Probably?
NELSON: We used to be more certain about that than we are now.
LAWRENCE: Are you saying then it used to be accepted that the more drugs were taken the more the body came to depend on them, but now there's some question whether that's true or not?
NELSON: That's it precisely.

LAWRENCE: Isn't it because the necessary work hasn't been done to verify the facts one way or the other?
NELSON: I'm afraid so.
LAWRENCE: Thank you, Doctor. No further questions.
D. A.: The people rest, Your Honor.

(*Interior courtroom. Day.* DR. HARTOG *on the witness stand.*)
LAWRENCE: Dr. Hartog, could you tell the court and jury the kind of work you do.
HARTOG: I'm chairman of the Joint Research Council on Drug Addiction.
LAWRENCE: And whom does the Council represent?
HARTOG: We're a national, voluntary organization. We have a medical advisory board made up of leading physicians, psychiatrists, and professors of medicine throughout the country. Our national advisory board has on it educators, law enforcement officials, judges, a United States Senator—a very distinguished panel.
LAWRENCE: And how would you define the aims of the Council?
HARTOG: Well, quite simply we want to help solve the problem of drug addiction in this country.
LAWRENCE: Do you really think that can be done?
HARTOG: Oh, definitely.
LAWRENCE: What progress is being made toward that end?
HARTOG: Very little. The number of known addicts increases every year, so I don't think there's any question that the problem's getting worse rather than better.
LAWRENCE: Even with all the new laws we've been putting on the books? How is that possible?
(*The* D. A. *rises. He starts forward.*)
D. A.: Your Honor, I've been listening patiently to this line of questioning because I assumed I'd understand soon enough what it had to do with the guilt or innocence of the accused.
(KEN *leans to* EDDIE.)
KEN: It took him longer than I thought.
(EDDIE *turns to look for* ANNE. *She looks nervous, distraught.* EDDIE *is worried.*)
D. A.'S VOICE: I'd like to enter an objection on the grounds that nothing the witness has testified to is relevant to this trial.
JUDGE: Mr. Preston, would you care to explain what your purpose is in calling this witness?
LAWRENCE: The defense intends to prove, Your Honor, that by no stretch of the language or the imagination can Edward Clark be considered a narcotics peddler in the conventional sense. It intends to prove that he is innocent of any wrong-doing within the broader meaning and intent of the statutes. In order to do this, however, it's necessary to show the jury that the defendant's attitudes toward drug addiction aren't unique

or anti-social . . . that in fact they're shared by some of the country's most respected citizens.

JUDGE: Are we really interested in the defendant's attitudes?

LAWRENCE: We are if we want to understand his motives. If the jury's to pass a really considered judgment upon Edward Clark, they have to understand why he acted as he did.

JUDGE: Mr. Wolfe, will you join me in my chambers? Mr. Preston . . . The Court will be in recess for ten minutes. (*He stands and starts off.* LAWRENCE *turns toward* EDDIE *and* KEN. *His expression might be interpreted as "so far so good."* KEN *nods.* EDDIE *again turns to seek out* ANNE.)

(*Interior Judge's chamber. Day. The* JUDGE, LAWRENCE, *and the* D. A.)

D. A.: It just seems like very weird procedure to me. I mean all we're here for is to find out if this guy sold narcotics without prescriptions.

JUDGE: Or wouldn't another way to put it be that we're here to see that justice is done?

D. A.: Yes sir, only stop me if I'm wrong, but I assumed justice is done when the people who break laws are punished for it.

JUDGE: Mr. Preston, something tells me the District Attorney isn't a man to be much impressed with long views when short ones are so much clearer and more attainable. What do you say?

LAWRENCE: I say to send Edward Clark to jail would be a gross distortion of justice. He didn't make a nickel on his sales, and we can prove that. He's no more a dope pusher than one of us is.

D. A.: Do you mean because his intentions were good we should pat him on the back and tell him to go home and take care of his addicts? I'm sorry, Sir, but I don't get that. (*He is as deferential as ever, much to* LAWRENCE'S *annoyance.*)

LAWRENCE: Of course not. You can take his license away from him and stop him cold. But I think what happened to this man could happen to anybody. He's much less a criminal than he is a victim of a repressive body of law. This country has some of the toughest narcotics laws in the world. It also has some of the highest incidence of addiction. Now I don't know if the two are connected, but it strikes me as something to think about.

D. A.: Yes, I know all that. I still don't see what that has to do with this case. I mean what was your big point with Nelson this morning about does dependency increase on or doesn't it? If I'm not imposing on your strategy, how does Clark fit into that?

LAWRENCE: My point was to establish how little we really know about the nature of addiction . . . that in fact we *don't* know what we're talking about.

D. A.: So swell . . . I'm with you. Let's find out more. Meanwhile, we have to control it, right?

LAWRENCE: Not if our efforts to control it prevent us from finding out more.

D. A. (*patronizing*): I'm sorry, but . . . I don't see what one has to do with the other . . . why can't you have control and research at the same time.

LAWRENCE: For one thing—and I'm sure you know this better than anybody—control doesn't work. You don't cure a disease by locking up its victims. Not smallpox, not leprosy, and not drug addiction. You tell me: how many addicts who go through the courts show up again?

D. A.: I know, I know. The relapse rate's around ninety-five per cent.

LAWRENCE: All this vast law enforcement machinery just to succeed with about five? Hardly seems worth it.

D. A.: So why don't your researchers come up with the answer?

LAWRENCE: Because they're afraid.

D. A.: Oh, I find that hard to believe. Who's going to touch a doctor if he's legitimate?

LAWRENCE: Over 25,000 M. D.'s have been arraigned since 1914. And three thousand of them have received prison sentences for violating the narcotics laws. Do you really think there were three thousand doctors pushing dope?

(*The* D. A. *broods silently.*)

JUDGE: You gentlemen obviously aren't going to resolve your differences in the few minutes we've got to make a decision. Mr. Wolfe, let me tell you the way I feel about it. You and I come into this court day in and day out and preside over the ritual of trying and sentencing narcotics offenders. It's all so cut and dried and apparently endless . . . I think we both get a little discouraged. Suddenly we've got a defendant—and I don't mean to pre-judge—who *seems* to be different and who's raising fundamental questions about what we're doing here. I agree with you that, strictly speaking, Mr. Preston is stretching procedure, and if you insist, I'll sustain your objection. But otherwise, my inclination is to give Clark a break—let Preston develop his case.

(*The* D. A. *hesitates, then shrugs.*)

D. A. (*sarcastically*): Who am I to stand in the way of progress and enlightenment for dope peddlers? Sure, go ahead. It's all right with me—after I make a phone call and clear it.

(*The* JUDGE *and* LAWRENCE *respond with satisfaction.*)

JUDGE: You can even use my phone.

D. A. (*to* LAWRENCE): But I still think I'm going to beat you.

LAWRENCE: I expect you to try.

(*Interior courtroom. Day.* EDDIE *and* ANNE *are seated on a back bench during the recess. Both are tense and therefore awkward.*)

EDDIE: It's going much better than I dared to expect, don't you think?

ANNE: Yes, I think so.

EDDIE: Can I get you something? A glass of water or something?

ANNE: No—why?

EDDIE: No reason, Anne.
ANNE: I don't look well, do I?
EDDIE: You look fine. Really.
ANNE: I'm trembling.
EDDIE: Well, under the circumstances that's only natural. We've got a great deal at stake here, haven't we? (*He holds out his hand.*) See! I'm trembling too.
ANNE: I have no more, Eddie.
EDDIE (*trying to ignore what she's said*): I imagine courtrooms have the same effect on most people . . .
ANNE: Did you hear me, Eddie?
EDDIE (*nodding*): Yes.
ANNE: I took the last pill I had last night. I was saving it for today. I knew I'd need it and I was hoarding it, like some miserable miser. But I woke up during the night, scared, petrified, knowing it was my last one, thinking about today. I couldn't help myself, Eddie. I had to take it.
EDDIE: Maybe you ought to go home now.
ANNE: Don't, Eddie. Please. You need me here. I need to be here. I'll be all right, you'll see. This is just a form of stage fright. Once Mr. Preston puts me on that witness stand, I'll see that it isn't so bad and I'll get over this shakiness. That's all it is, shakiness. You'll see, Eddie.

(*Interior courtroom. Day.* HARTOG *is testifying.*)
LAWRENCE'S VOICE: Doctor Hartog, what makes a drug addict?
HARTOG: The sad truth is no one knows what addiction really is. We believe that every addict has a personality disorder of some kind. That doesn't mean you have to be wildly disturbed to become an addict. The tensions of . . . just plain modern living are usually enough to predispose many to addiction. Those tensions are greatest among minority groups, and of course a great many addicts are members of such groups. But an addict can be any age, race, class, or sex.
LAWRENCE: What else is needed for addiction to occur?
HARTOG: A supply of narcotics. I'm not being facetious. It's the ready availability of narcotics, mainly heroin, on the illegal market that constitutes a big cause of addiction.
LAWRENCE: What is the reason for this availability?
HARTOG: The profits you can make selling the stuff. A drug addict will pay anything he has to get what he wants, so of course the profits are tremendous.
LAWRENCE: But why should heroin cost so much. Is it that rare?
HARTOG: No. It's very cheap to produce. It's just a question of supply and demand. The supply is limited because it's against the law. But the demand from any single addict is as big as his habit.
LAWRENCE: And the threat of long prison sentences and in some states even death doesn't stop the suppliers?

HARTOG: We know it doesn't. There seems to be always somebody willing to take a chance to make that kind of money.
(LAWRENCE *goes to his table, takes up a sheet of paper from a sizable stack of pamphlets, books, etc.*)
LAWRENCE: I have here a summary of testimony given to the President's Advisory Commission on Narcotic and Drug Abuse. I'm quoting now, "There are less than five hundred known opiate addicts in Great Britain where the situation has remained remarkably benign. There are practically no serious crimes committed by addicts in that country. There is hardly any illicit traffic in narcotics and the problem hasn't spread to juveniles to any significant degree." Are you acquainted with the British approach to this problem, Doctor?
HARTOG: Yes, they permit their doctors to treat addict patients as they see fit.
LAWRENCE: In other words they say it's a problem for doctors to handle and not for police.
HARTOG: That's right. Physicians are allowed to prescribe maintenance doses for drug addicts as long as the ultimate aim is to secure withdrawal. And I emphasize "ultimate." They recognize that withdrawal isn't always something that can be done just like that. But they too do not withhold drugs from sick people who'll do anything for relief. People are forced by a misguided society to steal, to mug, to kill, to commit crimes of violence to maintain a habit which should only cost perhaps a dollar a day. (*He snaps his fingers.*)
(*The* D. A. *is engaged in cross-examining* HARTOG.)
D. A.: Do you mean to say you advocate allowing anybody who wants to just walk into a doctor's office, get a shot of heroin or whatever, and walk out?
(HARTOG's *been taking a pretty good hammering and his back is up.*)
HARTOG: No I don't mean that at all.
D. A.: It certainly sounded like it.
HARTOG: Not from anything I said.
D. A.: But you don't see anything wrong in addicts being kept on maintenance doses by their doctors for months or maybe years?
HARTOG: Not if the doctor, in his professional opinion, determines that to be the best course of treatment. After all, the police don't tell doctors how to treat their pneumonia patients or their arthritis patients or their cardiac patients.
D. A.: But isn't a doctor only responsible for a drug addict when he's in his office? And isn't it the police who have the problem all the rest of the time?
HARTOG (*exasperated*): But that's just the point! There isn't *necessarily* a problem . . .
D. A. (*cutting in*): Oh, really? Do you have any idea how much crime is committed in this country by addicts?

HARTOG: Do you have any idea of how much crime would be omitted if we stopped treating addicts as criminals.

(TOM GRAFTON *has taken the witness stand. He is nervous but doing pretty well.*)

TOM: All I paid was a few cents per pill. He couldn't have made any profit from me.

LAWRENCE: Did Mr. Clark ever ask you for more money?

TOM: No.

(ANNE *is very distraught. Her face is perspiring, the tension more than she can bear.*)

LAWRENCE'S VOICE: Would you have paid more if he had asked for it? That is, could he have made a profit from the sale of narcotics had he chosen to?

TOM: Sure, he could have, but . . . well, the question doesn't really apply to me.

LAWRENCE: Why not?

TOM: Mr. Clark knew right from the start that I had the habit. I mean it wasn't a question of starting me off cheap until I got hooked and then boosting the price . . . you know the way a pusher would. No, he never said anything about money. I had to ask him the first time how much I owed him.

LAWRENCE: Did he put any conditions at all on the transactions, or did he just give you the pills with no strings attached?

TOM: No, he was very strict about what I had to do . . . about what he called my end of the bargain.

LAWRENCE: And what was your end of the bargain, Tom?

TOM: I had to agree to go to a psychiatrist regularly and do everything I could to straighten myself out.

(KEN *looks troubled as he rises to his feet. And taps* LAWRENCE *on the shoulder.*)

LAWRENCE: May I have a moment, Your Honor?

JUDGE: Yes.

LAWRENCE (*to* KEN): What is it?

KEN: Do you still plan to call Mrs. Clark?

LAWRENCE: Without her, we don't have a motive. Sure I do.

KEN: How soon?

LAWRENCE: Right after Tom Grafton. Why?

KEN: She's gone.

(LAWRENCE *turns to look to* ANNE'S *empty chair.* EDDIE *is tormented with worry.*)

ACT FOUR

(*Interior drugstore. Day.* ANNE—*her eyes betray her fear. She is trying very hard to appear normal. She manages a weak smile.*)

ANNE: I'm on my way to Court now. I felt a headache coming on and thought I'd stop by and take something for it.

(STANLEY—*the substitute pharmacist, mid-twenties, brash, insensitive.*)

STANLEY: Sure thing, Mrs. Clark. Help yourself. I'm sure you remember where it is. I'll get you some water.

(*As he leaves,* ANNE *slips behind the counter, a key in her hand, fumbles with the door to a small safe under the counter. Her hands shake, making the task doubly difficult.*)

STANLEY'S VOICE: What are you doing back there, Mrs. Clark?

ANNE (*startled*): I . . . I thought it looked open.

(*She stands abruptly as* STANLEY *hurries up with a paper cup filled with water.*)

ANNE: The safe looked open.

STANLEY: Not a chance. You don't have to worry about me. I'm tremendously careful. I mean I'm sure not going to make Mr. Clark sorry he gave me this chance. Matter of fact, we got a shipment in a little while ago, and I'm going to put it away right now . . . not wait till we close.

(*He busies himself opening the safe, pulling over a small carton, tearing it open.*)

STANLEY: Oh, did you get something for your headache?

ANNE: Yes . . . thanks.

STANLEY: No . . . please . . . when you see Mr. Clark tell him he shouldn't worry about anything up here, will you do that?

(ANNE *stares at the open carton as* STANLEY, *a handful at a time, takes out small boxes—the kind that contain bottles of pills—and places them in the open safe.*)

ANNE: Let me help you . . .

(*She suddenly reaches down, takes one of the boxes from the carton.* STANLEY *pays little attention.*)

STANLEY: Oh, no . . . that's okay . . .

(*She takes the bottle from the box, her hands trembling.*)

STANLEY'S VOICE: You got more to do today than help around here. Thanks . . . (*He holds his hand for the bottle.*)

ANNE: Oh . . . (*As if by accident, she lets the bottle fall. It breaks. The pills scatter.* ANNE *crouches, reaches for a pill that rolls around the end of the counter. A man's foot moves in, stops the pill. Surprised,* ANNE *looks up.* KEN *looks down at her.*)

KEN: What's the matter? (*He bends, picks up the pill.*)

(ANNE *remains crouched, staring at* KEN, *frozen.* STANLEY *stands up from behind the counter, brushes his hands off.*)

STANLEY: Had a little accident. Can I help you?

KEN: I just stopped in to see Mrs. Clark. (*He helps her to her feet.*)

STANLEY: Oh, well, give my best to Mr. Clark.

(*He disappears again behind the counter.* KEN *leads* ANNE *toward the front of the store. They speak quietly so that* STANLEY *won't overhear.*)
KEN: How about it? Are you going to testify or not?
ANNE: Yes, I am . . . if I can just have something first. You don't know what it's been like in there.
KEN: I can't help you, Mrs. Clark.
(*She looks steadily at him. Suddenly the plea in her eyes changes. She smiles a little. Her tone is suggestive. She touches the button on his jacket.*)
ANNE: Listen, you must know somebody . . . a doctor who'll give you a prescription. Then I'll be great . . . and very appreciative. Honest . . . I'll do anything if you'll help me . . . please . . . (*It's meant of course to be seductive, but it's only grotesque.* KEN *is sickened, turns aside. The half-parted lips congeal. She suddenly covers her face with her hands.*) Oh God . . .
(KEN *is deeply moved by compassion for her.*)
KEN: Don't . . . please . . . you didn't mean that. It's already forgotten . . .
(*After a moment she takes her hands away. Slowly. Her face is distorted with contempt for herself, with self-hatred.*)
ANNE: I . . . can't stand myself.
(*He takes her gently by the arm.*)
KEN: Come on . . . let's go back . . .
ANNE (*sudden panic*): Go back? What do you mean?
KEN: To the court. You are going to testify, aren't you?
ANNE: No! I can't! You don't know . . . (*beginning to weep*) I'm sorry . . . I'm sorry . . .
(KEN *wants to argue, and yet he realizes how futile it would be to say anything. And too, he is overwhelmed with pity.*)
ANNE: I want to do it . . . I just can't . . .
(*The woman's suffering is more than* KEN *can bear. He raises his clenched fist, opens it. In his palm, the white tablet he picked up from the floor.* ANNE'S *eyes stare at the pill, then, wide with surprise, up to* KEN.)

(*Interior courtroom. Day.*)
LAWRENCE: What is your relationship to the accused, Edward Clark?
ANNE: I'm his wife.
LAWRENCE: How long have you and Mr. Clark been married?
ANNE: Seven years.
LAWRENCE: Are you a drug addict, Mrs. Clark?
ANNE: Yes, I am.
LAWRENCE: What drug are you addicted to?
ANNE: Morphine.
LAWRENCE: And how long have you been an addict?

ANNE: A little over a year.

LAWRENCE: Are you under the influence of morphine at this moment, Mrs. Clark?

ANNE (*after a beat*): Yes.

(*There is a barely audible catching of breaths throughout the court.*)

LAWRENCE: Will you please tell the court what it's like to be under the influence of morphine?

ANNE: What it's like?

LAWRENCE: Yes. What do you see? What do you hear?

ANNE: The same thing everybody else sees. You . . . Eddie . . . the other people . . .

LAWRENCE: Really? No satyrs? No lurid fantasies? You don't hear any devil's tom-toms or celestial harps?

ANNE: No.

LAWRENCE: Then why do you bother taking morphine at all? If you only experience the same sensations the rest of us do, what's the point?

ANNE: Because . . . if I don't take it, I . . .

(*She stops.* LAWRENCE *leans in.*)

LAWRENCE: Go on, Mrs. Clark . . . what happens if you don't take it?

ANNE: For one thing, if I hadn't had morphine, I couldn't be here.

LAWRENCE: Why not?

ANNE: I just couldn't, that's all. I couldn't get up from that chair and walk across the room in front of these people and sit down.

LAWRENCE: What would happen if you did though? If someone made you do it?

ANNE: I'm afraid I'd make a pretty bad spectacle of myself. It's very hard to explain . . .

LAWRENCE: I know it is. I want you to try.

ANNE: The thing is . . . with me, at least . . . that I lose control. I can't . . . stop crying for one thing. I just can't stop. And I can't sit still . . . I can't hold still. Have you ever had a fever and felt you always had to move . . . to turn . . . to move your legs and your head? It's something like that. Only with me at the time I'm moving, I'm not moving right. What I mean is I lurch, I fall a lot, bump into things. When I reach for something, I almost always knock it over. And then my skin becomes very sensitive . . . as though it were raw or burned. When I touch something it feels like getting a shock . . . you know, from a wire. And my clothes become . . . well, not tight so much as . . . tormenting, I guess. They just hurt me. Everything hurts me. (*beat*) So that's why I say I couldn't have made it from over there to here. Not in a million years.

LAWRENCE: And when you take morphine? What happens then?

ANNE: In the first place everything slows down. It doesn't really, I guess, but it seems to. The falling stops, the burning stops. Things become slow and easy and reasonable. I can handle myself again. I can pick something up. I can even . . . be content with myself a little. That's the best part . . . not to despise yourself for a while.

LAWRENCE: In other words, at those times you feel quite normal.

ANNE (*with growing fervor*): Not "quite" normal! Normal. Just like anybody else. That's what you people don't know about us; what you refuse to understand. You're not addicted. You don't know, you can't know—or you wouldn't do this to us. You'd stop punishing us, degrading us, treating us like filth. Whom does it hurt if we take a drug that spares us from torture? That allows us to remain human, that allows us to think and feel and love and be loved—and be normal. Because we are.

LAWRENCE: Would you like to step down for a few moments, Mrs. Clark?

ANNE: No. Please go on.

LAWRENCE: When did your husband first give you morphine without a prescription?

ANNE: I think it was last . . . September or October.

LAWRENCE: What took place just prior to that?

ANNE: I tried to kill myself.

(ANNE *has spoken quietly. There has been an unnatural stillness in the court. Even now it is a moment before anyone can move.*)

LAWRENCE: Mrs. Clark, you said you're under the influence of morphine now.

ANNE: Yes.

LAWRENCE: Did you acquire it legally? By prescription?

(EDDIE *fears the worst.*)

ANNE'S VOICE: No.

LAWRENCE'S VOICE: Then . . . do you have a supply?

ANNE: I don't have any more, and I don't know how to get any more.

LAWRENCE: What . . . do you intend to do?

ANNE: I don't know. I hope someone does. I hope someone does.

LAWRENCE: Thank you. Your witness.

(*He turns, walks away.*)

(D. A. *stands, hesitates for some moments.*)

D. A.: I have no questions.

(*He sits.*)

(EDDIE *on the stand.*)

EDDIE: I found her on the floor of the bathroom. I called the doctor and got the bleeding stopped . . . and then I didn't say anything to her . . . just got dressed and went over to the store and got a bottle of morphine sulphate, changed the amounts on some prescriptions to cover it and gave it to her.

LAWRENCE: And you supplied her ever since?

EDDIE: Except for two periods when she tried to stop.

LAWRENCE: Has she been under the care of a doctor the whole time?

EDDIE: A psychiatrist.
LAWRENCE: But she still needs drugs.
EDDIE: Yes.
LAWRENCE: And you'd be willing to keep supplying her with them?
EDDIE: As long as I could. As long as she needed them.
LAWRENCE: Knowing you would be committing a crime?
EDDIE: I don't believe it's a crime.
LAWRENCE: You do know it's against the law?
EDDIE: Yes.
LAWRENCE: And that your punishment for breaking that law could be extremely severe?
EDDIE: I don't care about that.
LAWRENCE: About law and order?
EDDIE: About anything that deliberately destroys my wife.
LAWRENCE: Thank you, Mr. Clark. That's all.
(D. A.: *rises, advances on* EDDIE.)
D. A.: Mr. Clark, you didn't supply illegal opiates only to your wife did you? We know that others were also beneficiaries of your . . . generosity. And how many others were there?
EDDIE: Three.
D. A.: Only three? By your standard, there must be thousands of people who qualify for the . . . Edward Clark treatment for drug addiction.
EDDIE: I suppose there are. I don't know them.
D. A.: But if you did, you'd give drugs to them too, is that right?
EDDIE: No . . . I don't know . . . I didn't want to help anybody except Anne. The others just happened . . . each one for its own reasons I guess.
D. A.: Did you ever turn down anybody? Did you ever say to anybody who came to you for help . . . did you ever say: "No. It's against the law and there's nothing I can do for you."?
EDDIE: No.
D. A.: Why not? Isn't that what other pharmacists do?
EDDIE: I suppose so.
D. A.: Does that mean they're all heartless and you're the only member of your profession who's got feelings and who likes to help people?
EDDIE: No. I did the same thing for years. Or at least I would have if the problem had ever come up.
D. A.: You mean there was a time when you respected the laws of the state and the codes and ethics of your profession.
EDDIE: I still do.
D. A.: How is that possible, Mr. Clark? How can you have respect for the law and at the same time systematically break it? Will you explain that to us?
(EDDIE *is feeling boxed, harrassed.*)

EDDIE: I don't know . . . I respect the law, that's all. I try to do what's right . . .
D. A.: Willfully defying the law? Is that what you call doing what's right?
EDDIE: All I know is I kept my wife alive when there wasn't any other way to do it. Can that be wrong? I took an oath when I got married, didn't I? To protect her in sickness? That's what I did. I gave her medicine so that . . .
D. A.: You gave her narcotic drugs which better qualified people than you have found to be harmful.
EDDIE: Drugs, medicine . . . call it what you want . . .
D. A.: No! The function of medicines is to cure. What you gave your wife only makes her sicker.
EDDIE (*suddenly furious*): That's not true! You don't know that! What I gave her kept her going, kept her functioning while a doctor tried to cure her. What about insulin? Isn't that a medicine? What does insulin cure? All it does is keep people with diabetes alive and functioning. They depend on it. Without it they don't survive. With it they lead a normal life. That's exactly what morphine does for my wife. Exactly! So what's really the difference? Will you tell me that? Will somebody tell me that?
(*He looks around, baffled, a small man caught in a large anomaly.*)

(*Interior courtroom. Day.* LAWRENCE *approaches the jury to begin his summation.* JUDGE, EDDIE, KEN, D. A., ANNE *are in their respective places.*)
LAWRENCE: Edward Clark told you he respects the law. For evidence you have a lifetime of good citizenship. And yet Edward Clark, as the District Attorney put it, willfully and systematically broke the law. Forced to choose between the law and his wife's health, Edward Clark broke the law which makes it possible for a man to be confronted with such a choice. The Harrison Act was passed by Congress in 1914. It was a simple revenue and regulatory measure. It placed a tax on narcotics and required importers and druggists and doctors to keep records. That act is still the basis for the vast enforcement system we have today. Nothing in the act was ever intended to make it a crime to be a drug addict. And yet from that modest beginning has grown a huge police apparatus, the Federal Bureau of Narcotics. And today, despite the Bureau's efforts, we find ourselves more troubled by the narcotics problem than ever.
(LAWRENCE *walks to his seat where* KEN *hands him a document, opened and underlined.*)
LAWRENCE: We find the New York Academy of Medicine able to report as recently as May 1963: "Obviously there are defects in a method that in execution fails to catch the real criminals, the key men in the syndicates, but makes statutory criminals of sick persons, succeeds in bringing some of them to docket, places some in jail, fails to provide proper

medical care for them, and instead erects almost insuperable barriers to medical management." We find ourselves listening to an expert such as Doctor Hartog make the startling statement that "no one knows what addiction really is." Why? Because until very recently, our Narcotics Agents had put the fear of God into any doctor who would have liked to find out what addicton was.

(*He holds out his hand, and* KEN *places in it another document.*)

LAWRENCE: "The nature of administrative enforcement of the Harrison Act is such that physicians are deterred from performance of their ethical duties." An advisory council of judges said that only months ago. In other words, the medical profession was bullied and intimidated into turning its back on the problem of drug addiction, and the whole field was left in the benevolent hands of the enforcers. So that's the history. That's why your lives and Edward Clark's have come together at this time, in this place. Forty years ago we allowed a policeman to come between the doctor and his patient, and a seed took root. Forty years later a neighborhood druggist harvested the fruit of fear and ignorance. Forty years from now we'll all be ashamed.

(*He looks at the members of the jury, then turns away.*)

(D. A. *is making his summation. He carries a copy of the* Journal of the American Medical Association.)

D. A.: We've heard a lot about doctors in this case . . . about the difference between what they believe and how they're permitted to practice. According to Mr. Preston, the accused only did what doctors would have done if the law let them. But is it really that simple? Let me tell you what the American Medical Association says about it. "Continued administration of drugs for the maintenance of addiction is not a bona fide attempt at cure, nor is it ethical treatment . . ."

(LAWRENCE *reacts with annoyance and frustration. He would like to respond, to point out the fallacies in the argument, but of course must keep his peace.*)

D. A.'S VOICE: In other words, what the accused did is specifically condemned by the American Medical Association.

D. A.: Now as to this business of doctors being intimidated, scared off by the Bureau of Narcotics, let me quote from the Joint Statement on Narcotic Addiction by the American Medical Association and the National Research Council dated May 14, 1962: "Historically, society has found it necessary to employ legal controls to prevent the spread of certain types of illness that constitute a hazard to the public health. Drug addiction is such a hazard." Does that sound like the doctors are suffering under a lot of intolerable restrictions? Do you really get the feeling from that that doctors want to do away with controls in this business of narcotics? Of course not. In fact, throughout this entire report, the A.M.A. repeatedly says it is anxious to cooperate with

the Bureau of Narcotics. So much, I hope, for the spectre of the quaking doctor so effectively raised by counsel for the defense. Finally, ladies and gentlemen, we're left with one fact that no amount of argument, no amount of persuasion, can change: the accused, Edward Clark, deliberately and systematically chose to place himself above the law.
(EDDIE *is standing beside his chair. He turns to seek out* ANNE. *He smiles at her reassuringly.* ANNE *smiles back reassuringly at her husband, seemingly in control. But her hands, out of* EDDIE's *line of sight, are trembling as they twist a lace handkerchief.*)
(*Jury filing in.* EDDIE, LAWRENCE, KEN *seated at the defense table.* EDDIE *tenses as he turns and watches the jury file in.*)
CLERK: Ladies and gentlemen of the jury, have you reached a verdict?
(*The* FOREMAN *rises.*)
FOREMAN: We have.
CLERK: What is your verdict?
FOREMAN: We find the defendant guilty as charged.
(EDDIE *is stunned.*)
(ANNE's *handkerchief—tearing in two under the strain of her convulsive grip.* ANNE—*her face lifeless. Rising slowly—almost somnambulistically.*)
(EDDIE *is staring ahead in disbelief. In the background* ANNE *is moving woodenly up the aisle toward the door.* LAWRENCE *is standing.*)
CLERK: You, the jury, say you find the defendant, Edward Clark, guilty of the crime as charged in the indictment. And so say you all.
FOREMAN: Yes.
LAWRENCE: Your Honor, I ask that the jury be polled.
JUDGE: The clerk will poll the jury.
(KEN—*turning to look for* ANNE *and seeing her gone. Then seeing her leaving.* KEN *rises and starts up the aisle after* ANNE.)

(*Corridor outside courtroom. As* ANNE *emerges from courtroom and walks mechanically toward the exit.* KEN *appears a moment later, crosses to her quickly, stops her by taking her arm firmly. She doesn't turn to see who it is; she knows.*)
ANNE: I can't face him.
KEN: He doesn't blame you for what happened.
ANNE: What's happened is past. He'll want to know what's going to happen to me. And we all know the answer to that one, don't we?
KEN: Maybe we all just think we do.
(ANNE *turns and looks at* KEN *closely, deeply appreciative.*)
ANNE: Thank you for that, Mr. Preston. But I couldn't change now . . . I know I couldn't. I'm a drug addict—and that's what I'll always be. And I couldn't promise Eddie anything else.
KEN: Eddie knows that, Mrs. Clark. Better than anyone else.

(ANNE *looks toward the courtroom door.*)
ANNE (*pointing toward door*): Is he still in there?
KEN: Yes. Come on.
(*They cross.* KEN *opens door as* ANNE *approaches. In the deep background* EDDIE *and* LAWRENCE *are standing.* EDDIE *is looking toward* ANNE. *The courtroom is empty except for* EDDIE's *guard.*)
(EDDIE—*his face lighting up as he sees* ANNE *in the doorway.* EDDIE *starts up the aisle toward her.*)
(ANNE—*looking at* EDDIE. *Her eyes wet. She starts toward him. Reaching each other, embracing.*)
EDDIE: Come on now. Mr. Preston thinks the judge will go easy on me when he sentences. If he does—and I behave myself—you'll have me back in just a couple of years.
ANNE (*bleakly*): A couple of years.
EDDIE: Do you think you can—wait? They'll be watching you now. Waiting for you to make a mistake. Waiting for you to drive yourself into their courts, into their jails.
ANNE: I'll try. That's the most I can promise.
(D. A.—*entering from counsel room. He seems a little embarrassed at seeing the Clarks. The Clarks kiss.* EDDIE *turns and exits with the guard.*)
D. A. (*to* ANNE): I'm sorry.
ANNE: Everybody is. But that hasn't solved anything, has it? (*She walks up the aisle and exits.*)
D. A. (*to* LAWRENCE): I thought you might like to know when Clark comes up for sentencing, we're going to recommend a light one.
LAWRENCE: What about Mrs. Clark? What have we done about her sentence? Eddie will get what? Three years? Three months? The question is: what will *she* do tonight? Where will she be when that last pill wears off? What will she do? Where can she turn? Who's going to hear her screams of agony, and who's going to care? Why must she be made to endure torture to satisfy our law, our morality? She may not be able to stand it. In just a few hours she may go out and steal—or prostitute herself—or kill herself. Tonight! We may have convicted a man who broke a law but we may have made a criminal of his wife in the process. Does that give you a sense of accomplishment, Sam?
(LAWRENCE *and* KEN *leave the* D. A. *standing there without an answer.*)

Questions

1. Why is the play called *The Pill Man* and not, for example, *The Dope Peddler*? Is this distinction in the use of language employed within the play?
2. What do the following characters contribute to the development of the ideas in the play: Anne Clark, Tom Grafton, Dr. Nelson, Dr. Hartog?
3. What limitations on the development of the issues involved does the dramatic form impose?

4. Could this play be considered propaganda? Why or why not?
5. Which side of the question are the authors on?
6. Does the particular case of Eddie Clark confuse or clarify the more general issues involved? How?
7. Is the question raised by the play a medical or a legal one? Explain your conclusion.
8. Summarize the approaches to the drug problem represented in the play by Eddie, by Dr. Hartog, by the D. A., and by Tom's father.

Assignments

1. Compare the British and the American methods of handling the problem of narcotics addiction.
2. Review the play, discussing its success in treating the ideological problem that it raises.
3. Analyze the major points on each side of the narcotics argument.
4. Separate the economic, the medical, the legal, and the political aspects of the narcotics problem in the United States today. Describe these aspects of the question and argue which of them is, in your judgment, most important.
5. Argue for or against one of the following propositions:
   a. Narcotics laws have proved to be just another unsuccessful attempt to legislate morality.
   b. The use of drugs is a personal, not a social, question.
   c. Doctors should be given the freedom to prescribe drugs for addicts.
6. Using this play, and any other literary works which you think appropriate, discuss whether or not propaganda can be art.

Additional Reading

The problem of drug addiction is receiving increasing attention from all points of view. The major issue raised in *The Pill Man,* on the legal and medical aspects of the problem, has also been discussed in "Addiction: An Illness, Not a Sin or Crime," *Science News Letter,* LXXXI (January 6, 1963), 8; J. Kobler, "Narcotics Dilemma: Crime or Disease?" *Saturday Evening Post,* CCXXXV (September 8, 1962), 64–66 ff; W. Sparks, "Narcotics and the Law," *Commonweal,* LXXIV (August 25, 1961), 467–469. There have also been official statements and conferences which have studied the problem. Nat Hentoff's article, "Drug Addiction: Crime or Disease?" *Reporter,* XXIV (May 11, 1961), 52–53, discusses the Reports of the Joint Committee of the American Bar Association and the American Medical Association on Narcotic Drugs. A. R. Lindesmith, in "Addiction: Beginnings of Wisdom," *Nation,* CXCVI (January 19, 1963), 49–52, discusses the White House Conference on Narcotic and Drug Abuse.

Three recent books provide more thorough studies of various aspects of the problem: David W. Maurer and Victor H. Vogel, *Narcotics and Narcotic Addiction* (Springfield, Illinois, 1962), William Butler Eldridge, *Narcotics and Law: A Critique of the American Experiment in Narcotic Drug Control* (New York, 1962); and Isidor Chein, Donald L. Gerard, Robert S. Lee, and Eva Rosenfeld, *The Road to H: Narcotics, Delinquency, and Social Policy* (New York, 1964).

SECTION SEVEN

The Spoils of City Planning

Modern City Planning: The Victory Over Vitality

JANE JACOBS

There is a wistful myth that if only we had enough money to spend—the figure is usually put at $100,000,000,000—America could wipe out all her slums in ten years, reverse decay in the great, dull Gray Belts that were yesterday's and day-before-yesterday's suburbs, anchor the wandering middle class and its wandering tax money, and perhaps even solve the traffic problem.

But look what we have built with the first several billions: Low-income housing projects that become worse centers of delinquency, vandalism and general social hopelessness than the slums they were supposed to replace. Middle-income housing projects which are perfect marvels of dullness and regimentation, sealed against any buoyancy or urban vitality. Luxury housing projects that mitigate their inanity, or try to, with a vapid vulgarity. "Cultural centers" that are unable to support a good book store. "Civic centers" that are avoided by everyone but the leisured indigent, who have fewer choices of loitering place than others. "Commercial centers" that are lackluster imitations of standardized suburban chain emporia. Promenades that go from no place to nowhere and have no promenaders. Expressways that eviscerate the metropolis.

This is not the rebuilding of cities. This is the sacking of cities.

These accomplishments are poorer than their poor pretentious surfaces. They seldom aid the city around them, as in theory they are supposed to do.

Columbia University Forum, IV (Fall 1961), 19–26. © Copyright 1961 by Jane Jacobs. This material appears in another version in *The Death and Life of Great American Cities*, by Jane Jacobs. Reprinted by permission of Random House, Inc.

The amputated neighborhoods around them typically develop galloping gangrene. To house people in this planned fashion, price tags are fastened to the population, and each sorted-out chunk comes to live in growing suspicion and tension against the surrounding city. When two or more such hostile islands are juxtaposed, the result is called "a balanced neighborhood." Monopolistic shopping centers and monumental cultural centers cloak, under the public relations hoo-ha, the subtraction of commerce, and of culture too, from the intimate and casual life of cities.

To accomplish such wonders as these, it is necessary to push about the people marked with the planners' hex, to uproot them much as if they were the subjects of a conquering power. Thousands upon thousands of small businesses are destroyed, and their proprietors ruined, with hardly a gesture at compensation. Whole communities are ripped apart and sown to the winds, with a harvest of cynicism, resentment and despair that must be heard and seen to be believed. A group of clergymen in Chicago, appalled at the fruits of planned city-rebuilding there, asked, "Could Job have been thinking of Chicago when he wrote:

> Here are men that alter their neighbor's landmark . . . shoulder the poor aside, conspire to oppress the friendless.
> Reap they the field that is none of theirs, strip the vineyard wrongfully seized from its owner . . .
> A cry goes up from the city streets, where wounded men lie groaning . . ."

If so, he was also thinking of New York, Philadelphia, Boston, Washington, St. Louis, San Francisco, and a number of other places.

The economic rationale of current city rebuilding does not rest solely and soundly on reasoned investment of public tax subsidies, as the theory of "urban renewal" proclaims, but also on vast, involuntary subsidies wrung out of helpless site victims. And the increased tax returns from such sites, accruing to the cities as a result of this "investment," are a mirage, a pitiful gesture against the ever-increasing sums of public money needed to combat the disintegration and instability that flow from the cruelly shaken-up city. The means to planned city-rebuilding are as deplorable as the ends.

Meantime, all the art and science of city planning seem to be helpless to stem decay—and the spiritlessness that precedes decay—in ever more massive swathes. Nor can this decay be laid, reassuringly, to lack of opportunity for the arts of planning. It seems to matter little whether they are applied or not. The foregoing is what I believe they have achieved. And the history of the most influential ideas informing orthodox city planning—and urban architecture—seem by their very nature to predict this awful achievement.

The most important thread of influence may be said to begin with Ebenezer Howard, an English court reporter for whom planning was an avocation. Howard looked at the living conditions of the poor in late nineteenth-century

London and understandably did not like what he smelled, saw or heard. It was not simply that he hated the wrongs and mistakes of the city, he hated the city. He thought it an outright evil and an affront to nature that so many people should get themselves into an agglomeration. His prescription for saving the people was to do the city in.

The program he proposed, in 1898, was to halt the growth of London and also repopulate the declining country villages by building a new kind of town—the Garden City, where the city poor might again live close to nature. So they might earn their livings, industry was to be set up in the Garden City, for while Howard was not planning cities, he was not planning dormitory suburbs either. His aim was the creation of self-sufficient small towns—very nice towns if the citizen were docile, had no plans of his own and did not mind spending his life among others with no plans of their own. For, as in all Utopias, the right to have originality and force of any significance belonged only to the planners in charge. The Garden City was to be encircled with a belt of agriculture. Industry was to be in its planned preserves; schools, housing and greens in their planned preserves; and in the center were to be commercial, club and cultural places, held in common. The town and greenbelt, in their totality, were to be permanently controlled by the public authority under which the town was developed, to prevent speculation or supposedly irrational changes in land use, and also to do away with temptations to increase its density—in brief, to prevent it from ever becoming a city. The maximum population was to be held to thirty thousand.

Nathan Glazer has summed up the vision well in *Architectural Forum:* "The image was the English country town—with the manor house and its park replaced by a community center, and with some factories hidden behind a screen of trees, to supply work."

The closest American equivalent would probably be the model company town, but with profit-sharing, and the Parent-Teacher Associations in charge of the routine, custodial political life. For Ebenezer Howard was envisioning not simply a new physical environment and social life, but a paternalistic political and economic society.

Nevertheless, as Glazer has pointed out, the Garden City was essentially "conceived as an alternative to the city, and as a solution to city problems this was, and is still, the foundation of its immense power as a planning idea." Howard managed to get two garden cities built, Letchworth and Welwyn, and of course England and Sweden have, since the War, built a number of satellite towns based on Garden City principles. In the United States, the suburb of Radburn, N. J., and the depression-built, Government-sponsored greenbelt towns (actually suburbs) were all modifications on the idea. But Howard's success in the literal, or reasonably literal, acceptance of his program was as nothing compared to his success in influencing American city planning today. City planners and designers with no interest in the Garden City pure are thoroughly governed by its underlying principles.

Howard set spinning powerful and city-destroying ideas: He conceived that the way to deal with the city's functions was to sort and sift out of the whole certain simple land-uses, and to arrange each of these in relative self-containment. He believed the provision of wholesome housing to be the central problem, to which everything else was subsidiary; further, he defined wholesome housing according to suburban physical qualities and small-town social qualities. He conceived of commerce as the routine, standardized supply of goods, and as serving a self-limited market. He conceived of good planning as a settling of things once for all; in each case, the plan must anticipate all that is needed and be protected, after it is executed, against any but the most minor subsequent changes. He conceived of planning also as essentially paternalistic, if not authoritarian. He was uninterested in those aspects of the city which could not be abstracted to serve his Utopia. In particular, he simply wrote off the intricate, many-faceted, cultural life of the metropolis. He was uninterested in such problems as the way great cities unofficially police themselves, or allow for the exchange of ideas, or operate politically, or invent new economic arrangements. In short, he was not designing for city life at all.

Howard's influence on American city planning converged on the city from two directions: from town and regional planners on the one hand, and from architects on the other. Along the avenue of planning, Sir Patrick Geddes, a Scots biologist and philosopher, saw the Garden City idea not as a fortuitous way to absorb population growth otherwise destined for a great city, but as the starting point of a much grander and more encompassing pattern. He thought of the planning of cities as part of the planning of whole regions. Under regional planning, Garden Cities would be rationally distributed throughout large territories, dovetailing into natural resources, balanced against agriculture and woodland, forming one far-flung logical whole.

Howard's and Geddes' ideas were enthusiastically adopted in America during the 1920's, and developed further by a group of extraordinarily effective and dedicated people—among them Lewis Mumford, Clarence Stein, the late Henry Wright, and Catherine Bauer. While they thought of themselves as regional planners, Catherine Bauer has more recently called this group the "Decentrists," and this name is more apt, for the primary result of regional planning, as they saw it, would be to decentralize great cities, thin them out, and disperse their enterprises and populations into smaller, separated cities, or, better yet, towns. At the time, it appeared that the American population was both leveling off in numbers and increasing in median age, and the problem appeared to be not one of accommodating a rapidly growing population, but simply of redistributing a static one.

As with Howard, this group's effect was less in getting literal acceptance of its program—that got nowhere—than in influencing city planning, and legislation affecting housing and housing finance. Model housing schemes by Stein and Wright, built mainly in suburban settings or at the fringes of cities, together with the writings, diagrams, sketches and photographs presented by Mumford and Bauer, demonstrated and popularized ideas such as these, which are now taken for granted in orthodox planning:

1) The street is bad as an environment for humans; houses should be turned away from it and faced inward, toward sheltered greens.

2) Frequent streets are wasteful, of advantage only to real estate speculators who measure value by the front foot.

3) The basic unit of city design is not the street, but the block and more particularly the superblock.

4) Commerce should be segregated from residences and greens.

5) A neighborhood's demand for goods should be calculated "scientifically," and this much and no more commercial space allocated.

6) The presence of many other people is, at best, a necessary evil, and good city planning must aim for at least an illusion of isolation and quasi-suburban privacy. The Decentrists also hammered home, and with equal success, Howard's basic premises that the planned community must be islanded off as a self-contained unit, that it must resist future change, and that every significant detail must be controlled by the planners from the start and then stuck to. In short, good planning was project planning.

To reinforce and dramatize the necessity for the new order of things, the Decentrists incessantly cried down the bad old city.

They were incurious about its successes. They were interested only in failures, and all was failure. A book like Mumford's *The Culture of Cities* was largely a morbid and biased catalogue of ills. The great city was Megalopolis, Tyrannopolis, Necropolis, a monstrosity, a tyranny, a living death. New York's midtown was "solidified chaos" (Mumford). The shape and appearance of cities was nothing but "a chaotic accident . . . the summation of the haphazard, antagonistic whims of many self-centered, ill-advised individuals" (Stein). The centers of cities amounted to "a foreground of noise, dirt, beggars, souvenirs and shrill competitive advertising" (Bauer).

How could anything so bad be worth the attempt to understand it? And in the schools of planning and architecture, and in Congress, state legislatures and City Halls too, the Decentrists' ideas were gradually accepted as basic doctrine for working *constructively*.

The man with the most dramatic idea of how to get all this anti-city planning right into the cities themselves was the European architect Le Corbusier. He devised in the 1920's a dream city, which he called the Radiant City, composed not of the low buildings beloved of the Decentrists, but instead mainly of skyscrapers within a park. "Suppose we are entering the city by way of the Great Park," Le Corbusier wrote. "Our fast car takes the special elevated motor track between the majestic skyscrapers: as we approach nearer, there is seen the repetition against the sky of the twenty-four skyscrapers; to our left and right on the outskirts of each particular area are the municipal and administrative buildings; and enclosing the space are the museums and university buildings. The whole city is a Park." In Le Corbusier's vertical city, the common run of mankind was to be housed at 1,200 inhabitants to the acre, a fantastically high city density. But by building up so high, planners could leave 95 per cent of the ground open. The skyscrapers would occupy only 5 per cent of the ground. The high-income inhabitants would be in lower, luxury housing around courts, with 85 per cent of their ground left open. Here and there would be restaurants and theaters.

Le Corbusier was planning not only a physical environment, he was planning for a social Utopia as well. Le Corbusier's Utopia was a state of what he called maximum individual liberty, by which he seems to have meant not liberty to do anything much, but liberty from ordinary responsibility. In his Radiant City nobody, presumably, was going to have to be his brother's keeper anymore. Nobody was going to have to struggle with plans of his own. Nobody was going to be tied down.

The Decentrists and other loyal advocates of the Garden City were aghast at Le Corbusier's city of towers in a park, and still are. Their reaction to it was, and remains, much like that of progressive nursery school teachers confronting an utterly institutional orphanage. And yet, ironically, the Radiant City comes directly out of the Garden City. Le Corbusier accepted the Garden City's fundamental image, and worked to make it practical for high densities. He described his creation as the Garden City made attainable.

In another sense, too, in its relatively easy public reception, Le Corbusier's Radiant City depended upon the Garden City. The Garden City planners and their ever-increasing following among housing reformers, students and architects were tirelessly popularizing the idea of the superblock, the project neighborhood, the unchangeable plan, and grass, grass, grass. Le Corbusier really did not have to justify his vision in either humane or functional terms. The Decentrists' cries of institutionalization, mechanization, depersonalization seemed to others foolishly sectarian.

Le Corbusier's dream city has had an immense effect on our own cities. It was hailed deliriously by architects, and has gradually been embodied in scores of projects, ranging from low-income public housing to office building projects. Aside from making at least the superficial Garden City principle superficially practicable in dense cities, Le Corbusier attempted to make the automobile an integral part of his scheme, and this was, in the 1920's and early 1930's, a new and exciting idea. He included great arterial roads for express one-way traffic. He cut the number of streets because "crossroads are an enemy to traffic." He proposed underground streets for heavy vehicles and deliveries, and of course, like the Garden City planners, he kept the pedestrians off the streets and in the parks. It was like a wonderful mechanical toy. Furthermore, his conception, as an architectural work, had a dazzling clarity, simplicity and harmony. It was orderly, visible, easy to understand. It said everything in a flash, like a good advertisement. This vision and its bold symbolism have been all but irresistible to planners, housers, designers, and to developers, lenders and mayors too. It exerts a great pull on "progressive" zoners, who write rules calculated to encourage non-project builders to reflect, if only a little, the dream.

Although the Decentrists, with their devotion to the ideal of a cozy town life, have never made peace with the Le Corbusier vision, most of their disciples have. Virtually all sophisticated city designers today combine the two conceptions in various permutations. The rebuilding technique variously known as "selective removal" or "spot removal" or "renewal planning" or "planned conservation"—meaning that total clearance of an area is avoided—is largely the trick of seeing how many old buildings can be left standing and the area still converted into a passable version of Radiant Garden City. Zoners, highway planners, legislators, land-use planners, and park and playground planners—none of whom live in an ideological vacuum—constantly use, as fixed points of reference, these two powerful visions and the more sophisticated merged vision. They may wander from the visions, they may compromise, they may vulgarize, but these are the points of departure.

Let us look briefly at one other, less important, line of ancestry in orthodox planning. This one begins, more or less, with the great Columbian Exposition in Chicago in 1893, just about the same time that Howard was formulating his Garden City ideas. The Chicago fair snubbed the exciting modern architecture which had begun to emerge in Chicago and instead dramatized a retrogressive imitation-Renaissance style. One heavy, grandiose monument after another was arrayed in the exposition park, like frosted pastries on a tray, in a sort of squat, decorated forecast of Le Corbusier's later repetitive ranks of towers in a park. This ensemble of the rich and monumental captured the imagination of both planners and public. It gave impetus to a movement called the City Beautiful, and indeed the planning of the exposition was dominated by the man who became the leading City Beautiful planner, Daniel Burnham of Chicago.

The aim of the City Beautiful was the City Monumental. Great schemes were drawn up for systems of baroque boulevards, which mainly came to nothing. What did come out of the movement was the Center Monumental, modeled on the fair. City after city built its Civic Center or its Cultural Center. These buildings were arranged along a boulevard (as at Benjamin Franklin Parkway in Philadelphia), or along a mall (as is the Government Center in Cleveland), or were bordered by park (as is the Civic Center at St. Louis), or were interspersed with park (as is the Civic Center at San Francisco). However they were arranged, the important point was that the monuments had been sorted out from the rest of the city, and assembled into the grandest effect thought possible, a complete unit, separate and well defined.

People were proud of them, but the Centers were not a success. Invariably the ordinary city around them ran down instead of being uplifted, and they always acquired an incongruous rim of tattoo parlors and second-hand clothing stores, or else just nondescript, dispirited decay. The people stayed away from them remarkably. Somehow, when the fair became part of the city, it did not work like the fair.

The architecture of the City Beautiful centers went out of style. But the idea behind the centers was not questioned, and it has never had more force than it does today. The idea of sorting out certain cultural or public functions and decontaminating their relationship with the workaday city dovetailed nicely with the Garden City teachings. The conceptions have harmoniously merged, much as the Garden City and the Radiant City merged, into a sort of Radiant Garden City Beautiful. Witness the immense Lincoln Square project for New York, in which a Monumental City Beautiful cultural center is one among a series of adjoining Radiant City and Radiant Garden City housing, shopping and campus centers.

And by analogy, the principles of sorting out—and of bringing order by repression of all plans but the planners'—have been easily extended to all manner of city functions, until today a land-use master plan for a big city is largely a matter of the proposed placement of many series of decontaminated sortings.

From beginning to end, from Howard and Burnham to the latest amendment to Urban Renewal law, the entire concoction is, of course, quite irrelevant to the workings of genuine cities.

When we deal with cities we are dealing with life at a complex and intense level. Because this is so, there is a basic esthetic limitation on what can be done: *A city cannot be a work of art.*

Art has its own peculiar forms of order, and they are rigorous. Artists, whatever their medium, *make selections* from the abounding materials of life, and organize these selections into works that are under the control of the artist. The rather miraculous result of this work—if the selectivity, the organization and the control are consistent within themselves—can be art. But the essence of such work is disciplined, highly discriminatory selectivity *from* life. In relation to the inclusiveness and the literally endless intricacy of life, art is arbitrary, symbolic and abstracted. That is its value and the source of its own kind of order and coherence.

To approach a city, or even a city neighborhood, as if it were a larger architectural problem, capable of being given order by converting it into a disciplined work of art, is to make the mistake of attempting to substitute art for life. The results of such profound confusion between art and life are neither life nor art. They are taxidermy.

Nineteenth-century Utopians, with their revulsion at urbanized and industrialized society, and with their inheritance of eighteenth-century romanticist ideas about the nobility and simplicity of "natural" or primitive man, were much attracted to the idea of simple environments that were works of art by a harmonious consensus. To get back to this condition has been one of the hopes incorporated in our tradition of Utopian reform.

This futile (and deeply reactionary) hope tinctured the Utopianism of the Garden City planning movement too, and, at least ideologically, somewhat gentled its more dominant theme of harmony and order imposed and frozen by authoritarian planning.

The hope for an eventual, simple environment formed of art-by-consensus—or rather, a ghostly vestige of that hope—has continued to flit through Garden City planning theory when it has kept itself pure from Radiant City and City Beautiful planning. Thus, as late as the 1930's, Lewis Mumford in *The Culture of Cities* gave an importance (which would be puzzling indeed in the absence of this tradition) to pursuits like basket-weaving, pottery-making and blacksmithing in the planned communities he envisioned for us. As late as the 1950's, Clarence Stein, the leading American Garden City planner, on the occasion of receiving the American Institute of Architects' gold medal for his contributions to architectural progress, was casting about for some object which might suitably be created by harmonious consensus in the ideal communities he envisioned. He suggested that citizens could be allowed to build a nursery school with their own hands. Aside from the conceded nursery school, the complete physical environment of a community and all the arrangements that compose it must be in the total, absolute and unchallenged control of the project's architects.

This is, of course, no different from the Radiant City and City Beautiful assumptions.

Like the housers who face a blank if they try to think what to build besides income-sorting projects, or the highwaymen who face a blank if they try to think what to do besides accommodate more cars, just so, architects who venture into city design often face a blank in trying to create order in cities except by substituting the order of art for the very different order of life.

We are constantly being told simple-minded lies about cities, being assured that duplication represents order. It is the easiest thing in the world to seize hold of a few forms, give them a regimented regularity, and try to palm them off in the name of order. Yet regimented regularity and significant systems of functional order are seldom coincident in this world.

To see complex systems of functional order as order, and not as chaos, takes understanding. The leaves dropping from the trees in the autumn, the interior of an airplane engine, the entrails of a dissected rabbit, all appear to be chaos if they are seen without comprehension. Once they are understood as systems of order, they actually *look* different.

When city designers and planners try to find a design device that will express, in a clear and easy way, the "skeleton" of city structure (expressways and promenades are current favorites), they are on the wrong track. A city is not put together like a mammal or a steel frame building, or even like a honeycomb or a coral. *A city's very structure consists of mixture of uses, and we get closest to its structural secrets when we deal with the conditions that generate diversity.*

If the slippery shorthand of analogy can help, perhaps the best analogy is this: imagine a large field in darkness. In the field, many fires are burning. They are of many sizes, some great, others small; some far apart, others dotted close together; some are brightening, some are slowly going out. Each fire, large or small, extends its radiance into the surrounding murk, and thereby carves out a space. But the space and the shape of that space exist only to the extent that the light from the fire creates it.

The murk has no shape or pattern except where it is carved into space by the light. Where the murk between the lights becomes deep and undefinable and shapeless, the only way to give it form or structure is to kindle new fires in the murk or sufficiently enlarge the nearest existing fires.

Only intricacy and use give to the parts of a city appropriate structure and shape. Wherever the fires of use and vitality fail to extend in a city is a place in the murk, a place essentially without city form and structure. Without that vital light, no seeking for "skeletons" or "frameworks" or "cells" can bring a city into form.

These metaphoric space-defining fires are formed—to get back to tangible realities—by areas where *diverse* city uses and users give each other close and lively support. This is the essential order which city design can assist. These areas of vitality need to have their remarkable functional order clarified. As cities have more such areas, and less gray area or murk, the need and the opportunities for clarification of this order will increase.

Whatever is done to clarify this order, this intricate life, has to be done mainly by tactics of emphasis and suggestion. Instead of attempting to substitute art for life, city designers should return to a strategy ennobling both to art and to life: a strategy of illuminating and clarifying life and helping to explain to us its meanings and order—in this case, helping to illuminate, clarify and explain the spontaneous order of cities.

All the various tactics for capturing city order are concerned with bits and pieces—bits and pieces which are, to be sure, knit into a city fabric of use that is as continuous and little cut apart as possible. Emphasis on bits and pieces is of the essence: this is what a city is, bits and pieces that supplement each other and support each other.

Perhaps this all seems very commonplace compared with the sweep and swoop of highways, or the eerily beautiful beehive huts of tribal kraals. But what we have to express in expressing our cities is not to be scorned. Their intricate order—a manifestation of the freedom of countless numbers of people to make and carry out countless plans—is in many ways a great wonder; we ought not to be reluctant to make this living collection of interdependent uses, this freedom, this life, more understandable for what it is, nor so unaware that we do not know what it is.

Mother Jacobs' Home Remedies

LEWIS MUMFORD

Ever since 1949, when the national Housing Act was passed, the cities of this country have been assaulted by a series of vast federally aided building operations. These large-scale operations have brought only small-scale benefits to our city. The people who gain by the government's handouts are not the displaced slum dwellers but the new investors and occupants. In the name of slum clearance, many quarters of Greater New York that would still have been decently habitable with a modest expenditure of capital have been razed, and their inhabitants, along with the shopkeepers and tavern keepers who served them, have been booted out, to resettle in even slummier quarters. Even in municipal projects designed to rehouse the displaced slum dwellers or people of equivalent low income, the physical improvements have been only partial and the social conditions of the inhabitants have been worsened through further social stratification—segregation, actually—of people by their income levels. The standard form of housing favored by the federal government and big-city administrators is high-rise slabs—bleak structures of ten to twenty stories. Superficially, these new buildings are an immense improvement over both the foul Old Law tenements of New York and the New Law (1901) tenements that covered the newer sections of the Bronx and the upper West Side up to 1930. The latest model buildings are only two rooms deep; all the flats have outside exposure; the structures are widely spaced around small play areas and patches of fenced grass spotted with benches. Not merely are the buildings open to the sun and air on all sides but they are as bugproof and verminproof as concrete floors and brick walls can make them; they have steam heat, hot and cold water, standard bathroom equipment, and practically everything a well-to-do family could demand except large rooms and doors for their closets; the absence of the latter is an idiotic economy achieved at the expense of the tenants, who must provide curtains.

New Yorker, XXXVIII (December 1, 1962), 148–179. Reprinted by permission; © 1962 The New Yorker Magazine, Inc.

These buildings, with all their palpable hygienic virtues, are the response to a whole century of investigation of the conditions of housing among the lower-income groups in the big cities, particularly New York. Shortly after 1835, when the first slum tenement deliberately designed for congestion was built, on Cherry Street, the Health Commissioner of New York noted the appallingly high incidence of infant mortality and infectious diseases among the poor, and he correlated this with overcrowding of rooms, overcrowding of building plots, poor ventilation, lack of running water and indoor toilet facilities. For a large part of the nineteenth century, in all big cities, housing conditions worsened, even for the upper classes, despite the common boast that this was "the Century of Progress." It was only because of a tremendous effort by physicians, sanitarians, housing reformers, and architects that legislation established minimum standards for light, air, constructional soundness, and human decency.

Unfortunately, it turned out that better housing was more expensive housing, and at the rents the lower-income groups could afford no landlord could be tempted to invest. The most profitable rentals came from congested slum housing. So pressing were the economic and sanitary problems in urban housing that when finally government aid on a large scale was secured, the dominant concept of good lower-income housing was naturally centered on physical improvements. Our current high-rise housing projects find their sanction in the need to wipe out more than a century of vile housing and provide space for people who have been living in slums holding three hundred to seven hundred people an acre. On sound hygienic terms, the one way of meeting this demand within the limited areas provided is the erection of tall buildings, whose grim walls are overshadowing ever-larger sections of Manhattan. There is nothing wrong with these buildings except that, humanly speaking, they stink. What is worse, after a few years of occupancy, some of them stink in an olfactory sense. Not only that, but the young have found the automatic elevators marvellous instruments for annoying adults; putting them out of order or stalling them has become a universal form of play. London County Council administrators have told me the same story about the conflict between high-rise urban aesthetics and what Jane Adams called the spirit of youth in city streets—or, rather, here, in city elevator shafts. By the very nature of the high-rise slab, its inhabitants are cut off from the surveillance and protection of neighbors and passersby, particularly when they are in elevators. In some housing projects, the possibility of casual violence, rape, even murder—a rising menace in all our big cities—is conspicuously present. The daily life of the inhabitants, besides being subject to the insistent bureaucratic regulation of the management, labors under a further handicap. Because of a long-standing rule, only lately removed, urban-renewal projects could not provide marketing facilities to replace those they had wiped out; often the housewife has to trundle her heavy shopping bags many blocks and is denied the convenience of sending a small member of the family to the corner store. In short, though the hygiene of these new structures was incomparably superior to anything the market had offered in the past—and in sunlight, air, and view definitely superior to the congested super-slums of the rich on Park Avenue—most of the other desirable facilities and opportunities had descended to a lower level.

From time to time in this column I have pointed out these deficiencies in public housing in New York; as far back as 1942, when one of the first high-rise projects opened, in the Navy Yard area of Brooklyn, I foretold that it would become the slum that it now notoriously is. But the person who has lately followed through on *all* the dismal results of current public housing and has stirringly presented them is Mrs. Jane Jacobs, whose book, "The Death and Life of Great American Cities" (Random House), has been an exciting theme for dinner-table conversation all over the country this past year. Though her examples of desirable urban quarters are drawn chiefly from New York—indeed, largely from a few tiny pockets of New York—the bad fashionable patterns she points to are universal. A few years ago, Mrs. Jacobs stepped into prominence at a planners' conference at Harvard. Into the foggy atmosphere of professional jargon that usually envelops such meetings, she blew like a fresh offshore breeze to present a picture, dramatic but not distorted, of the results of displacing large neighborhood populations to facilitate large-scale rebuilding. She pointed out a fact to which many planners and administrators had been indifferent—that a neighborhood is not just a collection of buildings but a tissue of social relations and a cluster of warm personal sentiments, associated with the familiar faces of the doctor and the priest, the butcher and the baker and the candlestick maker, not least with the idea of "home." Sanitary steam-heated apartments, she observed, are no substitute for warmhearted neighbors, even if they live in verminous cold-water flats. The chat across the air shaft, the little changes of scene as a woman walks her baby or tells her troubles with her husband to the druggist, the little flirtations that often attend the purchase of a few oranges or potatoes, all season the housewife's day and mean more than mere physical shelter. It is no real gain to supplant the sustaining intimacies of long neighborhood association with the professional advice of a social worker or a psychiatrist, attempting by a wholly inadequate therapy to combat the trauma of social dislocation. Mrs. Jacobs gave firm shape to a misgiving that many people had begun to express. But she saw more deeply into the plight of both those who were evicted and those who came back to live in homogenized and sterilized barracks that had been conceived in terms of bureaucratic regimentation, financial finagling, and administrative convenience, without sufficient thought for the diverse needs of personal and family life, thus producing a human void that matched the new architectural void. In this process, even valuable buildings have often been destroyed, though cherished landmarks in the life of the community, so that the operation may "start clean," without any encumbrances.

Mrs. Jacobs' criticism established her as a person to be reckoned with.

Here was a new kind of "expert," very refreshing in current planning circles, where minds unduly fascinated by computers carefully confine themselves to asking only the kind of question that computers can answer and are completely negligent of the human contents or the human results. This able woman had used her eyes and, even more admirably, her heart to assay the human result of large-scale housing, and she was saying, in effect, that these toplofty barracks that now crowd the city's sky line and overshadow its streets are not fit for human habitation. For her, the new pattern of high-rise urban housing was all one—whether undertaken by municipal authorities to rehouse low-income groups displaced from their destroyed slum quarters, or by insurance companies to house, somewhat more spaciously and elegantly, carefully selected members of the middle classes and provide a safe, reasonably high return, or by speculative investors and builders taking advantage of government aid to feather their private nests.

From a mind so big with a fresh point of view and pertinent ideas, one naturally expected a book of equally large dimensions. But whereas "Sense and Sensibility" could have been the title of her Harvard talk, what she sets forth in "The Death and Life of Great American Cities" comes close to deserving the secondary title of "Pride and Prejudice." The shrewd critic of dehumanized housing and faulty design is still evident, and has applied some of her sharp observations and her municipal political experience to the analysis of urban activities as a whole. But this excellent clinical analyst has been joined by a character who has patched together out of the bits and pieces of her local personal observations nothing less than a universal theory about the life and death of our great—by "great," Mrs. Jacobs seems always to mean "big"—American cities. This new costume of theory, though not quite as airy as the Emperor's clothes, exposes such large areas of naked unawareness that it devaluates Mrs. Jacobs' many sound statements. Some of her boldest planning proposals, indeed, rest on faulty data, inadequate evidence, and startling miscomprehensions of views contrary to hers. This does not make her book easy to appraise.

Before seeking to do justice to Mrs. Jacobs' work as a whole, I must say a word about her first chapter, in which she does not do justice to herself. Ironically, this doughty opponent of urban-renewal projects turns out to have a huge private urban-renewal project of her own. Like a construction gang bulldozing the site clean of all habitations, good or bad, she gaily bulldozes out of existence every desirable innovation in urban planning during the last century and every competing idea, without even a pretense of critical evaluation. She is opposed to sterile high-rise projects, but she is even more opposed to the best present examples of urban residential planning, such as Chatham Village, in Pittsburgh, and she seems wholly to misunderstand their nature, their purpose, and their achievement. Her misapprehension of any plans she regards as subversive of her own concepts of urban planning leads her to astounding statements, and she even attempts to liquidate possible opponents by treating those who have attempted to improve the design of cities by methods not her own as if such people were determined enemies of the city. To wipe out her most dangerous rival, she concentrates her attack on Sir Ebenezer Howard, the founder of the New Towns (Garden City) movement in England. Her handling of him is, for those who know anything of his biography, comic. Howard, it happens, devoted the last quarter century of his life to the improvement of cities, seeking to find by actual experiment the right form and size, and the right balance between urban needs and purposes and those of the rural environment. Under the rubric of the "garden city," he reintroduced into city building two important ideas: the notion that there is a limit to the area and population of a city, and the notion of providing for continued population growth by founding more towns, which would form "town clusters," to perform the more complex functions of a metropolis without wiping out the open recreational spaces and the rural activities of the intervening countryside. Fifteen such communities exist in England today as partial embodiments of his principle, mostly with populations ranging from sixty to ninety thousand—a group of towns that will eventually hold a vast number of people working not as commuters to London but in their local factories and business enterprises. During the last year three more such towns have been founded in Britain alone.

Ebenezer Howard, Mrs. Jacobs insists, "set spinning powerful and city-destroying ideas: He conceived that the way to deal with the city's functions was to sort and sift out of the whole certain simple uses, and to arrange each of these in relative self-containment. He focussed on the provision of wholesome housing as the central problem, to which everything else was subsidiary." But this characterization brashly contradicts Howard's clearly formulated idea of the garden city as a balanced, many-sided urban community. In the same vein, Mrs. Jacobs' dislike of nearly everything about current town planning is concentrated in one omnibus epithet, expressive of her utmost contempt: "Radiant Garden City Beautiful." Obviously, neither radiance (sunlight) nor gardens nor spaciousness nor beauty has any place in Mrs. Jacobs' picture of a great city.

I shall say no more of Mrs. Jacobs' historical knowledge and scholarly scruple except that her innocence of easily ascertainable facts is rather frequent. An English reviewer has charitably called her an *enfant terrible;* terrible or not, she has become a rampant public figure in the cities movement, and she has a sufficiently large uncritical following even among supposedly knowledgeable professors of planning to require a rigorous appraisal of her work lest all of it be accepted as holy writ.

"This book is an attack on current city planning and rebuilding." With these brave words Mrs. Jacobs introduces herself. An exhaustive critical analysis and appraisal of the torrent of urban renewal that has been reducing areas of New York and other cities to gargantuan nonentities of high-rise buildings has been long overdue. To have someone look over the situation with her rude, fresh eye seemed almost a gift from Heaven. Unfortunately, her assault on current planning rests on an odd view of the nature and function and structure of big cities. Underneath her thesis—that the sidewalk, the street, and the neighborhood, in all their higgledy-piggledy unplanned casualness, are the very core of a dynamic urban life—lies a preoccupation that is almost an obsession: the prevention of criminal violence in big cities.

In judging Mrs. Jacobs' interpretations, I speak as a born and bred New Yorker, who in his time has walked almost every street in Manhattan, and who has lived in every kind of neighborhood and in every type of housing, from a private row house on the West Side to an Old Law dumbbell railroad flat, from a grim walkup apartment off Washington Square to the thirtieth floor of an East Side hotel, from a block of row houses with no shops on Brooklyn Heights to a two-room flat in the same neighborhood over a lunchroom, with the odor of stale fat filtering through the windows, and with a tailor, a laundry, a florist, grocery store, and restaurants—Mrs. Jacobs' favorite constellation for "urban liveliness"—immediately at hand. Like a majority of my fellow-citizens, I am still unregenerate enough to prefer the quiet flat with a back garden and a handsome church beyond it in Hicks Street or a row house backing on a green common in Sunnyside Gardens to all the dingy "liveliness" of Clinton Street as it was back in the twenties.

"I shall mainly be writing about common ordinary things: for instance, what kinds of city streets are safe and what kinds are not; why some city parks are marvellous and others are vice traps and death traps," Mrs. Jacobs says. This reveals an overruling fear of living in the big city she so openly adores, and, as all New Yorkers know, she has considerable reason for fear. Her underlying animus fosters some of her most sensitive interpretations of the quality of life in a genuine neighborhood, but it also fosters a series of amateurish planning proposals that will not stand up under the most forbearing statistical examination. From her point of view, one of the chief mischiefs of contemporary planning is that it reduces the number of streets by creating superblocks reserved almost exclusively for pedestrian movement, free from through wheeled traffic, with the space once preëmpted by unnecessary paved streets turned into open areas for play or provided with benches and plantations for the sedentary enjoyment of adults. Such a separation of automobile and pedestrian runs counter to her private directives for a safe and animated neighborhood; namely, to multiply the number of cross streets, to greatly widen the sidewalks, to reduce all other open spaces, and to place many types of shops and services on streets now devoted solely to residences. The street is her patent substitute for the more diversified meeting places that traditional cities have always boasted. What is behind Mrs. Jacobs' idea of assigning exclusively to the street the mixed functions and varied activities of a well-balanced neighborhood unit? The answer, I repeat, is simple: Her ideal city is mainly an organization for the prevention of crime. To her, the best way to overcome criminal violence is such a mixture of economic and social activities at every hour of the day that the streets will never be empty of pedestrians, and that each shopkeeper, each householder, compelled to find both his main occupations and his recreations on the street, will serve as watchman and policeman, each knowing who is to be trusted and who is not, who is defiant of the law and who upholds it, who can be taken in for a cup of coffee and who must be kept at bay.

This is indeed an original theory of the city, and a new order of city planning. It comes pretty close to saying that if the planners had kept blocks as small and irregular as they are in many old quarters of Manhattan below Fourteenth Street, and had made universal the mixture of shops and tenement houses that long characterized the main avenues, the blight and corrosion and violence that have now spread over the whole city could have been avoided. By concentrating upon the street and upon such neighborhood activities as the street promotes, Mrs. Jacobs holds, we shall go a long way toward producing a metropolis that shall be at once "fantastically dynamic"—the phrase is hers—and humanly safe. But if this remedy were a sound one, eighteenth-century London, which met all of Mrs. Jacobs' planning prescriptions, would not have been the nest of violence and delinquency it actually was.

As one who has spent more than fifty years in New York, I must remind Mrs. Jacobs that many parts of the city she denounces because they do not conform to her standards were for over the better part of a century both economically quite sound and humanly secure. In the urban range of my boyhood, there were occasional rowdy gangs even half a century ago—we always ran for cover when the West Ninety-eight Street gang invaded our street—but their more lethal activities were confined largely to their own little ghettos and nearby territory: Hell's Kitchen, the Gas House District. With the policeman on his beat, a woman could go home alone at any time of the night on a purely residential street without apprehension. (She could even, astonishingly, trust the policeman.) Mrs. Jacobs treats the great parks she fears are an invitation to crime (she also disparages them as a recreation space) on the strange ground that no one any longer can safely use them, as if they were an original sin and a chronic ailment, although this is a state of affairs that would have seemed incredible as late as 1935. Until the present Age of Extermination, Mrs. Jacobs' plans for abating violence would not have been called for—not even by Mrs. Jacobs. Certainly it was not Frederick Olmsted's mistake in long ago laying out Riverside Drive, Morningside Park, and St. Nicholas Park that has made these large parks unusable shambles today. What is responsible for their present emptiness is something Mrs. Jacobs disregards: the increasing pathology of the whole mode of life in the great metropolis, a pathology that is directly proportionate to its overgrowth, its purposeless materialism, its congestion, and its insensate disorder—the very conditions she vehemently upholds as marks of urban vitality. That sinister state manifests itself not merely in the statistics of crime and mental disorder but in the enormous sums spent on narcotics, sedatives, stimulants, hypnotics, and tranquillizers to keep the population of our "great" cities from coming to terms with the vacuous desperation of their daily lives and with the even more vacuous horrors that their rulers and scientific advisers seem to regard as a reasonable terminus for the human race. Lacking any sense of an intelligible purpose or a desirable goal, the inhabitants of our great American cities are simply "waiting for Godot."

Mrs. Jacobs is at her best in dealing with small, intimate urban areas. She understands that the very life of a neighborhood depends upon the maintenance of the human scale, for it fosters what the philosopher Martin Buber calls I-and-thou relations between visible people who share a common environment, who meet face to face without intermediaries, who are aware of their personal identity and their common interests even though they may not exchange a word. This sense of belonging rests, however, not on a metropolitan dynamism but on continuity and stability—the special virtues of the village. These virtues remain conspicuous features of Greenwich Village—the area Mrs. Jacobs favors as a paragon of healthy urban design. By the beginning of the nineteenth century this part of the city, the old Ninth Ward, was so well defined, so individualized, that the City Planning Commissioners of 1811 did not dare to make it conform to the gridiron pattern they imposed with geometric rigor on the rest of the city.

The larger part of this homogeneous area consisted of two- and three-story red brick houses with white porticoes, some of the best of which, those on Varick and King Streets, were destroyed to make way for the Seventh Avenue extension. For long, a loyal population clung to these quarters partly because—as an old friend of mine who lived there remembers—though the residents of the oldest houses had to draw their supply of water from a common pump in the back yard, they were far cheaper than more up-to-date accommodations. This historic enclave would have lost most of the very features Mrs. Jacobs admires, including its short streets, if it had been sufficiently "dynamic." The Village's two special characteristics, indeed, make mock of her "new" principles—its original low density of population and its well-defined architectural character, which graciously set it off from the up-and-coming brownstone-front city that leaped beyond it. In short, old Greenwich Village was almost as much a coherent, concrete entity, with definite boundary lines, as a planned neighborhood unit in a British New Town.

The contradiction between Mrs. Jacobs' perceptions of the intimate values of neighborhood life and her unqualified adoration of metropolitan bigness and dynamism remains unreconciled largely because she rejects the principles of urban design that would unite these complementary qualities. Her ultimate criteria of sound metropolitan planning are dynamism, density, and diversity, but she never allows herself to contemplate the unfortunate last term in the series—disintegration. Yet her concern for local habits and conventions points her in the right direction for overcoming this ultimate disintegration: the recognition of the neighborhood as a vital urban entity, whose stability and continuity are necessary for rebuilding the kind of life that the metropolis, in all its cataclysmic economic voracity ("cataclysmic" is Mrs. Jacobs' happy epithet), has destroyed. She recognizes that a city is more than buildings, but she fails to perceive that a neighborhood is more than its streets, or that the static geometrical order of the gridiron plan and the old-fashioned rectangular block has long been one of the chief obstacles to an effective neighborhood life. The new street system she proposes, with twice the number of intersecting north-and-south streets, would do nothing to give visible reality to the social functions of a neighborhood—those performed by school, church, market, clinic, park, library, eating house, theatre. Mrs. Jacobs has no use for the orderly distribution of these activities or the handsome design of their necessary structures; she prefers the hit-and-miss distribution of the present city. No wonder she opposes the admirable work of Clarence Stein and Henry Wright. These pioneer planners have repeatedly demonstrated—in Sunnyside Gardens; in Radburn, New Jersey; in Chatham Village—how much superior a well-planned, visibly homogeneous neighborhood can be to the sort of random community she advocates. In the multi-dimensional order of the city she favors, beauty does not have a place. Yet it is the beauty of great urban cathedrals and palaces, the order of the great monastic and university precincts of Oxford and Cambridge, the serenity and spaciousness of the great squares of Paris, London, Rome, Edinburgh, that have preserved intact the urban cores of truly great cities over many centuries. Meanwhile, the sordid dynamism of the dingier parts of these same cities has constantly proved uneconomic, inefficient, and self-destructive. Instead of asking what are the best possible urban patterns today for renovating our disordered cities, Mrs. Jacobs asks only under what conditions can existing slums and blighted areas preserve their congenial humane features without any radical changes in their physical structure or their mode of life. Her simple formula does not suggest that her eyes have ever been hurt by ugliness, sordor, confusion, or her ears offended by the roar of trucks smashing through a once quiet residential neighborhood, or her nose assaulted by the chronic odors of ill-ventilated, unsunned housing at the slum standards of congestion that alone meet her ideal standards for residential density. If people are housed in sufficiently congested quarters—provided only that the buildings are not set within superblocks—and if there is a sufficient mish-mash of functions and activities, all her social and aesthetic demands are satisfied. She has exposed these convictions in a flat statement: "A city cannot be a work of art." The citizens of Florence, Siena, Venice, and Turin should take note. But, of course, Mrs. Jacobs might have her own peculiar answer to this: If these places are beautiful they are not and never were cities. What has happened is that she has jumped from the quite defensible position that good physical structures and handsome design are not everything in city planning to the callow notion that they do not matter at all. That beauty, order, spaciousness, clarity of purpose may be worth having for their direct effect on the human spirit, even if they do not promote dynamism or reduce criminal violence, seems not to occur to her. This is the aesthetics of social realism with a vengeance.

Mrs. Jacobs' most original proposal, then, as a theorist of metropolitan development is to turn its chronic symptom of disorder—excessive congestion—into a remedy, by deliberately enlarging the scope of the disease. It is her belief, unshaken by irrefutable counter-evidence, that congestion and disorder are the normal, indeed the desirable, conditions of life in cities. But it is now a well-established fact in biology that overcrowded quarters produce stress even in animals, a state marked by anxiety and hostility. Elbow room is a general requisite for even animal health. Since her obstinate belief in high population density underlies Mrs. Jacobs' entire argument, it gratuitously vitiates even her valid contributions.

Yet despite its blind spots and omissions, her book at times offers a valuable look at the complex activities of the city—especially those urban functions that flourish precisely because of all the interchanges that take place, by chance no less than by plan, most frequently in cities that have reached a certain order of bigness and complexity. Unlike the big corporations and research laboratories that are stampeding into suburbia, Mrs. Jacobs recognizes how much of value they will leave behind, in exchange for temporary access to a golf course, a private airfield, or a few domestic acres. She also recognizes, by observation and experience, the communal nucleus of the city—the value of the spontaneous "primary" association of families and neighbors, upon which all the later complexities of urban life are based. And though she dislikes the notion of a planned "neighborhood unit," she chooses for her normal neighborhood the size that Clarence Perry, in his studies for the Regional Plan for New York back in the twenties, hit upon as roughly the proper size for such a unit—about five thousand people. "We shall have something solid to chew on," she observes, "if we think of city neighborhoods as mundane organs of self-government. Our failures with city neighborhoods are ultimately, failures in localized self-government. And our successes are successes at localized self-government. I am using self-government in its broadest sense, meaning both the informal and formal self-management of society." Excellent. But, as against Mrs. Jacobs, many of us hold that such activities would be furthered by deliberately designed structures and that a planned architectural neighborhood unity will give firmness to its common functions, as it does in the classic example of Venice.

Venice was one of the few cities that, from the Middle Ages onward, were deliberately planned and practically organized on the neighborhood principle, each parish with the little *campo* at the center—occupied by a café, and shops, and a fountain—and its guildhall and its church, a building that might boast as fine a Tintoretto as the ducal palace. There is still plenty of variety and domestic vitality in such neighborhoods despite their long decay, but they do not follow Mrs. Jacobs' formula of shops and factories strewn all over the quarter. Her overvaluation of the now archaic street pattern leads to her naïve remedy for combatting random violence. And her prescription ("eyes on the street") is a result of wishful thinking. Since when has the idea of shopkeepers as substitute policemen kept even them from being held up and knifed? And what makes Mrs. Jacobs think that even policemen are immune to murderous attack? But about the long-term remoralization of this demoralized metropolitan community, she is emphatically right; the stabilities of the family and the neighborhood are the basic sources of all higher forms of morality, and when they are lacking, the whole edifice of civilization is threatened. When no one cares for anyone else, because we have all become mere telephone digits or Social Security numbers, the elaborate fabric of urban life breaks down. Out of this rejection and isolation and emptiness comes, probably, the purposeless hostility of the juvenile delinquent.

Mrs. Jacobs' concern for the smallest unit of urban life is, then, pertinent and well directed. Unhappily, the main tendency of the metropolitan economy she ardently supports is to turn all business over to big commercial enterprises increasingly automatic in operation and automatically increasing in size. The huge, impersonal supermarket is symbolically the ultimate goal of unregulated metropolitan expansion. Mrs. Jacobs wishes to fight new forms of economic organization that are wiping out choice and variety. But the notion of achieving this by multiplying the number of short streets and increasing the number of marginal small enterprises absurdly ignores the larger forces that must be controlled and humanized. The dominant economic institutions in our cities deliberately work to curtail freedom and reduce autonomy. There is no dividing line between the dynamic forces Mrs. Jacobs favors and the cataclysmic forces she opposes, for they have the same origin—an obsessive concern for power and profit, and an indifference to more humane interests.

In passing from that now barely recognizable unit of urban life, the neighborhood, to the larger problems of the city, Mrs. Jacobs again approaches but never reaches a desirable goal. She has had enough political experience to recognize that the city, by its very size, has got out of hand, particularly out of the hands of its own citizens, and that its hugeness causes it to be misplanned and misadministered. Because they lack any integral organs for formulating policies or making decisions, or even contesting the proposals of the Mayor, the City Planning Commissioners, the Borough Presidents, or Mr. Moses, the political pressure exerted by local areas is feeble and sporadic, and achieved only with great effort through *ad-hoc* organizations. The result has been a docile conformity by our governing agencies to other influences, unconcerned with the common good. Mrs. Jacobs realizes that if public officials are to be made more responsive to public opinion and be prevented from making wanton changes in neighborhoods to favor lending institutions, big contractors, and rich tenants instead of the old residents, politics must be organized on a local basis. So, too, her proposed new neighborhood organ of government, like the English borough and unlike the purely formal area of an Assembly District, must have some coherence and integrity as an economic and social unit. Functions that were once pushed to the periphery of the city, or packed into specialized enclaves, like the Seventh Avenue garment district, should be distributed over wider areas in these local-government units. For smaller metropolises, like Baltimore, she suggests that thirty thousand would be the right population for such units, while for cities as big as Chicago and New York, she chooses a hundred to two hundred thousand, and she recognizes that to form these boroughs into active municipal entities, industry and business must be established in these sub-centers. (See "The Roaring Traffic's Boom," in *The New Yorker* of April 16, 1953, for a similar proposal.)

I take a certain mischievous delight in pointing out that the thirty thousand she has hit on for a self-governing district is precisely the figure Leonardo da Vinci, the first advocate of New Towns, suggested to the Duke of Milan when he proposed to overcome the congestion and sordor of that city of three hundred thousand people by designing ten component cities of thirty thousand, the same number, I repeat, that Ebenezer Howard—the archvillain in Mrs. Jacobs' private urban melodrama—tentatively chose for his original garden city. Nor do I think less of her proposals because the great Leonardo and the wise Howard got there before Mrs. Jacobs. But the recent Royal Commission in Great Britain on the government of London concluded that a hundred thousand to two hundred and fifty thousand was the desirable population for the boroughs of Metropolitan London. If Mrs. Jacobs errs in laying down the ideal number for a borough in ordinary metropolises, she errs in favor of the smaller unit. I salute her as a reluctant ally of old Ebenezer Howard.

Mrs. Jacobs innocently believes that complexity and diversity are impossible without the kind of intense congestion that has in fact been emptying out the big city, hurling masses of people into those vast, curdled suburban Milky Ways. In the desire to enjoy amenities unattainable at even a quarter of the density of population she considers desirable, millions of people are giving up the delights and stimulations of genuine city life. It is quite ordinary people who cherish such suburban desires, not followers of Ebenezer Howard or Clarence Stein. Now, it is this massive, century-old drift to suburbia, not the building of superblocks or garden cities, that is mainly responsibile for the dilapidation and the near-death of big American cities. This movement toward the rural periphery in search of things that were the proud posession of every pre-mechanized city has been helped by the most active enemies of the city—the overbudgeted highway engineers who have riddled metropolitan areas with their gaping expressways and transformed civic cores into parking lots. Those who leave the city wish to escape its snarling violence and its sickening perversions of life, its traffic in narcotics and its gangster-organized lewdness, which break into the lives even of children. Not least, the suburban exiles seek to find some nightly surcease from constant bureaucratic regimentation: Punch the time clock! Watch your step! Curb your dog! Do not spit! No parking! Get in line for a ticket! Move on! Keep off the grass! Follow the green line! Wait for the next train! Buy now, pay later! Don't buck the system! Take what you get! The refugees who leave the metropolis may not keep even the fleeting illusion of freedom and security and a normal family life for long. But their reaction is evidence of their own spontaneous vitality and a quickened desire for autonomy, which most of their working life as members of an overcongested, necessarily impersonal hive defeats. Strangely, the city that so insistently drives its population into the suburbs is the very same city that Mrs. Jacobs quaintly describes as "vital." She forgets that in organisms there is no tissue quite as "vital" or "dynamic" as cancer growths.

But if "The Death and Life of Great American Cities," taken as a critique of modern city planning, is a mingling of sense and sentimentality, of mature judgments and schoolgirl howlers, how does it stand as an interpretation of the larger issues of urban development and urban renewal, which the title itself so boldly points to? Here again Mrs. Jacobs heads her argument in the right direction, toward matters that have been insufficiently appreciated or misinterpreted. No one has surpassed her in understanding the reasons for the great metropolis's complexity and the effect of this complexity, with its divisions of labor, its differentiations of occupations and interests, its valuable racial, national, and cultural variety, upon its daily activities. She recognizes that one cannot handle such a multi-dimensional social organization as one might handle a simple machine, designed for a single function. "A growing number of people have begun, gradually," she notes, "to think of cities as problems in organized complexity—organisms that are replete with unexamined, but obviously intricately interconnected, and surely understandable, relationships." An admirable observation, but the author has forgotten the most essential characteristic of all organic growth—to maintain diversity and balance, the organism must not exceed the norm of its species. Any ecological association eventually reaches the "climax stage," beyond which growth without deterioration is not possible. Despite Mrs. Jacobs' recognition of organic complexity in the abstract, she has a very inadequate appreciation of the ecological setting of cities and neighborhoods; she brusquely turns her back to all but the segregated local environment. Yet the overgrowth of our big cities has destroyed those special environmental qualities that made their setting desirable and fostered their growth in the first place. The obvious result of the large-scale metropolitan congestion she advocates—the poisoning of the human system with carbon monoxide and the two hundred known cancer-producing substances usually in the air, the muffling of the vital ultraviolet rays by smog, the befouling of streams and oceanside (once used for fishing and bathing) with human and industrial waste—is flatly ignored. This is worse than an oversight; it points to a basic defect in her thinking, a failure to take in the environment as a whole.

Mrs. Jacobs approvingly quotes Dr. Karl Menninger's observation that the best remedies for delinquency are "plentiful contacts with other people; work, including even drudgery; and violent play." But the kind of congested conglomeration she advocates would provide no room for violent play, and no sufficient opportunity to find relief from the monotonous and depressing regimentation of the big city. From the days of Ur onward, city dwellers have always had the countryside close at hand. There their homicidal impulses could be exorcised by digging and delving, or by shooting at destructive animals, and there their need for spontaneous muscular exercise could be satisfied by swimming and boating and climbing rather than by knives, brass knuckles, and rumbles. (Emerson long ago prescribed a pasture and a wood lot as the best cure for juvenile village mischief; they didn't call it "juvenile delinquency" in his day.)

When they have reached a point long ago overpassed by New York, Chicago, London, Tokyo, and Moscow, big cities are under the necessity to expand their operations to a more capacious container—the region. The forces that have formed our cities in the past are now almost automatically, by their insensate dynamism, wrecking them and threatening to destroy whole countries and continents. Against this background, the problem of policing public thoroughfares to prevent violence is minor; violence and vice are symptoms of those far graver forms of disorder that Mrs. Jacobs rules out of consideration, because they challenge her rosily sentimental picture of the "great American city." To blame the conditions in the congested, overgrown metropolis of today on the monumental scale and human hollowness of its urban-renewal projects is preposterous, for this draws attention from the grim, enveloping realities that our whole metropolitan civilization confronts. The prevailing economic and technological forces in the big city have broken away from the ecological pattern, as well as from the moral inhibitions and the social codes and the religious ideas that once, however imperfectly, kept them under some sort of control, and reduced their power to human dimensions. Just as there is no limit to the power assigned to those who build nuclear weapons and rockets, who plan space shots and lunatic-cool mass exterminations, so there is no limit to those who multiply motor roads for the sake of selling more motorcars and gasoline, who push on the market every variety of drug, narcotic, chemical, and biotic agent, without regard to the effect on the landscape or upon any form of organic life. Under this "cataclysmic" eruption of power, with its lack of any goal but its own expansion, as Henry Adams presciently predicted half a century ago, law disappears as a priori principle and gives place to force, morality becomes police, disintegration overcomes integration. The present metropolitan explosion is both the symbol and the agent of this uncontrolled power.

Failing to appraise the larger sources of urban disintegration, or to trace the connection between our major adult and our minor juvenile forms of delinquency, Mrs. Jacobs mistakenly regards those who may have a better grasp of the situation as enemies of metropolitan life. Now, under more normal circumstances, the special virtue of the great city was that it tended to keep any one idea or institution or group from dominating. Today military power, scientific power, technical power, financial power, and, in fact, "cataclysmic" power in every manifestation, to operate most successfully on their own terms, wipe out urban diversity and do away with every mode of organic growth, ecological partnership, and autonomous activity. "Silent Spring" came to the big city long before it visited the countryside. No planning proposal now makes sense unless it is conceived in terms of truly human—that is, self-limited and self-directed—purposes. The command of this unlimited, automatically expanding power is, again as Henry Adams wisely pointed out half a century ago, the central problem of our civilization. For Mrs. Jacobs to imagine that the horrifying human by-products of the city's disordered life can be eliminated by a few tricks of planning is as foolish as for her to imagine that too generous open spaces and superblocks fostered these symptoms.

If our urban civilization is to escape progressive dissolution, we shall have to rebuild it from the ground up. Certainly we shall have to do far more than alter street plans, humanize housing projects, and give wider geographic distribution to economic activities. Since such a general transformation will affect every aspect of life, urban politics and planning must play an active and significant part. But it is the formative, stabilizing, coherent, order-making forces, not the dynamic ones, that need special encouragement. One cannot control destructive automatisms at the top unless one begins with the smallest units and restores choice and initiative to them—to the person as a responsible human being, to the neighborhood as the primary organ not merely of social life but of moral behavior, and finally to the city as an organic embodiment of the common life, in ecological balance with other cities, big and little, within the larger region in which they lie. A quick, purely local answer to these problems is no better than applying a homemade poultice for the cure of a cancer. And that, I am afraid, is what the more original proposals of "The Death and Life of Great American Cities" come to.

*City Planning and Urban Realities**

HERBERT J. GANS

American intellectuals have begun to rediscover the city. Not since the days of the muckrakers has there been so much interest in local politics and in the "physical" features of the city—the problems of slums and urban renewal,

* A review of *The Death and Life of Great American Cities*, by Jane Jacobs (Random House, 458 pp., $7.50).

Commentary, XXXIII (February 1962), 170–175. Copyright © 1962 by the American Jewish Committee. Reprinted by permission of *Commentary* and the author.

middle-income housing, the lack of open space, the plight of the downtown business district, and the ever-increasing traffic congestion. The new concern with questions usually relegated to architects and planners has been stimulated especially by two recent changes in city life. The rapid influx of Negro and Puerto Rican immigrants has created slums in some neighborhoods where intellectuals live, forcing them to choose between fighting for neighborhood improvement or joining the rest of the middle class in flight. At the same time, the postwar building boom—in office buildings as well as residential projects—is altering and destroying some favorite intellectual haunts like New York's Greenwich Village and Chicago's Near North Side.

This change has provided new material for one of the basic themes of the ongoing critique of American society—the destruction of tradition by mass-produced modernity. During the 1950's, the critique centered on the ravages produced by mass culture and by suburbia. In the 1960's it is likely to focus on the destruction of traditional urbanity by new forms of city building.

Many of the ideas behind the new urban critique have come from the writings of Jane Jacobs, an associate editor of *Architectural Forum*. Now she has put her ideas into a book which seems destined to spearhead the attack, just as another book by an editor of another Luce magazine—I refer to William H. Whyte's *The Organization Man*—spearheaded the attack on suburbia. *The Death and Life of Great American Cities* is a thoughtful and imaginative tract on behalf of the traditional city, an analysis of the principles that make it desirable, an attack on the city planner—whom Mrs. Jacobs takes to be the agent of its transformation—and a program of new planning principles that she believes will create vital cities and vital neighborhoods.

The vital neighborhood—and vitality is Jane Jacobs' central aim—should be diverse in its use of land and in the people who inhabit it. Every district should be a mixture of residences, business, and industry; of old buildings and new; of young people and old; of rich and poor. Mrs. Jacobs argues that people want diversity, and in neighborhoods where it exists, they strike roots and participate in community life, thus generating vitality. When diversity is lacking, when neighborhoods are scourged by what she calls the great blight of dullness, residents who are free to leave do so, and are replaced by the poverty-stricken, who have no other choice, and the areas soon turn into slums.

According to Mrs. Jacobs, the most important component of vitality is an abundant street life. Neighborhoods that are designed to encourage people to use the streets, or to watch what goes on in them, make desirable quarters for residence, work, and play. Moreover, where there is street life, there is little crime, for the people on the street and in the buildings which overlook it watch and protect each other, thus discouraging criminal acts more efficiently than police patrols.

The abundance of street life, Mrs. Jacobs argues, is brought about by planning principles which are diametrically opposed to those practiced by orthodox city planners. First, a district must have several functions, so that its buildings and streets are used at all times of the day, and do not (like Wall Street) stand empty in off-hours. The area should be built up densely with structures close to the street and low enough in number of stories to encourage both street life and street watching. Blocks should be short, for corners invite stores, and these bring people out into the streets for shopping and socializing. Sidewalks should be wide enough for pavement socials and children's play; streets should be narrow enough to prevent intensive and high-speed automobile traffic, for the automobile frightens away pedestrians. Small parks and playgrounds are desirable, but large open spaces—especially those intended only for decoration and not for use—not only deaden a district by separating people from each other but also invite criminals. Buildings should be both old and new, expensive and cheap, for low rents invite diversity in the form of new industries, shops, and artists' studios.

Neighborhoods which are designed on the basis of these principles—and which provide Mrs. Jacobs with concrete evidence for her argument—are areas like New York's Greenwich Village and San Francisco's Telegraph Hill (where residences of all types, prices, and ages mix with small business, industry, and cultural facilities), and low-income ethnic quarters like Boston's North End and Chicago's Back-of-the-Yards district.

The new forms of city building, Mrs. Jacobs says, discourage street life, and create only dullness. High-rise apartment buildings, whether in public housing or private luxury flats, are standardized, architecturally undistinguished, and institutional in appearance if not operation. They house homogeneous populations, segregating people by income, race, and often even age, and isolating them in purely residential quarters. Elevators, and the separation of the building from the street by a moat of useless open space, frustrate maternal supervision of children, thus keeping children off the street. Often there are no real streets at all, because prime access is by car. Nor is there any reason for people to use the streets, for instead of large numbers of small stores fronting on a street, there are shopping centers containing a small number of large stores—usually chains—each of which has a monopoly in its line. The small merchant, who watches the street and provides a center for neighborhood communication and social life, is absent here. In such projects, the residents have no place to meet each other, and there is no spontaneous neighborhood life. As a result, people have no feeling for their neighbors, and no identification with the area. In luxury buildings, doormen watch the empty streets and discourage the criminal visitor, but in public housing projects, there are no doormen, and the interior streets and elevators invite rape, theft, and vandalism. Areas like this are blighted by dullness from the start, and are destined to become slums before their time.

The major responsibility for the new forms of city building Mrs. Jacobs places on the city planner and on two theories of city form: Ebenezer Howard's low-density Garden City, and Le Corbusier's high-rise apartment complex, the Radiant City. The planner is an artist who wants to restructure life by principles applicable only to art. By putting these principles into action, he is methodically destroying the features that produce vitality. His planning theories have also influenced the policy makers, and especially realtors, bankers, and other sources of mortgage funds. As a result, they refuse to lend money to older but still vital areas which are trying to rehabilitate themselves, thus encouraging further deterioration of the structures until they are ripe for slum clearance, redevelopment with projects—and inevitable dullness.

Anyone who has ever wandered through New York's Greenwich Village or Boston's North End is bound to respond to Mrs. Jacobs' conception of a vital city. Her analysis of the mechanics of street life, and of the ways in which people use buildings, streets, and vacant spaces in such areas is eye-opening. The principles of neighborhood planning which derive from her observations—she is herself a resident of Greenwich Village—are far more closely attuned to how people actually live than are those of orthodox city planning. It would be easy to succumb to the charm of the neighborhoods she describes, and to read her book only as a persuasive appeal for their retention. But since Mrs. Jacobs is out to reform all of city planning, it is necessary to examine her central ideas more closely.

Her argument is built on three fundamental assumptions: that people desire diversity; that diversity is ultimately what makes cities live and that the lack of it makes them die; and that buildings, streets, and the planning principles on which they are based, shape human behavior. The first two of these assumptions are not entirely supported by the facts of the areas she describes. The last assumption, which she shares with the planners whom she attacks, might be called the physical fallacy, and it leads her to ignore the social, cultural, and economic factors that contribute to vitality or dullness. It also blinds her to less visible kinds of neighborhood vitality and to the true causes of the city's problems.

Ethnic neighborhoods like the North End, or the Italian and Irish sections of Greenwich Village, are not diverse, but quite homogeneous in population as well as in building type. The street life of these areas stems not so much from their physical character as from the working-class culture of their inhabitants. In this culture, the home is reserved for the family, so that much social life takes place outdoors. Also, children are not kept indoors as frequently as in the middle class, and since they are less closely supervised in their play, they too wind up in the streets.

If such districts are near the downtown area, they may attract intellectuals, artists, and bohemian types, who also tend to spend a good deal of time outside their apartments, contributing further to the street life. The street life, the small stores that traditionally serve ethnic groups and other cultural minorities, and the area's exotic flavor then draw visitors and tourists, whose presence helps to make the district even livelier. The resulting blend of unusual cultures makes for a highly visible kind of vitality. It helps if the district is old and basically European in architecture, but traditional-looking frontages can be superimposed by today's clever builder.

In other working-class neighborhoods, especially those far away from the downtown area, street life is also abundant, but the people and the stores are neither ethnic nor esoteric. In middle-class neighborhoods, there is no street life, for all social activities take place inside the home, children play less often on the sidewalks, and the street is used only for transportation. Such neighborhoods look dull, notably to the visitor, and therefore they seem to be less vital than their ethnic and bohemian counterparts. But visibility is not the only measure of vitality, and areas that are uninteresting to the visitor may be quite vital to the people who live in them.

This possibility must also be considered for the new luxury and middle-class housing projects. Since they are largely occupied by childless middle-class people, they look even duller than other areas, just as their newness makes them seem more standardized to the visitor than older areas in which the initial homogeneity of buildings has been altered by conversion or just covered by the accretions of dirt and age. It is clear that we need to learn how residents live in such projects before we can be sure of the validity of Mrs. Jacobs' charges.

In proposing that cities be planned to stimulate an abundant street life, Mrs. Jacobs not only overestimates the power of planning in shaping behavior, but she in effect demands that middle-class people adopt working-class styles of family life, child rearing, and sociability. The truth is that the new forms of residential building—in suburb as well as city—are not products of orthodox planning theory, but expressions of the middle-class culture which guides the housing market, and which planners also serve. Often the planners serve it too loyally, and they ignore the needs of a working-class population. Thus, Jane Jacobs' criticism is most relevant to the planning of public housing projects, for its middle-class designers have made no provision for the street life that these particular tenants probably want.

But middle-class people, especially those raising children, do not want working-class—or even bohemian—neighborhoods. They do not want the visible vitality of a North End, but rather the quiet and the privacy obtainable in low-density neighborhoods and elevator apartment houses. Little of their social life involves neighbors, and their friends may be scattered all over the metropolitan area, as are the commercial and recreational facilities which they frequent. For this, they want a car, expressways, and all the freedom of movement that expressways create when properly planned. Middle-class people tend to value status over convenience, and thus they reject neighborhoods in which residence and business are mixed—or in which there is any real diversity in population. Having no love for walking or for riding public transit, they have brought shopping centers into being. Nor does their life style leave much room for the small merchant. Since their tastes are no longer ethnic but not yet esoteric, they prefer the supermarket to the small store, for it does provide more choice—if only among prosaic items—and its wider aisles facilitate gossip with neighbors.

One can quarrel with some of these tastes, but the fact is that the areas about which Mrs. Jacobs writes were built for a style of life which is going out of fashion with the large majority of Americans who are free to choose their place of residence. The North End and the Back-of-the-Yards district are not holding their young people, who tend to move to the suburbs as soon as they have children to raise. Even in Europe, the old working-class districts invariably empty out when prosperity reaches the blue-collar workers.

The middle-class visitor does not see these cultural changes. Nor does he see that the houses in these traditional districts are often hard to maintain, that parking is often impossible, that noise and dirt are ever-present, that some of the neighbors watch too much, and that not all the shopkeepers are kind. Because the traditional districts are so different from his own neighborhood, and because he is a visitor, he sees only their charm and excitement. He therefore is most understandably reluctant to see them disappear.

But for the planning of cities, the visitor's wishes are less important than the inhabitant's. One cannot design all neighborhoods for a traditional style of life if only a few people want to live this way. Nevertheless, areas like the North End and the Village are worth saving. They provide low-rent housing for people with low incomes; they give pleasure to visitors, and may even attract tourists; and they are appealing reminders of our European heritage and our pre-automobile past. The city would be a poorer place without them.

Even so, the future of the American city is not going to be determined by the life or death of the North Ends and the Greenwich Villages. The real problems lie elsewhere. Mrs. Jacobs' concentration on these areas diverts her from properly analyzing the more fundamental problems, even while she makes some highly pertinent comments. This can best be illustrated by examining her discussion of slums and her proposals for urban renewal.

As noted earlier, she argues that slums are caused ultimately by lack of diversity. Homogeneous and dull areas are deserted by residents who have the resources to go elsewhere, and are replaced by people who have no other choice, and who, for reasons of poverty and racial discrimination, are forced to live in overcrowded conditions. She suggests that if these areas could be made more diverse, the initial occupants might not leave, and owners would then be able to rehabilitate the buildings.

This analysis is too simple. People leave such areas not to seek diversity but to practice new life styles, and additional diversity would not persuade them to stay. It is true that some areas occupied by non-mobile ethnic groups, notably the North End and Back-of-the-Yards, hold their residents longer than other areas. It is also true that these areas are not slums; they are low-rent districts, and Mrs. Jacobs is right in insisting on the distinction. Slums (she calls them perpetual slums) are areas in which housing and other facilities are physically and socially harmful to the inhabitants and to the larger community, primarily because of overcrowding. Low-rent areas (which she calls unslumming slums) may look equally dilapidated to the casual observer—and planners sometimes base their decisions only on casual observation—but they are not overcrowded and they are not harmful. Mrs. Jacobs criticizes urban renewal—and rightly so—for confusing such areas with real slums, and clearing them needlessly with grievous hurt to their inhabitants. She proposes that they can be rehabilitated by providing home and tenement owners with easier access to mortgage funds, and by planning for greater diversity. This proposal has merit, although landlords probably would not undertake as much rehabilitation as she envisages unless the area were attracting middle-class people with quasi-bohemian tastes—as in the case of the Village and Philadelphia's West Rittenhouse Square district.

But such neighborhoods—and purely working-class ones like the North End—are numerically unimportant in most cities. It is also no coincidence that they are occupied almost exclusively by whites. Their improvement cannot solve the problem of the real slums. These slums are not caused by dullness—they are often similar in plan and architecture to low-rent areas—but by the overcrowding of buildings already old by poverty-stricken and otherwise deprived non-whites, who have no other place to go. To be sure, such people usually move into areas being deserted by their previous residents, but even when the older residents are not leaving, the same thing can happen. Chicago's Hyde Park district was not being deserted by its middle-class residents, but portions of it became a slum because the Negro Black Belt to the north simply could not accommodate any more migrants.

Once an area becomes an overcrowded slum, rehabilitating the structures is no solution. The crucial step in rehabilitation is the uncrowding of the buildings. But slum structures are owned by absentee landlords who have no incentive to rehabilitate because they reap immense profits from overcrowding. Even if they were willing to convert rooming houses back to apartments, most of the slum dwellers who would then have to move would not be able to do so. They cannot afford to pay the rentals demanded for an apartment, and since they are non-white, other districts of the city are unwilling to accept them even if there are vacant apartments, which is rarely the case.

The slums cannot be emptied unless and until there is more low-cost housing elsewhere. Private enterprise cannot afford to build such housing. The traditional solution has been to rely on public housing, but thanks to the opposition of the real-estate men and the private builders, it has never been supplied in large enough amounts. Even then, it had to be located in the slums, because other city districts were unwilling to give over vacant or industrial land. In order to minimize clearance, public housing has had to resort to elevator buildings, and in order to protect itself from the surrounding slums, it has constructed fenced-in projects. In order to satisfy its powerful opponents that it was not wasting tax money on ne'er-do-wells, it has had to impose institutional restrictions on its hapless occupants, and in order to avoid competition with the private housing market, it has been forced to expel tenants whose income rises above a certain level.

Mrs. Jacobs suggests that the government stop building public housing, and instead subsidize builders to make their units available to low-income tenants. This is a useful suggestion, and one that has been proposed by planners and public housing advocates before. But earlier attempts to scatter low-income housing in other ways have been rejected by the recipient neighborhoods. Mrs. Jacobs' scheme has more merit than some earlier ones, but I doubt whether middle-class areas in the city and suburbs will make room for the large number of non-white poor who need to be taken out of overcrowded slums.

The sad fact is that until we abolish poverty and discrimination—or until the middle class becomes tolerant of poor non-white neighbors—the government is probably going to have to build more low-income ghettos.

Unfortunately, Mrs. Jacobs' anger with the planners is so intense that she blames them for the sins of private enterprise and the middle class, and she is eager to return functions to private enterprise which it has shown itself unable and unwilling to perform. She also forgets that private enterprise— acting through the well-heeled builder and realtor lobby in Washington—is responsible for some of the more obnoxious features of the urban renewal laws, and for hamstringing public housing in the ways I have indicated. Her blanket indictment of planners detracts from the persuasiveness of her other proposals, and antagonizes people who might agree with her on many points. More important, it is likely to win her the support of those who profit from the status quo, of the nostalgic who want to bring back the city and the society of the 18th and 19th centuries, and of the ultra-right-wing groups who oppose planning—and all government action—whether good or bad.

Orthodox city planning deserves considerable criticism for its anti-urban bias, for giving higher priority to buildings, plans, and design concepts than to the needs of people, and for trying to transform ways of living before even examining how people live or want to live. But not all the planners think this way—actually, much of the theory Mrs. Jacobs rejects was developed by architects and architecturally-trained planners—and some of her ideas have in fact been set forth by planners themselves.

No one, it is true, has stated these ideas as forcefully as she, or integrated them into an over-all approach before. The neighborhoods with which she is most concerned cannot serve as models for future planning, but the way in which she has observed them, the insights she has derived, and the principles she has inferred from her observations can—and ought to be—adapted for use in planning cities and suburbs in the future. Her book is a pathbreaking achievement, and because it is so often right, I am all the more disappointed by the fact that it is also so often wrong.

City Centres Die at Six

WYNDHAM THOMAS

On a fine evening last spring, full of curiosity, I boarded one of Stockholm's fast, clean electric trains. I wanted to see Vällingby, a new semi-detached suburb of Stockholm, which has won a lot of praise from British architects and planners. In no time I was climbing the wide stairs from Vällingby station up into the town centre directly above. The centre is given over almost completely to pedestrians, and contains all the shops, offices, a cinema, a theatre, and several other buildings. And arranged closely around it are the high and low blocks of flats in which Vällingby's 25,000 people live.

    What I had been told by my architect friends about Vällingby's centre—the whole point of my curiosity—was that having all the population housed so close to it meant that it did not die, as our centres are said to do, when the shops close at six; rather, this was a signal for a new burst of human activity, so that it became a gay, bustling, attractive place, giving a heart and a soul to the suburb. I was interested because this, we are all the time being urged, is what we should make of our old and new town centres. The matter is an important one, because it may be taken for granted that the centre of any town or city, whatever its size, unless it is a new town, is going to be largely or completely redesigned and rebuilt in the next ten years or so. In addition, mainly because of the expected increase of 8,000,000 in our population by the nineteen-eighties, we shall have to build at least another twenty new towns and expand a great many more. Even if this scale of population growth does not come about—as I for one fervently hope it does not—we shall still have to have many more new towns to relieve overcrowding in our overgrown cities.

    How, then, should we plan these old and new town centres? We are all agreed that they must be safe for pedestrians, attractive to look at, and pleasing to walk about in. Anyone who has visited one of the new towns, or the rebuilt city centre of Coventry, will have some idea of how a modern centre might look. But in the minds of many architect-planners glow visions

---

    The Listener, LXXI (February 13, 1964), 263–264. Reprinted by permission of the author.

of the centre as the warm, vibrant heart of a single large community. With the shutting of the last shop door, a new way of life will take over. Concerts, films, plays; people dancing, bowling, skating, eating, drinking, strolling, arguing, flirting—each night an endless round of fun and culture. As a picture of human happiness it appeals strongly to the romantic in me. But there are two or three things wrong about it, I think.

The first I learned at Vällingby. For an hour I walked round this most pleasant centre. I admired the superb designs of the furniture, the glassware, and the toys in the shops. I observed everything with care. But I saw about as much life and gaiety as you would find, say, in Wick on a wet Wednesday night. The lesson to me was that if people have good, comfortable homes they are more likely to stay in of an evening than go out, especially in our kind of climate, and even if the centre is outside their front door.

The other mistake many people make is to assume that civilization is the art of living in cities; and that the hallmarks of civilization are theatres, opera-houses, art galleries, cinemas for foreign films, and smart cafés and clubs. This is to confuse civilized behaviour among us all with the cultivated tastes and habits of a small minority; and the great danger of this confusion, in my view, is that a large population is needed close at hand to provide the small minority who will take part in these highly specialized activities. For the sad truth is that the majority among us care little for the live theatre, highbrow music, ballet, or classical art. A friend of mine has worked out that the average Londoner visits the National Gallery once every 200 years.

Further, if you take the view that the best city centre is the one that has the widest range of choice for all sorts of specialized cultural pursuits, it is only a short step to claim that the bigger the city the better; and that London is the best place of all.

I oppose this view passionately. First, you can indulge a wide range of cultural tastes—through radio, television, books, journals, and record-players—while living in a country cottage. But people who equate a piling up of population with social wealth and creative vitality tend to ignore the conditions of life of the large numbers of ordinary families who make up a big city's population.

The following paragraph is from a book by an American, Susan Langer:

> The ordinary city dweller knows nothing of the earth's productivity; he does not know the sunrise and rarely notices when the sun sets; ask him what phase the moon is in or when the tide in the harbour is high, and likely as not he cannot answer. Seed time and harvest are nothing to him. If he has never witnessed an earthquake, a great flood or a hurricane, he probably does not feel the power of nature as a reality at all. His realities are the motors that run elevators . . . and cars, the steady feed of water and gas through the mains and of electricity over the wires, the crates of foodstuffs that arrive at night . . . the concrete and brick, bright steel and dingy woodwork that take the place of earth and waterside and sheltering roof for him . . . Nature, as man has always known it, he knows no more.

Miss Langer thinks that technical progress and the impersonal character of the great clumsy machine called the city are 'putting man's freedom of mind in jeopardy'. There is even greater foreboding in the words of William Parker, chief of police in Los Angeles, who said recently that the trend towards concentrating masses of humanity in big cities is terrible, because these places are conducive to anti-social behavior, and the breakdown of family life and of social order.

Things in Britain may not be that bad—anyway, not yet. We are at least trying to prevent the further outward growth of our largest cities and to reduce, or hold down, the level of population within them. But every time we appear to be making progress towards humanizing our cities, up comes another vision of what glorious places we could make them if only we had the will and would spend the money. This happened recently with the Buchanan report on Traffic in Towns. The report did not advance any particular plans, but it did carry drawings to illustrate possibilities. One showed the city motorist of 1984 gliding along a wide highway, while above and around him rose tiers of concrete decks linked by escalators and pierced by soaring buildings. Perhaps most of us were excited by this particular vision, not because of its architectural quality but because it suggested man's total and permanent control of city form and functioning. Controlled human purposes would have taken over from the crude economic forces which have made so much of our cities shabby, ugly, and oppressive.

One of the clearest conclusions I draw from the Buchanan report is that the smaller the town the easier and cheaper per head of population it is to provide a highway system for 100 per cent. car use. Another is that, given two towns of equal area, it is easier and cheaper to deal with the less densely developed and populated one. Leeds, which is studied in the report, could have a far more adequate road system and would be a far superior place to live and work in if its population could be reduced to 400,000 from 500,000. And how much better London would be if 6,000,000 people lived in it instead of 8,000,000 and if 3,000,000 people worked there instead of 4,000,000. All the logic of the Buchanan report points towards strict limitation of the size of all our big cities, and a reduction of concentration within them—particularly for housing, industry and commerce. Traffic volume is directly related to the size of a city and the degree of concentration within it.

As for city centres, is it not time we dropped the notion that they should cater for almost every kind of urban activity? The centre is a rag-bag holding the large and specialized shops, offices, civic buildings, concert hall, cinemas, cafés, hotels, dance halls, bowling rinks, markets, and flats. As new cars flood on to the roads at the rate of 1,000,000 a year, such a centre will continue to work only if we provide multi-storey car parks and a central road system of enormous scale and cost. Wouldn't life be easier for all of us who live and work in large towns and cities if we sited some of these activities at key points outside the main centre? Say a civic area at one point, an entertainment centre at another, an educational centre at a third, and so on. It would take time to organize the rearrangement, but that matters less than having a coherent guiding plan and as ratepayers spending our money to the best advantage.

The great need still is to make our cities and towns much better places for family life, and especially for women and children. In his report, Professor Buchanan advocated a policy of designing the town's primary road system to create what he calls 'environmental areas'. In this way, housing neighbourhoods would be clearly defined, and only traffic having business in them would enter them. This would make them safer, more peaceful, more humane, as they are in the new towns we are building. The same thing was said twenty years ago by Lewis Mumford, the authority on city design and change. Writing about the post-war plans for Britain, he said that our largest cities, to become fine cities must first become country towns. What he meant was that we must open them out to provide the houses, the parks, the shops and the schools in a series of separate communities together making up the single entity of the city. And the city could then hold an even richer store of cultural, recreational, and educational facilities. The surest way to destroy the city is to allow it to become more congested with people, vehicles, and buildings.

So look carefully at the rebuilding plans for your town, and also at the plans for new towns or cities. Many of them will have their priorities right, and aim first of all to reshape or create cities for families, not the reverse. Look especially closely at plans to crowd people closer together. Ask yourself if any magic would be worked for you—whether you would become happier and more neighbourly—if the whole town were designed to throw you into face-to-face contact with your fellow-citizens the moment you step outside. And whenever you see the words 'exciting' or 'dramatic' to describe some proposal of monumental scale—and every architect wants to build his own monument—recall the words of Truthful James in Brett Hart's [sic] verse:

> Do I sleep, do I dream,
> Do I wonder and doubt?
> Are things what they seem,
> Or is visions about?

Questions

1. Why does Mrs. Jacobs separate the two sentences of paragraph three of her article from paragraph two?
2. To what extent does Mrs. Jacobs use loaded words in her descriptions of the city planners? Are "suburban," "small town," and "paternalistic" in her discussion of Howard loaded? Do Mumford and Gans make use of similar terms? To what extent?
3. Explain Mrs. Jacobs' use of the "fires and murk" analogy.
4. Does Mrs. Jacobs' use of alliteration increase the effectiveness of her style?

5. Is Gans correct in suggesting that our suburbs and cities are not so much the result of bad planning, as Mrs. Jacobs argues, but "expressions of . . . middle-class culture"? Do you have to be a sociologist to discuss this point?
6. Analyze the various schools of planning described by Mrs. Jacobs and Mumford, looking at them from the social class point-of-view which Gans suggests. Does your analysis support Gans's argument?
7. Discuss the ways in which Mumford uses allusion and analogy.
8. Do Gans and Mumford agree on the virtues of Mrs. Jacobs' book?
9. What does Mumford mean by the comment, " 'Silent Spring' came to the big city long before it visited the countryside" ?
10. Does Mumford fall into what Gans describes as "the physical fallacy" ?
11. Mrs. Jacobs describes Lewis Mumford as one of the "Decentrists." Does his essay about her book give evidence that her description is right?
12. Wyndham Thomas' article does not discuss Jane Jacobs' argument. Could his discussion be taken to support, modify, or refute her point of view? Explain.

Assignments

1. Mrs. Jacobs claims that Howard's concept prevented the Garden City from "ever becoming a city." What is her definition of "city"? How does it differ from the definitions of Mumford and Gans? After reading the essays, give your definition of "city."
2. Discuss the relationship between city planning and architecture. Is architecture a branch of city planning or city planning a branch of architecture?
3. Define and compare the position of Mrs. Jacobs and that of Mumford on the relation between life and art.
4. Compare and contrast the three writers' views on the role of the city planner.
5. Gans suggests that newness may make new housing projects and apartment blocks appear more homogeneous and more standardized than older areas. One architect has described the process of modification and differentiation which individualizes the units of a housing project as "folk art." Take an older housing development and describe the folk art which has differentiated it and given it character.
6. Analyze the planning evident in the composition of a city you know well.
7. Describe the methods by which city planning is achieved in the United States today and discuss the effectiveness of these methods.
8. Describe your experience of a particular city. Which writer in this section describes the city in terms closest to yours?

Additional Reading

Jane Jacobs' book, *The Death and Life of Great American Cities* (New York, 1961), has created more controversy among city planners and architects than any other recent book. Comments on the book in periodicals devoted to architecture and the arts include M. Mannes, *Architectural Forum*, CXV (December 1961), 149; E. Goble, *Architectural Record*, CXXX (November 1961), 9; R. Banham, *Arts*, XXXVI (April 1962), 73. A more extensive comment can be found in S. Moholy-Nagy's article, "In Defense of Architecture; Jane Jacobs' Book," *Architectural Forum*, CXVI (April 1962), 19.

Among the classics of city planning, Sir Ebenezer Howard's *Garden Cities of Tomorrow* (reprinted in London, 1951), Frank Lloyd Wright's *The Living City* (New York, 1958), and Le Corbusier's *Concerning Town Planning* (New Haven, Connecticut, 1948) are important.

Lewis Mumford's recent study *The City in History* (New York, 1961) and his earlier *The Culture of Cities* (New York, 1938) and *The Exploding Metropolis* (Garden City, New York, 1958), a concise survey of our urban planning problems by the editors of *Fortune,* provide interesting investigations of various aspects of the city. A recent collection, *City and Country in America* by David R. Weimer (New York, 1962), offers an excellent survey of significant materials on city planning.

IV
Science and Technology

SECTION ONE | The Quick and the Dead on the American Highway

An Analysis of Highway Safety Strategies

WILLIAM HADDON, JR., M.D., M.P.H., AND JAMES L. GODDARD, M.D., M.P.H.

One of the remarkably stable characteristics of highway safety activity is the continuing and chaotic profusions of its claims and programs, all supported vociferously, usually without reference to any reasonably logical and specific conceptual framework within which their general relevance can be evaluated. There is almost invariably a fatal weakness in the link between the specifics of many such activities and the documentation of the ways in which the results claimed for them are supposed to come about. The very dogmatism of the pronouncements, for example with respect to "strict enforcement" and "stricter licensing," to name but two of the customary panaceas, nicely camouflages not only the depth of our ignorance but also the vagueness inherent in such generalizations.

Despite its complexity, there is nothing particularly abstruse about the highway safety area, and it should not be particularly difficult to devise a comprehensive framework within which its various aspects could be classified and their interrelationships and differences at least partially defined. Needless to say, such a framework must necessarily encompass some aspects of the problem previously considered by others, including several of those represented at this conference. Nonetheless, a diligent review of the literature has

From *Passenger Car Design and Highway Safety* (New York: Association for Crippled Children and Consumer's Union of U. S., Inc., 1962), pp. 6–11. Reprinted by permission of the Association for Crippled Children and the authors. The concepts presented in this selection have been extended and further developed in William Haddon, Jr., E. A. Suchman, and D. Klein, *Accident Research—Methods and Approaches* (New York: Harper and Row, 1964), 752 pp.

failed to reveal the formulation of any adequately comprehensive and logical framework within which may be classified *all* of the measures now proposed or in use. Consequently, it is the purpose of this paper to present such a framework in a condensed form and to suggest that through its use it is possible to define the tactics for a logical and scientifically weighted approach to the highway safety problem.[1]

There are four basic strategies that may be used in attempting to reduce property damage, injury, and death. These represent attempts to interfere with the causal sequence at four consecutive levels in the progression of events that produces the undesirable end results. Analogous strategies are widely employed with respect to other major public health problems. These four strategies are listed by title in Table I.

TABLE I. *Over-all Strategies for the Prevention of Property Damage, Injury, and Death*

    I   Modify Vehicle Use.
   II   Reduce Accidents.
  III   Modify Immediate Effects of Accidents.
  IV   Modify Subsequent Effects of Accidents.

Most discussion of highway safety measures has centered on the second of these and, to a much smaller extent, on the third, particularly from the standpoint of crash injury prevention.

In discussing any safety measure, it is essential that its position in this framework be clearly recognized and defined, and it is hoped that this suggestion will be followed throughout this conference. This is particularly the case, since the vehicle enters into consideration not only with respect to accident prevention (Strategy II), property damage, and crash injury reduction (Strategy III), but also with respect to both Strategy I and, particularly, Strategy IV. It should be noted that the listing of any strategy, substrategy, or tactic carries with it no presumption of either pertinence or practical value, since such questions can be answered only at the subsequent stage of the evaluation of the significance and potential utility of the accumulated scientific evidence relative to each point.

Table II summarizes substrategies and tactics under Strategy I, the modification of vehicle use.

TABLE II. *Substrategies and Sample Tactics for the Modification of Vehicle Use*

    1. Decrease *amount* of use (*e.g.*, encourage use of trains; ban motor vehicles).
    2. Alter *circumstances* of use (*e.g.*, taxis for cocktail parties; police drive revelers home).
    3. Alter *manner* of use (*e.g.*, use governors to limit speed).

---

[1] The analytical framework employed represents an expansion of a similar analysis prepared in August 1960 by W. Haddon, Jr. and D. P. Moynihan for use in The Public Executive, a course given in the Management Development Institute of the Maxwell Graduate School, Syracuse University.

4. Alter *place* of use (*e.g.*, circumferential highways).
5. Alter *time* of use (*e.g.*, stagger business and shopping hours).

It is readily seen that though there are current practices which illustrate most of these approaches, insufficient data are available to make possible an objective assessment of the possibilities they offer. For example, it might seem reasonable to expect theoretically on a priori grounds that the total elimination of the substantial morning vehicular commuter traffic into New York would result in a substantial decrease in accidental death, but this supposition is not supported by the fact that of a series of 43 fatal accidents in New York City involving drivers of passenger cars only one occurred in the three hours ending at 9 A.M.[2] (This suggests, incidentally, that the denominator of vehicle mileage, otherwise unqualified, may be a poor measure for highway safety purposes.) In short, so sparse is the evidence with respect to this group of approaches that it is not possible at present to estimate its potential, a situation not dissimilar to that encountered in the other areas to be discussed.

Table III summarizes substrategies and tactics under the reduction of accident occurrence.

TABLE III. *Substrategies and Sample Tactics for the Reduction of Accidents*

1. Highway (*e.g.*, eliminate railroad crossings; sand icy spots; limit access).
2. Vehicle (*e.g.*, eliminate blowouts and brake failures).
3. Driver (*e.g.*, eliminate drunks; educate drivers; change social and cultural environment with respect to drinking; eliminate roadhouses).
4. Pedestrian (*e.g.*, supervise children; educate the elderly; restrain drunks).
5. Interaction of above (*e.g.*, increase efficiency of driver-machine relationship: "human engineering"; separate pedestrian from vehicle traffic).

Here, too, although many current measures fall into this group, adequate evidence with respect to their efficacy is lacking. However, rather than anticipate the subsequent conference discussion with respect to the vehicle *per se*, let us consider an unrelated example which well demonstrates the extent to which conclusions used to justify major highway safety measures may be based at least in part upon inappropriate evidence.

This example stems from the widespread use of the lower injury and death rates per vehicle mile driven on limited access highways as the basis of estimates of the number of lives to be saved through their construction. Unfortunately, it is quite possible that differences in the characteristics of the users of such roads in comparison with the users of adjacent local roads account for at least a portion of the rate differences observed, a point which has yet to be investigated. For example, it is likely that party-goers and bar-hoppers tend to use differentially the local roads, with the result that their accidents are to a corresponding extent not represented in the limited-access

[2] "A Controlled Study of Fatal Automobile Accidents in New York City," by J. R. McCarroll and W. Haddon, Jr. In press: *Journal of Chronic Diseases.*

rates. Further, such rates are based upon deaths and injuries per *vehicle* mile and have yet to be reduced to a *passenger* mile basis. Since there are probably differences in the average number of persons at risk per vehicle in the two types of exposure, the vehicle-mile figure may be biased to an unknown extent.

Table IV*a* summarizes the substrategies and tactics for decreasing the severity of the collision of the vehicle with its environment. Table IV*b* summarizes the substrategies and tactics for decreasing the severity of the "second accident"—*i.e.*, the collision of the occupant or pedestrian with the vehicle.

TABLE IV*a*. *Substrategies and Sample Tactics for Decreasing Severity and Abruptness of Collision of Vehicle with its Environment*

1. Highway environment (*e.g.*, no trees along sides; shield abutments).
2. Vehicle (*e.g.*, strengthening the "package"; provision for energy absorption).
3. Driver (*e.g.*, training in "crash landing").

TABLE IV*b*. *Substrategies and Sample Tactics for Decreasing Severity of Collision of Occupant or Pedestrian with Vehicle*

1. Interior vehicle design:
    a. passive (*e.g.*, crash padding; eliminate low-radius curves; energy-absorbing glass).
    b. active (*e.g.*, seat belts).
2. Exterior vehicle design (*e.g.*, elimination of sharp hood ornaments, headlight hoods, and low radius curves; energy-absorbing impact points).
3. Occupant selection (*e.g.*, eliminate fragile old ladies).
4. Occupant armor (*e.g.*, crash helmets).

Although these groupings might be discussed at length, one point is particularly noteworthy. This is the distinction between "active" and "passive" means of reducing the severity of the "second accident"—the collision of the passenger or pedestrian with the vehicle. It has been the consistent experience of public health agencies concerned with the reduction of other causes of morbidity and mortality that measures which do not require the continued, active cooperation of the public are much more efficacious than those which do. Consequently, a much higher value and, hence, priority should be placed on proven measures in the "passive" than in the "active" area. This also implies that the introduction of such measures as energy-absorbing steering wheels, for example, should not be made dependent upon public demand.

Table V*a* summarizes substrategies and tactics concerned with decreasing costs of repairs and replacements, and V*b* those concerned with decreasing human and financial costs of injury.

Since Table V*a* concerns the vehicle, its contents will be left for subsequent discussion during the conference. With respect to the reduction of the

TABLE va. *Substrategies and Sample Tactics for Decreasing Cost of Repair and Replacement*

1. Vehicle (*e.g.*, more standardization of parts; design for easier, quicker replacement and lower cost).
2. Environment (*e.g.*, move shop fronts out of range to reduce cost of repairs).

TABLE vb. *Substrategies and Sample Tactics for Decreasing Human and Financial Cost of Injury*

1. Improve availability and quality of emergency medical care to reduce acute and chronic results.
2. Improve availability and quality of rehabilitation.
3. Decrease costs of medical care and rehabilitation.
4. Develop more successful treatment for results of injury (*e.g.*, better facial plastic surgery and better treatment for epilepsy resulting from traumatic brain damage, a not uncommon result of motor-vehicle accidents).

results of injury, however, suffice it to say that much remains to be done. Among the most important problems is the provision of better emergency care in view of the fact that relatively few of those fatally injured live more than a few hours. However, since a very large majority are dead within minutes of their accidents, such deaths can be prevented only by strategies aimed at earlier points in the sequence of which death is the frequent end result.[3]

The preceding discussion presents a logical analysis of possible highway safety measures. It cannot by itself resolve the next problem: that of choosing priorities among the tactics to which it points, because choice of priorities must depend upon acceptable evidence weighed in the practical context. It is the purpose of Dr. Bross's presentation, which follows, to outline some of the scientific ground rules under which evidence must be evaluated, and it is the purpose of the later presentations to give that evidence with respect to the vehicle in its manifold potential contributions to highway safety.

Speed Regulation

SPEED AND ACCIDENTS

1. Most accidents are the result of two or more contributing factors or circumstances. Improper speed is frequently one of these whether it be speed in excess of legal limits, or other speed too fast or too slow for conditions.

---

[3] *Ibid.*

From *Speed Regulation*, Report of the Committee on Speed Traffic and Transportation Conferences (Chicago: National Safety Council, 1965), pp. 3–8. Reprinted by permission of the National Safety Council.

2. Speeds much higher than those of normal traffic make it more difficult to avoid accidents in an emergency, bring the motorist to a point of conflict sooner than other motorists and pedestrians expect, and increase the severity of the resulting injury and/or damage.

3. Many accidents occur at locations and at times where relatively low speeds are too fast for conditions. Since accidents occur over the entire speed range, the speed control program must be directed at speed too fast for conditions, as well as at speed in excess of the legal limits.

4. Slow moving vehicles are an accident hazard on a busy highway because they impede the free flow of traffic and frequently induce other vehicles to pass at locations and at times where the maneuver cannot be made with safety.

5. Improper speed is especially important as a contributing factor in those accidents involving only one motor vehicle, and is even more important in single motor vehicle accidents where the motor vehicle leaves the roadway.

6. In accidents involving two or more vehicles, one of which was traveling at improper speed, actions of other drivers are often important contributing causes. Violations by these non-speeding drivers set up situations which drivers of vehicles being operated at an improper speed cannot avoid without accident.

LEGISLATION

7. The speed provisions of the Uniform Vehicle Code and Model Traffic Ordinance should be used as a guide in preparing speed legislation for consideration by states and cities.

EDUCATION

8. Education is an essential portion of the speed control program for cities and states. It is imperative that the public realize the dangers of improper speed, understand the speed laws, the meaning of speed signs and how to adjust their speeds to conditions of driver, vehicle and roadway.

ENGINEERING

9. Street and highway improvements through engineering redesign are the responsibility of public officials. Speed zoning at hazardous locations does not release officials from this responsibility.

10. Speed zoning is required on all arterial streets according to the Uniform Vehicle Code and is recommended for use at other locations where the general speed limits are not appropriate.

11. State traffic engineering authorities should prepare procedures and warrants for the establishment of speed zones.

12. Numerical limits for speed zones should be determined by an

engineering and traffic investigation. But no person should drive a vehicle on a highway at a speed greater than is reasonable and prudent under the conditions and having regard to the actual and potential hazards then existing.

13. The latest edition of the Manual on Uniform Traffic Control Devices for Streets and Highways should be used as a guide by states and cities for proper signs and posting of speed limits.

14. Controlled access facilities permit traffic operation at higher speeds and with heavier volumes than do more conventional highways. In spite of higher speeds, accident and fatality rates on such facilities are lower provided there is adequate supervision.

15. Any contention that vehicle horsepower has a bearing on accident rates can be resolved only by further study. It would appear, however, that if speed itself can be considered as having a direct bearing on accident rates, almost any standard production vehicle, regardless of horsepower, is capable of attaining dangerous speeds.

ENFORCEMENT

16. The speed enforcement program must promote the belief among road users that speed laws and enforcement policies are reasonable, that the police are always present, that detected violations will result in police action, and that punishment will be certain and adequate. While the police cannot do this alone, they must do all within their means to effect it, working through courts which understand and support enforcement objectives.

17. An effective enforcement program should provide a proper balance between speed enforcement and speed as a causative factor in accidents. A substantial number of on-view enforcement actions should be taken for speeding which is improper or unsafe, even though not in excess of posted limits. Speed violations in accidents need to be pinpointed, both for effective identification of accident causes and to enable specific corrective enforcement action where speed violations are apparent.

18. Written warnings, if properly recorded and followed up, are useful in limited cases, but should not be used in place of arrests or citations for violation of basic speed laws or rules of the road. Oral instruction is useful in helping drivers whose minor misbehavior is clearly due to inexperience or lack of information, but this should not be considered as a "warning."

19. Tolerances for violations of fixed speed limits should be only in the amount necessary to compensate for reasonable human and mechanical errors in determining speed. In pacing with a patrol vehicle, or in using approved fixed-position speed measurement techniques, a margin of five miles per hour is reasonable. Any additional "allowance" is an extension or distortion of the law.

20. The term "speed trap" for legitimate enforcement activities should

not be used. The use of fixed-position speed measuring devices, because they increase enforcement potential five to ten-fold, requires that extreme care be exercised as to type of device used, adequate public information in advance of enforcement use, and proper techniques be followed to assure accuracy. Primarily such devices should be used to supplement other enforcement methods. Their use should not lessen speed enforcement efforts by moving patrols, or give undue emphasis to speed violations in the total enforcement program.

21. Enforcement should not be expected to compensate entirely for inadequacies of other essential control elements, especially legislation and traffic engineering.

The Speed Problem

Speed and its control is one of the most important, difficult and controversial problems of traffic safety. It is important because speed violation is the most frequent violation noted on reports of fatal accidents today. It is difficult because there is usually no way of knowing definitely whether vehicles were going at an unsafe speed prior to being involved in accidents.

The Committee has recognized the basic concept that the speed control program must permit motorists to go to their destinations as rapidly as possible with safety. This is necessary if we are to have efficient transportation. The problem must be approached from a factual basis, first finding out what dangerous speed is, and what speeds are safe for various combinations of conditions. The speed control program should endeavor to do away with unsafe speed without unduly restricting drivers at times and at places where higher speeds can be permitted with safety.

The following section deals with the evaluation of speed as a factor in accidents. The remainder of the study deals with the determination of safe speeds, and the elements in a reasonable speed control action program, including legislation, engineering, education and enforcement.

Speed as a Factor in Accidents

Speed, as velocity, is an element in every accident, since if cars did not move, accidents would not occur. The higher the speed, the greater the chance for an accident because there is less time to maneuver or to stop to avoid one. However, speed may not be a contributing factor unless it is improper because of the physical, traffic and weather conditions present.

A speed is considered "too fast for conditions" when it is higher than the maximum speed at which the average prudent motorist would drive under the same conditions at the same location. The speed may not be a high speed, and in some cases may not be as fast as the legal speed limit.

High speed is usually considered as speed in excess of some arbitrary value such as 60 miles per hour. High speed may be excessive under some conditions and not excessive under others. Similarly, speeds in excess of legal limits are not necessarily speeds "too fast for conditions."

FREQUENCY OF REPORTED SPEED VIOLATIONS *

About three out of 10 drivers in fatal accidents were violating a speed law, according to reports from 18 states. Specifically, violations were reported for 32 per cent of the drivers (22 per cent were exceeding stated speed limits, and 10 per cent were exceeding safe speeds although traveling at less than the stated speed limits or on roads where no stated limits existed).

These speed violations were factors in 38 per cent of the fatal accidents, even though only 32 per cent of the drivers were violating. In some two-vehicle accidents only one driver was speeding, so speed was reported for a higher percentage of accidents than of drivers.

City accident summaries showed only 21 per cent of the drivers in fatal accidents violating speed laws, compared with rural summaries which showed 38 per cent. However, since accident summaries are based partly on reports of drivers, who often believe low speeds are safe regardless of conditions, differences in urban and rural per cents must be interpreted with caution.

REPORTED VIOLATIONS PER 100 DRIVERS

Excessive speed was the most important driver violation in both urban and rural areas. Failure to yield right of way was next in urban areas. Failure to keep to right of center line was next in rural areas. [See Figure I.]

APPROXIMATE SPEED AT TIME OF ACCIDENT

The table below gives the distribution by reported speed of vehicles involved in fatal accidents in 1956. The figures are based on reports from the following numbers of states: statewide—18, urban—9, rural—14.

The figures do not indicate the relative hazard of driving at each speed, because information is not available on the per cent of all cars on the road being driven at each speed.

Distribution of Vehicles in Fatal Accidents by Reported Speed

AREA	TOTAL	Standing	1–10 mph.	11–20 mph.	21–30 mph.	31–40 mph.	41–50 mph.	51–60 mph.	61–70 mph.	71 and over mph.
Statewide	100%	3%	6%	9%	12%	16%	20%	15%	10%	9%
Urban	100%	4%	10%	20%	28%	18%	9%	6%	3%	2%
Rural	100%	3%	5%	6%	8%	16%	22%	18%	11%	11%

* 1957 "Accident Facts," National Safety Council.

FIGURE I

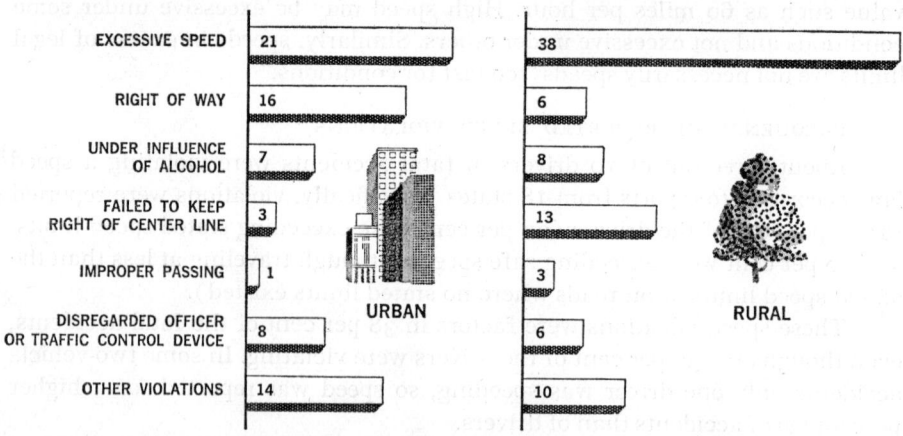

(SOURCE: 1957 "Accident Facts," National Safety Council)

SPEED AND ACCIDENT SEVERITY *

The following table shows the ratio of fatal accidents to all accidents for different reported speeds. Ratios are partly estimated on the basis of state reports.

Reported Speed (Miles per Hour)	Chance of Someone Being Killed If an Accident Happens **	
	All Accidents †	Rural Accidents ‡
25	1 in 300	1 in 125
35	1 in 115	1 in 75
45	1 in 70	1 in 50
55	1 in 40	1 in 30
65	1 in 20	1 in 15
75	1 in 8	1 in 7

Speeds used in this section are determined from summaries of motor vehicle accident reports submitted to the National Safety Council by the cities and states. Accident reports are completed by drivers involved and by Enforcement officials. Speeds reported are in most cases estimated speed at moment preceding accident.

* 1957 "Accident Facts."
** Ratios do not indicate chances of an accident happening at different speeds—only the chances of someone being killed if an accident does happen.
† Based on reports from 19 states.
‡ Based on reports from 11 states.

SPEED AND INJURY

In the annual report published by Cornell University Medical College on Automotive Crash Injury Research, and covering the period ending March 31, 1957, the following findings of a survey studying over 2,000 injury-producing accidents were reported:
1. Approximately 75 per cent of the cars were traveling at speeds under 60 mph. About 85 per cent *impacted* at speeds under 60 mph.
2. The relationship between increases in speeds and the frequency of dangerous or fatal injuries in these injury-producing accidents were examined; these findings resulted:
    a. An overall view of all speed ranges showed steady increases in the frequency of these grades of injury as impact or traveling speeds increased.
    b. The increases in these grades of injury were relatively small in the ranges progressing up to 50 mph. impact speeds and 60 mph. traveling speeds. Beyond these points the increases in dangerous or fatal grades of injury became more marked.
    c. Among all the persons traveling below 60 mph. (or impacting below 50 mph.), 6 per cent sustained dangerous or fatal grades of injury. Among all the persons traveling above 60 mph. (or impacting above 50 mph.), 17 per cent sustained such injuries. However, this near-tripling of the risk of dangerous or fatal grades of injury seen when the speeds were in the "high" ranges applied only to the occupants of 25 per cent of all cars studied.
3. Many factors other than speed operated to produce injury. Even if it had been possible to control completely the speeds to a maximum of 49 mph., 60 per cent of the dangerous or fatal injuries would still have occurred.
4. Other factors influencing injury were ejection from automobile, seat area occupied (driver, center front, left rear, etc.), and external site of crash impact.
5. Interpretation of the data also brought these two hypotheses about injury-producing accidents:
    a. Dangerous or fatal injuries observed in accidents where the traveling speed was less than 60 mph. are influenced far more by the design characteristics of objects which the occupant may contact than by the speed at which the cars were traveling before the accident.
    b. Those injuries in accidents where the speeds were above 60 mph. are closely associated with speed *plus* interior design characteristics and possibly other accident-injury variables such as type of accident, area of impact, etc.

Additional studies are being made by Cornell University Medical College since results of the first study have indicated that control of speed without simultaneous control of interior component design imposes severe limitations on the extent of injury reduction possible.

The Case for Fast Drivers

ROBERT L. SCHWARTZ

More than a clutch of my fellow Americans seem seized with the notion that we live at the mercy of maniacal speed demons who are making death traps of our highway system.

The myth about "the dangerous high-speed driver" is almost a perfect example of a mass search for a scapegoat: there *must* be someone at fault in the complicated, depressing highway-accident situation—sure enough, it's the high-speed driver. A substantial set of "facts" supports the myth. The facts, all completely wrong, usually go like this: (1) Auto deaths are increasing at a tremendous rate. (2) The resulting highway carnage is practically a national disgrace. (3) The chief cause is high-speed driving. (4) The "horsepower race"—the reckless insistence of automobile manufacturers on building cars with more and more powerful engines—is a major supporting cause. (5) A hard core of fast drivers is particularly dangerous. (6) Constant safety campaigns to increase public awareness of danger are important. (7) The real solution, however, is lower speed limits.

These truths are all false. The actual facts are these.

Auto deaths are not increasing. In absolute terms, the annual death toll has not only risen but fallen several times during the past three decades. Its highs were 39,969 in 1941 and 40,900 in 1962; its low, 23,823 in 1943. And in relative terms, the toll has decreased markedly. Although more Americans drive more every year, the rate of deaths per mile driven has been cut by better than two thirds over the past thirty years—from a high of 16.7 deaths per 100 million vehicle miles in 1934 to a current 5.3 deaths per 100 million vehicle miles. Traffic deaths once accounted for 3 per cent of all U. S. fatalities; they are now less than 2 per cent.

The annual death toll from highway accidents in the United States is lower than the death toll from pneumonia. This is not "carnage."

Over 85 per cent of all U. S. traffic accidents are caused by factors other than high speed. More than half of the fatal auto accidents in the U. S. happen at speeds below 40 mph. If no one in the country drove over 50 mph last year, 60 per cent of all fatalities would still have occurred.

The greater a car's horsepower, the less likely it is to become involved in an accident. Statistics prove that there is a direct relationship at every level between higher horsepower and fewer accidents.

There are practically no "high-speed drivers" as a constant group; a man's own driving speeds vary more from hour to hour or from day to day than they do from those of other motorists. A man killed at 40 mph today on a rural highway was going 65 mph yesterday—and he was safer then by 300 per cent.

Safety campaigns are more than a bore. They're a menace. By scaring the timid and by emotionalizing danger, they only add another disturbing ingredient to the highway problem.

Finally, and perhaps most surprising, there is evidence that lowering speed limits tends to *induce* accidents, while raising the limits prevents them.

These disclosures make a mockery of most of the nation's speed laws, speed limits, and speed enforcement, under which some three million Americans were arrested for speeding last year. Local traffic cops, safety officials, and police-court judges may, indeed, be causing more automobile fatalities than they prevent.

Most of this information comes from a survey submitted to Congress in February 1959 by the Bureau of Public Roads of the Department of Commerce. Called "The Federal Role in Highway Safety," it reports on a massive study of rural driving authorized by the Federal-Aid Highway Act of 1956—the same law that provided for the huge interstate highway system now under construction. The survey, the most comprehensive of its kind ever made, covered 600 miles of highway in eleven states and included roadside interviews with no fewer than 290,000 drivers. It amassed statistics on 3.7 billion miles of travel and on accidents involving 10,000 vehicles. It took three years to complete, and when it was finished there was so much data that conclusions had to be obtained by feeding the figures into a high-speed computer.

Its findings have subsequently been supported by independent studies conducted by several states—a few of which have quietly changed their speed laws as a result.* Nevertheless the report has been widely overlooked by traffic officials and entirely ignored by the public at large, possibly because the most dramatic conclusions were buried deep in an otherwise unremarkable government pamphlet.

Statistically the study is beyond reproach. Indeed, it is the only study to have measured the percentages of motorists traveling at different speeds, so

---

* Among the more enlightened traffic experts and highway officials who have urged changes as a result of the study, often after confirming state studies of their own: Wilbur S. Smith, Connecticut; J. Edward Johnston, Utah; J. C. Womack, California; J. E. P. Darrell, Minnesota; Martin E. Bruening, Wisconsin; J. P. Mills, Jr., Virginia; Burton W. Marsh, AAA; John E. Baerwald, University of Illinois; Harold L. Michael, Purdue.

that it is possible to reach conclusions like this one: A motorist driving at 65 mph on a main rural highway will go almost three times as far before a fatality (22 million miles) as a man going 35 mph (8 million miles). In other words, more people aren't killed at 35 mph because more are driving at 35 mph; more are killed because 35 is a less safe speed on a main rural highway than 65, mile by mile.

The logic to this seeming paradox is simple: a sustained high-speed traffic flow is far safer than a shifting current of fast- and slow-moving vehicles. It is best to set and maintain a speed limit which acknowledges the desire of most motorists to get where they're going within an increasingly shorter time.

Let Fast Drivers Rule

What would happen if the speed limits on all U. S. main rural highways were lowered to 40 mph? By hypothetically projecting the available data, we come up with a national death toll from auto accidents of 90,000—well over double the present figure. Grim support for such an estimate comes from the Pennsylvania Turnpike statistics: when a 1942 Presidential directive reduced Turnpike speeds from 70 to 35, in order to save wartime gas and tires, the Turnpike death toll shot up to its highest accident and fatality level—before or since.

Raising rural speed limits to 70, on the other hand, would probably cut the national death toll by as much as 5,000. In the New York City area today, the high-speed Garden State Parkway (60 mph, casually enforced) has less than half as many fatalities, mile for mile, as the less crowded, nearby Palisades Interstate Parkway (45 mph, rigidly enforced).

Tickets, under our present system, usually go to the safest drivers. As state surveys have repeatedly shown, the fast drivers are the ones who tend to go at safe speeds, regardless of the rules. Sensibly, many states have taken this lesson to heart and begun to let the drivers themselves determine speed limits. Assuming that, though most motorists ignore unreasonable curbs, they still have a strong, sane interest in their own survival, officials of these states set the maximum speed being used by 85 per cent of motorists as the limit. Most drivers respond to such adult treatment by slightly *lowering* their previous speed.

Where Illinois officials did a statewide test of this theory in 45 low-speed-limit areas, the obedience rate rose by 119 per cent, the average speed declined from 42.6 to 42.4 mph, and accidents declined 36 per cent from 62 a year to 40.

Results in Utah were much the same. On a two-lane highway west of Salt Lake City, the 85 percentile figure indicated a proper limit of 60, not the posted 40, which was being ignored by 95 per cent of motorists. Despite a huge public outcry because school buses were loaded in one section of the area and because the accident rate was already high, the authorities pressed ahead. What happened? Though speed limits had been raised 20 mph, the average speed through the area was reduced, legal limits were observed by 95 per cent of motorists instead of 5 per cent, and accidents declined in one year from 10 to 3 on this highway.

Similarly, when the Nebraska Highway Department raised the speed limits on Highway U. S. 30 as it went through twenty-eight Nebraska villages and towns, the accident rate fell 34 per cent.

In Oregon and in Virginia, merely the observance of speed limits was tested. The finding: in every one of nearly 1,000 cases where speed limits were *raised*, traffic speeds declined.

These findings fly in the face of all previous "logic" about speed, speed limits, and accidents. Perhaps it will pay to look at the earlier "logic" in action. Which brings us to "Safe Driving Day." This long-planned, widely heralded effort occurred on December 1, 1955. Sponsored by a Presidential committee with over two hundred cooperating national organizations, it was the nation's most massive attempt at an emotional approach to traffic safety. Unfortunately, the death toll climbed 10 per cent on "Safe Driving Day." Since a prior "dry-run" also increased the traffic toll, and the final performance confirmed it, the plan has been abandoned.

Another emotional effort for safety was a 1960 one-hour CBS television documentary called "The Great Holiday Massacre," narrated by Edward R. Murrow. Though thoughtfully done, the show featured screaming sirens, injured children, sheet-covered victims, and other emotion-loaded scenes. A subsequent audience poll by the National Safety Council found that the number of people who felt personally involved in the auto-accident problem had declined by 50 per cent; most viewers could not personally "identify" with the gore, and instead "transferred" their feelings of involvement to certain bad drivers featured on the show.

Emotional approaches to traffic safety, accompanied by our fixation with speed, have done still more serious damage by drying up any interest, and any funds, for a truly scientific study of auto accidents. As a result, practically nothing is known about them. Post-accident investigation is almost nonexistent. The police do little more than see that victims are sent to morgue or hospital and wreckage is cleared from the highway. Detailed mechanical, engineering, medical, and psychological studies are not attempted. The simplest report for a policeman to make is "Driving too fast," and, being human, he usually makes it.

In court, most motorists charged with speeding are understandably readier to plead guilty and leave than to plead not guilty and extend the proceedings. Thus the traffic court doesn't act as a corrective or a teaching influence either. What it does do is bring in money. Since contemporary folklore regards the arrest of speeders as almost noble, and since it is clearly profitable, there is a subtle pressure to keep low speed limits for their income potential—which is enormous. In 1951, for example, 47,000 summonses issued to speeders on the New York City parkway system brought in almost half a million dollars in fines.

Is Life Worth $5?

The saddest and heaviest loss caused by the traffic myths is in research. Quite possibly, more money has been spent on scientific study of any *one* major air crash than has been spent on the serious study of *all* of several million typical auto accidents. An average of $100,000 per victim goes into air-crash research. An average of less than five dollars per victim goes for auto fatalities. The difference in quality of the research is even greater than the difference in dollars.

Private and government studies continually lead to changes in airline procedures, techniques, and equipment (the Boeing 707 and the Douglas DC-8 have each had over 250 design modifications for increased safety—and more will come). But a typical auto "safety" effort usually leads absolutely nowhere. In 1960, for instance, the "coveted Alfred P. Sloan radio and TV award for distinguished public service in highway safety" was given to radio station WCCC in Hartford, Connecticut. What did the station do? It gave schoolteachers three thousand apples, each with a cellophane wrapper plugging safety—and also plugging radio station WCCC.

The incredible truth of the matter is that there is not one single study of the causes of the typical automobile accident, despite the millions of dollars spent for promoting highway safety. (Useful work done at Cornell, Minnesota, and the University of California, Los Angeles, is excluded since it deals with impact, seat belts, and other factors affecting survival *after* an accident. It does not attempt to study the *cause* of the accident. Hardly anybody does.)

The only serious study worthy of respect is one now under way at the Harvard Medical School, under a grant from the U. S. Public Health Service, and this study, as massive, complex, and thoughtful as it is, deals only with a fraction of highway accidents: those which are fatal. One of the earliest things learned by the Harvard group was that the fatal accident is a wholly different breed of animal from the nonfatal accident. Thus the typical or nonfatal accident is still unstudied and uncharted.

Researchers at Harvard investigate fatal auto accidents in the same painstaking detail as is used after air crashes. A team of scientists from many fields pores over the accident site, examining and recording everything. A mechanical and engineering group studies the wrecked cars, the highway, the collision course. An automotive engineer looks for possible auto malfunctioning prior to the crash. Another group of scientists studies the victims involved. This group includes a pathologist, chemist, technician, sociologist, internist, psychiatrist, ophthalmologist, optometrist, statistician, clergyman, and attorney. They examine survivors, witnesses, and others knowing the past history of the principals in the accident. In most cases, they do an autopsy on dead drivers to study (a) possible death or physical impairment prior to accident, (b) influence of alcohol, medication, or drugs, if any, and (c) actual cause of death.

Granted funds to study accidents in depth over a five-year period, the group has examined over two hundred fatal accidents so far. No overall results are yet available, but the fractional returns are interesting and enlightening.

Deadly Simple Slipups

Among the first things that became clear about fatal accidents was that generally accepted "causes" won't stand up. For instance, the three most widely believed accident causes are speed, traffic violations, and lack of courtesy. These turned out to be without significance.

What does produce accidents? The answer is very simple—and very complex. Fatal accidents are caused by small things, simple, everyday human or mechanical or highway failures. But they always team up. A list of the causes of any hundred fatal accidents would run over two hundred items.

Let us take one of the fatal accidents studied by the Harvard group. On the police records, the cause was "speeding," and there was a belief that intoxicants were a factor. The case was thus ended for police purposes.

There were actually four "causes" of the fatalities. Here, with names and locale changed, is what happened:

At 2:00 P.M. of a clear October afternoon, Miss Jane Smith and Miss Mabel Jones were returning to Boston from a trip to Gloucester. As they came over the crest of a hill on Route 128, they were in the left (high-speed) lane but were actually within the speed limit (50 mph). At this moment (Cause Number 1) the right-front tire of Miss Smith's car lost all its air. This was not a blowout; this was a *maintenance failure*. Some weeks earlier, Miss Smith's practically new tubeless tire had been cut by a rock and had gone slowly flat. The gas-station man "fixed" it by pouring some rubber-like glop over the inside of the scar. But the cut "sawed" back and forth on itself, and finally sawed through the repair compound. (The tire should have been thrown away. Did Miss Smith insist on repair instead of replacement? Did the garageman recommend repair as adequate? Or did he tell her he'd replaced her tire when he'd only "fixed" it? No one knows.)

At this point, Miss Smith was not in real trouble. At her speed and with the low density of traffic around her, she should have had no difficulty taking her car slowly off the road and gently braking to a stop. But Miss Smith (Cause Number 2) had *inadequate driving skills* for this situation. She promptly turned a minor problem into a major crisis. She vigorously grabbed the wheel to straighten the wobbly course of her car, and she slammed on the brakes. A straight-line "panic stop" with a flat tire is virtually impossible. Miss Smith's car swerved way to the right and went up on the wide, grassy berm alongside the road. Happy day! Miss Smith was now safely out of traffic, pointed in the right direction, and had one-half mile of grass paralleling the road in which to roll gently to a stop with moderate periodic braking. But Miss Smith didn't know about stopping gently with a blowout. She kept her brakes on hard. And now she was on grass. Her car swung back left and headed across her side of the highway toward the dividing grassy mall in the center.

At this point, no one still need have died. But Cause Number 3 was looming ahead. The mall was too narrow and had no guardrail to separate opposing traffic. If (Cause Number 3) *inadequate highway environment* had not been a factor, Miss Smith might have bounced along a retaining barrier and come to a noisy, fender-bending halt, hurt but still alive. (Divider barriers on roads with center malls drastically reduce fatalities by preventing head-on collisions.)

But by now, (1) Bad Maintenance (2) Inadequate Driving Skills, and (3) Inadequate Highway Environment had already gone a long way toward causing a fatal accident. At this point, one and possibly two persons were apparently doomed to death, but Cause Number 4 was still to take an additional life.

Miss Smith went across the mall and into the path of a car being driven by David Brown, returning from the beach with his family of four. Brown was in the fast lane and was going approximately 50 mph. Miss Smith, her speed now down to, say, 40, smashed at an angle right into the middle of the front bumper of Brown's car.

A head-on collision is always serious because of the combined speeds of the two cars, in this case, approximately 90 mph. What happened was predictable—though little understood and quite startling. Both cars hit each other four times. In an action much like the bouncing ping-g-g-g when a hammer strikes an anvil, the two cars impacted again and again and again, with such force that one bolt of the Smith car made four distinct, close-together dents in the bumper of the other car. (Passengers are also subject to this injury-producing series of impacts.) In the instant that this was happening, the rears of both cars rose high in the air. An impacting car, whether it hits a tree, a wall, or another car, always goes down in the front and way up in the rear. This action flipped Miss Smith and Miss Jones right through the windshield of their car and sent Miss Jones completely over the Browns' car and into the windshield of a third car, trailing behind Brown. This windshield did not break, but splintered, and the driver, braking hard but without success, smashed under the raised rear end of the Browns' car, still off the ground from impact. So quickly did all this occur that Miss Jones was dead against the windshield of the third car before Brown's car had even settled to the ground.

When the noise and dust had settled, Miss Smith and Miss Jones were dead, Brown, the driver of the second car, was mortally injured (he would die twenty-nine days later while apparently recovering), and all six other passengers were injured.

One safety device almost saved Brown; another saved the driver of the third car. Brown would have died instantly but for the deep-dish steering wheel (a product of Cornell research) which cushioned his impact against the steering column. The driver of the third car would have been killed by the arrival of Miss Jones through his windshield if it had not been safety glass of high-strength modern construction. As it was, no one—neither police nor survivors—would believe that Miss Jones had actually hit that windshield until the Harvard researchers showed lab tests proving the hair on it was hers. The police also (a) would not believe Miss Smith wasn't speeding, (b) would not accept the wobbly brake marks as indicating she had had a flat tire prior to impact, (c) were indifferent to the cut-and-repaired tire as additional evidence, and (d) preferred to ignore an autopsy report showing no alcohol in Miss Smith's blood. Instead, they accepted the "direct evidence" of their observation that Miss Smith was found with beer cans all around her. No one was interested in the Harvard lab report showing that Miss Smith's body finally came to rest among some half-rusted beer cans that had been on the mall for at least one month.

Miss Jones and Mr. Brown would be alive today if there had not been (Cause Number 4) *lack of restraining devices*. If all persons involved had been wearing seat beats, two of three deaths would have been prevented and more than half the injuries. This confirmed a typical Harvard finding: the group has never investigated a multiple-death accident without finding that at least *half* the deaths could have been prevented with seat belts. Yet only a small minority of Americans wear them.

"Keep It Moving"

Thus, like most of the accidents studied at Harvard, this one had not one cause, but many. None of them was high speed. It rarely is—and Americans are going to have to dismiss the comfortable, but inadequate, myth that "speeders" and "reckless madmen" are the principal cause of accidents.

Indeed, the high-speed myth, though still given credence by local police and magistrates (for whom it is a significant source of power and income) is given little importance by sophisticated thinkers about the problem.

Listen to Howard Pyle, President, National Safety Council: "Speed by itself decidedly has been overemphasized as a major cause of traffic deaths."

And to Russell E. Singer, Executive Vice President of the AAA: "Purely routine speed-checking is futile and wasteful of enforcement officers' time. It clogs the courts on matters that have a minimum relation to real traffic safety."

And to J. E. Johnston, Traffic Safety Engineer (addressing the Institute of Traffic Engineers): "Publicity . . . for the past thirty years has all been aimed at 'speed' as being the major cause of accidents, when nothing could be further from the truth."

Or to John D. Williams, Head of the Mathematics Division of the Rand Corporation (the Air Force "think factory" where both civilian and military problems are pondered by civilian eggheads): "The physical and social structure of the country would be almost frozen in its present attitude were we to freeze the speed of the automobile. Speed is one of the really crucial factors in our society. I cannot help but believe that we would manage better if we were conscious of the need for more speed, rather than believing the exact contrary. Our laws tend to be aimed at the limitation of speed rather than at the promotion of traffic flow. If one recognizes that the central problem is to promote the smooth and rapid flow of lots of traffic, one is likely to devise measures that will in fact operate in this direction—and it will probably have reasonable safety.

"The motto of everyone concerned with traffic should be 'Keep It Moving.' The odds are that no matter what one does to that end, something good will come of it. The odds are that whatever one does that is contrary to the motto will have a detrimental effect."

America produces jet aircraft, space missiles, and over 60 per cent of the world's automobiles. It is about time we produced—dispassionately and scientifically—some useful information about vehicular traffic accidents. Outmoded myths about speed can lead us nowhere.

Questions

1. Does the National Safety Council blame speed alone as a cause of major accidents? What other factors are listed as causes of accident and injury?
2. The National Safety Council's report on speed and Schwartz's article seem to agree on the basic statistics. Where do they disagree? What is the significance of this disagreement?
3. What does Schwartz mean when he writes: "The incredible truth of the matter is that there is not one single study of the causes of the typical automobile accident, despite the millions of dollars spent for promoting highway safety"? On the basis of what you have read, what would you do to cut down the number of accidents, injuries, and fatalities in your state?
4. What are the differences in tone, style, emphasis, and presentation of statistics between Schwartz's article and the selection from *Passenger Car Design and Highway Safety*?
5. Why do the various experts discussing the question of highway safety differ so in their approaches and in their conclusions?

Assignments

1. Using the material from Schwartz, the National Safety Council, and *Passenger Car Design and Highway Safety,* propose a program which would scientifically

test the efficacy of certain devices in cutting down highway injury and fatality.
2. Summarize in detail the points on which the three articles agree and disagree.
3. Argue for or against the proposition that automobiles should be totally outlawed in this country and that all transportation should be performed by trains, planes, buses, or other public means.

Additional Reading

Passenger Car Design and Highway Safety, from which a selection has been republished here, offers a full discussion of the subject. Although the various contributions to this publication are technical, the material is still not impossible for the layman to handle. The footnotes and bibliographical information provide additional technical reading on the subject. More popular discussions of the problem may be found in the regular issues of publications devoted to automobiles. Another point of view can be found in Edwin L. Kirby's "Let's Be Realistic about Speed Limits," *Traffic Safety,* June, 1963, pp. 8 ff. The annual automobile issue of *Consumer Reports* usually contains detailed descriptions of the safety features of the new models.

SECTION TWO
Public or Private Medicine

Report to the President, 1948

OSCAR R. EWING

Six main arguments have been raised against a system of Government health insurance. To the extent that they are valid objections, they may be considered to constitute disadvantages of the plan.

Briefly, the six arguments are these: (1) That Government health insurance is socialized or state medicine, (2) that it is compulsory, (3) that it would be highly centralized and would concentrate too much power in Federal Government, (4) that there are not sufficient personnel and facilities to make it effective, (5) that it would cost too much, and (6) that it would open the way to overuse and other abuses and would lower the quality of medical services.

Let us consider these arguments, one by one.

Argument of Socialization

Little is gained by arguments that Government health insurance is or is not socialized medicine. This is a quarrel of definitions. Certainly, Government health insurance as proposed here is not socialized or state medicine. Basically, socialized or state medicine means that the Government owns and operates all hospitals, and that practicing physicians are employed by the Government on a salary basis. They, like firemen or policemen, are on Government payrolls and come under full Government supervision.

Clearly, no such system is proposed under the plan for Government insurance laid down in this report.

From *The Federal Government's Role in Providing Medical Care to Citizens of the United States*, Senate Document No. 31, 88th Congress, 1st Session 3–8 (1963).

Full freedom of choice should be left to doctors, hospitals, and all other instrumentalities of health as to whether they will participate. The method and rate of payment should be a matter for negotiation. Literally, the only change proposed by advocates of national health insurance is that, instead of the patient paying as he has money available, he would receive a service for which the doctor would be paid by the insurance system at a rate and by a method to which he had agreed. This is a thoroughly American system, resting upon insurance principles which have been part of our national fabric for generations.

Similar practices already exist in this country under voluntary plans. Likewise, today in this Nation, doctors are paid stipulated fees for performing tasks of service to the public health, for example, in administering immunization treatments or in venereal disease therapy.

Argument of Compulsion

The compulsory quality of Government health insurance has been greatly exaggerated. The proposed plan is compulsory in only a single aspect—all persons in certain categories to be determined by their representatives in the Congress would pay a stipulated percentage of their income in exchange for services and benefits under a system of insurance. It would be compulsory in the same way that payments for unemployment insurance or old-age and survivors insurance are compulsory. The benefits of these systems are well established and they are an accepted and valuable part of our American way of living.

Argument of Centralization

It has been charged that under a system of Government health insurance, all control would be lodged in the Federal Government, in one agency, or in the hands of one man. No such system is proposed in this report, and the intent is that actual administration of the program should rest mainly with the States and localities. The Federal Government's part would be to aid the State programs and to handle the finance of the total system, with a carefully designed system of checks and balances.

Adequacy of Resources

The statement has been made that Government health insurance could not be instituted because there are not sufficient personnel or facilities available to provide essential care. Two possible results are foreseen: One, that the Government would promise to supply care that could not be given because of shortage of personnel and facilities; two, that the increased patient load would reduce the standards of care.

This objection must be taken more seriously than others that have been raised. It is acknowledged that we do not now have enough personnel, enough hospitals, and other resources and services to satisfy all the people's needs. This has long been recognized, and it is one important reason for the timetable approach to health insurance suggested in this report. The tooling-up period could do something to break the bottleneck of shortages, particularly in accomplishing better distribution of manpower and facilities. Concerted steps could be taken by rural or impoverished areas to provide facilities and attract personnel with the assurance that, on a given future date, insurance would provide a stable financial basis for medical and health services. This, and the data on resources in this report, make it reasonably certain that there would be enough resources and services available, after the suggested tooling-up period, to give basic medical care benefits to millions who do not now have them.

The insurance system could not, of course, supply fully comprehensive services for everyone until there are enough physicians, dentists, nurses, hospitals, and supporting personnel, and until these resources and facilities are more evenly distributed throughout the country; until there is a proper organization and coordination of services everywhere.

Because of this fact, it has been argued that a health insurance program should not be instituted until it can provide all necessary services to all people. The proposal, under this line of thinking, would be first to develop the resources and services and then to find a method of enabling people to have the purchasing power to buy them.

It is totally unrealistic to think of eliminating the deficits ahead of solving financial problems. It puts the cart before the horse. Facilities and manpower expand in response to effective demand, and demand depends on total group purchasing power. This principle of supply and demand operates throughout our economy.

It is acknowledged that there is a shortage of both personnel and facilities and that this constitutes a limitation on the amount of services that can be rendered at the outset. The plan as outlined here takes full account of this factor, and arranges to cut the pattern to fit the cloth. But it does more than this, and so far as I can determine it is the only plan which does so—it will provide the funds and generate the steady and increased demand which will assure us enough medical manpower and facilities in the foreseeable future.

Argument of Cost

The question of greater cost has been raised in two areas: One, that medical and health services would require a greater national expenditure under a system of Government health insurance; two, that administrative costs would be excessive.

The answer to the first part of this issue is simple and is supported by this entire report: The Nation needs to spend more for health. This is the only way in which national levels of health can be improved. But a large part of the expenditures under health insurance would not be added expenditures; money normally expended in direct payments for medical care during illness would be distributed by small payments over longer periods of time. All people under the plan would pay periodically and consequently the burden of sickness—ordinarily concentrated upon a small part of the population in any given year—would be spread over more time and over more people.

So far as administrative costs are concerned, there is no reason to believe that the total expenses would be as large in relation to premiums collected as in the nonprofit plans, where the expense runs to approximately 12 percent. Actually, administration by Government should prove less costly. An important part of the administrative cost incurred by voluntary plans is the expense of soliciting and retaining members—a situation that would not apply to the Government.

I can find no valid disadvantage to the plan on the question of cost.

Quality of Service

The most serious charge made against a system of Government health insurance is that it would inevitably lower the quality of medical service. It is asserted that under such a program, (1) individuals would not have free choice of doctor; (2) that doctors would have to treat so many patients that they would not have time to give good and careful service; (3) that physicians would lose certain freedoms which they now have—such as the right to reject patients and to determine the fees to be charged; (4) that there would be abuses which would increase costs and lessen quality of care; (5) that the remuneration would be insufficient to give incentives to doctors to provide good service, that this weakens the doctor's interest in his patient, and destroys the important doctor-patient relationship; and (6) that there would be political interference—all to the detriment of quality of service.

Because these are questions of extreme importance, I am going to discuss them in some detail, taking up the various points in order. It is important to emphasize, in this connection, that quality of service has two aspects—quality of service for the community or the Nation at large; and quality of service accorded the individual. National interest demands that both be improved.

It must also be mentioned that this and many of the other problems of a Government health insurance plan also exist in voluntary plans and have to be solved by these plans also.

Free Choice of Doctors

1. The charge that individuals would not have free choice of doctor.

The Nation.—Many people today do not have free choice of physician, for two reasons; (1) in many sections of the country, there are not enough doctors to meet the needs, and (2) many millions of people do not have the money to pay doctors.

Under these circumstances, it is ridiculous to discuss "freedom of choice" for these people. Those in areas that have few, if any physicians, those who cannot afford to pay a doctor, have equally no choice in the matter. In one case, they must "choose" the doctor that is available; in the other they must "choose" the doctor that charity provides.

A prepaid plan of Government health insurance would certainly provide greater freedom of choice for the millions of people included in both these categories because it would help assure a better supply of physicians in underprivileged areas, and because prepayment would entitle millions who cannot now pay to have the services of a doctor of their choice.

Individuals.—If legislation is drawn up in the terms suggested in this chapter, the individual would be guaranteed under the law the privilege of choosing the doctor he wishes, and of changing doctors if he should so desire, subject to the doctor's right to reject patients.

Doctor's Burden

2. The charge that doctors would have to treat so many patients that they would have no time to give good and careful service.

The Nation.—It is proposed that legislation provide that the amount of benefits available in any area of the country be limited to the resources—doctors, hospitals, and so on—that can be provided for that area during the "tooling-up" period. It is proposed, further, that benefits should be increased only as local resources are increased, with the proviso that all efforts be bent toward increasing both as rapidly as possible. This commonsense approach to the problem offers the best overall guarantee that doctors will not be overburdened.

Individuals.—The suggested legislative provision is that the individual doctor have the right to reject or accept patients as he pleases, and on the same bases as now. This would certainly enable the individual doctor to limit his practice to the number of people he could care for. The individual patient, equally, would have the privilege of choosing any particular doctor or of changing doctors—he could change from a doctor who had too many patients. Difficulties for a popular doctor would undoubtedly arise as they do under the present system, but he would be under no greater compulsion than at present to care for all patients who come to him.

Doctor's Freedom

3. The charge that doctors would lose certain freedoms that they have now—such as the right to reject patients or to determine the fees to be charged.

The freedom to reject patients, as stated, would be reserved to doctors. As to fees, doctors would make an individual decision to participate in, or stay outside, the insurance plan. Those who wished to participate, and their representatives, would help make all decisions on rates of payment for services, as they have under voluntary plans in a number of the States. Flexibility of fees might be lost for the individual doctor who wished to participate, but this could operate to his advantage. Instead of charging one man $250 and another $25, according to the patient's individual ability to pay, the doctor would receive a uniform fee for a particular service. It is a fair assumption that, under a system of equal pay to the individual doctor for equal service, the total income of most doctors would be greater. Charity cases would be virtually eliminated.

Abuses of Services

4. The charge that "malingering" patients and some physicians would overuse services.

The experience of many voluntary health insurance plans in this country, and of compulsory plans in other countries, has shown that these abuses are greatly exaggerated and can be controlled either by organized action on the part of the physicians themselves, or by administrative procedures that have been tested by experience, or by a combination of both professional and administrative action.

Doctor's Incentives

5. The charge that the remuneration would be insufficient to give incentives to doctors to provide good services, that this weakens the doctor's interest in his patient and destroys the important doctor-patient relationship.

The clear implication of this assertion is that the doctor's chief interest in the patient is the fee that he collects for his services. Granted that doctors, like everyone else, have to be assured of their livelihood, I still cannot accept this purely financial interpretation of the intimate doctor-patient relationship. But, in any case as pointed out, most doctors could expect to earn better incomes under an insurance system than they do now. Large incomes are rare among doctors. Those few doctors whose incomes would not be increased under insurance probably would not participate. Reduction of income of the medical profession as a whole is, therefore, not an issue.

Granted an adequate income, the chief interest of any doctor is in practicing the best possible quality of scientific medicine, of providing the best care to his patients, and in having adequate facilities for his patient's needs. He will want to improve his skill and his knowledge by refresher courses and by contact with other leaders in medicine. Health insurance will help the doctor to do these things by assuring stability of income and by encouraging such coordination of services as would make possible a physician's release from practice in order to study.

If being paid by a third party, instead of the patient, would undermine the doctor-patient relationship and reduce the doctor's incentive, we might expect to find this situation at its worst where the doctor is paid on a salary basis, where he is not answerable to the patient but to his employer. In many of our best university medical schools and hospitals and in many of our most famous clinics, doctors are paid salaries by the institution—not fees by the patient. Yet those institutions are famous for quality of care, probably the best to be found anywhere in the world.

Political Issue

6. The charge that there would be political interference in the practice of medicine.

The system of Government health insurance which I suggest offers no opportunity for "politics," as I understand the term, to enter in. Political parties—Democrats, Republicans, or whatnot—do not come into the picture. The role of the Federal Government would be to collect the insurance premiums, distribute the money among the States in accordance with a law passed by the Congress, and prescribe standards which State plans should meet. State governments would adopt statewide plans but would have little, if anything, to do with administration. Administration would be left in the hands of local boards composed of doctors and laymen. Neither doctors nor patients would have any contact with the Federal Government and only rarely with their State governments. The local administrative boards would not change with political upheavals. Under the Selective Service Act, local administrative boards were remarkably free from political influences. There is every reason to believe that local boards to administer health insurance would be equally free of "politics."

It is pure poppycock and deliberately misleading to say that Government health insurance would make medicine a "political football," that doctors would be victims of the spoils system, that they would be subject to orders of untrained lay clerks, that doctors could expect no advancement because of professional merit but only through political pull, etc., etc. Under the suggested law, professional men are guaranteed the fullest possible latitude and protection, and a system of administrative and judicial appeals would be set up.

It is clear to me, and it certainly is implicit in the pattern of legislation recommended herein, that the insurance system should be fully insulated from "politics" of all sorts, so that purely medical concerns are left in the hands of the physicians and there is no unwarranted interference or "political control of medicine."

What Constitutes Quality?

Many of the elements that make up high-quality medical care as it relates to doctors have become apparent in this discussion of a Government system of prepaid insurance. But high-quality care is made up of more than the doctor-patient relationship, important though that is. Good medical care has been defined as "the application of all necessary services of modern scientific medicine to the needs of all the people."

Fundamental to achieving this standard is the availability of adequate numbers of physicians and other professional personnel, of hospitals and other facilities for diagnosis and care. The quality of the training of medical personnel is critical. The changing and expanding science of medicine requires that patients have access to specialists in various fields of medicine and, at need, to special equipment and facilities.

As measured against these standards, this report has shown that very few of the people—probably only the well-to-do in large urban centers—have access to good medical care. The question arises of what health insurance, under the terms proposed, would do to make all necessary services of scientific medicine available to all the people.

The assistance that insurance would give in creating greater supplies of manpower, toward increasing facilities and toward achieving more equitable distribution of both throughout the country, has been explained. The advantages of coordinated services, particularly in providing modern medical care, are reviewed in chapter 9. The discussion shows clearly that both group practice and integration of hospital services—highly desirable developments—would be stimulated by health insurance. All of these results would assist in providing the elements of better medical care to more people.

In the light of all these facts, it is difficult to see how the plan given here for a Government system of prepaid insurance would lower the quality of medical care. It seems clear to me that the reverse is true; that for the Nation as a whole, it would work toward a vast improvement in quality. This is not to say that there will not be difficulties, but there are none that careful planning and fairminded cooperation cannot overcome.

I am the more convinced of this because of the experience in some 34 States where voluntary insurance plans for medical care are in operation. In six of the States, 15 percent or more of the population is enrolled—in Delaware, 43 percent. In none of the States, so far as I can ascertain, has any serious charge been made that those voluntary plans have lowered the quality of medical care.

Only one essential difference exists between the program as proposed here and the voluntary insurance plans of the various States: The voluntary insurance plans cover only a percentage of the population—in 27 such plans, less than 10 percent; the Government plan ultimately would cover everyone in every State.

While it is true that a bad health insurance system can certainly lower the quality of service, the program as set forth here has taken the fullest possible cognizance of these problems and is designed to prevent any lowering of quality, as well as to accomplish the aims that have been set forth.

Summary

In conclusion, I recognize fully that Government health insurance is a highly controversial issue. The program as outlined here is not 100 percent perfect and is not a final answer to the health needs of the people. Some of the disadvantages of such a system present serious difficulties which, plan as we will, we cannot fully eliminate in advance. I am equally sure that, with good will and faith, and with energetic and continuing effort toward improvement, we can make Government health insurance workable and successful.

The compelling argument, however, that drives me to an advocacy of national health insurance is that I see no other possible way of bringing adequate medical service to fully half of the American people. It would, obviously, be nice if we could find some other way that would arouse less opposition from many members of the medical profession. But I see none. And seeing none, I am not willing to abandon my advocacy of a program that I believe will bring more adequate medical services to fully 70 million people just because some members of the medical profession prefer to maintain the status quo. It seems to me impossible to argue fairly for the status quo in the face of the fact that there are more than 300,000 deaths each year that we have the knowledge and skills to prevent.

I, therefore, recommend that the President continue to urge upon the Congress the earliest possible enactment of Government health insurance in some such terms as outlined in this report.

The Case Against Federalized Medicine

DR. GEORGE M. FISTER

The American Medical Association last November adopted a statement reaffirming its previous policy that the medical profession "will not be a willing party to implementing any system [of medical care] which it believes to be detrimental to the public welfare." This statement was aimed at the Administration-sponsored proposal for a government-controlled program of

Saturday Evening Post, CCXXXVI (February 23, 1963), 8–9. © 1963 The Curtis Publishing Company. Reprinted by permission of the author.

health care for the aged financed by increased payroll taxes on the nation's workers and employers. It was prompted by the belief that this proposal, which the Administration will attempt to force through Congress again this year, would seriously undermine professional freedom.

Doctors want to be free to give their patients the best medical care they are capable of giving. With few exceptions, they are convinced that only if medicine remains a free institution can it serve the people of America to the limits of its capacity. It will not be the medical profession that will deprive the people of high-quality medical care and the fruits of progress in medical science. That will come when government begins meddling and interfering with medical freedom.

If the victories and achievements of American medicine over the last 25 or 30 years had been compressed into a single year, they would have electrified the world. Death is regularly cheated in hospital operating rooms by surgical procedures developed by American physicians that could not have been performed 20 or 30 years ago, even if physicians of that era had dared to try. This country has marked up more important drug discoveries in the last two decades than the rest of the world together. It is engaged in more extensive and more varied medical research by far than any other nation, and it has produced more winners of the Nobel Prize in medicine in the last 15 years than all other countries combined. In less than a generation the United States has emerged as the world center of medical education as well as research. And in step with medical progress, it has had the foresight to provide the facilities necessary to bring the fruits of modern medicine to the people. An average of more than 50 new hospitals, for example, has been built here every year for the past 15 years.

This catalogue of achievements in medicine is a tribute to thousands of dedicated men and women who have had the opportunity to think, to work, to excel in a nation where government has not yet erected artificial and unnatural barriers to the freedom of medicine to pursue its goals.

Medicine is a science that advances by experimenting with new ideas and questioning old concepts. It is a science that flourishes best in freedom. Consequently, it is a strange and disturbing fact that American medicine, which has accomplished so much for the benefit of the people because it has been free, is in danger of losing its freedom. More disquieting still is the fact that the strongest threat comes from the Federal Government which, in a nation surrounded by the Communist doctrine of enslavement, ought to be medical freedom's greatest defender, not its executioner.

The U. S. vs. doctors

But the power of the Federal Government has been mercilessly employed in an attempt to intimidate the medical profession as a means of gaining a political end, in this case a government-controlled health-care program both wasteful and unnecessary and at the same time potentially harmful to the nation's health. Rarely has this country witnessed such bold use of government power to set a nation against a minority group. Physicians as represented by the American Medical Association have in effect been accused of being enemies of the people.

The immediate issues in the conflict are actually simple and clear-cut. On the one hand, the medical profession believes in helping those who need help, utilizing tax funds where they may be required. The medical profession also contends that citizens of whatever age who are financially able to take care of themselves should not become a burden on the taxpayers. The A.M.A., which represents 90 percent of the practicing physicians in the country, has repeatedly affirmed its position that no one in America will be denied medical care solely because he cannot pay for it.

On the other hand, the Administration and those who support its position argue that it is right and proper to force the nation's workers and their employers to pay higher taxes to buy hospitalization and nursing-home care for virtually everyone over 65 regardless of their financial need, the wealthy and well-to-do included.

Such a program would be difficult to justify either morally or economically, even if the needs of the aged for financial help in meeting medical bills were as severe in general as they have been portrayed, which they are not, and even if better programs were not available, which they are.

The spectacular growth of voluntary health insurance and the prepayment plans—one of the great social phenomena of our times—has brought within the reach of millions of people over 65 an increasing selection of flexible programs adaptable to their own needs and resources in guarding against the cost of unexpected illness or injury. Advocates of government-operated health care for the aged claim that private health insurance is inadequate and too costly for people over 65. The argument would appear to lack substance in light of the fact that most policies are far more comprehensive than the Administration's scheme would be and that more than 9,500,000 people over 65 have purchased health-insurance coverage with a wide range of benefits. Policies are available covering hospitalization as well as physicians' fees. The number insured represents nearly 70 percent of all the elderly who either need or want health insurance, since many can afford to be without it and many thousands of others already get medical care through welfare programs.

Voluntary health insurance and the prepayment plans are doing an increasingly effective job for the elderly who are financially able to provide for themselves without help from the taxpayers. And for those who are honestly in need of assistance in paying for medical care, Congress already has extended the helping hand of government by passage of the Kerr-Mills Medical Aid for the Aged Law in 1960. Both of these programs—voluntary health insurance and the Kerr-Mills Law—are vigorously and actively supported by the medical profession.

The Kerr-Mills Law is in substance a partnership program between the states and the Federal Government, offering Federal funds to the states to help finance medical care for everyone over 65 who needs it. It is a flexible program, adaptable to the varying requirements of the states and authorizing a full range of medical care to the aged who qualify for its benefits.

Kerr-Mills dovetails neatly into the traditional pattern of other assistance programs—Federal financial contributions, but state control and state determination of what is required to discharge government responsibility to its citizens.

There is no demonstrable need for any other program. And if there were, it would be folly to embark on a wasteful and extravagant scheme, as proposed by the Administration, which rests on the unsupportable assumption that everyone becomes ill and destitute at that point in time when he passes his 65th birthday. No one disputes the fact that many of the elderly do need help in meeting their medical bills, but to argue that poverty is a universal condition of the aged flays common sense as well as fact.

Surveys of the economic condition of American families have proved repeatedly that the aged as a group are better off than most of the younger workers who would be burdened with new taxes under the Administration's proposal. The latest survey, conducted by the University of Michigan Survey Research Center, verified others which have shown that the aged on the average have double the assets of younger age groups, have substantially less debt and fewer family obligations. They also enjoy numerous tax advantages denied the younger families. Of major significance to the oft-repeated claim that medical costs are a crushing burden on the aged, the Michigan University survey found that 96 percent of the elderly questioned owed no bills whatever for doctor, dentist or hospital. It is true that older families generally have less income, but when all the factors are weighed and income is measured against need, the aged families are not substantially worse off than younger families. While those over 65 comprise 9 percent of the population, they receive 8 percent of the U. S. income.

Persuasive evidence exists, furthermore, that the economic condition of the aged is improving year by year and that their financial problems are diminishing and will decline even more in the future. In 1949, for example, more than 23 percent of the entire population over 65 was receiving old-age assistance. Only about 12 percent are on old-age rolls today.

Another barometer of the rising fortunes of the aged is contained in a recent report of the Census Bureau revealing that during 1961 the median income of families headed by a person over 65 increased by 4.5 percent while median income of all U. S. families gained by only 2 percent. Still another factor favoring the aged deserves more recognition than it has been accorded in evaluating the needs of the aged. While a large percentage of the elderly now retired does not enjoy the security of a private pension plan, increasing millions of today's workers are covered by private retirement programs.

No one really argues with much conviction anymore that the Administration-sponsored scheme would not be the first step in an expanding program of government-controlled medicine eventually embracing the entire population. No principle exists by which the Government can claim responsibility for hospitalization and nursing-home care for the elderly and not their doctor bills, for drugs supplied in a hospital but not those purchased at the corner drugstore—or for medical expenses of the elderly but not for everyone else.

But even if that were not the ultimate objective, the Administration's proposal is still unwise. In the name of humanitarianism, it would confer on an agency of government the power to impose and enforce arbitrary rules and regulations governing the administration and the practice of medicine in the nation's hospitals and permit laymen in government to make medical decisions affecting the health of 17 million Americans. Despite denials that no one in the expansive environs of the Department of Health, Education and Welfare would covet such authority, the grant of power would be both explicit and implied by the fact that the Government, footing the bill, would be obligated to set the terms, conditions and standards governing the expenditure of the tax funds.

Vetoing doctor's orders

All the proposals so far advanced implicitly confer on agents of government the authority to determine who would be admitted to a participating hospital, how long they could remain, what services could be provided by the hospital to the patient and whether a course of treatment prescribed for an elderly patient by a physician was necessary. It is clear enough that someone appointed or employed by a government agency would be permitted to exercise a veto over the judgment of the family physician.

What would happen if the cost of this program began to get out of hand because the cost had been grossly underestimated as there is every reason to believe it has? The power to control would then become the power to deprive. Some of the elderly would inevitably be denied hospital care because there wasn't enough money to go around. For the same reason, some family doctor inevitably would be told that the course of treatment he had prescribed for an elderly patient was unnecessary and the patient removed from the hospital.

Those who are incessantly pushing this kind of program are doing citizens 65 and over a disservice by constantly setting them apart from the rest of the population, giving them a group or class identity they neither want nor deserve simply because they have reached the age of 65. They are individuals, with likes and dislikes, aspirations and hopes and fears and capabilities as varied as their numbers. This identification of them as a 17-million-member national problem does them no good and perhaps much harm.

In short, the government-sponsored medical program is bad medicine for both patients and doctors.

America's Medical Future: A Briton's View

LORD TAYLOR

Discussions on medicare sometimes lead to echoes of Billy Bones's opinion in *Treasure Island* that "Doctors is all swabs." Having known a good many on both sides of the Atlantic, I would say with confidence that this ain't so. Every profession everywhere has its share of black sheep and psychopaths, but medicine gets less than the average, for the simple reason that the hard work involved makes little appeal to the really bad eggs.

American doctors compare well with doctors anywhere else in the world. Technically, their level of achievement is generally excellent. As individuals, most of them are fine men, with high standards of personal and professional ethics, with wide humanity and understanding of their patients, and a rugged independence and individuality which are essential for good doctoring. As individuals, most are popular with their patients. But collectively, the image is a divided one. As the white-gowned servant of humanity, the American doctor is a hero, a figure of romance, with science and his own personal skill as weapons in a never-ending battle against disease. His offense in the eyes of his detractors is that he is rich, and is determined to stay that way. In a society dedicated to achievement on a sound cash basis, unpopularity on this score is surprising.

The trouble is that the doctor is not very good at putting his own case. This is partly because he has not thought it out thoroughly himself, and partly because good doctors everywhere prefer doctoring to medical politics. So in his collective capacity he appears as the affluent enemy of progress, which is far from being the case.

In Britain, the broad pros and cons of medicare are no longer argued. We are almost all of us pretty sure we have moved in the right direction. That is not to say that we have got all the answers; indeed we haven't. But more than 90 per cent of us like our National Health Service well enough to use it, even though we don't have to. And almost all our best doctors are in fact practicing within the service. There are still genuine difficulties to be solved, for both patients and doctors, not least of which is our failure to create new medical schools. We are shorter of doctors than ever before, yet at the same time there are more boys and girls wanting to become doctors than ever before. Medical schools get more than thirty applicants for every vacancy, a sufficient testimony that the National Health Service has not destroyed the popularity of medicine as a career. The wail which goes up in America from disgruntled Englishmen, most of whom have failed at home to get the jobs they want, is quite unrepresentative. Anyone seeking an objective picture of Britain's National Health Service should turn to an excellent book by an American, Almont Lindsey, entitled *Socialized Medicine in England and Wales* (University of North Carolina Press, 1962).

The case for medicare is so strong that it is bound to spread the world over—America included. But it carries with it risks and dangers to patients and doctors alike. These must not be minimized; rather they must be examined carefully, so that they can be avoided. The benefits of medicare are obvious, the risks subtle. In the public mind, therefore, only the benefits will be seen. It is up to the experts, medical and non-medical, to concentrate their thoughts on the real risks and dangers and not waste their energy fighting where the case is hopeless.

The arguments in favor of medicare are simple and overwhelming. Good medical care is, and is bound to be, expensive. In the years ahead, as the science of medicine expands, it will become more expensive. It follows that most people will be unable to pay the full cost in cash at the time they receive treatment. Common sense tells us to spread the cost of our episodes of illness over our entire earning life. This means we must insure. But for most of us the heaviest costs are inevitably in infancy and old age, outside our normal working and earning span. This means family and whole-life insurance. During a period of, say, forty working years, we have to pay for risks spread over seventy or more years. But there is another difficulty. Because of their heredity or upbringing or work some people are better risks than others. Through no fault of their own, the bad risks simply cannot carry their own burden. Nor indeed is it possible to isolate the bad risks in advance. The only fair thing to do is to pool all our risks. But even if we do this, a flat per capita payment will be unfair. A uniform flat payment will have little effect on the $40,000 a year man, but will seriously reduce the standard of living of the man earning one-tenth of this amount, and this in turn may reduce his family's level of health. It follows that, if we want everyone to have the best possible medical care at his time of need, everyone must pay according to his capacity throughout his entire earning life. In a modern society this presents no inherent technical difficulty. It simply means that the cost of medicare is added to the income tax or other graduated taxes. That is what we have done in Britain. Of our weekly per capita contributions of about $2 for national insurance, a small part only goes toward the cost of the health service. Something like seven-eighths of the cost of the service comes out of general taxation—mainly income tax, purchase (or sales) tax and excise tax.

In a sense, this idea, which is generally accepted in Britain, is foreign to the American philosophy of self-help and the devil take the hindmost. There is much to be said for the American doctrine of self-reliance, of giving and getting value for money, of working hard and taking both the rewards of success and the knocks inevitable in comparative failure. But with medical care, this philosophy in America has already broken down. Sickness insurance is already widespread. But, to the outside observer, the picture is chaotic, with the commercial insurance firms seeking to skim off the low-risk cream and the nonprofit-making organizations being left with the high-risk, high-cost residue.

As a matter of common humanity, medicare for older people has a great deal to commend it. But in terms of national economics, it presents special problems. This is the high-risk group, so the cost to the community per year of risk covered will be relatively far higher than the cost of covering everybody. Medicare for the old may be humane common sense; it may be politically practical; but its effects will be far more dramatic than is generally realized. The great bulk of serious medicine and surgery in advanced societies is now done on older people. So, in effect, medicare for senior citizens will mean that a substantial part of most doctors' work will be for medicare patients. It follows that medicare for senior citizens presents almost as great an administrative challenge, and almost as many potential risks and dangers, as medicare for all.

Properly run, medicare can convey great benefits to patients and doctors alike. The risk is the destruction of the freedom and independence of the medical profession, with a corresponding fall in the quality of service rendered to the public. Instinctively doctors realize this, but they have not faced the problem. I do not think most American doctors have any inherent objection to prepaid medical schemes, provided that the payments are a proper return for work done, and do not involve unnecessary form-filling and outside control of the doctor's work. Here I would say they are right. A whole-time salaried medical service would be a disaster for America, as it would be for Britain. We pay our general practitioners by capitation fee and our specialists by part-time salary. Both groups remain free to practice medicine as they think fit, and neither is restricted, as are civil servants, in their freedom of speech or political action. Doctors working in the National Health Service criticize every aspect of it freely, and they can and do serve as members of Parliament, as municipal councilors, and as members of the many committees which run the service. Nor has the National Health Service been handed over to the Public Health Services. Within its legislative framework, it is largely a self-governing association of physicians, and herein lies its strength.

I am certain that medicare in America will involve payment of most doctors on a fee-for-service basis. Whether this will be direct, from federal or state agencies, or via some noncommercial buffer like Blue Shield, is a secondary matter. Since the risks to be covered are universal, payments are bound to be through taxation. No government can properly farm out its tax-collecting function. But there should be no compulsion on citizens to use, or doctors to participate in, medicare schemes.

As a result of the growth of insurance practice in the States, the custom of "charging what the traffic will bear" is dying a natural death. Fees are, in fact, becoming standardized, despite resistance to the establishment of recognized fee schedules. Nevertheless, there would seem to be a case for three levels of schedule—one for the general practitioner, a second for the specialist, and a third for what might be called the super-specialist. Many doctors who are now classed as GPs might well be graded as specialists for certain types of work, and vice versa (for example, the internist who sews up a cut finger or sets a fracture).

America, like Britain, suffers from under-doctoring in its less attractive areas and over-doctoring in its more pleasant spots. Over-doctoring might be justifiable if there were a total surplus of doctors, though its effects on the profession in the over-doctored areas are on the whole bad. For under-doctoring there is no excuse. In Britain, we have managed to avoid "direction" of doctors as to where they should practice by two simple measures. First, we offer extra cash incentives to doctors who set up practices in under-doctored areas. Second, additional practitioners are forbidden to set up new Health Service practices in over-doctored areas, though they can of course start private practices anywhere they like. These controls apart, there is freedom to practice wherever a doctor wishes. It is fair to add, however, that British patients change their doctor far less readily than do Americans. As a result, most doctors enter practice as assistants or partners with established doctors. So opportunities for practice are limited by patient behavior rather than by law.

Medicare, then, involves two incursions into the doctor's freedom. First, he cannot fix his own fee for his medicare patients; he must accept a negotiated scale, which should, however, have regard to his degree of competence and experience. Second, until all areas have enough doctors, he cannot set up in medicare practice in over-doctored areas. These restrictions apart, he should be able to continue to practice precisely as at present, without state interference in his professional work.

Hospitals in the United States display a remarkable diversity in both ownership and quality. There are church and community hospitals, municipal and veterans' hospitals, proprietary private hospitals and so-called convalescent homes. Most are excellent, but many are very poor indeed. Any medicare plan must involve some measure of hospital planning over wide regions. Without this, patients who need highly specialized care cannot receive it. Hospital planning means surveys of both quantity and quality. An effective hospital service means upgrading of the less good to the level of the best, and the provision of new facilities where they are most needed and not necessarily where enthusiastic citizen groups would like to put them.

In Britain, all hospitals have been nationalized. This has greatly simplified hospital planning and upgrading. I doubt if so drastic a solution is needed in America. Indeed, there would be many practical disadvantages, arising largely from the size of the country. In each state or region, the minimum requirement is that there should be a hospital planning authority, with sufficient powers and incentives to achieve what is needed. Such an authority should cover all types of hospital—charitable and municipal, mental and psychiatric, long-stay for the aged and chronically sick, as well as the proprietary hospitals and convalescent homes. A firmly operated licensing system could prevent the proliferation of unnecessary hospitals. Upgrading could be achieved by the adjustment of capital and maintenance grants through the hospital planning authorities.

I have said nothing thus far about the future of group medical practice or the existing prepayment schemes. The former will probably continue to grow under their own momentum; but they should certainly not be imposed generally on an unwilling profession. The latter will inevitably go out of business as collectors of contributions, but could well continue as payers of benefits or providers of facilities, assuming they are genuinely nonprofit-making. On the other hand, it is hard to see how commercial insurance companies could perform any useful role in the provision of medicare on a universal (or nearly universal) scale.

Accurate social prognosis is hard enough in one's own country. To attempt the same thing in another country is even more difficult. On medicare, the people of America will make their own decisions. My excuse for this incursion is to try to illuminate some of the problems we met and dealt with, when we trod the same road fifteen years ago. I have tried to put them into the context of modern American medicine. In so doing, I have been guilty of both dogmatism and over-simplification. But these faults have at least the virtue of showing up the difficulties with greater clarity. No one can study the American scene without being impressed by the quality of the civil service, the public health and hospital administrators, and above all the doctors, in general and specialized practice. Among them, I have little doubt, they will find better answers to the problems of tomorrow than I have been able to suggest. It is high time they got together to examine the real challenges and risks inherent in any medicare program.

New US Patterns

ROBERT S. MORISON, M.D.

The most dangerous feature of greater government participation in medical care now is the probability that it would serve to solidify patterns of practice

New Republic, CXLIX (November 9, 1963), 38-41. © 1963 *New Republic*. Reprinted by permission of *New Republic*.

that are becoming increasingly obsolete every day. Since most of the enemies of greater government participation in medical care are by and large the enemies of change in general, this argument is little used by those who oppose the growth of a government role in medical care. But the general public should be more aware than it is that the establishment of a single nationwide scheme for meeting the costs of medical care is more than likely to retard the development of new and suitable forms of medical practice.

Take what has happened in England. As Mrs. Somers noted in her report, it is simply not true that the quality of medical care provided by the National Health Service is inferior to that available to the great majority of Englishmen before the scheme went into effect. All competent observers agree that it is better, especially perhaps in the far more equitable provision of specialists throughout the country. Nevertheless, it is not nearly so good as it could and should be. Its more glaring defects, however, are the result not of radical innovation but of a tendency to prolong and even intensify the defects of the past.

The heavy emphasis on general practice, the almost complete separation of the general practitioner from the hospital and the specialist, the tendency to prescribe some sort of drug at every visit whether the patient needs it or not, even the chronic shortage of hospital beds were all characteristic of British practice before the scheme. The operation of the scheme has only reinforced them.

This is not the place to argue the pros and cons of general practice, and I will not attempt to do so. I will simply assert that the rapid growth of medical knowledge is making it increasingly difficult for a single individual to offer anything more than a small fraction of what medicine as a whole has to offer the general public. This fact was reasonably well recognized by experts in medical care when the British scheme was being founded some 20 years ago. Nevertheless, it was felt desirable for several practical and political reasons to preserve the traditional merits of the general practitioner together with the sacred doctor-patient relationship and the free choice of a physician. In pursuit of these objectives and in order to preserve something of the old incentives, the GP in Britain is compensated according to the number of patients he attracts. Even though there is a ceiling (3,500) on the total number who can sign up, the ordinary doctor must usually confine himself to the following activities: (1) taking care as rapidly as possible of ordinary aches and pains; (2) certifying patients for disability compensation; (3) trying to identify the occasional case which is serious enough to justify referral to the hospital with its group of specialist consultants.

The British hospital is another world from the GP's office. It is staffed entirely by specialists with some of the highest qualifications to be found anywhere. Although there has been a deplorable lag in the provision of physical facilities, the level of professional services available is without much doubt more consistently high than in the US. At the risk of making a dangerous oversimplification, one might say that English medicine is more or less uniformly mediocre as practiced outside the hospital and uniformly very good at the hospital level. In the US, quality is much more variable both inside and outside the hospital, ranging from rather poor to excellent in both cases. Over-all, the advantages and disadvantages seem to cancel themselves out, so that such measures of effectiveness as infant mortality and life expectancy are strikingly similar in the two countries. What this country's lack of system allows which the British scheme makes rather difficult is continued experimentation with new forms of practice appropriate to the rapidly evolving nature of medical science.

Thus an increasing number of physicians in the US are serving as what in England would be called hospital consultants on full- or part-time salaries. Indeed if one includes industry, the Veterans Administration, the Armed Services, group practice clinics, and the various provisions for the medically indigent, very nearly a third of US professional medical work is already conducted on a salaried rather than fee-for-service basis so sacred to the AMA. Perhaps even more important and more peculiarly American is the evolution of private office practice from the individual general practitioner to the group of qualified specialists. On the purely economic side there is an accompanying evolution of private and public insurance schemes—Blue Cross, Blue Shield, and the increasingly popular plans elaborated by private insurance companies for dealing with major medical costs or "catastrophes."

It is ironical that almost every step in this evolution has been vigorously opposed by the same forces that oppose the adoption of any over-all national medical plan. For as I have tried to show, it is the failure to establish a national plan that allows the evolution of these new forms to proceed.

There is still a lot of evolving to be done both along paths already started as well as on some that are as yet scarcely descried. Premature emphasis on schemes for paying medical costs tends to obscure the question of what is being paid for and why it costs so much. Since good health is thought of as almost literally priceless, it is in any case embarrassing to ask about costs. When a surgeon may actually save a life by the timely removal of an appendix, it seems pretty small-minded to ask why he should charge 10 times as much as the internist who spends perhaps three times the effort trying to arrive at a difficult diagnosis. When specialist obstetricians working in marvelous hospitals do such a fine job, it seems at best impolite to ask how Holland manages to have a majority of its deliveries at home (most of them by midwives). Costs may be 20 times as much in the US, but it is hard to say that Americans are getting anything better for their money. Maternal mortality rates may be a tiny bit higher in Holland, but the US infant mortality rate is higher by a half.

Several years ago a comparative study showed that Swedish hospitals employ about two-thirds the number of people to take care of the same number of patients that American hospitals do. Admittedly, the study was relatively small scale and was published in a rather obscure way, but much the same point has been made over and over again by the easily available statistics on doctor-patient ratios in the two countries. The amazing thing is that so few people have ever tried to find out how the Swedes do it, and whether such facts have any bearing on hospital planning in this country.

At regular intervals since the last war the US has had a series of reports on medical care, its costs, and its needs. All of them include estimates of the need for various categories of personnel. In most cases these are simply extrapolations of existing trends. In no case have the authors seriously tried to find out how other countries manage to do such a good job at far less cost in terms of both money and personnel. In no case has the possibility of reducing US requirements for more surgeons by reducing the amount of unnecessary surgery even been suggested. Although many of these reports contain estimates of the probable need for what is known as ancillary or paramedical personnel, no serious attempt has ever been made to show how changes in the training and utilization of such personnel might be used to reduce requirements for the most expensive sort of professionals.

Public discussion of the medical care program has centered almost entirely on where the money is to come from and in what form it is to be paid. Think of the almost endless hours of discussions on such matters as fee-for-service versus salary, insurance plans which provide service (Blue Cross) versus those which provide cash payment, and last but not least whether old peoples' care should be paid for from general tax funds or by a special social security tax.

Occasionally, such discussions reach points which have some bearing on the cost and quality of medical care, as when it is pointed out that payment on an annual basis tends to increase service at the patient's option whereas fee-for-service tends to increase it at the physician's. For the most part, however, energy is burnt up in an endless defense of abstractions or irrelevancies. The current bickering over social security versus general tax funds as a source is only the most recent and perhaps the most absurd of these preoccupations.

One useful, though negative, result has been achieved by all this talk: by failing to adopt a national health plan of any sort, the US has at least preserved its freedom to experiment. There is no doubt that further experimentation is necessary before arrangements capable of providing a high level of care for all at a cost the country can afford are elaborated.

Some of the questions that should be looked into have already been mentioned—the fact that other countries achieve better results with fewer doctors, the encouragement the present American system gives to performance of unnecessary procedures at the physician's option, the wide variation in quality between the best and the poorest hospitals, the ridiculous disparity between surgical and medical fees—a disparity which among other things encourages the ugly business of fee splitting and ghost surgery. These and other problems have been dealt with in more detail in accompanying articles. The only purpose of my remarks is to remind ourselves that the primary problem is not one of finding new means of paying for what American citizens are getting now. First, our policy-makers should be sure that when a means of payment is worked out, all Americans will be getting the best care possible, and at a cost which makes the most efficient use of all available resources. The country is not even close to either objective today.

Questions

1. Why does Ewing describe the insurance system as "a thoroughly American system"? What does he mean?
2. Does the order in which Ewing arranges his points have a rationale?
3. In the logical development of Dr. Fister's argument, what is the role of the third paragraph?
4. Define the word "freedom" as Dr. Fister uses it.
5. Describe the tone of paragraph six in Dr. Fister's essay. How is this tone established?
6. Reread this statement from Dr. Fister's article carefully. "The number insured represents nearly 70 percent of all the elderly who either need or want health insurance, since many can afford to be without it and many thousands of others already get medical care through welfare programs." What are the criteria for "need and want"? How large a percentage of those who need medical care is this 70 percent? Is the statement an effective argument?
7. Does Lord Taylor's statement that "the doctor is not very good at putting his own case" apply to Dr. Fister? To Dr. Morison?
8. Would Dr. Fister agree on the "two incursions [necessitated by medicare] into the doctor's freedom" described by Lord Taylor?
9. Can Lord Taylor's article be considered merely social prognosis?
10. Does Dr. Morison's phrase "enemies of change in general" fit Dr. Fister?
11. What does Dr. Fister mean when he says a medicare program for the aged "would be difficult to justify . . . morally"?
12. Both Dr. Morison and Lord Taylor seem to assume that "government medicine" is inevitable. Do they adequately support this view? List their reasons for offering this view.
13. What is the difference between national health insurance and socialized medicine. Do all four writers distinguish between the two?
14. Which writer is most objective toward the subject? Why? Which is least objective? Why?

Assignments

1. Nearly everyone accepts the necessity of some government activity in matters of health. Control of epidemics, for example, is considered a public concern. Discuss the extent to which health should be a public concern.
2. Describe the major issues involved in the medicare controversy.
3. Defend or oppose one of the following propositions:
    a. Medicare was inevitable.
    b. The AMA opposition to medicare was the result of a fear of change.
    c. Socialized medicine is superior to medicare.

4. Write a legislative history of medicare bills in Congress.
5. Compare two European medicare schemes.

Additional Reading

Comment on government health insurance and socialized medical plans has been voluminous, discussing not only the theoretical considerations but also the issues involved in the various bills which have been placed before Congress. Particular points of view are offered in the materials distributed by interested parties, for example, Congressmen, the AMA, and insurance companies. Any of the periodical indexes will provide a substantial bibliography of magazine articles. A collection on the subject, *The Federal Government's Role in Providing Medical Care to Citizens of the United States* (Washington, 1963), prepared by the government for use in schools and by debating societies, includes comments on both sides of the controversies over a number of medicare bills. Two recent scholarly books throw considerable light on important aspects of the controversy. Seymour Harris, a Harvard economist, has done an intensive study of *The Economics of American Medicine* (New York, 1964), which describes in detail the present economic conditions in American medicine. Almont Lindsey's book *Socialized Medicine in England and Wales, The National Health Service, 1948–1961* (Chapel Hill, North Carolina, 1962) provides a thorough and objective account of the British system, which almost inevitably comes into American discussions of government health care.

SECTION THREE | Smoking, Cancer, and Statistics

Smoking and Health

A. BACKGROUND AND HIGHLIGHTS

In previous studies, the use of tobacco, especially cigarette smoking, has been causally linked to several diseases. Such use has been associated with increased deaths from lung cancer and other diseases, notably coronary artery disease, chronic bronchitis, and emphysema. These widely reported findings, which have been the cause of much public concern over the past decade, have been accepted in many countries by official health agencies, medical associations, and voluntary health organizations.

The potential hazard is great because these diseases are major causes of death and disability. In 1962, over 500,000 people in the United States died of arteriosclerotic heart disease (principally coronary artery disease), 41,000 died of lung cancer, and 15,000 died of bronchitis and emphysema.

The numbers of deaths in some important disease categories that have been reported to have a relationship with tobacco use are shown in Table 1. This table presents one aspect of the size of the potential hazard; the degree of association with the use of tobacco will be discussed later.

Another cause for concern is that deaths from some of these diseases have been increasing with great rapidity over the past few decades.

Lung cancer deaths, less than 3,000 in 1930, increased to 18,000 in 1950. In the short period since 1955, deaths from lung cancer rose from less than 27,000 to the 1962 total of 41,000. This extraordinary rise has not been recorded for cancer of any other site. While part of the rising trend for lung

From *Smoking and Health*, Report of the Advisory Committee to the Surgeon General of the Public Health Service (Washington: U. S. Department of Health, Education, and Welfare, 1964), pp. 25–40.

cancer is attributable to improvements in diagnosis and the changing age-composition and size of the population, the evidence leaves little doubt that a true increase in lung cancer has taken place.

Deaths from arteriosclerotic, coronary, and degenerative heart disease rose from 273,000 in 1940, to 396,000 in 1950, and to 578,000 in 1962.

Reported deaths from chronic bronchitis and emphysema rose from 2,300 in 1945 to 15,000 in 1962.

The changing patterns and extent of tobacco use are a pertinent aspect of the tobacco-health problem.

TABLE I. *Deaths from Selected Disease Categories, United States, 1962*

Cause of death *	Total	Males	Females
Degenerative and arteriosclerotic heart disease, including coronary disease (420,422)	577,918	348,604	229,314
Hypertensive heart disease (440–3)	62,176	26,654	35,522
Cancer of lung (162–3)	41,376	35,312	6,064
Cirrhosis of liver (581)	21,824	14,329	7,495
Bronchitis and emphysema (502, 527.1)	15,104	12,937	2,167
Stomach and duodenal ulcers (540–1)	12,228	8,836	3,392
Cancer of bladder (181)	8,081	5,575	2,506
Cancer of oral cavity (140–8)	6,481	4,920	1,561
Cancer of esophagus (150)	5,088	3,973	1,115
Cancer of larynx (161)	2,417	2,172	245
All above causes	752,693	463,312	289,381
All other causes	1,004,027	531,477	472,550
All causes	1,756,720	994,789	761,931

* International Statistical Classification numbers in parentheses.

Nearly 70 million people in the United States consume tobacco regularly. Cigarette consumption in the United States has increased markedly since the turn of the century, when per capita consumption was less than 50 cigarettes a year. Since 1910, when cigarette consumption per person (15 years and older) was 138, it rose to 1,365 in 1930, to 1,828 in 1940, to 3,322 in 1950, and to a peak of 3,986 in 1961. The 1955 Current Population Survey showed that 68 percent of the male population and 32.4 percent of the female population 18 years of age and over were regular smokers of cigarettes.

In contrast with this sharp increase in cigarette smoking, per capita use of tobacco in other forms has gone down. Per capita consumption of cigars declined from 117 in 1920 to 55 in 1962. Consumption of pipe tobacco, which reached a peak of 2½ lbs. per person in 1910, fell to a little more than half a pound per person in 1962. Use of chewing tobacco has declined from about four pounds per person in 1900 to half a pound in 1962.

The background for the Committee's study thus included much general information and findings from previous investigations which associated the increase in cigarette smoking with increased deaths in a number of major disease categories. It was in this setting that the Committee began its work to assess the nature and magnitude of the health hazard attributable to smoking.

KINDS OF EVIDENCE

In order to judge whether smoking and other tobacco uses are injurious to health or related to specific diseases, the Committee evaluated three main kinds of scientific evidence:

1. *Animal experiments.* In numerous studies, animals have been exposed to tobacco smoke and tars, and to the various chemical compounds they contain. Seven of these compounds (polycyclic aromatic compounds) have been established as cancer-producing (carcinogenic). Other substances in tobacco and smoke, though not carcinogenic themselves, promote cancer production or lower the threshold to a known carcinogen. Several toxic or irritant gases contained in tobacco smoke produce experimentally the kinds of non-cancerous damage seen in the tissues and cells of heavy smokers. This includes suppression of ciliary action that normally cleanses the trachea and bronchi, damage to the lung air sacs, and to mucous glands and goblet cells which produce mucus.

2. *Clinical and autopsy studies.* Observations of thousands of patients and autopsy studies of smokers and non-smokers show that many kinds of damage to body functions and to organs, cells, and tissues occur more frequently and severely in smokers. Three kinds of cellular changes—loss of ciliated cells, thickening (more than two layers of basal cells), and presence of atypical cells—are much more common in the lining layer (epithelium) of the trachea and bronchi of cigarette smokers than of non-smokers. Some of the advanced lesions seen in the bronchi of cigarette smokers are probably premalignant. Cellular changes regularly found at autopsy in patients with chronic bronchitis are more often present in the bronchi of smokers than non-smokers. Pathological changes in the air sacs and other functional tissue of the lung (parenchyma) have a remarkably close association with past history of cigarette smoking.

3. *Population studies.* Another kind of evidence regarding an association between smoking and disease comes from epidemiological studies.

In retrospective studies, the smoking histories of persons with a specified disease (for example, lung cancer) are compared with those of appropriate control groups without the disease. For lung cancer alone, 29 such retrospective studies have been made in recent years. Despite many variations in design and method, all but one (which dealt with females) showed that proportionately more cigarette smokers are found among the lung cancer patients than in the control populations without lung cancer.

Extensive retrospective studies of the prevalence of specific symptoms and signs—chronic cough, sputum production, breathlessness, chest illness, and decreased lung function—consistently show that these occur more often in cigarette smokers than in non-smokers. Some of these signs and symptoms are the clinical expressions of chronic bronchitis, and some are associated more with emphysema; in general, they increase with amount of smoking and decrease after cessation of smoking.

Another type of epidemiological evidence on the relation of smoking and mortality comes from seven prospective studies which have been conducted since 1951. In these studies, large numbers of men answered questions about their smoking or non-smoking habits. Death certificates have been obtained for those who died since entering the studies, permitting total death rates and death rates by cause to be computed for smokers of various types as well as for non-smokers. The prospective studies thus add several important dimensions to information on the smoking-health problem. Their data permit direct comparisons of the death rates of smokers and non-smokers, both overall and for individual causes of death, and indicate the strength of the association between smoking and specific diseases.

Each of these three lines of evidence was evaluated and then considered together in drawing conclusions. The Committee was aware that the mere establishment of a statistical association between the use of tobacco and a disease is not enough. The causal significance of the use of tobacco in relation to the disease is the crucial question. For such judgments all three lines of evidence are essential, as discussed in more detail on pages 26–27 of this Chapter, and in Chapter 3.

The experimental, clinical, and pathological evidence, as well as data from population studies, is highlighted in Section B of this Chapter, which in turn refers the reader to specific places in Part II of the Report where this evidence is presented in detail.

In the paragraphs which follow, the Committee has chosen to summarize the results of the seven prospective population studies which, as noted above, constitute only one type of evidence. They illustrate the nature and potential magnitude of the smoking-health problem, and bring out a number of factors which are involved.

EVIDENCE FROM THE COMBINED RESULTS OF PROSPECTIVE STUDIES

The Committee examined the seven prospective studies separately as well as their combined results. Considerable weight was attached to the consistency of findings among the several studies. However, to simplify presentation, only the combined results are highlighted here.

Of the 1,123,000 men who entered the seven prospective studies and who provided usable histories of smoking habits (and other characteristics such as age), 37,391 men died during the subsequent months or years of the studies. No analyses of data for females from prospective studies are presently available.

To permit ready comparison of the mortality experience of smokers and non-smokers, two concepts are widely used in the studies—excess deaths of smokers compared with non-smokers, and mortality ratio. After adjustments for differences in age and the number of cigarette smokers and non-smokers, an expected number of deaths of smokers is derived on the basis of deaths among non-smokers. Excess deaths are thus the number of actual (observed) deaths among smokers in excess of the number expected. The mortality ratio, for which the method of computation is described in Chapter 8, measures the relative death rates of smokers and non-smokers. If the age-adjusted death rates are the same, the mortality ratio will be 1.0; if the death rates of smokers are double those of non-smokers, the mortality ratio will be 2.0. (Expressed as a percentage, this example would be equivalent to a 100 percent increase.)

Table 2 presents the accumulated and combined data on 14 disease categories for which the mortality ratio of cigarette smokers to non-smokers was 1.5 or greater.

The mortality ratio for male cigarette smokers compared with non-smokers, for all causes of death taken together, is 1.68, representing a total death rate nearly 70 percent higher than for non-smokers. (This ratio includes death rates for diseases not listed in the table as well as for the 14 disease categories shown.)

In the combined results from the seven studies, the mortality ratio of cigarette smokers over non-smokers was particularly high for a number of

TABLE 2.[1] *Expected and Observed Deaths for Smokers of Cigarettes Only and Mortality Ratios in Seven Prospective Studies*

Underlying cause of death	Expected deaths	Observed deaths	Mortality ratio
Cancer of lung (162–3) [2]	170.3	1,833	10.8
Bronchitis and emphysema (502, 521.1)	89.5	546	6.1
Cancer of larynx (161)	14.0	75	5.4
Oral cancer (140–8)	37.0	152	4.1
Cancer of esophagus (150)	33.7	113	3.4
Stomach and duodenal ulcers (540, 541)	105.1	294	2.8
Other circulatory diseases (451–68)	254.0	649	2.6
Cirrhosis of liver (581)	169.2	379	2.2
Cancer of bladder (181)	111.6	216	1.9
Coronary artery disease (420)	6,430.7	11,177	1.7
Other heart diseases (421–2, 430–4)	526.0	868	1.7
Hypertensive heart (440–3)	409.2	631	1.5
General arteriosclerosis (450)	210.7	310	1.5
Cancer of kidney (180)	79.0	120	1.5
All causes [3]	15,653.9	23,223	1.68

[1] Abridged from Table 26, Chapter 8, Mortality.
[2] International Statistical Classification numbers in parentheses.
[3] Includes all other causes of death as well as those listed above.

diseases: cancer of the lung (10.8), bronchitis and emphysema (6.1), cancer of the larynx (5.4), oral cancer (4.1), cancer of the esophagus (3.4), peptic ulcer (2.8), and the group of other circulatory diseases (2.6). For coronary artery disease the mortality ratio was 1.7.

Expressed in percentage-form, this is equivalent to a statement that for coronary artery disease, the leading cause of death in this country, the death rate is 70 percent higher for cigarette smokers. For chronic bronchitis and emphysema, which are among the leading causes of severe disability, the death rate for cigarette smokers is 500 percent higher than for non-smokers. For lung cancer, the most frequent site of cancer in men, the death rate is nearly 1,000 percent higher.

OTHER FINDINGS OF THE PROSPECTIVE STUDIES

In general, the greater number of cigarettes smoked daily, the higher the death rate. For men who smoke fewer than 10 cigarettes a day, according to the seven prospective studies, the death rate from all causes is about 40 percent higher than for non-smokers. For those who smoke from 10 to 19 cigarettes a day, it is about 70 percent higher than for non-smokers; for those who smoke 20 to 39 a day, 90 percent higher; and for those who smoke 40 or more, it is 120 percent higher.

Cigarette smokers who stopped smoking before enrolling in the seven studies have a death rate about 40 percent higher than non-smokers, as against 70 percent higher for current cigarette smokers. Men who began smoking before age 20 have a substantially higher death rate than those who began after age 25. Compared with non-smokers, the mortality risk of cigarette smokers, after adjustments for differences in age, increases with duration of smoking (number of years), and is higher in those who stopped after age 55 than for those who stopped at an earlier age.

In two studies which recorded the degree of inhalation, the mortality ratio for a given amount of smoking was greater for inhalers than for non-inhalers.

The ratio of the death rates of smokers to that of non-smokers is highest at the earlier ages (40–50) represented in these studies, and declines with increasing age.

Possible relationships of death rates and other forms of tobacco use were also investigated in the seven studies. The death rates for men smoking less than 5 cigars a day are about the same as for non-smokers. For men smoking more than 5 cigars daily, death rates are slightly higher. There is some indication that these higher death rates occur primarily in men who have been smoking more than 30 years and who inhale the smoke to some degree. The death rates for pipe smokers are little if at all higher than for non-smokers, even for men who smoke 10 or more pipefuls a day and for men who have smoked pipes more than 30 years.

EXCESS MORTALITY

Several of the reports previously published on the prospective studies included a table showing the distribution of the excess number of deaths of cigarette smokers among the principal causes of death. The hazard must be measured not only by the mortality ratio of deaths in smokers and non-smokers, but also by the importance of a particular disease as a cause of death.

In all seven studies, coronary artery disease is the chief contributor to the excess number of deaths of cigarette smokers over non-smokers, with lung cancer uniformly in second place. For all seven studies combined, coronary artery disease (with a mortality ratio of 1.7) accounts for 45 percent of the excess deaths among cigarette smokers, whereas lung cancer (with a ratio of 10.8) accounts for 16 percent.

Some of the other categories of diseases that contribute to the higher death rates for cigarette smokers over non-smokers are diseases of the heart and blood vessels, other than coronary artery disease, 14 percent; cancer sites other than lung, 8 percent; and chronic bronchitis and emphysema, 4 percent.

Since these diseases as a group are responsible for more than 85 percent of the higher death rate among cigarette smokers, they are of particular interest to public health authorities and the medical profession.

Associations and Causality

The array of information from the prospective and restrospective studies of smokers and non-smokers clearly establishes an association between cigarette smoking and substantially higher death rates. The mortality ratios in Table 2 provide an approximate index of the relative strength of this association, for all causes of death and for 14 disease categories.

In this inquiry the epidemiologic method was used extensively in the assessment of causal factors in the relationship of smoking to health among human beings upon whom direct experimentation could not be imposed. Clinical, pathological, and experimental evidence was thoroughly considered and often served to suggest an hypothesis or confirm or contradict other findings. When coupled with the other data, results from the epidemiologic studies can provide the basis upon which judgments of causality may be made.

It is recognized that no simple cause-and-effect relationship is likely to exist between a complex product like tobacco smoke and a specific disease in the variable human organism. It is also recognized that often the coexistence of several factors is required for the occurrence of a disease, and that one of the factors may play a determinant role; that is, without it, the other factors (such as genetic susceptibility) seldom lead to the occurrence of the disease.

The Effects of Smoking: Principal Findings

Cigarette smoking is associated with a 70 percent increase in the age-specific death rates of males. The total number of excess deaths causally related to cigarette smoking in the U. S. population cannot be accurately estimated. In view of the continuing and mounting evidence from many sources, it is the judgment of the Committee that cigarette smoking contributes substantially to mortality from certain specific diseases and to the overall death rate.

LUNG CANCER

Cigarette smoking is causally related to lung cancer in men; the magnitude of the effect of cigarette smoking far outweighs all other factors. The data for women, though less extensive, point in the same direction.

The risk of developing lung cancer increases with duration of smoking and the number of cigarettes smoked per day, and is diminished by discontinuing smoking. In comparison with non-smokers, average male smokers of cigarettes have approximately a 9- to 10-fold risk of developing lung cancer and heavy smokers at least a 20-fold risk.

The risk of developing cancer of the lung for the combined group of pipe smokers, cigar smokers, and pipe and cigar smokers is greater than for non-smokers, but much less than for cigarette smokers.

Cigarette smoking is much more important than occupational exposures in the causation of lung cancer in the general population.

CHRONIC BRONCHITIS AND EMPHYSEMA

Cigarette smoking is the most important of the causes of chronic bronchitis in the United States, and increases the risk of dying from chronic bronchitis and emphysema. A relationship exists between cigarette smoking and emphysema but it has not been established that the relationship is causal. Studies demonstrate that fatalities from this disease are infrequent among non-smokers.

For the bulk of the population of the United States, the relative importance of cigarette smoking as a cause of chronic broncho-pulmonary disease is much greater than atmospheric pollution or occupational exposures.

CARDIOVASCULAR DISEASES

It is established that male cigarette smokers have a higher death rate from coronary artery disease than non-smoking males. Although the causative role of cigarette smoking in deaths from coronary disease is not proven, the Committee considers it more prudent from the public health viewpoint to assume that the established association has causative meaning than to suspend judgment until no uncertainty remains.

Although a causal relationship has not been established, higher mortality of cigarette smokers is associated with many other cardiovascular diseases, including miscellaneous circulatory diseases, other heart diseases, hypertensive heart disease, and general arteriosclerosis.

OTHER CANCER SITES

Pipe smoking appears to be causally related to lip cancer. Cigarette smoking is a significant factor in the causation of cancer of the larynx. The evidence supports the belief that an association exists between tobacco use and cancer of the esophagus, and between cigarette smoking and cancer of the urinary bladder in men, but the data are not adequate to decide whether these relationships are causal. Data on an association between smoking and cancer of the stomach are contradictory and incomplete.

The Tobacco Habit and Nicotine

The habitual use of tobacco is related primarily to psychological and social drives, reinforced and perpetuated by the pharmacological actions of nicotine.

Social stimulation appears to play a major role in a young person's early and first experiments with smoking. No scientific evidence supports the popular hypothesis that smoking among adolescents is an expression of rebellion against authority. Individual stress appears to be associated more with fluctuations in the amount of smoking than with the prevalence of smoking. The overwhelming evidence indicates that smoking—its beginning, habituation, and occasional discontinuation—is to a very large extent psychologically and socially determined.

Nicotine is rapidly changed in the body to relatively inactive substances with low toxicity. The chronic toxicity of small doses of nicotine is low in experimental animals. These two facts, when taken in conjunction with the low mortality ratios of pipe and cigar smokers, indicate that the chronic toxicity of nicotine in quantites absorbed from smoking and other methods of tobacco use is very low and probably does not represent an important health hazard.

The significant beneficial effects of smoking occur primarily in the area of mental health, and the habit originates in a search for contentment. Since no means of measuring the quantity of these benefits is apparent, the Committee finds no basis for a judgment which would weigh benefits against hazards of smoking as it may apply to the general population.

The Committee's Judgment in Brief

On the basis of prolonged study and evaluation of many lines of converging evidence, the Committee makes the following judgment:

Cigarette smoking is a health hazard of sufficient importance in the United States to warrant appropriate remedial action.

B. COMMENTS AND DETAILED CONCLUSIONS

(A Guide to Part II of the Report)

All conclusions formally adopted by the Committee are presented at the end of this section in bold-faced type for convenience of reference. In the interest of conciseness, the documentation and most of the discussion are omitted from this condensation. Together with the tables of contents which appear at the beginning of each chapter in Part II, it is intended as a guide to the Report.

Chemistry and Carcinogenicity of Tobacco and Tobacco Smoke

Condensates of tobacco smoke are carcinogenic when tested by application to the skin of mice and rabbits and by subcutaneous injection in rats (Chapter 9, pp. 143–145). Bronchogenic carcinoma has not been produced by the application of tobacco extracts, smoke, or condensates to the lung or the tracheobronchial tree of experimental animals with the possible exception of dogs (Chapter 9, p. 165).

Bronchogenic carcinoma has been produced in laboratory animals by the administration of polycyclic aromatic hydrocarbons, certain metals, radioactive substances, and viruses. The histopathologic characteristics of the tumors produced are similar to those observed in man and are predominantly of the squamous variety (Chapter 9, pp. 166–167).

Seven polycyclic hydrocarbon compounds isolated from cigarette smoke have been established to be carcinogenic in laboratory animals. The results of a number of assays for carcinogenicity of tobacco smoke tars present a puzzling anomaly: the total tar from cigarettes has many times the carcinogenic potency of benzo (a) pyrene present in the tar. The other carcinogens known to be present in tobacco smoke are, with the exception of dibenzo (a,i) pyrene, much less potent than benzo (a) pyrene and they are present in smaller amounts. Apparently, therefore, the whole is greater than the sum of the known parts. This discrepancy may possibly be due to the presence of cocarcinogens in tobacco smoke, and/or damage to mucus production and ciliary transport mechanism (Chapter 6, p. 61, Chapter 9, p. 144 and Chapter 10, pp. 267–269).

There is abundant evidence that cancer of the skin can be induced in man by industrial exposure to soots, coal tar, pitch, and mineral oils. All of these contain various polycyclic aromatic hydrocarbons proved to be carcinogenic in many species of animals. Some of these hydrocarbons are also present in tobacco smoke. It is reasonable to assume that these can be carcinogenic for man also (Chapter 9, pp. 146–148).

Genetic factors play a significant role in the development of pulmonary adenomas in mice. It is possible that genetic factors can influence the smoking habit and the response in man to carcinogens in smoke. However, there is no evidence that they have played an appreciable role in the great increase of lung cancer in man since the beginning of this century (Chapter 9, p. 190).

Components of the gas phase of cigarette smoke have been shown to produce various undesirable effects on test animals or organs. One of these effects is suppression of ciliary transport activity, an important cleansing function in the trachea and bronchi (Chapter 6, p. 61 and Chapter 10, pp. 267–270).

Characterization of the Tobacco Habit

The habitual use of tobacco is related primarily to psychological and social drives, reinforced and perpetuated by the pharmacological actions of nicotine on the central nervous system. Nicotine-free tobacco or other plant materials do not satisfy the needs of those who acquire the tobacco habit (Chapter 13, p. 354).

The tobacco habit should be characterized as an habituation rather than an addiction. Discontinuation of smoking, although possessing the difficulties attendant upon extinction of any conditioned reflex, is accomplished best by reinforcing factors which interrupt the psychogenic drives. Nicotine substitutes or supplementary medications have not been proven to be of major benefit in breaking the habit (Chapter 13, p. 354).

Pathology and Morphology

Several types of epithelial changes are much more common in the trachea and bronchi of cigarette smokers, with or without lung cancer, than of non-smokers and of patients without lung cancer. These epithelial changes are (a) loss of cilia, (b) basal cell hyperplasia, and (c) appearance of atypical cells with irregular hyperchromatic nuclei. The degree of each of the epithelial changes in general increases with the number of cigarettes smoked. Extensive atypical changes have been seen most frequently in men who smoked two or more packs of cigarettes a day.

Women cigarette smokers, in general, have the same epithelial changes as men smokers. However, at given levels of cigarette use, women appear to show fewer atypical cells than do men. Older men smokers have more atypical cells than younger men smokers. Men who smoke either pipes or cigars have more epithelial changes than non-smokers, but have fewer changes than cigarette smokers consuming approximately the same amount of tobacco. Male ex-cigarette smokers have less hyperplasia and fewer atypical cells than current cigarette smokers.

It may be concluded, on the basis of human and experimental evidence, that some of the advanced epithelial hyperplastic lesions with many atypical cells, as seen in the bronchi of cigarette smokers, are probably premalignant (Chapter 9, pp. 167–173).

Typing of Tumors.—Squamous and oval-cell carcinomas (Group I of Kreyberg's classification) comprise the predominant types associated with the increase of lung cancer in the male population. In several studies, adenocarcinomas (Group II) have also shown a definite increase, although to a much lesser degree. The histological typing of lung cancer is reliable, but the use of the ratio of histological types as an index of the magnitude of increase in lung cancer is of limited value (Chapter 9, pp. 173–175).

Functional and Pathological Changes.—Cigarette smoke produces significant functional alterations in the trachea, bronchus, and lung. Like several other agents, cigarette smoke can reduce or abolish ciliary motility in experimental animals. Postmortem examination of bronchi from smokers shows a decrease in the number of ciliated cells, shortening of the remaining cilia, and changes in goblet cells and mucous glands. The implication of these morphological observations is that functional impairment would result.

In animal experiments, cigarette smoke appears to affect the physical characteristics of the lung-lining layer and to impair alveolar (air sac) stability. Alveolar phagocytes ingest tobacco smoke components and assist in their removal from the lung. This phagocytic clearance mechanism breaks down under the stress of protracted high-level exposure to cigarette smoke, and smoke components accumulate in the lungs of experimental animals (Chapter 10, pp. 269–270).

The chronic effects of cigarette smoking upon pulmonary function are manifested mainly by a reduction in ventilatory function as measured by the forced expiratory volume (Chapter 10, pp. 289–292).

Histopathological alterations occur as a result of tobacco smoke exposure in the tracheobronchial tree and in the lung parenchyma of man. Changes regularly found in chronic bronchitis—increase in the number of goblet cells, and hypertrophy and hyperplasia of bronchial mucous glands—are more often present in the bronchi of smokers than non-smokers. Cigarette smoke produces significant functional alterations in the upper and lower airways to the lungs. Such alterations could be expected to interfere with the cleansing mechanisms of the lung.

Pathological changes in pulmonary parenchyma, such as rupture of alveolar septa (partitions of the air sacs) and fibrosis, have a remarkably close association with past history of cigarette smoking. These latter changes cannot be related with certainty to emphysema or other recognized diseases at the present time (Chapter 10, pp. 270–275).

Mortality

The death rate for smokers of cigarettes only, who were smoking at the time of entry into the particular prospective study, is about 70 percent higher than that for non-smokers. The death rates increase with the amount smoked. For groups of men smoking less than 10, 10–19, 20–39, and 40 cigarettes and over per day, respectively, the death rates are about 40 percent, 70 percent, 90 percent, and 120 percent higher than for non-smokers. The ratio of the death rates of smokers to non-smokers is highest at the earlier ages (40–50) represented in these studies, and declines with increasing age. The same effect appears to hold for the ratio of the death rate of heavy smokers to that of light smokers. In the studies that provided this information, the mortality ratio of cigarette smokers to non-smokers was substantially higher for men who started to smoke under age 20 than for men who started after age 25. The mortality ratio was increased as the number of years of smoking increased. In two studies which recorded the degree of inhalation, the mortality ratio for a given amount of smoking was greater for inhalers than for non-inhalers. Cigarette smokers who had stopped smoking prior to enrollment in the study had mortality ratios about 1.4 as against 1.7 for current cigarette smokers. The mortality ratio of ex-cigarette smokers increased with the number of years of smoking and was higher for those who stopped after age 55 than for those who stopped at an earlier age (Chapter 8, p. 93).

The biases from non-response and from errors of measurement that are difficult to avoid in mass studies may have resulted in some over-estimation of the true mortality ratios for the complete populations. In our judgment, however, such biases can account for only a part of the elevation in mortality ratios found for cigarette smokers (Chapter 8, p. 96).

Death rates of cigar smokers are about the same as those of non-smokers for men smoking less than five cigars daily. For men smoking five or more cigars daily, death rates were slightly higher (9 percent to 27 percent) than for non-smokers in the four studies that gave this information. There is some indication that this higher death rate occurs primarily in men who have been smoking for more than 30 years and in men who stated that they inhaled the smoke to some degree. Death rates for current pipe smokers were little if at all higher than for non-smokers, even with men smoking 10 or more pipefuls per day and with men who had smoked pipes for more than 30 years. Ex-cigar and ex-pipe smokers, on the other hand, showed higher death rates than both non-smokers and current pipe or cigar smokers in four out of five studies (Chapter 8, p. 94). The explanation is not clear but may be that a substantial number of such smokers stopped because of illness.

Mortality by Cause of Death. In the combined results from the seven prospective studies, the mortality ratio of cigarette smokers was particularly high for a number of diseases. There is a further group of diseases, including some of the most important chronic diseases, for which the mortality ratio for cigarette smokers lay between 1.2 and 2.0. The explanation of the moderate elevations in mortality ratios in this large group of causes is not clear. Part may be due to the sources of bias previously mentioned or to some constitutional and genetic difference between cigarette smokers and non-smokers. There is also the possibility that cigarette smoking has some general debilitating effect, although no medical evidence that clearly supports this hypothesis can be cited (Chapter 8, p. 105).

In all seven studies, coronary artery disease is the chief contributor to the excess number of deaths of cigarette smokers over non-smokers, with lung cancer uniformly in second place (Chapter 8, p. 108).

For cigar and pipe smokers combined, there was a suggestion of high mortality ratios for cancers of the mouth, esophagus, larynx and lung, and for stomach and duodenal ulcers. These ratios are, however, based on small numbers of deaths (Chapter 8, p. 107).

Cancer by Site

LUNG CANCER

Cigarette smoking is causally related to lung cancer in men; the magnitude of the effect of cigarette smoking far outweighs all other factors. The data for women, though less extensive, point in the same direction.

The risk of developing lung cancer increases with duration of smoking and the number of cigarettes smoked per day, and is diminished by discontinuing smoking.

The risk of developing cancer of the lung for the combined group of pipe smokers, cigar smokers, and pipe and cigar smokers, is greater than for non-smokers, but much less than for cigarette smokers. The data are insufficient to warrant a conclusion for each group individually (Chapter 9, p. 196).

ORAL CANCER

The causal relationship of the smoking of pipes to the development of cancer of the lip appears to be established.

Although there are suggestions of relationships between cancer of other specific sites of the oral cavity and the several forms of tobacco use, their causal implications cannot at present be stated (Chapter 9, pp. 204–205).

CANCER OF THE LARYNX

Evaluation of the evidence leads to the judgment that cigarette smoking is a significant factor in the causation of laryngeal cancer in the male (Chapter 9, p. 212).

CANCER OF THE ESOPHAGUS

The evidence on the tobacco-esophageal cancer relationship supports the belief that an association exists. However, the data are not adequate to decide whether the relationship is causal (Chapter 9, p. 218).

CANCER OF THE URINARY BLADDER

Available data suggest an association between cigarette smoking and urinary bladder cancer in the male but are not sufficient to support a judgment on the causal significance of this association (Chapter 9, p. 225).

STOMACH CANCER

No relationship has been established between tobacco use and stomach cancer (Chapter 9, p. 229).

Non-Neoplastic Respiratory Diseases, Particularly Chronic Bronchitis and Pulmonary Emphysema

Cigarette smoking is the most important of the causes of chronic bronchitis in the United States, and increases the risk of dying from chronic bronchitis.

A relationship exists between pulmonary emphysema and cigarette smoking but it has not been established that the relationship is causal. The smoking of cigarettes is associated with an increased risk of dying from pulmonary emphysema.

For the bulk of the population of the United States, the importance of cigarette smoking as a cause of chronic bronchopulmonary disease is much greater than that of atmospheric pollution or occupational exposures.

Cough, sputum production, or the two combined are consistently more frequent among cigarette smokers than among non-smokers.

Cigarette smoking is associated with a reduction in ventilatory function. Among males, cigarette smokers have a greater prevalence of breathlessness than non-smokers.

Cigarette smoking does not appear to cause asthma.

Although death certification shows that cigarette smokers have a moderately increased risk of death from influenza and pneumonia, an association of cigarette smoking and infectious diseases is not otherwise substantiated (Chapter 10, p. 302).

Cardiovascular Disease

Smoking and nicotine administration cause acute cardiovascular effects similar to those induced by stimulation of the autonomic nervous system, but these effects do not account well for the observed association between cigarette smoking and coronary disease. It is established that male cigarette smokers have a higher death rate from coronary disease than non-smoking males. The association of smoking with other cardiovascular disorders is less well established. If cigarette smoking actually caused the higher death rate from coronary disease, it would on this account be responsible for many deaths of middle-aged and elderly males in the United States. Other factors such as high blood pressure, high serum cholesterol, and excessive obesity are also known to be associated with an unusually high death rate from coronary disease. The causative role of these factors in coronary disease, though not proven, is suspected strongly enough to be a major reason for taking countermeasures against them. It is also more prudent to assume that the established association between cigarette smoking and coronary disease has causative meaning than to suspend judgment until no uncertainty remains (Chapter 11, p. 327).

Male cigarette smokers have a higher death rate from coronary artery disease than non-smoking males, but it is not clear that the association has causal significance.

Other Conditions

PEPTIC ULCER

Epidemiological studies indicate an association between cigarette smoking and peptic ulcer which is greater for gastric than for duodenal ulcer (Chapter 12, p. 340).

TOBACCO AMBLYOPIA

Tobacco amblyopia (dimness of vision unexplained by an organic lesion) has been related to pipe and cigar smoking by clinical impressions. The association has not been substantiated by epidemiological or experimental studies (Chapter 12, p. 342).

CIRRHOSIS OF THE LIVER

Increased mortality of smokers from cirrhosis of the liver has been shown in the prospective studies. The data are not sufficient to support a direct or causal association (Chapter 12, p. 342).

MATERNAL SMOKING AND INFANT BIRTH WEIGHT

Women who smoke cigarettes during pregnancy tend to have babies of lower birth weight.

Information is lacking on the mechanism by which this decrease in birth weight is produced.

It is not known whether this decrease in birth weight has any influence on the biological fitness of the newborn (Chapter 12, p. 343).

SMOKING AND ACCIDENTS

Smoking is associated with accidental deaths from fires in the home.

No conclusive information is available on the effects of smoking on traffic accidents (Chapter 12, p. 345).

Morphological Constitution of Smokers

The available evidence suggests the existence of some morphological differences between smokers and non-smokers, but is too meager to permit a conclusion (Chapter 15, p. 387).

Psycho-Social Aspects of Smoking

A clear cut smoker's personality has not emerged from the results so far published. While smokers differ from non-smokers in a variety of characteristics, none of the studies has shown a single variable which is found solely in one group and is completely absent in another. Nor has any single variable been verified in a sufficiently large proportion of smokers and in sufficiently few non-smokers to consider it an "essential" aspect of smoking.

The overwhelming evidence points to the conclusion that smoking—its beginning, habituation, and occasional discontinuation—is to a large extent psychologically and socially determined. This does not rule out physiological factors, especially in respect to habituation, nor the existence of predisposing constitutional or hereditary factors (Chapter 14, p. 377).

Smoking and Health: *Other Side of the Report*

ALAN S. DONNAHOE

The recent report of the Surgeon General's advisory committee is based largely on statistics of highly questionable nature, and is shot through with inconsistencies and contradictions.

If we are to accept the major conclusion that cigaret smoking is a major cause of lung cancer, we must also accept other illogical and sometimes downright ridiculous conclusions that evolve from the same statistical evidence.

In this analysis, no attempt will be made to review all of the evidence in the lengthy report. Rather, an effort will be made to review some of the more

Richmond *Times-Dispatch*, January 19, 1964, p. B–13. Reprinted by permission of the author.

glaring contradictions in this evidence, which up to this time have received little emphasis or publicity.

This discussion will be confined to the report itself. No attempt will be made to consider any other evidence, outside the report, even though some of this is quite dramatic in its apparent refutation of the committee's main conclusion.

The advisory committee included eight doctors, one chemist, and one statistician. In view of the fact that most of the available evidence was statistical, it is unfortunate that more statisticians were not included on the committee.

This is particularly important, it would seem, inasmuch as the committee did not undertake any original research but rather confined itself to a review and evaluation of research conducted by others. Such a review of statistical work performed by others is especially difficult for anyone other than a highly competent statistician.

The major evidence before the committee evolved from seven statistical surveys, sponsored by a variety of agencies. In terms of basic methodology, by the committee's own admission, these surveys leave much to be desired. Here is the description applied by the committee itself:

"Various reasons dictated the choices made of the seven study populations, considerations of feasibility playing an important role. None of the populations was designed, in particular, to be representative of the United States male population. An answer to the question 'to what general population of men can the results be applied?', must involve an element of unverifiable judgment. The seven studies differ considerably in size. They vary also in the extent to which they are free from methodological weakness."

What this means, in non-technical language, is that the findings of these various surveys, as a matter of sound statistical procedure, cannot be considered as representative of any known population of any kind. Statistically speaking, this is a serious indictment of any survey.

On this subject, a further comment by the committee, dealing with the percentage of individuals who failed to respond to survey questionnaires, is quite significant:

"In the two American Cancer Society studies it is not possible to present meaningful percentages, since each research volunteer selected her own small part of the study population from among her own acquaintances."

One need not be a statistician to recognize the dangers involved in selecting any sample from among one's own "acquaintances." It would be difficult to suggest a more unscientific sampling procedure.

But this is not all. The committee goes on to say:

"In all five studies that had a clearly defined target population, sizeable proportions of the population were omitted. The major reason was failure to answer the questionnaire; in addition, certain replies were rejected as too incomplete."

Individuals who failed to respond in point of fact, represented 15, 32, 32, 43, and 44 per cent in the five studies. This, again, is a major statistical deficiency, raising the possibility of serious bias in the results. This possibility, at least in part, is acknowledged by the committee.

When we consider both of these factors: (1) the fact that respondents were selected on a haphazard or volunteer basis, and hence were not representative of any known population; and (2) the large percentage of non-response encountered—the result is a statistical melange of unknown and unknowable reliability.

This may account for some of the strange and unexplainable results produced by these surveys. In most instances, for example, the mortality rate after adjustment for age is far below the national average—not only for non-smokers, but often for heavy cigaret smokers as well. In three of the seven studies, the age-adjusted mortality rate of heavy cigaret smokers was lower than the average for all males in the United States population, and in one survey was almost 30 per cent lower than the national average!

The committee comments on this as follows:

"It is clear that the seven . . . studies involve populations which are healthier than United States males as a whole. Secondly, the low death rates for non-smokers suggest the possibility that the studies recruited unusually healthy groups of non-smokers."

After pointing out that the exclusion of hospitalized and seriously ill individuals might account for some of this variation, the committee admits that "the sizes of the differences appear surprising." All things considered, this would seem to be a rather remarkable understatement.

There are other oddities in the statistical evidence, such as one finding that men from 80 to 89 who are heavy cigaret smokers have about 40 per cent less mortality than non-smokers, and still another finding in one of the surveys that men smoking less than 15 years have a slightly lower mortality rate than non-smokers.

It is possible that these freakish results evolve from the use of small samples in these sub-categories; but this cannot account for another and far more significant paradox.

If the statistical evidence before the committee is to be accepted and believed in full, then we must conclude that cigaret smoking not only causes lung cancer, but is also a major cause of almost every other type of death from all diseases of all kinds!

The astonishing fact—if we are to believe the statistical evidence cited by the committee—is that lung cancer accounts for only 15 to 20 per cent of the excess deaths attributable to cigaret smoking. About half of the excess is to be found in heart disease, and another quarter of the excess in other chronic diseases of various kinds.

Altogether, if projected to the United States population, this would mean that some 250,000 people die every year from some disease induced by cigaret smoking, and that this occurs without a single one of these deaths being noted as such by clinical test of any kind. As one statistician puts it: only by their numbers are they known!

This rather staggers the imagination, and particularly so when the committee finds no causal connection between these various diseases and cigaret smoking.

The committee does consider some hypotheses that have been offered on the subject—that smokers differ physically from non-smokers, or perhaps that cigarets have a generally debilitating effect—but it passes no judgment on any of these.

The statistical evidence is equally paradoxical on the matter of pipe smoking. Here is what the committee has to say on this subject:

"Death rates for current pipe smokers were little if at all higher than from non-smokers, even with men smoking 10 or more pipefuls per day and with all men who had smoked pipes for more than 30 years. Ex-pipe smokers, on the other hand, showed higher death rates than both non-smokers and current smokers in four out of five studies. The epidemiological studies on ex-cigar and ex-pipe smokers are inadequate to explain this puzzling phenomenon."

In other words, the statistical evidence would indicate that it is quite safe to smoke a pipe, but highly dangerous to discontinue the practice! This is indeed a puzzling phenomenon, but if we are to accept the other statistical findings in the report, we must accept this one as well.

Another curious finding in the report shows the relative mortality from all causes, in relation to cigaret smoking and other factors. While such smoking would appear to raise the mortality rate in every instance, the other factors also appear quite potent.

For example, cigaret smokers who take heavy exercise have a lower mortality rate than non-smokers who take none. Similarly, cigaret smokers among married men have just about the same mortality rate as non-smokers who are single. If cigaret smokers are so fortunate as to have long-lived parents and grandparents, their mortality rate is about the same as for non-smokers with short-lived ancestors.

From other data shown in the commission report, it appears that the incidence of certain types of cancer tends to vary from one region of the country to another, and even by individual city, and is inversely related to income level. Among males in the lowest income class, for example, the lung cancer rate is double that of high income males. None of this would seem to have any relationship to cigaret smoking. Other instances cited in the commission report:

Bartenders, waiters and others engaged in the alcoholic beverage trade have double the average mortality rate for lung cancer. This, presumably, has nothing to do with their consumption of cigarets.

Among American citizens, men and women born in Ireland have high death rates from oral and esophageal cancers. Polish-born Americans have pronounced excess mortality for esophageal and gastric cancers, and Polish males rank first in lung cancer. Russian-born individuals show high death rates for stomach and (among women only) esophageal cancer. English-born Americans have above-average lung cancer risks.

Whereas none of this would deny a possible relationship with cigaret smoking, it does clearly indicate that the causes of cancer are complex in their origin, and that we are still far from any real understanding of the subject.

Perhaps more significant, in terms of the report under discussion, are its findings with respect to the incidence of lung cancer in other countries. Although the finding is that there is some correlation with cigaret smoking, the data might well justify the opposite interpretation.

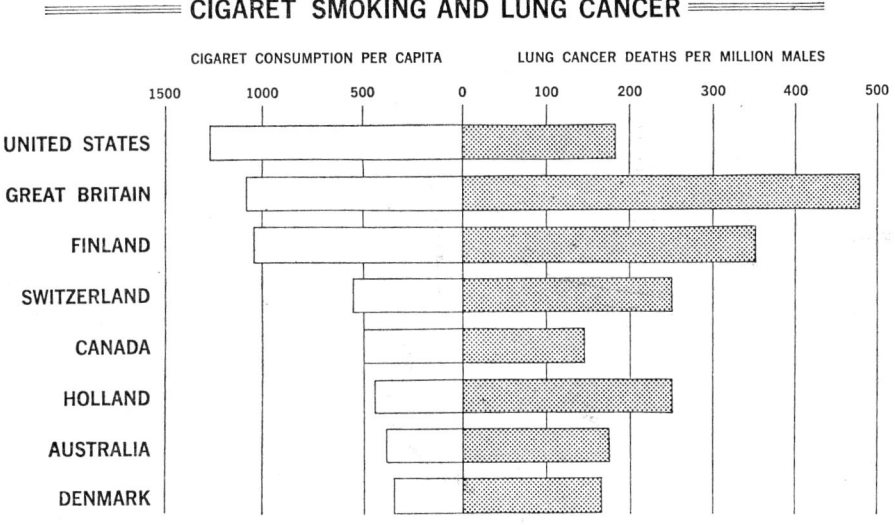

From Data Reported on Page 176 of "Smoking and Health." Lung Cancer Rates for 1950, Per Capita Consumption of Cigarets for 1930, in Selected Countries.

For example, the report shows that Holland, Switzerland, Finland and Great Britain have a lower per capita consumption of cigarets than the United States, but that all have higher mortality from lung cancer. Indeed, in the case of Great Britain, the mortality rate is more than double that of the United States. Similarly, Canada, Australia and Denmark all have about one-half the United States per capita consumption of cigarets, but show about the same mortality rate from lung cancer.

Finally, the report is not impressive in the evidence presented to supplement its statistical findings. One would think that the best evidence would be obtained by direct experimentation. In other words, to ascertain the effect of cigaret smoking, experimental animals would be subjected to such smoke for extended periods of time, to see if cancer were induced.

On this subject, the committee's report is succinct and to the point:

"Few attempts have been made to produce bronchogenic carcinoma in experimental animals with tobacco extracts, smoke or smoke condensates. With one possible exception, none has been successful.

"The production of bronchogenic carcinomas has not been reported by any investigator exposing experimental animals to tobacco smoke."

In view of the fact that perhaps a billion dollars has been spent on cancer research in the last decade, this would seem to be an astonishing statement. Why have there been so "few attempts" at what would seem to be the most direct experimental approach to the subject?

A possible explanation for this strange lack of effort in what would seem to be the most logical, direct, and persuasive form of research may be found in a statement attributed to Einstein. He is quoted as having once remarked that the only way to discover what scientists really believe is not by what they say, but by what they do.

Certainly any scientist who could offer experimental proof of the causal effect of cigaret smoking on any type of cancer would doubtless win a brace of Nobel prizes. Why, then, so little effort in this particular experimental field? The apparent answer: scientists do not believe they can establish any such relationship, and hence are not willing to waste their time in this type of effort.

This may or may not be true, but it is surprising that the advisory committee made no significant comment on the question, and offered no adequate explanation of why more work had not been done in this more relevant and highly important research area.

The reader who has had the hardihood to follow this discussion in full may now well inquire: what does it all mean? The only honest answer would seem to be that no one can say precisely what it all means, which perhaps is the most significant conclusion of all.

Surely this report raises a strong inference that cigaret smoking has an adverse influence on health; but at this stage, it is simply that: an inference, no more and no less, and this it must remain until it can be verified experimentally.

By the nature of public statements, it is to be expected that the major conclusions of the advisory committee would be heavily publicized and widely noted. By the same token, it is to be expected that little attention would be given to the oddities and paradoxes in the report, even though these are quite astonishing in many surprising ways, and yet must be accepted in full if we are to accept the remainder of the report.

It is doubtful that the public will be aware, for example, that one of the most distinguished medical statisticians in the nation, Dr. Joseph Berkson of the Mayo Clinic, has raised many of the questions discussed here, as well as others, and expressed serious doubt about the statistical evidence on the effects of cigaret smoking, in various articles published by the American Statistical Association.

If, for example, we are willing to assume that non-smokers tend to differ physically and otherwise from smokers—in such ways, for example, as self-protective instinct; and we are further willing to assume certain biases among those who responded and failed to respond to these surveys; then the same type of survey findings could be obtained without any true correlation whatsoever between smoking and health.

In other words, these factors are sufficient to generate the appearance of correlation, although none in fact exists.

In many ways, this is a more plausible hypothesis and is more consistent with much of the evidence available than the one adopted in the advisory committee report. It at least avoids the collateral inference that cigaret smoking is adversely related to almost every known type of disease: a fantastic assumption which cannot be supported by the slightest shred of clinical or experimental evidence of any kind.

In any case, these are things that should be considered, to arrive at any proper perspective on the report issued by the advisory committee. It would be a tragedy if, on the basis of this report, the public were to decide that the issue had been resolved when, in point of fact, the report raises more questions than it answers.

Two immediate steps would seem to be in order. First, an official request to the American Statistical Association to appoint a committee of distinguished statisticians to review and evaluate all statistical evidence on the subject. This committee should also be asked to suggest the framework for all future studies, to insure cogency, significance, and reliability of results.

Second, increased emphasis by all interested agencies, supported by such funds as may be required, on experimental research of all kinds, and particularly on the effects of continuous exposure to tobacco smoke on the lungs of animals: the type of research where, in the words of the committee, there have been "few attempts" up to now. In this, as in all medical areas of knowledge, there can be no certainty until hypotheses have been verified by actual experimentation or clinical test.

In the history of science, many theories have been created and fully accepted for long periods, only to be abandoned, sometimes centuries later, on the basis of new and contradictory evidence. In this light, it may be appropriate to suggest that the final word has not yet been written, by the Surgeon General's committee or otherwise, on the subject of smoking and health.

Questions

1. Why is the statistical approach so basic to the question of whether cigarette smoking causes lung cancer? What are some of the objections Donnahoe

makes to the statistical methods described in the Surgeon General's report? Do these objections make sense?
2. Does Donnahoe refute all the evidence represented in the Surgeon General's report? What is Donnahoe's method of argument?
3. What has a smoker's personality got to do with his smoking? Might there be some way of determining that personality from a close analysis of the appeals made in newspaper, magazine, radio, and television cigarette advertising? How would you go about it?
4. What does Donnahoe mean when he says that the Surgeon General's report merely "raises a strong inference that cigarette smoking has an adverse influence on health"? Do you suppose it is possible that this inference might be disproved?
5. Dr. Charles Mayo, of the Mayo Clinic, was reported to have said about the report: "I hear these things [statistics] all the time. I don't think you can legislate against tobacco any more than you can legislate against sex or alcohol. We got into so much trouble with Prohibition before that we should have learned a lesson from that experience." What has legislation to do with the issue?
6. How do the methods of investigation and of argument in the two selections impress you? Are you convinced by either side? What reservations do you have?
7. Can you determine from the Surgeon General's report how the investigators went about getting their information? What weight would you give to evidence gained in the laboratory (experiments with animals, for instance) as opposed to evidence gained from questionnaires?
8. What is meant by "reliability"? "Validity"? "Correlation"? Why are these terms important in scientific studies?
9. What hypothesis did the investigators start with? How did they proceed? Would different procedures have been just as valid?
10. Which piece of writing is easier to read, the Surgeon General's report or Donnahoe's analysis? Why? Which carries more weight? Why?
11. What arguments beside the medical ones can be raised against smoking? What arguments are there to defend smoking?

Assignments

1. Without taking sides, summarize Donnahoe's statistical objections to the Surgeon General's report.
2. Design an experiment that would either prove or disprove that the excessive eating of candy causes lung cancer. Prepare your experiment in outline form, explaining what each step is supposed to establish.
3. Many persons turn around when they realize that someone is staring at them. First, stare steadily at the backs of the heads of several classmates, and report your findings. Second, interview several other persons to find out whether they have ever turned around when they thought someone was staring at them. Discuss the two different ways of getting information. Analyze your findings and propose a hypothesis—for example, "some persons can tell better than others when someone is looking at the backs of their heads."
4. On the basis of the material in this section, describe scientific method and scientific hypothesis. Show how your descriptions apply to one other section in this text.
5. Speculate on how it is possible for some perfectly respectable and well-trained

persons in a discipline to disagree with a majority of their colleagues. Consider the question, at least in passing, as to what extent scientific method and theory may be affected by social pressures.

6. Separate the scientific, the social, and the economic aspects of the cigarette smoking-lung cancer problem.

Additional Reading

The Surgeon General's report, *Smoking and Health* (Washington, 1964), offers the fullest treatment to date of the relation between cigarette smoking and lung cancer. The references in parentheses in the selection here refer to the full material in the text. The report also contains a very extensive bibliography. A more popular discussion, which also includes a survey of the tobacco industry's handling of the lung cancer problem, was published by Consumers Union: *Smoking and the Public Interest* (New York, 1963). In the March 1964 *Consumer Reports,* the organization relates its study to the Surgeon General's report.

While the focus in this section has been mainly on the scientific aspects of the problem, it is plain that the problem has many social and financial implications, involving government, the tobacco and advertising industries, as well as individuals. The New York *Times* index will indicate many news articles having to do with the several aspects of tobacco smoking.

For the possibility that lung cancer may have causes other than smoking, see the New York *Times* of March 8, 1964, p. 4, which carries a report by Arthur J. Olsen of an article published that month in the *Journal of Cancer Research,* in Düsseldorf, claiming that a careful and extensive analysis of lung cancer cases in the state of North-Rhine Westphalia indicated that air pollution was the more likely cause of the cancers than smoking. Edith Iglauer's article "Fifteen Thousand Quarts of Air," *New Yorker,* XL (March 7, 1964), 54–117, also discusses, among other things, the dangerous consequences of air pollution, including the damage done to lungs.

Two recent reports by the Associate Scientific Director of the Tobacco Industry Research Committee (150 East 42nd Street, New York 17, New York), Robert C. Hockett, Ph.D., survey the arguments against the exclusive correlating of smoking with disease: *Current Knowledge of Tobacco and Health* (New York, 1962) and "Cigarettes—Why More Research?" *Yale Scientific Magazine,* XXXVIII (April 1964), 5–9.

SECTION FOUR
Ethics and Population Control

Population Problems and the Control of Fertility

HUDSON HOAGLAND

The Decline in the Death Rate

Knowledge of itself is ethically neutral, but the uses to which it is put may have far-reaching consequences for good and evil. Major contributions of science of great significance often carry with them dangerous and quite unforeseen consequences. Examples of such ambivalences readily come to mind.

One of the most interesting examples is posed by the advances in the medical sciences in the last hundred years, which have brought a remarkable alleviation of human suffering and extension of the life span. In the Greco-Roman world of some two thousand years ago, the life expectancy of an infant at birth was only about 25 years, and in general it was even lower in Europe during the Middle Ages. At about 1850, the life expectancy in Western Europe and the United States had risen to only 40 years. But then a remarkable change occurred. In the past hundred years, life expectancy has climbed steadily so that it is now about 70 years in the United States—a gain of 30 years in the past century compared to 15 years in the previous twenty centuries.

Maurice Tainter [1] has given a good account of these changes and the

---

[1] Maurice L. Tainter, "Medicine's Golden Age: The Triumph of the Experimental Method," *Transactions of the New York Academy of Sciences*, 18 (1956), pp. 206–227.

Daedalus, Journal of the American Academy of Arts and Sciences, LXXXVIII (Summer 1959), 425–443. Reprinted by permission of *Daedalus* and the author.

major factors involved. The sudden increase of the life span, beginning about 1860 (see Figure 1) was the result primarily of the introduction of experimental procedures in physiology involving the study of living laboratory animals under controlled conditions. The name of the French physiologist Claude Bernard stands out above others here. A brilliant student of Magendie, he was a friend of Pasteur, who was in turn greatly influenced by him. Bernard's impact on professional biologists and medical men—for example, through his *Introduction to Experimental Medicine* (1865)—may be compared to that of Darwin.

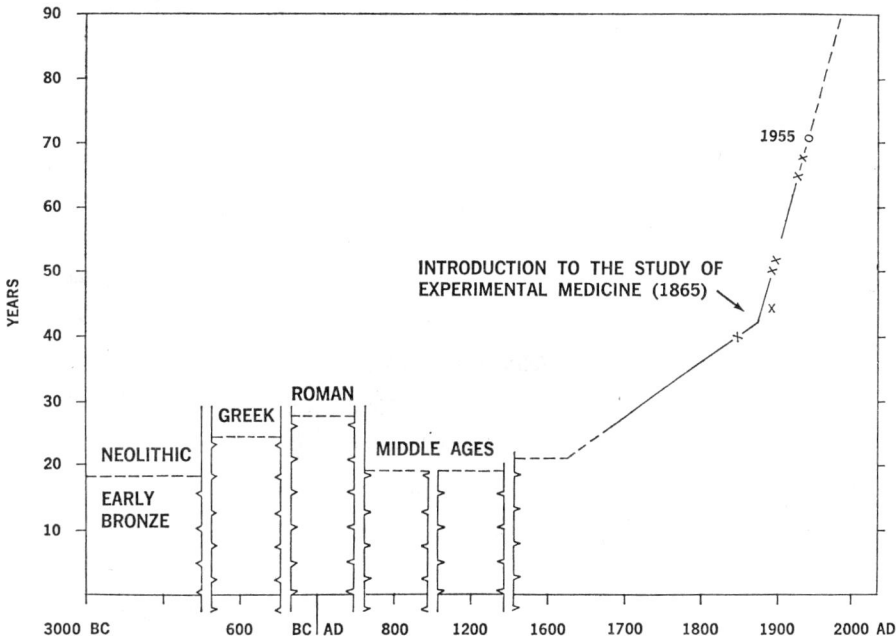

FIGURE 1. *Life Expectancy at Birth (Average of White Male and Female Population)*. Based on Maurice L. Tainter, *op. cit.*

A factor of comparable importance in advancing the medical sciences was the accumulation of knowledge about the carbon compounds, beginning early in the nineteenth century. The great development of organic chemistry and of its later offshoot biochemistry in the twentieth century has revolutionized the theory and practice of medicine. Starting with Pasteur, the bacteriological sciences and the sciences of immunology and sanitary practices have rapidly brought many infectious diseases under control. Within recent decades sulfa drugs, antibiotics, and insecticides have greatly extended this conquest through the happy conjunction of work of microbiologists, organic chemists, physiologists, biochemists, and clinicians. Thus, for example, from 1937 to 1955, a span of eighteen years, the over-all death rate in the United States dropped 18 per cent. In the eleven years from 1944 to 1955 the death rate from rheumatic fever dropped 77 per cent; that from pneumonia, 37 per cent; that from influenza, 90 per cent; that from maternal deaths, 77 per cent. The death rate from kidney diseases fell 65 per cent, and infant mortality rates declined 33 per cent.[2]

The result is that today the United States and Western Europe have relatively older populations increasingly susceptible to metabolic disorders more characteristic of the aged. We are told that one in three die of cardiovascular diseases, and one in five of cancer. It has also been pointed out that one out of one of us will die. Those who have been spared the bacteria and viruses have other unpleasant things in store, and consequently much of the medical research of today is directed against metabolic diseases and degenerative processes, which will further extend life expectancy.

The Population Expansion

The declining death rate throughout the world has resulted in an explosive increase in population. The United Nations (see Figure 2) estimates

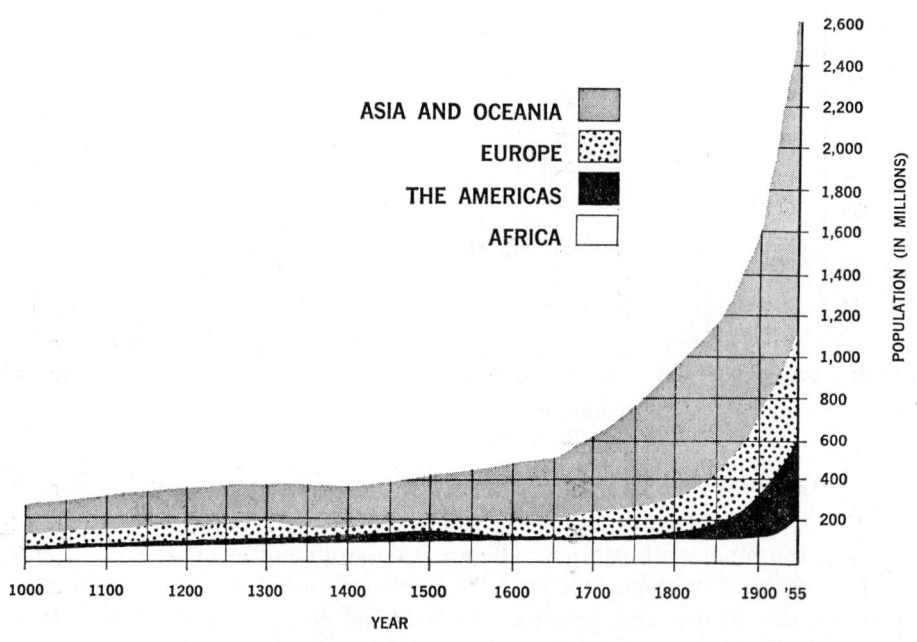

FIGURE 2. *World Population Growth, 1000–1955*

that the world population, now over 2.7 billion, is currently increasing by 40 million per year, or about 100,000 per day.[3] Thus the population is doubling

[2] *The National Health Education Committee, Inc., 1957 Report*, New York.
[3] United Nations Bureau of Social Affairs, *Report on the World Social Situation*. New York, United Nations, 1957.

about every forty years. China has a present population of about 650 million, and a current growth rate of over 2 per cent per annum. At this rate it will reach 5 billion a hundred years from now. This indicates about twice the present population of the world for one country alone. . . . Murray Luck in a well-documented paper has recently written that "to judge from the trends of the past 25 years a world population of 9 billion and a U. S. population of 600 million by the year 2050 are almost inevitable."[4] This appears to be a conservative estimate. Kingsley Davis [5] has estimated a world population of 13 billion by 2050.

The effects of decreasing death rates are most pronounced in economically underdeveloped countries. The introduction of sanitation and medical and prenatal care rapidly lowers the death rate, while the birth rate holds constant or increases, at least for a few generations. The population of Egypt has thus increased from 7 to 23 million in the last two generations. Primarily by the use of insecticides and the elimination of malaria, Ceylon recently cut its death rate 70 per cent in ten years. In Malaya the birth rate has been constant since World War II, while the death rate dropped approximately 40 per cent between 1946 and 1954. These figures are typical of many Asian, African, and Latin-American countries.[6,7]

The Consequences of the Rapid Expansion of Population

In contrast to countries like the United States, in which improved control of infant mortality is an accomplishment of past generations, the present population gains in underdeveloped countries are maximal among the young—in infants and children. Thus in Algeria, according to Kingsley Davis,[8] 52 per cent of the Moslems are less than 20 years of age, in contrast to only 37 per cent of people less than 20 in the United States and 31 per cent less than 20 years of age in France. Opportunities for jobs and education for these waves of youth are inadequate, and they can therefore fall prey the more easily to demagogues and revolutionary leaders. Under these circumstances, aggressive nationalism becomes especially appealing; if the leaders are incapable of sound economic statesmanship and are ambitious for power, they can play faction against faction and hate against hate as in the Middle East today. Here lies one of the most dangerous consequences of the rapid expansion of population.

In time, usually a matter of generations, following a population expansion resulting from an increased life expectancy in a region, the birth rate

[4] J. Murray Luck, "Man Against his Environment; the Next Hundred Years," *Science*, 126 (1957), pp. 903–908.
[5] Kingsley Davis, *The New York Times Magazine*, 22 September 1957.
[6] Robert C. Cook, ed., "World Population Summary," *Population Bulletin*, 13, No. 8 (December 1957).
[7] Karl Sax, "The Population Explosion," *Headline Series*, No. 120. New York, Foreign Policy Association, 1956.
[8] Davis, *op. cit.*

may be expected to fall slowly as primitive agricultural economy, requiring many sons for farming, shifts to industrial economy, and as the standards of living and education improve. But with the present unprecedented increase in populations, the accumulation of capital and credits for modernization is exceedingly difficult, and the lack of freely available areas for the expansion of peoples into new territories makes the situation grim indeed. It has been estimated that on the present American standard of living, this planet could support a population of only 900 million, or about a third of the present world population. According to J. G. Harrar,[9] the American people, constituting only 6 per cent of the world's population, consume 3100 calories per capita daily, while 55 per cent of the world's population are underfed on a daily consumption of 2200 calories per capita. Leallyn Clapp [10] has pointed out that the United States consumes eighteen tons of the world's resources per capita per year (food, metals, building materials, fuel) in contrast to two tons per person per year for the rest of the Free World. The conservative prediction of nine billion for a world population a century hence will be ten times the number now estimated to be supportable in terms of the current American standard of living. Only by a radical scaling down of ambitions for a decent standard of living, or by discoveries of quite new and cheap forms of food and sources of power, can the world maintain its ever increasing population burden, and at that, only within circumscribed limits. Unchecked increases in population seem clearly a source of misery and a potential cause of wars. It is indeed ironical that this situation has resulted primarily from the success of scientific, medical, and public-health advances, which in themselves are potentially beneficial to every individual.

Murray Luck has reviewed the possibility of feeding 9 billion people in the year 2050. He thinks it will be barely possible, although inequities in distribution will be accentuated. He points out that by bringing under control—at great expense—vast arable land areas not now utilized for agricultural purposes, and with the application of known mechanical techniques for producing food, one may hope for a doubling of world food production as a goal for feeding a tripled population. In addition, he believes that much of our essential food, especially some of the indispensable amino acids, will have to be produced in factories. There is little likelihood that we can long continue to enjoy the luxury of food from domestic animals; the production of animal food for human consumption is an inefficient process, requiring great quantities of food for the animals in order to produce relatively small amounts of protein and fats for human consumption. About 50 per cent of the crops grown are used by animals. Only 3 to 5 per cent of the food that animals eat is converted to food for man. Synthetic amino acids would thus have to substitute for animal-protein amino acids to a large

[9] J. G. Harrar, "Food, Science and People," *Transactions of the New York Academy of Sciences, Series II*, 20 (1958), pp. 263–267.
[10] Leallyn B. Clapp, "Science and Human Want," *American Scientist*, 46 (June 1958), pp. 176–190.

degree. In addition, protein material extracted from leaves and grown from algae, such as *Chlorella* in fresh-water ponds, might come to supply much of the needed food protein. Luck writes:

> It is also reasonably certain that our society will become so complex because of the evolving patterns in industry, the pressure of high population density, and the inevitable increase of controls of all sorts designed to husband our diminishing resources, and to keep us at peace with our neighbors, that governments will become more and more pervasive and domineering; the precious freedoms of the individual will diminish.[11]

Food production has been increasing substantially in recent years, but the population has increased more rapidly. According to the United Nations Food and Agriculture Organization,[12] even though the world's production of food as of 1951 had increased by 9 per cent since 1934–1938, the population had increased by 12 per cent. As a result, the mean world per capita calorie consumption dropped from 2380 calories per day to 2260 calories, and hunger and food shortages increased in many areas. To meet the rapidly increasing demands for food, vast sums will have to be expended in land reclamation and the prevention of further erosion, in the manufacture of fertilizers, and in the husbanding of nitrogen- and phosphorus-containing wastes. Fisheries will have to be greatly extended, especially in the southern hemisphere, and much of the food supply will have to be harvested from the ocean and from fresh water via the cultivation of bacteria, yeasts, and photosynthetic algae.

There are some who take a much more optimistic view of the potentialities of science and technology to keep up adequately with our burgeoning populations. But even with all techniques known or predicted at present, the outlook for feeding 9 to 13 billion people a century hence is most serious. Only in a closely interlocking industrial and agricultural community would it seem at all possible. A war with modern weapons would so disintegrate such a complex society that effective food supply and distribution would become impossible, and a large fraction of those escaping the bombs might perish from hunger.

Measures to Decrease the Birth Rate

There is one clear solution to the problem resulting from decreased death rates; a decrease in the birth rates. In short, I believe that birth control is not only desirable but morally necessary if men are to live in civilized societies and not destroy each other in competition for resources. Fortunately, the governments of some Asian countries are alert to the danger. Thus India has built into its second five-year plan provisions for research into population control. The Province of Kerala has offered approximately five dollars to each

---

[11] Luck, *op. cit.*
[12] *World Food Problems, No. 2*, "Man and Hunger." Rome, Food and Agriculture Organization of the United Nations, 1957.

of its male citizens who submits to sterilization. On 16 February 1959 *The New York Times* reported that the Indian government had decided to provide facilities in all hospitals to carry out sterilization operations for all who wished to restrict the size of their families. At first these facilities were to be available only for the sterilization of males. Several years ago Mao Tse-tung stated that China's population would be stabilized at 600 million and birth-control clinics were established extensively in that country. Recently, however, this sensible policy has been reversed, amid propaganda claims that China should and could support double its present population. The Japanese have succeeded in checking their accelerating population growth since the war by the drastic use of legalized abortion clinics.[13] In 1920 the population of Japan was 51 million: in 1957 it had increased to 91 million, in a country the size of Montana. In 1948, the annual birth rate was 34 per thousand and the death rate 12 per thousand. This would have doubled the population in thirty-two years. As a result, in 1948, the Japanese Diet legalized abortion, and established 800 health centers and 30,000 birth-control guidance offices. As a consequence, the birth rate fell to 19.4 per thousand in 1955, cutting the rate of population growth almost in half and bringing it below that of the United States.

To counteract the consequence of what has been referred to as the "population bomb," greatly improved methods of contraception are needed, for current methods are unreliable, inconvenient, and expensive. For some years, two sure forms of surgical contraception have been available. But in women, salpingectomy (cutting ovarian tubes) is a major operation, expensive and irreversible, one not used to prevent childbearing except under unusual medical circumstances. On the other hand, vasectomy in men (cutting the spermatic duct) can be performed under local anesthesia by a physician in half an hour in his office. This procedure sterilizes the male without in any way affecting his sexual potency or the sex act. But the irreversible nature of this process and its confusion with castration in the lay mind, together with social and religious taboos, have precluded its use to any significant degree by men who wish to prevent further pregnancies on the part of their wives. What is most needed is a contraceptive that can be taken by mouth so as to prevent pregnancy during the time of its action in the body. Such a substance must produce no untoward side effects and must not block future normal pregnancies after the withdrawal of medication. It must also be very inexpensive if it is to be widely used in underdeveloped countries, where its need is most urgent.

Fertility Control With Oral Medication

Valuable work on oral contraceptives has been carried out over the past five years at The Worcester Foundation for experimental Biology under the direction of my colleague, Dr. Gregory Pincus, who, with Dr. Min-Chueh Chang

[13] Cook, *op. cit.*

of our staff, has done much basic work in the field of mammalian reproduction. Pincus and Chang, with the clinical collaboration of Dr. John Rock and Dr. Ramón García of the Harvard Medical School and the Brookline Free Hospital for Women, have demonstrated several synthetic steroid hormone-like substances of great promise, which can be used as oral contraceptives. The credit should go to Dr. Pincus for the discovery that the group of synthetic steroids of the 19-nor type block ovulation and are therefore effective as oral contraceptives.

Fertility-preventing procedures may operate on different parts of the complex mammalian reproductive system. Conventional methods are aimed at preventing the sperm from reaching the egg. These procedures have psychological drawbacks and may also at times be ineffective. Chemical agents may be considered, whose function is to prevent ovulation or to prevent the implantation of the fertilized egg, or to inactivate the sperm before it can reach the egg in the tubes or to cause abortion of the very early embryo soon after implantation in the uterine wall. The discovery of Pincus and his collaborators falls into the first classification; it involves the use of substances that prevent the release of eggs from the ovary and so prevent pregnancy.

In the human female, in the years between puberty and the menopause, there normally occurs the release of an egg about every twenty-eight days from one of the two ovaries. The egg migrates down the Fallopian tube into the uterus, which has been prepared to receive it by the action of hormones. If the egg is fertilized by meeting a sperm, it becomes implanted in the uterine wall, and pregnancy ensues. If fertilization does not occur, the egg degenerates and is discharged along with the prepared lining of the uterus in the form of the menses. If fertilization and implantation of the ovum take place, a biochemical signal in the form of a steroid hormone called progesterone is released, which prevents the further discharge of eggs from the ovary at the time of subsequent ovulation periods. It does this by suppressing the release of a gonadotrophic hormone secreted by the pituitary gland located at the base of the brain. Several pituitary gonadotrophins in the form of specific protein hormones regulate the normal sex cycle and also control pregnancy and lactation. They regulate the female sex cycle by controlling the release of several forms of steroid sex hormones from the ovary and from the egg follicle. Suppression of the pituitary by progesterone suppresses the action of ovarian estrogens involved in menstruation and ovulation. Were this not to happen, further pregnancies might occur, with disastrous consequences during the development of the earlier embryo. One may say that during the period of pregnancy progesterone acts as nature's own contraceptive.

Since progesterone endogenously released during pregnancy inhibits ovulation, one might expect that its injection would have a similar blocking action. Makepeace et al.[14] in 1937 demonstrated that progesterone when

---

[14] A. W. Makepeace, G. L. Weinstein, and M. H. Friedman, "Effect of Progestin and Progesterone on Ovulation," *American Journal of Physiology*, 119 (1937), pp. 512–516.

injected into rabbits inhibited ovulation.* In 1953, this was confirmed by Pincus and Chang,[15] who showed in addition a quantitative relationship between the duration of inhibition and the amount of progesterone injected. Substances that have progesterone-like effects on the lining of the uterus in animals or other progestational activities are referred to as progestins. Pincus and Chang also found that an orally administered progestin (17-a-ethynyl testosterone) was effective in blocking ovulation; 17-a-methyl progesterone was effective when it was injected, but not when administered orally. Eleven other progesterone derivatives were found to be ineffective as ovulation inhibitors. Further work by these investigators showed similar effects of these three active steroids in blocking fertility in the rat.

Encouraged by these results, Pincus and Chang proceeded to test the effect of a still larger number of steroid substances on the fertility of female rabbits and rats. In the course of examining some sixty compounds, they investigated a class of steroid substances known as the 19-nor steroids, so named because they lack the usual methyl group on the number 19 carbon of the steroid skeleton. These are synthetic steroids with progestational activity.[16] Three of these 19-nor progestins (referred to here as I, II, and III) † were selected by Pincus and Chang [17,18] because they found them to have strong antifertility properties in very small concentration. A summary of the findings [19,20] demonstrates that these substances when given orally to rabbits and rats are much more effective in very low doses than is progesterone itself, not only in regard to the inhibition of ovulation but also in other indices of progestational activities on tissues of the animals. It was found that in the rabbit the inhibition of ovulation induced by the progestins could easily be

* Menstrual cycles are characteristic only of females of the higher primates, and differ from the oestrous cycles of other animals. But without digressing into comparative physiology, it is sufficient for our purposes to point out that both menstrual and oestrus cycles are regulated by a similar interplay of protein hormones from the pituitary gland and of steroid hormones from ovary and egg follicles.

[15] G. Pincus and M. C. Chang, "The Effects of Progesterone and Related Compounds on Ovulation and Early Development in the Rabbit," *Acta Physiologica Latinoamericana*, 3 (1953), pp. 177–183.

[16] M. Ehrenstein in 1944 was the first to produce a mixture of amorphous 19-nor progesterone, and in 1950 A. J. Birch synthesized and isolated specific compounds. Since 1950 a number of biologically active 19-nor steroids have been produced. A description of these compounds and their biological activities is contained in the symposium, "New Steroid Compounds and Progestational Activity," *Annals of the New York Academy of Science*, 71 (1958), pp. 479–806.

† These substances are: I, norethesterone or 17-a-ethynyl-19-nortestosterone; II, norethynodrel or 17-a-ethinylestra-(5,10)-eneolone; III, norethylsterone or 17-a-ethyl-19-nortestosterone. Their trade names are: I, Norlutin; II, Enovid; and III, Nilevar.

[17] G. Pincus, "Some Effects of Progesterone and Related Compounds upon Reproduction and Early Development in Mammals," *Fifth International Conference Planned Parenthood*, Tokyo (October 1955), pp. 175–184.

[18] ———, "Some Effects of Progesterone and Related Compounds upon Reproduction and Early Development in Mammals," *Acta Endocrinologica*, Supplement 28 (1956).

[19] G. Pincus, M. C. Chang, E. S. E. Hafez, M. X. Zarrow, and A. Merrill, "Effect of Certain 19-nor Steroids on Reproductive Processes in Animals," *Science*, 124 (1956), pp. 890–891.

[20] G. Pincus et al., "Studies of the Biological Activity of Certain 19-nor Steroids in Female Animals," *Endocrinology*, 59 (1956), pp. 695–707.

overcome by the administration of pituitary gonadotrophin to the ovulation-blocked female. Moreover, following the withdrawal of the steroid medication, normal reproductive function resumes.[21] This was true both for rabbits and for rats, conception taking place following regular coitus in all cases 25 to 28 days after the cessation of medication.

The Inhibition of Ovulation in Women

As a result of the findings with animals, investigations were made of the comparative effects of progesterone and of these three 19-nor steroids on the inhibition of ovulation in women. In animals it had been found that five to twenty times more progesterone was required when administered by mouth than when given by injection to block ovulation. Normally ovulating and menstruating women served as subjects, and the following procedure of medication was carried out in collaboration with Dr. Rock and Dr. García. Following a period of control observations of each individual's cycle, 300 milligrams of progesterone were taken orally in one series of studies, and in another series 10-milligram tablets of the 19-nor steroids were used. These hormones were taken daily from the fifth through the twenty-fourth day of each menstrual cycle. This span of medication covers the possible range of ovulation time, and also assures bleeding comparable to normal menstruation following the withdrawal of the progesterone or of the synthetic progestins. Thus the subject could experience normal menstrual periods under this procedure, but if the medication were effective she would not ovulate. In all of the early tests daily records were obtained of two indices of ovulation. These were basal body temperature measurements and vaginal smears. In addition, an endometrial biopsy test for ovulation was made on one day between the nineteenth and twenty-first days of the cycle. These days were chosen to correspond to the maximum expected activity of the progesterone released from the corpus luteum. Determinations of urinary concentration of creatinine, pregnanediol (a metabolite of progesterone) and 17-ketosteroid were made on forty-eight-hour urine samples collected during days 19 to 21. From endometrial biopsies, vaginal smears, and temperature data, gynecologists can determine with reasonable assurance whether or not ovulation has occurred. Pregnanediol reflects the possible suppression of a gonadotrophic release of eggs via their corpora lutea and the consequent suppression of endogenous progesterone. The 17-ketosteroid determinations were used primarily as an index of adrenocortical function, since for the most part they are metabolites of adrenocortical steroid hormones.

The first investigation consisted of a study of thirty subjects given daily doses of 300 milligrams of progesterone itself for thirty control and sixty medication cycles.[22] Ovulation was found to be inhibited from 75 to 80 per

[21] Pincus and Chang, *op. cit.*
[22] "New Steroid Compounds," *loc. cit.;* Pincus, *opera cit.*

cent in the first cycle of progesterone medication, from 75 to 100 per cent in the second cycle, and from 87.5 to 100 per cent in the third cycle. Some significant shortening in the mean cycle lengths during this medication period were found as a result of early menstrual bleeding in about 30 per cent of the cases taking progesterone.

As a result of the findings with animals of the superior oral activity of the 19-nor steroids they were next employed in a medication series similar to that described for progesterone, involving fifty women (forty women received either I or II and ten received III). Ten-milligram daily doses of the substances were administered; no alterations occurred in the mean cycle length with the 19-nor steroids. Ovulation was inhibited in from 88 to 100 per cent of the cycles by any of the criteria studied. No significant change in 17-ketosteroid excretion was seen, but there was a marked drop in pregnanediol output, suggesting an absence of corpora lutea. Observations indicated that, following medication with these compounds in the first treatment cycle, there may be a delay of several days in the resumption of normal cyclical activities of the ovary. No conceptions occurred in the fifty women during the 125 medication cycles, although normal sexual activities continued. Seven of the women became pregnant within five months after the cessation of treatment.[23]

The most extensive and revealing investigations have been carried out in Puerto Rico and Haiti, under the direction of Dr. Pincus, using the 19-nor steroid II (norethynodrel) in Enovid tablets.* These studies have involved investigations of 830 women followed for 8133 menstrual cycles, equivalent to 635 woman-years. Many of these women have taken the 19-nor steroid in 10-milligram doses from the fifth to the twenty-fifth day of the menstrual cycle for a period of over three years.[24] Each subject was given a bottle containing twenty tablets, with instructions to take one each day from the fifth through the twenty-fourth days of her menstrual cycle. Social workers visited the subjects and recorded any occasions on which tablet-taking was missed as checked by the count of pills in the bottle. This study was carried out by four separate groups in the Caribbean area—three in Puerto Rico and one in Haiti. All four groups reported similar effects of the medication. The important finding has been that norethynodrel is 100 per cent effective if taken according to the prescribed regimen.

[23] J. Rock, C. R. García, and G. Pincus, "Synthetic Progestins in the Normal Human Menstrual Cycle," *Recent Progress in Hormone Research*, 13 (1957), pp. 323–346. In a further study (G. Pincus, "Long Term Administration of Enovid to Human Subjects," *Proceedings of a Symposium on 19-Nor Progestational Steroids* [Chicago, Searle Research Laboratories, 1957], p. 105), no contra-indications for the use of 19-nor steroids could be found.

* Each Enovid tablet contains, in addition to 10 milligrams of norethynodrel, 0.15 milligrams of an estrogen (ethynyl estradiol 3-methyl ether). This estrogen supplement was added for the adequate maintenance of the endometrium, thus preventing premature menstrual bleeding, since this progestin by itself was sometimes, in some women, inadequate for this purpose.

[24] G. Pincus, "Field Trials with Norethynodrel as an Oral Contraceptive," *Proceedings of the Sixth International Planned Parenthood Conference, 1959* (in press).

Study of Secondary Effects

The contraceptive effects of the tablets do not diminish when medication is continued over long-time spans. The menstrual cycles of women taking these tablets are of normal length, and are actually more regular than those not taking the tablets, unless tablet-taking is missed. When tablet-taking is missed, a certain amount of menstrual bleeding may be precipitated upon withdrawal of the medication, and this may be blocked by remedication, thus lengthening the cycles. A certain amount of premature menstrual bleeding was found to occur in a small percentage of medication cycles, despite regular tablet-taking. This was highest in the first cycle of medication, and it declined progressively to very low levels of occurrence by the fifth cycle. In only 0.7 to 3.2 per cent of the medication cycles did menstruation fail to occur promptly after withdrawal of the tablets.

In questioning the total group of subjects, the great majority reported no change in the quantity of menstrual flow during the medication cycles. In some cases there was a decrease, and the frequency of this decrease of flow was the same in the early as in the late medication cycles. Painful menstruation, normally characteristic of a considerable number of women, was considerably decreased during the periods of medication. A certain percentage complained of nausea, dizziness, and headache. Such reactions ranged from 6.3 per cent for one of the Caribbean groups to 18.3 per cent for another. The reactions were highest in the first medication cycle, declining thereafter to much lower levels—to zero by the twentieth cycle in the Puerto Rican group showing the early mean of 6.3 per cent, and to 9.0 per cent in the group showing the early incidence of 18.3 per cent.

A study was performed on those reporting these complaints, in which the effects of placebos and medication were compared.* The occurrence of the side reaction was a little greater for the group on the medication, but the differences were not statistically significant. The absence of admonition to the subjects about the possibility of the occurrence of reactions also markedly decreased the side effects. It was concluded that these side reactions are probably psychogenic in origin.

Some gains in weight were reported in the majority of women taking the medication. In this connection it should be borne in mind that, compared to women in the United States, the normal calorie consumption of most of these Puerto Rican and Haitian subjects is relatively low. When questioned, about a third of the subjects reported increased well-being, and less than 10 per cent reported decreased well-being.

Most of the subjects reported no change in libido during medication, but an examination of reports of the frequency of coitus indicated an increase in frequency in the first twelve medication cycles, and a sustainment of these

---

* This was a "double-blind" study, in that neither the subject nor the observer knew whether the pill was a placebo or medication, since it was administered according to a code by a third person.

increased frequencies in later cycles. Such a result might be expected to follow from a decrease in the fear of pregnancy. Gynecological examinations carried out on a number of the women at different periods of the medication cycles indicated no pathological changes. There seemed to be a mild growth stimulus to the uterus in a few cases and improvement in vaginal tone. Liver-function tests were made on 148 subjects in various cycles of medication and were compared to 20 unmedicated controls. The data indicated an entirely normal liver function following the medication.

These findings fully confirmed the contraceptive effect of norethynodrel reported in early studies. The normal pregnancy rate without medication established for women of the mean age range of 28 years (an age range corresponding to that of the 830 women of the study) is one pregnancy per 1.48 woman-years. But in these experiments—including those women who did not take the medication faithfully—the over-all rate was one pregnancy per 37 woman-years. This is equivalent to a 96 per cent reduction in the normal premedication pregnancy rate. Furthermore, if in this comparison one eliminates the times during which the women would have been pregnant in the premedication years, one finds a 98.9 per cent reduction in pregnancy rate.

Data were carefully kept of the number of tablets missed by the women. The group of faithful tablet-takers (87.5 per cent of the 830 women, who missed none of the twenty days per cycle for their medication periods) showed only one case of pregnancy, and in this case it was not certain that tablets had not been missed. The pregnancy rate was thus essentially zero for those following the regimen. For those who missed taking one to five tablets (9.4 per cent of the total), there were five pregnancies, and for those missing six to nineteen tablets (3.6 per cent of the total), there were eleven pregnancies. An analysis of the frequency with which medication was missed during the 8133 cycles indicated a tendency to miss tablet-taking more frequently in the earlier cycles, with correspondingly higher frequencies of conception.

Fertility subsequent to the withdrawal of medication was determined by follow-up data on 86 subjects. Pregnancies developed in 83 per cent of those failing to use more means of contraception in a mean exposure period of 6.1 months, and in 15 per cent of those regularly using other contraceptives over a mean exposure period of 52 months. The mean pregnancy rate for those not using contraceptives was 193 per 100 exposure years, and for the latter group—i. e., those using conventional contraceptives—it was 37 per 100 exposure years. The value of 193 pregnancies per 100 exposure years is of the same magnitude as the value of 242 pregnancies per 100 exposure years previously found in a group of Puerto Rican women who had used no contraceptives. It is thus clear that the medication had no inhibiting effect on subsequent pregnancies throughout the twenty cycles for those observed in this follow-up study.

An investigation was also made of the effects of administering one-half and one-quarter the daily 10-milligram dosages of medication. No pregnancies were reported in the subjects taking these lower doses. Adequate sustainment of menstrual cyclic activity was fully maintained on a 5-milligram dose, but a tendency for early menstrual bleeding in some patients occurred on the 2.5-milligram dose.

Data have been obtained on sectioned ovaries of a group of nine women who took the medication for periods of two to twenty months (unpublished). The ovaries were removed for reasons that had nothing to do with the medication, and the operations were planned before the women engaged in the experiment. The ovaries were compared to those obtained from eight women who had not received medication. The ovaries of the women of the experimental group showed absence of corpora lutea and large follicles but an entirely normal count of primordial follicles, indicating a lack of damage from the steroids to the basic egg-producing process. There were no pathological signs in the ovaries. A similar prolonged study of rats receiving 19-nor steroids for very long periods gave similar data, as well as normal returns to fertility after a latent period.

In conclusion it appears, on the basis of data on nearly 1000 women to date, that Enovid is 100 per cent effective as an oral contraceptive when taken regularly from the fifth to the twenty-fifth day of the menstrual cycle, and that side effects, such as nausea, dizziness, and headache are absent in most cases and probably of psychogenic origin in the small fraction of cases who have these symptoms. No signs of pathology of the reproductive tract attributable to medication have emerged in women who have taken it. It is, of course, to be anticipated from known statistics that pathology of the reproductive tract may ultimately develop in a significant number of any sample of 1000 women irrespective of medication. The use of the substances tends to regularize menstruation, reduce menstrual pain, promote a feeling of well-being, and increase female libido.[25]

Implications for the Population Problems

What are the implications of these findings in relation to the problems of overpopulation? Science can only make inventions available. It is the public

[25] Carl G. Heller, W. M. Laidlaw, H. T. Harvey, and W. O. Nelson ("Effects of Progestational Compounds on the Reproductive Processes of the Human Male," *Annals of the New York Academy of Sciences*, 71 [1958], pp. 649–665) have studied effects of progesterone and the three 19-nor steroids used by Pincus on nineteen normal men. All four compounds were found progressively to lower the sperm count to zero after some seven to ten weeks. The 19-nor steroids were given orally in two 15-milligram doses per day, and the progesterone was injected intramuscularly in a dose of 50 milligrams daily. Accompanying the failure of sperm, there was a loss of libido on the part of the men.

Biopsies of testicular tissue at the time of the failure of sperm production showed corresponding tissue damage in the Enovid and Norlutin therapy groups. However, such damage was not seen in the progesterone and Nilevar studies, despite failure of spermatogenesis. Within a relatively brief time following cessation of medication, the sperm count returned to normal or exceeded its pretreatment levels. While these steroids may be effective contraceptives in the male, their prolonged use is not acceptable.

that determines their use, and in general the American public is remarkably apathetic to threats inherent in unlimited expansion of populations. Population pressures and the unrest they help generate are abrasive factors in international relations. The Communists are effectively exploiting the increasing poverty and unrest in Asia, Africa, and the Near East. But the right to unlimited procreation is assumed to be inviolate, and the question is shunned by politicians.

The fear is sometimes expressed that sexual promiscuity would increase and the family would be endangered if in time simple and highly effective methods of contraception become generally available. This issue must be balanced against the consequences of continued and rapid population growth. Moreover, it might be pointed out that birth control of some sort is widely practiced, especially among the better educated and economically favored. To what extent fear of pregnancy is a deterrent to extramarital sexual relations has never been determined. Nor have we any data as to whether efficient contraceptives, instead of inefficient ones in which people nonetheless have confidence, may increase promiscuity. In relation to the problem of promiscuity, it should be noted that the tablets must be taken for some days to assure blockade of ovulation. This would eliminate their use as rapid, temporary, and transient protectors against conception even if they were to become freely available.

New drug applications of the 19-nor steroids I, II, and III have been allowed for use by physicians under the authority of the Pure Food and Drug Act. These substances are available to the public only by prescription, and I and II are used by gynecologists primarily to correct menstrual abnormalities. The physician is warned that they also block ovulation. They are not being recommended or sold by the manufacturers as contraceptives. The attitude of the manufacturers and of many physicians is to consider that more data are necessary to make certain that there would be no adverse effects from the daily use of the substances over periods of many years. General consensus is lacking as to criteria to assure the complete harmlessness of the medication. Views on this matter depend upon many psychological variables and prejudices operating in the persons expressing opinion.

The investigations of Dr. Pincus and his collaborators have been financed primarily through generous gifts from Mrs. Stanley McCormick made to the Worcester Foundation for Experimental Biology. The work has also been aided by grants from the Josiah Macy, Jr., Foundation and from the Planned Parenthood Federations of America. Patents for manufacture of the 19-nor steroids are owned by pharmaceutical companies whose chemists had synthesized them before their antifertility use was discovered, and the substances were made available by the manufacturers for purposes of investigation.

There is universal consensus in favor of medical and public-health measures that increase health and life expectancy throughout the world. Since life expectancy will probably be further prolonged by research, we must decrease birth rates if we are to control runaway populations. The 19-nor steroids reversibly block pregnancy without the destruction of life, and do this by acting after the manner of the natural hormone progesterone. Clearly, this is a better way to deal with the problem than the desperate measure of extensive abortions that the Japanese have found necessary to halt their runaway population growth. It is in countries where population pressures in relation to resources are especially acute that these substances may find an early use. Those concerned with human welfare may well hope that these or related substances may come to play a significant role in the control of world populations.

The Catholic Position on Population Control

JOHN L. THOMAS, S.J.

The formulation of any position related to ethical issues necessarily implies a set of definite assumptions concerning the nature of the human agent and the requisite qualities of right moral conduct. In practice, Catholic ethical positions tend to be formulated on the basis of principles derived from both reason and faith, though Catholic thinkers have consistently vindicated man's natural ability to discover the basic principles and norms requisite for right moral conduct.[1] Since the divine law is manifested in the natures of things, the life of grace itself must build upon nature. Hence, however high above nature Christian ideals may stand, their foundations remain rooted in the laws of nature. The God who is conceived as the model of all perfection is also the God whose laws are manifested in the natures of things.[2]

Because the area of human activity is extremely complex, and because we acquire our knowledge of human nature and its essential tendencies through observation, there is ample room for development in ethical perspective. The basic premise that good is to be done and evil avoided is readily grasped in experience, but the application of this principle to specific human acts, depending as it must upon our limited knowledge of tendencies and purposes, is subject to imperfection, error, and development as we proceed to evaluate the more complex areas of human activity. Ethical judgments are practical judgments based upon insights into human situations. Although we

[1] The official Catholic position is clearly stated in the Vatican Council, Session III, Cap. 2, and in the encyclical *Humani Generis* of Pius XII, *Acta Apostolicae Sedis*, 42 (1950), 561–578; English translation, *Catholic Mind*, 48 (November 1950), 688–700.
[2] For an interesting discussion of some of the implications of this view, see H. Richard Niebuhr, *Christ and Culture* (New York, Harper & Brothers, 1951), pp. 143 ff.

Daedalus, Journal of the American Academy of Arts and Sciences, LXXXVIII (Summer 1959), 444–453. Reprinted by permission of *Daedalus* and the author.

benefit from the accumulated insights of the past, we must proceed with caution and humility in seeking to evaluate the evolving complex relationships of the present.

An intelligent judgment concerning the morality of birth control must be based on the logical application of general moral principles to this specific human act. It follows that those who base their considerations in this matter upon different moral principles will necessarily reach different conclusions. For example, the Christian who believes that the human person is a unity of body and soul, endowed with faculties of intellect and will, and possessing an essential relationship of origin, dependence, and destiny to his Creator, will judge the morality of birth control differently from one who maintains that man has no essential qualitative difference from other higher forms of animal life. This point appears to be all too frequently forgotten in current controversy. Disagreements concerning the licitness of birth control must logically be based on differences concerning basic moral principles, and since these are based on our concept of the nature, origin, and destiny of man, any worthwhile discussion of disagreements must ultimately center on this point.

The premises upon which the Catholic position is based may be summarized briefly as follows. First, there is order in the world, established by a creative intelligence and revealed in the inherent purposes of things as discovered by observing their normal tendencies and operations. Second, as a creature endowed with reason, man achieves the development and perfection of his nature by using things in accord with the order established by the Creator. Third, it follows that men act reasonably when they use for their self-development and perfection all those things in nature which have been placed under their direct dominion. Fourth, the Creator alone is the author and source of life. He has not placed life or the faculties furnishing the co-principles of life under the creature's absolute dominion. Men hold these in trust from the Creator, so that they must respect their own lives and those of others, nor may they destroy them for their own personal satisfaction. They must also respect the integrity of their reproductive faculties and the normal process of the generative act in which they furnish the co-principles of life. The function of sex (the possession and use of faculties involving the co-principles of life) has been entrusted to men for the good of the species, and right reason demands that it be employed accordingly. Although the sexual act is designed for the propagation of the human race by the Creator, it is also a manifestation of conjugal love and creativity, a means of maintaining a stable, balanced, and affectionate union. Thus, the act has unique symbolic significance.

Population Problems

The praiseworthy success of medical science in achieving the postponement of death has dramatically upset a balance that mankind has hitherto taken generally for granted. What Malthus termed "the prevalence of people" is becoming one of the major challenges we face. Throughout much of the world, unprecedented annual increments of population are creating problems that bid fair to tax human ingenuity and available natural resources to their utmost. Not that we lack either know-how or necessary materials; nature is not as niggardly as the older classical economists appeared to believe. But a world sharply divided between rich and poor nations, rampant with rising nationalism, historically dichotomized into East and West, and ideologically polarized round Communism and capitalism, scarcely offers a propitious climate in which to tackle our population problems.[3]

In discussing issues related to population control, we must distinguish between the speculative, over-all problem of world population *vs.* world resources on the one hand, and specific, practical population-resource problems existing in various countries on the other. Among the latter, we must distinguish the problems of industrialized nations like the United States, where the management of large annual surpluses is an outstanding problem, from the problems of underdeveloped countries, where factors not directly related to the economy have induced and promise to maintain increases in population that place a serious strain on available resources. We must also recognize that population problems are not primarily economic, for economic factors make their impact felt on changes in the size of the population only through sociopsychological processes highly complex in their origin and operation. Finally, we must distinguish between known facts and more or less educated guesses. For example, Merrill Bennett, Director of the Food Research Institute at Stanford University, has pointed out some of the questionable assumptions and norms currently used to estimate past and present trends in per capita calorie consumption and world food supply;[4] while Philip Hauser, head of the Population Research Center, University of Chicago, has ably summarized the gaps in our knowledge of the relationships between population trends and socioeconomic conditions.[5]

---

[3] "When we take the very long view of man's world in the next century we see that the main problems are less those of technology than they are those of men's getting along with other men, communicating with other men, and organizing themselves in such a way that their genius and imagination can be vigorously applied to the problems that confront them. Our major problems involve the enriching, enlarging, improving, and mobilizing of our intellectual forces." (Harrison Brown, James Bonner, and John Weir, *The Next Hundred Years* [New York, The Viking Press, 1957], p. 153.)

[4] Merrill Bennett, *The World's Food* (New York, Harper & Brothers, 1954).

[5] "Our ignorance can be described in several dimensions. First, it may be stated that basic population data—statistics of the type derived from censuses, sample surveys, and birth and death registration systems—are entirely inadequate for most of the world's population. Second, and this is not unrelated to the first point, demographic theory is oversimplified and often obsolete. Third, we have only a limited ability to predict the specific demographic consequences of particular economic or social changes, and even less ability to make predictions in the opposite direction. Fourth, we have hardly begun to use such limited predictive knowledge as we have to trace a sequence of interrelated demographic, social, and economic changes. Fifth, we are particularly ill-equipped to provide policy makers and administrators with an adequate factual basis for social engineering purposes. The many gaps in our knowledge are dramatized by the Committee in its fifty recommendations for studies designed to dissipate ignorance in important areas." (Philip Hauser, in *Proceedings of the World Population Conference, Rome, 31 August— 10 September 1954,* Summary Report, United Nations, Department of Economic and Social Affairs, New York, 1955, p. 176.)

Considering the dimensions of our ignorance, together with the known variety and complexity of the variables involved, it is best to proceed cautiously when developing policies related to population control. As the Swedish population expert, Alva Myrdal, reminds us, "The population problem concerns the very foundation of the social structure," and if we are not on our guard, "there is a palpable danger that population policy will be irrationally narrowed down and forced into remedial quackery."[6]

The Catholic View of Parenthood

Catholic teaching has always maintained that those who choose the vocation of marriage find in children the divinely designed means of achieving full self-realization and perfection as mature Christians. Although children constitute one of the major blessings of marriage, their ideal number is relative to the capacities and peculiar circumstances of the individual couple who must bear and rear them to maturity.

In this connection, Catholic thinkers offer two observations. First, marriage, considered as a status, is a divinely designed institution through which men and women cooperate with the Creator in the propagation and education of the race. Marriage partners who habitually make use of the rights and privileges of this status implicitly accept the obligation of achieving its purpose; if they always avoided the possibility of pregnancy throughout their married life, they would show that they either did not understand the blessings of parenthood or were acting on motives alien to Christian standards. Second, in determining the extent of these obligations, the general principle applies that an affirmative law does not bind if its fulfillment involves proportionately grave inconvenience extrinsic to the law. Pius XII has enumerated under the general headings of medical, eugenic, economic, and social "indications" some of the sources from which such inconveniences might arise. As long as these exist, whether for a time or throughout marriage, the couple are excused from the obligation.[7]

Means of Population Control

In the light of these observations, we may conclude that, since Catholic thinkers seek roughly the same human goals and must rely on the same information as others in defining their position on population control, the distinguishing traits in their approach will be found in the means they judge to be ethically acceptable. Stated briefly, the means for population control that

---

[6] Alva Myrdal, *Nation and Family* (London, Kegan Paul, Trench, Trubner and Company, Ltd., 1945), p. 2.

[7] Pius XII, address to the Italian Catholic Union of Midwives, *Acta Apostolicae Sedis*, 18 (1951), pp. 835–854; for a good English translation, see *The Clergy Review*, 36 (December 1951), 379–391; for an excellent commentary, see Francis Hurth, *De Re Matrimoniali*, Rome, Gregorian University Press, 1955.

they reject are direct abortion, sterilization, and all deliberate acts aimed solely and directly at the antecedent frustration or hindrance of the fecundity of the conjugal act, once it is freely initiated. They reject these means for the following reasons.

First, in regard to abortion, they view direct, deliberately induced abortion as murder. An abortion is direct when the sole immediate result of the procedure is the termination of pregnancy before viability. The Catholic position is based on the principle that human life is sacred and must be respected in the unborn as well as in others. Any operation that directly kills either the mother or the child is judged immoral.

Catholic moralists distinguish direct from indirect abortions. An abortion is indirect when it is the by-product of a procedure immediately directed to the cure of a serious pathological condition of the mother. In this case the interruption of the pregnancy is the undesired effect of a procedure immediately directed to secure some other good purpose, such as the stopping of a hemorrhage or the removal of a cancer. In deciding such cases, moralists apply the well-known principle of the double effect, which may be stated as follows: it is licit to perform an action which has good and bad effects, provided (a) that the action itself is not morally bad; (b) that the evil effect is sincerely not desired, but merely tolerated; (c) that the evil is not the means of obtaining the good effect; and (d) that the good effect is sufficiently important to balance or outweigh the harmful effect.

The second means of population control rejected by Catholic thinkers includes all deliberate acts aimed directly at the antecedent frustration or hindrance of the fecundity of the conjugal act. Such acts are commonly included under the broad term "birth control," but it is well to note that birth control may have many meanings, ranging from the planned limitation of offspring through periodic or absolute continence, to the control of fertility through the use of contraceptive devices. We shall use the term to include all deliberate acts that aim at depriving the conjugal act of its normal procreative quality or finality (e.g., the practice of *coitus interruptus* or the use of a condom).

It should be noted that birth control is considered illicit, not because its effect is the prevention of a possible conception, but because the act itself is judged to be contrary to the order of right reason. Marriage partners who use birth control do not act as reasonable persons since they will to perform an act essentially implying the fulfillment of this initial stage, yet at the same time they do not will its fulfillment. Such action constitutes a clear contradiction in the practical order and is consequently a violation of the order of right reason. The act itself is considered intrinsically vitiated and thus unethical. It follows that the practice of birth control differs essentially from the use of rhythm, inasmuch as the latter does not vitiate the nature of the conjugal act.

Family limitation achieved through the observance of either absolute or periodic continence is considered licit by Catholic thinkers. They readily admit that the observance of absolute continence among normal couples may become extremely difficult and calls for a high degree of self-control. However, it is maintained that when marital situations calling for the observance of absolute continence arise, this becomes possible provided the couple have adequate psychological insight and motivation, and seek additional aid through prayer and the sacraments.

The observance of periodic continence based on rhythm [8] offers a somewhat easier means of the control of conception, since it is estimated that the period of ovulation can be predicted or ascertained with a fair degree of accuracy in roughly 80 per cent of married women. There seems little doubt that medical science will make further advances in this area.

Third, Catholic thinkers regard direct sterilization, whether permanent or temporary, whether performed for eugenic or contraceptive purposes, as morally wrong. Direct sterilization, as the term is used here, includes every interference with the generative function in which sterility itself, either perpetual or temporary, is intended as an end in itself or as a means to a further end. Direct sterilization is rejected because it is regarded as an unreasonable mutilation.

Sterilization is termed indirect when the resultant sterility is an unintentional by-product of a genuine therapeutic procedure—for example, when a cancerous uterus is removed. Indirect sterilization is judged morally permissible under certain conditions. A widely used principle in medical ethics, sometimes called the principle of "totality," applies here: the individual has the right to use the services of his organism as a whole and consequently may allow individual parts to be destroyed or mutilated when and to the extent necessary for the good of his being as a whole. The conditions required for licit mutilation, whether by the removal of an organ or by the suppression of its function, are these: (a) the preservation of the organ or its functioning must be a source of actual harm or constitute a threat to the total well-being of the person; (b) there must be a well-founded assurance that the proposed mutilation will either remove or notably diminish the harm, and that this effect cannot be obtained without the mutilation; and (c) there must be a reasonable estimate that the good to be effected, e.g., by removing the harm, reducing pain, etc., will compensate for the evil effects consequent on the loss of the organ or function.[9]

In developing their position on the licit use of a pill to prevent ovulation, Catholic thinkers apply these general principles to the specific instance in question. Thus, if the use of the pill constituted *direct* sterilization as defined above, the action would be judged unethical; if its use resulted in *indirect* sterilization, the principle of totality would apply. It follows that such a pill could licitly be used to alleviate or eliminate various malfunctions or patho-

---

[8] For a detailed treatment of this problem, see John L. Thomas, *Marriage and Rhythm*. Westminster, Maryland, The Newman Press, 1957.

[9] See Gerald Kelly, S. J., "Medico-Moral Notes," *Linacre Quarterly*, 20 November 1953, pp. 106–107.

logical conditions in the human system. Further, if a suitable means could be discovered to control anabolic disorders or marked irregularities in the menstrual cycle, its use for this purpose would be permissible.

Conclusion

The Catholic position on the licit means of population control is sometimes regarded as a cultural residue surviving from an unscientific, agrarian past and one incapable of meeting the practical exigencies of the modern world situation. For their part, Catholic thinkers point out that ethical short cuts are bound to be self-defeating in the long run. Their approach calls for greater understanding and appreciation of the significance of sex, marriage, and parenthood. Since man is the most valuable productive agent, cultural progress can best be promoted by creating conditions favorable to his highest development. Inasmuch as such progress implies self-discipline, a sense of responsibility, self-control, and the disposition to postpone present satisfactions for future gains, the widespread use of unethical forms of population control would hinder rather than promote requisite cultural changes. The different aspects of man's personality tend to be interrelated: one cannot exempt the important area of sexual activity from mastery and control, while expecting the individual to display these same qualities in other sectors of human endeavor. The control of man's basic drives according to the order of reason constitutes the necessary precondition both for personal development and for productive social endeavor.

What practical solutions to the present population problems do Catholic thinkers propose? First, in regard to the over-all problem of world population *vs.* world resources, they maintain that our answers must remain highly speculative. We can only guess at future long-range trends in science and population growth, but we appear to have sufficient resources in energy and food to handle foreseeable population increases, provided we are willing to develop the means of production required to use them.

Second, in regard to the complex, varied problems of the underdeveloped countries, Catholic thinkers advocate a multifaceted approach, including emphasis on universal education, social and economic reforms, capital investment that will make the best use of the abundant labor supply, and needed marketing and trade reforms. They also insist that the goods of the earth have been created for the use of all mankind, so that the resource-adequate nations now have a serious obligation to aid the resource-needy regions through financial and technical assistance to the extent that this appears feasible.

Third, they maintain that present population pressures in many contemporary danger spots could be relieved considerably by migration, better opportunities for trade, and freer access to needed raw materials, together with financial and technical help from richer nations.

Finally, in defining the modern dimensions of the Malthusian dilemma in underdeveloped economics, they point out that functioning social systems are integrated systems, so that gradual or piecemeal reforms such as birth control offer no solution to existing population problems. As cultural anthropologists insist, people can live with reasonable satisfaction in an archaic peasant society or in an adapted urbanized industrial one, but not in a halfway house. In other words, when the death rate is rapidly lowered by the introduction of alien techniques and practices that do not affect the traditional social or economic situations of underdeveloped countries, these societies must choose either an immediate conversion to an intensive industrial development, or increasing poverty and decline. Piecemeal reforms such as birth control are ineffective, both because they are not aimed at changing traditional social and economic situations and because they will not prove acceptable until such changes occur.

The basic issue we face is not primarily population growth or resources, but man's ability to modify his cultural and social systems so that the fullest exploitation of the world's resources becomes possible. This calls for the elimination of traditional methods of exploitation by the more powerful nations in world trade and by the more powerful classes within each nation—in short, it calls for cooperation, organization, and serious personal effort.

Protestant Ethics and Population Control

JOHN C. BENNETT

The problem of population has become an acute ethical problem, whether one is thinking of the world-wide increase of population and its effect upon the standard of living of nations and upon peace and international order, or whether one is concerned chiefly about the welfare of the individual family, the health of mothers, and the opportunities open to children. Protestantism has no specific moral laws that inhibit either family planning by individual parents or large-scale policies by which nations, and even the United Nations, may encourage such family planning. The spectacular lowering of the death rate, especially among infants, which has been effected by medical science makes it obligatory for us to find effective ways of reducing the birth rate. It has been well said that death control makes birth control a necessity.

I have been asked to write as a Protestant. Therefore I shall outline briefly the nature of Protestant ethics as I understand it. The difference between my views and those of Roman Catholic writers can be understood only against the background of a Protestant conception of ethics. There is no *cumulative* body of moral laws related to specific situations by means of a tradition of casuistry. Individual theologians and leaders have laid down the law in no uncertain terms about many matters, but I put the emphasis on the word "cumulative." Protestant systems of ethics have their day and lose force, and Protestants are brought back again to the central imperatives of Christian faith without much concrete guidance on specific dilemmas. The various forms of Puritan legalism have faded away, although there is today renewed appreciation of the Puritan sense of responsibility to God that was deeper than the legalism. Also there has been a return to some of the moral insights of Puritanism, especially those associated with the rise of democracy, which were best expressed in the debates in Cromwell's army. Neither Luther nor Calvin can be said to be a guide on specific moral issues, except in this highly selective way.

Protestantism is today very much preoccupied with ethical problems, but the main emphasis is on the ultimate imperative of love, on the sources of motive and power for ethical living, and on the correctives for ethical distortion that are provided by the key doctrine of justification by faith. This doctrine means that the Christian himself is forgiven rather than fully righteous; it is the basis for all warnings against perfectionist or utopian illusions and against the danger of self-righteousness. There has been a strategic overemphasis in recent Protestant theology on the way self-righteousness becomes the source of hardness and cruel fanaticism. This has led to a widespread tendency to discount a direct concern for moral discipline as "moralism."

Protestantism has a great deal of pragmatism in its ethics. Judgments have to be made after the best thinking we can do about the probable consequences of our choices. Love intends the best available combination of consequences for all neighbors, and it should not be concerned primarily with the avoidance of particular acts that are absolutely condemned in advance by a law whose full applications are known. This pragmatism is not the sign of complete relativism, for the ultimate motive is known and there are criteria by which the consequences should be judged, although the fact that the criteria are in tension with each other leaves room for flexibility.[1]

As a result of this type of ethical thinking, Protestants expect to disagree on many issues. Yet they are in continuous conversation with one another, and there does develop from time to time a considerable consensus on

---

[1] This is not the place to compare Protestant ethics with Catholic ethics, but it might help to say that on most issues Catholic laws are related to one another and to the situation by the use of "prudence," and that this relation provides much flexibility in practice. But there are in Catholic ethics a few areas where the absolute law on a particular matter seems to Protestants to be given a too privileged position in the context. This is especially true of the spheres of sex and medicine.

important matters. The consensus does not extend to all members of the Churches; it is not a matter of taking a Gallup poll. It is rather a trend of thinking that characterizes those who take initiative in thought and in leadership and whose responsibility it is to emphasize the relationship of current thinking to the sources of the revelation, and who are able to transcend to some extent local and even national cultural pressures. This may appear to be very vague, but there is a process of ethical clarification, especially on social objectives, that does exist. Where there is no consensus about immediate action, there are at least boundaries within which the most serious ethical thinking is done. This process has been going on for some time on problems of racial and economic justice and on some international issues, and the boundaries within which ethical thinking should be done in those areas have become at least visible. On those issues there are no characteristic Protestant, as opposed to Roman Catholic, ethical judgments. But when we move into the area of population control we find a growing Protestant consensus and, unfortunately, a serious conflict between Protestant and Roman Catholic convictions.

Protestants generally favor the use of contraceptives. They advise married couples to use them conscientiously, and—although they have given much less thought to this aspect of the problem—they usually favor government policies that make effective contraceptives available to the population as a whole.

Protestants generally believe that the spacing of children in a family, or at least the limitation of their number by choice, is important for the welfare of the children and for the health of the mother. Moreover, Protestants generally hold that it is neither possible nor right to depend on long periods of sexual abstinence to achieve this result. The assumption underlying this view is that of the two purposes of sexual intercourse—the expression of love between husband and wife, and the procreation of children—the first should not be subordinated to the second. This assumption presents perhaps the clearest difference between Protestant and official Catholic teaching. Whereas Catholics believe that any "unnatural" frustration of the second purpose makes it against natural law to seek realization of the first, I know of no Protestant thinker of wide influence who would agree.

Since it is so often suggested that the Protestant view is merely a way of following the line of least resistance, a concession to man's sinful desires, I want to emphasize that Protestants increasingly believe the use of methods of birth control to be a duty for many people. *It may be a moral obligation to limit the number of births in a family, and it may also be morally wrong to advise a married couple to refrain from intercourse for long periods.* There are strains enough in marriage without adding this one, with all the mutual resentment or hostility it may create, if there is not full and willing assent to the practice by both partners. Moreover, even conscious assent may not necessarily prevent this kind of strain.

Dietrich Bonhoeffer, a Protestant theologian deeply admired both for his martyrdom in the struggle against the Nazis and for his contribution as a thinker, has written strongly on this subject in his *Ethics*. Many others have taken the same position, but I quote him because, while there is often boldness in his thought, he cannot be accused of being a mere follower of modern trends. He wrote:

> But as a matter of principle Catholic morality recognizes only one means for the achievement of this purpose [the limitation of the number of children in a family], namely total abstention. But in this way it undermines the physical basis of marriage and threatens marriage itself with nullification and destruction by robbing it of its fundamental right. . . . It certainly eliminates the unnatural act of preventing conception, but this is replaced by the unnatural state of a marriage without bodily union.[2]

Protestants also believe that birth control should not be practiced as an escape from parenthood in the normal marriage. Usually there is a responsibility to have children as well as to limit their number. Either to give birth to children or to prevent the birth of children may be irresponsible. The individual should approach such decisions conscientiously, prayerfully, in the spirit of obedience to God. I realize that when the issue is taken out of the sphere of conscientious personal decision and becomes a factor in public policy and in mass education, it is more difficult to prevent the irresponsible use of contraceptives. But this danger must be weighed against the danger of overpopulation.

I have spoken of an approximate Protestant consensus on the general question of birth control. Several American denominations, including the Methodist Church, the United Lutheran Church, and the Augustana Lutheran Church, have expressed themselves decisively on the matter. Others are at present preparing statements under the immediate pressure of the threat of "population explosion." The most significant development is the gradual change of convictions among the Anglican bishops, as presented through the reports of the Lambeth Conferences. In 1908 they spoke out unambiguously against the use of contraceptives. In 1920 they were still opposed, but Bishop Kirk, the leading Anglican authority of moral theology, sensed the beginnings of permissiveness on the subject.[3] The Lambeth Conference gave clear permission for the conscientious use of contraceptives in 1930, and was even more forthright in 1958 in presenting the case for birth control. This development is significant, partly because Anglican bishops are not reckless innovators and partly because they look for guidance to a considerable extent to the Catholic tradition of moral theology and are often cautious about taking any action that widens the separation between their Church and the Roman Church.

[2] Dietrich Bonhoeffer, *Ethics*, tr. Eberhard Bethge (New York, The Macmillan Company, 1955), p. 133.
[3] K. E. Kirk, *Conscience and Its Problems* (New York, Longmans, Green & Co., Inc., 1927), p. 292.

The Protestant theologians of widest influence generally give moral support for the conscientious use of contraceptives. Sometimes this is done with a degree of reluctance, but, all things considered, it is recognized that the use of contraceptives may be necessary. Increasingly the stress is on the positive values for marriage if sexual intercourse can at times be separated from procreation.[4]

The problem of population involves not only the quantity but also the quality of the world's future inhabitants. The effect of man-made radiation on the population to come requires close study, although the prevention of the genetic deterioration of the race from this cause now depends chiefly on political decisions not directly related to any kind of genetic planning. What does Protestant ethics have to say about forms of genetic planning, about the voluntary or, in extreme cases, the compulsory sterilization of those who by any standards are unfit to pass on their biological characteristics to future generations? Protestant ethics knows no law against such genetic planning, but I think that most Protestants would be very sensitive to the dangers in any elaboration of state policy in this field. To some extent the availability of effective and easily used birth-control methods would enable society to deal with this problem through education and voluntary action.

In principle, provision by the law of the state for the sterilization of those whose genetic unfitness is clear would be widely supported by Protestants. But there is danger in this kind of human engineering as it gains momentum. We cannot reject it, but we must beware of what might develop if society were to decide explicitly what sorts of human beings should or should not be born. There is here a threat to the liberties of the individual in the area of his most intimate personal life, where his freedom has been most secure from political interference.

The Protestant student of ethics knows no absolute law or principle that should control the solution of this deep and vexing problem. There must be freedom for each generation to deal with it with the sensitivity that love should inspire—sensitivity to the liberties of living persons and to the sufferings and frustrations of those who may be born with grievous physical and mental handicaps. I mentioned earlier the concept of boundaries within which ethical action should be taken, rather than fixed laws that should dictate particular decisions. This is the best that Protestants can offer. But action within these boundaries should always be directed by men who are open to the inspiration and judgment of God as He had made Himself known

---

[4] The following references provide examples of Protestant theological opinion: Emil Brunner, *The Divine Imperative* (Philadelphia, Westminster Press, 1947), pp. 368–371; Reinhold Niebuhr, "A Protestant Looks at Catholics," in *Catholicism in America* (New York, Harcourt, Brace & Co., 1953), pp. 31–34; Karl Barth, *Kirchliche Dogmatik*, III, part 4, pp. 306 ff; Dietrich Bonhoeffer, *op. cit.*, pp. 131–135; Otto Piper, *The Christian Interpretation of Sex* (New York, Charles Scribner's Sons, 1941), pp. 144–147; George F. Thomas, *Christian Ethics and Moral Philosophy* (New York, Charles Scribner's Sons, 1955), pp. 234–235.

in revelation—by men who are sensitive to the needs and aspirations of their neighbors, and especially of those who have least power to defend themselves.

American Population Growth in 1963

METROPOLITAN LIFE INSURANCE COMPANY

Both the United States and Canada experienced a substantial growth in population during 1963, bringing the total for the two countries to nearly 210,000,000 by the end of the year. In the United States, the population increase was 2,670,000 and raised the total, including the Armed Forces overseas, to 190,820,000. This increment of 1.4 percent compared with an average annual increase of 1.7 percent in the ten years since January 1954. Canada added over 330,000 inhabitants last year, bringing its population to 19,100,000. However, the increase of 1.8 percent in 1963 was well below the average annual increment of 2.4 percent recorded in the past decade.

The dominant factor in the recent population growth of the United States has been the unprecedented number of births. During each of the past 10 years, live births exceeded 4 million. There were almost 4,100,000 births registered in 1963 and 4,167,000 the year before; the all-time high of 4,280,000 occurred in 1957. The births in 1963 correspond to a rate of 21.7 per 1,000 population, compared with 22.4 in 1962 and 23.3 in 1961.

Reflecting the high level of births in the United States during the postwar years, the most rapid growth in population occurred at ages under 21 years. Between January 1954 and the end of 1963, this age group increased from 59.4 to 77.9 million, a rise of 18.5 million, or 31 percent; these figures include Alaska and Hawaii as well as the Armed Forces overseas. During the same period, the population at ages 65 and over rose from 13.9 million to 17.8 million. While the relative growth of this older population group was 28 percent—virtually the same as for the population under 21—the number of elders added to the population was only about one fifth the corresponding increment at the younger ages.

The population at ages 45–64 has also increased substantially in the past decade, from 32.6 million to 38.2 million, or 17 percent. However, persons in the early adult years—ages 21–44—have increased by only 1 percent reach-

Statistical Bulletin, XLV (January 1964), 1–4. Reprinted by permission of the Metropolitan Life Insurance Company.

TABLE 1 Population of the United States by Geographic Area, 1954–1964

Area	Number in Thousands				Annual Percent Increase † During	
	January 1, 1964	January 1, 1963	April 1, 1960	January 1, 1954	January 1954 to 1963	January 1963 *
UNITED STATES						
Including Armed Forces overseas	190,820	188,151	180,007	161,690	1.4	1.7
Excluding Armed Forces overseas	190,130	187,421	179,323	160,492	1.4	1.7
New England	10,812	10,743	10,509	9,640	.6	1.2
Maine	984	981	969	911	.3	.8
New Hampshire	630	626	607	551	.6	1.4
Vermont	390	390	390	376	.0	.4
Massachusetts	5,228	5,213	5,149	4,817	.3	.9
Rhode Island	890	883	859	815	.8	.9
Connecticut	2,690	2,650	2,535	2,170	1.5	2.2
Middle Atlantic	35,870	35,478	34,168	31,558	1.1	1.3
New York	17,880	17,634	16,782	15,657	1.4	1.3
New Jersey	6,544	6,424	6,067	5,196	1.9	2.4
Pennsylvania	11,446	11,420	11,319	10,704	.2	.7
East North Central	37,382	37,090	36,225	32,503	.8	1.5
Ohio	10,250	10,121	9,706	8,774	1.3	1.6
Indiana	4,698	4,686	4,662	4,238	.3	1.1
Illinois	10,194	10,154	10,081	9,016	.4	1.3
Michigan	8,163	8,083	7,823	6,924	1.0	1.7
Wisconsin	4,077	4,046	3,952	3,551	.8	1.5
West North Central	15,707	15,633	15,394	14,447	.5	.9
Minnesota	3,510	3,486	3,414	3,096	.7	1.3
Iowa	2,784	2,780	2,758	2,635	.1	.6
Missouri	4,330	4,327	4,320	4,110	.1	.6
North Dakota	634	633	632	621	.2	.2
South Dakota	747	730	681	658	2.3	1.2
Nebraska	1,467	1,454	1,411	1,320	.9	1.1
Kansas	2,235	2,223	2,179	2,007	.5	1.1
South Atlantic	28,023	27,474	25,972	22,615	2.0	2.2
Delaware	480	471	446	357	1.9	3.1
Maryland	3,322	3,265	3,101	2,595	1.7	2.6
District of Columbia	803	796	764	827	.9	− .4
Virginia	4,400	4,295	3,967	3,506	2.4	2.3
West Virginia	1,765	1,789	1,860	1,938	−1.3	− .9
North Carolina	4,800	4,737	4,556	4,177	1.3	1.4
South Carolina	2,503	2,464	2,383	2,226	1.6	1.1

Georgia	4,180	4,114	3,943	3,614	1.6	1.5
Florida	5,770	5,543	4,952	3,375	4.1	5.7
East South Central	12,498	12,386	12,050	11,446	.9	.9
Kentucky	3,108	3,093	3,038	2,916	.5	.7
Tennessee	3,718	3,677	3,567	3,347	1.1	1.1
Alabama	3,362	3,336	3,267	3,078	.8	.9
Mississippi	2,310	2,280	2,178	2,105	1.3	.9
West South Central	18,282	17,962	16,951	15,246	1.8	1.8
Arkansas	1,871	1,855	1,786	1,800	.9	.3
Louisiana	3,445	3,401	3,257	2,889	1.3	1.8
Oklahoma	2,516	2,471	2,328	2,147	1.8	1.6
Texas	10,450	10,235	9,580	8,410	2.1	2.2
Mountain	7,773	7,528	6,855	5,625	3.3	3.3
Montana	712	702	675	611	1.4	1.6
Idaho	720	707	667	589	1.8	2.0
Wyoming	338	334	330	298	1.2	1.3
Colorado	1,990	1,920	1,754	1,478	3.6	2.9
New Mexico	1,030	1,010	951	778	2.0	2.9
Arizona	1,602	1,524	1,302	912	5.1	5.9
Utah	998	971	891	755	2.8	2.8
Nevada	383	360	285	204	6.4	6.5
Pacific	23,783	23,127	21,198	17,412	2.8	3.2
Washington	3,082	3,040	2,853	2,506	1.4	2.2
Oregon	1,835	1,820	1,769	1,638	.8	1.2
California	17,910	17,326	15,717	12,543	3.4	3.7
Alaska	251	244	226	213	2.9	1.5
Hawaii	705	697	633	512	1.1	3.5

* Geometric average annual rate. †Minus sign (−) denotes decrease.
Note: Figures for divisions and States exclude population in the Armed Forces overseas. Each 1960 figure has been independently rounded; hence, the sums of parts may differ slightly from the totals.
Source: Figures for 1960, from the decennial census; those for other years, estimated by the Statistical Bureau of the Metropolitan Life Insurance Company from data published by the Bureau of the Census and the National Center for Health Statistics.

ing 56.9 million at the end of 1963. As a result, the population at these ages has decreased from 34½ percent to 30 percent of the total.

The babies born in the United States during 1963 had an excellent start in life. Infant mortality for the year established a new minimum of 25.0 per 1,000 live births; the previous low was 25.3 in 1961 and 1962. The current death rate among infants is one tenth below that recorded a decade ago, and only half the rate of a quarter century ago.

Unlike the experience among infants and children, persons aged 20 and over experienced moderate increases in mortality in 1963, primarily as a result of the widespread outbreaks of acute respiratory disease in the early months of the year. The crude death rate for the total population was 9.6 per 1,000 in 1963, compared with 9.5 the year before and with the all-time low of 9.2 in 1954. The number of deaths last year rose to a new high of about 1,810,000.

The number of registered births exceeded deaths by about 2,280,000 in 1963, a smaller natural increase than in any year since 1950. The United States also gained about 330,000 persons through migration last year, or about the same as the annual average in 1960–62.

Each geographic division of the United States gained population during 1963, as may be seen in Table 1. Continuing the trend of earlier years, the Mountain States experienced the most rapid rate of growth, namely, 3.3 percent. This was appreciably more than twice the national rate. Nevada and Arizona outranked all other States, with increases of 6.4 and 5.1 percent, respectively.

Equally noteworthy was the sustained high rate of population growth in California, as a result of which California edged New York State out of its leading position toward the end of November. It is estimated that at the close of 1963 California had about 17,910,000 residents, compared with approximately 17,880,000 in New York.

East of the Rocky Mountains, population growth continued to be most marked in Florida, where the increase amounted to 4.1 percent in 1963. Florida has gained about 2.4 million residents since January 1954, and is outranked only by California in this respect. New York and Texas complete the short list of States that added over 2 million people in the past ten years.

Most States recorded a slowing down in population growth during 1963. Exceptions to this general pattern were largely concentrated in the South—Arkansas, Georgia, Mississippi, Oklahoma, South Carolina, Virginia, and the District of Columbia. The population in the District of Columbia had been declining prior to 1960, but has since increased slowly. Nevertheless, fewer people are living there now than a decade ago. The loss of population has been even more pronounced in West Virginia—the only State with a decrease in population during 1963. In the past decade, the population of West Virginia has decreased by almost 1 percent annually, and is now down to about 1,765,000.

Canada's population growth in 1963 was due almost entirely to its excess of births over deaths, the gain by migration amounting to only a few thousand. There were about 468,000 births in 1963, compared with 469,700 the year before and with the all-time high of 479,275 in 1959. The birth rate in 1963 was below 25 per 1,000 population for the first time since 1945. With almost 148,000 deaths during the year, the death rate was 7.8 per 1,000 population, or only slightly above the low of 7.7 registered in 1961 and 1962.

In 1963, as in earlier years, Ontario and Quebec accounted for about two thirds of the total population increase in Canada; the details by Province are shown in Table 2. Ontario added about 120,000 residents during 1963, raising its population above 6,520,000 by the end of the year; Quebec's population increased by more than 90,000 to a total of about 5,522,000. All the other Provinces also gained population during the year, the increases ranging up to about 29,000 in Alberta and 36,000 in British Columbia.

TABLE 2 *Population of Canada by Province, 1954–1964*

Province	Number in Thousands				Annual Percent Increase During	
	January 1, 1964	January 1, 1963	June 1, 1961	January 1, 1954	1963	January 1954 to January 1963 *
CANADA	19,100	18,767	18,238	15,105	1.8	2.4
Newfoundland	488	477	458	390	2.3	2.3
Prince Edward Island	108	107	105	101	.9	.6
Nova Scotia	764	750	737	670	1.9	1.3
New Brunswick	617	611	598	538	1.0	1.4
Quebec	5,522	5,430	5,259	4,340	1.7	2.5
Ontario	6,522	6,401	6,236	5,041	1.9	2.7
Manitoba	960	944	922	818	1.7	1.6
Saskatchewan	935	930	925	869	.5	.8
Alberta	1,423	1,394	1,332	1,037	2.1	3.3
British Columbia	1,720	1,684	1,629	1,275	2.1	3.1
Yukon and Northwest Territories	41	39	38	26	5.1	4.6

* Geometric average annual rate.
Note: Each 1961 figure has been independently rounded; hence, the sum of parts may differ slightly from the total.
Source: 1961 Census and 1963 estimates, from the Dominion Bureau of Statistics; estimates for 1954 and 1964, by the Statistical Bureau of the Metropolitan Life Insurance Company.

Questions

1. Is the "population explosion" aptly named?
2. Explain the difference between ethics and morals.
3. What is the connection between the two halves of Hoagland's paper?
4. Is the population explosion primarily a problem of underdeveloped countries? Why? Do the problems raised by it differ in developed and underdeveloped countries? How?
5. Bennett claims that "it has been well said that death control makes birth control a necessity." Is he right?
6. What does Bennett mean by the term "pragmatic"?
7. Bennett says that "the clearest difference between Protestant and official Catholic teaching" concerns the priority of the "two purposes of sexual intercourse." Would Thomas agree?
8. Would Bennett agree with Thomas' conclusion that "the basic issue . . . is not primarily population growth or resources, but man's ability to modify his cultural and social systems so that the fullest exploitation of the world's resources becomes possible"? Would Hoagland agree?

9. The opposing positions on birth control are usually taken to be Catholic and Protestant. Are there any other positions that might be represented on this issue?

Assignments

1. Both Thomas and Bennett are concerned with the ethical questions involving birth control that arise from the population explosion. Discuss some of the other problems, scientific and ethical, that arise from the changes in population described by Hoagland.
2. Make a list of the ways in which Hoagland qualifies his statements to indicate the limits of his conclusions or the tentativeness of a particular point. Discuss briefly the reasons for precision in scientific style and the methods of achieving it.
3. After studying the footnotes in the three essays, make a list of the various uses that can be made of the footnote.
4. Discuss the alternative solutions to the population problem suggested by Thomas. Do they provide more realistic approaches than birth control?
5. Analyze the points of fundamental difference between Catholics and Protestants in their approach to ethical questions. In what ways do they agree?

Additional Reading

No discussion of the population explosion fails to mention Thomas Malthus. In *An Essay on the Principle of Population* (1798), he established the lines of argument on the problem which have prevailed ever since and, as one solution, suggested birth control. In a recent volume, *Three Essays on Population* (New York, 1960), Malthus' essay has been reprinted along with two modern discussions, Julian Huxley's (1955) and Frederick Osborn's (1960).

Other recent discussions of the question include John Rock, *The Time Has Come* (New York, 1963), a discussion by a Catholic physician; Dennis H. Wrong, *Population and Society* (New York, 1961), an objective, detailed survey of a demographer; and George F. Meir, ed., *Studies in Population* (Princeton, 1949), a collection of studies by various hands.

SECTION FIVE | Psychology and Science

The Dark Ages of Psychology

ARTHUR KOESTLER

For the last fifty years the dominant trend in academic psychology has been a pseudo-science called Behaviourism. Its pioneer was John B. Watson, Professor at John Hopkins University in Baltimore. In his first paper, published in 1913, Watson proclaimed: 'The time has come when psychology must discard all reference to consciousness . . . its sole task is the prediction and control of behaviour; and introspection can form no part of its method'. By 'behaviour', Watson meant observable activities—what the physicist calls 'public events'. Since all mental events are private events which can be made public only by introspective statements, they had to be excluded from the domain of psychology. Accordingly, terms like 'consciousness', 'sensation', 'imagination', 'purpose' were declared to be dirty words and banned from the vocabulary.

Watson on Behaviourism

If you look up the article on Behaviourism in the 1955 edition of the *Encyclopaedia Britannica*, you will find five columns of eulogy for Watson. His books, we are told, 'demonstrate the possibility of writing an adequate, comprehensive account of human and animal behaviour without the use of the philosophical concept of mind or consciousness'. Since few people, and that includes Behaviourists, have read Watson in the original, let me quote as an example his views on artistic creativity. Chapter X of Watson's textbook, *Behaviourism,* is called 'Talking and Thinking'. It has a long sub-title which

The Listener, LXXI (May 14, 1964), 785–787. Reprinted by permission of the BBC and the author.

reads: 'Talking and Thinking—Which, When Rightly Understood, Go Far in Breaking down the Fiction that there is any such Thing as "Mental" Life'. But if there is no such thing as mental life, how do books get written? Watson's answer is as follows:

> One natural question often raised is, how do we ever get new verbal creations such as a poem or a brilliant essay? The answer is that we get them by manipulating words, shifting them about until a new pattern is hit upon . . . How do you suppose Patou builds a new gown? Has he any 'picture in his mind' of what the gown is to look like when it is finished? He has not. . . . He calls his model in, picks up a new piece of silk, throws it around her, he pulls it in here, he pulls it out there . . . He manipulates the material until it takes on the semblance of a dress . . . The painter plies his trade in the same way, nor can the poet boast of any other method.

The key-word is 'manipulation'. Watson defines it as 'an instinctive tendency sometimes exalted in calling it constructiveness'. He explains how it works in children and in rats. Children have the tendency 'to reach out for objects, to scrape them along the floor, to pick them up, put them into the mouth, throw them down upon the floor', and so on. A rat put into a maze rushes to and fro, it manipulates its own legs in random fashion until it hits upon the food, in the same way as Patou manipulates the silk until he hits upon a new model; likewise the poet or novelist shifts about words until a new pattern is 'hit upon'. At the moment of the lucky hit the stimulus 'to arouse admiration and commendation' ceases to be active, and manipulation stops: 'the equivalent', Watson says, 'of the rat finding food'. Here you have what the *Encyclopaedia Britannica* calls 'an adequate and comprehensive account' of how *Hamlet* or the Sistine Chapel came into being.

Unfortunately, Watsonian Behaviourism is not a historical curiosity, but the foundation on which the more sophisticated and immensely influential neo-Behaviourist systems of Professors Guthrie, Clark Hull, and Skinner were built. The more blatant absurdities of Watson are forgotten or slurred over, but the philosophy of Behaviourism has remained the same.

Slot machines on the campus

I have called it a pseudo-science because it is an anachronism based on the crudely mechanistic conceptions of the nineteenth century which have been abandoned in all other branches of contemporary science, from physics to biology. Its basic doctrine is that all actions of animals and men can be analysed into elementary building blocks, into atoms of behaviour variously called conditioned reflexes or S-R units, where S stands for stimulus, R for response. Thus in the latest American textbook for college students † that has come my way, written by a galaxy of university professors, it is once more dogmatically asserted that any complex activity, such as writing a poem or

† *Psychology*, edited by Allen D. Calvin: Boston, 1961

carrying on a conversation, consists in the 'chaining together' of a linear series of S-R units. To illustrate this crucial point, the textbook gives the following example of a conversation:

> *He:* What time is it?
> *She:* Twelve o'clock.
> *He:* Thank you.
> *She:* Don't mention it.
> *He:* How about lunch?
> *She:* Fine.

The author, who is Chairman of the Department of Psychology of a well-known college, comments on it as follows:

> Now, this conversation can be analysed into separate S-R units. 'He' makes the first response, which is emitted probably to the stimulus of the sight of 'She'. When 'He' emits the operant 'What time is it?', the muscular activity, of course, produces a sound which also serves as a stimulus for 'She'. On the receipt of the stimulus, 'She' emits an operant herself, 'twelve o'clock', which in turn produces a stimulus to 'He', and so on. . . .

As I was reading this text, I had the vision of two cute automatic slot-machines facing each other on the campus, feeding each other with stimulus coins and popping out responses. And that is precisely the Behaviourist image of man.

Man as a Heath Robinson contraption

Do not misunderstand me. My objection to that image has nothing to do with the old question whether man is an 'automaton' in the broad sense of being subject to natural laws which determine his actions, or whether he has some freedom of choice. I cannot know whether my skull houses a computing machine made of soft-ware, or a machine plus something else. Personally I like to believe that there is something else, but I cannot prove it, and it has nothing to do with the subject I am discussing. I do not say that the Behaviourists are wrong in viewing man as a machine. I am saying that the *kind* of machine which they postulate is built on demonstrably false principles: it is not even a computer, but a Heath Robinson contraption.

Take an obvious example. As I am talking during this broadcast I am, according to the textbook that I have just quoted, unwinding a chain of S-R units, where each word, once uttered, acts as a stimulus which calls forth the next. I am of course doing nothing of the sort. When I was asked to deliver these talks, I first decided on the general theme, then sketched out a rough list of the particular subjects to be treated, then worked out each of these sub-headings in more detail; and the choice and manipulation of individual phrases and words came at the end. It is a process like the arborization of a tree trunk into branches, branches into twigs—and not a process of threading beads or making a daisy-chain. Moreover, if by tomorrow you still happen to remember anything of what I am now saying, you will not remember the actual words, but only the meaning and maybe my funny accent. The actual words, the so-called units of my verbal behaviour, are to a large extent replaceable by other units without much altering the meaning, and to a lesser extent my examples and sub-themes are also replaceable by others. Thus if you apply the Behaviourist programme and break down this complex operation into its simple, elementary units of behaviour, you will have learned next to nothing that is relevant—just as the examination of bricks and mortar will tell you nothing about the architecture of the building. Yet over the last fifty years, most of the work done in psychological laboratories consisted in analysing bricks and mortar in the hope that by patient effort somehow one day it would tell you what a cathedral looks like.

Unfolding complex activities

To repeat: complex activities are not what Behaviourists pretend them to be, that is, series of stimulus-response units chained together. They unfold as a tree grows, or as a military operation takes place: first the general strategy is conceived at headquarters, then the technical details are successively filled in on successively lower echelons of the hierarchy. This description applies not only to complex tasks like writing an essay; the principles of hierarchic organization, where the whole controls the sub-wholes and these their sub-sub-wholes, and so on, is found everywhere in organic life. A motor-car is put together on the assembly belt bit by bit (though even here there is an overall plan); but an embryo grows from a single fertilized cell which contains the blueprint of the whole, through successive stages of differentiation, each of which fills in more details of the final pattern. To revert to Watson's example, before Patou or Dior called in the model, he had, of course, a sketch of the new dress down on paper or in his head; the manipulation of the silk came only afterwards to fill in the final details. A pianist in a night club seems to conform to the Behaviourist canon when he reels off a tune like an S-R chain—but in fact he does not, because he can transpose the same tune into a different key where the units and the intervals form a different chain; he has learned not a linear series but a pattern.

The same considerations apply, as we shall see in a minute, to the experimental psychologist's favourite object of study, the white albino rat. You can hardly visit a psychological laboratory without seeing a rat disporting itself in a so-called Skinner box—a contraption invented in the nineteen-thirties by Professor Skinner of Harvard University. The box is equipped with a food tray, an electric bulb, and a bar which can be pushed down like the lever of a slot machine. When the rat presses it down with its paws, a food pellet falls into the dish. This experimental procedure is called 'operant conditioning' because the rat 'operates' on its environment—whereas in so-called 'classical conditioning' by the Pavlovian method, the dog is immobilized in its restraining harness. The purpose of the box is to enable the experimenter to measure behaviour by quantitative methods. The number of times the rat presses the lever in a given period of time is counted, plotted on a chart, and regarded as a measure of 'operant strength'; the food pellet is called a 'reinforcer'; withholding the food pellet after lever-pressing is a 'negative reinforcer'; the alternation of the two is 'intermittent reinforcement'; the light bulb is a 'secondary reinforcer', and so on.

Pavlov counted the number of drops which his dogs salivated through their artificial fistulae, and distilled them into a philosophy of man too crude even for American Behaviourists; Professors Skinner, Hull, and their followers took an equally heroic short cut from the rat in the box to the human condition. Skinner's two best-known books are called *The Behaviour of Organisms* and *Science and Human Behaviour*. Nothing in their resounding titles indicates that the data in them are mainly derived from conditioning experiments on rats and pigeons—which he then converted, by primitive analogies, into confident assertions about the political, religious, and ethical problems of human society. Similarly, Hull attempted to construct an all-embracing system of psychology based on the axiom 'that all behaviour of all species of mammalia, including man, occurs according to the same set of primary laws'. These primary laws or units of behaviour he, too, saw epitomized in the lever-pressing activities of the rat, on which most of Hull's later work was based.

A ratomorphic view of man

There was once a time when naturalists were inclined to hold anthropomorphic views, to attribute to animals reasoning powers and emotions similar to man's. In 1894, Lloyd Morgan postulated a principle which became a kind of eleventh commandment for psychologists, known as 'Lloyd Morgan's canon'. It says that one should not interpret an animal's actions in terms of human mental processes if the action can be explained in terms of simpler processes on lower levels. Behaviourist psychology reversed this principle. It refuses to attribute to man any mental processes which cannot be shown to occur in lower animals. In other words, for the anthropomorphic view of the rat, Behaviourism has substituted a ratomorphic view of man.

To complete the picture, I must mention that Professor Skinner has also invented another box, a labour-saving, air-conditioned cubicle with a glass front and built-in automatic sanitation in which, he recommends, human babies should be kept for most of the time during their first year. The baby in the box is naked, it needs no adult supervision, and there is no problem about diapers. He has actually tried the method on one of his own daughters, and several hundred American families have bought the box and followed his example. He has sponsored an automatic learning machine too: a series of questions appear successively in a slot; the pupil punches his answers on a tape, and, on examining the tape, can judge his progress. Neither of the two contraptions is quite as crazy as it sounds, but I cannot go into their merits and demerits. I am sorry to have to pick at Professor Skinner—who personally is a gentle soul, a kind of ratomorphic idealist; yet I cannot help feeling that he and his school symbolize in an extreme form the trend towards the dehumanization of man. They have even re-named psychology, once the science of the mind, and call it 'the Science of Behaviour'. It was a demonstrative act of semantic self-castration, and in keeping with Skinner's references to education as 'behavioural engineering'. As Sir Cyril Burt has written 'A cynical onlooker might be tempted to say that psychology having first bargained away its soul and then gone out of its mind, seems now, as it faces an untimely end, to have lost all consciousness'.

Lip service to senility

The picture which I have so far drawn is not exaggerated, but it is one-sided. Behaviourism has dominated the stage throughout the dark ages of psychology, and is still dominant in the groves of Academe, but it never had the stage all to itself. In the first place there have always been voices in the wilderness, lone figures from an older generation, such as Cyril Burt, whom I have just quoted, or Woodworth and his school in America. In the second place, there is Gestalt psychology, which for a couple of decades was a serious rival to Behaviourism. And, lastly, there is a new generation of brilliant young neurophysiologists and communication theorists who regard academic S-R psychology as senile, but have to pay lip service to it and adopt its jargon if they want to make a career.

The historic merit of the Gestalt school was its emphasis on the organism as a functional whole—and not merely the sum of its component parts. It rejected the atomistic approach of Behaviourism and asserted that psychology must concentrate on the Gestalt aspect—the pattern or configuration of phenomena—instead of searching for the illusory units or elements of behaviour. The central battlefield was the field of learning theory. According to the Behaviourist doctrine, all learning occurs by the hit-and-miss or trial-and-error method. The correct response to a given stimulus is hit upon by chance, and has a rewarding or, as the jargon has it, reinforcing effect; if the reinforcement is strong or repeated often enough, the response will be 'stamped in' and an S-R bond, a stimulus and response link is formed. Thus all mental development of the individual is supposed to be the result of random tries preserved through reinforcements—as the biological evolution of the species is supposed to be the outcome of random mutations preserved by natural selection. Originality and creativeness have no place in this system. We have heard Watson's view of how the poet and painter ply their trade. According to Guthrie, the original solution of a problem 'must be in the category of luck, and hence lie outside of science'. In Skinner's view, as in

Watson's, the method of solving a problem is 'merely that of manipulating variables which may lead to the emission of the response. No new factor of originality is involved'.

Astonishing chimpanzees

As against this view, the Gestalt school held that all true learning and problem-solving is based on spontaneous insight. In a series of famous experiments, Wolfgang Köhler has shown what astonishing feats chimpanzees are capable of; and I mean not circus tricks like riding a bicycle, but self-taught, spontaneous discoveries in the making and using of tools. A chimpanzee is of course vastly superior in intelligence to a rat, but that alone does not explain the contrast; it is primarily due to the different type of problem which each school sets its animals. Watson and his followers put rats into mazes, where they could only learn to find their way by exploring every blind alley, and then concluded that *all* learning is derived from trial and error. But as somebody has said, not even a Newton could learn a maze by any other method. On the other hand, Tolman and his followers were able to demonstrate that when a rat has learned its way about the maze, it does not simply reel off a chain of reflexes—such as second turn to the right, third left, first right, etc.—but carries a kind of mental map in its head; for when the normal path to the food is blocked, it will instantly choose an alternative path. In other words, though the rat had to learn by trial and error, it has nevertheless acquired insight into the topography of the maze.

But the great expectations which the Gestalt school had aroused were only partly fulfilled, and its limitations soon became apparent. The result was a kind of abortive renaissance followed by a counter-reformation. The neo-Behaviourists, having incorporated some of the Gestaltists' experimental findings into their theories, had indeed a remarkable come-back. The main reason was the ambiguity of the Gestalt school's central concept of 'insight'. They used this word sometimes in the sense of intelligence and understanding in general; but at other times to refer specifically to the sudden flash of inspiration, the moment of truth, the discovery of *new* insights.

Insight in the first sense—in the sense of intelligence and understanding—is a matter of degrees; we could say that even the dog in Pavlov's laboratory, who has been conditioned to salivate at the sound of the bell which always precedes the arrival of food, has gained a degree of insight into the situation by a process akin to the type of scientific reasoning called empirical induction. If the dog could speak it would say that the food follows the bell, as thunder follows lightning, for such is the law of the universe; and the dog's statement would be correct though incomplete, for it could not have known that the laws of his universe were decreed by God Pavlov. Similarly, the trial-and-error learning of the rat can display various degrees of insight, from random tries to the exploration and elimination of a series of tentative 'hypotheses', as Krechevsky and others have shown. But this kind of inductive process does not explain the phenomenon of the sudden dramatic emergence of the right solution all in one piece, the act of original creation. And although Gestalt proclaimed just this suddenness and completeness of the solution to be the prototype of all insightful learning in animal and man, this is demonstrably untrue, and its explanations were wholly inadequate. They were mostly derived from rather spurious analogies with visual perception. Thus for instance when we look at a figure presented in an incomplete outline, we tend to complete it in the mind's eye, that is, to *close* the gap; and according to Gestalt theory, we solve abstract problems by applying the 'closure principle'; the solution closes the gap.

The brain and the outside world

This is true enough, as far as it goes; but it is a metaphor, not an explanation. It tells us nothing specific about the kind of process by which Kepler discovered that the planets move in elliptical orbits, or by which Jenner discovered that vaccination with a dose of cowpox immunizes a person against smallpox. The tentative answers which the Gestalt school proposed boiled down roughly to this: that just as the eye takes in a whole figure at a glance, so the mind has the innate faculty of taking in at a glance the causal relations underlying complex phenomena—thanks to some pre-existing correspondence between processes in the brain and events in the outside world. It can be shown that this metaphysical assumption leads us ultimately back to Plato's 'eyes of the soul' whereas Behaviourism leads us ultimately back to the primitive atomism of Democritus. Neither of them has much bearing on the problem of creativity.

It is a fascinating question for the historian of science how it could happen that just at the time, in the nineteen-twenties, when the mechanistic theories of classical physics were abandoned, the concept of man as a rigid slot-machine activated by chain-reflexes became fashionable in cultures as different as the United States and the Soviet Union. In the end, the atoms of behaviour proved as elusive and volatile as the physicist's hard little lumps of matter. Heisenberg, one of the greatest theoretical physicists, said recently, 'nature is unpredictable'. It would be absurd to deny the living organism even that degree of unpredictability which quantum physics accords inanimate nature; and processes on the quantum level occur both in evolutionary genetics and in the nervous system.

Trivial predictions

Three years ago, I published in *The Observer* a series of articles on contemporary developments in psychology, which led to a protracted controversy in its correspondence columns. One well-known experimental psychologist in Oxford wrote: 'If Koestler wishes to be convinced of the predictability of human behaviour, including his own, I will undertake to make ten predictions about Koestler's behaviour over the next week, and send these in a sealed envelope to the Editor. I would be prepared to stake a large sum of money that Koestler's behaviour will conform to my predictions'.

Here was at last a chance to settle an age-old problem by a crucial experiment. I hastened to accept the bet, on condition, of course, that it should exclude trivial predictions of the type: 'Koestler will eat, sleep, exhale carbon dioxide, etc.'. Otherwise, I said, I would prefer to stick to the predictions of my favourite palm reader. Thereupon the Oxford psychologist called the bet off, with the disarming comment that he 'did not claim to be able to predict any but trivial behaviour'.

This seems to me a perfect summing up of the achievements of fifty years of ratomorphic psychology.

Outside the Cave

NEVILLE MORAY

'When I use a word, it means just what I choose it to mean—neither more nor less'. Thus Humpty Dumpty, talking to Alice in Looking Glass Lane—and thus, too, I am very much afraid, Arthur Koestler informing, if I may use the word loosely, informing us all about the nature of modern psychology.

The three talks that Mr Koestler recently gave on the Third Programme * formed an introduction to the book he has written about the nature of the creative act and his theory of artistic creativity. But for some reason he gave over the whole of his first talk to an attack on the aims, nature, and achievements of what he called 'modern academic psychology'. I suppose that by this phrase he means the kind of thing we teach our students at universities, but I must say that there is extraordinarily little similarity between Koestler's account and what actually goes on in departments of psychology. That is why I have dared to tackle him—because the subject I teach and the research I do is not the poor, sterile, bankrupt thing he described, and I do not like seeing it so misrepresented.

At the end of his first talk, which he called 'The dark ages of psychology',

* Printed in *The Listener*, May 14, 21, and 28.

The Listener, LXXI (June 25, 1964), 1028–1029. Reprinted by permission of the BBC and the author.

I thought that he was merely ill-informed, but after listening to the others and reading his book I am not so sure. He talked about modern psychology and how it has been dominated by what he called the 'ratomorphic' school. He pointed out some of the silly things about language and creativity which can be found among the writings of prominent contemporary psychologists. And then he went on to emphasize that all academic psychology is dominated by the so-called 'S-R' (or stimulus-response) theorists who draw their influence from Watson back in the nineteen-twenties. He said that there was a short-lived attempt to oust them by the Gestalt psychologists, who did not want to explain all human behaviour by means of chains of conditioned reflexes, but, as he put it:

> The great expectations which the Gestalt school had aroused were only partly fulfilled, and its limitations soon became apparent. The result was a kind of abortive renaissance followed by a counter-reformation.

And that, it appears, was more or less that. Academic psychology has been under the paw of rat psychology ever since. But is Mr Koestler's account historically accurate? What were those Dark Ages of psychology really like?

It is true that in America there have always been several 'schools' occupied with learning theory, and leaning heavily on work with rats. But the vast majority of psychologists have never been involved in that sort of work. After all, we study personality, social psychology, industrial processes, human engineering, vocational guidance, education, and so on. From what Koestler said you would think that in the nineteen-twenties and 'thirties the mainstream of psychology consisted entirely of two or three men—Watson, Hull, and Skinner, perhaps—and several thousand rats; but in Hamelin there were other citizens of some importance apart from the Pied Piper.

Concentrating on the 'rat men'

It is true that if you simply concentrate on the more outrageous claims of some of the rat men you might well conclude that Koestler was right. Studying psychology, like the practice of journalism, is no guarantee that you will not become drunk with the splendour of your own theories; but you might as well try to study medicine by keeping in touch only with the work on, say, drugs to stop hay fever. Think back, for example, to what Koestler said about emotions. He talked of 'self-assertive tendencies', and of a 'participatory tendency' in opposition to it. He complained, because all through the dark ages of psychology, the nineteen-twenties, no one had studied the emotions, particularly these complex ones. But the very phrase 'self-assertive tendencies', and long comments about its nature, and about all the other emotions in man, had come from the pen of William McDougall in the middle of those 'dark ages', just when Mr Koestler says no one was doing any work on them.

McDougall gave perhaps the most extensive account of the emotional life of man that has ever been attempted. He was one of the most famous psychologists of his day, one of the outstanding figures in the history of psychology, and the exact opposite of the rat men such as Watson. Koestler's writings on these topics could be mistaken for McDougall himself, yet Koestler said, in his second talk, that the neglect of them 'throughout the dark ages of psychology is one of the reasons why it has so little to tell us about the phenomena of creativity in science and art'.

Mr Koestler mentioned the name of Woodworth twice as 'a voice in the wilderness', 'a lonely figure of his generation'; but any student quickly discovers that the writings of Woodworth have far more importance than those of Watson, or even, in most departments, than Hull or Skinner; and leading American psychologists will tell you that in the nineteen-thirties Woodworth was perhaps the greatest figure in academic psychology—far more important than the ratomorphs.

Again, Koestler uses the idea of the 'schema' to discuss memory, but he does not mention that Bartlett, the doyen of the British academic psychologists of his day, wrote a whole book, a classic work on memory, precisely to develop that very idea. Again and again Koestler uses psychoanalytic terms, 'sublimation of instincts', 'regression', 'identification', and so on. Are we meant to think this has nothing to do with academic psychology? One might as well say that medicine has nothing to do with biochemistry because one is a form of therapy and the other an academic subject. No, as a history of academic psychology Mr Koestler's account just will not do.

An unrecognizable travesty

I was even more surprised to find that Koestler's account of psychology as it is practised today is as wrong as his history. He goes so far as to say that brilliant young scientists of our own day have to pay lip service to rat psychology and adopt its jargon if they want to make a career. That is what Koestler explicitly said, and it is entirely untrue. To anyone like me who has recently been a student in a British laboratory, it is an unrecognizable travesty of the situation. My undergraduate memories are still vivid. We were taught very little 'ratomorphism'. When we were taught it, it was as a method for studying the nervous system—certainly not as the be all and end all of psychology, the golden key to unlock the secrets of the human heart. Far less was it raised up as an over-all philosophy—Behaviourism with a capital 'B'. And I am sure this is true of most psychology departments. We learnt at least as much about, say, psychoanalytic theory as about learning theory. And seeing how many psychoanalytic terms Koestler uses in his book I should think he would be delighted about that.

So the picture he draws of modern psychology, too, is factually a false one. Indeed, judging by that first talk of his, you might think that he visited only those laboratories, read only those books, which would provide him with ammunition for his attack. What is so unfortunate is that a man as well known as Mr Koestler should so misrepresent us; for psychologists have a constant struggle to convince people that they are hard-working scientists tackling very difficult problems, and not bearded men leaning eagerly over couches. We are just beginning to get rid of that travesty, and here is the birth of a new one.

What is even more worrying, though, now that I have read his book, is that I cannot see any conclusion except that Koestler is not ignorant about modern psychology, but simply gave a distorted picture of it in his talks. That may sound rather strong, but I am really forced to it. For throughout his broadcasts, he used the findings of modern psychology again and again, although he did not then acknowledge their sources; and in his book there are about 250 pages which describe and make use of all sorts of data from the very academic psychology which he has attacked. If he really does know what we have been doing all these years, why then did he attempt to mislead his radio audience about modern psychology? One rather gets the impression that he dislikes the idea of a science of human behaviour so much that he cannot help being unfair to it even where it has been moderately successful, and indeed where it has helped him.

Psychology a 'pseudoscience'?

He calls it a 'pseudoscience' and pretends to reject all the terms and findings of modern psychology as valueless. But all those of us who are interested in Mr Koestler's work on creativity will recall another book—the brilliant monograph on artistic creativity by E. H. Gombrich, called *Art and Illusion*. Gombrich used experimental psychology as one of his strongest threads when he wove that outstanding study. Indeed the work of J. J. Gibson and Bartlett, two psychologists of the 'dark ages' of Koestler, is indispensable to Gombrich's argument in that book. Take, for example, the research on visual constancy—Koestler himself quotes it in these words:

> Hold your left hand six inches, the other twelve inches, away from your eyes: they will look about the same size although the retinal image of the left is twice the size of the right. Seeing is a complex skill, it enables us to recognize that the size, shape and colour of objects remain the same even though their retinal image changes all the time.

I have not read a better description of this in any of our psychology text books, and it is just one example of the way in which Koestler's own book, and his talks, are chock-a-block with our research and our language. 'Coding', 'sensory motor skills', 'motor hierarchy', 'matrix', 'ensemble', 'subskills'—the list is endless, or to be more accurate it takes up about 250 pages; and it is a major portion of modern British academic psychology.

I could go on for quite a time. I must say I find the whole thing very puzzling. It is true, sure enough, that psychologists have not yet offered much in the way of theories about creativity. And so we have instead now Mr Koestler's theory, pure and untainted by the beasts and bestialities of behaviourist psychology—a sort of Dornford Yates heroine over whom the pawing and lustful hands of the enemy have passed (after all, you can see the marks all over her) without ever violating her essential innocence. But what is this we find in Mr Koestler's second talk?

> In a series of classic experiments, Lashley has shown that if a rat's optical cortex is removed by surgery, other parts of the brain will, after a while, take over its function. And if a rat has learned to run a maze, and parts of its motor cortex are removed so that it cannot execute a right turn, it will execute a three-quarter turn to the left instead.

The work of Lashley, the man whose work is in many ways greater than Watson's, Hull's, or even Skinner's, the rat man to end all rat men, straight out of the 'dark ages'! At this rate our virginal theory may not prove so averse to animal studies after all. Before we know where we are, she will be coming home with a story about meeting Zeus in the form of a swan, to account for her act of creation.

Still, to be fair, thinking back to the S-R theories quoted by Koestler, what they had to say was arid stuff compared with the richness of his own theory. Just compare it with some of his comments: 'The participatory emotions make him feel included in some higher unity which transcends the boundaries of the self'; or: 'The Who is Who of the unconscious seems to be printed with coloured ink on blotting paper'; or 'In the aesthetic experience, on the other hand, the juxtaposition of some trivial experience or familiar object with a matrix of higher emotive potential leads to the quiet catharsis of the "oceanic feeling" '. I would be the first to admit that no theory of mine would ever sound like that.

Let us be clear that I have great admiration for anyone who is prepared to tackle such a complicated and difficult problem as the wellsprings of creativity; but even the construction of a successful theory would not excuse a gratuitous misrepresentation of a whole science.

Where does that leave us? With the best will in the world I have had to conclude that Koestler's account of academic psychology is very inaccurate. Why does he dislike it so? I think that the clue to his attitude may lie in the word 'behaviourism'. It is true that Watson raised behaviourism to the status almost of a philosophy—Behaviourism with a capital 'B' as I called it. But that was long ago. We now talk of 'behaviourism' with a small 'b' and it is a method, not a philosophy. I do not think that Mr Koestler has noticed this change.

The method of studying behaviour is perfectly valid. Humans show all sorts of patterns of behaviour which are repeatable, regular, and can be observed and analysed. But this does not mean the psychologists all believe that there is 'nothing but' behaviour. Some individual psychologists may say so, but when they do they are talking not as psychologists but as philosophers, and rather out-of-date philosophers at that. Whether or not you can investigate man's behaviour usefully (and obviously you can) is quite another matter from whether you are a materialist, a spiritualist, or whatever.

But this distinction between behaviourism as a method in science, and Behaviourism as a philosophy seems to have escaped Mr Koestler's notice. He speaks as if all of us who study behaviour are as a matter of course out to try to refute his idea that there is 'something more' than 'mere' mechanism to man's nature. This is laughable. You will find Christians and atheists, saints and sinners, all alike in departments of psychology—and probably in about the same proportion as among those who write big books on creativity.

I think that Mr Koestler has been frightened by something nasty in the behavioural woodshed; or perhaps, since he does seem to be living in the dark ages of psychology, it was the shadows on the back of his cave which scared him. But with the strange compulsion of one trapped in a particular vision he is unable to turn round and see what goes on in the real world.

Those of us to whom it is given to walk in the countryside of modern psychology find it beautiful, exciting, exacting, intellectually challenging. It enriches our understanding of human nature and increases our feeling of wonder at the extraordinary capacities of men. It is this, not ratomorphism, that most of us try to share with our students, and it is this that we enjoy doing with our lives.

The proper study of mankind is indeed man, not rats. But neither is it a jehad against straw men, nor the refusal to admit that shadows on the wall are only shadows on the wall, not the substance of the world. Do come out of your cave, Mr Koestler—it is such fun in the sunlight.

Questions

1. What are the major differences that Koestler finds between the Behaviorists and the Gestaltists?
2. Are Koestler's examples well-chosen? How effective are they rhetorically? Do they provide adequate evidence for his argument?
3. Why does Koestler choose the *Encyclopaedia Britannica* as his basis for the discussion of Behaviorism in the second paragraph? Is Einbinder's discussion of the *Britannica* (See part II, 2) relevant here?
4. What does Koestler's conclusion add to his discussion? How does it aid his argument?
5. To what point or points made by Koestler does Moray object most strongly? Are there any of Koestler's arguments with which he might agree?
6. What kinds of evidence does Moray use to refute Koestler? Is his evidence, on the whole, stronger or weaker than Koestler's?
7. Which argument of Moray's is most strongly made? Why? Which is his weakest argument? Why?

Assignments

1. Evaluate the reliability of the *Encyclopaedia Britannica*'s article on Behaviorism. Choose another encyclopedia and compare its discussion of Behaviorism with that in the *Britannica*.
2. Choose some area of academic study—for example, the "new criticism," content analysis, or statistical quantification in sociology—and attack or defend its validity and usefulness.
3. Choose an area of study with which you are familiar and describe the various schools of thought about or approaches to it.
4. Discuss this topic: Current methods in sociology (or psychology, psychotherapy, economics) are scientifically valid (or invalid).

Additional Reading

Koestler's questioning of the validity of contemporary psychology and his book *The Act of Creation* (New York, 1964) grew out of his investigations into the nature of creativity. Reviews of the book offer valuable commentary on Koestler's psychological concerns. *The Creative Process* (New York, 1952), an anthology edited by Brewster Ghiselin, provides an interesting selection of statements about the creative act. Also relevant are two essays by Lionel Trilling, "Freud and Literature" and "Art and Neurosis," from *The Liberal Imagination* (New York, 1952), in which Trilling analyzes critically the Freudian notion that the creative artist must have a "wound" to stimulate his creativity.

The introductions to most elementary textbooks in psychology contain discussions of scientific method in relation to psychology. Also, most surveys of the history or philosophy of science discuss scientific method as it applies to various fields. Interesting studies have appeared in general and scholarly journals on attempts to study creativity scientifically, most notably by J. P. Guilford and Frank Barron. Related articles on the subject are B. F. Skinner, "A Critique of Psychoanalytic Concepts and Theories," *Scientific Monthly*, LXXIX (1954), 300–305; J. F. Brown, "The Position of Psychoanalysis in the Science of Psychology," *Journal of Abnormal and Social Psychology*, XXXV (1940), 29–44; Lillian Blumberg McCall, "Does Psychoanalysis Cure?" *Commentary*, X (November 1950), 486–494 (which contains references to psychoanalytic literature); and McCall, "The Hidden Springs of Sigmund Freud," *Commentary*, XVIII (August 1954), 102–110.

SECTION SIX | Racing to the Moon

Why Land on the Moon?

ROBERT JASTROW AND HOMER E. NEWELL

Congress has been asked to provide $5.7 billion for the programs of the National Aeronautics and Space Administration during the current fiscal year, roughly 6 cents of every federal tax dollar. This level of expenditure has produced demands for a re-evaluation of the space program. Critics ask whether the exploration of the solar system is a valid enterprise for the United States to undertake at this time; or, granting the ultimate importance of the step, whether it must be carried out at the present pace.

The focal point of the criticism is the Apollo project for manned lunar landing, which absorbs $3.7 billion out of the $5.7 billion in the projected NASA budget. The Apollo budget which has produced the current outcry stems from a decision made in 1961. At that time the man-in-space program was expanded beyond the limited Mercury effort to a full-scale attack on the problems of manned flight to the moon and planets. The impetus for the decision came from a series of Soviet achievements in February and March of 1961, when the U.S.S.R. launched in rapid succession four spacecraft, each weighing 10,000 pounds or more. These were followed on April 12, 1961, by the successful orbiting of Major Gagarin in a 14,000-pound spacecraft and his safe recovery after a circuit of the earth in one hour and forty-seven minutes. Thus, the world saw the Soviet Union achieve man's first flight in space.

On May 26, 1961, President Kennedy laid the Soviet challenge before the American people. He urged the nation to commit itself to the goal of landing a

Atlantic Monthly, CCXII (August 1963), 41–45. Reprinted by permission of the authors.

man on the moon and returning him safely to earth before the decade was out. The President's message suggested the reasons underlying this recommendation: we faced the gloomy prospect of standing second to the U.S.S.R. in manned flight for years to come; the manned lunar landing would be the first major space achievement in which the U. S. effort could reach its full strength; a vigorous effort could achieve a manned lunar landing by the end of this decade; and if the United States set 1970 as its target date for the lunar landing, it would have a good chance to reach this goal before the U.S.S.R.

President Kennedy asked for a careful examination of the proposed commitment: "I think every citizen of this country as well as the Members of Congress should consider the matter carefully in making their judgment . . . there is no sense in agreeing, or desiring that the United States take an affirmative position in outer space unless we are prepared to do the work and bear the burdens."

In July, 1961, the Congress voted overwhelmingly for the funds requested to move the space program into high gear. In 1962 Congress reaffirmed its support by doubling the budget of the previous year. Now, in 1963, we see the substantial fruits of our increased labors in space. The manned-flight program is rapidly advancing through its intermediate objectives toward the milestone of the lunar landing. The space-flight program as a whole has produced a great volume of scientific research, as well as economically important applications to weather forecasting and communications.

At the same time, the Russians continue to show great vigor in their man-in-space program. The single-orbit flight of Gagarin was followed rapidly by Titov's seventeen-orbit mission, by other multi-orbit flights, and by the formidable accomplishment of a near rendezvous between pairs of cosmonauts. The Soviet science program in space has also been stepped up to a high level after a lull of some years, with eighteen Kosmos scientific satellites, a lunar probe, and a Mars probe launched during the last year. There appears to be no letup in the Soviet space challenge to the United States.

What, then, is the basis for the questioning of the commitment to the expanded U. S. space program?

Thoughtful critics, concerned over the allocation of limited national resources, ask whether this is a good way in which to spend funds that might otherwise be used for the betterment of man's lot on the surface of the earth. Could some of the money going into space research be diverted into other programs of public interest—medical research, education, housing, technical aid to emerging nations—a variety of projects contributing to the welfare of our society?

This question implies that public funds are transferable. However, the reduction of support for one national program does not carry a guarantee of increased support for other projects. President Kennedy remarked recently, "Some people say we should take the money we are putting into space and put it into housing or education. . . . My judgment is that what would happen would be that they would cut the space program and you would not get additional funds for education."

But if space money cannot readily be rerouted into other channels, that negative consideration in itself is not a reason for these large expenditures. What are the positive values which we derive from this investment?

The nation can expect the following consequences of the space program: the fruits of research into fundamental problems of science; economic benefits from the application of satellites to communications and weather forecasting; long-range technological benefits accruing to industry; a general stimulus to science and to science education; and, most important, the security which comes from U. S. leadership in space.

Scientific administrators ask, granted these benefits, can we afford the cost of the space program in technical manpower? Their concern is heightened by the fact that federal activities in defense, space, and atomic energy together consume nearly half of the science and engineering talent available in the United States. But is the space agency the major consumer of trained manpower within this federal complex of technical agencies? In actuality, NASA will be using 6 percent of the national manpower pool in science and engineering through its contracts with private industry, plus an additional one percent in government laboratories. If the space program has substantial value, this is not an overwhelming drain.

But scientists who see the benefits of space exploration are opposed to the timetable of the man-in-space program, and particularly the schedule set for landing men on the moon. They suggest that the objectives of space research can be realized by robot instruments, with the manned-flight program carried out at a slower pace.

This question requires a further exploration of the motives underlying the United States space effort. Is it primarily a scientific program? Or is it motivated by a broader concern with national interests and national goals? Looking back to the overwhelming support given the new space program by the Congress in 1961, it seems clear that this support was not tendered for purely scientific reasons, but came from a deep-seated conviction that the expanded program will make an important contribution to our future welfare and security. We believe that this is the reason why the people have supported the enlarged space program and the Congress has voted for it. That brings us to the point on which we take serious issue with some of our scientific colleagues, who complain, "The scientific exploration of the moon has been accorded a secondary priority in the lunar program." This remark is based on the premise that science should have top priority in the space program. However, while science plays an important role in lunar exploration, it was never intended to be the primary objective of that project. The impetus of the lunar program is derived from its place in the long-range U. S. program for exploration of the solar system. The heart of that program is man in space, the extension of man's control over his physical environment. The science and technology of space flight are ancillary developments which support the main thrust of manned exploration, while at the same time they bring valuable returns to our economy and our culture. The science which we do in space provides the equivalent of the gold and spices recovered from earlier voyages of exploration. It is the return to the taxpayer for his investment in his nation's future. But the driving force of the program is not in scientific research alone, valuable though that may be in the long run. Thus, the pace of the program must be set not by the measured patterns of scientific research, but by the urgencies of the response to the national challenge.

In these remarks we express our views as citizens confident in the destiny of this nation. Now, as scientists, we wish to turn to the scientific objectives of the lunar program. What are the important questions which may be illuminated by lunar exploration? One of the classical problems of science concerns the origin of the solar system—how we came to be here in the physical sense. It is a question which has occupied the mind of man for centuries, and a matter of the deepest scientific interest and philosophical importance. It is also an inquiry to which the space program can make a unique contribution, for, surprisingly, the exploration of the moon has a direct bearing on this basic problem.

In order to understand the relevance of lunar exploration, we must back off to supply the general context of the new ideas on the way in which a star, such as our sun, is formed, and how the planets may have been formed around it. The story will carry us through ten billion years of stellar history.

According to the current picture in astrophysics, a star is born when some chance fluctuation in density draws together the particles of gas and dust which make up interstellar matter; the gravitational attractions among the particles then act to draw them still closer together, building a very strong condensation at the center, with very high temperatures and pressures. When the temperature reaches about ten million degrees, the situation is ripe for the ignition of a thermonuclear reaction, in which the hydrogen nuclei combine or fuse to form helium nuclei, releasing at the same time enormous amounts of energy. This release of energy prevents the star from collapsing further under the force of gravity. But eventually the hydrogen fuel is used up, and the star again contracts, until a temperature of 100 million degrees is reached. At this point, the helium nuclei fuse to form the single heavier nucleus of carbon. From carbon, oxygen is formed, and then still other elements.

In this way, successively heavier elements are built up from the original hydrogen. The whole table of elements is developed step by step in this cooking process within the center of the star—a synthesis of all the elements of the universe out of the basic building block of hydrogen. We have duplicated this process for brief moments in the explosion of the hydrogen bomb, but we have not yet succeeded in producing it under controlled conditions.

Toward the end of the life of the star all available fuel has been consumed, and no further energy release can occur to support it against the massive pressure of the overlying layers. A collapse results, followed by an explosion and destruction of the star. The exploding star is called a supernova.

In a supernova explosion, most of the matter of the star, including the elements that were synthesized in it during its lifetime, is sprayed out into space. These elements join with the hydrogen of interstellar space to form an enriched mixture including the carbon, oxygen, iron, and other elements that were manufactured previously. The enriched mixture may then be drawn together in the body of another star later in the history of the galaxy.

Presumably our sun was formed in such a process. The planets are believed to have been formed as minor nuclei of condensation in the cloud of gas and dust around the primitive sun. If our own planet earth was formed in this way, then everything in the earth, including the constituents of our bodies, was once manufactured within other stars, dispersed to space, and condensed again to dust and solid matter.

We believe that all this happened 4.5 billion years ago, but we do not know precisely how it happened, or exactly what the tangled complex of events was which surrounded the genesis of the sun and the planets. The problem is a fascinating one and has been the object of much scientific effort during recent years.

In the study of this question the exploration of the moon plays a very special role because it is a body whose surface has preserved the record of its history for an exceptionally long time. On the earth the atmosphere and the oceans wear away surface features in 10 to 50 million years. Mountain-building activity turns over large areas of the surface in about the same time. There is little left on the surface of the earth of features that existed several hundred million or a billion years ago, and the same is probably true of Mars and Venus, whose properties resemble those of the earth. But on the moon there are no oceans and atmosphere to destroy the surface, and there is little if any of the mountain-building which rapidly changes the face of the earth.

For these reasons the moon has retained a record which probably goes back billions of years to the infancy of the solar system. The moon is the Rosetta stone of the solar system, and to the student of the origin of the earth and planets, this lifeless body is even more important than Mars and Venus.

The internal structure of the moon can also provide clues to the origin of the solar system, quite apart from the study of its surface features. One of the two principal theories for the formation of the planets, which is still generally popular, holds that they were created during a near collision between our sun and another star, in which the gravitational forces between these two massive bodies tore out huge streams of flaming gas. As the second star receded, the masses of gas which happened to be near the sun were captured by it into orbits in which they eventually cooled and solidified to form the planets.

If such a collision was the way in which the solar system was formed, the moon and the planets must have been very hot at an earlier stage in their histories. In that case, the heavy elements in their interiors would melt and run to the center to form a dense core. Iron is the most abundant of the heavy elements, and all planetary bodies would therefore have iron cores, according to this theory.

The other leading theory holds that the planets were formed out of condensations of gas and dust around the primitive sun. We know that stars themselves are probably formed in this way, by the condensation of interstellar gas and dust.

If the moon and planets were indeed condensed out of cold gas and dust, the iron in their interiors would not necessarily melt and flow to the center. Planets as large as the earth might be expected to melt completely, as a result of the heating due to decay of radioactive elements in the interior, and thus to develop iron cores in any case. But the moon is smaller, and if it was formed cold, enough heat could be lost from the lunar surface to prevent subsequent melting. As a result, the moon would not form an iron core but would retain a structure in which bits of iron were distributed through the main body of rock, like raisins in a fruitcake.

So, during the lunar exploration program we will study this and other questions related to the internal structure of the moon, by landing on its surface instruments of the kind used to study the interior of the earth. These will include a seismometer for the study of the internal structure directly, and radioactivity detectors, which have an indirect bearing on the problem by indicating the amount of heat released within the moon by decay of radioactive uranium and other elements. This radioactive heat supplements the heat of the moon at its formation and must be known before the early history can be deduced from the internal structure. The radioactivity detector and seismometer are included among the experiments being developed for the Surveyor spacecraft, an unmanned craft scheduled for landing on the moon in the 1964–1965 period. Through this variety of experiments on the moon, first using unmanned instruments and later with trained human observers, we expect to deduce information bearing on the origin of planetary bodies.

The answers to these questions are interesting not only to people trained in the problems of science. They also have great philosophical and general importance, because they relate to the origin of life and the probability of other living organisms in the universe.

For, if the moon and planets were formed in the near collision of two stars, then life must be very unusual, and possibly unique, because space is nearly empty and collisions between stars are extremely rare. The following analogy demonstrates the void of space: if the sun is the size of an orange, in New York, then the next nearest star is another orange 3000 miles away in Los Angeles. This is the emptiness of space—a distribution of oranges 3000 miles apart. Under these circumstances we can estimate that only ten stellar collisions such as would have produced planets can have occurred during the 15-billion-year lifetime of the galaxy.

On the other hand, if the planets were formed as a natural accompaniment to the condensation processes in which our sun was born, the creation of planets must have accompanied the formation of nearly every star in the universe. Since most of these stars are expected to have planets around them, there must be many cases in which the size of one of the planets and its distance from the star are suitable for the development of life in a form somewhat as we know it.

These are the fundamental questions involving the physical origin of our solar system and its living organisms, on which a powerful attack can now be made with the aid of lunar and planetary exploration. They provide the scientific motivation for both the unmanned and the manned projects in the lunar program. But some scientists feel that most facts of scientific interest about the moon and planets can be learned by remote-control instruments alone, at less cost than manned operations. An editorial in *Science,* the journal of the American Association for the Advancement of Science, estimates that robot instrument landings on the moon will see us through all the important phases of the lunar exploration program at one percent of the cost of the man-in-space budget. Actually, an inspection of the NASA budget indicates that the Surveyor project for unmanned lunar landings is more nearly 10 percent of the cost of the Apollo project, including the development costs in each program. On a per-flight basis in the long-range continuing programs, the cost ratio is 16 percent. When allowance is made for the increased chance of success in the mission which results from plugging man into the control systems, the comparison of costs is still more favorable to manned operations.

But a comparison of costs is not the only issue. The question is, will a robot instrument do everything that man can do?

The answer is that in early stages the simplest observations can be made by remote control. In later stages, when more difficult experiments are attempted for answers to the important questions, the trained human observer brings to the supervision of these experiments the ability to deal with unforeseen difficulties. The automatic instrument in this advanced stage of the program must be designed with great complexity, at a heavy price in reliability and cost of development, to achieve even a crude imitation of human sophistication and flexibility. The balance of cost and reliability then tips in favor of the human participant, expensive though it is to bring him to the scene.

Apart from these specific investigations, space exploration also has a general consequence for the physical sciences as a whole, and for science education. Scientists working on problems related to the exploration of space often refer to their field as space science. What is this new field? Is it physics or astronomy or geology? The answer is that it is the collection of all the problems of the physical sciences to which space-flight experiments can make a unique contribution not obtainable on the ground. Those are questions which encompass large segments of physics, astronomy, and the earth sciences. These fields, which together constitute what was once known as natural philosophy, split apart several hundred years ago in the flowering of the scientific revolution. Now, for the first time in centuries, we feel again a unity in our efforts as we draw together people of widely different backgrounds, all united by a general interest in the external physical world, in natural events on a large scale and their causes. Out of this interest and activity a separate discipline is forming with a distinct character and integrity. We call it space science, and that name will probably persist. But the development also represents a renaissance of the older tradition of natural philosophy, as well as a move away from the specialization that has characterized science in these past years toward a broader spirit of inquiry into the physical surroundings of man. This revival of the spirit of catholicity in science is an important accompaniment to space research.

Even more valuable for the future welfare of the nation, the space program has a pronounced effect on young people. It appeals to the imagination of the student and provides him with an additional stimulus to remain in school, to discipline his energies to the attainment of constructive ends, and to acquire the training necessary for advanced scientific and technical work. This can be one of the greatest contributions of space research—that through its general interest it may assist in the transformation of values which is so badly needed for the realization of the full potential of talent and energy in the United States.

These are the specific values of space exploration: the benefits of basic research, economically valuable applications of satellites, contributions to industrial technology, a general stimulus to education and to the younger generation, and the strengthening of our international position by our acceptance of leadership in a historic human enterprise. The current discussion of these values of the space program has served the United States well in directing its attention to questions of national purpose. But, however we may try to break the program down into its elements and to attempt a detailed balancing of debits and credits, the fact remains that the space effort is greater than the sum of its parts. It is a great adventure and a great enterprise, not only for the United States but for all humanity. We have the power and resources to play a leading role in this effort, and it is inconceivable that we should stand aside.

The Costs and the Choices

FRANKLIN A. LINDSAY

Man's exploration of space is both the greatest adventure and the greatest challenge for a technological society. But precisely because of this, it can also be of great danger to a society such as ours. The successful conquest of space can inadvertently provide us with easy diversions from the really tough problems on earth and ready excuses for not facing and solving them. For three days, Gordon Cooper's dramatic space flight in the *Faith 7* diverted public attention from the integration problem in Birmingham and provided us all a convenient excuse to forget about our shortcomings on earth. In the long run, if we fail to make reasonable progress on the problems at home, victory in space will taste bitter indeed.

Getting a man to the moon is a very expensive proposition, but given the funds, it is not a forbiddingly hard problem to solve. Solving the problems of economic growth and unemployment, or of urban renewal and education, will probably be equally expensive but much tougher and less glamorous than the exploration of space. Yet our space programs will have their impacts, some positive and some negative, on all these other problems.

Obviously, we are not faced with the alternatives of a full-scale space program on the one hand and no program at all on the other. But where can we reasonably begin, and how can we progress in an orderly and well-conceived way so that the dangers are minimized and the potentially great contributions of space are actually realized?

First, space can provide revolutionary new ways to carry out a variety of important peaceful activities more efficiently and less expensively than conventional earthbound methods. Radio relay satellites will provide effective intercontinental communications at significantly less cost per voice channel than present undersea cables. For the past two years the remarkably successful Tiros satellite system has been providing global coverage of the world's weather, and an improved weather satellite series, Nimbus, is about to be put into operation. As these and more advanced systems become operational, weather forecasting will become an even more effective tool for economic management. The economic payoff in crop planning, harvest scheduling, pest control, and water supply management can potentially add several billion

Atlantic Monthly, CCXII (August 1963), 51–54. Reprinted by permission of the author.

dollars' worth of food to the world economy. Photographic satellites can provide the underdeveloped areas of the world with maps, mineral and forest resource surveys, and even human and animal population surveys far faster, cheaper, and more accurately than any other available means. The more developed countries can benefit from satellite photography through accurate and timely indexes of economic activity, such as new housing starts, industrial activity levels, transportation activity, and crop forecasts. The resulting improvements in planning and use of resources can add significantly to the real wealth of these nations.

Another valuable potential contribution of satellite photography is in the area of arms control, where orbiting cameras can provide effective means of inspection for international agreements with minimum reliance on troublesome and tension-producing ground inspection. Cuba has shown the importance of aerial photography, even in the absence of an arms-control agreement. Soon it may even be possible to detect clandestine underground nuclear explosions with satellite cameras that can observe subtle changes in the surface of the ground above the point of detonation.

Basic research on the nature of space and its gravitational and magnetic fields, as well as on the fundamental nature of matter and its distribution in space, is being advanced very greatly by use of special instrumentation carried aboard spacecraft. Earth-based astronomy, for instance, is seriously hampered by the atmosphere. The earthbound astronomer is like a man standing at the bottom of a pool of murky water, trying to observe what goes on above the surface. While the seventy-five-mile-thick envelope of air and dust surrounding the earth effectively protects living organisms from lethal radiation coming from the sun and other sources in space, this same layer severely limits our ability to observe much of outer space by optical or radio telescopes. What light does get through the atmosphere is often so seriously distorted that the image of a distant star appears as though it were observed through the turbulent air rising above a hot pavement on a sunny day. Space astronomy, by freeing scientific observation from the earth's atmosphere, will increase manyfold the knowledge that can be gained from the solar system and intergalactic space. In ways that are yet unknown, this new knowledge will surely be of great benefit to mankind. For it is significant that the basic laws of Newtonian mechanics, without which the machine age could never have occurred, were evolved from astronomical observations; and the basic concepts of the atomic age were developed by Einstein and others from observations of stars and planets.

A further advantage of spacecraft is that they offer the only known means of creating a weightless environment, and scientists believe that fundamentally new knowledge of the nature of life will be gained by observing human and other biological life in such a space laboratory.

A major issue, now hotly debated, is whether man can accomplish more in space than can unattended instruments. There is a heavy weight (and therefore, cost) penalty for sending man and his elaborate life-support systems into space, and it is technically worthwhile only if he pays his way by being able to accomplish more than could an equal payload of instruments. The space-borne man must be protected from radiation by heavy shielding; he must carry oxygen and air conditioning, and travel in a pressurized vessel; and, finally, he must be brought back home through intensive heat. For every pound of man and his life-support equipment sent to the moon and back, very many added pounds of booster rocket will be required.

Dr. Edward Purcell of Harvard University has suggested that only the equivalent of man's eyeball and hands need be sent into space, leaving heart, lungs, brain, and other vital but noncontributing parts safely on the ground. Through a television extension of man's vision, it is possible to couple a television camera in space to the movements of his eyes on the ground so that he can see as clearly from the ground that which he would be able to see from space, simply by shifting the direction of his gaze. Similarly he could, from the ground, manipulate mechanical hands in space. Through remote radio control, it is likely he could thus accomplish most, if not all, of the operations he could perform from within the spacecraft.

Although a great deal has been said about the versatility of the human astronaut, it seems unlikely that in the foreseeable future there will be much opportunity for such human functions as repairs and maintenance in space. Reliability will be achieved primarily by designing and building better equipment. On the other hand, important missions may evolve which only a human can perform, and it is therefore important to develop now the capabilities for human travel in space.

This raises the inevitable question about one of our most ambitious and expensive space programs, Project Apollo. No one can help but share the tremendous pride of a successful human assault upon Mt. Everest or a dramatic conclusion to a multi-orbit Mercury trip. It is only when the cost becomes so great that other important things will have to be deferred or relinquished that many begin to question such a major space venture.

As the cost estimates to put a man on the moon mount from $20 to $40 billion to accomplish this feat before 1970, more and more protests are being heard that we are diverting too large a share of our resources from urgent but less glamorous problems on earth. This mammoth program is the most expensive single program ever undertaken by man. Warren Weaver, vice president of the Alfred P. Sloan Foundation, has made some dramatic comparisons between the cost of the moon race and more earthly projects.

> The sum of $30 billion, which is undoubtedly an underestimate of the total cost of "putting a man on the moon," is a sum so large that the ordinary human being simply cannot grasp its magnitude. . . .
> With that sum one could give a 10 percent raise in salary, over a 10-year period, to every teacher in the United States from kindergarten through uni-

versities (about $9.8 billion required); could give $10 million each to 200 of the better smaller colleges ($2 billion required); could finance seven-year fellowships (freshmen through Ph.D.) at $4,000 per person per year for 50,000 new scientists and engineers ($1.4 billion required); could contribute $200 million each toward the creation of 10 new medical schools ($2 billion required); could build and largely endow complete universities with liberal arts, medical, engineering, and agricultural faculties for all 53 of the nations which have been added to the United Nations since its original founding ($13.2 billion required); could create three more permanent Rockefeller Foundations ($1.5 billion required); and one would still have left $100 million for a program of informing the public about science.

Some of the arguments in favor of pursuing the moon program are, however, compelling. Champions of the program point out that we are in a race with the Soviets, and the nation which first lands on the moon will reap incredible rewards in cold war prestige and world leadership. They also say that the people of the United States need a new frontier to consume their energies. A dynamic society must maintain its momentum by heroic assaults on new obstacles. Further, it is suggested that the space race can be a psychological substitute for man's natural instinct to make war.

It is undoubtedly true that the United States will gain immensely in world prestige if we are first to the moon, and lose if we are second, or if we do not get there at all. This is especially true now because of the President's public commitment to realize this goal within the decade. There is no question that this is a worthwhile goal. Its opponents, however, point to the immense price tag—a price that must be paid not only in money, but in skilled manpower.

Clearly, NASA could not be expected to solve the integration problem, or the school problem, or the balance-of-payments problem, or the urban-renewal problem, or the underdeveloped-nations problem. Nevertheless, some argue that since most of the dollars going into the NASA moon program will be for construction, test equipment, and fuels and engines, much of the human and material resources could be used on other programs. The construction industry could just as well be used to build new schools and new university research buildings. The vast array of computers and their programmers could be of great value if employed to support economists in a deep analysis of the complexities of our economy and its lagging growth. The physicians, physicists, and engineers building the equipment to support human life in a space capsule could also be employed in finding solutions to pressing medical and air-pollution problems on earth.

One of the most difficult problems raised by the increasing level of space activities is the potential diversion of scientists and engineers from teaching and other professional careers. We are entering a period which will be characterized by a great increase in the college population. If the present teacher-student ratio is to be maintained, our universities will, over the next several years, have to retain about two thirds of their Ph.D. output instead of the present one third. Thus, the flow in new Ph.D.'s to government and industry would have to be cut roughly in half. It is just at this critical point in time that NASA's requirements will be peaking. And it appears that there will not be a sufficient supply to meet the requirements of both an expanding space program and a mushrooming college demand, as well as to meet the needs of the rest of society. Hard decisions will have to be made on where to cut.

A further major issue is the degree to which we will need to create a military space capability. Barring an effective international agreement, there will be an inevitable requirement for military space capabilities. The military use of airplanes evolved from that of passive observation platforms during World War I to the full-fledged military doctrine of control of the air as a prerequisite to ground operations in World War II. Similarly, the use of spacecraft will evolve from today's passive observation platforms to a requirement for the control of space, at least in close proximity to earth and perhaps as far as the moon.

Spacecraft are already being used as relay points for worldwide communications, as television platforms for coverage of the world's weather and terrain, and as ultra-accurate navigational and survey systems. Each of these functions has important military applications, and we will become increasingly reliant upon them to maintain our deterrent capability. In periods of extreme tension, as in the Cuban crisis, or in times of actual conflict, it will be vital for the United States to be able to protect these information and communication services against disablement or destruction by the Soviets.

On the other hand, the United States must develop capabilities for identifying Soviet spacecraft, intercepting them, inspecting them, and, if necessary, rendering them harmless. Thus, it seems almost inevitable that the United States and the U.S.S.R. will find themselves in a race to develop defensive and counteroffensive capabilities in space, for the nation which first achieves the capability of freely operating in space while denying that privilege to all others will win a substantial strategic and political cold war advantage.

Whether there are real advantages to orbiting nuclear bombs is not so clear. Intercontinental missiles, based on land or under the sea, can probably form a much less expensive, more accurate, and more swift-reacting nuclear force than anything orbiting in space. There is the remote possibility, however, that the Soviets will consider orbiting a several-hundred-megaton bomb. Detonated at an altitude of fifty to a hundred miles, it would be possible with one such bomb literally to incinerate an area of several tens of thousands of square miles. In the light of this possibility, and in the absence of effective international controls, it seems imperative that we develop effective means of inspecting and disarming orbiting weapons.

Another critical space issue, but one which has received much less public attention than the glamorous moon program or the hair-raising military question, is the possibility of inadvertently upsetting the delicate natural energy balance between the earth and outer space. Rachel Carson has pointed out the dangers of upsetting the biological balances on earth. The danger may be equally great in space, and could conceivably result in catastrophic changes on earth. The balance between the energy received by the earth from the sun and the radiation emitted by the earth is so delicate that a very small change in the balance could ultimately result in the return of the Ice Age or the melting of the polar ice caps and the consequent flooding of the earth's lowlands.

No one can now be certain about the complex mechanisms of energy transfer in space, but competent scientists have expressed fears that the exhaust gases from a relatively few burned-out rocket engines could seriously alter the rate at which solar energy is trapped and held within the earth's atmosphere. Similarly, the explosions of nuclear weapons in space are believed by some to endanger this balance by altering the chemical equilibrium in the ionosphere, which in turn may affect the absorption of high-energy radiation by the earth. These possibilities have been of serious concern to NASA, and research on this problem is being undertaken. It may be prudent, however, to spend even more time and effort studying the exact nature of this energy-transfer process before launching extensive new space efforts.

The proponents of the space program argue that new technologies of great significance will be evolved and that these technologies will give the economy a major boost. Critics of such a program agree that new technologies, such as miniature electronics or heat-resistant materials, will develop and will contribute to the economy and the advancement of society as a whole. But they say that this should not be a principal justification of the space program. If our economy needs new technologies as the basis for expansion, the critics argue, a greater result will undoubtedly occur if these problems are attacked directly rather than sought as a by-product of a space program. The massive research and development expenditures during and since World War II for defense and atomic energy have not, as yet, produced the stimulus to boost the rate of growth of the economy that has been predicted.

The important issues of space thus are not those that can be solved internally by the Department of Defense or by NASA. These agencies are both engaged in carrying out with dispatch programs that have been given them by the Congress and the Administration. Rather, the problems are such that they must be resolved by the nation as a whole. They are these questions:

1. How fast must we proceed in order to be the first to put men on the moon; how important a national goal is it; and what risks should be run in the process?

2. What is the proper balance between this essentially political objective and scientific research in space, and how large a premium should we pay for political ends?

3. What is the proper balance between military and nonmilitary space activities?

4. Finally, what is the proper balance between all of our space activities, on the one hand, and the other important objectives of our society, on the other hand?

It is not, then, a matter of massive program versus little or no program. Into the balance of rockets, satellites, man in space, and bombs must be placed schools, hospitals, medical research, and consumer products. The dramatic success of the Mercury program, where we elevated man into space, must be balanced against our failure to elevate large segments of our own society to the level of equal opportunity. Certainly we could not solve our earthly problems by turning our backs on space, but we should be very careful before we turn our backs on earth.

That Moon Trip: Debate Sharpens

EDWIN DIAMOND

Answer "true" or "false":

The United States Apollo program to send men to the moon at an estimated cost of $20 billion is:

(1) A giant moondoggle; a contest with the Soviet Union on the level of a teen-agers' drag race; a vastly overrated propaganda stunt; a great drain on the economy.

(2) An austere, carefully worked-out plan; a competition that will demonstrate the fitness of the United States to lead the free world; one of the greatest adventures of all time; a program whose practical by-products will be incalculable.

During the past few months, Americans have been asked to choose between these wildly contradictory descriptions of the Kennedy Administration's plan to land astronauts on the moon and to return them to earth in this decade. To compound public confusion, these characterizations of the moon program have been made by presumably knowledgeable insiders—on the one hand, former President Eisenhower, noted scientists and Congressmen, and on the other hand, President Kennedy and other equally noted scientists and Congressmen. Yet, what the taxpayer needs most at present is clarity, for at

New York Times Magazine, July 28, 1963, pp. 10, 23, 25. © 1963 by The New York Times Company. Reprinted by permission of The New York *Times* and the author.

issue in this choice is the pace, direction and, indeed, the fate of the entire space program.

Two years ago, on May 25, 1961, in his special message to the Congress on "urgent national needs," Mr. Kennedy asked that men on the moon be made a national goal for the United States. "No single space project will be more exciting, more impressive or more important," he said, "and none will be so difficult or expensive to accomplish." Today, although all the major Apollo contracts have been awarded, the new team of nine astronauts selected and the giant booster rockets and spaceships put under construction at plants around the country, a great—and belated—re-examination of the lunar landing goal is under way.

In general, three factions are taking a vociferous part in the lunar debate. They are the critics, the big boosters and the moderate boosters.

One of the chief complaints that the critics have against the lunar program is the $20 billion cost. And one of the chief complainants is Mr. Eisenhower, who in the two years since he left office has been increasingly critical of what he calls the Kennedy Administration's "fiscal recklessness." With the National Aeronautics and Space Administration's budget growing so spectacularly—the last NASA budget request was for $5.7 billion, almost six times greater than the final Republican space budget—Mr. Eisenhower has found it an obvious target for attack. "I have never believed," Mr. Eisenhower declared recently, "that a spectacular dash to the moon, vastly deepening our debt, is worth the added tax burden it will eventually impose upon our citizens. . . . I suggest that our enthusiasm here be tempered in the interest of fiscal soundness."

To dramatize the cost of the manned space program (which accounts for over 50 per cent of the over-all NASA budget this year), one physicist suggested, jokingly, that if some means could be found to weld 20 billion silver dollars together, an astronaut could walk to the moon. This uneasiness about the high cost of space is heightened by the suspicion that the moon is regarded, in some quarters at least, as another form of pork barrel, like the rivers-and-harbors bills. Matters weren't helped any in this respect when NASA selected Houston, Tex., the home district of Representative Albert Thomas (chairman of the House committee which oversees NASA's budget) as the site of its new $150 million Manned Spaceflight Center, and then announced that it planned to give Boston a $50 million award for an electronics center just a few months after Edward M. Kennedy had campaigned successfully on the promise that he could do more for Massachusetts.

The second major complaint leveled against the space program is that it is a waste not only of money but of brainpower—an even more precious commodity. Each year, American universities graduate about 3,000 new Ph.D.'s in science and engineering. Citing NASA's own estimates of its trained manpower needs through the decade, Prof. Barry Commoner of Washington University, St. Louis, says that the space agency will require the services of one in every four United States scientists by 1970. Commoner called this a "spectacular balancing act—education supported by science, science by space, and space by the man on the moon," and he asked: "Will it work?" The answer of the critics is a worried "No." With the talented scientific cream—and perhaps most of the milk—skimmed off each year, they believe that other urgent scientific tasks will suffer.

In a similar vein, Senator Kenneth Keating of New York cited the "disparity of spending and effort" between the 9,821 scientists currently engaged in NASA space projects and the 1,316 scientists working on heart disease, mental disorders and cancer research at the National Institute of Health.

The third major issue raised is one of priorities. The critics maintain that it is more important, in Sir John Cockcroft's phrase, to invest a greater effort toward "making a go" of things on earth before rocketing off into space. Democratic Senator J. W. Fulbright, for example, recently put such earth priorities as education and urban renewal ahead of such space priorities as men on the moon. The course of history, he suggests, is more likely to be influenced by how the United States deals with the unemployed than the unexplored.

The critics also challenge the prestige value of getting to the moon ahead of the Soviet Union. The first lunar landing, Dr. Philip H. Abelson, a noted chemist and editor of the journal Science, wrote a few months ago, will be a great occasion, but "subsequent boredom is inevitable." And in a recent pamphlet, the staff of the Senate Republican Policy Committee placed the cost of the lunar venture at double the NASA figure. "Estimates vary from day to day and scientist to scientist," the pamphlet charged, suggesting that "it is hardly worth $40 billion to get a few weeks of headlines."

Finally, the lunar program is questioned on technical grounds. The United States has yet to land one of its small Ranger space vehicles on the moon successfully, while the Soviet Union has bungled 14 consecutive shots in its lunar and interplanetary program, including three tries at the moon this year. Yet the United States is formally committed to the infinitely more ambitious goal of transporting men to the moon and back.

The Russians, perhaps significantly, have never officially announced that they have any lunar landing program under way. Indeed, when Sir Bernard Lovell, director of England's Jodrell Bank Radio-Astronomy Observatory, returned earlier this month from the Soviet Union, he reported that the Soviet

Academy of Sciences was still debating at this late date whether "it will ever be worthwhile getting a man on the moon." In this respect, at least, the Soviet scientists are more conservative than the most conservative of the American lunar critics.

True, both nations have sent men into space on prolonged voyages, but the critics of the Apollo program argue that these orbital accomplishments fail to provide a measure of the enormous difficulties involved in the lunar project.

To get to the moon, putting a man into space is only the first step. Once in orbit, the Apollo must accelerate to an escape velocity of 25,000 miles an hour, make the 240,000-mile lunar transit, go into orbit around the moon and finally detach a small landing bug to set two men on the lunar surface. Then, after exploring the surface, the two explorers must link up with the third man whirling around in his lunar orbit "bus," retrace their path and, finally, after the 500,000-mile trip, thread through a tiny re-entry corridor at the top of the earth's atmosphere.

Weighing all these difficulties, the British astronomer, Fred Hoyle, considers that 50 years, rather than five, is a more realistic estimate of the time span it may take to get men on the moon. Further, say the critics, even if space exploration were to proceed at a more leisurely pace, there would still be the danger of catastrophic failure. If the precedents for live coverage established by the Mercury flights were followed, disaster could unfold horrifyingly before a world-wide television and radio audience.

As an alternative to this ultimate TV sensation, the critics, including Dr. Vannevar Bush and Philip Abelson, have proposed sending instruments, instead of men. Small, unmanned, one-way lunar vehicles, they estimate, might cost only about 1 per cent of the cost of a manned vehicle, yet perform much the same surface-sampling experiments.

As the attack on the Administration's lunar program has accelerated, the task of defending the Apollo project has fallen principally on the second faction, the big boosters: President Kennedy, Vice President Johnson and NASA Administrator James E. Webb.

On the cost of Apollo, Webb has maintained that the budget is "austere" and "realistic," that the "fat" has been trimmed away and that flights have been planned "at the lowest price consistent with the target dates." The $20 billion figure is now described as firm. This means, in effect, that each American will be contributing about 60 cents a week for the next few years to support the lunar program. To put this figure in perspective, Vice President Johnson argues, Americans should remember that they spend more on cigarettes, alcohol and recreation. In 1962, he says, the nation "bet more on horse races than on space."

Yet, even granting that lunar exploration is expensive, the boosters cite four reasons, in ascending order of importance, which they feel compel the United States to press the Apollo program.

The first is the desire for scientific knowledge. Preserved on the surface of the moon—like pages in a book, in the arresting phrase of NASA physicist Robert Jastrow—is a pristine record of its history that could yield precious information about the origins of the solar system. Robot instruments are effective for simple observations, but only men can deal with the unexpected opportunities that might be encountered.

Second, there are the demands of national security. In his speeches and news conferences, Mr. Kennedy has referred to space as the "new ocean," and stresses the need for the United States to occupy a position of pre-eminence there so that the nation can help to decide whether space will be "a sea of peace or a new terrifying theater of war."

Third, there are the "down-to-earth" benefits of space. The billions for the moon program, NASA officials are fond of saying, will be spent here on earth. Administrator Webb speaks of "spin-off"—the creation of new jobs, new industries, new services—in areas where the space effort touches down, and of technological "fall-out" in the form of new space inventions, products and devices that have practical commercial applications.

The final reason offered in support of a vigorous lunar program—and probably its main justification in Mr. Kennedy's mind—is the need for the United States to demonstrate its leadership before the eyes of the world. Space exploration, Mr. Kennedy declared when he visited the new Manned Spaceflight Center in Houston last year, "is one of the great adventures of our time, and no nation which expects to be the leader of other nations can expect to stay behind. . . ."

In this view, the race to the moon is a test of national vitality. The nation that comes in first constantly renews and strengthens its leadership.

As often happens in political controversy, the arguments of both critics and supporters of the lunar program have tended to deteriorate into emotional or extravagant rhetoric. The Senate Republican Policy Committee pamphlet, for example, demands: "Is it more important to have a man on the moon than to conquer cancer, which will take the lives of 40 million Americans now living?"

The question is specious on several counts. Aside from the fact that no one has suggested that the moon is more important than a cancer cure, there is no basis for assuming that the space program is hurting medical research: mere cash and mere numbers cannot speed up cancer research—a point emphasized by officials of the National Institutes of Health in their annual testimony to Congress. Indeed, as such different observers as The Economist of London and The Bulletin of The Atomic Scientists have noted, the whole priorities issue may be phony. Money cut from the space budget by the fiscal conservatives in Congress isn't likely to be allocated by these same men for better schools, urban renewal or other welfare measures.

For their part, the Administration's space boosters have also been guilty of some fuzzy talk. There was a certain presumption in defending as perfect and inviolate a $5.7 billion budget which was drawn up almost a year before and which embraced scores of highly experimental and "blue-sky" projects. And the grandiose predictions about the "fall-out" of space inventions have proved, to date at least, to be overoptimistic.

Midway between the critics and big boosters in the lunar debate is a third faction of realists and key scientists, who give the program qualified support. They frankly recognize that pork-barrel politics and private profit probably inflate costs; they agree that there is little immediate scientific knowledge or military advantage to be obtained by men on the moon, and they admit that there is, in the caustic words of Prof. Colin Pittendrigh of Princeton, "an unfortunate association of the subject with comic books and cereal boxes." They also deplore the costly and divisive psychology of the "space race," preferring instead to halve the expense and take the moon out of the cold war—in much the same way that Antarctica has been made a scientific preserve.

Nevertheless, they appreciate the facts of political life enough to know that scientific endeavor doesn't exist in a vacuum. Their backing of the Administration's program can give it a decisive lift. Not long ago, eight eminent scientists, including Nobel Prizemen Joshua Lederberg, Willard F. Libby and Harold C. Urey, issued a timely press release offering a cogent rebuttal to the Abelson editorial in Science.

"Man-in-space makes an essential contribution to the scientific objectives of lunar exploration," it read in part, but "the pace of the program cannot be set only by the steady flow of scientific developments. It is essential that it be influenced also by the urgencies of the response to the national challenge."

The ultimate outcome of the national controversy over the way to the moon is more likely to be resolved by arguments like this than by hyperbole.

Over the next few years, attitudes toward the program will probably be erratic—with a sudden emphasis on some programs in response to Soviet success and sudden cutbacks in others as elections near or the Congressional mood changes. But there is reason to hope that a more balanced outlook will prevail. In a remarkable statement to the House Committee on Science and Astronautics earlier this year, Lee A. Du Bridge, president of the California Institute of Technology, suggested what that attitude might be:

"I think this committee and the Congress can have a broader and deeper view toward the space program than only to beat the Russians, or beat them to the moon. Think of it as one of the great scientific achievements or enterprises of all time. Its impact on the future of the world and mankind is simply beyond calculation at the present time.

"Let us keep our eye very definitely on the fact that in every space expedition we undertake we must learn something, and we should undertake whatever space expedition we can which does add to the sum of human knowledge."

Now It's an Agonizing Reappraisal of the Moon Race

RICHARD AUSTIN SMITH

It is probably too much to say, as some of NASA's more panicky partisans have, that the whole U.S. space program now stands in mortal peril. The $600 million that Congress has so far whacked out of NASA's $5.7-billion budget request seems intended to put the portly giant on combat rations, not a starvation diet. Capitol Hill's tougher, more critical attitude toward NASA appears confined to counting the cost of our achieving preeminence in space rather than challenging the aspiration. A halt has simply been called to issuing the agency any further blank checks and this in turn ends Congress' indulgent custom, begun in 1961, of encouraging NASA to double its budget every year. Nevertheless, NASA and the space program have reached a critical stage in their evolution; the next two years could very well see a realignment and re-evaluation as sweeping as that which rocked NASA a little over two years ago when President Kennedy suddenly committed the nation to a $20-billion to $40-billion program of beating the Russians to the moon.

This time, as before, the moon race lies at the heart of the re-evaluation and this time the President again appears as a prime mover in bringing about the reappraisal. By accident or design, he clearly signaled a change in pace in the United Nations speech inviting the Russians to make manned exploration of the moon a joint venture instead of a competition. True, the U.N. proposal had all the earmarks of a trial balloon hurriedly inflated at the eleventh hour to make a headline. But those who knew what had been going on in the lunar program found strong support for their view that reappraisal was now inevitable. So astonishing an invitation from the man who had

Fortune, LXVIII (November 1963), pp. 125–128, 268, 270, 273, 274, 276, 278, 280. Reprinted from *Fortune* Magazine by Special Permission; © 1963 Time Inc.

started the race in the first place implied at least a new Washington view about the urgency of *winning*.

The fact is the President has been keenly aware of growing skepticism in many quarters. Among scientists the initial enchantment has faded before the mounting costs and the fear of heavy drain on other fields of scientific endeavor. Less and less is heard of the military urgency of exploring and "conquering" the moon; on second thought even the Air Force has decided its interests lie more in "inner-space" capability (up to 500 miles) than in the moon. Even some of those who put enormous emphasis on being *first* to the moon for reasons of national prestige are beginning to question whether an orderly development of space capability is being sacrificed just to achieve a prestige victory.

To be sure, the space race still has plenty of powerful adherents. Congressional support has been fortified by the judicious spreading of Apollo contracts among congressional districts; many citizens still want to beat the Russians to the moon at any cost; some scientists retain an almost mystical attachment to Apollo as a stimulating challenge and the greatest of adventures. And the race idea might regain powerful support overnight should the Russians pull off another space spectacular. But even so, the problems of the moon race as now conceived are of the kind that will progressively worsen.

The trouble stems from the simple fact that the Apollo program as a *race* is a far different undertaking from Apollo pursued at a reasonable pace. The race timetable calls for bringing it to a culmination in 1967 or 1968 instead of sometime in the Seventies, as NASA originally planned; this speedup has increased the cost by around $8 billion. The drain on scientific manpower has gone up commensurately; the original time schedule envisioned recruitment of personnel through an expanded educational program, while the race schedule demands a rising percentage of scientific and technological talent in the pool today. Moreover, the preeminence given Apollo has made it virtually impossible for NASA to achieve orderly progress in other lines of space endeavor. Such a balanced approach has to give way as Apollo gets the best men, the highest priorities, and the bulk of the money. Apollo has become, not surprisingly, the tail that wags the dog.

Nobody is more aware of the possibility of a drastic realignment in space than NASA Administrator James Webb himself. Though Webb is a consummate high-level operator and takes his breaks as they come, he is, at the same time, one of Washington's more experienced administrators, which means that he has learned to be cautious. He has always seen the practical wisdom of a balanced, orderly program. His enormous management problems would be reason enough. Even before the advent of Apollo he had been hard pressed handling an agency that was at best a loose collection of research centers—Ames, Lewis, Langley, Edwards—plus one development center, Huntsville. Huntsville had been inherited from the Army, which in the post-Sputnik era was accustomed to letting Director Wernher von Braun write his own ticket.

The research centers had been inherited from the old NACA, perhaps the most loosely run organization in the government. But tough as things were in the early days of NASA, the saddling of this shaky management structure with the moon race seemed to magnify every problem. The agency virtually exploded. Its $915-million budget for fiscal 1961 shot up to $1.8 billion in fiscal 1962, more than doubled again in 1963 ($3.7 billion); personnel increased from the 17,500 people of 1961 to 28,500 in 1963.

Webb established the Office of Manned Space Flight with responsibility for the Apollo project and tried to bring the major centers under control, but the best he could work out was a kind of informal council. The centers, which had always had considerable autonomy, helped themselves to more of it, using the pressure of the race to justify their doing pretty much as they pleased. The Office of Manned Space Flight itself rapidly became an overbalancing element of the organization (claiming 60 percent of NASA's 1963 and 1964 budgets and getting 90 percent of all the publicity), with its own separate Washington offices and a director rivaling the Administrator in importance.

To be sure, Webb is well aware that the idea of beating the Russians at anything has great utility in loosening up the congressional purse strings—and he has made the most of this. The U.S., he admonished a congressional committee early this year, could not hope to get to the moon in this decade if NASA's requested $5.7-billion budget for 1964 were seriously cut. Yet, somewhat ambivalently—and much to the exasperation of those in direct charge of Apollo—he went out of his way to point out that the U.S. was no longer trying to be first to the moon. In a most remarkable statement this March he told the Congress, in essence, that it should take its cue from what the President had *not* said in an important speech on our space effort the previous fall. "The President," Webb emphasized, "did not say that our national goal is that of landing the first man on the moon or for that matter of being first with respect to any single achievement in space. We have done many things first and we will do many other things first including, we hope, sending the first explorers to the moon, but this is not the objective the President stated. Rather he forcefully declared our determination to attain 'a position of preeminence' in space and to 'become the world's leading space-faring nation.'" Was Webb even then signaling an end to the moon race in favor of something eloquently if vaguely described as "space-faring"?

The Cosmonaut and the Bay of Pigs

To keep the current reappraisal in perspective, it is worth remembering that even as late as January, 1961, a moon shot was not NASA's primary objective; it was instead a goal toward which the agency would judiciously move as its knowledge of space developed through more fundamental programs. Those programs were described by the NASA Administrator at the time as being: (1) the early application of earth satellites to practical uses, (2) the study of the space environment and celestial bodies to gain specific knowledge, (3) the determination of man's capacity to function usefully in space, *in order to open the way to* manned exploration of space, the moon, and the planets. What had changed all this, of course, were the events of April, 1961. On the twelfth, the Russians won a second epochal triumph in space, cosmonaut Yuri Gagarin becoming the first human being to orbit the earth. On the nineteenth, U.S. prestige suffered a humiliating setback when the invasion of Cuba ended in disaster at the Bay of Pigs.

An aroused President had then asked NASA what we could possibly do to surpass the Russians in space. It was not an easy question to answer. The demonstrated Soviet superiority in booster power foredoomed our chances of beating them in any middle-range achievements such as a manned space station or a manned circumnavigation of the moon; the U.S., NASA reasoned, would have to pick a goal that was so far in the future as to diminish the importance of the present Russian advantage. After a month of feverish pencil work within NASA and soul-searching within the White House's Space Council, it was finally decided that a crash program of manned lunar exploration, using specially developed boosters, the Saturns, was the earliest venture on which the U.S. could reasonably hope to come out ahead. The point to be noted, in the light of reappraisal, is that the moon race was chosen not because the moon itself had a special value but because a moon landing—out of several other ventures seriously considered—offered the first important space victory the U.S. could hope for.

On May 25, 1961, Kennedy officially launched the moon race in his Special Message on Urgent National Needs. We were confronted, he said, by the need to embark on "a great new enterprise . . . to take a clearly leading role in space achievement," and the heart of the enterprise was landing a man on the moon and returning him safely to earth "before this decade is out." From then on, Project Apollo was a reality. The combination of national prestige, scintillating new horizons, and pork in the sky pushed the venture through Congress with unexampled speed. By July 20, with hardly a dissenting vote, Congress authorized a space budget 60 percent bigger than Eisenhower's January request. Kennedy's moon race became a national goal with a DX (top) priority.

The effect of this decision on NASA is without a parallel in government since the crises of the great depression. Even in war—the $2-billion Manhattan Project comes most readily to mind—NASA's ordeal would have been virtually without peer as an organizational convulsion. Its job was to take a project on which *feasibility studies* had been completed only the week before Kennedy's speech and proceed to major hardware development at top speed.

Whole new facilities had to be planned, built, and staffed, existing programs such as Mercury had to be revamped to speed Apollo, new intermediate programs like Gemini (the two-man space capsule) had to be initiated, and hundreds of other projects that should have been done sequentially had to be done concurrently because of the tremendous pressures of time—e.g., the program for unmanned exploration of the moon, previously intended to precede manned exploration by five or six years, went forward almost hand in hand with the development of the hardware for manned lunar capability. By the same token NASA's methodical examination of alternate avenues of development had to be sacrificed to the demands of the time schedule. Principal case in point: because the big liquid-fueled rockets had been under development for four years at Huntsville, they offered a greater prospect of successful performance than giant solid-fueled boosters, so the moon shot was built around them—though the military interest lay in easily stored, instantly ready solids. Some hint of the breakneck speed is reflected in the fact that $630 million worth of contracts were signed in the six months following Kennedy's speech, $921 million more in the next six months.

All this made trouble enough, but NASA's Apollo problems were compounded by an additional handicap: while it was hiring hordes of new people and letting hundreds of millions of dollars worth of contracts, the agency still had to operate in the dark. NASA had only the most general notion of how it would get to the moon or what would be found there. Was a direct ascent to the moon and a "soft" landing there the best method? Or should two vehicles be put into earth orbit and the moon capsule launched from them? Or should the lunar craft go into temporary orbit around the moon and put off a capsule that could land, then rendezvous later with the space ship for a return to earth? Was the lunar surface a sea of electrostatically charged dust that might engulf the capsule, was it a collapsible crust, or one continually riddled by "shrapnel" from ricocheting meteorites?

Lacking the time to find out because of the frantic speedup, NASA made time the governing consideration and proceeded accordingly. North American was awarded the prime contract for Apollo ($400 million) in November, 1961, without even knowing what mode would be chosen for going to the moon. When the lunar-orbit-and-rendezvous method was finally decided upon almost a year later (it was the quickest), the budgeted amount for that contract had to be increased 200 percent ($1.2 billion). Even as late as this year Grumman Aircraft was awarded a $390-million contract to design the lunar landing module without having the foggiest notion what kind of surface it would be required to land on; the hurry-up Ranger probes, five so far, have all failed to bring back this essential information.

Despite the absurdities and inequities of this situation, things were going fine, so far as the public or the average Congressman could see, because of the momentum generated by the old program. Navigation and communication via American satellites were thrilling the world. The secrets of the weather were being unfolded every day by the Tiros meteorological satellites. The Mercury program was a whole series of splendid accomplishments—four men into orbit, four successful missions. Yet at the very time the national enthusiasm for space was at its height, in the months following Colonel John Glenn's flight, a secret reappraisal was actually going on—and going on in NASA itself.

The affair surfaced in a climactic battle between Webb and Brainerd Holmes, then director of Manned Space Flight. The two had been personally at odds for some time—Webb wanting to stay top dog in NASA and Holmes aspiring to that spot—but the struggle centered on a $400-million supplemental appropriation Holmes wanted to help speed up the slipping Gemini and Apollo programs. Thus the question at issue was really the pace of the lunar race. Holmes maintains Webb had assured him early in 1962 that he would put in for the $400 million. Webb declares he never made any such commitment. Another member of NASA's top brass describes the contretemps as simply "a case where Brainerd Holmes had to learn that the public expressions of the President did not mean a blank check. He took it to mean encouraging the contractors to go ahead faster."

In any event, when August rolled around, Webb refused to authorize the $400-million supplemental and Holmes found himself in an unpleasant situation. With Apollo's DX priority and beating the Russians always in mind, he had urged the contractors to go for broke; they had put on more people and he had stepped up the spending rate. Now without the supplemental there would not be sufficient funds to maintain the pace and the contractors would have to cut back. Cutbacks, of course, mean layoffs and layoffs set political wires to humming. So a month later, in September, the issue of the supplemental came before the President.

Kennedy had practically invited Holmes to ask for the extra funds during his tour of the space centers earlier that month, according to one Congressman, by asking directly if there were any place money could be put to speed up Apollo. But when the matter of Apollo's pace landed on his desk as an issue, he decided it was worth reconsideration. Webb was dead set against granting the extra funds and made plain his disagreement over the importance and priority given the manned space program. A White House poll of key space people on Capitol Hill, including the late Senator Robert S. Kerr, Chairman George Miller of the House's Science and Astronautics Committee, and Chairman Olin ("Tiger") Teague of the House Subcommittee on Manned Space, disclosed them to be as sharply split as Webb and Holmes. The request was quietly shelved. The President, patently, was having some second thoughts too. The extent of Kennedy's subsequent reservations about the pace of the moon race can be read in the fact that in June, 1963, when a recrudescence of the Holmes-Webb split gave him another opportunity to back an impatient Holmes or a circumspect Webb, he went along with Webb —and Holmes returned to private industry.

The Case Against the Race

What had no doubt impressed the President were growing signs of disenchantment with the moon race both inside and outside the NASA enclave. It was no secret in Washington that the White House science adviser, Jerome Wiesner, has been increasingly critical of Apollo, and Wiesner reflected a growing and important sector of the scientific community. New Mexico's Senator Clinton Anderson took note of the situation last June by convening his Committee on Aeronautical and Space Sciences to hear what a dozen scientists had to say about space goals. To a certain extent the disenchantment was a predictable reaction to the initial moon-race "sell," to a certain extent it represented a victory for the unpersuaded who had never liked space much anyway, but principally it could be explained as the kind of second thought that was bound to come.

The attack on the scientific value of the race has occurred at three levels. On the first level are those unpersuaded scientists who believe that the investment of money and talent in Apollo is out of all proportion to the foreseeable benefits, if weighed against what those resources might accomplish in other fields. The most effective spokesman for this school is Dr. Warren Weaver, vice president of the Alfred P. Sloan Foundation, who has a lively concern about some of the things that might be done with the $20 billion to $40 billion of the moon race. With $30 billion, he wrote in the *Bulletin of the Atomic Scientists*, "we could give a 10 percent raise in salary, over a ten-year period, to every teacher in the U.S. from kindergarten through universities (about $9.8 billion); give $10 million each to 200 of the best smaller colleges ($2 billion); finance seven-year fellowships (freshman through Ph.D.) at $4,000 per person per year for 50,000 new scientists and engineers ($1.4 billion); contribute $200 million each toward the creation of ten new medical schools ($2 billion); build and largely endow complete universities with medical, engineering, and agricultural faculties for . . . fifty-three of the nations which have been added to the United Nations since its original founding ($13.2 billion); create three more permanent Rockefeller Foundations ($1.5 billion); and still have $100 million left over to popularize science."

The Threat to the Satellites

The second level of attack on Apollo comes from scientists who are enthusiastic about a major exploratory effort in space but fear that Apollo and other man-in-space programs will swallow all the funds from the really important *scientific* programs, those that can be effectively accomplished with instruments. These minimally financed *un*manned space flights have contributed by far and away the bulk of the scientific information obtained to date. The discovery of the Van Allen belts, universally regarded as the outstanding accomplishment of the Space Age, was the result of an initial investment of at most $1 million; the Orbiting Solar Observatory and Nerv experiments have also been conspicuous successes for penny-ante outlays.

The third level of attack on Apollo comes from the growing number of scientists who have reached the conclusion that the race just isn't worth it. Dr. Philip Abelson, director of the Carnegie Institution's Geophysical Laboratory and editor of *Science*, official journal of the American Association for the Advancement of Science (membership: 76,000), recently conducted an informal straw poll among scientists not connected with NASA. The vote was 110 to 3 against the manned lunar program. "How one views Apollo," he says, "depends on what you think the basic values are. If you figure, as I do, that the yield is going to be awfully darned small, then you're going to be considerably more critical than if you think it's a big deal. I think very little in the way of enduring value is going to come out of putting a man on the moon—two or three television spectaculars—and that's that. If there's no military value—and people admit there isn't—and no scientific value—and no economic return, it'll mean we've put in a lot of engineering talent and research and wound up being the laughingstock of the world."

Dr. Polykarp Kusch of Columbia University, a Nobel laureate in physics, predicted to Senator Anderson's committee that the impact of the lunar program on research and development would be "extremely small." "I don't think," he declared, "we are going to get anything of the dimensions of the theory of chemical valence, which has been an enormously productive intellectual construct, or anything as effective as the quantum theory of physics, or anything as effective as the picture which the contemporary biologist has of genetic processes . . . I very much doubt the prospective purely scientific results are reasonably commensurate with the investment. I am commenting not only of the funding but also of the investment of men, which no amount of funding can replace."

The Cost in Brainpower

This latter aspect of the moon race, the drain of scarce manpower, has led some scientists to the conclusion that the program may actually render a *disservice* to science. NASA's requirement for men in the physical sciences, even taking the agency's own estimates, will siphon off 7 to 10 percent of the nation's physicists—enough, some think, to hamstring effort in other fields of research. NASA's Apollo demands will certainly clash head on with the program to educate more scientists. The universities and colleges will need twice the number of Ph.D.'s they formerly retained on their staffs if they are to meet the tremendously expanded college enrollments of the middle Sixties. Yet the college requirements for more Ph.D.'s will be reaching a peak just at the time NASA's are too. (The moon program alone is expected to demand the services of 350,000 people, many of them scientists and engineers.)

On the other hand, if NASA were to get the *first-rate* scientists, which it needs, then the effect might be even more pervasive. For the percentage of really creative and imaginative men in science is not considered to have kept pace with the rapid growth of competent technicians; the former are a very scarce commodity, perhaps numbering no more than 200 to 300, whose diversion to the new field of space would inevitably rob an established discipline of leadership. "We have a limited pool of genius," Dr. Abelson explains. "If we transfer genius in one direction, that genius isn't going to be available elsewhere. These fellows who have genius are transferable. They can learn physics and know all about nuclear physics, and then with a few years of study they can begin making important contributions in biology."

It should be noted that on space, as on practically every other issue, the views of the scientific community are far from monolithic. As critics of the NASA program have found voice, defenders also have spoken up. Last spring chemists Harold Urey and Willard Libby, and geneticist Joshua Lederberg, Nobel Prize winners all, joined five equally distinguished scientists in a special press release disputing Dr. Abelson. Man-in-space, they stated, is essential to "the scientific objectives of lunar exploration," and the pace of the program must be geared to "the urgencies of the response to the national challenge." But they did not specifically underwrite Apollo as a scientific proposition. And the fact that they felt it necessary to rally behind a program that, a year ago, needed no defenders indicates how severely scientific support for the moon race has eroded.

The Military's New Look

Something of the same re-evaluation has been going on in the military areas. In the first burst of space enthusiasm some military pundits seized on the moon as everything from the "high ground" so cherished by infantrymen to an indispensable Gibraltar guarding the portals to the universe. Under close examination the military theories about the moon have undergone a significant deflation. Prime example: use of the moon for a missile base. Moon-based missiles—shot on a trajectory of 240,000 miles from a moving launching pad diverging from its earthly target at speeds up to 1,000 miles per hour— have been found wanting when compared to earth-based ICBM's, which are only a few thousand miles from their targets.

The military's prime interest at this time is not the moon but operating capability in "inner space"—the zone up to 500 miles above the earth. Even here, however, its pace is exploratory rather than headlong. Last February, General Curtis E. LeMay, Chief of Staff of the Air Force, told the House Armed Services Committee: "We can't really define an offensive weapon for use in space that will be more efficient and less costly than one we could do the same job with on the ground or in the air."

Dr. Lawrence Kavanau, until recently space specialist with the Defense

Department's Office of Defense Research and Engineering, goes one step beyond LeMay to point out that no really new military space missions have been discovered since 1958 and even a few of the 1958 items were described as early as 1946. The emphasis is rather on assembling new technological "building blocks," the broad base on which future systems may be built.

Even the young space colonels of the Air Force never saw much utility in Apollo. The plain fact is that if Apollo and all the other programs that made up NASA's $5.7-billion budget request for 1964 were to be suddenly scrapped, the military (which has a $1.7-billion space program of its own) would have to spend only an additional $500 million to make up for whatever help NASA had been giving.

A Matter of the Inner Man

The most persistent justification for the moon race, of course, is that of prestige. Those Americans who never will forget the awesome sight of Sputnik streaking through the night sky simply feel in their bones that we must beat the Russians to the moon as a global demonstration of the superiority of our system. But has the U.S. so little to offer the world in other fields than space that our prestige would really be blighted if Russia beat us to the moon? Would the splendor of another American breakthrough like the Salk vaccine go into eclipse because a Soviet spaceship touched down on the lunar surface before we did?

"Everyone especially wants to be sure that the U.S. is ahead of the Soviet Union," said President Lee DuBridge of the California Institute of Technology, "but the wholly unanswerable question, I fear, is this: How much prestige can we buy for $1 billion, for $5 billion, for $30 billion, or $100 billion? We just do not know. At least I do not know. And even if we did know, we still do not know whether $1 billion will buy more prestige if invested in space or in housing or in education or medicine or military power or foreign-aid programs . . ."

Perhaps the only certain thing about the prestige issue is that the pattern of our recent competition with the Soviets should have made it plain, if it has not, that a lunar landing by either side will not be the clear-cut propaganda coup of Sputnik I. Regardless of who gets there first, the other will doubtless have something ready to steal some of the thunder of the feat —e.g., an interplanetary probe.

Even those who put more stock in space prestige than DuBridge raise questions of what kind of space prestige is best. The overriding question is simply whether the spectacular first of a moon shot is as important as a solid second built on space capability. Apollo, it should be remembered, is a tremendous but very narrowly defined engineering effort, strictly designed for the purpose of getting a man to the moon and back. The Saturn V rockets are larger than needed for inner-space use, too slow in launching for regular military use, too expensive for logistical supply, and too small for practical use in manned shots beyond the moon. Moreover, their ever larger bundles of liquid-fueled engines offer little to the advancement of the state of the art. As Dr. Donald Hornig, a member of the President's Science Advisory Committee, observed, the lunar race has put us "in the position of the airplane designers of 1925 who suggested that we put a hundred engines on an airplane to make it carry big loads."

The Coming Squeeze

The logic of events is working powerfully for a formal reappraisal of the moon-race goal. On the one hand, Congress is starting to cut NASA's budgets, on the other NASA sticks by its commitment to the moon race. For various reasons Apollo is falling behind schedule. Gemini, the program that is expected to work out the rendezvous techniques for Apollo in a series of two-man orbits, has already "slipped" some six months. The first manned flight around the earth in the Apollo capsule is now nine to eleven months behind schedule and is not expected to take place before 1966. This has moved the lunar shot itself from 1967 to 1968 at the earliest, but difficulties with the F-1 engines of the Saturn may make for additional slippage. If NASA is still saddled with Apollo as a top (DX) national priority, it will simply have to pour on more money in an effort to buy back the lost time and thereby stay in the race. Yet if Congress refuses to grant any over-all increase in NASA's total budget, on grounds that $5.7 billion or even $5.1 billion is a big enough commitment of national resources for space, then it is likely that Apollo will encroach on the meager $1.5 billion of NASA's budget for *un*manned space applications. Thus, lacking a deliberate change in plan, NASA will be spending less and less on the kind of balanced approach that more and more people want.

There is another reason why the lunar-race question is bound to come into clear focus in the months ahead: the real impact of Apollo on NASA's wobbly management structure is becoming increasingly evident. Webb tacitly acknowledged the deepened misgivings about NASA management in a well-publicized reorganization program introduced early last month. But it is doubtful that shifts in the chain of command can cure what ails an Apollo-oriented NASA. For example, the Houston center, which is supposed to co-ordinate the work of the contractors in bringing Apollo to completion, is itself in urgent need of coordination; its managerial group is one of the weakest within NASA and during the period of explosive growth—the center grew from 800 in 1961 to 3,500 people in 1963—has found little time to set its own house in order. Yet NASA in Washington still lacks the kind of top management that can step in and take over if Houston should bungle this all-important job of coordination.

Dr. George Mueller, Brainerd Holmes's successor as head of the Office of Manned Space Flight, is a technical man, a distinguished one, and a fine teacher as well; yet his gentle, almost diffident temperament and lack of administrative experience hardly suggest that his office will be run even as forcefully as Brainerd Holmes ran it. The latter, in the opinion of many qualified to judge, did a fine job at Manned Space Flight but he had to do it by joining forces with Houston and the other centers rather than establishing his office's hegemony over them. Now, under the pressure of the final phases of the moon race, effective intervention by Washington would seem even tougher. The greater the urgency to meet the deadlines, the greater will be the temptation for the centers to insist on a completely free hand.

Jim Webb's strength lies in his powerful connections with Congress, constantly reinforced with a judiciously distributed outpouring of space funds. When pressed on his budget he wastes little time in arguing the case for Apollo; instead he tells congressional critics rather baldly that the first effect of budget cutting will be a cutback in contracts already awarded. He has won the enormous gratitude of such powerful Texans as Vice President Lyndon Johnson and Congressman Albert Thomas, chairman of the House subcommittee in charge of NASA's appropriations, for his stirring defense of the estimated $250-million Houston center; he carries great weight as well with Senator Clinton Anderson and Congressman George Miller. But even these worthies cannot protect Webb on the management front. As will become increasingly clear, NASA's demands have been more than he has been able to cope with, and, under the crushing load of Apollo, perhaps more than anybody is able to cope with.

As Webb's day of reckoning approaches, he will probably get considerable personal support from the companies with large NASA contracts. But the contractors are perhaps more conversant with his management problems than anybody else. They know that they must make their principal connections with the powerful centers. However, much as they would like to deal with Webb, they have discovered the hard way that their livelihood depends on those in the centers who are the most effective challengers to Webb's authority.

The Failure of Fallout

Webb has also lost a substantial amount of support outside the aerospace industry. His lecture-tour promises of a broad industrial fallout from the lunar race have just not panned out. Experience with close tolerances and working with new materials have undoubted value to industry, but the very nature of the moon race militates against their wide usage or inexpensive acquisition. A recent study on "The Commercial Applications of Missile/Space Technology," prepared for NASA by the University of Denver, found it was "too early" to look for commercial byproducts. When would the right time be? About a decade from now.

An Orderly Program

The two and a half years that have elapsed since the President decreed the moon race have, in short, added perspective to the other elements of an epochal human undertaking. It is inconceivable that Americans, having taken the first steps into space, could ever be dissuaded from going on. But it is more and more doubtful that the orderly approach to an undertaking that—to use FORTUNE's words of June, 1962—is "hitching the economy to the infinite" will be served by a moon *race* that is hitched to an unrealistic timetable. Even such an Apollo enthusiast as Brainerd Holmes concedes that "the lunar program makes sense only if we go on from there—" to the planets. So let's take our time doing it. The crash timetable should be abandoned in favor of one that places the moon in perspective: i.e., as one way station in the sequential development of space. NASA will then have a chance to shake down and the nation will be better prepared for the immense costs involved. For make no mistake, the outlays that are so dismayingly big on today's research and development will be dwarfed by tomorrow's costs of maintaining a station in space or on the moon.

Such a revision in goals will, of course, bring a considerable outcry from those who have a large stake in Apollo—principally the NASA centers and the contractors—on grounds that a stretch-out will cost more in the long run. But it need not, given some judicious shifting of manpower to other projects, an end to the buildup of Apollo's overhead, and the obvious savings that will result from not having to do everything on a crash basis. To postpone the decision will cost even more because the biggest spending on Apollo is just about to start: during fiscal 1964 and 1965, NASA hopes to sink about $4 billion a year in the moon race and keep this rate in 1966 as well if the program runs into trouble. Instead the present lunar program could be continued through Gemini to determine such useful things as rendezvous techniques. Apollo and the costly hardware phase of the Saturn V's, however, would wait on the more complete explorations of "inner space."

Once the distorting influence of Apollo's high priority is reduced, we could then redefine the goal of developing a broad capability in space. For $2.5 billion to $3 billion it should be possible to have the sort of program that Caltech's President DuBridge outlined to a congressional committee: sending up many instrumented satellites to measure the Van Allen layers, cosmic rays, magnetic and gravitational fields. Some would observe weather patterns, carry communication systems and optical or radio telescopes for observations unimpeded by the troublesome atmosphere of the earth. The program would move forward at a slower pace than NASA does now in order to allow for the proper assimilation of material. (Data from the weather satellites, for example, is coming in faster than its meaning can be interpreted and applied.) In essence it would be like the present NASA program but with these all-important differences: (1) it would be a balanced effort, free of the dislocation caused by the emphasis on Apollo, (2) it would be free of the pressure of time, which increases costs and reduces benefits, (3) it would be subject to periodic reappraisal, substituting flexibility for the rigidities now characteristic of Apollo.

Whether such a program would get us to the moon ahead of the Russians would seem to be beside the point. The important thing is that when we did touch down on the lunar surface it would not be just a stunt. Behind our achievement would be the kind of deep knowledge that can take 240,000 miles in stride and not even breathe hard. We would have won the only race really worth winning, leading the Russians and the rest of the earth to a broad capability in space.

Questions

1. Diamond writes: "In general, three factions are taking a vociferous part in the lunar debate. They are the critics, the big boosters and the moderate boosters." What are some of the leading arguments offered by each of the three factions? To which faction does Lindsay belong? Jastrow and Newell?
2. Lindsay concludes: "Certainly we could not solve our earthly problems by turning our backs on space, but we should be very careful before we turn our backs on earth." Why should we not turn our backs on earth? What connection does part IV, 4, in the population explosion, have to do with a comment like Lindsay's? Or part III, 7, on city planning?
3. How do the selections in this section differ from one another in style, tone, coverage? Why do Lindsay, Jastrow, and Newell confine themselves to narrow areas of the whole subject? Why do Diamond and Smith range so broadly? Which selection is easiest to read? Most difficult? Why?
4. Why does Diamond say that "the second major complaint leveled against the space program is that it is a waste not only of money but of brainpower"? Is this a valid complaint?
5. Why do the writers in this section rely so much on statistics and quotations? What portion of each article is devoted to reporting and what portion to the writer's own speculation? Can you tell when the objective parts of the articles stop and the subjective ones begin? What can you learn for your own writing from the writers' ways of intermingling fact and opinion?
6. What do the following terms mean: "radio relay satellites," "energy balance," "inner space," "urban renewal," "pork-barrel politics," "astrophysics," "unmanned space flight," "penny-ante outlays," "orbiting solar observatory"? Can you determine the meanings from the contexts in which the terms appear? Where might you find definitions or explanations for them?

Assignments

1. In two columns, list the principal reasons for and against continuing Project Apollo. Try to balance a pro argument with a relevant con argument. Evaluate each of the columns in statements of about 300 words each.
2. Using part IV, 4, on the population explosion, as a starting point, argue either for continuation of space exploration or for its complete cessation. (You

might start with the following points: the continuing increase in the birth rate makes it imperative to find whether other planets are habitable by earth men; the continuing increase in the birth rate makes it imperative to devote all our energies, talents, and resources to solving the problems created by it.)
3. In a straight, newspaperlike account, summarize the substance of either Jastrow and Newell's article or Lindsay's, pretending that each had been delivered as a speech the night before.
4. Make up a glossary of at least ten technical terms that seem to be limited to the subject of landing on the moon.
5. Using the usual outline form, show the organization of one of the selections.

Additional Reading

The question of the moon shot is, of course, a current one, and articles appear regularly on the subject in such periodicals as the *Atlantic Monthly, Harper's,* and *The New York Times Magazine.* These are indexed in the usual periodical guides. One of the more provocative pieces on the question is "Martyrs on the Moon?" by Carl Dreher, in *Harper's,* CCXXVI (March 1963), 33–38. The title suggests the approach although Mr. Dreher writes: "Let me make it plain that I am not one of those opposed to the moon venture as such. I am in favor of it. Nor should we be squeamish about the certain loss of life in space exploration." A survey of the work done in the whole area is *A Review of Space Research* (Washington, 1963). The *General Electric Forum* of July–September 1962 is devoted to "Man's Opportunities in Space." Edwin Diamond, whose article "The Moon Trip: Debate Sharpens" appears in this section, elaborates on the subject in his book *The Rise and Fall of the Space Age* (New York, 1964).